Web Security, Privacy, and Commerce

SECOND EDITION

Web Security, Privacy, and Commerce

Simson Garfinkel
with Gene Spafford

O'REILLY®

Beijing · Cambridge · Farnham · Köln · Paris · Sebastopol · Taipei · Tokyo

Web Security, Privacy, and Commerce, Second Edition
by Simson Garfinkel, with Gene Spafford

Published by O'Reilly & Associates, Inc., 1005 Gravenstein Highway North, Sebastopol, CA 95472.

Editor:	Deborah Russell
Production Editor:	Colleen Gorman
Cover Designer:	Edie Freedman
Interior Designer:	David Futato

Printing History:

June 1997:	First Edition.
January 2002:	Second Edition.

Library of Congress Cataloging-in-Publication Data

Garfinkel, Simson.
   Web security, privacy & commerce/Simson Garfinkel with Gene Spafford.—2nd ed. p. cm.
   Includes index.
   Rev. ed. of: Web security & commerce. 1997.
   ISBN 0-596-00045-6
   1. Computer networks—Security measures. 2. World Wide Web—Security measures. 3. Web
   sites—Security measures. I. Spafford, Gene. II. Title.
TK5105.59.G37 2001
005.8—dc21   2001052375

ISBN: 0-596-00045-6
[M]

Table of Contents

Preface . . . . **xi**

Part I.   Web Technology

1. **The Web Security Landscape** **3**
   The Web Security Problem   3
   Risk Analysis and Best Practices   10

2. **The Architecture of the World Wide Web** **13**
   History and Terminology   13
   A Packet's Tour of the Web   20
   Who Owns the Internet?   33

3. **Cryptography Basics** **46**
   Understanding Cryptography   46
   Symmetric Key Algorithms   53
   Public Key Algorithms   65
   Message Digest Functions   71

4. **Cryptography and the Web** **78**
   Cryptography and Web Security   78
   Working Cryptographic Systems and Protocols   81
   What Cryptography Can't Do   88
   Legal Restrictions on Cryptography   90

5. **Understanding SSL and TLS** **107**
   What Is SSL?   107
   SSL: The User's Point of View   115

 6. **Digital Identification I: Passwords, Biometrics, and Digital Signatures** ... **119**
    Physical Identification 119
    Using Public Keys for Identification 130
    Real-World Public Key Examples 140

 7. **Digital Identification II: Digital Certificates, CAs, and PKI** **153**
    Understanding Digital Certificates with PGP 153
    Certification Authorities: Third-Party Registrars 160
    Public Key Infrastructure 174
    Open Policy Issues 187

Part II. Privacy and Security for Users

 8. **The Web's War on Your Privacy** **203**
    Understanding Privacy 204
    User-Provided Information 207
    Log Files 210
    Understanding Cookies 216
    Web Bugs 225
    Conclusion 229

 9. **Privacy-Protecting Techniques** **230**
    Choosing a Good Service Provider 230
    Picking a Great Password 231
    Cleaning Up After Yourself 242
    Avoiding Spam and Junk Email 252
    Identity Theft 256

10. **Privacy-Protecting Technologies** **262**
    Blocking Ads and Crushing Cookies 262
    Anonymous Browsing 268
    Secure Email 275

11. **Backups and Antitheft** **284**
    Using Backups to Protect Your Data 284
    Preventing Theft 295

12. **Mobile Code I: Plug-Ins, ActiveX, and Visual Basic** **298**
    When Good Browsers Go Bad 299
    Helper Applications and Plug-ins 304

Microsoft's ActiveX   308
The Risks of Downloaded Code   318
Conclusion   326

13. Mobile Code II: Java, JavaScript, Flash, and Shockwave **327**
Java   327
JavaScript   346
Flash and Shockwave   358
Conclusion   359

Part III. Web Server Security

14. Physical Security for Servers **363**
Planning for the Forgotten Threats   363
Protecting Computer Hardware   366
Protecting Your Data   381
Personnel   392
Story: A Failed Site Inspection   392

15. Host Security for Servers **396**
Current Host Security Problems   397
Securing the Host Computer   405
Minimizing Risk by Minimizing Services   411
Operating Securely   413
Secure Remote Access and Content Updating   423
Firewalls and the Web   431
Conclusion   433

16. Securing Web Applications **435**
A Legacy of Extensibility and Risk   435
Rules to Code By   443
Securely Using Fields, Hidden Fields, and Cookies   448
Rules for Programming Languages   454
Using PHP Securely   457
Writing Scripts That Run with Additional Privileges   467
Connecting to Databases   468
Conclusion   471

17. Deploying SSL Server Certificates **472**
Planning for Your SSL Server   472
Creating SSL Servers with FreeBSD   477
Installing an SSL Certificate on Microsoft IIS   501
Obtaining a Certificate from a Commercial CA   503
When Things Go Wrong   506

18. Securing Your Web Service **510**
Protecting Via Redundancy   510
Protecting Your DNS   514
Protecting Your Domain Registration   515

19. Computer Crime **517**
Your Legal Options After a Break-In   517
Criminal Hazards   523
Criminal Subject Matter   526

Part IV.   Security for Content Providers

20. Controlling Access to Your Web Content **533**
Access Control Strategies   533
Controlling Access with Apache   538
Controlling Access with Microsoft IIS   545

21. Client-Side Digital Certificates **550**
Client Certificates   550
A Tour of the VeriSign Digital ID Center   553

22. Code Signing and Microsoft's Authenticode **560**
Why Code Signing?   560
Microsoft's Authenticode Technology   564
Obtaining a Software Publishing Certificate   577
Other Code Signing Methods   577

23. Pornography, Filtering Software, and Censorship **579**
Pornography Filtering   579
PICS   582
RSACi   589
Conclusion   591

24. Privacy Policies, Legislation, and P3P **592**
    Policies That Protect Privacy and Privacy Policies   592
    Children's Online Privacy Protection Act   601
    P3P   606
    Conclusion   609

25. Digital Payments **610**
    Charga-Plates, Diners Club, and Credit Cards   610
    Internet-Based Payment Systems   620
    How to Evaluate a Credit Card Payment System   640

26. Intellectual Property and Actionable Content **642**
    Copyright   642
    Patents   645
    Trademarks   646
    Actionable Content   650

Part V.   Appendixes

A. Lessons from Vineyard.NET **655**

B. The SSL/TLS Protocol **688**

C. P3P: The Platform for Privacy Preferences Project **699**

D. The PICS Specification **708**

E. References **716**

Index **735**

Preface

The World Wide Web has changed our world. More than half the people in the United States now use the Web on a regular basis. We use it to read today's news, to check tomorrow's weather, and to search for events that have happened in the distant past. And increasingly, the Web is the focus of the 21st century economy. Whether it's the purchase of a $50 radio or the consummation of a $5 million business-to-business transaction, the Web is where the action is.

But the Web is not without its risks. Hand-in-hand with stories of the Internet's gold rush are constant reminders that the 21st century Internet has all the safety and security of the U.S. Wild West of the 1860s. Consider:

- In February 2000, web sites belonging to Yahoo, Buy.com, Amazon.com, CNN, E*Trade, and others were shut down for hours, the result of a massive coordinated attack launched simultaneously from thousands of different computers. Although most of the sites were back up within hours, the attacks were quite costly. Yahoo, for instance, claimed to have lost more than a million dollars per minute in advertising revenue during the attack.

- In December 1999, an attacker identifying himself as a 19-year-old Russian named "Maxim" broke into the CDUniverse web store operated by eUniverse Inc. and copied more than 300,000 credit card numbers. Maxim then sent a fax to eUniverse threatening to post the stolen credit cards on the Internet if the store didn't pay him $100,000.* On December 25, when the company refused to bow to the blackmail attack, Maxim posted more than 25,000 of the numbers on the hacker web site "Maxus Credit Card Pipeline."† This led to instances of credit card fraud and abuse. Many of those credit card numbers were then canceled by the issuing banks, causing inconvenience to the legitimate holders of

---

* *http://www.wired.com/news/technology/0,1282,33539,00.html*
† *http://www.cnn.com/2000/TECH/computing/01/10/credit.card.crack.2/*

those cards.* Similar break-ins and credit card thefts that year affected Real-Names,† CreditCards.com, EggHead.Com, and many other corporations.

- In October 2000, a student at Harvard University discovered that he could view the names, addresses, and phone numbers of thousands of Buy.com's customers by simply modifying a URL that the company sent to customers seeking to return merchandise. "This blatant disregard for security seems pretty inexcusable," the student, Ben Edelman, told *Wired News*.‡

- Attacks on the Internet aren't only limited to e-commerce sites. A significant number of high-profile web sites have had their pages rewritten during attacks. Those attacked include the U.S. Department of Justice, the U.S. Central Intelligence Agency (see Figure P-1), the U.S. Air Force, UNICEF, and the *New York Times*. An archive of more than 325 hacked home pages is online at *http://www.antionline.com/archives/pages/*.

Attacks on web servers are not the only risks we face on the electronic frontier:

- On August 25, 2000, a fraudulent press release was uploaded to the computer of Internet Wire, an Internet news agency. The press release claimed to be from Emulex Corporation, a maker of computer hardware, and claimed that the company's chief executive officer had resigned and that the company would have to adjust its most recent quarterly earnings to reflect a loss, instead of a profit. The next morning, Emulex's share price plunged by more than 60%: within a few hours, the multi-billion-dollar company had lost roughly half its value. A few days later, authorities announced the Emulex caper had been pulled off by a single person—an ex-employee of the online news service, who had made a profit of nearly $250,000 by selling Emulex stock short before the release was issued.

- Within hours of its release on May 4, 2000, a fast-moving computer worm called the "Love Bug" touched tens of millions of computers throughout the Internet and caused untold damage. Written in Microsoft Visual Basic Scripting Language (VBS), the worm was spread by people running the Microsoft Outlook email program. When executed, the worm would mail copies of itself to every email address in the victim's address book, then destroy every MP3 and JPEG file that it could locate on the victim's machine.

- A growing number of computer "worms" scan the victim's hard disk for Microsoft Word and Excel files. These files are infected and then sent by email to recipients in the victim's address book. Not only are infections potentially started more often, but confidential documents may be sent to inappropriate recipients.

---

* Including one of the authors of this book.
† *http://www.thestandard.com/article/display/0,1151,9743,00.html*
‡ *http://www.wired.com/news/technology/0,1282,39438,00.html*

Figure P-1. On September 18, 1996, a group of Swedish hackers broke into the Central Intelligence Agency's web site (http://www.odci.gov/cia) and altered the home page, proclaiming that the Agency was the Central Stupidity Agency.

The Web doesn't merely represent a threat for corporations. There are cyberstalkers, who use the Web to learn personal information and harass their victims. There are pedophiles, who start relationships with children and lure them away from home. Even users of apparently anonymous chat services aren't safe: In February 1999, the defense contracting giant Raytheon filed suit against 21 unnamed individuals who made disparaging comments about the company on one of Yahoo's online chat boards. Raytheon insisted that the 21 were current employees who had leaked confidential information; the company demanded that the Yahoo company reveal the identities behind the email addresses. Yahoo complied in May 1999. A few days later, Raytheon announced that four of the identified employees had "resigned," and the lawsuit was dropped.*

---

* *http://www.netlitigation.com/netlitigation/cases/raytheon.html*

Even using apparently "anonymous" services on the Web may jeopardize your privacy and personal information. A study of the 21 most visited health-related web sites on the Internet (prepared for the California HealthCare Foundation) discovered that personal information provided at many of the sites was being inadvertently leaked to third-parties, including advertisers. In many cases, these data transfers were in violation of the web sites' own stated privacy policies.* A similar information leak, which sent the results of home mortgage calculations to the Internet advertising firm DoubleClick, was discovered on Intuit's Quicken.com personal finance site.†

Web Security: Is Our Luck Running Out?

We have been incredibly lucky. Despite the numerous businesses, government organizations, and individuals that have found danger lurking on the Web, there have been remarkably few large-scale electronic attacks on the systems that make up the Web. Despite the fact that credit card numbers are not properly protected, there is surprisingly little traffic in stolen financial information. We are vulnerable, yet the sky hasn't fallen.

Today most Net-based attackers seem to be satisfied with the publicity that their assaults generate. Although there have been online criminal heists, there are so few that they still make the news. Security is weak, but the vast majority of Internet users still play by the rules.

Likewise, attackers have been quite limited in their aims. To the best of our knowledge, there have been no large-scale attempts to permanently crash the Internet or to undermine fundamental trust in society, the Internet, or specific corporations. The *New York Times* had its web site hacked, but the attackers didn't plant false stories into the newspaper's web pages. Millions of credit card numbers have been stolen by hackers, but there are few cases in which these numbers have been directly used to commit large-scale credit fraud.

Indeed, despite the public humiliation resulting from the well-publicized Internet break-ins, none of the victimized organizations have suffered lasting harm. The Central Intelligence Agency, the U.S. Air Force, and UNICEF all still operate web servers, even though all of these organizations have suffered embarrassing break-ins. Even better, none of these organizations actually lost sensitive information as a result of the break-ins, because that information was stored on different machines. A few days after each organization's incident, their servers were up and running again—this time, we hope, with the security problems fixed.

* *http://admin.chcf.org/documents/ehealth/privacywebreport.pdf*
† *http://news.cnet.com/news/0-1007-200-1562341.html*

The same can be said of the dozens of security holes and design flaws that have been reported with Microsoft's Internet Explorer and Netscape Navigator. Despite attacks that could have allowed the operator of some "rogue web site" to read any file from some victim's computer—or even worse, to execute arbitrary code on that machine—surprisingly few scams or attacks make use of these failings.[*] This is true despite the fact that the majority of Internet users do not download the security patches and fixes that vendors make available.

Beyond the Point of No Return

In the world of security it is often difficult to tell the difference between actual threats and hype. There were more than 200 years of commerce in North America before Allan Pinkerton started his detective and security agency in 1850,[†] and another nine years more before Perry Brink started his armored car service.[‡] It took a while for the crooks to realize that there was a lot of unprotected money floating around.

The same is true on the Internet, but with each passing year we are witnessing larger and larger crimes. It used to be that hackers simply defaced web sites; then they started stealing credit card numbers and demanding ransom; in December 2000, a report by MSNBC detailed how thousands of consumers had been bilked of between $5 and $25 on their credit cards by a group of Russian telecommunications and Internet companies; the charges were small so most of the victims didn't recognize the fraud and didn't bother to report the theft.[§]

Many security analysts believe things are going to get much worse. In March 2001, the market research firm Gartner predicted there would be "at least one incident of economic mass victimization of thousands of Internet users . . . by the end of 2002."[**]

> "Converging technology trends are creating economies of scale that enable a new class of cybercrimes aimed at mass victimization," explain[ed] Richard Hunter, Gartner Research Fellow. More importantly, Hunter add[ed], global law enforcement agencies are poorly positioned to combat these trends, leaving thousands of consumers vulnerable to online theft. "Using mundane, readily available technologies that have already been deployed by both legitimate and illegitimate businesses, cybercriminals can now surreptitiously steal millions of dollars, a few dollars at a time, from millions of individuals simultaneously. Moreover, they are very likely to get away with the crime."

---

[*] More accurately, there have been very few reported incidents. It is possible that there have been some widespread incidents, but the victims have either been unaware of them, or unwilling to report them.

[†] *http://www.pinkertons.com/companyinfo/history/pinkerton/index.asp*

[‡] *http://www.brinksireland.com/history/history.htm*

[§] *http://www.zdnet.com/zdnn/stories/news/0,4586,2668427,00.html*

[**] *http://www.businesswire.com/webbox/bw.033001/210892234.htm*

Despite these obvious risks, our society and economy has likely passed a point of no return: having some presence on the World Wide Web now seems to have become a fundamental requirement for businesses, governments, and other organizations.

Building in Security

It's difficult for many Bostonians to get to the Massachusetts Registry of Motor Vehicles to renew their car registrations; it's easy to click into the RMV's web site, type a registration number and a credit card number, and have the registration automatically processed. And it's easier for the RMV as well: their web site is connected to the RMV computers, eliminating the need to have the information typed by RMV employees. That's why the Massachusetts RMV gives a $5 discount to registrations made over the Internet.

Likewise, we have found that the amount of money we spend on buying books has increased dramatically since Amazon.com and other online booksellers have opened their web sites for business. The reason is obvious: it's much easier for us to type the name of a book on our keyboards and have it delivered than it is for us to make a special trip to the nearest bookstore. Thus, we've been purchasing many more books on impulse—for example, after hearing an interview with an author or reading about the book in a magazine.

Are the web sites operated by the Massachusetts RMV and Amazon.com really *secure*? Answering this question depends both on your definition of the word "secure," and on a careful analysis of the computers involved in the entire renewal or purchasing process.

In the early days of the World Wide Web, the word "secure" was promoted by Netscape Communications to denote any web site that used Netscape's proprietary encryption protocols. Security was equated with encryption—an equation that's remained foremost in many people's minds. Indeed, as Figure P-2 clearly demonstrates, web sites such as Amazon.com haven't changed their language very much. Amazon.com invites people to "Sign in using our secure server," but is their server really "secure"? Amazon uses the word "secure" because the company's web server uses the SSL (Secure Sockets Layer) encryption protocol. But if you click the link that says "Forgot your password? Click here," Amazon will create a new password for your account and send it to your email address. Does this policy make Amazon's web site more secure or less?

Over the Web's brief history, we've learned that security is more than simply another word for cryptographic data protection. Today we know that to be protected, an organization needs to adopt an holistic approach to guarding both its computer systems and the data that those systems collect. Using encryption is clearly important, but it's equally important to verify the identity of a customer before showing that customer his purchase history and financial information. If you send out email, it's

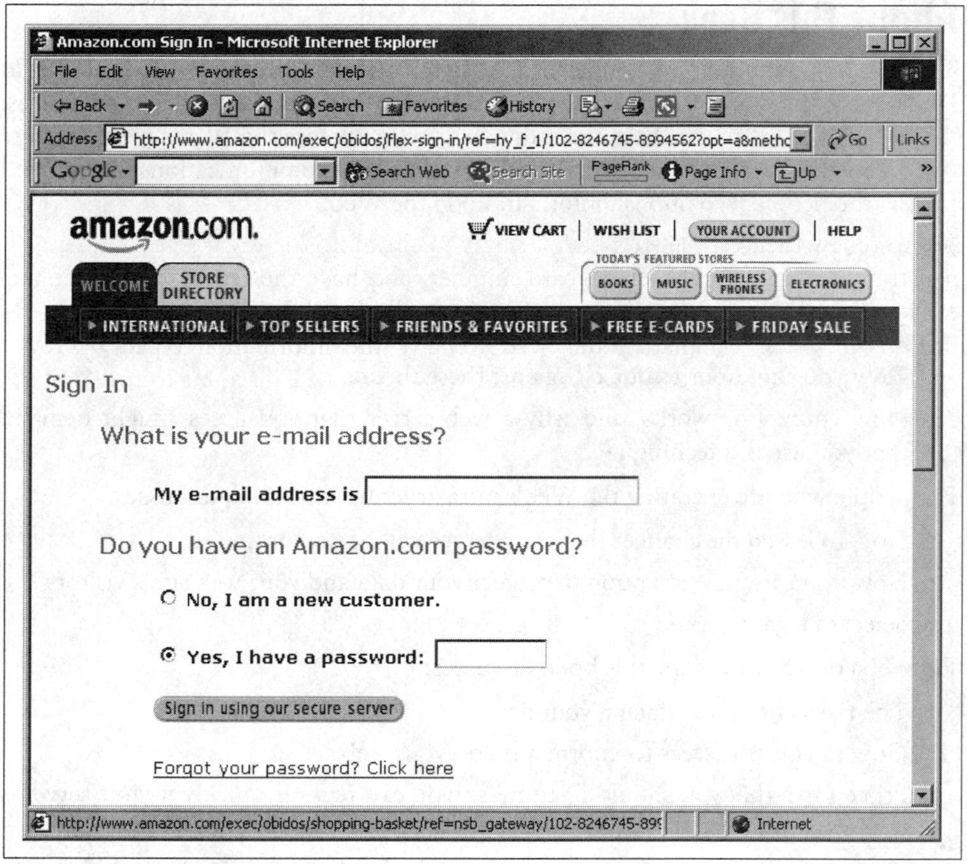

Figure P-2. Amazon.com describes their server as "secure," but the practice of emailing forgotten passwords to customers is hardly a secure one.

important to make sure that the email doesn't contain viruses—but it is equally important to make sure that you are not sending the email to the wrong person, or sending it out against the recipient's wishes. It's important to make sure that credit card numbers are encrypted before they are sent over the Internet, but it's equally important to make sure that the numbers are kept secure *after* they are decrypted at the other end.

The World Wide Web has both promises and dangers. The promise is that the Web can dramatically lower costs to organizations for distributing information, products, and services. The danger is that the computers that make up the Web are vulnerable. These computers have been compromised in the past, and they will be compromised in the future. Even worse, as more commerce is conducted in the online world, as more value flows over the Internet, as more people use the network for more of their daily financial activities, the more inviting a target these computers all become.

About This Book

This is a book about how to enhance security, privacy, and commerce on the World Wide Web. Information in this book is aimed at three distinct but related audiences: the ordinary users of the Web, the individuals who operate the Web's infrastructure (web servers, hosts, routers, and long-distance data communications links), and finally, the people who publish information on the Web.

For users, this book explains:

- How the Web works
- The threats to your privacy and your computer that await you on the Web
- How you can protect yourself against these threats
- How encryption works, and why a web server that you access might demand that you use this technique

For people who are operating the Web's infrastructure, this book discusses:

- How to lessen the chances that your server will be compromised
- How you can use encryption to protect your data and your web site's visitors
- Selected legal issues

For web content providers, this book discusses:

- The risks and threats facing your data
- How to control access to information on your web server
- Procedures that you should institute so you can recover quickly if your server is compromised
- Security issues arising from the use of Java, JavaScript, ActiveX, and Netscape plug-ins

This book covers the fundamentals of web security, but it is not designed to be a primer on computer security, operating systems, or the World Wide Web. For that, we have many recommendations.

Some especially good O'Reilly books on security- and web-related topics include the following: Æleen Frisch's *Essential System Administration*, Chuck Musciano and Bill Kennedy's *HTML & XHTML: The Definitive Guide,* Shishir Gundavaram's *CGI Programming on the World Wide Web*, Elizabeth Zwicky, Simon Cooper, and Brent Chapman's *Building Internet Firewalls*, and finally our own book, *Practical Unix & Internet Security*.

We also have some recommendations for books from other publishers. For in-depth information on cryptography, we heartily recommend Bruce Schneier's excellent book *Applied Cryptography*. For detailed information on configuring the Apache web server, we recommend Lincoln Stein's *Web Security*. And for a general overview of security engineering and practices, we recommend Ross Anderson's *Security Engineering*.

These books and other helpful references are listed Appendix E.

Organization of This Book

This book is divided into five parts; it includes 27 chapters and 5 appendixes:

Part I, *Web Technology*, examines the underlying technology that makes up today's World Wide Web and the Internet in general.

Chapter 1, *The Web Security Landscape*, examines the basics of web security—the risks inherent in running a web server, in using the Web to distribute information or services, and finally, the risks of being a user on the Internet.

Chapter 2, *The Architecture of the World Wide Web*, is a detailed exploration of computers, communications links, and protocols that make up the Web. It provides a technical introduction to the systems that will be discussed throughout the rest of the book and that underlie web security concepts.

Chapter 3, *Cryptography Basics*, introduces the science and mathematics of cryptography, with a particular emphasis on public key encryption.

Chapter 4, *Cryptography and the Web*, specifically looks at the encryption algorithms that are used on the Web today.

Chapter 5, *Understanding SSL and TLS*, looks more closely at the Secure Sockets Layer (SSL) and the Transport Layer Security (TLS) system that are used by "secure" web servers.

Chapter 6, *Digital Identification I: Passwords, Biometrics, and Digital Signatures*, introduces the topic of authentication and gives an overview of several classes of authentication systems in use on the Internet.

Chapter 7, *Digital Identification II: Digital Certificates, CAs, and PKI*, focuses on the use of digital certificates for authentication and introduces certification authorities (CAs) and the public key infrastructure (PKI).

Part II, *Privacy and Security for Users*, looks at the concerns of people using the Web to access information—that is, anybody who runs a web browser.

Chapter 8, *The Web's War on Your Privacy*, discusses the technical means by which personal information can be compromised on the Web.

Chapter 9, *Privacy-Protecting Techniques*, explores techniques that you can follow to increase your privacy while using the Web.

Chapter 10, *Privacy-Protecting Technologies*, continues the discussion of privacy self-help, by exploring programs and services that can further enhance your privacy.

Chapter 11, *Backups and Antitheft*, shows you how to protect against data loss and theft of both data and equipment.

Chapter 12, *Mobile Code I: Plug-Ins, ActiveX, and Visual Basic*, explores how programs that travel over the Web can threaten your computer system and your personal information. This chapter focuses on the most dangerous programs that can be downloaded with email or through web pages.

Chapter 13, *Mobile Code II: Java, JavaScript, Flash, and Shockwave*, continues the discussion of mobile programs that can threaten computer users. This chapter focuses on the "safer" technologies that, it turns out, still have some security implications.

Part III, *Web Server Security*, is addressed to people and organizations that are operating servers attached to the Internet. The chapters in this part focus on the mechanics of web server operation. They are particularly relevant to corporations that operate their own web servers, administrators at Internet service providers (ISPs), and home users who run their own servers at the end of cable modems or DSL lines.

Chapter 14, *Physical Security for Servers*, addresses one of the most important but frequently overlooked topics—how to protect your computer's physical well-being.

Chapter 15, *Host Security for Servers*, explores security having to do with your computer's operating system.

Chapter 16, *Securing Web Applications*, discusses the added security issues that arise when running web servers that can execute programs or scripts.

Chapter 17, *Deploying SSL Server Certificates*, gives step-by-step instructions for enabling SSL on the Apache and Internet Information Services (IIS) web servers.

Chapter 18, *Securing Your Web Service*, broadens the security discussion to show how to defend your service against problems resulting from your ISP or the Internet's Domain Name Service (DNS).

Chapter 19, *Computer Crime*, explores the specific legal options available to you after your computer system has been broken into, as well as other legal issues of concern to administrators.

Part IV, *Security for Content Providers*, focuses on issues surrounding the content of the web server, rather than the mechanics of the web server's operation.

Chapter 20, *Controlling Access to Your Web Content*, looks at techniques for controlling information to "private" areas of your web server.

Chapter 21, *Client-Side Digital Certificates*, expands on the access control techniques described in Chapter 20 by discussing how you can use digital certificates for access control and secure messaging.

Chapter 22, *Code Signing and Microsoft's Authenticode*, shows how you can sign Windows binaries, including ActiveX controls and *.EXE* files, using Microsoft's Authenticode technology.

Chapter 23, *Pornography, Filtering Software, and Censorship*, discusses the politics and the technology of controlling pornography on the Internet.

Chapter 24, *Privacy Policies, Legislation, and P3P*, explores the concept of data protection and discusses legislative and self-regulatory techniques for controlling the use of personal information.

Chapter 25, *Digital Payments*, is a how-to guide for sending and receiving money over the Internet. For those interested in e-commerce history, this chapter also discusses a number of failed digital payment systems.

Chapter 26, *Intellectual Property and Actionable Content*, discusses trademarks, copyright, and patents—all legal structures that can be used to protect information.

Part V, *Appendixes*, is filled with lists and nitty-gritty technical information that is too detailed for the main body of this book.

Appendix A, *Lessons from Vineyard.NET*, is a first-person account of the first five years of operation of Vineyard.NET, the oldest, largest, and currently only ISP that offers service exclusively on Martha's Vineyard.

Appendix B, *The SSL/TLS Protocol*, contains more detailed information about the SSL and TLS protocols. This chapter won't give you enough information to write your own SSL or TLS implementation, but it will give you an understanding of what is happening on the wire.

Appendix C, *P3P: The Platform for Privacy Preferences Project*, is a detailed introduction to the P3P specification. This chapter, written by Lorrie Faith Cranor and included with permission, includes information on how to write your own P3P policy.

Appendix D, *The PICS Specification*, provides detailed information on the PICS specification. Although PICS appears largely dead today, an implementation is included in Microsoft's Internet Explorer, so PICS is still there for anybody who wants to use it.

Appendix E, *References*, lists books, articles, and web sites containing further helpful information about web security, privacy, and commerce.

What You Should Know

Web security is a complex topic that touches on many aspects of traditional computer security, computer architecture, system design, software engineering, Internet technology, mathematics, and the law. To keep the size of this book under control, we have focused on conveying information and techniques that are not readily found elsewhere.

To get the most out of this book, you should already be familiar with the operation and management of a networked computer. You should know how to connect your computer to the Internet; how to obtain, install, and maintain computer software; and how to perform routine system management tasks, such as backups. You should have a working knowledge of the World Wide Web, and know how to install and maintain your organization's web server.

That is not to say that this is a book written solely for "propeller-heads" and security geeks. Great effort has been made to make this book useful for people who have a working familiarity with computers and the Web, but who are not familiar with the nitty-gritty details of computer security. That's why we have included introductory chapters on such topics as cryptography and SSL.

Web Software Covered by This Book

A major difficulty in writing a book on web security is that the field moves incredibly quickly. Configuration information and screen shots that look up-to-date one month seem antiquated and obsolete a few months later. This is partially the result of the steady release of new software versions, and the integration of new features into commonly-used software. The difficulty in keeping current is complicated by the steady drumbeat of warnings from vendors and organizations such as SANS and CERT/CC, announcing a significant new security vulnerability every few days— often caused by the vendors' rush to deliver all those new features without carefully testing them for security flaws!

But in fact, the field of web security is not moving as fast as it may seem. Although new vulnerabilities have been created and discovered, the underlying concepts of web security have changed little since the first edition of this book was published in the spring of 1997. We have therefore refrained from updating all of our screenshots and code examples simply to match the latest revisions of Microsoft and Netscape's offerings. If a point is well made by a screenshot that featured an older version of a product, we have generally opted to leave the screenshot in place.

To avoid the planned obsolescence that seems to beset many computer books, this book concentrates on teaching concepts and principles, rather than specific sequences of commands and keystrokes.

In writing this book, we used a wide variety of software. Examples in this book are drawn primarily from two web servers:

Apache
> Apache is one of the most popular web servers currently in use. Apache runs on a wide variety of computers, including most versions of Unix and Windows NT. When combined with the *mod_ssl* encryption module, Apache can be the basis for creating an extremely sophisticated web publishing system. Apache is freely available in both source code and precompiled form; it is even preinstalled on many computer systems.

Microsoft Internet Information Server
> IIS is Microsoft's cryptographically enabled web server that is bundled with the Windows NT Server and Windows 2000 operating systems.

The following web browsers were used in the creation of this book:

Netscape Navigator
> Netscape Navigator is the web browser that ignited the commercialization of the Internet. Versions 1, 2, 3, 4, and 6 were used in the preparation of this book. Navigator is available on a wide variety of computer platforms, including various versions of Windows, Unix, Linux, and the Macintosh.

Microsoft Internet Explorer
> The Microsoft Internet Explorer is a cryptographically enabled web browser that is deeply interconnected with the Microsoft Windows operating system, and is also available for Macintosh computers. Versions 3, 4, 5, and 6 were used in the preparation of this book.

Opera
> We also used Opera Software's browser, "the fastest browser on earth." Opera is available for BeOS, EPOC, Linux, Mac, OS/2, and Windows.

Conventions Used in This Book

The following conventions are used in this book:

Italic is used for file and directory names and for URLs. It is also used to emphasize new terms and concepts when they are introduced.

`Constant Width` is used for code examples and system output.

`Constant Width Italic` is used in examples for variable input or output (e.g., a filename).

`Constant Width Bold` is used in examples for user input.

<u>Underlining</u> is used occasionally in examples to highlight code being discussed.

~~Strike-through~~ is used in examples to show input typed by the user that is not echoed by the computer. This is mainly for passwords and passphrases that are typed.

CTRL-X or ^X indicates the use of control characters. It means hold down the CONTROL key while typing the character "X".

All command examples are followed by RETURN unless otherwise indicated.

Indicates a tip, suggestion, or general note.

Indicates a warning or caution.

Comments and Questions

We have tested and verified all of the information in this book to the best of our ability, but you may find that features have changed, that typos have crept in, or that we have made a mistake. Please let us know about what you find, as well as your suggestions for future editions, by contacting:

O'Reilly & Associates, Inc.
1005 Gravenstein Highway North
Sebastopol, CA 95472
(800)998-9938 (in the U.S. or Canada)
(707)829-0515 (international/local)
(707)829-0104 (fax)

You can also send us messages electronically. To be put on the mailing list or request a catalog, send email to:

info@oreilly.com

To ask technical questions or comment on the book, send email to:

bookquestions@oreilly.com

We have a web site for the book, where we'll list examples, errata, and any plans for future editions. You can access this page at:

http://www.oreilly.com/catalog/websec2/

For more information about this book and others, see the O'Reilly web site:

http://www.oreilly.com

History and Acknowledgments

In June 1991, O'Reilly & Associates published our first book, *Practical Unix Security*. The book was 450 pages and contained state-of-the-art information on securing Unix computers on the Internet. Five years later, we published the revised edition of our book, now entitled *Practical Unix & Internet Security*. During the intervening years, the field of computer security had grown substantially. Not surprisingly, so had our page count. The new volume was 1000 pages long.

In 1996, our editor Debby Russell suggested that we create a revised version of *Practical Unix & Internet Security* that was aimed at the growing community of web users and service providers. But because the book was already so long, we decided to write a new book that would focus on SSL encryption, client-side digital signature certificates, and special issues pertaining to electronic commerce. That book, *Web Security and Commerce*, was published in 1997.

In the spring of 2000, Debby approached us again, asking if we would like to rewrite either of the security books. We looked them over and started on this project. Originally we thought that we would simply remove the material from *Web Security and Commerce* that was no longer relevant—alternatives that had been rejected by the marketplace. And certainly, some screen shots and configuration information needed to be revised. But as we looked more deeply at the project, we realized that a total rewrite and a significant expansion of the book was required. The result of that complete rewrite is this second edition.

Second Edition

For help in creating this second edition of the book, we wish to offer our special thanks to:

- Aaron Goldfeder at Microsoft. Over more than six months, Aaron proved to be a godsend, able to find out the answers to all sorts of questions having to do with Internet Explorer, Internet Information Services, Authenticode, and even Veri-Sign. Many errors were headed off at the pass by Aaron's gracious responses to our email. And thanks to Charles Fitzgerald for putting us in touch with Stephen Purpura, who put us in touch with Aaron!

- Andy Cervantes and the Privacy Foundation, who provided us with information regarding hostile browser helpers.

- Ann Wiles and CardWeb.com, who provided us with information about credit card fraud.

- Aaron S. Cope at Vineyard.NET, who provided all-around question-answering and web-searching capabilities.

- Bert-Jaap Koops, who answered questions about his Crypto Law Survey and allowed us to reprint its findings.

- Bradford Biddle, now at Intel, who answered many questions about PKI and public key issues and provided us with material for Chapter 7.

- Christopher D. Hunter, who provided information about online privacy issues.

- D.A. Smith at Sandstorm Enterprises, whose constant reading and summarization of Bugtraq and other mailing lists saved the authors a tremendous amount of time.

- David Flanagan, who answered questions on JavaScript security.

- Elisabeth Cohen, formerly at Merrit Group, VeriSign's PR agency, who helped set up an interview that proved useful.

- Eric Pollard at Earthlink, who put us in touch with one of our reviewers, Lisa Hoyt.

- Karl Auerbach at ICANN, who provided needed details regarding the organization's formation.

- Jane Winn, who answered many questions about digital signatures and wrote a terrific article about E-SIGN.

- Jeff Morrow of Switch and Data, which provided us with a photograph of their Internet data center.

- Jeff Ubois at Omniva Policy Systems, who sent us many messages that self-destructed.

- Joe Chou at Sun and the Mozilla project, who verified for us that JavaScripts downloaded by SSL are not treated as signed JavaScripts (despite claims to the contrary in the documentation). Also thanks to George Drapeau at Sun and Norris Boyd at ATG, and John Gable at Netscape, who worked on the same issue.

- John Lambert at Microsoft, who found out for us the process for getting a root certificate bundled into Microsoft Internet Explorer.

- Kevin Fu at MIT, whose knowledge of cookies and cryptography proved invaluable.

- Lorrie Cranor, who answered all things relating to P3P, and even wrote our appendix on the subject.

- Michael Baum, who took time out of his busy flying schedule to answer some questions about digital signatures and the law.

- Michael Froomkin, who answered questions about digital signatures and put us in touch with Jane Winn.

- Mitchell Stoltz, who answered even more questions about signed JavaScripts in Netscape 6.

- Shaun Clowes for providing very helpful information on PHP security.

- Stephen Wu of VeriSign, who caught and helped us to correct many inaccurate statements regarding his company.

- Trista Haugen at Surety, who answered questions about the company's current offerings.

- Veronica at Lycos.com's Product Support Analysis Team, who really tried to find out for us what HotBot's cookies do, but ended up simply telling us how to disable cookies in our browser.

This book was reviewed by Norris Boyd at ATG, Carl Ellison at Intel, Kevin Fu at MIT, Lisa Hoyt at Earthlink, Reuven Lerner, Radia Perlman at Sun Microsystems, Mitch Stoltz at Netscape, Rich Wellner, and Stephen Wu at VeriSign. Many thanks to all of you.

Our editor Debby Russell did yet another fabulous job editing this book. Rob Romano created illustrations that helped convey some of the more difficult ideas. Many thanks to Colleen Gorman, the production editor for this book; Edie Freedman and Ellie Volckhausen, who designed the front cover; Emma Colby, who designed the back cover,

David Futato, who designed the interior format; Audrey Doyle, the copyeditor; Mary Brady, Phil Dangler, Maureen Dempsey, Derek Di Matteo, Catherine Morris, and Edie Shapiro, who entered edits; and John Bickelhaupt, who indexed the book.

First Edition

We want to reiterate our thanks to the people who helped us in creating the original edition of *Web Security & Commerce*. We received help from many people in the computer industry, including:*

- At Consensus, Christopher Allen and Tim Dierks reviewed our chapters on SSL.

- At Cybercash, Carl Ellison sent us many email messages about the role and usefulness of certificates.

- At First Virtual, Marshall Rose and Lee Stein gave us lots of juicy information about what they were doing.

- At JavaSoft, David Brownell answered many questions regarding Java and Java's interaction with digital signatures.

- At Microsoft, we had tremendous help from Charles Fitzgerald, Barbara Fox, Rick Johnson, Thomas Reardon, and Michael Toutonghi, who spent a great number of days and nights acquainting us with the issues of SET, Java, JavaScript, and ActiveX security.

- At Netscape, Frank Chen, Eric Greenberg, Jeff Treuhaft, and Tom Weinstein provided us with many technical insights.

- At VeriSign, Michael Baum, Gina Jorasch, Kelly M. Ryan, Arn Schaeffer, Stratton Sclavos, and Peter Williams were very patient, answering many questions.

- At the World Wide Web Consortium (W3C), Paul Resnick reviewed the chapter on PICS and made several helpful suggestions.

Adam Cain at UIUC provided interesting timing information about SSL for the SSL chapter. Brad Wood from Sandia National Labs gave us excellent comments about the role of encryption in securing web servers. John Guinasso at Netcom gave us interesting insights into the human problems facing ISPs. Mark Shuttleworth at Thawte and Sameer Parekh at Community ConneXion told us more about web servers and dealing with VeriSign than we ever imagined we might need to know. Nessa Feddis at the American Banker's Association straightened us out about many banking regulations. Eric Young, the author of SSLeay, answered many questions about his program and other aspects of SSL. Jon Orwant looked over the Perl code and answered questions for us.

---

* The companies and organizational affiliations listed here were accurate as of the writing of the first edition; many of these companies may no longer exist, and most of these people have moved on to other opportunities.

We would like to thank our reviewers, who made this a better book by scanning the draft text for inaccuracies and confusions. Special thanks are due to Michael Baum, David Brownell, Carl Ellison, Barbara Fox, Lamont Granquist, Eric Greenberg, John Guinasso, Peter Neumann, Marshall Rose, Lincoln Stein, Ilane Marie Walberg, Dan Wallach, and David Waitzman. Special thanks to Kevin Dowd, who provided information on Windows NT host security, to Bradford Biddle, who gave us permission to include digital signature policy information, and to Bert-Jaap Koops, who let us use his table on export restrictions.

## PART I

Web Technology

This part of the book examines the underlying technology that makes up today's World Wide Web and the Internet in general.

Chapter 1, *The Web Security Landscape*, looks at the basics of web security—the risks inherent in running a web server, in using the Web to distribute information or services, and finally, the risks of being a user on the Internet.

Chapter 2, *The Architecture of the World Wide Web*, is a detailed exploration of computers, communications links, and protocols that make up the Web. It provides a technical introduction to the systems that will be discussed throughout the rest of the book and that underlie web security concepts.

Chapter 3, *Cryptography Basics*, introduces the science and mathematics of cryptography, with a particular emphasis on public key encryption.

Chapter 4, *Cryptography and the Web*, specifically looks at the encryption algorithms that are used on the Web today.

Chapter 5, *Understanding SSL and TLS*, looks more closely at the Secure Sockets Layer (SSL) and the Transport Layer Security (TLS) system that are used by "secure" web servers.

Chapter 6, *Digital Identification I: Passwords, Biometrics, and Digital Signatures*, introduces the topic of authentication and gives an overview of several classes of authentication systems in use on the Internet.

Chapter 7, *Digital Identification II: Digital Certificates, CAs, and PKI*, focuses on the use of digital certificates for authentication and introduces certification authorities (CAs) and the public key infrastructure (PKI).

CHAPTER 1
The Web Security Landscape

This chapter looks at the basics of web security. We'll discuss the risks of running a web server on the Internet and give you a framework for understanding how to mitigate those risks. We'll look at the risks that the Web poses for users—people who simply want to use the Web to get information or participate in online communities. And we'll look at the hype surrounding web security, analyze what companies (probably) mean when they use the phrase "secure web server," and discuss overall strategies for reducing the risks associated with the World Wide Web.

The Web Security Problem

When we published the first edition of *Practical Unix Security* in 1991, we gave a simple definition of computer security:

> A computer is secure if you can depend on it and its software to behave as you expect.

This definition has stood the test of time. Whether you are talking about a complex attack such as cross-site scripting, or you are discussing the age-old problem of password sharing, the fundamental goal of computer security is to minimize surprise and to have computers behave as we expect them to behave. Our definition puts forth a holistic approach to protecting computers and the information that they contain: a web site is as dead if it is compromised by an attacker as it is if the sole web server on which the site resides washes away in a flood. Web security, then, is a set of procedures, practices, and technologies for assuring the reliable, predictable operation of web servers, web browsers, other programs that communicate with web servers, and the surrounding Internet infrastructure. Unfortunately, the sheer scale and complexity of the Web makes the problem of web security dramatically more complex than the problem of Internet security in general.

Today's web security problem has three primary facets:

Securing the web server and the data that is on it
> You need to be sure that the server can continue its operation, that the information on the server cannot be modified without authorization, and that the information is only distributed to those individuals to whom you want it distributed.

Securing information that travels between the web server and the user
> You would like to assure that information the user supplies to the web server (usernames, passwords, financial information, the names of web pages visited, etc.) cannot be read, modified, or destroyed by any third parties. You want similar protection for the information that flows back from the web servers to the users. It is also important to assure that the link between the user and the web server cannot be easily disrupted.

Securing the end user's computer and other devices that people use to access the Internet
> Finally, web security requires that the end user's computer be reasonably secured. Users need to run their web browsers and other software on a secure computing platform that is free of viruses and other hostile software. Users also need protections for their privacy and personal information, to make sure that it is not compromised either on their own computers or by their online services.

Each of these tasks, in turn, can be broken down into many others. For example, in the case of a web publisher, the goal of securing the web server used in electronic banking might include the following tasks:

- Devising and implementing a system for verifying the identity of users who connect to the web server to view their bank statements, a process also known as *authentication*. One approach to authentication involves implementing a system of usernames and passwords, devising a technique for distributing the initial passwords to the users, and creating a mechanism for users to securely change their passwords or obtain new passwords when their old passwords are forgotten.

- Analyzing the programs and scripts that operate the web site for flaws and vulnerabilities (e.g., making sure that a web page that leads to the display of one user's account can't be tricked into displaying the account of another user).

- Providing for secure, off-site backup of user information.

- Creating a secure logging and auditing facility that can be used for billing, conflict resolution, and so-called "nonrepudiation" (see the note in the section "Roles for Cryptography" in Chapter 4), and investigation of misuse.

- Balancing the load among multiple servers to protect against usage spikes and hardware failures, and to provide responsive service.

- Creating a second data center so that in the event of a disaster (e.g., an earthquake, blizzard, explosion, or invasion from outer space) affecting the primary data center, services will continue.

- Providing for redundant Internet connections, using multiple service providers, to minimize the chances that a service disruption on the Internet will prevent users from reaching the web site.

- Securing your Domain Name Service (DNS) service so that an attacker can't change the domain name to point to another organization's server.

- Protecting your billing records so customers will be charged accurately for services rendered.
- Creating a 24-hour Network Operations Center, or employing the services of an outside monitoring organization, so that if there is a security incident the bank will be able to respond to it in a timely fashion.
- Providing for the physical security of your site and servers.
- Providing adequate training for your personnel so they know what to do in an emergency and can resist a social engineering attack.

As you can see, the items on this list include technology that needs to be created and deployed, procedures that need to be followed, and policies that need to be developed. Security is not an additional feature that can be purchased after-the-fact and simply bolted on to an existing system. Neither is security a set of policies that can be implemented within an organization by a single person who has the mandate to be Chief Security Officer. Building a secure computing environment is an involved undertaking that requires careful planning and continued vigilance. The reward is a computing infrastructure that continues to function in the face of adversity—whether that adversity results from man-made attacks or natural disasters.

What Do Attackers Want?

Nearly all attackers on the World Wide Web have the same goal: they want to make your computers do things that you don't want them to do. For example:

- They want to scan your system for confidential documents, which they will transmit to other systems.
- They want to corrupt the information on your computer, or even reformat your computer's hard disk drive.
- They want to use your system to store pirated software, MP3 music files, or pornographic images for later access by them and their friends.
- They want to modify your computer's operating system, leaving traps, creating new security holes, or simply causing your system to crash.
- They want to use home-banking applications or credit card numbers residing on your computer to transfer money from your bank account to theirs.
- They want to be able to selectively block access to your system as they wish, or use it in a coordinated attack to deny access to someone else.
- They want to install some form of server, such as an IRC (Internet Relay Chat) server they can access without slowing down their own machines.
- They want to see the press coverage that results from their triumphs and your misfortune.

Securing the Web Server

Securing the web server is a three-part process. First, the computer itself must be secured using traditional computer security techniques. Second, special programs that provide web service must be secured. Finally, you need to examine the operating system and the web service to see if there are any unexpected interactions between the two that might compromise the system's overall security.

Server security is complicated because most web servers run on traditional multi-purpose operating systems, such as Unix or Windows NT. The web server can be used to exploit bugs in the host security, and failings in host security can be used to probe for problems with the web server. Consider these two typical attacks:

- A poorly written script or application may make it possible to change a web server's configuration file, which can then be modified so that the web server runs with excess privileges. By exploiting a host security flaw, an attacker could then create a privileged script that would lead to the attacker's obtaining full access to the entire computer system.

- A web server may have well-written scripts and be running on a secure operating system, but a related database server may contain a default account that allows full access to anyone on the Internet. By connecting to the database server and typing a few commands, an attacker may be able to get access to the names, email addresses, and credit card numbers of every customer who has purchased something from the web site.

The first part of server security, securing the underlying computer system, involves a complete examination of the computer's hardware, its operating system, and add-on programs. The goal of this process is to make sure that authorized users of the system have sufficient capabilities or privileges necessary to perform their work, and nothing more. For example, you may wish to allow all users to read the contents of the server's main web page, but you probably do not wish to give any unidentified user the ability to shut down the computer or alter the system accounting files. Traditional computer security techniques are also designed to secure the system so that people on the Internet cannot break into it and gain control. Chapter 15 presents an overview of several generic techniques; the references in Appendix E contain many more.

To secure the computer's web service, you first need to understand how the program that serves web pages works and how it is configured. Examine the server's configuration to make sure that the correct levels of privilege and authorization are granted for the files that are on the server. Next, examine the scripts—be they CGIs written in Perl, ASP pages written with VBScript, or stand-alone programs written in C—to make sure that each script properly follows your security policy and that it cannot be exploited by a malicious Internet user. Information on how to do this is in Chapter 16.

Finally, you need to look for possible interactions among all of the various components that are running on the computer. This can be a difficult and tedious process to perform. Generally speaking, the best way to minimize interactions is to minimize dependencies between different components that make up your system, and to make sure that each component makes few assumptions about the environment in which it is operating.

Simplification of services

One of the best strategies for improving a web server's security is to minimize the number of services provided by the host on which the web server is running. If you need to provide both a mail server and a web server, the safest strategy is to put them on different computers. On the system that runs your web service, design the system to run only your web services, choose an underlying operating system and web server that don't come with lots of extra defaults and unnecessary options, and remove all the services and options you know you don't need. The more complex the system, the more interactions, and the more that can go wrong . . . or be abused by an attacker.

Another good strategy for securing the information on the web server is to restrict access to the web server. The server should be located in a secure location, so that unauthorized people do not have physical access to the equipment. You should limit the number of users who have the ability to log into the computer. The server should be used only for your single application; otherwise, people who have access to the server might obtain access to your information, or accidentally change something that allows others to gain access. And you should make sure that people who remotely access the server for administrative purposes do so using secure means such as SSH, SecureID, or S/Key.

Policing copyright

Many web developers also want to protect the information that they put on their web sites from unauthorized use. Companies putting pay-per-view information on a web site would like to prevent users from downloading this information and sharing it with others who have not paid for the service. Most web sites that provide information freely to the public prefer that each Internet user pick up the data for themselves, so that the sites can track the number of downloads and possibly show an advertisement at the same time. Some web sites have threatened legal action—and there have even been a few lawsuits—when one web site displays information that is taken from another, even if that other web site distributes the same information "for free."

It is impossible to impose technical solutions that limit the spread of information once it has been provided to the user. If the data is viewed on the user's screen, that information can simply be copied off the screen and either printed or saved in a file. At the very least, the screen can be photographed and the photograph later scanned. "Copy protected" sound can be recorded with a tape recorder and redigitized.

Although a number of copy protection systems for web data have been proposed (and marketed), they can all be subverted by a sufficiently-motivated attacker. As an alternative to technical measures that prevent copying, some web sites have instead invested in a technique called *digital watermarking*. This involves making very small, hidden alterations to the data to store a form of identification of the material. The alterations can't be noticed by the user, and are done in a special fashion to defeat attempts to remove them. Images, sound files, and other watermarked data can be examined with programs that find and display the identifying information, showing the true owner and possibly the name of the person for whom the copy was first produced.

Securing Information in Transit

Much of the initial emphasis in the field of web security involved the problem of protecting information as it traveled over the Internet from a web server to the end user's computer. The concern was that someone eavesdropping on the network (at intermediate nodes) might copy sensitive information, or alter information in transit.

There are many ways to protect information from eavesdropping as it travels through a network:

- Physically secure the network, so that eavesdropping is impossible.
- Hide the information that you wish to secure within information that appears innocuous.
- Encrypt the information so that it cannot be decoded by any party who is not in possession of the proper key.

Of these techniques, encryption is the only technique that is practical on a large-scale public network. Physically securing the Internet is impossible. Information hiding only works if the people you are hiding the information from do not know it is hidden. Additionally, encryption can prevent outside alteration, or make it obvious when the information has been changed.

One of the pivotal events in the launch of the World Wide Web was Netscape Communications' development of an easy-to-use system for sending encrypted information over the Internet. Called the Secure Sockets Layer (SSL), this system made it possible for unsophisticated users to employ cryptographic security similar to what had previously been reserved for banks and governments. The encryption provided by SSL made it possible for people to transmit credit card numbers securely over the Internet using the Web, which many people at the time said was a prerequisite for electronic commerce. That's why Netscape is generally credited with launching the commercialization of the Internet and the Web.

In fact, there were no real barriers to Internet commerce solved by SSL. Before SSL, consumers routinely purchased items by sending credit card numbers by email.

Under U.S. regulations, consumers are only liable for $50 in fraud on credit cards: they had little to fear. But large merchants and the credit card companies were worried about the apparent lack of online security and wanted to do something that would address this perceived vulnerability. What Netscape really did to advance Internet commerce was to create a reasonably good browser and then distribute it widely, creating an audience for web sites.

Indeed, SSL is only one component of web security. SSL makes it possible to send usernames, passwords, and credit card numbers securely over the Internet, but SSL doesn't provide protection for the information at the two ends of the connection.

Another risk to information in transit is a denial-of-service attack resulting from a disruption in the network. A denial-of-service can result from a physical event, such as a fiber cut, or a logical event, such as a bug in the Internet routing tables. In February 2000, a large-scale denial-of-service attack against several prominent Internet sites made the front pages of newspapers around the world; this event resulted from a sustained attack against these servers by computers all over the Internet. One of the most common attacks involved in this incident simply repeated requests for web pages—thousands every second, from hundreds of different servers.

Today there is no practical way for an individual to defend against denial-of-service attacks, although redundancy, high-capacity connections, and backup systems can help to minimize their impact. Ultimately, it will take effective use of the legal system to pursue and prosecute attackers to make these attacks less frequent.

Securing the User's Computer

Security threats facing users have become front-page news—but these threats have not materialized in the way that was widely expected.

For the first five years of the Web's existence, web security was largely an academic exercise. Companies including Netscape, Microsoft, and Macromedia distributed browser software, while computer researchers at universities such as UC Berkeley and Princeton found flaws in those programs. Each new vulnerability in a web browser generated a front-page story in the *New York Times* with ominous warnings of how the flaw could be exploited by a "hostile" web site. A few days later, the embarrassed vendor would distribute an update. It all made for good newscopy, but in fact only a small percentage of computer users actually downloaded the fixes; most users remain vulnerable. Nevertheless, few losses to date are attributable to any browser flaw.

Over that same period, millions of computer users suffered billions of dollars in losses from real attacks experienced over the Internet. Most of the damages were caused by fast-moving computer viruses and worms that traveled by email, or that involved automated exploitation of flaws in network service programs.

Computer security professionals had long maintained that *education* was the most effective way to secure end users' computers. The theory was that if you could teach users how to make reasonable decisions about their computer's security, and if you could teach them to recognize unusual situations, then the users would be far more effective at protecting their own security than any program or computer could ever be.

In recent years, however, some people have revised their opinions, and are now putting their hopes for strong end user computer security in technology, rather than in a massive education effort. The reason is that computer systems are simply too complex for most end users to make rational security decisions. A good example comes from the history of computer worms and viruses. In the late 1990s, users at large organizations were instructed to never run a program that was emailed by somebody that they didn't know. Unfortunately, this advice left these users wide open to attack from computer worms such as ILOVEYOU (discussed in Chapter 12). These worms propagated automatically by sending copies of themselves to everyone in the victim's address book. To the people receiving copies of this worm, the email messages appeared to come from somebody they knew, and so the individuals who received the worm frequently ran them—which resulted in files being deleted and the worm propagating to other victims.

Risk Analysis and Best Practices

Security is most often viewed as a process that is designed to *prevent* something from happening. As a result, people often approach computer security by thinking about the risks that they face and then formulating strategies for minimizing or mitigating these risks. One traditional way to approach this problem is with the process of *risk analysis*, a technique that involves gauging the likelihood of each risk, evaluating the potential for damage that each risk entails, and addressing the risks in some kind of systematic order.

Risk analysis has a long and successful history in the fields of public safety and civil engineering. Consider the construction of a suspension bridge. It's a relatively straightforward matter to determine how much stress cars, trucks, and weather on a bridge will place on the bridge's cables. Knowing the anticipated stress, an engineer can compute the chance that the bridge will collapse over the course of its life given certain design and construction choices. Given the bridge's width, length, height, anticipated traffic, and other factors, an engineer can compute the projected destruction to life, property, and commuting patterns that would result from the bridge's failure. All of this information can be used to calculate cost-effective design decisions and a reasonable maintenance schedule for the bridge's owners to follow.

Unfortunately, the application of risk analysis to the field of computer security has been less successful. Risk analysis depends on the ability to gauge the likelihood of each risk, identify the factors that enable those risks, and calculate the potential

What Is a "Secure Web Server?"

In recent years, the phrase *secure web server* has come to mean different things to different people:

- For the software vendors that sell them, a secure web server is a program that implements certain cryptographic protocols, so that information transferred between a web server and a web browser cannot be eavesdropped upon.

- For users, a secure web server is one that will safeguard any personal information that is received or collected. It's one that supports users' privacy and won't subvert their browsers to download viruses or other rogue programs onto their computers.

- For a company that runs one, a secure web server is one that is resistant to a determined attack over the Internet or from corporate insiders.

A secure web server is all of these things, and more. It's a server that is reliable. It's a server that is mirrored or backed up, so that it can be reconstituted quickly in the event of a hardware or software failure. It's a server that is expandable, so that it can adequately service large amounts of traffic.

Unfortunately, when vendors use the phrase "secure web server," they almost always are referring to a web server that implements the SSL cryptographic protocol. These protocols allow web browsers and servers to exchange information without the risk of eavesdropping by parties with access to the messages in transit. Such encryption is widely regarded as a prerequisite for commerce on the Internet.

As this book demonstrates, while cryptographic protocols are certainly useful for protecting information that is sent over the Internet from eavesdropping, they are not strictly necessary for web security, nor are they sufficient to ensure it. Many of the most dramatic computer security problems of recent years involved web servers that implemented cryptographic protocols: the attackers simply stole the credit card numbers *after* they had been decrypted by the web server and stored in a relational database.

To avoid confusion, this book uses the term *cryptographically enabled web server*, rather than "secure web server," to describe a web server that implements cryptographic protocols. As we'll see, web security requires far more than mere cryptographic protection against simple eavesdropping.

impact of various choices—figures that are devilishly hard to pin down. How do you calculate the risk that an attacker will be able to obtain system administrator privileges on your web server? Does this risk increase over time, as new security vulnerabilities are discovered, or does it decrease over time, as the vulnerabilities are publicized and corrected? Does a well-maintained system become less secure or more secure over time? And how do you calculate the likely damages of a successful penetration? Unfortunately, few statistical, scientific studies have been performed on these questions. Many people think they know the answers to these questions, but research has shown that people badly estimate risk based on personal experience.

Because of the difficulty inherent in risk analysis, another approach for securing computers has emerged in recent years called *best practices*, or *due care*. This approach consists of a series of recommendations, procedures, and policies that are generally accepted within the community of security practitioners to give organizations a reasonable level of overall security and risk mitigation at a reasonable cost. Best practices can be thought of as "rules of thumb" for implementing sound security measures.

The best practices approach is not without its problems. The biggest problem is that there really is no one set of "best practices" that is applicable to all web sites and web users. The best practices for a web site that manages financial information might have similarities to the best practices for a web site that publishes a community newsletter, but the financial web site would likely have additional security measures.

Following best practices does not assure that your system will not suffer a security-related incident. Most best practices require that an organization's security office monitor the Internet for news of new attacks and download patches from vendors when they are made available. But even if you follow this regimen, an attacker might still be able to use a novel, unpublished attack to compromise your computer system.

The very idea that tens of thousands of organizations could or even should implement the "best" techniques available to secure their computers is problematical. The "best" techniques available are simply not appropriate or cost-effective for all organizations. Many organizations that claim to be following best practices are actually adopting the minimum standards commonly used for securing systems. In practice, most best practices really aren't.

We recommend a combination of risk analysis and best practices. Starting from a body of best practices, an educated designer should evaluate risks and trade-offs, and pick reasonable solutions for a particular configuration and management. Web servers should be hosted on isolated machines, and configured with an operating system and software providing the minimally-required functionality. The operators should be vigilant for changes, keep up-to-date on patches, and prepare for the unexpected. Doing this well takes a solid understanding of how the Web works, and what happens when it doesn't work. This is the approach that we will explain in the chapters that follow.

In this chapter:
- History and Terminology
- A Packet's Tour of the Web
- Who Owns the Internet?

## CHAPTER 2

The Architecture of the World Wide Web

In this chapter, we'll look at the technological underpinnings of The World Wide Web and of the Internet, the computer network on which the Web is based.

Before we begin our detailed discussion of web security, it is important to explain the basic mechanics of how the Internet and the Web work. It's also important to introduce the terminology that this book uses. And finally, to understand where the Web is today, it's useful to review the history of basic networking and the Internet.

History and Terminology

The success of the Internet has been nothing short of phenomenal. It's difficult to remember that the Internet is more than 25 years old and that the Web has existed for more than a decade. Although it's increasingly difficult to remember what business was like in the age before the Internet, the vast majority of today's Internet users have had email and dialup access to the World Wide Web for less than five years, and more than half probably gained their first access during the last 18 months.

It's easy to attribute the success of the Internet and the Web to a combination of market need, determinism, and consumerism. It's possible to argue that the critical mass of reasonably powerful desktop computers, reasonably fast modems, and reasonably sophisticated computer users made it inevitable that something like the Web would be deployed in the mid-1990s and that it would gain mass appeal. The world was ripe for the Web.

It's also possible to argue that the Web was pushed on the world by companies including IBM, Cisco, Dell, and Compaq—companies that engaged in huge advertising campaigns designed to convince business leaders that they would fail if they did not go online. Certainly, the apparent success of a large number of venture capital-financed Internet startups such as Amazon.com, Yahoo, and VeriSign helped to create a climate of fear among many "old economy" CEOs at the end of the 20th century; the rapid growth of the Internet-based firms, and their astonishing valuations by Wall Street, made many firms feel that their only choice for continued survival was to go online.

But such arguments are almost certainly flawed. It is a mistake to attribute the success of the Internet and the Web to a combination of timing and market forces. After all, the Internet was just one of many large-scale computer networks that were deployed in the 1970s, 80s, and 90s—and it was never considered the network "most likely to succeed." Instead, for many years most industry watchers were placing their bets on a network called the Open System Interconnection (OSI). As examples, IBM and HP spent hundreds of millions of dollars developing OSI products; OSI was mandated by the U.S. government, which even in the 1990s saw the Internet and TCP/IP as a transitional step.

Likewise, it was hardly preordained that the World Wide Web, with its HyperText Transfer Protocol (HTTP) and HyperText Markup Language (HTML) would become the world's universal information library at the start of the 21st century. The last thirty years have seen dozens of different information retrieval and hypertext systems come and go, from Ted Nelson's Xanadu (circa 1960!), to the Gopher and Archie networks of the early 1990s, to the Z39.50 "Information Retrieval: Application Service Definition and Protocol Specification" that was being widely deployed by the Library of Congress and other organizations when the Web first showed up.

In our opinion, the fact that the Internet and the Web have been so tremendously successful is not the result of marketing or timing, but largely a result of their design—a design that was technically superior to its competitors, extraordinarily open to developers, easy for people to use, and free for the taking.

Building the Internet

The Internet dates back to the late 1960s. Funded by the Advanced Research Projects Agency (ARPA) of the U.S. Department of Defense, the goal of the network was to develop robust packet switching technology. As such, it is probably the most successful project that ARPA has ever funded.

Packet switching started with the simple goal of making telephone and teletype networks more reliable. Imagine that you had a military command center, Alpha, and two outlying bases, Bravo and Charlie (see Figure 2-1). Now imagine that each of these bases has telephone lines running between them, but the lines between Alpha and Bravo travel over a bridge. An enemy wanting to disrupt communications might try bombing the bridge to disrupt the communications. In theory, a packet-switched network would be able to detect this sort of attack and automatically re-establish communications between Alpha and Bravo by way of the lines connecting both bases with command center Charlie.

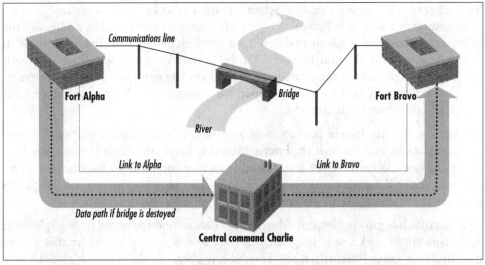

Figure 2-1. *Packet switching was developed to allow computers on a network to communicate with each other even if the direct connections between two computers are rendered inoperative*

This sort of self-healing network seems obvious today, but it wasn't in 1966 when work on the ARPA packet-switched network started. Back then, phone lines basically went point-to-point, and a telephone conversation used up an entire channel. With such a network, the only way for commanders at Alpha and Bravo to communicate, if their phone lines were down, would be for an operator at base Charlie to manually link together two trunk lines.

Packets and postcards

Packet switching solves the problem of connecting different parts of a network even when direct communication lines are disrupted. In a packet-switched network, every piece of information that travels over the network, be it a simple email message or an hour-long streaming video, is divided into compact pieces called *packets*. In addition to the data that it carries, each packet contains the address of its source and the address of its destination. These addresses are the key to making the packet-switched network operate properly.

You can think of a packet as a postcard, because each packet contains a little bit of information as well as the address of its intended destination and the address of the computer that sent the packet (also called the *source address*). Each card also contains a sequence number, so if the cards arrive out of sequence they can be read in the proper order.*

---

* This metaphor dates back to Dr. Vint Cerf who is widely credited with being one of the Internet's founders.

To return to our military example, when a computer at base Alpha wishes to communicate with a system at Bravo, it creates a few packets that have the address of the Bravo computers and sends them down the direct link between the two computers. If the link between Alpha and Bravo is disrupted, the computers at Alpha automatically send the packets to the computers at Charlie. The computers at Charlie examine the packets, see that they are destined for computers at Bravo, and resend the packets to their correct destination.

It turns out that the idea of packets as little postcards is an extremely apt metaphor, because packets hop through the Internet the way postcards move through the U.S. Postal Service. As each packet gets passed from one computer to another, the computer receiving the packet picks it up, reads the destination address, and then passes the packet to the next computer on the way to the packet's destination.

The Internet has grown a lot since the first packets were transmitted in 1969, but the basic concept of packet switching remains the same. Basically, the Internet is a huge machine that takes Internet packets created anywhere on the network and delivers them to their intended destination. Everything else is details.

Protocols

For computers on the Internet to be able to get packets to their intended destinations, they need to communicate with each other. Similar to how people trying to communicate with each other need to speak the same *language*, computers or other machines trying to communicate with each other need to use the same (or compatible) *protocols*. Protocols specify all of the details of how systems (hardware and software) communicate and with what means.

Today's Internet uses thousands of different protocols at different points. There are protocols for very low-level details, such as how two computers attached to the same wire can determine whose turn it is to send data, and there are protocols for very high-level details, such as how to transfer $50 in anonymous digital cash from one person's bank account to another.

The most fundamental protocols on the Internet govern how the Internet itself functions—that is, they control the format of packets and how packets are moved from one computer to another. This protocol is the Internet Protocol, sometimes called IP, but more often (and somewhat erroneously) called the IP Protocol.

IP is an evolving protocol. The current version, IPv4, has been in use since 1983. A new version, IPv6, was developed in the 1990s and is slowly being deployed. The primary advantage of IPv6 is that it provides for addressing many more individual computers than IPv4. While the two protocols are not strictly compatible with each other, it is possible for the two protocols to interoperate.

So how big are these packets, anyway? On the Internet of 2001 the average packet is between 400 and 600 bytes long; packets rarely exceed 1500 bytes in length—the limit imposed by the ubiquitous Ethernet local area network technology. Thus, packets are quite small; an email message that's a few screens long might not fit into fewer than five or six packets. The way that data is divided up and reassembled is specified by higher layers of the Internet Protocol. Email, web pages, and files are typically sent using the Transmission Control Protocol (TCP/IP), which is optimized for efficiently transmitting large blocks of information without error. But while TCP/IP works well for transmitting web pages, it's not optimal for streaming media, such as sending audio and video. These applications typically rely on the User Datagram Protocol (UDP), a protocol that allows applications to control the transmission and reception of information packet-by-packet.

Hosts, gateways, and firewalls

Over the past thirty years, the people who build and use the Internet have created a precise but at times confusing terminology for describing various network pieces.

Computers can be connected to one or more networks. Computers that are connected to at least one network are called *hosts*. A *computer network* is a collection of computers that are physically and logically connected together to exchange information. Figure 2-2 shows a network with several hosts and a *router* that connects the network to the Internet.

Firewalls are special kinds of computers that are connected to two networks but that selectively forward information. There are essentially two kinds of firewalls. A *packet-filtering firewall* decides packet-by-packet whether a packet should be copied from one network to another. Firewalls can also be built from application-level *proxies*, which operate at a higher level. Because they can exercise precise control over what information is passed between two networks, firewalls are thought to improve computer security.*

The client/server model

Most Internet services are based on the *client/server* model. Under this model, one program, called the *client,* requests service from another program, called the *server.* For example, if you read your mail on a desktop computer using a program such as Eudora or Outlook Express, the desktop mail program is a *mail client*, and the computer from which it downloads your email runs a program called a *mail server*, as

---

* Firewall construction is difficult to get correct. Furthermore, organizations often forget about internal security after a firewall is installed. And firewalls generally do nothing to protect against insider misuse, viruses, or other internal problems. Thus, many firewalls only provide the illusion of better security, and the networks of many organizations are actually *less* secure several months after a firewall is installed, because the network's users and administrators grow careless.

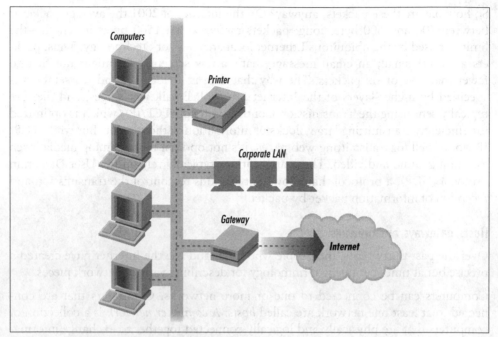

Figure 2-2. A simple corporate network with several hosts connected by a gateway to the greater network

shown in Figure 2-3. Often, the words "client" and "server" are used to describe the computers as well, although this terminology is technically incorrect: the computer on which the mail server resides might be a single-purpose computer, or it might run many other servers at the same time.

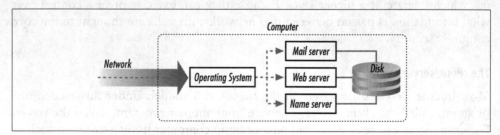

Figure 2-3. Servers are programs that provide special services, such as email, to other computers

The vast majority of client software is run on desktop computers,* such as machines running the Windows, Linux, or Mac OS operating systems, and the majority of

---

* It's tempting to call these personal computers, but the average computer in use today within homes is shared by whole families, and the computers in universities or businesses may be shared by dozens of users running distributed services. We may lapse in places and call these systems "PCs," but bear in mind that they are usually shared resources—and this introduces security concerns that a real PC doesn't have.

server software tends to run on computers running a version of the Unix or Windows operating system. But these operating system distinctions are not too useful because it is also possible to run servers on personal computers, and most computers that run network servers also support numerous clients that are used to request information from still other machines.

Weaving the Web

The World Wide Web was invented in 1990 by Tim Berners-Lee while at the Swiss-based European Laboratory for Particle Physics (CERN). The original purpose of the Web was to give physicists a convenient way to publish their papers on the Internet. There were also several databases at CERN, such as the laboratory's phone list, which Berners-Lee wanted to make easily accessible over the Internet.

In 1990 there were plenty of ways of moving information over the Internet and accessing remote databases. For example, a physicist who wanted to download a paper from Stanford's Linear Accelerator (SLAC) could use the FTP (File Transfer Protocol) protocol and software to connect to the computer *ftp.slac.stanford.edu*. The physicist could then use FTP's reasonably cryptic commands named *ls, cd, binary,* and *get* to find the particular directory that he wanted, find the particular file, and finally download it. Once the file was on his computer, the physicist could use various obscure Unix commands such as *dvi2ps* and *lpr* to convert the file into a format that could be handled by his computer's printer. And if our fictional physicist wanted to look up the phone number or email address of an associate at SLAC, there was a program named *finger* that could search the SLAC administrative directory.

The genius of Tim Berners-Lee was twofold. First, Berners-Lee realized that the growing collection of information on the Internet needed a single addressing scheme, so that any piece of information could be named with an unambiguous address. All other successful large-scale communications systems have these kinds of addresses; for the telephone system, it is the country code, city code, and phone number. For the postal system, we use a person's name, street address, city, state, postal code, and country. For the Internet, Berners-Lee created the *URL*, the Uniform Resource Locator. URLs are familiar to anyone who has used the Internet. As an example, consider *http://www.whitehouse.gov/index.html*. A URL consists of a protocol (in this case, *http:*), the name of a computer (*www.whitehouse.gov*), followed by the name of a document or an object on that computer (*index.html*).

The second great insight of Berners-Lee was the realization that Internet addresses could be embedded within other documents. In this way, documents on the Internet could contain references, or *links*, to other documents. This desire to link information together was only natural for a system that was designed to publish physics articles, as one article will typically cite several others. By making the links URLs, and then devising an unobtrusive technique for embedding these links into text, Berners-Lee created a system that could be used both to present information and to present indexes or lists of other information repositories. That is, the power of the URL and the *Hyper-Text Markup Language* (HTML) is that people are free to create their own web pages and link them together, all without prior consent or approval.

Of course, the Web is more than simply two good ideas; it is software. To prove his ideas, Berners-Lee created two programs: a web server, which received requests for documents over the Internet and served them up, and a web browser, which displayed those documents on a computer's screen.[*]

The Web might have remained an academic curiosity were it not for the National Center for Supercomputer Applications (NCSA) at the University of Illinois at Champaign-Urbana. There, a team headed by Mark Andreessen developed a web browser for the Macintosh, Windows, and Unix operating systems named Mosaic. Jim Clark, a successful Silicon Valley businessman, realized the commercial potential for the new technology and started a company called Mosaic Communications to commercialize it. Clark asked Mark Andreessen and his team to join Mosaic. The company created a web browser with the code name Mozilla. As a result of trademark conflicts, Clark's company was soon renamed Netscape Communications and the web browser was renamed Netscape Navigator.

A Packet's Tour of the Web

The easiest way to explain the functioning of the Web today is to explore what happens when you start a web browser and attempt to view a page on the Internet.

Booting Up Your PC

Every computer[†] manufactured today is equipped with a small memory chip that holds its information even when the computer is turned off. When you turn on your computer, the computer's microprocessor starts executing a small program that is stored on this memory chip. The program is called the computer's Basic Input Output System, or BIOS. The BIOS has the ability to display simple information on the computer's screen, to read keystrokes from the keyboard, to determine how much memory is in the computer, and to copy the first few blocks of the computer's disk drive into memory and execute them.

---

[*] As an interesting historical sidenote, Berners-Lee developed all of these programs on his workstation, a black cube manufactured by NeXT Computers, Inc. Without the easy-to-program NeXT operating system, the descendant of which is the Macintosh MacOS X, the Web might not have been created.

[†] Most people on the Web today are using Windows-based computers, so this example will use them as well. However, much of what is said here about Windows-based computers applies in approximately the same way to computers running Unix or Linux operating systems, Macintosh computers, and a variety of other systems.

The first few blocks of the computer's hard drive contain a program called the *bootstrap loader*.* The bootstrap loader reads in the first part of the computer's operating system from storage (on a disk or CD-ROM), which loads in the rest of the computer's operating system, which starts a multitude of individual programs running. Some of these programs configure the computer's hardware to run the operating system, others perform basic housekeeping, and still others are run for historical reasons—whether that is to assure compatibility with previous generations of operating systems, or because developers at the company that created the operating system forgot to take the programs out of the system before it was shipped.

The computer may finally prompt you for a username and password. This information is used to "log in" (*authenticate*) to the computer—that is, to set up the computer for a particular user's preferences and personal information, and possibly to gain access to network resources shared with other computers local to your organization. Finally, the computer starts up a graphical user interface, which displays the computer's *desktop*. Simson's desktop computer's screen is shown in Figure 2-4.

PC to LAN to Internet

What your computer knows about the Internet after it boots depends on how your computer is connected to the Internet. A *computer network* is a collection of computers that are physically and logically connected together to exchange information. To exchange information with other computers in an orderly fashion, each computer has to have a unique address on each network where it has a direct connection. Addresses on a computer network are conceptually similar to telephone numbers on the telephone network.

A large number of people who use the Internet today do so using a dial-up connection and the Point-to-Point Protocol (PPP). Their computers use a device called a *modem* for dialing the telephone and communicating with a remote system. Other forms of connection, including DSL† and ISDN,‡ also use a modem to connect to remote systems using telephone lines.

If your computer accesses the Internet by dialing a modem, your computer probably does not have an address assigned until it actually connects to the network.§ If your

---

* The phrase *bootstrap loader* comes from the expression "to pull oneself up by one's bootstraps." Starting a computer operating system is a tricky thing to do, because the only way to load a program into a computer's memory is by using another program, and when the computer starts operating it doesn't have a program in memory.

† Digital Subscriber Loop, a technology for providing high-speed data connections on ordinary telephone lines.

‡ Integrated Services Digital Network, another technology for providing data connections on telephone lines.

§ These simple generalizations are frequently more complex in practice. For example, some Internet service providers assign permanent addresses to dialup users. Others are using dialup protocols such as PPP over local area networks—a technique called Point-to-Point Protocol over Ethernet, or PPPoF. The users have the appearance of "dialing" the Internet, but their computers are in fact always connected.

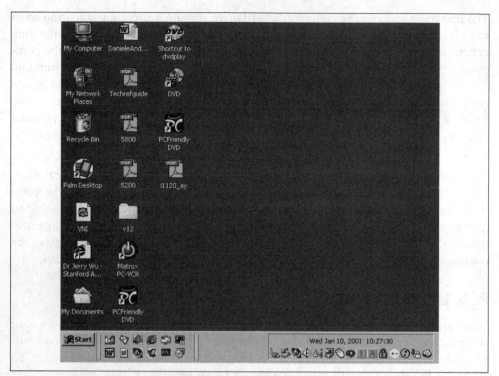

Figure 2-4. When your operating system starts up, the computer doesn't know anything about the Internet

computer is connected to a *local area network* (LAN) at an office or in many homes, then your computer probably has an IP address and the ability to transmit and receive packets on the LAN at any time.

Dialing up the Internet

Computers that use dial-up Internet connections have two distinct modes of operation. When they start up, they are not connected to the Internet. To connect to the Internet, the computer runs a program called a *dialer*. The dialer sends codes to the computer's modem that cause the modem to go "off hook," dial the phone, and initiate a data connection with the remote system.

When the modem of the local computer can exchange information with the remote system, the dialer starts the PPP subsystem. PPP is a sophisticated protocol that lets two computers that are on either end of a communications link exchange packets. First, PPP determines the capabilities of the system on each end. When dialing up an Internet service provider, the next thing that typically happens is that the called system asks the calling system to provide a valid username and password. If the username and password provided are correct, the called system will assign the caller an

IP address. From this point on, the two computers can exchange IP packets as if they were on the same network.

Connected by LAN

Computers that are connected to the Internet by a LAN typically do not need to "dial up the Internet," because they are already connected. Instead, computers with permanent connections usually have preassigned addresses; when they wish to send a packet over the Internet, they simply send the packet over the LAN to the nearest gateway.* When the gateway receives a packet, it retransmits the packet along the desired path.

The Walden Network

Most of the examples in this book are based on the Walden Network, a small local area network that Simson created for his house on Walden Street in Cambridge.

The Walden Street network was built with several computers connected to a 10/100 Ethernet hub. Every computer in the house has an Ethernet interface card, and each card has an IP address on the home LAN. The computers include Simson's desktop computer, his wife's computer, and a small server in their living room that they also call Walden.†

Walden the computer is a rack-mounted PC running FreeBSD, a Unix-like operating system that's similar to Linux and Sun's Solaris. Walden has a pair of 75-gigabyte hard drives on which Simson stores all of his files. The computer actually has three Ethernet cards; one has an IP address on the network that communicates with the cable modem, one has an IP address on the network that communicates with the DSL bridge, and the third has an IP address for the internal LAN. The computer sends and receives email on the Internet. Walden runs the web server that houses his home page *http://www.simson.net/*. Finally, Walden is a firewall: it isolates the home network from the Internet at large. Figure 2-5 shows a schematic picture of the Walden network.

As we hinted previously, the Walden network actually has two connections to the Internet. The primary connection is a cable modem. The cable modem is pretty fast: in Simson's testing, he got roughly 600 kilobits per second (kbps) in both directions. This is nearly 20 times faster than a traditional dial-up modem. The second connection is a DSL line. The DSL line is slower—it only runs at 200 kbps—and it costs more than three times as much ($150/month, versus $41.50/month).

---

* Some computers on a LAN use the Dynamic Host Configuration Protocol (DHCP) to get a dynamically assigned IP address when they start up or before they need to use the network.

† Gene also has an Ethernet LAN in his house, along with a wireless network. However, his wife won't let him put a computer in the living room. Yet.

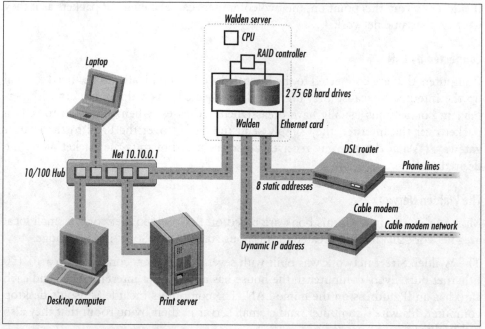

Figure 2-5. Simson's home network

So why have the DSL line? The most important reason has to do with Internet addressing. Simson's cable company gives him what's called a *dynamically assigned IP address*. This means that the IP address that his computer gets from the cable modem can change at any time. (In fact, it seems to change about once every two or three months.) For the DSL line, he pays extra money to get a *static IP address*, meaning that the IP address does not change.

But there is another reason why Simson has two Internet connections. That reason is *redundancy*. In the two years since he has had his cable modem, he's lost service on more than a dozen occasions. Usually lost service was no big deal, but sometimes it was a major inconvenience. And when he started running his own mail server, losing service resulted in mail's being bounced. This caused a huge problem for him—and to make matters worse, the cable modem company would never answer his questions or tell him why the service was down or when service would be restored. In the end, Simson decided that if he wanted to have a reliable service, he would need to pay for that reliability the same way that big companies do: by obtaining redundant Internet connections from separate companies, and then designing his network so that if one connection went down, the other connection would be used in its place.*

---

* One complication of having multiple Internet service providers is dealing with multiple IP addresses. Each ISP will typically give their customers IP addresses particular to the ISP. (Large organizations handle the complexity by getting their own IP address space and having this space "announced" by their upstream providers.) On the Walden Street network, this issue is resolved by putting *both* sets of IP addresses on the Walden computer and using DNS techniques so that incoming connections arrive through the appropriate network.

We've gone into this level of detail because the Walden network is actually quite similar to the networks operated by many small businesses. When the computer on Simson's desktop creates a packet bound for the outside network, it puts the packet on the home LAN. This packet is picked up by the gateway, which retransmits the packets out to the Internet. When packets come back from the Internet, the cable modem or the DSL modem transmits the packet to the gateway, and from there to the LAN, and from the LAN to his desktop.

The Domain Name Service

There's a very important part of the Internet's infrastructure that hasn't been discussed until now—the machinery that converts Internet domain names that people use (e.g., *www.aol.com* or *www.simson.net*) into the IP address that the Internet's underlying transport network can use (e.g., 205.188.160.121 or 64.7.15.234). The machinery that does this is called the *Domain Name Service* (DNS).

Think of the DNS as a huge phone book that lists every computer that resides on the network. But whereas a traditional phone book has a list of names and phone numbers, the DNS has a list of computer names and IP addresses.

For example, the internal phone book for a small organization might look like this:

```
Front desk              617-555-1212
Fax                     x101
Mail Room               x102
Publications            x103
```

The DNS for that same organization might look like this:

```
192.168.0.1             router.company.com
192.168.0.2             faxserver.company.com
192.168.0.3             mail.company.com
192.168.0.4             www.company.com
```

In this example, the organization's domain is *company.com*, and the names *router*, *faxserver*, *mail* and *www* represent computers operating within that domain.*

It's easy to get confused between local area networks and domains, because computers on the same local area network are usually in the same domain, and vice versa.

But this doesn't have to be the case. For example, the company in the previous example might pay for a large ISP to run its web server. In this case, the IP address

---

* This example, and most of the other examples in this book, draws its IP addresses from the set of unroutable IP addresses that were established by the Internet Engineering Task Force in RFC 1918. These IP addresses are designed for test networks. Increasingly, they are also used by organizations for internal addressing behind a firewall or NAT (Network Address Translation) converter. The three blocks of unroutable IP addresses are 10.0.0.0–10.255.255.255, 172.16.0.0–172.31.255.255, and 192.168.0.0–192.168.255.255.

for the web server would probably be on a different local area network, and the DNS table for the organization might look like this instead:

```
192.168.0.1        router.company.com
192.168.0.2        faxserver.company.com
192.168.0.3        mail.company.com
172.16.10.100      www.company.com
```

DNS wasn't part of the original Internet design. For the first ten years of operation, the Internet was small enough so that all of the host names and IP addresses could fit in a single file—a file that was aptly named *HOSTS.TXT*. But by the mid-1980s this file had grown to be tens of thousands of lines long, and it needed to be changed on a daily basis. The Internet's creators realized that instead of having all of the hosts located in a single file, the network itself needed to provide some sort of host name resolution service.

Instead of a single centralized host service, the Internet uses a distributed database. This system allows each organization to be responsible for its own piece of the global namespace. The system is based upon programs called *nameservers* that translate Internet host names (e.g., *www.company.com*) to IP addresses (e.g., 172.16.10.100).

How DNS works

Host name resolution is the process by which computers on the Internet translate Internet host names to IP addresses. When your computer needs to translate a host name to an IP address, it creates a special kind of packet called a *DNS request* and sends the packet to a nearby nameserver; your system is normally configured (manually or dynamically during dialup) to know of several nameservers.

The nameserver that your computer contacts will sometimes know the answer to the request. If so, the DNS response is sent back to your computer. If the nameserver doesn't have the information, it will usually attempt to discover the answer and then report it back to your system.

Let's see how this works in practice. To do this, we'll use the *ping* program on a Windows desktop PC and the *tcpdump* network monitoring tool on a Unix server. The *ping* program sends out an ICMP ECHO packet to the remote system. The Unix *tcpdump* program displays packets as they move across the local area network.

For example, let's say we wish to ping the web server at the Internet Corporation for Assigned Names and Numbers (ICANN). (We'll discuss ICANN in some detail in the last section of this chapter.) From the Windows desktop, we might type:

```
C:\>ping www.icann.org

Pinging www.icann.org [192.0.34.65] with 32 bytes of data:

Reply from 192.0.34.65: bytes=32 time=101ms TTL=235
Reply from 192.0.34.65: bytes=32 time=99ms TTL=235
Reply from 192.0.34.65: bytes=32 time=100ms TTL=235
```

```
Reply from 192.0.34.65: bytes=32 time=99ms TTL=235

Ping statistics for 192.0.34.65:
    Packets: Sent = 4, Received = 4, Lost = 0 (0% loss),
Approximate round trip times in milli-seconds:
    Minimum = 96ms, Maximum =  104ms, Average =  100ms

C:\>
```

We can watch the packets as they flow across the local area network using the program *tcpdump*:

```
21:07:38.483377 desk.nitroba.com.2001 > walden.domain:  1+ A? www.icann.org. (31)
21:07:39.986319 desk.nitroba.com.2001 > walden.domain:  1+ A? www.icann.org. (31)
21:07:40.196762 b.domain > desk.nitroba.com.2001:  1* 1/6/9 A www.icann.org (365)
21:07:40.202501 desk.nitroba.com > www.icann.org: icmp: echo request
21:07:40.303782 www.icann.org > desk.nitroba.com: icmp: echo reply
21:07:41.206051 desk.nitroba.com > www.icann.org: icmp: echo request
21:07:41.304950 www.icann.org > desk.nitroba.com: icmp: echo reply
21:07:42.210855 desk.nitroba.com > www.icann.org: icmp: echo request
21:07:42.310785 www.icann.org > desk.nitroba.com: icmp: echo reply
21:07:43.215661 desk.nitroba.com > www.icann.org: icmp: echo request
21:07:43.315358 www.icann.org > desk.nitroba.com: icmp: echo reply
```

Each line of this printout corresponds to a packet sent across the local area network. Each column contains specific information about each packet. Let's explore the contents of the first line to understand the columns. Here it is:

```
21:07:38.483377 desk.nitroba.com.2001 > walden.domain:  1+ A? www.icann.org. (31)
```

The columns represent:

- The time (21:07:38.483377 on the first line corresponds to almost half a second past 9:07:38 p.m.).
- The computer that transmitted the packet (*desk.nitroba.com* is the desktop computer).
- The port from which the packet was sent. (In this case, port *2001*. This port was randomly chosen by the desktop computer and has no special significance; its sole purpose is to allow replies from the domain server to be sent to the correct program.)
- The computer to which the packet was sent (*walden*).
- The port on the receiving computer (in this case, the port is *domain*, the port of the DNS nameserver).
- The contents of the packet (*1+ A?* indicates a DNS request for an A record, which is the type of record that relates host names to IP addresses).

With this information, we can now decode the output from the *tcpdump* command. In the first line, a DNS request is sent from the desktop to *walden*. Walden doesn't respond to this request, and 1.5 seconds later another request is sent. This time

Walden responds with an A record containing the IP address of *www.icann.org*. After this response from the nameserver, Walden is no longer directly involved in the communications. Instead, the computer sends *www.icann.org* four ICMP ECHO REQUEST packets, and *www.icann.org* sends back four ICMP ECHO REPLY packets.

Although this seems complicated, what is actually going on behind the scenes is even more complicated. Look again at the first two lines. When *desk* asks *walden* for the IP address of *www.icann.org*, *walden* doesn't know the answer. But rather than replying "I don't know," *walden* attempts to find the answer. When the second request comes in, *walden* is deep in a conversation with a number of other computers on the Internet to find out precisely where *www.icann.org* resides. A few tenths of a second later, the conversation is finished and Walden knows the answer, which it then reports back to *desk*.

When *walden*'s nameserver starts up, all it knows is the addresses of the root nameservers. When the request comes in for *www.icann.org*, *walden*'s nameserver goes to the root nameserver and asks for the address of a nameserver that serves the *org* domain. *walden* then contacts that nameserver, asking for a nameserver that knows how to resolve the *icann.org* address. Finally, *walden* contacts the *icann.org* nameserver, asking for the address of *www.icann.org*.

Engaging the Web

When we type the address *http://www.icann.org/* into the web browser, we instruct the web browser to fetch the home page of the ICANN web server. As shown in the previous example, the first thing that the computer needs to do to reach a remote web server is to learn the IP address of the web server.

Once the IP address of the remote machine is known, the desktop computer attempts to open up a TCP/IP connection to the web server. This TCP/IP connection can be thought of as a two-way pipe: the connection allows the computer to send information to the remote system and to receive a response.

Opening a TCP/IP connection is a three-step process. First, the desktop computer sends a special packet (packet #1) called a *SYN packet* to the remote system. This SYN packet requests that a TCP/IP connection be opened. Once again, we can eavesdrop on the communications with the *tcpdump* packet monitor:*

```
packet #1:
21:54:28.956695 desk.nitroba.com.6636 > www.icann.org.http: S 2897261633:
2897261633(0) win 16384 <mss 1460,nop,nop,sackOK> (DF)
```

The (DF) at the end of the line indicates that this packet has the *don't fragment* option set. If the remote system is able to open the TCP/IP connection, it responds

---

* To simplify reading the output from the *tcpdump* program, we have inserted a blank line between each packet. To simplify the discussion, we've labeled each packet with a packet number.

with a SYN/ACK packet (packet #2). When the computer receives this SYN/ACK packet, it sends an ACK packet (packet #3). This three-packet exchange is known as a *three-way handshake*, and it is the way that every TCP/IP connection is started.

```
packet #2:
21:54:29.039502 www.icann.org.http > desk.nitroba.com.6636: S 3348123210:
3348123210(0) ack 2897261634 win 32120 <mss 1460,nop,nop,sackOK> (DF)
```

```
packet #3:
21:54:29.039711 desk.nitroba.com.6636 > www.icann.org.http: . ack 1 win 17520 (DF)
```

In the first line, packet #1 is sent from the computer's port 6636 to the remote system's "http" port. (Once again, the fact that the packet came from port 6636 has no actual significance; when a computer initiates a TCP/IP connection to a remote system, it uses a randomly-selected port, usually between 1024 and 65535.) This first packet contains a randomly-generated number, in this case 2897261633, which is known as the TCP/IP sequence number. The remote system responds with packet #2, a SYN carrying a sequence number of its own (3348123210). Finally, the desktop system sends packet #3, the ACK packet.

After the TCP/IP connection is set up, the desktop computer sends a single packet that contains the HTTP request:

```
packet #4:
21:54:29.041008 desk.nitroba.com.6636 > www.icann.org.http: P 1:304(303) ack 1 win
17520 (DF)
```

This packet consists of 303 bytes. The "P" indicates that the TCP/IP push option is set, which has the effect of telling the destination system (*www.icann.org*) that the data should be immediately transmitted to the receiving program on the remote system.

By using another Unix tool (the *strings*(1) command), it's possible to look inside the packet and display the text that it contains:*

```
GET / HTTP/1.0
Host: www.icann.org
Accept-Encoding: gzip, deflate
Accept: image/gif, image/x-xbitmap, image/jpeg, image/pjpeg, application/vnd.ms-
powerpoint, application/vnd.ms-excel, application/msword, */*
User-Agent: Mozilla/4.0 (compatible; MSIE 5.01; Windows NT 5.0)
Accept-Language: en-us
```

The first line of this packet indicates that it is requesting the root HTML page from the remote web server using HTTP protocol 1.0. The second line indicates that we wish to connect to the computer *www.icann.org* (the *Host:* line is useful when multiple

---

* If you count up the letters in the previous code fragment, you will see that there are only 289 characters. But there are six lines with text and one blank link, and each line is terminated by a carriage return/line feed pair. Adding 289+7+7=303, which is the number of bytes in the packet.

domains are served from a single IP address). Explanation of the remaining lines is beyond the scope of this discussion.

After this packet requests a page from the web server, the web server sends a stream of packets containing the web page back to the local computer. As the data is received, it is acknowledged by a series of ACK packets:

packet #5:
```
21:54:29.124031 www.icann.org.http > desk.nitroba.com.6636: . ack 304 win 31817 (DF)
```

packet #6:
```
21:54:29.132202 www.icann.org.http > desk.nitroba.com.6636: . 1:1461(1460) ack 304
win 32120 (DF)
```

packet #7:
```
21:54:29.258989 desk.nitroba.com.6636 > www.icann.org.http: . ack 1461 win 17520 (DF)
```

packet #8:
```
21:54:29.348034 www.icann.org.http > desk.nitroba.com.6636: . 1461:2921(1460) ack 304
win 32120 (DF)
```

packet #9:
```
21:54:29.348414 desk.nitroba.com.6636 > www.icann.org.http: . ack 2921 win 17520 (DF)
```

packet #10:
```
21:54:29.349575 www.icann.org.http > desk.nitroba.com.6636: . 2921:4381(1460) ack 304
win 32120 (DF)
```

packet #11:
```
21:54:29.438365 www.icann.org.http > desk.nitroba.com.6636: . 4381:5841(1460) ack 304
win 32120 (DF)
```

packet #12:
```
21:54:29.438760 desk.nitroba.com.6636 > www.icann.org.http: . ack 5841 win 17520 (DF)
```

packet #13:
```
21:54:29.442387 www.icann.org.http > desk.nitroba.com.6636: . 5841:7301(1460) ack 304
win 32120 (DF)
```

packet #14:
```
21:54:29.442743 desk.nitroba.com.6636 > www.icann.org.http: . ack 7301 win 17520 (DF)
```

packet #15:
```
21:54:29.528037 www.icann.org.http > desk.nitroba.com.6636: . 7301:8761(1460) ack 304
win 32120 (DF)
```

packet #16:
```
21:54:29.529545 www.icann.org.http > desk.nitroba.com.6636: . 8761:10221(1460) ack
304 win 32120 (DF)
```

packet #17:
```
21:54:29.529918 www.icann.org.http > desk.nitroba.com.6636: FP 10221:10703(482) ack
304 win 32120 (DF)
```

packet #18:
```
21:54:29.529958 desk.nitroba.com.6636 > www.icann.org.http: . ack 10221 win 17520
(DF)
```

packet #19:
```
21:54:29.530133 desk.nitroba.com.6636 > www.icann.org.http: . ack 10704 win 17038
(DF)
```

packet #20:
```
21:54:29.550608 desk.nitroba.com.6636 > www.icann.org.http: F 304:304(0) ack 10704
win 17038 (DF)
```

packet #21:
```
21:54:29.630469 www.icann.org.http > dhcp103.walden.vineyard.net.31-11: . ack 305 win
32120 (DF)
```

If a portion of the transmitted data is not acknowledged within a certain period of time, the remote system automatically retransmits that data. Acknowledging data sent over the network in this fashion assures that all of the data arrives at the remote system even if the Internet is overloaded and dropping packets.

Notice that the packets #17 and #20 both have the "F" bit set. Here the "F" means FIN. When a packet has its FIN bit set, this tells the remote system that no more data will be sent in that direction along the connection. Packet #17 sent from ICANN to *desk* says that the last byte sent is 10703 bytes into the data stream; *desk* then responds with packet #18, saying that it has processed through byte #10221, and packet #19, saying that it is ready for byte 10704. Of course, there will be no byte #10704, because the FIN has been sent.

This process repeats on packets #20 and #21. In packet #20, *desk* sends a packet to the remote system saying that 304 bytes have been sent and no more are coming. In packet #21, the remote system says that all of these bytes have been processed and it is ready for byte 305. Of course, that byte will not be coming either.

After packet #21 is sent, both sides have sent their FIN packets and both FIN packets have been acknowledged. The TCP/IP connection is presumed to be closed.

We can also look inside the contents of the packets that were sent from the ICANN web server to our desktop system. The first 30 lines look like this:

```
HTTP/1.1 200 OK
Date: Wed, 07 Feb 2001 02:54:29 GMT
Server: Apache/1.3.6 (Unix)  (Red Hat/Linux)
Last-Modified: Mon, 22 Jan 2001 01:10:54 GMT
ETag: "d183c-28c4-3a6b889e"
Accept-Ranges: bytes
Content-Length: 10436
Connection: close
Content-Type: text/html
<HTML>
<HEAD>
  <META NAME="GENERATOR" CONTENT="Adobe PageMill 3.0 Win">
```

```
<TITLE>ICANN | Home Page </TITLE>
<META CONTENT="text/html; charset=windows-1252" HTTP-EQUIV="Content-Type">
</HEAD>
<BODY BGCOLOR="#ffffff">
<P><CENTER><TABLE BORDER="0" CELLPADDING="0" CELLSPACING="2"
WIDTH="95%">
  <TBODY>
  <TR>
<TD WIDTH="12%"> </TD>
    <TD WIDTH="21%"><IMG SRC="/logos/icann-logo.gif" ALIGN="BOTTOM"
     ALT="ICANN Logo" HEIGHT="145" WIDTH="188" NATURALSIZEFLAG="0"></TD>
    <TD WIDTH="67%">
     <P><CENTER><STRONG><FONT SIZE="+2" FACE="Arial">The Internet
     Corporation <BR>
     for Assigned Names and Numbers</FONT></STRONG></CENTER></TD>
  </TR></TBODY>
</TABLE></CENTER></P>
<P><CENTER><HR NOSHADE SIZE="1" WIDTH="95%"><TABLE BORDER="0"
```

Finally, Figure 2-6 shows how the web page itself appears.

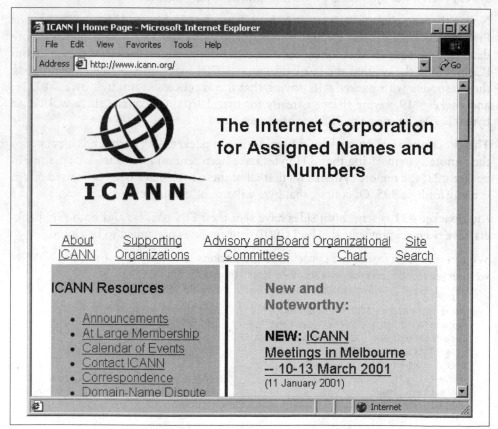

Figure 2-6. http://www.icann.org/

Who Owns the Internet?

Now that we've seen how the underlying Internet technology works, the next logical question to ask is, "Who do you complain to when the Internet stops working?" Another way of asking this question is, "Who runs the Internet?" And who owns it?

The Internet is a large, distributed network operated by millions of individuals and organizations. As such, it doesn't have a single owner—it has many of them. When your computer is connected to the Internet it literally becomes part of the network, so in a very real sense you are one of the Internet's owners. But don't get carried away: you only own a very small part.

Let's look at the various other "owners" of the Internet.

Your Local Internet Service Provider

There are many ways that you can connect to the Internet. You can use a dial-up modem, a DSL line, an ISDN connection, a cable modem, or even a wireless link through your cellular phone. But no matter what sort of digital pipe you use to make the connection, at the other end of the pipe there needs to be a computer that receives your packets and routes them to other computers on the network.

The organization that operates the equipment on the other side of your Internet connection is referred to as an Internet service provider (ISP). The first ISPs were universities and research labs. They provided Internet service for their employees, students, affiliates, and frequently friends and family of the system operators.

Over the past two decades, the world of ISPs has been transformed. In the late 1980s, before commercial use of the Internet was allowed, most ISPs were poorly-funded small businesses run by the early Internet entrepreneurs. In the 1990s some of these ISPs grew large enough on their own funds that they could service tens or hundreds of thousands of customers. Others arranged for outside funding. Still more ISPs were started by wealthy individuals, banks, or venture capital funds, all seeking to get in on the Internet gold rush.

Today many universities still provide Internet service to their staff and students, and there are thousands of relatively small ISPs that provide service to a few thousand customers. But by far the majority of people who use the Internet in the United States now get their Internet service from a large ISP. Some of these large ISPs are either owned outright or affiliated with existing telephone companies and cable TV companies.

It's convenient to think of ISPs as owning their own part of the Internet. That is, most ISPs operate equipment and telecommunications systems that provide Internet service. These machines are the ISP's responsibility and they are, for the most part, under the ISP's control. When they operate properly, the ISP makes money (in theory, at least). When these systems don't work, the ISP loses money, receives angry phone calls, and eventually loses customers.

A typical ISP might operate, own or lease some or all of the following systems:

- Domain nameservers, which translate host names to IP addresses.

- Web servers, which store the content of web pages and send them over the network when the information on the web pages is requested.

- Short and long distance data communications lines, which transmit Internet packets from one location to the other.

- Data centers, where the computers reside that run their portion of the Internet. (Data centers typically include equipment racks, cabling, power systems, air conditioning systems, and physical security systems. See Figure 2-7.)

- Network operations centers (NOCs), where the status and health of the network are monitored.

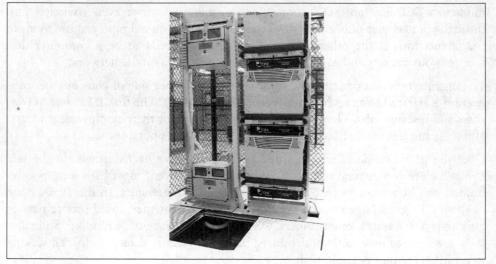

Figure 2-7. Two racks in a typical Internet data center (reprinted with permission of Switch and Data Corporation)

Network Access Points and Metropolitan Area Exchanges

For the Internet to function properly, packets must travel between ISPs. For example, the two ISPs serving the Walden network are AT&T, the cable ISP, and Megapath, the DSL ISP. But let's say that Simson wishes to send email to Debby, our editor at O'Reilly & Associates, which uses MCI WorldCom as its provider. There needs to be some place for the packets to travel from one of Simson's ISPs to O'Reilly's.

The easiest way for two ISPs to exchange Internet *traffic* with each other is for the ISPs to purchase a data circuit between a data center belonging to the first ISP and a data center belonging to the second ISP. But if more than a few ISPs wish to exchange traffic with each other, a much more cost-effective method is for the ISPs to rent space at a common location and to put multiple routers belonging to the different organizations on the same local area network.

In 1993, the National Science Foundation awarded MCI WorldCom a contract to set up a number of Network Access Points (NAPs) to facilitate communications between ISPs that were providing access to universities as part of the academic Internet. Since then, the number of Network Access Points has mushroomed. Two of the most successful are the Metropolitan Area Exchanges operated by MCI WorldCom in Northern Virginia (MAE East) and in San Jose (MAE West).

Once an ISP has rented space at a NAP or MAE and installed its equipment, two more important events need to take place before the ISP can exchange traffic. First, the ISP needs to lease or purchase one or more high-speed data circuits from the NAP or MAE to the ISP's own facilities. Second, the ISP needs to make a deal with one or more other ISPs to exchange the actual traffic. Such deals are referred to as either *peering agreements* or *transit agreements*.

Peering

Peering is the simplest way for two ISPs to interconnect. The two ISPs exchange electronic maps of each other's networks. Each ISP then programs its routers so that if the router receives a packet for the other ISP, the packet is automatically sent to the peering point and over the shared connection. Peering makes good financial and technical sense if two ISPs have a lot of users that typically access each other's services.* For example, in Cambridge, AT&T's cable modem network peers with the university networks for both MIT and Harvard. As a result, the round-trip time between the Walden network and the MIT network is less than 3 milliseconds:

```
walden% traceroute web.mit.edu
traceroute to web.mit.edu (18.7.21.70), 30 hops max, 40 byte packets
 1  24.147.16.1 (24.147.16.1)  2.309 ms  1.885 ms
 2  CMBRMA1-RTR01-CMBRMA1-RTR02.ne.mediaone.net (24.128.190.85)  3.394 ms  2.034 ms
 3  bsgsr01-srp4.rr.com (24.218.189.169)  2.481 ms  2.349 ms
 4  cmbrt01-srp3.rr.com (24.218.189.172)  2.391 ms  2.792 ms
 5  MIT-MEDIAONE.MIT.EDU (18.3.1.1)  2.692 ms  2.506 ms
 6  W92-RTR-1-BACKBONE.MIT.EDU (18.168.0.20)  3.499 ms  3.453 ms
 7  SALTICUS-PECKHAMAE.MIT.EDU (18.7.21.70) 3.245 ms 3.245 ms
walden%
```

The disadvantage of peering is that two ISPs that are in a peering agreement can only send traffic to each other that is destined for each other's network.

---

* Although the financial aspects of peering agreements are usually kept secret, they typically do not involve the exchange of money between the two peered ISPs. More frequently, peering agreements involve the exchange of favors between engineers or network architects at the ISPs—favors such as technical assistance, high-quality sushi dinners, or additional peering agreements.

Transit

The alternative to peering is called *transit*. You can think of transit as a promise between the two ISPs: the ISP providing the transit promises the second ISP that it will deliver the other's traffic to wherever the traffic is going on the Internet, no matter whether the traffic's ultimate destination is within the first ISP's network or on some other ISP's network.

Unlike peering, which is normally bartered, transit is invariably purchased. Typically, smaller ISPs purchase transit from larger ISPs. Like peering, the financial aspects of transit deals are usually secret. Unlike peering, transit is almost always very expensive.

The Walden DSL ISP appears to purchase transit from Exodus, a company that specializes in operating Internet data centers. We can determine this by looking at the traceroutes of packets sent between Simson's home network and the same web server at MIT:

```
Walden2% traceroute -q 2 web.mit.edu
traceroute to web.mit.edu (18.7.21.77), 30 hops max, 40 byte packets
  1  SIMSON.NET (64.7.15.233)  1.083 ms  1.040 ms
  2  sdsl-216-36-94-1.dsl.bos.megapath.net (216.36.94.1)  62.548 ms  32.031 ms
  3  64.28.72.98 (64.28.72.98)  20.712 ms  19.834 ms
  4  64.14.80.153 (64.14.80.153)  33.078 ms  16.630 ms
  5  ibr02-g2-0.wlhm01.exodus.net (64.14.70.69)  16.621 ms 27.349 ms
  6  p5-1.bstnma1-cr7.bbnplanet.net (4.24.92.101)  15.617 ms  15.742 ms
  7  p5-0.bstnma1-ba2.bbnplanet.net (4.24.4.225)  15.632 ms  15.818 ms
  8  p1-0.bstnma1-ba1.bbnplanet.net (4.24.4.193)  14.564 ms  14.410 ms
  9  p5-2.cambridge1-nbr1.bbnplanet.net (4.0.2.173)  15.337 ms  15.443 ms
 10  p1-0-0.cambridge1-br1.bbnplanet.net (4.0.1.22)  14.880 ms  14.812 ms
 11  h3-0.cambridge2-br2.bbnplanet.net (4.0.1.202)  16.325 ms  20.244 ms
 12  ihtfp.mit.edu (192.233.33.3)  20.664 ms  18.496 ms
 13  W92-RTR-1-BACKBONE.MIT.EDU (18.168.0.20)  33.733 ms 34.790 ms
 14  SICARIUS-SPATULATUS.MIT.EDU (18.7.21.77)  40.954 ms 53.178 ms
Walden2%
```

This traceroute was done a few minutes after the traceroute from Walden using the cable modem. As you can see, the network connection has tenfold higher latency than the preceding one. Part of the speed difference can be attributed to the difference between the cable modem connection and the DSL connection, but part of the difference is caused by the longer path that the packets need to follow.

The Root and Top-Level Nameservers

Most ISPs will operate DNS servers for their own customers. But that's only half the story. When Simson's desktop computer attempted to resolve the name *www.icann. org*, the computer first went to one of the root domain nameservers to get the address for the *org* domain nameserver. It then went to the *org* domain nameserver to get the address for the *icann.org* domain nameserver. Without root and top-level domain nameservers, the DNS could not function properly.

So how does a DNS server find the root nameservers to start the whole process? Currently, this information is distributed in a file that is provided with most Unix operating systems. (Overwhelmingly, it is Unix systems that run the Internet's DNS infrastructure.) The current root nameserver file contains 13 entries in this file, with the names *A.ROOT-SERVERS.NET* through *M.ROOT-SERVERS.NET*.

Who runs the root?

Perhaps nowhere is the Internet's history as a project between the U.S. Department of Defense and America's universities more evident than in the ownership and operation of these 13 nameservers. In February 2001, more than 25 years after the Internet's founding, six of the Internet's 13 root servers were still being operated by the U.S. military, U.S. government, U.S. universities, and U.S. military contractors. The list of root nameservers is in Table 2-1.

Table 2-1. Root nameservers on February 1, 2001

Official name	Original name	Operating agency
A.ROOT-SERVERS.NET.	NS.INTERNIC.NET	Network Solutions, Inc.
B.ROOT-SERVERS.NET.	NS1.ISI.EDU	University of Southern California Information Sciences Institute
C.ROOT-SERVERS.NET.	C.PSI.NET	PSINet, Inc
D.ROOT-SERVERS.NET.	TERP.UMD.EDU	University of Maryland
E.ROOT-SERVERS.NET.	NS.NASA.GOV	National Aeronautics and Space Administration
F.ROOT-SERVERS.NET.	NS.ISC.ORG	Internet Software Consortium
G.ROOT-SERVERS.NET.	NS.NIC.DDN.MIL	U.S. Department of Defense Defense Data Network
H.ROOT-SERVERS.NET.	AOS.ARL.ARMY.MIL	U.S. Army
I.ROOT-SERVERS.NET.	NIC.NORDU.NET	Nordic national networks for research and education
J.ROOT-SERVERS.NET.	–	Network Solutions, Inc.
K.ROOT-SERVERS.NET.	–	RIPE Network Coordination Centre
L.ROOT-SERVERS.NET.	–	University of Southern California Information Sciences Institute
M.ROOT-SERVERS.NET.	–	Asia Pacific Network Information Center

Each root domain server maintains a list of top-level generic domains (e.g., *.com*, *.net*, *.org*, *.gov*, and so on), and the roughly 250 top-level domains associated with country codes (e.g., *.uk* for the United Kingdom, *.ca* for Canada). With the exception of the master root server, *A.ROOT-SERVERS.NET*, all of the top-level domains are run on computers that are not directly associated with the master root servers.

An example

For example, if you ask the root server *A.ROOT-SERVERS.NET* for the address of *ICANN.ORG*'s domain server, you will get it:

```
% dig @a.root-servers.net icann.org

; <<>> DiG 8.3 <<>> @a.root-servers.net icann.org
; (1 server found)
;; res options: init recurs defnam dnsrch
;; got answer:
;; ->>HEADER<<- opcode: QUERY, status: NOERROR, id: 6
;; flags: qr rd; QUERY: 1, ANSWER: 0, AUTHORITY: 6, ADDITIONAL: 6
;; QUERY SECTION:
;;      icann.org, type = A, class = IN

;; AUTHORITY SECTION:
icann.org.              2D IN NS        NS.APNIC.NET.
icann.org.              2D IN NS        NS.ISI.EDU.
icann.org.              2D IN NS        VENERA.ISI.EDU.
icann.org.              2D IN NS        NS.RIPE.NET.
icann.org.              2D IN NS        RIP.PSG.COM.
icann.org.              2D IN NS        SVC00.APNIC.NET.

;; ADDITIONAL SECTION:
NS.APNIC.NET.           2D IN A         203.37.255.97
NS.ISI.EDU.             2D IN A         128.9.128.127
VENERA.ISI.EDU.         2D IN A         128.9.176.32
NS.RIPE.NET.            2D IN A         193.0.0.193
RIP.PSG.COM.            2D IN A         147.28.0.39
SVC00.APNIC.NET.        2D IN A         202.12.28.131

;; Total query time: 133 msec
;; FROM: r2.nitroba.com to SERVER: a.root-servers.net  198.41.0.4
;; WHEN: Wed Feb  7 11:17:14 2001
;; MSG SIZE  sent: 27  rcvd: 261

%
```

But if you ask the same question of the root server *C.ROOT-SERVERS.NET*, you will be advised to seek your answer elsewhere—at one of the generic top-level domain servers for the *org* domain:

```
% dig @c.root-servers.net icann.org

; <<>> DiG 8.3 <<>> @c.root-servers.net icann.org
; (1 server found)
;; res options: init recurs defnam dnsrch
;; got answer:
;; ->>HEADER<<- opcode: QUERY, status: NOERROR, id: 6
```

```
;; flags: qr rd; QUERY: 1, ANSWER: 0, AUTHORITY: 12, ADDITIONAL: 12
;; QUERY SECTION:
;;       icann.org, type = A, class = IN

;; AUTHORITY SECTION:
org.                    6D IN NS        A.ROOT-SERVERS.NET.
org.                    6D IN NS        E.GTLD-SERVERS.NET.
org.                    6D IN NS        F.GTLD-SERVERS.NET.
org.                    6D IN NS        J.GTLD-SERVERS.NET.
org.                    6D IN NS        K.GTLD-SERVERS.NET.
org.                    6D IN NS        A.GTLD-SERVERS.NET.
org.                    6D IN NS        M.GTLD-SERVERS.NET.
org.                    6D IN NS        G.GTLD-SERVERS.NET.
org.                    6D IN NS        C.GTLD-SERVERS.NET.
org.                    6D IN NS        I.GTLD-SERVERS.NET.
org.                    6D IN NS        B.GTLD-SERVERS.NET.
org.                    6D IN NS        D.GTLD-SERVERS.NET.

;; ADDITIONAL SECTION:
A.ROOT-SERVERS.NET.     5w6d16h IN A    198.41.0.4
E.GTLD-SERVERS.NET.     6D IN A         207.200.81.69
F.GTLD-SERVERS.NET.     6D IN A         198.17.208.67
J.GTLD-SERVERS.NET.     6D IN A         210.132.100.101
K.GTLD-SERVERS.NET.     6D IN A         213.177.194.5
A.GTLD-SERVERS.NET.     6D IN A         198.41.3.38
M.GTLD-SERVERS.NET.     6D IN A         202.153.114.101
G.GTLD-SERVERS.NET.     6D IN A         198.41.3.101
C.GTLD-SERVERS.NET.     6D IN A         205.188.185.18
I.GTLD-SERVERS.NET.     6D IN A         192.36.144.133
B.GTLD-SERVERS.NET.     6D IN A         203.181.106.5
D.GTLD-SERVERS.NET.     6D IN A         208.206.240.5

;; Total query time: 376 msec
;; FROM: r2.nitroba.com to SERVER: c.root-servers.net  192.33.4.12
;; WHEN: Wed Feb  7 11:18:33 2001
;; MSG SIZE  sent: 27  rcvd: 440

%
```

Finally, if you should ask *A.ROOT-SERVERS.NET* for the domain server of a
domain that is in England, you're likely to be referred to some nameservers on the
other side of the Atlantic:

```
% dig @a.root-servers.net virgin.co.uk

; <<>> DiG 8.3 <<>> @a.root-servers.net virgin.co.uk
; (1 server found)
;; res options: init recurs defnam dnsrch
;; got answer:
;; ->>HEADER<<- opcode: QUERY, status: NOERROR, id: 6
;; flags: qr rd; QUERY: 1, ANSWER: 0, AUTHORITY: 4, ADDITIONAL: 5
;; QUERY SECTION:
;;       virgin.co.uk, type = A, class = IN
```

```
;; AUTHORITY SECTION:
UK.                     2D IN NS        NS1.NIC.UK.
UK.                     2D IN NS        NS.EU.NET.
UK.                     2D IN NS        NS0.JA.NET.
UK.                     2D IN NS        NS.UU.NET.

;; ADDITIONAL SECTION:
NS1.NIC.UK.             2D IN A         195.66.240.130
NS.EU.NET.              2D IN A         192.16.202.11
NS0.JA.NET.             2D IN A         128.86.1.20
NS0.JA.NET.             2D IN A         193.63.94.20
NS.UU.NET.              2D IN A         137.39.1.3

;; Total query time: 136 msec
;; FROM: r2.nitroba.com to SERVER: a.root-servers.net  198.41.0.4
;; WHEN: Wed Feb  7 11:19:42 2001
;; MSG SIZE  sent: 30  rcvd: 198

%
```

For the most part, the ownership and operation of these domain nameservers is transparent to most of the Internet's users. The nameservers are an incredibly critical part of the Internet, and as a result they are carefully watched and maintained. Moreover, because there are 13 separate root nameservers, the majority of them can be down without significantly affecting the reliability of the Internet.

But every now and then there is a problem that affects all of the domain nameservers. When things go wrong, there is not much that most users of the Internet can do except wait for the outage to pass or fall back on using IP addresses instead of host names—provided that you know the IP address of the web server you wish to reach.

The Domain Registrars

The database of domain names and IP addresses for each top-level domain is maintained by an organization called an Internet *registrar*. These organizations maintain a database for their top-level domain and of all the subdomains, consisting of a list of all of the domains, the IP address for each domain server, and the names of the individuals who are authorized to make changes in the records.

For most of the 1990s, the Virginia-based government contractor Network Solutions, Inc., maintained registration services for the Internet's generic top-level domains as part of a contract that was issued by the National Science Foundation, and then later by the U.S. Department of Commerce. In 1999, the services provided by NSI were split into two pieces. Although Network Solutions maintained monopoly control over the backend database, the aspects of the business that involve taking orders and payments from the public were opened to a competitive process. There are now more than two dozen corporations that are authorized to register names in the top-level domains *com*, *net*, and *org*. We'll describe Network Solutions' role and history in greater detail in the final section of this chapter.

Internet Number Registries

Just as the proper functioning of the Internet relies on the fact that no two organizations can have the same domain name, proper functioning of the Internet also requires that no two organizations use the same IP address.

Most organizations and individuals that connect to the Internet use IP addresses that are borrowed from their upstream provider. But in some cases, it makes sense for organizations to have their own IP addresses. For example, a medium-to-large ISP that peers with a variety of other ISPs needs to have its own IP addresses for the peering and routing protocols to function properly. There are also many large organizations that want to have their own IP addresses so that their networks do not need to be renumbered if the organization changes Internet service providers.

Until 1996, Internet IP addresses were freely available for the asking. Since then, IP addresses have been distributed by regional Internet number registries. In North America, IP addresses allocations are controlled by ARIN, the American Registry of Internet Numbers.

The Internet Corporation for Assigned Names and Numbers

Created in 1998 by Joe Sims, an attorney in Washington, D.C., and later awarded a contract by the National Telecommunications and Information Administration (NTIA), the Internet Corporation for Assigned Names and Numbers (ICANN) is a nonprofit California corporation that has responsibility for assigning and managing IP address space, protocol parameters, the DNS root servers, and management in general of the Domain Name Service. This responsibility theoretically makes ICANN the arbitrator of all Internet policy issues having to do with allocation policy.*

You may wonder why the NTIA, a unit of the U.S. Department of Commerce, gave a California-based corporation that is controlled by a board of directors with extremely limited public accountability the power to manage a public resource such as the Internet. Or you may wonder how it came to be that a branch of the U.S. government had power over the Internet in the first place. Or you may wonder if ICANN is really in control of the Internet, because its authority comes by right of a contract that it was granted by the U.S. government, rather than from the Internet's actual owners, users, and operators.

ICANN's short and somewhat torturous history is the result of the origin of the Internet itself. Started as a Department of Defense research project, one of the original government contractors for the network development was the University of California at Los Angeles (UCLA). At UCLA, a graduate student, Jon Postel, took it upon

---

* Information in this section is from the ICANN web site *http://www.icann.org/*, and from the Center for Democracy and Technology's Domain Name Management Policy Report, *http://www.cdt.org/dns/icann/study/*.

himself to maintain the Internet's list of host names and to edit and maintain the Requests for Comments (RFCs) that were prepared by the ARPANET research. The original Internet had no central coordinating authority for names and numbers.

Postel was widely respected for both his technical skills and his ability as a technical mediator. In March 1977, Postel moved from UCLA to the Information Sciences Institute (ISI) at the University of Southern California. Postel devoted much of his work to documenting the design of protocols, the allocation of addresses, and the creation of procedures for the Internet, from its inception through its first three decades. As the task grew, Postel began to delegate the job to graduate students, but he maintained technical oversight. As the importance of this project became clear, Postel coined the term "Internet Assigned Numbers Authority" to describe the unincorporated, voluntary organization that coordinated the assignment process. His friends called him the "Numbers Czar."

IANA proved to be critical to the proper functioning of the Internet. The problem wasn't so much the rational allocation of scarce resources, but the coordination of multiple parties that needed unique addresses, identifiers, and port numbers. Consider that there are 65,535 TCP port numbers. That's quite a lot, considering that each port might be used for a different Internet protocol, and that only a few dozen protocols are widely used. The telnet protocol is assigned to port 23; the SMTP protocol is assigned to port 25; HTTP is assigned to port 80; and so on. But somebody needed to make sure that no two developers would accidentally choose the same port number for the same protocol. That was IANA's job. It did the same thing for IP address space and domain names—that is, it made sure that two different people didn't pick the same domain name.

As the Internet grew in the 1980s into thousands of hosts, the registration process became too much for Postel and his graduate students to handle. DARPA wrote a contract to SRI International for the management of the Network Information Center, which soon was known as SRI-NIC. When universities became the dominant users, management and funding of the NIC was transferred from DARPA to the National Science Foundation. In 1993, the NSF wrote three contracts for the management of the Internet. They were awarded to General Atomics, AT&T, and a new company called Network Solutions. The first two contracts were for managing different aspects of directory services—what would later become known as search engines. Both Atomics International and AT&T failed to produce anything tremendously interesting. The third contract was for the management of the DNS.

From the Internet's birth until the mid-1990s, Internet resources other than bandwidth, hardware, and consulting time were largely free. Specifically, neither IANA nor SRI-NIC charged for domain names or IP address space. But the one thing that was not free was the growing management burden. Network Solutions' contract was originally for a set fee plus an overhead cost. But in 1995, complaining that it simply could not keep up with the Internet's growth without substantial investment, Network Solutions sought and was granted permission to charge a $50/year fee for each newly registered domain name.* This charge was allowed under Amendment #4 of the original contract, rather than having a new contract put out for competitive bid. This fee proved to be a significant revenue source. Based on Network Solution's position as the Internet's sole registrar, the company achieved significant growth and investment, and in September 1997 staged a tremendously successful initial public offering (IPO) of its stock, with a 40% increase in value on the first day—despite the fact that its five-year contract to manage the NIC was due to expire in March 1998.

The growing wealth of Network Solutions and the power that the company enjoyed through its control of the Domain Name System was not lost upon policy makers in Washington, D.C. On July 1, 1997, President Clinton directed the Secretary of Commerce to privatize the Domain Name System in a manner that would "increase competition and facilitate international participation in its management."† The following day, the Department of Commerce issued a request for proposals on how the DNS administration should be redesigned. On January 30, 1998, the National Telecommunications and Information Administration (NTIA), an agency of the Department of Commerce, published "A Proposal to Improve the Technical Management of Internet Names and Addresses." This was published in the Federal Register on February 20, referred to as the "Green Paper," and put up for public comment. Six months later, the Department of Commerce issued a "White Paper," which largely codified the policy statements of the Green Paper.

The key goals of the Internet corporation envisioned by the Department of Commerce were:

Stability
"During the transition and thereafter, the stability of the Internet should be the first priority of any DNS management system."

Competition
"Where possible, market mechanisms that support competition and consumer choice should drive the management of the Internet because they will lower costs, promote innovation, encourage diversity, and enhance user choice and satisfaction."

Private sector, bottom-up coordination
"A private coordinating process is likely to be more flexible than government and to move rapidly enough to meet the changing needs of the Internet and of

---

* The $50 included a $35 fee and $15 that was provided to the U.S. government for "infrastructure." The $15 charge was declared to be an illegal tax, but Congress enacted special legislation to allow the fee to be retained rather than refunded.

† "Management of Internet Names and Addresses," U.S. Department of Commerce, Docket Number 980212036-8146-02. Currently archived at *http://www.icann.org/general/white-paper-05jun98.htm.*

Internet users. The private process should, as far as possible, reflect the bottom-up governance that has characterized development of the Internet to date."

Representation

"Management structures should reflect the functional and geographic diversity of the Internet and its users. Mechanisms should be established to ensure international participation in decision making."

Joe Sims was Postel's attorney. His law firm drafted the incorporation document and charter for an organization called the Internet Corporation for Assigned Names and Numbers (ICANN). The Department of Commerce accepted the proposal in September 1998. Then Postel suffered a heart attack and died on October 16, 1998.

In the days following Postel's death, Sims contacted a number of individuals and told them that they had been chosen for ICANN's board. Esther Dyson was chosen as ICANN's Interim Chairman of the Board and Michael M. Roberts was chosen as ICANN's Interim President and Chief Executive Officer. A board of directors was selected and the organization had its first board meeting at an airport in New York City. The first public meeting followed on November 14–15, 1998, in Cambridge, Massachusetts.

ICANN was not the only possibility for Internet governance. One was the International Forum on the White Paper, of which Michael Robers was one of the leaders (see *http://www.domainhandbook.com/ifwp.html*). Another was the Boston Working Group (see *http://www.cavebear.org/bwg*). The means by which NTIA chose the ICANN proposal over the others remains unclear.

Since its first meeting, ICANN has licensed additional companies to compete with Network Solutions for registration services (although NSI still operates the backend domain database), and the company has authorized the creation of several new top-level domains. ICANN has also organized a worldwide Internet election for its "at large" membership and has allowed that membership to elect a number of "at large directors."

As of this writing in September 2001, ICANN has not lived up to many of the white paper's goals. The DNS remains relatively stable—there have been no serious outages or interruptions of service. But attempts to create more than a token number of new top-level domains have been stymied by ICANN's go-slow approach. There is essentially no "bottom up," private sector coordination or "representation."

On the other hand, ICANN's power really does come from the consent of the governed. If the major ISPs wished to do so, they could do away with ICANN and set up a replacement organization. They could revise the way that the top-level domains are managed and the rules governing IP address assignment. The ISPs don't do this because ICANN works, overall—at least it works well and cheaply enough that the ISPs can afford to let it continue doing what it is doing while the ISPs concentrate on the task of making money.

Whether or not ICANN will suceed in the long run is unclear. But if ICANN fails, the ISPs will need to set up something a lot like ICANN to replace it, if for no other reason than to assure that people do not pick the same names and numbers for different computers and protocols.

CHAPTER 3
Cryptography Basics

In this chapter:
- Understanding Cryptography
- Symmetric Key Algorithms
- Public Key Algorithms
- Message Digest Functions

This chapter explains the basics of cryptography, on which many secure Internet protocols are based. Cryptography is a complex topic and in this chapter we're obviously presenting only a summary. Chapter 4 describes how cryptography is used today on the Web. For more complete information on cryptography concepts and algorithms, see the references in Appendix E.

Understanding Cryptography

Cryptography is a collection of mathematical techniques for protecting information. Using cryptography, you can transform written words and other kinds of messages so that they are unintelligible to anyone who does not possess a specific mathematical *key* necessary to unlock the message. The process of using cryptography to scramble a message is called *encryption*. The process of unscrambling the message by use of the appropriate key is called *decryption*. Figure 3-1 illustrates how these two processes fit together.

Cryptography is used to prevent information from being accessed by an unauthorized recipient. In theory, once a piece of information is encrypted, that information can be accidentally disclosed or intercepted by a third party without compromising the security of the information, provided that the key necessary to decrypt the information is not disclosed and that the method of encryption will resist attempts to decrypt the message without the key.

For example, here is a message that you might want to encrypt:

```
SSL is a cryptographic protocol
```

And here is the message after it has been encrypted:

```
Ç'@%[»FÇ«$TfiPΣ|x¿EÛóõÑ‰ß+ö˜•...aÜ˝BÆuâw
```

Because the decryption key is not shown, it should not be practical to take the preceding line of gibberish and turn it back into the original message.

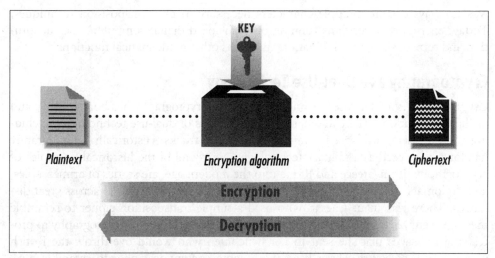

Figure 3-1. Encryption is a process that uses a key to transform a block of plaintext into an encrypted ciphertext. Decryption is the process that takes an encrypted ciphertext and a decryption key and produces the original plaintext.

Roots of Cryptography

The science of cryptography is thousands of years old. In his book *The Code Breakers*, David Kahn traces the roots of cryptography back to ancient Egypt, Greece, and Rome. For example, writes Kahn, Greek generals used cryptography to send coded messages to commanders who were in the field. In the event that a messenger was intercepted by the enemy, the message's content would not be revealed.

Most cryptographic systems have been based on two techniques: *substitution* and *transposition*:

Substitution

> Substitution is based on the principle of replacing each letter in the message you wish to encrypt with another one. The Caesar cipher, for example, substitutes the letter "a" with the letter "d," the letter "b" with the letter "e," and so on. Some substitution ciphers use the same substitution scheme for every letter in the message that is being encrypted; others use different schemes for different letters.

Transposition

> Transposition is based on scrambling the characters that are in the message. One transposition system involves writing a message into a table row-by-row, then reading it out column-by-column. Double transposition ciphers involve using two such transformations.

In the early part of the 20th century, a variety of electromechanical devices were built in Europe and the United States for the purpose of encrypting messages sent by telegraph or radio. These systems relied principally on substitution, because there was no way to store multiple characters necessary to use transposition techniques. Today, encryption algorithms running on high-speed digital computers use substitution and transposition in combination, as well as other mathematical functions.

Cryptography as a Dual-Use Technology

Cryptography is a "dual-use" technology—that is, cryptography has both military and civilian applications. There are many other examples of dual-use technologies, including carbon fibers, high-speed computers, and even trucks. Historically, cryptography has long been used as a military technology.* Nearly all of the historical examples of cryptography, from Greece and Rome into the modern age, are stories of armies, spies, and diplomats who used cryptography to shield messages transmitted across great distances. There was Julius Caesar, who used a simple transposition cipher to scramble messages sent back from Gaul. Mary, Queen of Scots, tried to use cryptography to protect the messages that she sent to her henchmen who would overthrow the British Crown. And, of course, Hitler used the Enigma encryption cipher to scramble messages sent by radio to the German armies and U-Boats during World War II.

There is also a tradition of nonmilitary use of cryptography that is many centuries old. There are records of people using cryptography to protect religious secrets, to hide secrets of science and industry, and to arrange clandestine romantic trysts. In Victorian England, lovers routinely communicated by printed encrypted advertisements in the London newspapers. Lovers again relied on encryption during World War I, when mail sent between the U.S. and foreign countries was routinely opened by Postal Service inspectors looking for communiques between spies. These encrypted letters, when they were intercepted, were sent to Herbert Yardley's offices in New York City, which made a point of decrypting each message before it was resealed and sent along its way. As Herbert Yardley wrote in his book *The American Black Chamber*, lovers accounted for many more encrypted letters than did spies— but almost invariably the lovers used weaker ciphers! The spies and the lovers both used cryptography for the same reason: they wanted to be assured that, in the event one of their messages was intercepted or opened by the wrong person, the letter's contents would remain secret. Cryptography was used to increase privacy.

In recent years, the use of cryptography in business and commerce appears to have far eclipsed all uses of cryptography by all the world's governments and militaries. These days, cryptography is used to scramble satellite television broadcasts, to protect automatic teller networks, and to guard the secrecy of practically every purchase made over the World Wide Web. Indeed, cryptography made the rapid commercialization of the Internet possible: without cryptography, it is doubtful that banks, businesses, and individuals would have felt safe doing business online. For all of its users, cryptography is a way of ensuring certainty and reducing risk in an uncertain world.

* Ironically, despite the fact that cryptography has been primarily used by the military, historically the strongest publicly known encryption systems were invented by civilians. For a discussion, see Carl Ellison's essay at *http://world.std.com/~cme/html/timeline.html* or read Kahn's book.

A Cryptographic Example

Let's return to the example introduced at the beginning of this chapter. Here is that sample piece of plaintext again:

```
SSL is a cryptographic protocol
```

This message can be encrypted with an *encryption algorithm* to produce an encrypted message. The encrypted message is called a *ciphertext*.

In the next example, the message is encrypted using the Data Encryption Standard (DES).[*] The DES is a symmetric algorithm, which means that it uses the same key for encryption as for decryption. The encryption key is *nosmis*:

```
% des -e < text > text.des
Enter key: nosmis
Enter key again: nosmis
%
```

The result of the encryption is this encrypted message:[†]

```
% cat text.des
Ç'@%[»FÇ«$TfiP∑|x¿EÛóõÑ‰ß+ö˜•...aÜ˜BÆuâw
```

As you can see, the encrypted message is nonsensical. But when this message is decrypted with the key *nosmis*, the original message is produced:

```
% des -d < text.des > text.decrypt
Enter key: nosmis
Enter key again: nosmis
% cat text.decrypt
SSL is a cryptographic protocol
%
```

If you try to decrypt the encrypted message with a different key, such as *gandalf*, the result is garbage:[‡]

```
% des -d < text.des > text.decrypt
Enter key: gandalf
Enter key again: gandalf
```

---

[*] To be precise, we will use the DEA, the Data Encryption Algorithm, which conforms to the DES. Nearly everyone refers to it as the DES instead of the DEA, however. Perhaps referring to the DEA makes too many programmers and cryptographers nervous?

[†] Modern encrypted messages are inherently binary data. Because of the limitations of paper, not all control characters are displayed.

[‡] In the example, the *des* command prints the message "Corrupted file or wrong key" when we attempt to decrypt the file *text.des* with the wrong key. How does the *des* command know that the key provided is incorrect? The answer has to do with the fact that DES is a block encryption algorithm, encrypting data in blocks of 64 bits at a time. When a file is not an even multiple of 64 bits, the *des* command pads the file with null characters (ASCII 0). It then inserts at the beginning of the file a small header indicating how long the original file "really was." During decryption, the *des* command checks the end of the file to make sure that the decrypted file is the same length as the original file. If it is not, then something is wrong: either the file was corrupted or the wrong key was used to decrypt the file. Thus, by trying all possible keys, it is possible to use the *des* command to experimentally determine which of the many possible keys is the correct one. But don't worry: there are a lot of keys to try.

```
Corrupted file or wrong key
% cat text.decrypt
±N%EÒR...f'"H;OªōO>˝„!_+í∞›
```

The only way to decrypt the encrypted message and get printable text is by knowing the secret key *nosmis*. If you don't know the key, and you need the contents of the message, one approach is to try to decrypt the message with every possible key. This approach is called a *key search attack* or a *brute force attack*.

How easy is a brute force attack? That depends on the length of the key. The message above was encrypted with the DES algorithm, which has a 56-bit key. Each bit in the 56-bit key can be a 1 or a 0. As a result, there are 2^{56}—that is, 72,057,594,037,900,000—different keys. Although this may seem like a lot of keys, it really isn't. If you could try a billion keys each second and you could recognize the correct key when you found it (quite possible with a network of modern computers), you could try all possible keys in a little less than 834 days.

And in fact, DES is even less secure than the example above implies. The Unix *des* command does a very poor job of transforming a typed "key" into the key that's actually used by the encryption algorithm. A typed key will typically only include the 96 printable characters, reducing the keyspace to 96^8 possible keys—this number is only one-tenth the size of 2^{56}. If you can search a billion keys a second, you could try all of these keys in only 83 days.

We'll discuss these issues more thoroughly in the section "Key Length with Symmetric Key Algorithms" later in this chapter.

Cryptographic Algorithms and Functions

There are fundamentally two kinds of encryption algorithms:

Symmetric key algorithms
> With these algorithms, the same key is used to encrypt and decrypt the message. The DES algorithm discussed earlier is a symmetric key algorithm. Symmetric key algorithms are sometimes called *secret key algorithms* and sometimes called *private key algorithms*. Unfortunately, both of these names are easily confused with public key algorithms, which are unrelated to symmetric key algorithms.

Asymmetric key algorithms
> With these algorithms, one key is used to encrypt the message and another key to decrypt it. The encryption key is normally called the *public key* in some algorithms because it can be made publicly available without compromising the secrecy of the message or the decryption key. The decryption key is normally called the *private key* or *secret key*. Systems that are used in this fashion are called *public key systems*. Sometimes, people call all asymmetric key systems "public key," but this is not correct—there is no requirement that one key be made public.

This technology was invented independently by academic cryptographers at Stanford University and by military cryptographers at England's GCHQ, who called the techniques *two-key cryptography*. (The U.S. National Security Agency may also have invented and shelved the technology as a novelty, notes Carl Ellison.) This technology is a recent development in the history of cryptography.

Symmetric key algorithms are the workhorses of modern cryptographic systems. They are generally much faster than public key algorithms. They are also somewhat easier to implement. And finally, it is generally easier for cryptographers to ascertain the strength of symmetric key algorithms. Unfortunately, symmetric key algorithms have three problems that limit their use in the real world:

- For two parties to securely exchange information using a symmetric key algorithm, those parties must first exchange an encryption key. Alas, exchanging an encryption key in a secure fashion can be quite difficult.

- As long as they wish to send or receive messages, both parties must keep a copy of the key. This doesn't seem like a significant problem, but it is. If one party's copy is compromised and the second party doesn't know this fact, then the second party might send a message to the first party—and that message could then be subverted using the compromised key.

- If each pair of parties wishes to communicate in private, then they need a unique key. This requires $(N^2-N)/2$ keys for N different users. For 10 users that is 45 keys. This may not seem like much, but consider the Internet with perhaps 300,000,000 users. If you wanted to be able to communicate with each of them, you'd need to store 299,999,999 keys on your system in advance. And if everyone wanted to communicate privately with everyone else, that would require 44,999,999,850,000,000 unique keys (almost 45 quadrillion)!

Public key algorithms overcome these problems. Instead of a single key, public key algorithms use two keys: one for encrypting the message, the other for decrypting the message. These keys are usually called the public key and the

private key.

In theory, public key technology (illustrated in Figure 3-2) makes it relatively easy to send somebody an encrypted message. People who wish to receive encrypted messages will typically publish their keys in directories or make their keys otherwise readily available. Then, to send somebody an encrypted message, all you have to do is get a copy of their public key, encrypt your message, and send it to them. With a good public key system, you know that the only person who can decrypt the message is the person who has possession of the matching private key. Furthermore, all you really need to store on your own machine are your own two keys.

Public key cryptography can also be used for creating *digital signatures*. Similar to a real signature, a digital signature is used to denote authenticity or intention. For example, you can sign a piece of electronic mail to indicate your authorship in a manner akin to signing a paper letter. And as with signing a bill of sale agreement, you can electronically sign a transaction to indicate that you wish to purchase or sell something. Using public key technology, you use the private key to create the digital signature; others can then use your matching public key to verify the signature.

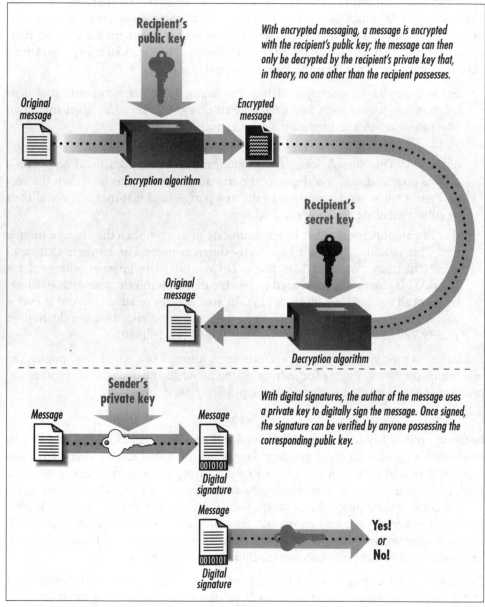

Recipient's public key

With encrypted messaging, a message is encrypted with the recipient's public key; the message can then only be decrypted by the recipient's private key that, in theory, no one other than the recipient possesses.

Original message

Encrypted message

Encryption algorithm

Recipient's secret key

Original message

Decryption algorithm

Sender's private key

With digital signatures, the author of the message uses a private key to digitally sign the message. Once signed, the signature can be verified by anyone possessing the corresponding public key.

Message

Message

0010101
Digital signature

Message

0010101
Digital signature

Yes! or **No!**

Figure 3-2. Public key cryptography can be used for encrypted messaging or for digital signatures

Unfortunately, public key algorithms have a significant problem of their own: they are computationally expensive.[*] In practice, public key encryption and decryption require as much as 1000 times more computer power than an equivalent symmetric key encryption algorithm.

To get both the benefits of public key technology and the speed of symmetric encryption systems, most modern encryption systems actually use a combination:

Hybrid public/private cryptosystems
> With these systems, slower public key cryptography is used to exchange a random *session key*, which is then used as the basis of a private (symmetric) key algorithm. (A session key is used only for a single encryption session and is then discarded.) Nearly all practical public key cryptography implementations are actually hybrid systems.

Finally, there is a special class of functions that are almost always used in conjunction with public key cryptography. These algorithms are not encryption algorithms at all. Instead, they are used to create a "fingerprint" of a file or a key:

Message digest functions
> A message digest function generates a seemingly random pattern of bits for a given input. The digest value is computed in such a way that finding a different input that will exactly generate the given digest is computationally infeasible. Message digests are often regarded as fingerprints for files. Most systems that perform digital signatures encrypt a message digest of the data rather than the actual file data itself.

The following sections look at these classes of algorithms in detail.

Symmetric Key Algorithms

Symmetric key algorithms are for the bulk encryption of data or data streams. These algorithms are designed to be very fast and have a large number of possible keys. The best symmetric key algorithms offer excellent secrecy; once data is encrypted with a given key, there is no fast way to decrypt the data without possessing the same key.

Symmetric key algorithms can be divided into two categories: block and stream. *Block algorithms* encrypt data a block (many bytes) at a time, while *stream algorithms* encrypt byte-by-byte (or even bit-by-bit).

---

[*] The previous edition of this book used the words "quite slow" instead of "computationally expensive." With modern computers, a public key operation can actually be quite fast—an encryption or decryption can frequently be performed in less than a second. But while that may seem fast, such a delay can be significant on a web server that is serving millions of web pages every day. This is why we use the phrase "computationally expensive."

Cryptographic Strength of Symmetric Algorithms

Different encryption algorithms are not equal. Some systems are not very good at protecting data, allowing encrypted information to be decrypted without knowledge of the requisite key. Others are quite resistant to even the most determined attack. The ability of a cryptographic system to protect information from attack is called its *strength*. Strength depends on many factors, including:

- The secrecy of the key.
- The difficulty of guessing the key or trying out all possible keys (a *key search*). Longer keys are generally more difficult to guess or find.
- The difficulty of inverting the encryption algorithm without knowing the encryption key (*breaking* the encryption algorithm).
- The existence (or lack) of *back doors*, or additional ways by which an encrypted file can be decrypted more easily without knowing the key.
- The ability to decrypt an entire encrypted message if you know the way that a portion of it decrypts (called a *known plaintext attack*).
- The properties of the plaintext and knowledge of those properties by an attacker. For example, a cryptographic system may be vulnerable to attack if all messages encrypted with it begin or end with a known piece of plaintext. These kinds of regularities were used by the Allies to crack the German Enigma cipher during World War II.

In general, cryptographic strength is not proven; it is only disproven. When a new encryption algorithm is proposed, the author of the algorithm almost always believes that the algorithm offers "perfect" security*—that is, the author believes there is no way to decrypt an encrypted message without possession of the corresponding key. After all, if the algorithm contained a known flaw, then the author would not propose the algorithm in the first place (or at least would not propose it in good conscience).

As part of proving the strength of an algorithm, a mathematician can show that the algorithm is resistant to specific kinds of attacks that have been previously shown to compromise other algorithms. Unfortunately, even an algorithm that is resistant to every known attack is not necessarily secure, because new attacks are constantly being developed.

From time to time, some individuals or corporations claim that they have invented new symmetric encryption algorithms that are dramatically more secure than existing algorithms. Generally, these algorithms should be avoided. As there are no known attacks against the encryption algorithms that are in wide use today, there is no reason to use new, unproven encryption algorithms—algorithms that might have lurking flaws.

---

* This is not to be confused with the formal term "perfect secrecy."

Key Length with Symmetric Key Algorithms

Among those who are not entirely familiar with the mathematics of cryptography, key length is a topic of continuing confusion. As we have seen, short keys can significantly compromise the security of encrypted messages, because an attacker can merely decrypt the message with every possible key so as to decipher the message's content. But while short keys provide comparatively little security, extremely long keys do not necessarily provide significantly more practical security than keys of moderate length. That is, while keys of 40 or 56 bits are not terribly secure, a key of 256 bits does not offer significantly more real security than a key of 168 bits, or even a key of 128 bits.

To understand this apparent contradiction, it is important to understand what is really meant by the words *key length*, and how a brute force attack actually works.

Inside a computer, a cryptographic key is represented as a string of binary digits. Each binary digit can be a 0 or a 1. Thus, if a key is 1 bit in length, there are two possible keys: 0 and 1. If a key is 2 bits in length, there are four possible keys: 00, 01, 10, and 11. If a key is 3 bits in length, there are eight possible keys: 000, 001, 010, 011, 100, 101, 110, and 111. In general, each added key bit doubles the number of keys. The mathematical equation that relates the number of possible keys to the number of bits is:

number of keys = $2^{(number\ of\ bits)}$

If you are attempting to decrypt a message and do not have a copy of the key, the simplest way to decrypt the message is to do a *brute force attack*. These attacks are also called *key search attacks*, because they involve trying every possible key to see if that key decrypts the message. If the key is selected at random, then on average, an attacker will need to try half of all the possible keys before finding the actual decryption key.

Fortunately for those of us who depend upon symmetric encryption algorithms, it is a fairly simple matter to use longer keys by adding a few bits. Each time a bit is added; the difficulty for an attacker attempting a brute force attack doubles.

The first widely used encryption algorithm, the Data Encryption Standard (DES), used a key that was 56 bits long. At the time that the DES was adopted, many academics said that 56 bits was not sufficient: they argued for a key that was twice as long. But it appears that the U.S. National Security Agency did not want a cipher with a longer key length widely deployed, most likely because such a secure cipher would significantly complicate its job of international surveillance.* To further reduce the

---

* The NSA operates a world-wide intelligence surveillance network. This network relies, to a large extent, on the fact that the majority of the information transmitted electronically is transmitted without encryption. The network is also used for obtaining information about the number of messages exchanged between various destinations, a technique called *traffic analysis*. Although it is widely assumed that the NSA has sufficient computer power to forcibly decrypt a few encrypted messages, not even the NSA has the computer power to routinely decrypt all of the world's electronic communications.

impact that the DES would have on its ability to collect international intelligence, U.S. corporations were forbidden from exporting products that implemented the DES algorithm.

In the early 1990s, a growing number of U.S. software publishers demanded the ability to export software that offered at least a modicum of security. As part of a compromise, a deal was brokered between the U.S. Department of Commerce, the National Security Agency, and the Software Publisher's Association. Under the terms of that agreement, U.S. companies were allowed to export mass-market software that incorporated encryption, provided that the products used a particular encryption algorithm and that the length of the key was limited to 40 bits. At the same time, some U.S. banks started using an algorithm called Triple-DES—basically, a threefold application of the DES algorithm, for encrypting some financial transactions. Triple-DES has a key size of 168 bits. Triple-DES is described in the following section.

In October 2000, the National Institute of Standards and Technology (NIST) approved the *Rinjdael* encryption algorithm as the new U.S. Advanced Encryption Standard. Rinjdael can be used with keys of 128, 192, or 256 bits. The algorithm's extremely fast speed combined with its status as the government-chosen standard, means that it will likely be used in preference to the DES, Triple-DES, and other algorithms in the future.

So how many bits is enough? That depends on how fast the attacker can try different keys and how long you wish to keep your information secure. As Table 3-1 shows, if an attacker can try only 10 keys per second, then a 40-bit key will protect a message for more than 3,484 years. Of course, today's computers can try many thousands of keys per second—and with special-purpose hardware and software, they can try hundreds of thousands. Key search speed can be further improved by running the same program on hundreds or thousands of computers at a time. Thus, it's possible to search a million keys per second or more using today's technology. If you have the ability to search a million keys per second, you can try all 40-bit keys in only 13 days.

If a key that is 40 bits long is clearly not sufficient to keep information secure, how many bits are necessary? In April 1993, the Clinton Administration introduced the Clipper encryption chip as part of its Escrowed Encryption Initiative (EEI). This chip used a key that was 80 bits long. As Table 3-1 shows, an 80-bit key is more than adequate for many applications. If you could search a billion keys per second, trying all 80-bit keys would still require 38 million years! Clipper was widely criticized not because of the key length, but because the Clipper encryption algorithm was kept secret by the National Security Agency, and because each Clipper chip came with a "back door" that allowed information encrypted by each Clipper chip to be decrypted by the U.S. government in support of law enforcement and intelligence needs.

Table 3-1. Estimated success of brute force attacks (for different numbers of bits in the key and number of keys that can be tried per second)

Length of key	Keys searched per second	Postulated key searching technology[a]	Approximate time to search all possible keys
40 bits[b]	10	10-year-old desktop computer	3,484 years
40 bits	1,000	Typical desktop computer today	35 years
40 bits	1 million	Small network of desktops	13 days
40 bits	1 billion	Medium-sized corporate network	18 minutes
56 bits	1 million	Desktop computer a few years from now	2,283 years
56 bits	1 billion	Medium-sized corporate network	2.3 years
56 bits[c]	100 billion	DES-cracking machine	8 days
64 bits	1 billion	Medium-sized corporate network	585 years
80 bits	1 million	Small network of desktops	38 billion years
80 bits	1 billion	Medium-sized corporate network	38 million years
128 bits	1 billion	Medium-sized corporate network	10^{22} years
128 bits	1 billion billion (1×10^{18})	Large-scale Internet project in the year 2005	10,783 billion years
128 bits	1×10^{23}	Special-purpose quantum computer, year 2015?	108 million years
192 bits	1 billion	Medium-sized corporate network	2×10^{41} years
192 bits	1 billion billion	Large-scale Internet project in the year 2005	2×10^{32} years
192 bits	1×10^{23}	Special-purpose quantum computer, year 2015?	2×10^{27} years
256 bits	1×10^{23}	Special-purpose quantum computer, year 2015?	3.7×10^{46} years
256 bits	1×10^{32}	Special-purpose quantum computer, year 2040?	3.7×10^{37} years

[a] Computing speeds assume that a typical desktop computer in the year 2001 can execute approximately 500 million instructions per second. This is roughly the speed of a 500 Mhz Pentium III computer.
[b] In 1997, a 40-bit key was cracked in only 3.5 hours.
[c] In 2000, a 56-bit key was cracked in less than 4 days.

Increasing the key size from 80 bits to 128 bits dramatically increases the amount of effort to guess the key. As the table shows, if there were a computer that could search a billion keys per second, and if you had a billion of these computers, it would still take 10,783 billion years to search all possible 128-bit keys. As our Sun is likely to become a red giant within the next 4 billion years and, in so doing, destroy the Earth, a 128-bit encryption key should be sufficient for most cryptographic uses, assuming that there are no other weaknesses in the algorithm used.

Lately, there's been considerable interest in the field of quantum computing. Scientists postulate that it should be possible to create atomic-sized computers specially designed to crack encryption keys. But while quantum computers could rapidly crack 56-bit DES keys, it's unlikely that a quantum computer could make a dent on a 128-bit encryption key within a reasonable time: even if you could crack 1×10^{23}

keys per second, it would still take 108 million years to try all possible 128-bit encryption keys.

It should be pretty clear at this point that there is no need, given the parameters of cryptography and physics as we understand them today, to use key lengths that are larger than 128 bits. Nevertheless, there seems to be a marketing push towards increasingly larger and larger keys. The Rinjdael algorithm can be operated with 128-bit, 192-bit, or 256-bit keys. If it turns out that there is an as-yet hidden flaw in the Rinjdael algorithm that gives away half the key bits, then the use of the longer keys might make sense. Otherwise, why you would want to use those longer key lengths isn't clear, but if you want them, they are there for you.

Common Symmetric Key Algorithms

There are many symmetric key algorithms in use today. Some of the algorithms that are commonly encountered in the field of web security are summarized in the following list; a more complete list of algorithms is in Table 3-2.

DES

The Data Encryption Standard was adopted as a U.S. government standard in 1977 and as an ANSI standard in 1981. The DES is a block cipher that uses a 56-bit key and has several different operating modes depending on the purpose for which it is employed. The DES is a strong algorithm, but today the short key length limits its use. Indeed, in 1998 a special-purpose machine for "cracking DES" was created by the Electronic Frontier Foundation (EFF) for under $250,000. In one demonstration, it found the key to an encrypted message in less than a day in conjunction with a coalition of computer users around the world.

Triple-DES

Triple-DES is a way to make the DES dramatically more secure by using the DES encryption algorithm three times with three different keys, for a total key length of 168 bits. Also called "3DES," this algorithm has been widely used by financial institutions and by the Secure Shell program (*ssh*). Simply using the DES twice with two different keys does not improve its security to the extent that one might at first suspect because of a theoretical kind of known plaintext attack called *meet-in-the-middle*, in which an attacker simultaneously attempts encrypting the plaintext with a single DES operation and decrypting the ciphertext with another single DES operation, until a match is made in the middle.

Blowfish

Blowfish is a fast, compact, and simple block encryption algorithm invented by Bruce Schneier. The algorithm allows a variable-length key, up to 448 bits, and is optimized for execution on 32- or 64-bit processors. The algorithm is unpatented and has been placed in the public domain. Blowfish is used in the Secure Shell and other programs.

IDEA

The International Data Encryption Algorithm (IDEA) was developed in Zurich, Switzerland, by James L. Massey and Xuejia Lai and published in 1990. IDEA uses a 128-bit key. IDEA is used by the popular program PGP to encrypt files and electronic mail. Unfortunately, wider use of IDEA has been hampered by a series of software patents on the algorithm, which are currently held by Ascom-Tech AG in Solothurn, Switzerland.[*]

RC2

This block cipher was originally developed by Ronald Rivest and kept as a trade secret by RSA Data Security. The algorithm was revealed by an anonymous Usenet posting in 1996 and appears to be reasonably strong (although there are some particular keys that are weak). RC2 allows keys between 1 and 2048 bits. The RC2 key length was traditionally limited to 40 bits in software that was sold for export to allow for decryption by the U.S. National Security Agency.[†]

RC4

This stream cipher was originally developed by Ronald Rivest and kept as a trade secret by RSA Data Security. This algorithm was also revealed by an anonymous Usenet posting in 1994 and appears to be reasonably strong. RC4 allows keys between 1 and 2048 bits. The RC4 key length was traditionally limited to 40 bits in software that was sold for export.

RC5

This block cipher was developed by Ronald Rivest and published in 1994. RC5 allows a user-defined key length, data block size, and number of encryption rounds.

Rinjdael (AES)

This block cipher was developed by Joan Daemen and Vincent Rijmen, and chosen in October 2000 by the National Institute of Standards and Technology to be the United State's new Advanced Encryption Standard. Rinjdael is an extraordinarily fast and compact cipher that can use keys that are 128, 192, or 256 bits long.

---

[*] Although we are generally in favor of intellectual property protection, we are opposed to the concept of software patents, in part because they hinder the development and use of innovative software by individuals and small companies. Software patents also tend to hinder some forms of experimental research and education.

[†] The 40-bit "exportable" implementation of SSL actually uses a 128-bit RC2 key, in which 88 bits are revealed, producing a "40-bit secret." Netscape claimed that the 88 bits provided protection against *code-book attacks*, in which all 2^{40} keys would be precomputed and the resulting encryption patterns stored. Other SSL implementors have suggested that using a 128-bit key in all cases and simply revealing 88 bits of key in exportable versions of Navigator made Netscape's SSL implementation easier to write.

Table 3-2. Common symmetric encryption algorithms

Algorithm	Description	Key Length	Rating
Blowfish	Block cipher developed by Schneier	1–448 bits	Λ
DES	Data Encryption Standard adopted as a U.S. government standard in 1977	56 bits	§
IDEA	Block cipher developed by Massey and Xuejia	128 bits	Λ
MARS	AES finalist developed by IBM	128–256 bits	ø
RC2	Block cipher developed by Rivest	1–2048 bits	Ω
RC4	Stream cipher developed by Rivest	1–2048 bits	Λ
RC5	Block cipher developed by Ronald Rivest and published in 1994	128–256 bits	ø
RC6	AES finalist developed by RSA Labs	128–256 bits	ø
Rijndael	NIST selection for AES, developed by Daemen and Rijmen	128–256 bits	Ω
Serpent	AES finalist developed by Anderson, Biham, and Knudsen	128–256 bits	ø
Triple-DES	A three-fold application of the DES algorithm	168 bits	Λ
Twofish	AES candidate developed by Schneier	128–256 bits	ø

Key to ratings:

Ω) Excellent algorithm. This algorithm is widely used and is believed to be secure, provided that keys of sufficient length are used.

Λ) Algorithm appears strong but is being phased out for other algorithms that are faster or thought to be more secure.

ø) Algorithm appears to be strong but will not be widely deployed because it was not chosen as the AES standard.

§) Use of this algorithm is no longer recommended because of short key length or mathematical weaknesses. Data encrypted with this algorithm should be reasonably secure from casual browsing, but would not withstand a determined attack by a moderately-funded attacker.

Attacks on Symmetric Encryption Algorithms

If you are going to use cryptography to protect information, then you must assume that people who you do not wish to access your information will be recording the encrypted data and attempting to decrypt it forcibly.[*] To be useful, your cryptographic system must be resistant to this kind of direct attack.

Attacks against encrypted information fall into three main categories. They are:

- Key search (brute force) attacks
- Cryptanalysis
- Systems-based attacks

---

[*] Whitfield Diffie has pointed out that if your data is not going to be subject to this sort of direct attack, then there is no need to encrypt it.

Key search (brute force) attacks

As we saw earlier, the simplest way to attack an encrypted message is simply to attempt to decrypt the message with every possible key. Most attempts will fail, but eventually one of the tries will succeed and either allow the cracker into the system or permit the ciphertext to be decrypted. These attacks, illustrated in Figure 3-3, are called key search or brute force attacks.

There's no way to defend against a key search attack, because there's no way to keep an attacker from trying to decrypt your message with every possible key.

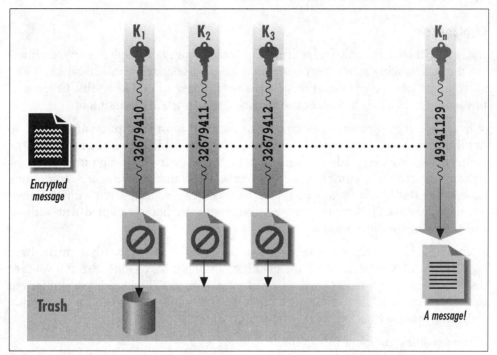

Figure 3-3. A key search attack

Key search attacks are not very efficient. And, as we showed earlier, if the chosen key is long enough, a key search attack is not even feasible: for instance, with a 128-bit key and any conceivable computing technology, life on Earth will cease to exist long before even a single key is likely to be cracked!

On the other hand, many key search attacks are made considerably simpler because most users pick keys based on small passwords with printable characters. For a 128-bit key to be truly secure, all 128 bits must be randomly chosen. That is, there must be 2^{128} distinct keys that could possibly be used to encrypt the data. If a "128-bit key" is actually derived from a password of four lower-case letters, then even though the key appears to be 128 bits long, there are really only $26 \times 26 \times 26 \times 26$, or 456,976 different keys that could actually be used. Instead of a 128-bit key, a key that is chosen from four lower-case letters has an effective key length between 18 bits and 19 bits! (This is because $2^{18} = 262,144$, while $2^{19} = 524,288$.)

From this simple analysis, it would appear that any of the strong algorithms described earlier with a 128-bit key length should be sufficient for most cryptographic needs—both now and forever more. Unfortunately, there are a number of factors that make this solution technically, legally, or politically unsuitable for many applications, as we'll see later in this chapter.

Cryptanalysis

If key length were the only factor determining the security of a cipher, everyone interested in exchanging secret messages would simply use codes with 128-bit keys, and all cryptanalysts (people who break codes) would have to find new jobs. Cryptography would be a solved branch of mathematics, similar to simple addition.

What keeps cryptography interesting is the fact that most encryption algorithms do not live up to our expectations. Key search attacks are seldom required to divulge the contents of an encrypted message. Instead, most encryption algorithms can be defeated by using a combination of sophisticated mathematics and computing power. The result is that many encrypted messages can be deciphered without knowing the key. A skillful cryptanalyst can sometimes decipher encrypted text without even knowing the encryption algorithm.

A cryptanalytic attack can have two possible goals. The cryptanalyst might have ciphertext and want to discover the plaintext, or might have ciphertext and want to discover the encryption key that was used to encrypt it. (These goals are similar but not quite the same.) The following attacks are commonly used when the encryption algorithm is known, and these may be applied to traffic on the Web:

Known plaintext attack
> In this type of attack, the cryptanalyst has a block of plaintext and a corresponding block of ciphertext. Although this may seem an unlikely occurrence, it is actually quite common when cryptography is used to protect electronic mail (with standard headers at the beginning of each message), standard forms, or hard disks (with known structures at predetermined locations on the disk). The goal of a known plaintext attack is to determine the cryptographic key (and possibly the algorithm), which can then be used to decrypt other messages.

Chosen plaintext attack
> In this type of attack, the cryptanalyst can have the subject of the attack (unknowingly) encrypt chosen blocks of data, creating a result that the cryptanalyst can then analyze. Chosen plaintext attacks are simpler to carry out than

they might appear. (For example, the subject of the attack might be a radio link that encrypts and retransmits messages received by telephone.) The goal of a chosen plaintext attack is to determine the cryptographic key, which can then be used to decrypt other messages.

Differential cryptanalysis

This attack, which is a form of chosen plaintext attack, involves encrypting many texts that are only slightly different from one another and comparing the results.

Differential fault analysis

This attack works against cryptographic systems that are built in hardware. The device is subjected to environmental factors (heat, stress, radiation) designed to coax the device into making mistakes during the encryption or decryption operation. These faults can be analyzed and from them the device's internal state, including the encryption key or algorithm, can possibly be learned.

Differential power analysis

This is another attack against cryptographic hardware—in particular, smart cards. By observing the power that a smart card uses to encrypt a chosen block of data, it is possible to learn a little bit of information about the structure of the secret key. By subjecting the smart card to a number of specially-chosen data blocks and carefully monitoring the power used, it is possible to determine the secret key.

Differential timing analysis

This attack is similar to differential power analysis, except that the attacker carefully monitors the time that the smart card takes to perform the requested encryption operations.

The only reliable way to determine if an algorithm is strong is to hire a stable of the world's best cryptographers and pay them to find a weakness. This is the approach used by the National Security Agency. Unfortunately, this approach is beyond the ability of most cryptographers, who instead settle on an alternative known as *peer review*.

Peer review is the process by which most mathematical and scientific truths are verified. First, a person comes up with a new idea or proposes a new theory. Next, the inventor attempts to test his idea or theory on his own. If the idea holds up, it is next published in an academic journal or otherwise publicized within a community of experts. If the experts are motivated, they might look at the idea and see if it has any worth. If the idea stands up over the passage of time, especially if many experts try and fail to disprove the idea, it comes to be regarded as truth.

Peer review of cryptographic algorithms and computer security software follows a similar process. As individuals or organizations come up with a new algorithm, the algorithm is published. If the algorithm is sufficiently interesting, cryptographers or other academics might be motivated to find flaws in it. If the algorithm can stand the test of time, it might be secure.

It's important to realize that simply publishing an algorithm or a piece of software does not guarantee that flaws will be found. The WEP (Wireless Encryption Protocol) encryption algorithm used by the 802.11 networking standard was published for many years before a significant flaw was found in the algorithm—the flaw had been there all along, but no one had bothered to look for it.

The peer review process isn't perfect, but it's better than the alternative: no review at all. Do not trust people who say they've developed a new encryption algorithm, but also say that they don't want to disclose how the algorithm works because such disclosure would compromise the strength of the algorithm. In practice, there is no way to keep an algorithm secret: if the algorithm is being used to store information that is valuable, an attacker will purchase (or steal) a copy of a program that implements the algorithm, disassemble the program, and figure out how it works.* True cryptographic security lies in openness and peer review, not in algorithmic secrecy.

Systems-based attacks

Another way of breaking a code is to attack the cryptographic system that uses the cryptographic algorithm, without actually attacking the algorithm itself.

One of the most spectacular cases of systems-based attacks was the VC-I video encryption algorithm used for early satellite TV broadcasts. For years, video pirates sold decoder boxes that could intercept the transmissions of keys and use them to decrypt the broadcasts. The VC-I encryption algorithm was sound, but the system as a whole was weak. (This case also demonstrates the fact that when a lot of money is at stake, people will often find the flaws in a weak encryption system and those flaws will be exploited.)

Many of the early attacks against Netscape's implementation of SSL were actually attacks on Netscape Navigator's implementation, rather than on the SSL protocol itself. In one published attack, researchers Wagner and Goldberg at the University of California at Berkeley discovered that Navigator's random number generator was not really random. It was possible for attackers to closely monitor the computer on which Navigator was running, predict the random number generator's starting configuration, and determine the randomly chosen key using a fairly straightforward method. In another attack, the researchers discovered that they could easily modify the Navigator program itself so that the random number generator would not be executed. This entirely eliminated the need to guess the key.

---

* In the case of the RC2 and RC4 encryption algorithm, the attackers went further and published source code for the reverse-engineered algorithms!

Public Key Algorithms

The existence of public key cryptography was first postulated in print in the fall of 1975 by Whitfield Diffie and Martin Hellman. The two researchers, then at Stanford University, wrote a paper in which they presupposed the existence of an encryption technique in which information encrypted with one key (the public key) could be decrypted by a second, apparently unrelated key (the private key). Robert Merkle, then a graduate student at Berkeley, had similar ideas at the same time, but because of the vagaries of the academic publication process, Merkle's papers were not published until the underlying principles and mathematics of the Diffie-Hellman algorithm were widely known.

Since that time, a variety of public key encryption systems have been developed. Unfortunately, there have been significantly fewer developments in public key algorithms than in symmetric key algorithms. The reason has to do with how these algorithms are created. Good symmetric key algorithms simply scramble their input depending on the input key; developing a new symmetric key algorithm requires coming up with new ways for performing that scrambling reliably. Public key algorithms tend to be based on number theory. Developing new public key algorithms requires identifying new mathematical equations with particular properties.

The following list summarizes the public key systems in common use today:

Diffie-Hellman key exchange

A system for exchanging cryptographic keys between active parties. Diffie-Hellman is not actually a method of encryption and decryption, but a method of developing and exchanging a shared private key over a public communications channel. In effect, the two parties agree to some common numerical values, and then each party creates a key. Mathematical transformations of the keys are exchanged. Each party can then calculate a third session key that cannot easily be derived by an attacker who knows both exchanged values.

DSA/DSS

The Digital Signature Standard (DSS) was developed by the National Security Agency and adopted as a Federal Information Processing Standard (FIPS) by the National Institute for Standards and Technology. DSS is based on the Digital Signature Algorithm (DSA). Although DSA allows keys of any length, only keys between 512 and 1024 bits are permitted under the DSS FIPS. As specified, DSS can be used only for digital signatures, although it is possible to use some DSA implementations for encryption as well.

Elliptic curves

Public key systems have traditionally been based on factoring (RSA), discrete logarithms (Diffie-Helman), and the knapsack problem. Elliptic curve cryptosystems are public key encryption systems that are based on an elliptic curve rather than on a traditional logarithmic function; that is, they are based on solutions to the equation $y^2 = x^3 + ax + b$. The advantage to using elliptic curve systems stems from the fact that there are no known subexponential algorithms for computing discrete logarithms of elliptic curves. Thus, short keys in elliptic curve cryptosystems can offer a high degree of privacy and security, while remaining very fast to calculate. Elliptic curves can be computed very efficiently in hardware. Certicom (*http://www.certicom.com*) has attempted to commercialize implementations of elliptic curve cryptosystems for use in mobile computing.

RSA

RSA is a well-known public key cryptography system developed in 1977 by three professors then at MIT: Ronald Rivest, Adi Shamir, and Leonard Adleman. RSA can be used both for encrypting information and as the basis of a digital signature system. Digital signatures can be used to prove the authorship and authenticity of digital information. The key may be any length, depending on the particular implementation used.

When Is 128 Bigger than 512?

Because the keys of symmetric and asymmetric encryption algorithms are used in fundamentally different ways, it is not possible to infer the relative cryptographic strength of these algorithms by comparing the length of their keys.

Traditionally, Internet-based cryptographic software has paired 512-bit RSA keys with 40-bit RC2 keys; 1024-bit RSA keys have been used with 128-bit RC2. But this does not mean that 512-bit RSA keys offer roughly the same strength as 40-bit RC2 keys, or that 1024-bit RSA keys offer roughly the strength of 128-bit RC2 keys.

As this book goes to press, 40-bit RC2 keys can be readily cracked using a small network of high-performance personal computers; there is even software that is commercially available for networking PCs together for the purpose of cracking 40-bit RC2 keys. At the same time, 512-bit RSA keys are right at the edge of the size of numbers that can be factored by large Internet-based factoring projects that employ tens of thousands of individual computers. Thus, a 512-bit RSA key offers considerably more security than the 40-bit RC2 key.

It is likely that within the next 20 years there will be many breakthroughs in the science of factoring large numbers. It is also clear that computers in 20 years' time will be dramatically faster than the computers of today. Thus, it might be reasonable to assume that it will be quite possible to factor a 1024-bit RSA key in the year 2020.

But as we have seen in this chapter, even if there are dramatic advances in the field of quantum computing, it is unlikely that it will be possible to do a brute-force attack on a 128-bit RC2 key within the course of human existence on the planet Earth. The reason that these numbers are so different from the 512-bit/40-bit numbers is that each increased bit of key for the RC2 algorithm doubles the difficulty of finding a new key, but each additional bit of key for the RSA algorithm only nominally increases the difficulty of factoring the composite number used by the algorithm, assuming some advances in our ability to identify prime numbers.

Thus, it's possible a 128-bit RC2 key is impossibly stronger than a 1024-bit RSA key.[a]

a. For more information on cryptographic key sizes, see "Selecting Cryptographic Key Sizes," by Arjen K. Lenstra and Eric R. Verheul, available from *http://cryptosavvy.com/cryptosizes.pdf* and *http://cryptosavvy.com/toc.pdf*.

Uses of Public Key Encryption

Two of the most common uses for public key cryptography are *encrypted messaging* and *digital signatures*:

- With encrypted messaging, a person who wishes to send an encrypted message to a particular recipient encrypts that message with the individual's public key. The message can then only be decrypted by the authorized recipient.

- With digital signatures, the sender of the message uses the public key algorithm and a private key to digitally sign a message. Anyone who receives the message can then validate the authenticity of the message by verifying the signature with the sender's public key.

In the following two sections we'll show examples of each.

Encrypted messaging

Encrypted messaging is a general term that is used to describe the sending and receiving of encrypted email and instant messages. In general, these systems use a public key to transform a message into an encrypted message. This message can only be decrypted by someone (or something) that has the public key's corresponding private key.

For example, here is a message:

```
this is a test message
```

And here is a small PGP public key:

```
-----BEGIN PGP PUBLIC KEY BLOCK-----
Version: PGP 6.5.8

mQGiBDqX9jwRBADakcIMfMhgvHCgeOJOXWqv7Lo8CtbqNpkvpRc98Z7dqjkhhcqC
4xol6rAv4zoZipMtCKOvR2jAOuqQIO5GGSnDdOFXeIXH7tW9oquljjwlRBUqWbTb
zAcZCOqyNCdStiKTOSZCFzdDGVHiomSYQ7OmOQP77ipjFnNwyQk5hmTBhQCg/1JE
sSl5O4X8tSf9vTglF5TvpyOD/1HtVqrrebkK7zPG2AKDoIOOdgtGvOPeJSJ76EWB
FHMKFm6hOBQjq4NSHUsxuCyO/mpLa31Hm57FHAY/4IbQ1RkFNdDAnpqXeOHWcAT2
Oy1OL/dMSy2OFOvlx/WUKEgz869CaxPBlq14C1R68P+eMp5t8FG8mPXMFyAyMBcA
rTLBA/9p6xZAOrxLhaOaPbQpNFSb78J89bs3Wb8dDzJONkUB2dpGUPy7YfAHoZR1
8GOkGk5+8CuhQ8xbOt5jr11/aCjSs2kzrORYpYiDJXprSTvVUHhLjqttXoBCMlsj
TlUNXvc5w+ONVD6Dq6HMNOHQldDcvGjeCCGBvF5kfYsyJEQGkrQbTXIuIFRlc3Qg
S2V5IDxOZXNOQGtleS5jb2O+iQBOBBARAgAOBQI6l/Y8BAsDAgECGQEACgkQGQai
QpjjHCxWlACbBw1H9gYMIuu6FZyXC+n8GcbiOzUAnjuE/UeTtKTWa+1U+cU6xRRR
2YxMuQENBDqX9jOQBADvKZeABrS2KagG6cDOmiUWiG4Y7VIq4CjsC9cdeQtbZ+FV
OoxAb9vz1pSmqdf8/RcvS5Tr5Wby+oBxlXRy33R72FO3J4wTOdfstzdnMEA87p/n
kIla4Quo4j5XoWCycMWAZ1w5/SHw+N2ESOCyvITY19dDjh2sJ8zsOg9rp4rNAwAC
AgP9F6N+z2baqrm/Wi2tTVoEpDL8Y+BF6Wz3FI7pdLZxOojEGI6ELfChH3P3VDoh
LjduRMt9VUyhD/9Sl7BmFJOlUczLuQICv3toOINtHlY6gH8KM2nh1dfcB8OGwg9V
oGE71lXO6T6wMNy6KmFxLYLscFh592ThpXsvn8GBPOfIZTCJAEYEGBECAAYFAjqX
9jOACgkQGQaiQpjjHCwJ1ACfWjQlxRaS+Xj/qv5z3cceMevCetgAoJFbuuMHXl/X
NTFrAkXTgoJ1MYVH
=Wx2A
-----END PGP PUBLIC KEY BLOCK-----
```

We can use the encryption key to encrypt the small message. Here is the result:

```
-----BEGIN PGP MESSAGE-----
Version: PGP 6.5.8

qANQR1DBwE4DZuAgjgADrN4QBADoJ9piydOc9fLS25Cya6NrtR1PrY4hOk7aZzlN
p1fZbOWptzb8Pn3gkrtY3H2OMWc2hhl3ER68CFwyC8BAB6EJqHwtpldB258D43iu
```

```
NffuB4vKTdu1caoT4AHSZgo2zX/Ao/JuEaOmwzhnxFGYhuvR26y2hVk7IlWyDJ6d
ZRfN3QQAx9opTjQRSjA3YJUKism8t+ba8VYEvIeRI7sukblzVF5OjG6vQW3m368V
udCWwfPDbC7XM3Hwfvuw054ImYGsz3BWWGPXjQfOeOBJzKVPXArUUDv+oKfVdp7w
V/sGEErhnly7s9Q2IqyeXPc7ug99zLhXb5FRtmPf3mASwwuhrQHJLRm3eWUfKn8z
IMehG2KU3kJrNQXEUORdWJ9gV72tQlyB6AD2tJK33tNk7gV+lw==
=5h+G
-----END PGP MESSAGE-----
```

Notice that the encrypted message is considerably longer than the original plaintext. Encrypted messages are almost always longer than the original plaintext because they usually contain header information and other details that are useful for the decryption process. This overhead is most noticeable when short messages are encrypted. In the case of PGP messages, the encrypted message contains (among other things) the ID code for each of the keys that can decipher the message.

Digital signatures

Instead of encrypting a message, we can use public key cryptography to digitally sign a message.

Consider the message from the previous example:

```
this is a test message
```

This message can be signed with a private key that corresponds to the public key shown. The result is a signed message:

```
-----BEGIN PGP SIGNED MESSAGE-----
Hash: SHA1

this is a test message

-----BEGIN PGP SIGNATURE-----
Version: PGP 6.5.8

iQA/AwUBOpf3DRkGokKY4xwsEQKQvQCg291aRcMYyjsdeTdIOQZ2dZOHpdkAn3z8
gT7Vd/OWadj1j+OnXLysXK+E
=CcHl
-----END PGP SIGNATURE-----
```

For detailed information about digital signatures, see Chapter 6. Additional information about public keys, digital signatures, and encrypted messaging can be found in the book *PGP: Pretty Good Privacy*, by Simson Garfinkel.

Attacks on Public Key Algorithms

Public key algorithms are theoretically easier to attack than symmetric key algorithms because the attacker (presumably) has a copy of the public key that was used to encrypt the message. The job of the attacker is further simplified because the message presumably identifies which public key encryption algorithm was used to encrypt the message.

Public key algorithm attacks generally fall into two categories: key search attacks and analytic attacks.

Key search attacks

Key search attacks are the most popular kind of attacks to mount on public key encrypted messages because they are the most easily understood. These attacks attempt to derive a private key from its corresponding public key.

In the case of the RSA public key system, key search attacks are performed by attempting to factor a large number that is associated with the public key. The number is the product of two prime numbers. Once the large composite number is factored, the private key can be readily derived from the public key.

Because of the widespread use of the RSA system, techniques for rapidly factoring large composite numbers have become of great interest to many mathematicians. But while there have been steady improvements in factoring techniques, mathematicians have not yet discovered a fast, general-purpose technique for factoring arbitrarily large numbers. Of course, the fact that no such factoring algorithm has been discovered should not be taken as proof that no such algorithm exists: there may come a time when factoring becomes a trivial problem and the world needs to discard RSA in favor of some other public key encryption algorithm.

The most famous factoring attack at the time of this writing was the factoring of the RSA-129 challenge number. The number, named "RSA-129" because it consisted of 129 decimal digits, was first published as a challenge to readers in the September 1977 issue of *Popular Science*. The number was factored in 1994 by an international team of volunteers coordinated by Arjen Lenstra, then at Bellcore (the research arm of the U.S. local telephone companies), Derek Atkins, Michael Graff, and Paul Leyland.

RSA Data Security publishes a list of additional factoring challenges, with cash rewards for people who are the first to factor the numbers. You can get a complete list of the RSA challenge numbers by sending a message to *challenge-rsa-list@rsa.com*.

Analytic attacks

The other way of attacking a public key encryption system is to find a fundamental flaw or weakness in the mathematical problem on which the encryption system is based. Don't scoff—this has been done at least once before. The first public key encryption system to be patented was based on a mathematical problem called the Superincreasing Knapsack Problem. A few years after this technique was suggested, a way was found to mathematically derive the secret key from the public key in a very short amount of time.

Known versus published methods

It is worth noting that there may always be a difference between the best *known* methods and the best *published* methods. If a major mathematical breakthrough in factoring were discovered, it might not be published for all to see. For example, if a new method were developed by a government agency, it might be kept secret to be used against encrypted messages sent by officials of other countries. Alternatively, if a new method were developed by someone with criminal tendencies, it might be kept secret to be used in future economic crimes involving existing encryption methods.

Implementation Strength

We would be remiss not to note that strong algorithms and good choices for keys are not sufficient to assure cryptographic strength. It is also vital that the implementation of the algorithm, along with any key generation and storage, be correct and carefully tested. A buggy implementation, poor random number generation, or sloppy handling of keys may all increase the exposure of your information.

It is also the case that the implementations are points of attack. Law enforcement, criminals, or members of your family may all be interested in what you are encrypting. If they can gain access to your software or hardware, they may be able to alter the system to capture your keys to decrypt your messages, or capture the unencrypted traffic. For one example of a hardware device to capture keys and text, you might look at the KeyGhost at *http://www.keyghost.com/*.

Message Digest Functions

Message digest functions distill the information contained in a file (small or large) into a single large number, typically between 128 and 256 bits in length. This is illustrated in Figure 3-4. The best message digest functions combine these mathematical properties:

- Every bit of the message digest function is potentially influenced by every bit of the function's input.
- If any given bit of the function's input is changed, every output bit has a 50 percent chance of changing.
- Given an input file and its corresponding message digest, it should be computationally infeasible to find another file with the same message digest value.

Message digests are also called one-way *hash functions* because they produce values that are difficult to invert, resistant to attack, effectively unique, and widely distributed.

Many message digest functions have been proposed and are now in use. Here are a few:

MD2
Message Digest #2, developed by Ronald Rivest. This message digest is probably the most secure of Rivest's message digest functions, but takes the longest to compute. As a result, MD2 is rarely used. MD2 produces a 128-bit digest.

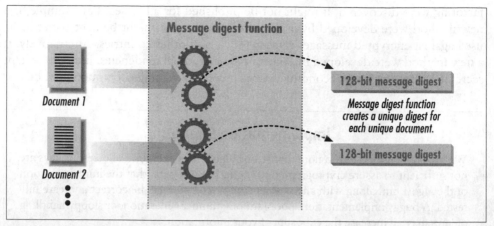

Figure 3-4. A message digest function

MD4

Message Digest #4, also developed by Rivest. This message digest algorithm was developed as a fast alternative to MD2. Subsequently, MD4 was shown to have a possible weakness. That is, it is possible to find a secured file that produces the same MD4 as a given file without requiring a brute force search (which would be infeasible for the same reason that it is infeasible to search a 128-bit keyspace). MD4 produces a 128-bit digest.

MD5

Message Digest #5, also developed by Rivest. MD5 is a modification of MD4 that includes techniques designed to make it more secure. Although widely used, in the summer of 1996 a few flaws were discovered in MD5 that allowed some kinds of *collisions* in a weakened form of the algorithm to be calculated (the next section explains what a collision is). As a result, MD5 is slowly falling out of favor. MD5 and SHA-1 are both used in SSL and Microsoft's Authenticode technology. MD5 produces a 128-bit digest.

SHA

The Secure Hash Algorithm, related to MD4 and designed for use with the National Institute for Standards and Technology's Digital Signature Standard (NIST's DSS). Shortly after the publication of the SHA, NIST announced that it was not suitable for use without a small change. SHA produces a 160-bit digest.

SHA-1

The revised Secure Hash Algorithm incorporates minor changes from SHA. It is not publicly known if these changes make SHA-1 more secure than SHA, although many people believe that it does. SHA-1 produces a 160-bit digest.

SHA-256, SHA-384, SHA-512

These are, respectively, 256-, 384-, and 512-bit hash functions designed to be used with 128-, 192-, and 256-bit encryption algorithms. These functions were proposed by NIST in 2001 for use with the Advanced Encryption Standard.

Besides these functions, it is also possible to use traditional symmetric block encryption systems such as the DES as message digest functions. To use an encryption function as a message digest function, simply run the encryption function in cipher feedback mode. For a key, use a key that is randomly chosen and specific to the application. Encrypt the entire input file. The last block of encrypted data is the message digest. Symmetric encryption algorithms produce excellent hashes, but they are significantly slower than the message digest functions described previously.

Message Digest Algorithms at Work

Message digest algorithms themselves are not generally used for encryption and decryption operations. Instead, they are used in the creation of digital signatures, the creation of message authentication codes (MACs), and the creation of encryption keys from passphrases.

The easiest way to understand message digest functions is to look at them at work. The following example shows some inputs to the MD5 function and the resulting MD5 codes:

```
MD5(The meeting last week was swell.)= 050f3905211cddf36107ffc361c23e3d
MD5(There is $1500 in the blue box.) = 05f8cfc03f4e58cbee731aa4a14b3f03
MD5(There is $1100 in the blue box.) = d6dee11aae89661a45eb9d21e30d34cb
```

Notice that all of these messages have dramatically different MD5 codes. Even the second and third messages, which differ by only a single character (and, within that character, by only a single binary bit), have completely different message digests. The message digest appears almost random, but it's not.

Let's look at a few more message digests:

```
MD5(There is $1500 in the blue bo)   = f80b3fde8ecbac1b515960b9058de7a1
MD5(There is $1500 in the blue box)  = a4a5471a0e019a4a502134d38fb64729
MD5(There is $1500 in the blue box.) = 05f8cfc03f4e58cbee731aa4a14b3f03
MD5(There is $1500 in the blue box!) = 4b36807076169572b804907735accd42
MD5(There is $1500 in the blue box..)= 3a7b4e07ae316eb60b5af4a1a2345931
```

Consider the third line of MD5 code in this example: you can see that it is *exactly the same* as the second line of the first MD5 example. This is because *the same text always produces the same MD5 code.*

Message digest functions are a powerful tool for detecting very small changes in very large files or messages; calculate the MD5 code for your message and set it aside. If you think that the file has been changed (either accidentally or on purpose), simply recalculate the MD5 code and compare it with the MD5 that you originally calculated. If they match, you can safely assume that the file was not modified.[*]

In theory, two different files can have the same message digest value. This is called a *collision*. For a message digest function to be secure, it should be computationally infeasible to find or produce these collisions.

Uses of Message Digest Functions

Message digest functions are widely used today for a number of reasons:

- Message digest functions are much faster to calculate than traditional symmetric key cryptographic functions but appear to share many of their strong cryptographic properties.

- There are no patent restrictions on any message digest functions that are currently in use.

- There are no export or import restrictions on message digest functions.

- Message digest functions appear to provide an excellent means of spreading the randomness (entropy) from an input among all of the function's output bits.[†]

- Using a message digest, you can easily transform a typed passphrase into an encryption key for use with a symmetric cipher. PGP uses this technique for computing the encryption key that is used to encrypt the user's private key.

- Message digests can be readily used for message authentication codes that use a shared secret between two parties to prove that a message is authentic. MACs are appended to the end of the message to be verified. (RFC 2104 describes how to use keyed hashing for message authentication. See the "HMAC" section later in this chapter.)

Because of their properties, message digest functions are also an important part of many cryptographic systems in use today:

- Message digests are the basis of most digital signature standards. Instead of signing the entire document, most digital signature standards specify that the message digest of the document be calculated. It is the message digest, rather than the entire document, which is actually signed.

---

[*] For any two files, there is of course a finite chance that the two files will have the same MD5 code. This chance is roughly equal to 1 in 2^{128}. As 2^{128} is such a large number, it is extraordinarily unlikely that any two files created by the human race that contain different contents will ever have the same MD5 codes.

[†] To generate a "random" number, simply take a whole bunch of data sources that seem to change over time, such as log files, time-of-date clocks, and user input, and run the information through a message digest function. If there are more bits of entropy in an input block than there are output bits of the hash, all of the output bits can be assumed to be independent and random, provided that the message digest function is secure.

- MACs based on message digests provide the "cryptographic" security for most of the Internet's routing protocols.
- Programs such as PGP (Pretty Good Privacy, described in Chapter 4) use message digests to transform a passphrase provided by a user into an encryption key that is used for symmetric encryption. (In the case of PGP, symmetric encryption is used for PGP's "conventional encryption" function as well as to encrypt the user's private key.)

Considering the widespread use of message digest functions, it is disconcerting that there is so little published theoretical basis behind most message digest functions.

HMAC

A Hash Message Authentication Code (HMAC) function is a technique for verifying the integrity of a message transmitted between two parties that agree on a shared secret key.

Essentially, HMAC combines the original message and a key to compute a message digest function of the two.* The sender of the message computes the HMAC of the message and the key and transmits the HMAC with the original message. The recipient recalculates the HMAC using the message and the sender's copy of the secret key, then compares the received HMAC with the calculated HMAC to see if they match. If the two HMACs match, then the recipient knows that the original message has not been modified, because the message digest hasn't changed, and that it is authentic, because the sender knew the shared key, which is presumed to be secret (see Figure 3-5).

HMACs can be used for many of the same things as digital signatures, and offer a number of advantages, including:

- HMACs are typically much faster to calculate and verify than digital signatures, because they use hash functions rather than public key mathematics. They are thus ideal for systems that require high performance, such as routers, or systems with very slow or small microprocessors, such as embedded systems.
- HMACs are much smaller than digital signatures, yet offer comparable signature security, because most digital signature algorithms are used to sign cryptographic hash residues rather than the original message.

---

* The simplest way to create a HMAC would be to concatenate the data with the key and compute the hash of the result. This is not the approach that is used by the IETF HMAC standard described in RFC 2104. Instead of simply concatenating the key behind the data, RFC 2104 specifies an algorithm that is designed to harden the HMAC against certain kinds of attacks that might be possible if the underlying MAC were not secure. As it turns out, HMAC is usually used with MD5 or SHA, two MAC algorithms that are currently believed to be quite secure. Nevertheless, the more complicated HMAC algorithm is part of the IETF standard, so that is what most people use.

- HMACs can be used in some jurisdictions where the use of public key cryptography is legally prohibited or in doubt.

However, HMACs do have an important disadvantage over digital signature systems: because HMACs are based on a key that is shared between the two parties, if either party's key is compromised, it will be possible for an attacker to create fraudulent messages.

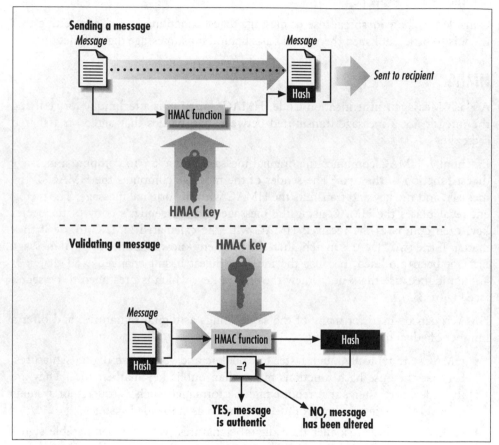

Figure 3-5. Using an HMAC to verify the authenticity and integrity of a message

Attacks on Message Digest Functions

There are two kinds of attacks on message digest functions. The first attack is to find two messages—any two messages—that have the same message digest. The second attack is significantly harder: given a particular message, find a second message that has the same message digest code. There's extra value if the second message is in a human-readable message, in the same language, and in the same word processor format as the first.

MD5 is probably secure enough to be used over the next five to ten years. Even if it becomes possible to find MD5 collisions at will, it will be very difficult to transform this knowledge into a general-purpose attack on SSL.

Nevertheless, to minimize the dependence on any one cryptographic algorithm, most modern cryptographic protocols negotiate the algorithms that they will use from a list of several possibilities. Thus, if a particular encryption algorithm or message digest function is compromised, it will be relatively simple to tell Internet servers to stop using the compromised algorithm and use others instead.

## CHAPTER 4

Cryptography and the Web

In this chapter:
- Cryptography and Web Security
- Working Cryptographic Systems and Protocols
- What Cryptography Can't Do
- Legal Restrictions on Cryptography

When you get right down to it, the Internet is an unsecure communications system. While the Internet was designed to be efficient and robust, it was not designed to be inherently secure. The Internet's original security was provided by simple access control: only trustworthy military installations, corporations, and schools were allowed to have access. At each of those organizations, only trustworthy individuals were allowed to have accounts. In theory, people who abused the network lost their access.

The idea of using access control to ensure security failed almost immediately. In December 1973, Robert Metcalfe noted that high school students had gained access to the Internet using stolen passwords; two computers had crashed under suspicious circumstances. In RFC 602 (reprinted on the following page) Metcalfe identified three key problems on the network of his day: sites were not secure against remote access; unauthorized people were using the network; and some ruffians were breaking into computers (and occasionally crashing those machines) simply for the fun of it.

Today, the Internet's overall security posture has changed significantly. As we saw in Chapter 2, the simple act of browsing a web page on a remote computer can involve sending packets of information to and receiving them from more than a dozen different computers operated by just as many different organizations. The division of responsibility among multiple organizations makes it possible for each of these organizations—and many more—to eavesdrop on your communications, or even to disrupt them.

Yet in many ways, today's Internet is more secure than the early network of the 1970s and 1980s. The reason is the widespread and growing use of cryptography.

Cryptography and Web Security

Today, cryptography is the fundamental technology used to protect information as it travels over the Internet. Every day, encryption is used to protect the content of web transactions, email, newsgroups, chat, web conferencing, and telephone calls as they

RFC 602

Arpa Network Working Group Bob Metcalfe (PARC-MAXC)
Request for Comments: 602 Dec 1973 NIC #21021

"The Stockings Were Hung by the Chimney with Care"

The ARPA Computer Network is susceptible to security violations for at least the three following reasons:

1. Individual sites, used to physical limitations on machine access, have not yet taken sufficient precautions toward securing their systems against unauthorized remote use. For example, many people still use passwords which are easy to guess: their first names, their initials, their host name spelled backwards, a string of characters which are easy to type in sequence (e.g., ZXCVBNM).

2. The TIP[a] allows access to the ARPANET to a much wider audience than is thought or intended. TIP phone numbers are posted, like those scribbled hastily on the walls of phone booths and men's rooms. The TIP requires no user identification before giving service. Thus, many people, including those who used to spend their time ripping off Ma Bell, get access to our stockings in a most anonymous way.

3. There is lingering affection for the challenge of breaking someone's system. This affection lingers despite the fact that everyone knows that it's easy to break systems—even easier to crash them.

All of this would be quite humorous and cause for raucous eye winking and elbow nudging if it weren't for the fact that in recent weeks at least two major serving hosts were crashed under suspicious circumstances by people who knew what they were risking; on yet a third system, the system wheel password was compromised—by two high school students in Los Angeles, no less.[b]

We suspect that the number of dangerous security violations is larger than any of us know and is growing. You are advised not to sit "in hope that Saint Nicholas would soon be there."

a. The Terminal Interface Processor was the ARPANET's anonymous dialup server.

b. The *wheel* password is the superuser password.

are sent over the Internet. Without encryption any crook, thief, Internet service provider, telephone company, hostile corporation, or government employee who has physical access to the wires that carry your data could eavesdrop upon its contents. With encryption, as we discussed in Chapter 3, it is possible to protect a message in such a way that all of the world's computers working in concert until the end of time would be unable to decipher its contents.

Cryptography can be used for more than scrambling messages. Increasingly, systems that employ cryptographic techniques are used to control access to computer systems and to sign digital messages. Cryptographic systems have also been devised to allow the anonymous exchange of digital money and even to facilitate fair and unforgeable online voting.

Roles for Cryptography

Security professionals have identified five different roles that encryption can play in modern information systems. In the interest of sharing a common terminology, each of these different roles is identified by a specific keyword. The roles are:

Authentication
> Digital signatures can be used to identify a participant in a web transaction or the author of an email message; people who receive a message that is signed by a digital signature can use it to verify the identity of the signer. Digital signatures can be used in conjunction with passwords and biometrics (see Chapter 6) or as an alternative to them.

Authorization
> Whereas authentication is used to determine the identity of a participant, authorization techniques are used to determine if that individual is authorized to engage in a particular transaction. Crytographic techniques can be used to disbribute a list of authorized users that is all but impossible to falsify.

Confidentiality
> Encryption is used to scramble information sent over networks and stored on servers so that eavesdroppers cannot access the data's content. Some people call this quality "privacy," but most professionals reserve that word for referring to the protection of personal information (whether confidential or not) from aggregation and improper use.

Integrity
> Methods that are used to verify that a message has not been modified while in transit. Often, this is done with digitally signed message digest codes.

Nonrepudiation
> Cryptographic receipts are created so that an author of a message cannot realistically deny sending a message (but see the discussion later in this section).

Strictly speaking, there is some overlap among these areas. For example, when a message is encrypted to provide confidentiality, an unexpected byproduct is often integrity. That's because many encrypted messages will not decrypt if they are altered. Current practices, however, dictate that it is better to use algorithms that are specifically designed to assure integrity for this purpose, rather than relying on integrity as a byproduct of other algorithms. Using separate algorithms allows finer control of the underlying processes. Using separate algorithms for confidentiality, authentication, and integrity also minimizes the impact of any legal restrictions that apply to cryptography, because these restrictions are usually aimed at confidentiality but not other cryptographic practices.

Nonrepudiation means adding assurance mechanisms to verify the identity and intent of the user. This is needed so the user cannot claim, after the fact, that she did not actually conduct the transaction. This claim may be phrased as a denial that the activity was ever conducted, or it may be a claim that someone else was using her account. Although nonrepudiation is often listed as one of the advantages of public key technology, the "nonrepudiation" provided by this technology is not true nonrepudiation. Public key technology can prove that a certain private key was used to create a digital signature, but it cannot prove the intent of the key's user.

"Nonrepudiation," as the term is commonly used by cryptographers, analysts, and even lawmakers, is simply not possible. Even if the cryptography is perfect, the person's computer might be infected with a virus that causes it to behave in a manner other than what's intended. Smart cards and biometrics do not solve the nonrepudiation problem either—you might insert your smart card into a reader, thinking you are signing an electronic check to subscribe to a magazine, only to discover that a hostile ActiveX control has noticed the insertion and used your smart card to authorize the transfer of $1000 out of your bank account. Or a crook may force your signature at gunpoint. People can *always* repudiate something that a computer has done on their behalf.

Working Cryptographic Systems and Protocols

A cryptographic *system* is a collection of software and hardware that can encrypt or decrypt information. A typical cryptographic system is the combination of a desktop computer, a web browser, a remote web server, and the computer on which the web server is running. A cryptographic *protocol*, by contrast, describes how information moves throughout the cryptographic system. In our examples, the web browser and the remote web server communicate using the Secure Sockets Layer (SSL) cryptographic protocol.

More than a dozen cryptographic protocols have been developed for Internet security and commerce. These systems fall into two categories. The first category of cryptographic programs and protocols is used for encryption of offline messages—mostly email. The second category of cryptographic protocols is used for confidentiality, authentication, integrity, and nonrepudiation for online communications.

Offline Encryption Systems

Offline encryption systems are designed to take a message, encrypt it, and either store the ciphertext or transmit it to another user on the Internet. Some popular programs that are used for email encryption are shown in Table 4-1 and described in the sections that follow.

Table 4-1. Cryptographic protocols for offline communications

Protocol	What does it do?	Widely deployed?	Programs and systems	URL
PGP/OpenPGP	Encryption and digital signatures for email and electronic documents	Yes	PGP (Network Associates)	*http://www.pgp.com/*
			Hushmail (Hush Communications)	*http://www.hushmail.com/*
			Veridis	*http://www.veridis.com/*
			Highware	*http://www.highware.com/*
			GNU Privacy Guard (GNU)	*http://www.gnupg.org/*
S/MIME	Encryption and digital signatures for email	No	Netscape Communicator (Netscape Communications)	*http://netscape.com/*
			Outlook (Microsoft)	
			Outlook Express (Microsoft)	*http://microsoft.com/*

PGP/OpenPGP

PGP (Pretty Good Privacy)* is a complete working system for the cryptographic protection of electronic mail and files. OpenPGP is a set of standards (RFC 2440) that describe the formats for encrypted messages, keys, and digital signatures. PGP offers confidentiality, integrity, and nonrepudiation.

PGP was the first widespread public key encryption program. The original version was written between 1990 and 1992 by Phil Zimmermann and released on the Internet in June 1991. Later versions were the result of efforts by Zimmermann and programmers around the world.

PGP is available in two ways: as a command-line program, which can be run on many different operating systems, and as an integrated application, which is limited to running on the Windows and Macintosh platforms. The integrated application comes with plug-in modules that allow it to integrate with popular email packages such as Microsoft Outlook, Outlook Express, Eudora, and Netscape Communicator. With these plug-ins, the standard email packages can automatically send and receive PGP-encrypted messages.

Current versions of PGP allow users to create two kinds of private keys: *encryption keys*, which are used for actually encrypting email messages, and *signing keys*, which are used for digitally signing messages. Older versions of PGP supported only a single key that was used for both encryption and signing.

Each PGP key consists of two parts: a person's name and the actual mathematical key that is used to perform cryptographic operations, as shown in Figure 4-1.

---

* *http://www.pgp.com/* and *http://www.pgpi.org/*

Key ID: 903C9265
Date Key Created: 1994/07/15

User ID's and Digital Signatures

User ID	Certified by
simson@acm.org	√ Ruth √ Jane
simson@mit.edu	√ Ruth √ Debby

PGP public key

Key information is part of the public key certificate, but does not play any role in the decryption of messages

Figure 4-1. PGP keys consist of the actual public key that is used to encrypt or decrypt information, one or more email addresses, and one or more digital signatures attached to each email address.

Because PGP keys have names, one logical question to ask is this: how do you know that a given PGP key really belongs to the person whose name is on that key? This can be a very difficult question to answer.

The simplest way to be sure of a key's authenticity is to get a copy of the key from its owner. Unlike other email encryption systems, every PGP user can certify any key that he wishes: if you have a key, it is up to you to decide if you believe that the key actually belongs to the person who is named on the key's certificate. When you get a person's key and add it to your PGP *key ring*, you can tell your copy of PGP whether or not to trust the key.

In practice, it is not always possible to have face-to-face meetings with people before you get their keys. As an alternative to face-to-face meetings, PGP has a provision for key signing. That is, one PGP key can be used to sign a second key. Essentially, this means that the first person is using his key to attest to the validity of the second person. I may not be able to meet directly with Sam, but if I trust Deborah, and I get a copy of Sam's key with Deborah's signature on the key attesting to the fact that Sam's key is valid, I may trust the key. This process is called *certification*. Certification is discussed in detail in Chapter 7. Chapter 6 contains additional discussion of PGP and provides examples of its use.

PGP's name-based system also assumes that everybody who signed and who uses the key thinks that the name on the key refers to the same person. This may be true for some names and email addresses, but it is certainly not true for others. There might be many John Smiths; several people might use the email address *president@company.com* over the course of a few years. On this issue, PGP is silent.

S/MIME

When you send an email with an attachment over the Internet, the attachment is encoded with a protocol called the Multipurpose Internet Mail Extensions,[*] or MIME. The MIME standard codifies the technique by which binary files, such as images or Microsoft Word documents, can be encoded in a format that can be sent by email.

Secure/MIME[†] (S/MIME) extends the MIME standard to allow for encrypted email. On the surface, S/MIME offers similar functionality to PGP; both allow email messages to be encrypted and digitally signed. But S/MIME is different from PGP in an important way: to send somebody a message that is encrypted with PGP you need a copy of that person's key. With S/MIME, on the other hand, to send somebody an encrypted message you need a copy of that person's S/MIME certificate. In general, people cannot create their own S/MIME certificates. Instead, these certificates are issued by third parties called *certification authorities*. This extra layer of complexity has somewhat limited the widespread adoption of S/MIME as a system for encrypted email.

Online Cryptographic Protocols and Systems

Online cryptographic protocols generally require real-time interplay between a client and a server to work properly. The most popular online protocol is SSL, which is used to protect information as it is sent between a web browser and a web server. Some popular systems that fall into this category are summarized in Table 4-2 and described in the following sections.

Table 4-2. Cryptographic protocols for online communications

Protocol	What does it do?	Widely deployed?	Programs and systems	URL
DNSSEC (Secure DNS)	Provides secure hostname to IP address resolution	No	BIND, Version 9 (Internet Software Consortium)	http://www.ietf.org/html.charters/dnsext-charter.html
IPsec and IPv6	Secures IP traffic	No		http://www.ietf.org/html.charters/ipsec-charter.html
Kerberos	Provides secure authentication and cryptographic key exchange for higher-level protocols	Somewhat	Kerberos (MIT) Windows 2000 (Microsoft)[a]	http://web.mit.edu/kerberos/www/
PCT (Private Communications Technology)	Provides privacy for web transactions	No	Internet Explorer (Microsoft) Internet Information Server (Microsoft)	http://www.graphcomp.com/info/specs/ms/pct.htm

[*] RFC 2045, RFC 2046, RFC 2047, RFC 2048, and RFC 2049.

[†] *http://www.ietf.org/html.charters/smime-charter.html*

Table 4-2. Cryptographic protocols for online communications (continued)

Protocol	What does it do?	Widely deployed?	Programs and systems	URL
SET (Secure Electronic Transactions)	Provides privacy and nonrepudiation for credit card transactions; prevents merchants from getting credit card numbers	No	Capital One Wallet	http://www.visa.com/set http://www.mastercard.com/set
SSH (Secure Shell)	Provides secure remote access (telnet) protocol and additional provisions for encrypting other protocols such as email and X Windows	Yes	SSH Version 1.x, 2.x	http://www.ssh.com
			OpenSSH	http://openssh.org
			Putty	http://www.chiark.greenend.org/uk/nsgtatham/putty/
			SecureCRT (Vandyke Communications)	htttp://www.vandyke.com/products/securecrt/
SSL (Secure Sockets Layer)	Encrypts stream communications; mostly used for downloading web pages and email	Yes	Apache Web Server	http://www.apache-ssl.org http://www.modssl.org/
			Internet Information Server (Microsoft)	http://www.microsoft.com/windows2000/technologies/web
			Commerce Server (Netscape)	http://home/netscape.com/eng/ssl3/
			Most web browsers	

^a The Microsoft version of Kerberos contains proprietary extensions not compatible with open standards.

SSL

The Secure Sockets Layer* (SSL) is a general-purpose web cryptographic protocol for securing bidirectional communication channels. SSL is commonly used with TCP/IP. SSL is the encryption system that is used by web browsers such as Netscape Navigator and Microsoft's Internet Explorer, but it can be used with any TCP/IP service.

SSL connections are usually initiated with a web browser using a special URL prefix. For example, the prefix https: is used to indicate an SSL-encrypted HTTP connection, whereas snews: is used to indicate an SSL-encrypted NNTP connection.

SSL offers confidentiality through the use of:

- User-specified encryption algorithms
- Integrity, through the use of user-specified cryptographic hash functions
- Authentication, through the use of X.509 v3 public key certificates
- Nonrepudiation, through the use of cryptographically signed messages

SSL is in the process of being replaced by the IETF Transport Layer Security† (TLS) protocol. The two protocols are described in depth in Chapter 5 and in Appendix B.

---

* *http://home.netscape.com/eng/ssl3/*

† *http://www.ietf.org/html.charters/tls-charter.html*

PCT

The Private Communications Technology (PCT) is a transport layer security protocol similar to SSL that was developed by Microsoft because of shortcomings in SSL 2.0. The SSL 2.0 problems were also addressed in SSL 3.0 and, as a result, use of PCT is decreasing. Nevertheless, Microsoft intends to continue supporting PCT because it is being used by several large Microsoft customers on their corporate intranets.

SET

The Secure Electronic Transaction* (SET) protocol is an online payment protocol designed to facilitate the use of credit cards on the Internet.

The fundamental motivation behind SET is to speed transactions while reducing fraud. To speed transactions, the protocol automates the "buy" process by having the consumer's computer automatically provide the consumer's credit card number and other payment information, rather than forcing the consumer to type this information into a form in a web browser. To reduce fraud, SET was designed so that the merchant would never have access to the consumer's actual credit card number. Instead, the merchant would receive an encrypted credit card number that could only be decrypted by the merchant's bank.

There are three parts to the SET system: an "electronic wallet" that resides on the user's computer; a server that runs at the merchant's web site; and the SET Payment Server that runs at the merchant's bank. All of these parts need to be operational before any transactions can be processed. Largely because of this complexity, SET has not been successful in the marketplace to date.

A more detailed explanation of SET appears in Chapter 25.

DNSSEC

The Domain Name Service Security (DNSSEC) standard† is a system designed to bring security to the Internet's Domain Name System (DNS). DNSSEC creates a parallel public key infrastructure built upon the DNS system. Each DNS domain is assigned a public key. A domain's public key can be obtained in a trusted manner from the parent domain or it can be preloaded into a DNS server using the server's "boot" file.

DNSSEC allows for secure updating of information stored in DNS servers, making it ideal for remote administration. The DNSSEC standard is built into the current version of *bind*, the DNS server that is distributed by the Internet Software Consortium.

---

* *http://www.visa.com/set* and *http://www.mastercard.com/set*
† *http://www.ietf.org/html.charters/dnsext-charter.html*

IPsec and IPv6

IPsec* is a cryptographic protocol designed by the Internet Engineering Task Force to provide end-to-end confidentiality for packets traveling over the Internet. IPsec works with IPv4, the standard version of IP used on today's Internet. IPv6, the "next generation" IP, includes IPsec.

IPsec does not provide for integrity, authentication, or nonrepudiation, but leaves these features to other protocols. Currently, the main use of IPsec seems to be as a multivendor protocol for creating virtual private networks (VPNs) over the Internet. But IPsec has the capacity to provide authentication, integrity, and optionally, data confidentiality for all communication that takes place over the Internet, provided that vendors widely implement the protocol and that governments allow its use.

Kerberos

Kerberos† is a network security system developed at MIT and used throughout the United States. Unlike the other systems mentioned in this chapter, Kerberos does not use public key technology.‡ Instead, Kerberos is based on symmetric ciphers and secrets that are shared between the Kerberos server and each individual user. Each user has his own password, and the Kerberos server uses this password to encrypt messages sent to that user so that they cannot be read by anyone else.

Support for Kerberos must be added to each program that is to be protected. Currently, "Kerberized" versions of Telnet, FTP, POP, SSH, and Sun RPC are in general use. Several systems that use Kerberos to provide authentication and confidentiality for HTTP have been developed but not widely deployed.

Kerberos is a difficult system to configure and administer. To operate a Kerberos system, each site must have a Kerberos server that is physically secure. The Kerberos server maintains a copy of every user's password. In the event that the Kerberos server is compromised, every user's password must be changed.

Despite the fact that Microsoft built support for Kerberos into its Windows 2000 operating system, to date Kerberos has not been widely deployed beyond a few academic environments. That Microsoft built proprietary, non-standard extensions into

---

* *http://www.ietf.org/html.charters/ipsec-charter.html*

† *http://web.mit.edu/kerberos/www/*

‡ Kerberos didn't adopt public key technology for two reasons. The first was that when Kerberos was developed in 1985, computers were much slower. The developers thought that public key encryptions and decryptions would be too slow to use Kerberos to authenticate logins and requests for email. The second reason was because of the Stanford and MIT patents. Kerberos' developers wanted to be able to distribute the code freely over the Internet. They were worried that they would have trouble if the system required the licensing of patents. (Phil Zimmermann struggled with this same issue six years later when he wrote PGP, but he resolved it differently.)

their version of Kerberos has probably worked against its interoperability and more general adoption.

SSH

The Secure Shell (SSH)[*] provides for cryptographically protected virtual terminal (*telnet*) and file transfer (*rcp*) operations. Originally developed as free software for Unix, a wide variety of both commercial and noncommercial programs that implement the SSH protocol are now available for Unix, Windows, Mac OS, and other platforms. These implementations also allow for the creation of cryptographically secured "tunnels" for other protocols.

What Cryptography Can't Do

Cryptography is an incredibly powerful technology for protecting information, but it is only one of many technologies that play a role in web security and commerce. Unfortunately, cryptography plays such an important role that many people assume that any computer system is automatically secure, and that any system that does not use encryption can't be made secure. As a matter of fact, the phrase *secure web server* is often used interchangeably with the phrase *cryptographically enabled web server*.

Encryption isn't all-powerful. You can use the best cryptography that's theoretically possible, but if other mistakes are made in either systems design or data handling, confidential information may still be revealed. For example, a document might be encrypted so that it could only be decoded by one person, but if that person prints out a document and then throws it out without first shredding the paper, the secrets that the document contains could still end up on the front page of the local newspaper.

Likewise, cryptography isn't an appropriate solution for many problems, including the following:

Cryptography can't protect your unencrypted documents
> Even if you set up your web server so that it only sends files to people using 1024-bit SSL, remember that the unencrypted originals still reside on your web server. Unless you separately encrypt them, those files are vulnerable. Somebody breaking into the computer on which your server is located will have access to the data.

Cryptography can't protect against stolen encryption keys
> The whole point of using encryption is to make it possible for people who have your encryption keys to decrypt your files or messages. Thus, any attacker who

---

[*] *http://www.ssh.com* and *http://openssh.org*

can steal or purchase your keys can decrypt your files and messages. That's important to remember when using SSL, because SSL keeps copies of the server's secret key on the computer's hard disk. (Normally it's encrypted, but it doesn't have to be.)

Cryptography can't protect against most denial-of-service attacks

Cryptographic protocols such as SSL are great for protecting information from eavesdropping. Unfortunately, attackers can have goals other than eavesdropping. In banking and related fields, an attacker can cause great amounts of damage and lost funds by simply disrupting your communications or deleting your encrypted files. Although there has been some research on techniques by which cryptography can guard against some specific denial-of-service attacks (such as client puzzles and SYN hash cookies), the results of this research are not generally applicable.

*Cryptography can't protect you against records of message traffic or the fact that a message was sent**

Suppose you send an encrypted message to Blake Johnson, and Blake murders your lover's spouse, and then Blake sends you an encrypted message back. A reasonable person might suspect that you have some involvement in the murder, even if that person can't read the contents of your messages. Or suppose there is a record of your sending large, encrypted messages from work to your company's competitor. If there is a mysterious deposit to your bank account two days after each transmission, an investigator is likely to draw some conclusions from this behavior.

Cryptography can't protect against a booby-trapped encryption program

Someone can modify your encryption program to make it worse than worthless. For example, an attacker could modify your copy of Netscape Navigator so that it always uses the same encryption key. (This is one of the attacks that was developed at the University of California at Berkeley.)

Unless you write or inspect all of the programs that run on your computer, there is no way to completely eliminate these possibilities.† They exist whether you are using encryption or not. However, you can minimize the risks by getting your cryptographic programs through trusted channels and minimizing the opportunity for your program to be modified. You can also use digital signatures and techniques such as code signing to detect changes to your encryption programs.

Cryptography can't protect you against a traitor or a mistake

Humans are the weakest link in your system. Your cryptography system can't protect you if your correspondent is sending your messages to the newspapers

---

* In cryptanalysis, the study of such information is called *traffic analysis*.

† And unless you are a stellar programmer, writing the programs yourself may put you at even greater risk from bugs and design errors.

after legitimately decrypting them. Your system also may not protect against one of your system administrators being tricked into revealing a password by a phone call purporting to be from the FBI.

Cryptography can't protect you against a passerby

If you leave your computer unlocked when you go to the bathroom or to get a cup of coffee, somebody can use your computer and do things with your private keys.

Thus, while cryptography is an important element of web security, it is not the only part. Cryptography can't guarantee the security of your computer if people can break into it through other means. But cryptography will shield your data, which should help to minimize the impact of a penetration if it does occur.

Legal Restrictions on Cryptography

The legal landscape of cryptography is complex and constantly changing. In recent years the legal restrictions on cryptography in the United States have largely eased, while the restrictions in other countries have increased somewhat.

In this section, we'll examine restrictions that result from patent law, trade secret law, import/export restrictions, and national security concerns.

 These regulations and laws are in a constant state of change, so be sure to consult with a competent attorney (or three) if you will be using cryptography commercially or internationally.

Cryptography and the Patent System

Patents applied to computer programs, frequently called *software patents*, have been accepted by the computer industry over the past thirty years—some grudgingly, and some with great zeal.

Some of the earliest and most important software patents granted by the U.S. Patent and Trademark Office were in the field of cryptography. These software patents go back to the late 1960s and early 1970s. Although computer algorithms were widely thought to be unpatentable at the time, the cryptography patents were allowed because they were written as patents on encryption devices that were built with hardware—computers at the time were too slow to perform meaningfully strong encryption in a usably short time. IBM's original patents on the algorithm that went on to become the U.S. Data Encryption Standard (DES) were, in fact, on a machine that implemented the encryption technique.

The *doctrine of equivalence* holds that if a new device operates in substantially the same way as a patented device and produces substantially the same result, then the new device infringes the original patent. As a result of this doctrine, which is one of the foundation principles of patent law, a program that implements a patented encryption technique will violate that patent, even if the original patent was on a machine built from discrete resistors, transistors, and other components. Thus, the advent of computers that were fast enough to implement basic logic circuits in software, combined with the acceptance of patent law and patents on electronic devices, assured that computer programs would also be the subject of patent law.

The public key patents

The underlying mathematical techniques that cover nearly all of the cryptography used on the Web today are called *public key cryptography*. This mathematics was largely worked out during the 1970s at Stanford University and the Massachusetts Institute of Technology. Both universities applied for patents on the algorithms and for the following two decades the existence of these patents was a major barrier to most individuals and corporations that wished to use the technology.

Today the public key patents have all expired. For historical interest, here they are:

Public Key Cryptographic Apparatus and Method (4,218,582)
> Martin E. Hellman and Ralph C. Merkle
>
> Expired August 19, 1997
>
> The Hellman-Merkle patent introduced the underlying technique of public key cryptography and described an implementation of that technology called the *knapsack algorithm*. Although the knapsack algorithm was later found to be not secure, the patent itself withstood several court challenges throughout the 1990s.

Cryptographic Apparatus and Method (4,200,700)
> Martin E. Hellman, Bailey W. Diffie, and Ralph C. Merkle
>
> Expired April 29, 1997
>
> This patent covers the Diffie-Hellman key exchange algorithm.

Cryptographic Communications System and Method (4,405,829)*
> Ronald L. Rivest, Adi Shamir, and Leonard M. Adleman
>
> Expired September 20, 2000.
>
> This patent covers the RSA encryption algorithm.

Other patented algorithms

Many other algorithms beyond initial public key algorithms have been patented. For example, the IDEA encryption algorithm used by PGP Version 2.0 is covered by U.S. patent 5,214,703; its use in PGP was by special arrangement with the patent holders, the Swiss Federal Institute of Technology (ETH) and a Swiss company called

---

* By sheer coincidence, the number 4,405,829 is prime.

Ascom-Tech AG. Because this patent does not expire until May 2011, the algorithm has not been widely adopted beyond PGP.

In addition to algorithms, cryptographic protocols can be protected by patent. In general, one of the results of patent protection appears to be reduced use of the invention. For example, deployment of the DigiCash digital cash system has been severely hampered by the existence of several patents (4,529,870, 4,759,063, 4,759,064, and others) that prohibit unlicensed implementations or uses of the technology.

The outlook for patents

Although new encryption algorithms that are protected by patents will continue to be invented, a wide variety of unpatented encryption algorithms now exist that are secure, fast, and widely accepted. Furthermore, there is no cryptographic operation in the field of Internet commerce that requires the use of a patented algorithm. As a result, it appears that the overwhelming influence of patent law in the fields of cryptography and e-commerce have finally come to an end.

Cryptography and Trade Secret Law

Until very recently, many nontechnical business leaders mistakenly believed that they could achieve additional security for their encrypted data by keeping the encryption algorithms themselves secret. Many companies boasted that their products featured *proprietary encryption algorithms*. These companies refused to publish their algorithms, saying that publication would weaken the security enjoyed by their users.

Today, most security professionals agree that this rationale for keeping an encryption algorithm secret is largely incorrect. That is, keeping an encryption algorithm secret does not significantly improve the security that the algorithm affords. Indeed, in many cases, secrecy actually decreases the overall security of an encryption algorithm.

There is a growing trend toward academic discourse on the topic of cryptographic algorithms. Significant algorithms that are published are routinely studied, analyzed, and occasionally found to be lacking. As a result of this process, many algorithms that were once trusted have been shown to have flaws. At the same time, a few algorithms have survived the rigorous process of academic analysis. These are the algorithms that are now widely used to protect data.

Some companies think they can short-circuit this review process by keeping their algorithms secret. Other companies have used algorithms that were secret but widely licensed as an attempt to gain market share and control.

But experience has shown that it is nearly impossible to keep the details of a successful encryption algorithm secret. If the algorithm is widely used, then it will ultimately be distributed in a form that can be analyzed and reverse-engineered.

Consider these examples:

- In the 1980s Ronald Rivest developed the RC2 and RC4 data encryption algorithms as an alternative to the DES. The big advantage of these algorithms was that they had a variable key length—the algorithms could support very short and unsecure keys, or keys that were very long and thus impossible to guess. The United States adopted an expedited export review process for products containing these algorithms, and as a result many companies wished to implement them. But RSA kept the RC2 and RC4 algorithms secret, in an effort to stimulate sales of its cryptographic toolkits. RSA Data Security widely licensed these encryption algorithms to Microsoft, Apple, Lotus, and many other companies. Then in 1994, the source code for a function claiming to implement the RC4 algorithm was anonymously published on the Internet. Although RSA Data Security at first denied that the function was in fact RC4, subsequent analysis by experts proved that it was 100 percent compatible with RC4. Privately, individuals close to RSA Data Security said that the function had apparently been "leaked" by an engineer at one of the many firms in Silicon Valley that had licensed the source code.

- Likewise, in 1996 the source code for a function claiming to implement the RC2 algorithm was published anonymously on the Internet. This source code appeared to be derived from a copy of Lotus Notes that had been disassembled.

- In the 1990s, the motion picture industry developed an encryption system called the Contents Scrambling System (CSS) to protect motion pictures that were distributed on DVD (an acronym that originally meant Digital Video Discs but now stands for Digital Versatile Discs in recognition of the fact that DVDs can hold information other than video images). Although the system was thought to be secure, in October 1999 a C program that could descramble DVDs was posted anonymously to an Internet mailing list. The original crack was due to a leaked key. Since then, cryptographers have analyzed the algorithm and found deep flaws that allow DVDs to be very easily descrambled. Numerous programs that can decrypt DVDs have now been published electronically, in print, on posters, and even on t-shirts.*

Because such attacks on successful algorithms are predictable, any algorithm that derives its security from secrecy is not likely to remain secure for very long. Nevertheless, algorithms that are not publicly revealed are protected by the trade secret provisions of state and federal law.

---

* Source code for the original CSS descrambling program can be found at *http://www.cs.cmu.edu/~dst/DeCSS/Gallery/*, or at least it could when this book went to press.

Regulation of Cryptography by International and National Law

In the past 50 years there has been a growing consensus among many governments of the world on the need to regulate cryptographic technology. The original motivation for regulation was military. During World War II, the ability to decipher the Nazi Enigma machine gave the Allied forces a tremendous advantage—Sir Harry Hinsley estimated that the Allied "ULTRA" project shortened the war in the Atlantic, Mediterranean, and Europe "by not less than two years and probably by four years."* As a result of this experience, military intelligence officials in the United States and the United Kingdom decided that they needed to control the spread of strong encryption technology—lest these countries find themselves in a future war in which they could not eavesdrop on the enemy's communications.

In the early 1990s, law enforcement organizations began to share the decades' old concerns of military intelligence planners. As cryptographic technology grew cheaper and more widespread, officials worried that their ability to conduct search warrants and wiretaps would soon be jeopardized. Agents imagined seizing computers and being unable to read the disks because of encryption. They envisioned obtaining a court-ordered wiretap, attaching their (virtual) alligator clips to the suspect's telephone line, and then hearing only static instead of criminal conspiracies. Their fears were made worse when crooks in New York City started using cellular phones, and the FBI discovered that the manufacturers of the cellular telephone equipment had made no provisions for executing wiretaps. Experiences like these strengthened the resolve of law enforcement and intelligence officials to delay or prevent the widespread adoption of unbreakable cryptography.

U.S. regulatory efforts and history

Export controls in the United States are enforced through the Defense Trade Regulations (formerly known as the International Traffic in Arms Regulation—ITAR). In the 1980s, any company wishing to export a machine or program that included cryptography needed a license from the U.S. government. Obtaining a license could be a difficult, costly, and time-consuming process.

In 1992, the Software Publishers Association opened negotiations with the State Department to create an expedited review process for mass-market consumer software. The agreement reached allowed the export of programs containing RSA Data Security's RC2 and RC4 algorithms, but only when the key size was set to 40 bits or less.

---

* "The Influence of ULTRA in the Second World War," lecture by Sir Harry Hinsley, Babbage Lecture Theatre, Computer Laboratory, University of Cambridge, Tuesday, 19 October 1993. A transcript of Sir Hinsley's talk can be found at *http://www.cl.cam.ac.uk/Research/Security/Historical/hinsley.html*.

Nobody was very happy with the 40-bit compromise. Many commentators noted that 40 bits was not sufficient to guarantee security. Indeed, the 40-bit limit was specifically chosen so the U.S. government could decrypt documents and messages encrypted with approved software. Law enforcement officials, meanwhile, were concerned that even 40-bit encryption could represent a serious challenge to wiretaps and other intelligence activities if the use of the encryption technology became widespread.

Following the 1992 compromise, the Clinton Administration made a series of proposals designed to allow consumers the ability to use full-strength cryptography to secure their communications and stored data, while still providing government officials relatively easy access to the plaintext, or the unencrypted data. These proposals were all based on a technique called *key escrow*. The first of these proposals was the administration's Escrowed Encryption Standard (EES), more commonly known as the Clipper chip.

The idea behind key escrow is relatively simple. Whenever the Clipper chip is asked to encrypt a message, it takes a copy of the key used to encrypt that message, encrypts that message key with a second key, and sends a copy of the encrypted key with the encrypted message. The key and message are stored in a block of data called the Law Enforcement Access Field (LEAF). Each Clipper chip has a second key that is unique to that particular Clipper chip, and the government has a copy of every one of them (or the ability to recreate them). If the Federal Bureau of Investigation, the National Security Agency, or the Central Intelligence Agency should intercept a communication that is encrypted with a Clipper chip, the government simply determines which key was used to encrypt the message, gets a copy of that chip's second key, and uses the second key to decrypt the LEAF. First, it decrypts the message key, and then uses the message key to decrypt the message. This is shown schematically in Figure 4-2.

The Clipper chip proposal was met with much hostility from industry and the general public (see Figure 4-3). Criticism centered upon two issues. The first objection was hardware oriented: PC vendors said that it would be prohibitively expensive to equip computers with a Clipper chip. The second objection was philosophical: many people thought that the government had no right mandating a back door into civilian encryption systems; Clipper was likened to living in a society where citizens had to give the police copies of their front door keys.

In early 1996, the Clinton Administration proposed a new system called *software key escrow*. Under this new system, companies would be allowed to export software that used keys up to 64 bits in size, but only under the condition that a copy of the key used by every program had been filed with an appropriate *escrow agent* within the United States, so that if law enforcement required, any files or transmission encrypted with the system could be easily decrypted. This proposal, in turn, was replaced with another one called *key recovery*, that didn't require escrowing keys at all, but that still

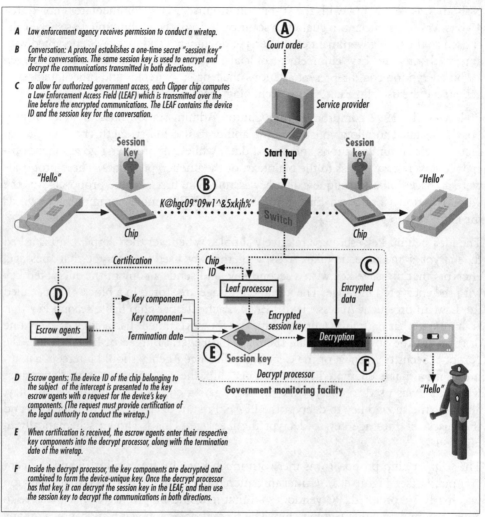

A Law enforcement agency receives permission to conduct a wiretap.

B Conversation: A protocol establishes a one-time secret "session key" for the conversations. The same session key is used to encrypt and decrypt the communications transmitted in both directions.

C To allow for authorized government access, each Clipper chip computes a Law Enforcement Access Field (LEAF) which is transmitted over the line before the encrypted communications. The LEAF contains the device ID and the session key for the conversation.

Ⓐ Court order

Service provider

Session Key

Start tap

"Hello"

Ⓑ

K@hgc09*09w1^&5xkjh%*

Chip

Switch

Session key

"Hello"

Chip

Certification

Chip ID

Ⓒ

Ⓓ

Leaf processor

Encrypted data

Key component

Escrow agents

Key component

Encrypted session key

Termination date

Ⓔ Session key

Decryption

Ⓕ

Decrypt processor

Government monitoring facility

"Hello"

D Escrow agents: The device ID of the chip belonging to the subject of the intercept is presented to the key escrow agents with a request for the device's key components. (The request must provide certification of the legal authority to conduct the wiretap.)

E When certification is received, the escrow agents enter their respective key components into the decrypt processor, along with the termination date of the wiretap.

F Inside the decrypt processor, the key components are decrypted and combined to form the device-unique key. Once the decrypt processor has that key, it can decrypt the session key in the LEAF, and then use the session key to decrypt the communications in both directions.

Figure 4-2. A copy of the key used to encrypt the message is included with the encrypted message in a block of data called the Law Enforcement Access Field (LEAF). Each LEAF is encrypted with a key that is unique to the particular Clipper chip. (Adapted with permission from a diagram prepared by SEARCH.)

gave the government a back door to access encrypted data. As an added incentive to adopt key recovery systems, the Clinton Administration announced that software publishers could immediately begin exporting mass-market software based on the popular DES algorithm (with 56 bits of security) if they committed to developing a system that included key recovery with a 64-bit encryption key.

None of these programs were successful. They all failed because of a combination of technical infeasibility, the lack of acceptance by the business community, and objections by both technologists and civil libertarians.

Figure 4-3. The "big brother inside" campaign attacked the Clinton Administration's Clipper chip proposal with a spoof on the successful "intel inside" marketing campaign.

In 1997, an ad hoc group of technologists and cryptographers issued a report detailing a number of specific risks regarding all of the proposed key recovery, key escrow, and trusted third-party encryption schemes (quotations are from the report):[*]

The potential for insider abuse

There is fundamentally no way to prevent the compromise of the system "by authorized individuals who abuse or misuse their positions. Users of a key recovery system must trust that the individuals designing, implementing, and running the key recovery operation are indeed trustworthy. An individual, or set of individuals, motivated by ideology, greed, or the threat of blackmail, may abuse the authority given to them. Abuse may compromise the secrets of individuals, particular corporations, or even of entire nations. There have been many examples in recent times of individuals in sensitive positions violating the trust placed in them. There is no reason to believe that key recovery systems can be managed with a higher degree of success."

The creation of new vulnerabilities and targets for attack

Securing a communications or data storage system is hard work; the key recovery systems proposed by the government would make the job of security significantly

---

[*] For a more detailed report, see "The Risks of Key Recovery, Key Escrow, and Trusted Third-Party Encryption," by Hal Abelson, Ross Anderson, Steven M. Bellovin, Josh Benaloh, Matt Blaze, Whitfield Diffie, John Gilmore, Peter G. Neumann, Ronald L. Rivest, Jeffrey I. Schiller, and Bruce Schneier, 27 May 1997 (*http://www.cdt.org/crypto/risks98/*).

harder because more systems would need to be secured to provide the same level of security.

Scaling might prevent the system from working at all

The envisioned key recovery system would have to work with thousands of products from hundreds of vendors; it would have to work with key recovery agents all over the world; it would have to accommodate tens of thousands of law enforcement agencies, tens of millions of public-private key pairs, and hundreds of billions of recoverable session keys: "The overall infrastructure needed to deploy and manage this system will be vast. Government agencies will need to certify products. Other agencies, both within the U.S. and in other countries, will need to oversee the operation and security of the highly-sensitive recovery agents—as well as ensure that law enforcement agencies get the timely and confidential access they desire. Any breakdown in security among these complex interactions will result in compromised keys and a greater potential for abuse or incorrect disclosures."

The difficulty of properly authenticating requests for keys

A functioning key recovery system would deal with hundreds of requests for keys every week coming from many difficult sources. How could all these requests be properly authenticated?

The cost

Operating a key recovery system would be incredibly expensive. These costs include the cost of designing products, engineering the key recovery center itself, actual operation costs of the center, and (we hope) government oversight costs. Invariably, these costs would be passed along to the end users, who would be further saddled with "both the expense of choosing, using, and managing key recovery systems and the losses from lessened security and mistaken or fraudulent disclosures of sensitive data."

On July 7, 1998, the U.S. Bureau of Export Administration (BXA) issued an interim rule giving banks and financial institutions permission to export non-voice encryption products without data-recovery features, after a one-time review. This was a major relaxation of export controls, and it was just a taste of what was to come. On September 16, 1998, the BXA announced a new policy that allowed the export of any program using 56-bit encryption (after a one-time review) to any country except a "terrorist country,"* export to subsidiaries of U.S. companies, export to health, medical, and insurance companies, and export to online merchants. This policy was implemented by an interim rule on December 31, 1998.†

---

* These countries consisted of Cuba, Iran, Iraq, Libya, North Korea, Sudan, and Syria as of March 2001.
† *http://jya.com/bxa123198.txt*

In August 1999, the President's Export Council Subcommittee on Encryption released its "Liberalization 2000" report, that recommended dramatic further relaxations of the export control laws. The Clinton Administration finally relented, and published new regulations on January 12, 2000. The new regulations allowed export of products using any key length after a technical review to any country that was not specifically listed as a "terrorist country." The regulations also allowed unrestricted exporting of encryption source code without technical review provided that the source code was publicly available. Encryption products can be exported to foreign subsidiaries of U.S. firms without review. Furthermore, the regulations implemented the provisions of the Wassenaar Arrangement (described in the next section, "International agreements on cryptography,") allowing export of all mass-market symmetric encryption software or hardware up to 64 bits. For most U.S. individuals and organizations intent on exporting encryption products, the U.S. export control regulations were essentially eliminated.*

In the final analysis, the U.S. export control regulations were largely successful at slowing the international spread of cryptographic technology. But the restrictions were also successful in causing the U.S. to lose its lead in the field of cryptography. The export control regulations created an atmosphere of both suspicion and excitement that caused many non-U.S. academics and programmers to take an interest in cryptography. The regulations created a market that many foreign firms were only too happy to fill. The widespread adoption of the Internet in the 1990s accelerated this trend, as the Internet made it possible for information about cryptography— from historical facts to current research—to be rapidly disseminated and discussed. It is no accident that when the U.S. National Institute of Standards and Technology decided upon its new Advanced Encryption Standard, the algorithm chosen was developed by a pair of Europeans. The U.S. export controls on cryptography were ultimately self-defeating. Nevertheless, an ongoing effort to regulate cryptography at the national and international level remains.

The *Crypto Law Survey* is a rather comprehensive survey of these competing legislative approaches compiled by Bert-Jaap Koops. The survey can be found on the Web at the location *http://cwis.kub.nl/~frw/people/koops/lawsurvy.htm*. The later sections on international laws, as well as parts from the preceding paragraphs, draw from Koops' January 2001 survey, which was used with his permission.

The Digital Millennium Copyright Act

There is a huge and growing market in digital media. Pictures, e-books, music files, movies, and more represent great effort and great value. Markets for these items are

---

* The actual regulations are somewhat more complex than can be detailed in this one paragraph. For a legal opinion on the applicability of the current export regulations to a particular product or software package, you should consult an attorney knowledgeable in import/export law and the Defense Trade Regulations.

projected to be in the billions of dollars per year. The Internet presents a great medium for the transmission, rental, sale, and display of this media. However, because the bits making up these items can be copied repeatedly, it is possible that fraud and theft can be committed easily by anyone with access to a copy of a digital item. This is copyright violation, and it is a serious concern for the vendors of intellectual property. Vendors of digital media are concerned that unauthorized copying will be rampant, and the failure of users to pay usage fees would be a catastrophic loss. The experience with Napster trading of MP3 music in 2000–2001 seemed to bear out this fear.

Firms creating and marketing digital media have attempted to create various protection schemes to prevent unauthorized copying of their products. By preventing copying, they would be able to collect license fees for new rentals, and thus preserve their expected revenue streams. However, to date, all of the software-only schemes in general use (most based on cryptographic methods) have been reverse-engineered and defeated. Often, the schemes are actually quite weak, and freeware programs have been posted that allow anyone to break the protection.

In response to this situation, major intellectual property creators and vendors lobbied Congress for protective legislation. The result, the Digital Millenium Copyright Act (DMCA), was passed in 1998, putatively as the implementation of treaty requirements for the World Intellectual Property Organization's international standardization of copyright law. However, the DMCA went far beyond the requirements of the WIPO, and added criminal and civil provisions against the development, sale, trafficking, or even discussion of tools or methods of reverse-engineering or circumventing any technology used to protect copyright. As of 2001, this has been shown to have unexpected side-effects and overbroad application. For example:

- A group of academic researchers were threatened with a lawsuit by the music industry for attempting to publish a refereed, scientific paper pointing out design flaws in a music watermarking scheme.
- A Russian programmer giving a security talk at a conference in the U.S. was arrested by the FBI because of a program manufactured and sold by the company for which he worked. The creation and sale of the program was legal in Russia, and he was not selling the program in the U.S. while he was visiting. He faces (as of 2001) significant jail time and fines.
- A publisher has been enjoined from even publishing URLs that link to pages containing software that can be used to play DVDs on Linux systems. The software is not industry-approved and is based on reverse-engineering of DVDs.
- Several notable security researchers have stopped research in forensic technologies for fear that their work cannot be published, or that they might be arrested for their research—despite those results being needed by law enforcement.
- Traditional fair use exemptions for library and archival copies of purchased materials cannot be exercised unless explicitly enabled in the product.

- Items that pass into the public domain after the copyright expires will not be available, as intended in the law, because the protection mechanisms will still be present.

Narrow exemptions were added to the law at the last moment allowing some research in encryption that might be used in copyright protection, but these exemptions are not broad enough to cover the full range of likely research. The exemptions did not cover reverse-engineering, in particular, so the development and sale of debuggers and disassemblers could be considered actionable under the law.

The DMCA is under legal challenge in several federal court venues as of late 2001. Grounds for the challenges include the fact that the law chills and imposes prior restraint on speech (and writing), which is a violation of the First Amendment to the U.S. Constitution.

If the law stands, besides inhibiting research in forensic tools (as mentioned above), it will also, paradoxically, lead to poorer security. If researchers and hobbyists are prohibited by law from looking for weaknesses in commonly used protocols, it is entirely possible that weak protocols will be deployed without legitimate researchers being able to alert the vendors and public to the weaknesses. If these protocols are also used in safety- and security-critical applications, they could result in danger to the public: criminals and terrorists will not likely be bound by the law, and might thus be in a position to penetrate the systems.

Whether or not the DMCA is overturned, it is clear that many of the major entertainment firms and publishers will be pressing for even greater restrictions to be legislated. These include attempts to put copyright protections on arbitrary collections of data and attempts to require hardware support for copyright protection mechanisms mandated in every computer system and storage device. These will also likely have unintended and potentially dangerous consequences.

As this is a topic area that changes rapidly, you may find current news and information at the web site of the Association for Computing Machinery (ACM) U.S. Public Policy Committee (*http://www.acm.org/usacm/*). The USACM has been active in trying to educate Congress about the dangers and unfortunate consequences of legislation that attempts to outlaw technology instead of penalizing infringing behavior. However, the entertainment industry has more money for lobbying than the technical associations, so we can expect more bad laws in the coming years.

International agreements on cryptography

International agreements on the control of cryptographic software (summarized in Table 4-3) date back to the days of COCOM (Coordinating Committee for Multilateral Export Controls), an international organization created to control the export and spread of military and dual-use products and technical data. COCOM's 17 member countries included Australia, Belgium, Canada, Denmark, France, Germany, Greece,

Italy, Japan, Luxemburg, The Netherlands, Norway, Portugal, Spain, Turkey, the United Kingdom, and the United States. Cooperating members included Austria, Finland, Hungary, Ireland, New Zealand, Poland, Singapore, Slovakia, South Korea, Sweden, Switzerland, and Taiwan.

In 1991, COCOM realized the difficulty of controlling the export of cryptographic software at a time when programs implementing strong cryptographic algorithms were increasingly being sold on the shelves of stores in the United States, Europe, and Asia. As a result, the organization decided to allow the export of mass-market cryptography software and public domain software. COCOM's pronouncements did not have the force of law, but were only recommendations to member countries. Most of COCOM's member countries followed COCOM's regulations, but the United States did not. COCOM was dissolved in March 1994.

In 1995, negotiations started for the follow-up control regime—the Wassenaar Arrangement on Export Controls for Conventional Arms and Dual-Use Goods and Technologies.* The Wassenaar treaty was signed in July 1996 by 31 countries: Argentina, Australia, Austria, Belgium, Canada, the Czech Republic, Denmark, Finland, France, Germany, Greece, Hungary, Ireland, Italy, Japan, Luxembourg, the Netherlands, New Zealand, Norway, Poland, Portugal, the Republic of Korea, Romania, the Russian Federation, the Slovak Republic, Spain, Sweden, Switzerland, Turkey, the United Kingdom, and the United States. Bulgaria and Ukraine later joined the Arrangement as well. The initial Wassenaar Arrangement mirrored COCOM's exemptions for mass-market and public-domain encryption software. In December 1998 the restrictions were broadened.

The Council of Europe is a 41-member intergovernmental organization that deals with policy matters in Europe not directly applicable to national law. On September 11, 1995, the Council of Europe adopted Recommendation R (95) 13 Concerning Problems of Criminal Procedure Law Connected with Information Technology, which stated, in part, that "measures should be considered to minimize the negative effects of the use of cryptography on the investigation of criminal offenses, without affecting its legitimate use more than is strictly necessary."

The European Union largely deregulated the transport of cryptographic items to other EU countries on September 29, 2000, with Council Regulation (EC) No 1334/2000 setting up a community regime for the control of exports of dual-use items and technology (Official Journal L159, 30.1.2000), although some items, such as cryptanalysis devices, are still regulated. Exports to Australia, Canada, the Czech Republic, Hungary, Japan, New Zealand, Norway, Poland, Switzerland, and the United States, may require a Community General Export Authorization (CGEA). Export to other countries may require a General National License for export to a specific country.

---

* See *http://www.wassenaar.org/* for further information on the Wassenaar Arrangement.

Table 4-3. International agreements on cryptography

Agreement	Date	Impact
COCOM (Coordinating Committees for Multilateral Export Controls)	1991–1994	Eased restrictions on cryptography to allow export of mass-market and public-domain cryptographic software.
Wassenaar Arrangement on Export Controls for Conventional Arms and Dual-Use Goods and Technologies	1996–present	Allows export of mass-market computer software and public-domain software. Other provisions allow export of all products that use encryption to protect intellectual property (such as copy protection systems).
Council of Europe	1995–present	Recommends that "measures should be considered to minimize the negative effects of the use of cryptography on investigations of criminal offenses, without affecting its legitimate use more than is strictly necessary."
European Union	2000–present	Export to other EU countries is largely unrestricted. Export to other countries may require a Community General Export Authorization (CGEA) or a General National License.

National regulations of cryptography throughout the world

Table 4-4 summarizes national restrictions on the import, export, and use of cryptography throughout the world as of March 2001.

Table 4-4. National restrictions on cryptography[a]

Country	Wassenaar signatory?	Import/export restrictions	Domestic use restrictions
Argentina	Yes	None.	None.
Australia	Yes	Export regulated in accordance with Wassenaar. Exemptions for public domain software and personal-use. Approval is also required for software that does not contain cryptography but includes a plug-in interface for adding cryptography.	None.
Austria	Yes	Follows EU regulations and Wassenaar Arrangement.	Laws forbid encrypting international radio transmissions of corporations and organizations.
Bangladesh		None apparent.	None apparent.
Belarus		Import and export requires license.	A license is required for design, production, sale, repair, and operation of cryptography.
Belgium	Yes	Requires license for exporting outside of the Benelux.	None currently, although regulations are under consideration.
Burma		None currently, but export and import may be regulated by the Myanmar Computer Science Development Council.	Use of cryptography may require license.
Brazil		None.	None.
Canada	Yes	Follows pre-December 1998 Wassenaar regulations. Public domain and mass-market software can be freely exported.	None.

Table 4-4. National restrictions on cryptography[a] (continued)

Country	Wassenaar signatory?	Import/export restrictions	Domestic use restrictions
Chile		None.	None.
People's Republic of China		Requires license by State Encryption Management Commission for hardware or software where the encryption is a core function.	Use of products for which cryptography is a core function is restricted to specific products using preapproved algorithms and key lengths.
Columbia		None.	None.
Costa Rica		None.	None.
Czech Republic	Yes	Import allowed if the product is not to be used "for production, development, collection or use of nuclear, chemical or biological weapons." Export controls are not enforced.	None.
Denmark	Yes	Some export controls in accordance with Wassenaar.	None.
Egypt		Importers must be registered.	None.
Estonia		Export controlled in accordance with Wassenaar.	
Finland	Yes	Export requires license in accordance with EU Recommendation and Wassenaar, although a license is not required for mass-market goods.	None.
France	Yes	Some imports and exports may require a license depending on intended function and key length.	France liberalized its domestic regulations in March 1999, allowing the use of keys up to 128 bits. Work is underway on a new law that will eliminate domestic restrictions on cryptography.
Germany	Yes	Follows EU regulations and Wassenaar; companies can decide for themselves if a product falls within the mass-market category.	None.
Greece	Yes	Follows pre-December 1998 Wassenaar.	None.
Hong Kong Special Administrative Region		License required for import and export.	None, although encryption products connected to public telecommunication networks must comply with the relevant Telecommunications Authority's network connection specifications.
Hungary	Yes	Mirror regulations requiring an import license if an export license is needed from Hungary. Mass-market encryption software is exempted.	None.
Iceland		None.	None.
India		License required for import.	None.
Indonesia		Unclear.	Unclear.

Table 4-4. National restrictions on cryptography[a] (continued)

Country	Wassenaar signatory?	Import/export restrictions	Domestic use restrictions
Ireland	Yes	No import controls. Export regulated under Wassenaar; no restrictions on the export of software with 64-bit key lengths.	Electronic Commerce Act 2000 gives judges the power to issue search warrants that require decryption.
Israel		Import and export require a license from the Director-General of the Ministry of Defense.	Use, manufacture, transport, and distribution of cryptography within Israel requires a license from the Director-General of the Ministry of Defense, although no prosecutions for using unlicensed cryptography are known and many Israeli users apparently do not have licenses.
Italy	Yes	Follows EU regulations.	Encrypted records must be accessible to the Treasury.
Japan		Export regulations mirror pre-December 1998 Wassenaar. Businesses must have approval for export of cryptography orders larger than 50,000 yen.	None.
Kazakhstan		Requires license.	License from the Committee of National Security required for research, development, manufacture, repair, and sale of cryptographic products.
Kyrgyzstan		None.	None.
Latvia		Mirrors EU regulations.	None.
Luxembourg	Yes	Follows pre-December 1998 Wassenaar.	None.
Malaysia		None.	None, although search warrants can be issued that require the decryption of encrypted messages.
Mexico		None.	None.
Moldova		Import and export requires a license from the Ministry of National Security.	Use requires a license from the Ministry of National Security.
The Netherlands	Yes	Follows Wassenaar. No license required for export to Belgium or Luxemburg.	Police can order the decryption of encrypted information, but not by the suspect.
New Zealand	Yes	Follows Wassenaar. Approval is also required for software that is designed for plug-in cryptography.	None.
Norway	Yes	Follows Wassenaar.	None.
Pakistan		None.	Sale and use of encryption requires prior approval.
Philippines		None.	Not clear.
Poland		Follows Wassenaar.	None.
Portugal	Yes	Follows pre-December 1998 Wassenaar.	None.

Table 4-4. National restrictions on cryptography[a] (continued)

Country	Wassenaar signatory?	Import/export restrictions	Domestic use restrictions
Romania	Yes	No import controls. Exports according to Wassenaar.	None.
Russia		License required for import and export.	Licenses required for some uses.
Saudi Arabia		None.	"It is reported that Saudi Arabia prohibits use of encryption, but that this is widely ignored."
Singapore		No restrictions.	Hardware equipment connected directly to the telecommunications infrastructure requires approval. Police, with the consent of the Public Prosecutor, may compel decryption of encrypted materials.
Slovakia	Yes	In accordance with pre-December 1998 Wassenaar.	None.
Slovenia		None.	None.
South Africa		Import and export controls only apply to military cryptography.	No regulations for commercial use or private organizations. Use by government bodies requires prior approval.
South Korea	Yes	Import of encryption devices forbidden by government policy, not legislation. Import of encryption software is not controlled. Export in accordance with Wassenaar.	None.
Spain		Export in accordance with Wassenaar and EU regulations.	None apparent.
Sweden		Export follows Wassenaar. Export of 128-bit symmetric mass-market software allowed to a list of 61 countries.	Use of equipment to decode encrypted radio and television transmissions is regulated.
Switzerland		Import is not controlled. Export mirrors Wassenaar.	Some uses may be regulated.
Turkey		Follows pre-December 1998 Wassenaar controls.	No obvious restrictions.
United Kingdom		Follows EU and Wassenaar restrictions on export.	Regulation of Investigatory Powers Act 2000 gives the government the power to disclose the content of encrypted data.
United States of America	Yes	Few export restrictions.	None.
Uruguay		None.	None.
Venezuela		None.	None.
Vietnam		Import requires license.	None.

[a] Source material for this table can be found at *http://cwis.kub.nl/~frw/people/koops/cls2.htm*.

In this chapter:
- What Is SSL?
- SSL: The User's Point of View

CHAPTER 5

Understanding SSL and TLS

SSL is the Secure Sockets Layer, a general-purpose protocol for sending encrypted information over the Internet. Developed by Netscape, SSL was first popularized by Netscape's web browser and web server. The idea was to stimulate the sales of the company's cryptographically enabled web servers by distributing a free client that implemented the same cryptographic protocols.

Since then, SSL has been incorporated into many other web servers and browsers, and by now support for SSL is no longer a competitive advantage but a necessity. SSL has gone through two major versions. In 1996 the Internet Engineering Task Force Transport Layer Security (TLS) was established to create an open stream encryption standard. The group started with SSL 3.0 and, in 1999, published RFC 2246, "TLS Protocol Version 1.0." RFC 2712 adds Kerberos authentication to TLS. RFC 2817 and 2818 apply to TLS using HTTP/1.1. This chapter introduces SSL and TLS. Appendix B provides detailed technical information.

What Is SSL?

SSL is a layer that exists between the raw TCP/IP protocol and the application layer. While the standard TCP/IP protocol simply sends an unauthenticated, error-free stream of information between two computers (or between two processes running on the same computer), SSL adds numerous features to that stream, including:

- Authentication of the server, using digital signatures
- Authentication of the client, using digital signatures
- Data confidentiality through the use of encryption
- Data integrity through the use of message authentication codes

Cryptography is a fast-moving field, and cryptographic protocols don't work unless both parties to the communication use the same algorithms. For that reason, SSL is an extensible and adaptive protocol. When one program using SSL attempts to contact another, the two programs electronically compare notes, determining the strongest cryptographic protocol that they share in common. And this exchange is called the *SSL Hello*.

SSL was designed for use worldwide, but it was developed in the United States when the U.S. restricted the export of strong cryptography. For this reason, SSL was designed with many features intended to conform with the U.S. government's older, more restrictive policies on the export of cryptographic systems (described in Chapter 4).

SSL Versions

The SSL protocol was designed by Netscape for use with Netscape Navigator. Version 1.0 of the protocol was used inside Netscape. Version 2.0 of the protocol shipped with Netscape Navigator Versions 1 and 2. After SSL 2.0 was published, Microsoft created a similar secure link protocol called PCT, which overcame some of SSL 2.0's shortcomings. The advances of PCT were echoed in SSL 3.0. The SSL 3.0 protocol is the basis for the TLS protocol developed by the IETF. Implementations of SSL 3.0/TLS are present in Netscape Navigator, Microsoft Windows, and the open source OpenSSL library.

This chapter describes SSL 3.0 and TLS, which are essentially the same protocol.[*]

SSL/TLS Features

SSL/TLS offers many features of both practical and theoretical interest:

Separation of duties
> SSL/TLS uses separate algorithms for encryption, authentication, and data integrity with different keys (called *secrets*) for each function. The primary advantage of this separation of duties is that the keys used for authentication and data integrity can be longer than the keys used for privacy. This was useful for products that were designed for export from the United States, because federal regulations formerly placed limitations on the lengths of keys used for confidentiality but not those used for data integrity and authentication.
>
> SSLv3 and TLS allow for connections that are not encrypted but are authenticated and protected against deliberate tampering by a sophisticated attacker. This might be useful in circumstances where encryption is forbidden or severely restricted by law.
>
> The choice of algorithms and key lengths is determined by the SSL server, but is limited by both the server and the client.

---

[*] TLS is actually version 3.1 of the SSL protocol.

Using SSL to Send Credit Card Numbers Securely

One of the most common questions asked by people new to SSL is, "How do I use SSL to send a credit card number securely?" The answer to this question is surprisingly straightforward—assuming that you have a web server that is cryptographically enabled.

The whole point of SSL is to hide the complexities of cryptography from both users and developers. If your users are using an SSL-aware web browser, such as Netscape Navigator or Microsoft's Internet Explorer, you can instruct the browser to create an encrypted connection to your server simply by replacing the http in your URLs with https.

For example, say you have a proprietary document located at this URL:

> *http://www.company.com/document.html*

Your users can obtain the document securely by requesting this URL:

> *https://www.company.com/document.html*

Likewise, if you have a CGI form which allows people to submit sensitive information (such as a credit card number), you can force the information to be submitted cryptographically by simply modifying the action= clause in your HTML file, again changing the http: to https:.

For example, if the <form> tag in your HTML file looks like this:

```
<form method="POST" action="http://www.company.com/cgi-bin/enter">
```

simply change it to look like this:

```
<form method="POST" action="https://www.company.com/cgi-bin/enter">
```

Efficiency

> Public key encryption and decryption is a time-consuming operation. Rather than repeat this process for every communication between a client and a server, SSL/TLS implementations can cache a "master secret" that is preserved between connections. This allows new connections to immediately begin secure communications, without the need to perform more public key operations.

Certificate-based authentication

> SSL/TLS provides for authentication of both the client and the server through the use of digital certificates and digitally signed challenges. SSLv3 and TLS use X.509 v3 certificates. Authentication is an optional part of the protocol, although server certificates are effectively mandated by today's client implementations.

Protocol agnostic

> Although SSL was designed to run on top of TCP/IP, it can in fact run on top of any reliable connection-oriented protocol, such as X.25 or OSI. The SSL protocol

cannot run on top of a nonreliable protocol such as the IP User Datagram Protocol (UDP). All SSL/TLS communication takes place over a single bidirectional stream. In the case of TCP/IP, the ports listed in Table 5-1 are commonly used.

Table 5-1. TCP/IP ports used by SSL-protected protocols

Keyword	Decimal port	Purpose
https	443/tcp	SSL/TLS-protected HTTP
ssmtp	465/tcp	SSL/TLS-protected SMTP (mail sending)
snews	563/tcp	SSL/TLS-protected Usenet news
ssl-ldap	636/tcp	SSL/TLS-protected LDAP
spop3	995/tcp	SSL-/TLS-protected POP3 (mail retrieving)

Protection against man-in-the-middle and replay attacks

The SSL/TLS protocol was specifically designed to protect against both man-in-the-middle and replay attacks. In a *man-in-the-middle attack*, an attacker intercepts all of the communications between two parties, making each think that it is communicating with the other (see Figure 5-1).

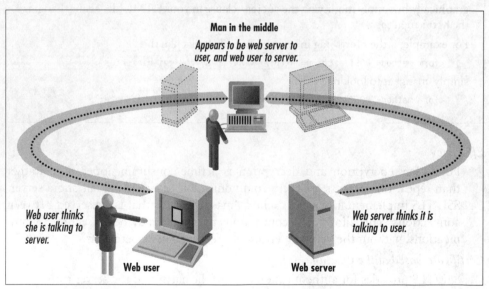

Figure 5-1. A man-in-the-middle attack

SSL/TLS protects against man-in-the-middle attacks by using digital certificates to allow the web user to learn the validated name of the web site. Unfortunately, every web browser used today hides this information, making it accessible only to users who use special, arcane commands. A better user interface would display the web site's validated name in the title bar of the web browser, or in some other obvious place.* Because the certificate information is normally hidden, SSL does a poor job protecting users from man-in-the-middle attacks. See the next section for a discussion of SSL's limitations.

In a *replay attack*, an attacker captures the communications between two parties and replays the messages. For example, an attacker might capture a message between a user and a financial institution instructing that an electronic payment be made; by replaying this attack, the attacker could cause several electronic payments to be made (see Figure 5-2).

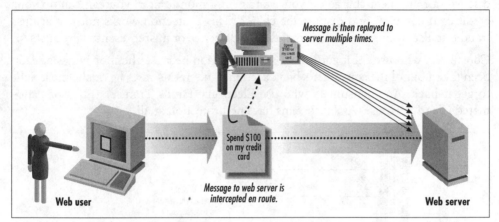

Figure 5-2. A replay attack

Support for compression
Because encrypted data cannot be compressed,† SSL/TLS provides for the ability to compress user data before it is encrypted. The protocol supports multiple compression algorithms.

Backwards compatibility with SSL 2.0
SSLv3.0 servers can receive connections from SSLv2.0 clients and automatically handle the message without forcing the client to reconnect.

What Does SSL Really Protect?

SSL actually does little to protect against the real attacks that consumers and merchants have experienced on the Internet—largely because SSL (and Netscape, by

---

* SSL does not protect against man-in-the-middle attacks when used in "encrypt-only" mode with any *SSL_DH_anon cipher* suite. That is because this mode allows neither the server nor the client to authenticate each other.

† Encrypted data cannot be compressed because good encryption effectively removes any of the repetition or self-similarity that is removed during compression. If your encrypted data can be compressed, then your encryption isn't very good!

extension) did not attempt to solve the hard security problems of Internet commerce, but instead focused on problems that were easy to solve. Figure 5-3 shows estimates of the ease of various types of attacks on e-commerce credit card transactions. Of these attacks, SSL provides no protection against what are by far the most common threats, attacks on clients and merchants.

Real consumer protection on the Internet comes from Regulation E and Regulation Z and the policies of companies like VISA, MasterCard, American Express, and others that implement these policies. If you shop on the Internet with your credit card, and discover a fraudulent charge on your statement a month later, you can call up your credit card company and dispute the charge. This protection works not just against fraud but also against merchants that deliver defective or misrepresented products.

Consumers who use debit cards have less protection because the money has already been taken out of the consumer's bank account, and in this case, he or she must fight to get it back. And consumers who use Electronic Funds Transfer (EFT) or Automated Clearing House (ACH) systems have no protection at all.

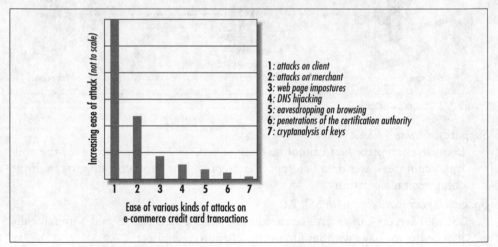

Figure 5-3. Estimated ease of various kinds of attacks on e-commerce credit card transactions

Digital Certificates

SSL/TLS makes extensive use of public key certificates to authenticate both the client and the server in SSL/TLS transactions. SSL/TLS makes use of both X.509 v3 certificates and Diffie-Helman certificates for holding encryption key pairs; SSL 3.0 also supports a modified X.509 certificate for holding public keys used by the U.S. Department of Defense Fortezza/DMS key exchange protocol.* Digital certificates are explained in detail in Chapter 7 and Chapter 17.

---

* Although SSLv3.0 supports the TLS U.S. Department of Defense Fortezza hardware encryption system, no such support is provided in the TLS standard.

SSL supports the following kinds of certificates:

- RSA public key certificates with public keys of arbitrary length
- RSA public key certificates that are limited to 512 bits, designed for use in jurisdictions to restrict the use, export, or import of strong cryptography.
- Signing-only RSA certificates, which contain RSA public keys that are used only for signing data, and not for encryption
- DSS certificates
- Diffie-Hellman certificates

Use of certificates is optional. SSL requires server certificates unless both the client and the server SSL implementations use the Diffie-Hellman key exchange protocol. Currently, Netscape products do not implement the Diffie-Hellman algorithms.

SSL Implementations

The Secure Sockets Layer was initially designed in July 1994. As we mentioned in Chapter 1, the protocol was fundamental to Netscape's business plans. As the plan was originally presented, Netscape intended to give away a great browser that had the added benefit of allowing the user to perform encrypted communications with Netscape's servers using Netscape's proprietary protocol.

SSL Netscape

The first implementation of SSL was located in Netscape's browsers and servers but never sold separately.

SSLRef and Mozilla Network Security Services

After the deployment of Netscape Navigator, Netscape produced a reference SSL implementation that would be distributable within the United States. That program, written in C, was called SSLRef. The 2.0 reference implementation was published in April 1995. Although the SSLRef source code was distributed freely within the United States on a noncommercial basis, it is no longer available. Netscape requests that individuals interested in SSLRef should instead use the Mozilla Network Security Services system.

Network Security Services (NSS) is a set of libraries designed to support cross-platform development of security-enabled server applications. Applications built with NSS can support SSLv2 and SSLv3, TLS, PKCS #5, PKCS #7, PKCS #11, PKCS #12, S/MIME, X.509 v3 certificates, and other security standards. NSS is the cryptographic package that powers Netscape Navigator 6.0, server products from *i*Planet E-Commerce Solutions, and other products. The source code is available for free and under a generous license agreement. For further information, consult *http://www. mozilla.org/projects/security/pki/nss/*.

SSLeay and OpenSSL

SSLeay was an independent implementation of SSL 3.0 developed by Eric A. Young and Tim Hudson, two computer programmers in Australia. It was made freely available around the world on a number of anonymous FTP sites.

SSLeay used implementations of the RC2 and RC4 encryption algorithms based on the algorithms that were anonymously published on the Usenet *sci.crypt* newsgroup in September 1994 (RC4) and February 1996 (RC2). Young and Hudson eventually took jobs with RSA Data Security and used their SSLeay implementation as the basis of RSA's SSL-C product. When they did, other volunteers took up the SSLeay project and renamed it OpenSSL.

OpenSSL is distributed under a generous license agreement. It is the basis of the SSL implementation in the Apache web server and numerous other products. It can be downloaded from *http://www.openssl.org/*.

SSL Java

There are also at least two implementations of SSL in Java:

- Many versions of Java include the Java Cryptography Extensions, which provide a standardized set of classes that will encrypt and decrypt user-provided data. Two class hierarchies to explore are *com.sun.crypto.provider.SunJCE* and *javax. crypto*. For more information see the book *Java Security* by Scott Oaks (O'Reilly).

- RSA Data Security offers JSAFE, a version of its BSAFE cryptography toolkit, but completely rewritten into Java. This toolkit includes high-speed implementations of the most popular encryption algorithms as well as RSA's proprietary algorithms (e.g., RC2).

SSL Performance

SSL noticeably slows the speed of transmitting information over the Internet. The performance degradation is primarily the result of the public key encryption and decryption that is required to initialize the first SSL connection. Compared with this, the additional overhead of encrypting and decrypting data using RC2, RC4, DES, or other algorithms is practically insignificant.

Users have reported performance degradations of approximately 50% when using SSL, compared to sending information in the clear. Users with current systems have reported that the public key encryption/decryption requires approximately less than three CPU seconds per user with a 1024-bit key.

This means there will be a few seconds pause between opening a connection to an SSL server and retrieving an HTML page from that server. Because SSL can cache the master key between sessions, the delay affects only the first SSL transaction between a client and a server.

If you have a fast computer and a relatively slow network connection—and who doesn't?—the overhead of SSL can be insignificant, especially if you are sending large amounts of information over a single SSL session or over multiple SSL sessions that use a shared master secret.

On the other hand, if you expect to be serving dozens or more SSL HTTP requests over the course of a minute, consider getting either an extremely fast computer or hardware assistance for the public key operations.

To minimize the impact of SSL, many organizations transmit the bulk of their information in the clear, and use SSL only for encrypting the sensitive data. Unfortunately, this leaves the user open to attack, because the unencrypted HTML can be modified in transit as it is sent from the client to the server by a sophisticated packet filtering and injection program. (Graduate students at the University of California at Berkeley have already demonstrated how such a program can modify an executable program delivered on the fly over the network.)

For example, the action tag in an HTML form could be changed so that instead of posting a credit card number to a transaction processing system, the number is posted to a pirate computer in South America. Assuming that the pirate system's operator can get a signed digital ID for his SSL server, it may be very difficult for a user duped in this manner to detect that she was the victim of an attack.

SSL/TLS URLs

Information about SSL can be found at:

http://www.ietf.org/rfc/rfc2246.txt
  The TLS 1.0 protocol.
http://www.openssl.org/
  The OpenSSL project.
http://www.mozilla.org/projects/security/pki/nss/
  The Network Security Services project.

SSL: The User's Point of View

Both Netscape Navigator and Microsoft's Internet Explorer contain extensive support for SSL and TLS. This section describes the support for transferring documents using encryption. SSL/TLS support for digital certificates is described in Chapter 17.

Netscape Navigator uses the term "secure document" as shorthand for the phrase "documents that are transmitted using SSL."

Of course, documents transmitted using SSL aren't any more secure or unsecure than documents that are sent in the clear. They are simply cryptographically protected against eavesdropping and modification while in transit. The SSL Protocol makes no assurance that the document itself was not modified on the web server—a far easier attack than intercepting and modifying the contents of a TCP/IP stream.

Browser Preferences

Netscape Navigator and Internet Explorer control their SSL behavior through the use of special control panels. Navigator calls this panel Security Preferences and it is accessed from Navigator's Preferences menu. Explorer calls this panel the Advanced Options panel and it is accessed from Explorer's Internet Options menu.

Navigator preferences

The Netscape Navigator 6.0 Security Preferences panel is shown in Figure 5-4.

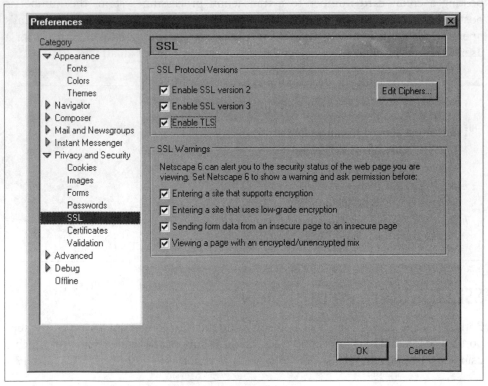

Figure 5-4. Netscape Navigator's Security Preferences panel

The controls listed under Navigator's General tab allow the user to choose when various alerts are displayed. Netscape Navigator can be configured to alert the user:

- When entering a site that uses SSL.
- When entering a site that uses "low-grade" encryption (that is, 40-bit symmetric ciphers or 512-bit RSA).
- When an HTML form is submitted (using GET or POST) without encryption.
- When a document that has a combination of encrypted and unencrypted elements is displayed.

Pressing the "Edit Ciphers . . . " button displays a panel (shown in Figure 5-5) allowing you to control which ciphers Netscape will offer to the remote SSL/TLS server.

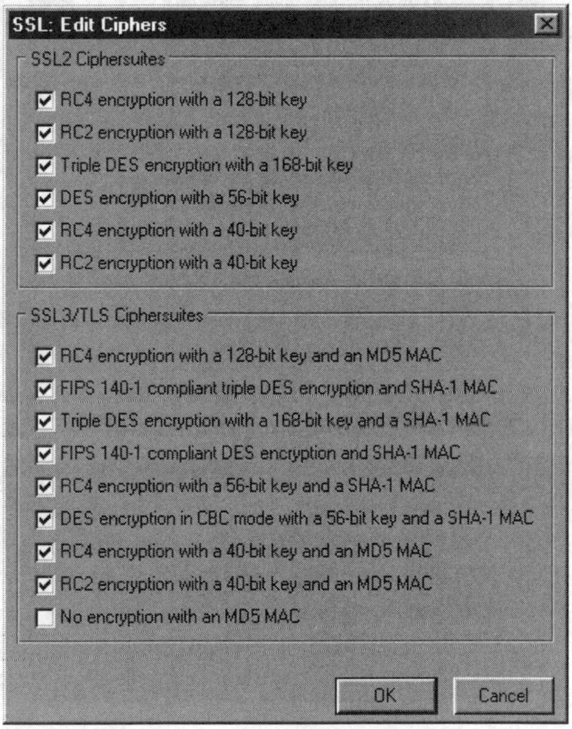

Figure 5-5. The Edit Ciphers panel allows you to control which encryption ciphers Netscape Navigator will offer to the remote system.

Netscape Navigator further allows you to prevent pages that are downloaded with SSL from being stored in the client's disk cache. Storing pages in the cache speeds performance, particularly over slow network connections. However, pages are stored without encryption on the user's computer. If the computer is likely to be stolen or accessed by an unauthorized individual, and the information on the encrypted pages is highly sensitive, you may wish to disable this option.

Internet Explorer preferences

The Internet Explorer 6.0 Options panel is shown in Figure 5-6. Explorer has many more options than Navigator. Specific options that are of interest include:

Check for publisher's certificate revocation

> Activates the software inside the Windows SSL implementation that checks for revoked certificates on Authenticode-signed controls.

Do not save encrypted pages to disk

> Prevents pages downloaded using SSL from being saved on your local hard disk.

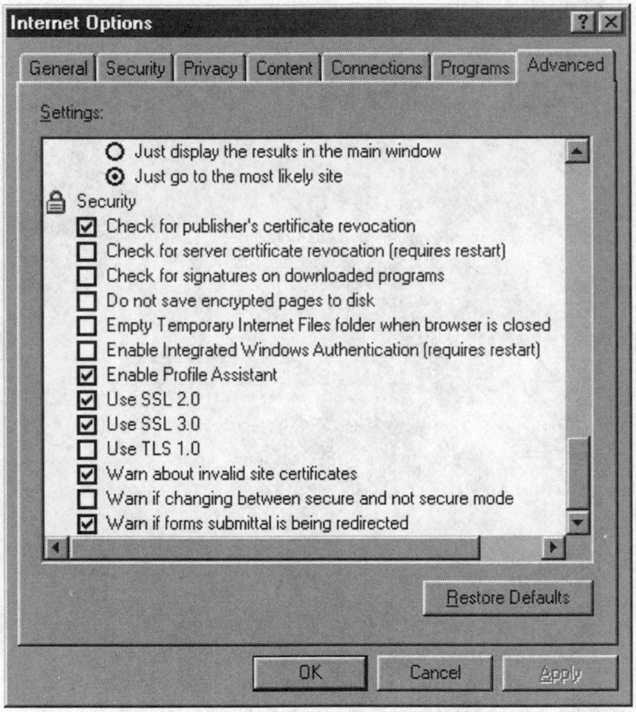

Figure 5-6. Internet Explorer's security preferences can be controlled from the Advanced tab of the Internet Options panel.

Browser Alerts

Both Netscape Navigator and Internet Explorer display a small padlock at the bottom of the browser to indicate the page currently viewed was downloaded using SSL.

CHAPTER 6

Digital Identification I: Passwords, Biometrics, and Digital Signatures

A variety of identification systems in use on the Web today are designed to provide the same sort of assurance in cyberspace that they offer in the real world. The simplest of the systems are based on usernames and passwords; others are based on special-purpose hardware that can measure unique distinguishing characteristics of different human beings. Finally, there are systems that are based on cryptography, relying on the public key cryptography techniques introduced in earlier chapters.

This chapter presents a survey of the various digital technologies that are available to identify people on and off the Internet. Chapter 7 describes the use of digital certificates and their use in the public key infrastructure (PKI).

Physical Identification

Fly to San Francisco International Airport, flash two pieces of plastic, and you can drive away with a brand new car worth more than $20,000. The only assurance the car rental agency has that you will return its automobile is your word—and the knowledge that if you break your word, they can destroy your credit rating and possibly have you thrown in jail.

Your word wouldn't mean much to the rental agency if they didn't know who you are. It's your driver's license and credit card, combined with a worldwide computer network, that allows the rental agency to determine in seconds if your credit card has been reported stolen, and that gives the firm and its insurance company the willingness to trust you.

As the rental car agency knows, the ability to identify people creates accountability, which helps to promote trust. Indeed, identification is an indispensable part of modern life. Large organizations use employee identification badges to help guards determine who should be let into buildings and who should be kept out. Governments use identification papers to help control their borders and provide taxpayer-funded benefits. And, increasingly, computers use various kinds of systems to determine the identity of their users and control access to information and services.

No identification techniques are foolproof. Fortunately, most of them don't have to be. The goal of most identification systems isn't to eliminate the possibility of impersonation, but to reduce to acceptable levels the risk of impersonation and the resulting losses. Another important goal of identification systems is to quantify the amount of risk that remains once the system has been deployed: quantifying the amount of residual risk allows an organization to make decisions about policies, the need or desirability of alternative identification systems, and even the amount of insurance coverage necessary to protect against the remaining amount of fraud.

Subtle Distinctions

Three related concepts that are often lumped together under the title "identification:"

- Identification: associating an identity with a subject
- Authentication: establishing the validity of something, such as an identity
- Authorization: associating rights or capabilities with a subject

All three of these concepts are important, but they are separable—you don't need to have all three in every situation. For instance, if someone presents a $20 bill to buy a loaf of bread at a grocery store, there is no need for the customer to identify or authenticate himself. If the purchase includes a six-pack of beer, then the customer's grey hair and facial wrinkles could be used to authenticate that he is over 21 years of age, without the need for identification.

As another example, if you are driving down the highway at 80 miles an hour, and a police car pulls you over, there is no immediate need to know the identity of the officer writing you a ticket. He has the authority as a uniformed patrol officer to issue a citation and his authentication is the uniform, badge, and ticket.

In both examples, the authentication can be false (e.g., a fake beard and latex face mask with wrinkles, or a costume shop police uniform). In fact, in any instance the authentication can be either falsified or incorrect. We simply set limits as to how much we will risk by accepting a particular form of authentication.

In the rest of this chapter, we may use the word "identification" as meaning both identification and authentication. But we know (and now you know) the distinction.

The Need for Identification Today

For much of human history, the way people proved their identity was by showing up.* People were born into their communities. They were educated, employed, married, and eventually buried. People had history and were known in their community by their faces, their word, and their actions. Identification was based on biometrics.

---

* Thanks to Carl Ellison for this lovely turn of phrase.

For much of the 20th century, driver's licenses, passports, and other kinds of identity cards have been the primary tools that people have used to prove their identities outside of their direct community—when personal identification based on knowledge and friendship fails. We use them when cashing checks, opening accounts with new businesses, applying for jobs, and buying property. We use them when we are cited by police for speeding or jaywalking, as an alternative to being arrested, taken to a police station, and held for a hearing. By reliably identifying who we are, these physical tokens make it possible for businesses to extend credit and trust to individuals with whom they are unfamiliar.

You might think that the alternative to identification systems is to do business solely with cash. But even when cash or other articles of value are used, strong identification is often required because of the possibility of fraud. Think about it: would *you* take three pounds of gold as payment for a new car without knowing the name of the person handing you the bullion? Given the opportunities for counterfeiting and fraud, most people wouldn't even take a stack of crisp new $100 bills.

Identification cards don't create a stable business environment by themselves: they work hand-in-hand with the legal system. If a person bounces a check or fails to carry through on the terms of a contract, the business knows that it ultimately has the option of going to court with its grievance. But a successful outcome in court is only possible if the business knows the true identity of the customer. This is one reason why it is a crime to create false identification papers.

Customers also need to be able to determine the identity of businesses when they are engaging in financial transactions. In the physical world, the assurance is usually provided by physical location: if Sara buys a book in Harvard Square and then for some reason decides that she has been cheated (she may take the book home only to discover that the book was water damaged and has become a moldering growth medium), she knows that she can walk back to Harvard Square and demand a replacement or a refund. And she knows that she can trust the bookstore, at least within reason, because the store has obviously spent a considerable amount of money on the accoutrements of business: books, shelves, carpets, cash registers, and so on. It's unrealistic to think that the bookstore would spend so much money and then cheat a few dollars on paperback purchases that would damage the store's reputation. And if the bookstore were a scam, at least Sara knows where the bookstore is based. In the worst case, Sara can always go to City Hall, look up the store's owner, and take him to court.

Things are not so neat and tidy on the Internet. Sara might go to an online auction and purchase a slightly used cell phone for $200. After she sends the check and receives the phone, Sara discovers that she can't get it activated because it has a "revenue lock" and can only be used in Seattle. When she sends email back to the person who sold her the phone, her mail bounces. When she contacts the email provider, she learns that the email address was for a web-based email system and that the company has no idea of the name or the address of the person who signed up. When Sara gets back her check, she finds that it was cashed at a large out-of-state bank that refuses to help her identify the perpetrator because $200 is below their "fraud limit."

Things can be just as difficult for online businesses attempting to determine the names of their customers—or trying to verify that the person at the other end of the web browser is actually the person that he or she claims to be. Consider an online stock trading company that gets an order from one of its customers to sell 500 shares of a stock. How does the trading house know that the "sell" order came from a bona fide customer and not from the customer's 10-year-old son—or from the son's best friend who happens to be visiting for the afternoon? What sort of proof is possible, when your only connection with your customer is over a 28.8-kbps modem?

Paper-Based Identification Techniques

The most common way of determining the identity of a person in the physical world is to examine documents that are issued from a trusted authority. Consider passports and driver's licenses. Governments issue these documents to show affiliation (e.g., citizenship) or privileges (e.g., the right to drive), but these documents are also commonly used to authenticate identity, because the issuing of these documents is carefully controlled, they show a person's name, and they are difficult to forge.

Verifying identity with physical documents

Paper-based identification systems are so commonplace that we rarely think about how they work. Consider a U.S. passport: this document has a photograph of the holder, the person's hair and eye color, date and place of birth, the person's a signature, and the seal of the United States government. (Figure 6-1 shows Simson's own passport.)

To verify the identity of a U.S. citizen, you start by examining the passport itself to see if it looks authentic. U.S. passports now have laminations with special seals, so you would check to make sure the lamination hasn't changed, and the markings are present as expected. If the passport looks good, the next step is to compare the person described by the passport with the person who is standing before you. Does the photograph in the passport look like the person? Because looks can be deceiving, this is actually a more difficult task than it seems.

If you have reason to be suspicious of the person standing before you, you can ask him to sign his name on a piece of paper and compare that signature with the one on the document. Or you can ask the person questions based on the information that the document contains—for example, you might ask him to describe the town where his passport says he was born.

However, it is possible that the picture on the passport is eight years old, the passport holder now has a tan and has lost a lot of weight (and hair), his hand is in a cast,

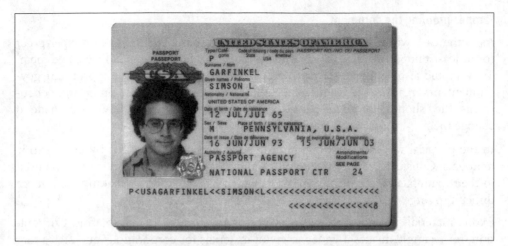

Figure 6-1. A driver's license, passport, or gym membership card is a credential that can be used to prove identification

and his family moved away from his town of birth when he was six months old. At some point, you need to make a decision based on what you have available to you.

Reputation of the issuing organization

One of the key items contributing to the success of paper-based identification systems is the reputation of the organization that issues the documents. How much care does the organization exercise before it issues an identification document? How carefully does the organization safeguard the stock of blank identification materials? Does the organization have internal controls to account for blank documents? How easy is it to bribe a member of the organization to produce a fraudulent document? If such documents are produced, what is the likelihood that they will be discovered? Is there a legal or extra-legal penalty for using fraudulent documents from the organization?

Consider a membership card for a local gymnasium. This card might have a photograph and name on it. But despite the fact that the card identifies the holder, few merchants would allow a person to cash a check using the gym membership card as the sole source of identification. That's because gymnasiums use lower standards of scrutiny when they issue membership cards than do governments when they issue passports and drivers licenses; it's easier to get a gym card with a bogus name than to get a fake passport.*

An identification document without an issuing organization is worthless—anybody can make an "identification card" that has a name, photograph, and signature.

---

* Although, realistically, many U.S. health clubs may actually exercise more due care issuing ID cards than many third-world government passport offices do in issuing passports. Furthermore, many U.S.businesses do not accept passports as identification because their clerks and cashiers are unfamiliar with the documents.

Tamper-proofing the document

As is the case with U.S. passports, good identification credentials are *tamper-proof* (or at least tamper-resistant) so that the person who holds them can't change them. They should also be *forgery-proof* to prevent anyone other than the appropriate government or organization from issuing them. And in the case of important documents, they should also be *tamper-evident* to signal that attempts have been made to change them.

In the physical world, tampering and forgery are usually prevented by using exotic materials. Consider U.S. passports: the binding, paper, printing, and lamination used in their manufacture are quite expensive, which has the effect of making them more difficult to forge or alter.

Exotic materials are not only the province of governments. The Polaroid Corporation, for example, makes a wide variety of materials for corporations and states that need to issue physical identification cards. Polaroid's Polacolor ID Ultraviolet Film is imprinted with a pattern in ultraviolet ink. This pattern can be seen and verified by waving an identification card printed with the Polacolor UV film underneath an ultraviolet light. If the identification photo or card is tampered with, the pattern is destroyed. To further improve security, the card can be sealed with PolaSeal laminate, which is designed to form a molecular bond with the top surface of the Polacolor UV film.

Tamper-proof systems are never perfect; they simply raise the cost of making a passable forgery. The Polaroid products make it very difficult to replace the photograph on an existing ID card, but it's still possible to issue fraudulent cards if the forger can get hold of his own UV film, laminate, and appropriate production equipment.

Another exotic material that has become commonplace is the security hologram. Originally used exclusively on credit cards, today you can find these metallic patches on software boxes, compact disks, and even some books and cereal boxes. Although it's fairly easy to make a hologram with film—you can make one in your basement for less than $1000—the equipment required to press a hologram onto a thin strip of aluminum is comparatively expensive. As the businesses that operate these machines tend to have close relationships with the banking industry, they don't look kindly on counterfeiters.

Computer-Based Identification Techniques

For more than fifty years, computers have been programmed with various means to identify their users. Users of the earliest punch-card systems were given account numbers so that each user's time spent on the computer could be automatically recorded and billed. Passwords were employed so that one user couldn't inadvertently (or intentionally) run up another's account. Usernames and passwords have been a part of large-scale computer systems ever since. Even personal computers, which lacked passwords for the first two decades of their existence, now come equipped with software that can control access using usernames and passwords.

There is a key difference that separates username/password systems from the document-based systems discussed earlier in this chapter. Whereas most identification documents are printed with the true name of the individual being identified, username/password-based systems are only interested in establishing that the person who is sitting at the keyboard is the authorized user of a particular account. Traditional paper-based systems concern themselves with *absolute identification,* whereas username/password systems are concerned with *relative identification* or the *continuity of identification.* Rather than proving that the person sitting at the keyboard is in fact John Smith, Jr. of Boston, MA, and having a database that says John Smith, Jr. of Boston is an authorized user, these systems avoid the absolute identification step.

Absolute identification is an extraordinarily difficult task for the typical computer system to perform. Instead, a plethora of relative identification systems have been fielded. Computer security professionals usually describe these systems as relying on "something that you know," "something that you have," or "something that you are." The following sections describe these three traditional approaches, as well as a newer one: "someplace where you are."

Password-based systems: something that you know

The earliest digital identification systems were based on passwords. Every user of the system is assigned a username and a password; to "prove" your identity to the computer, you simply type your password. If the password that you type matches the password that is stored on the computer, then the assumption is that you must be who you claim to be (see Figure 6-2).

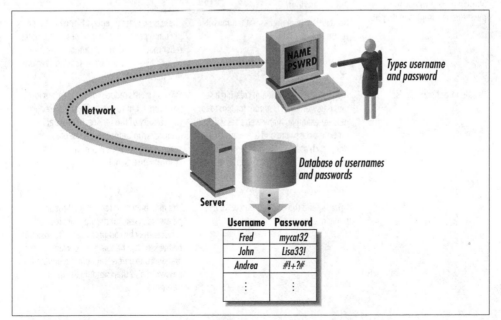

Figure 6-2. Using a username and a password to prove who you are

Because they are simple to use and require no special hardware, passwords continue to be the most popular authentication system used in the world today. As a result of this popularity, most of us now have dozens of passwords that we need to remember on an almost daily basis, including PINs (personal identification numbers) or passwords for accessing ATM cards, long-distance calling cards, voicemail systems, and answering machines, and for disabling "V-Chips" installed in modern televisions, unlocking cell phones, unlocking desktop computers, accessing dialup Internet service providers, downloading electronic mail, and accessing web sites.

As Table 6-1 shows, there are a number of problems with passwords, and many of these problems have no good solutions. However, despite these problems, passwords continue to be used because they do not require any special hardware or exotic programming.

Table 6-1. Problems with passwords and the commonly-used solutions

Password problem	Typical solutions	Risk of the solution
Before you can use a device, a computer, or an online service, you need a password.	Many systems are delivered with a default password or PIN (e.g., "0000" or "1234").	Default PINs are frequently not changed.
	Some systems are configured so that the first person who turns on the device can set a password.	There is no way to assure that the person who first turns on the device is in fact an authorized user. For example, a teenager might be the first person to turn on a family's television and program the V-Chip.
Your password can be intercepted when you send it to the computer. Somebody else who learns your password can impersonate you.	Encryption can be used to scramble a password as it is transmitted from one computer to another.	In practice, encryption is rarely used.
	No solution: in many cases it is impossible to use encryption!	There is no way to "encrypt" the PIN that a person types on the keypad of an automatic teller machine so that it cannot be deciphered by a second person looking over the first person's shoulder.
People forget passwords.	Give the user the option of creating a second password that is harder for him to forget. For example, many web sites will ask for both a password and a "security question," such as "What is your mother's maiden name?" If the password is forgotten, the answer to the question may be provided.	These systems reduce the problems of lost passwords, but they also invariably reduce the security of the service, because an attacker who cannot guess the password may be able to discern the answer to the "security question."
	Offer to send the person's password by paper mail or email.	The mail may be intercepted. If the same password is used at multiple services, other services may be compromised. (This risk can be avoided by changing the person's password to a new, randomly-generated password and then sending the new password.)

Table 6-1. Problems with passwords and the commonly-used solutions (continued)

Password problem	Typical solutions	Risk of the solution
People choose easily guessed passwords.	Require that passwords contain letters, numbers, and symbols. Do not allow passwords that contain a person's username or a word that is in the dictionary.	People are frequently angered or frustrated when they cannot choose a password that they wish to use. Many people use the same password for multiple purposes; if they cannot use their standard password, it is more likely that they will forget it.
People tell their passwords to other people so that others can access a restricted service.	Monitor the service for signs of use by more than one individual (e.g., simultaneous use from more than one location). If such use is detected, shut down the password or otherwise punish the user.	There may be a legitimate need for multiple people to access the same service at the same time, but there may be technical, political, or institutional reasons that prevent all of these people from obtaining their own usernames and passwords.

Physical tokens: something that you have

Another way that people can authenticate their identities is through the use of tokens—physical objects whose possession somehow proves identity. Figure 6-3 shows the Robocard sold by CryptoCard, Inc.

Figure 6-3. Using a token-based system to prove who you are (reprinted with permission)

Door keys have been used for centuries as physical access tokens; in many modern buildings, metal keys are supplemented with either magnetic or radio-frequency-based access card systems. To open a door, you simply hold the card up to a reader. Systems that use radio frequencies to sense the card are generally more secure than magnetic-strip-based systems because the cards are more difficult to forge or copy.

Access card systems are superior to metal-key-based systems because every card can have a unique number that is tied to an identity. The system, in turn, has a list of the cards authorized to open various doors. Time-based restrictions can be added as well, so that a low-level clerk's card can't be used to gain access to an office after-hours. One of the nice features of token-based systems is that they tend to be self-policing: users quickly report cards that are lost or stolen because they need their cards to gain access; when a card is reported missing, that card can be deactivated and a new card issued to the holder. This is an improvement over a keypad-based system, where individuals can share their PIN codes without losing their own access.

As with passwords, tokens have problems as well:

- The token doesn't really "prove" who you are. Anybody who has physical possession of the token can gain access to the restricted area.
- If a person loses a token, that person cannot enter the restricted area, even though that person's identity hasn't changed.
- Some tokens are easily copied or forged.

Token-based systems don't really authorize or identify individuals: they authorize the tokens. This is especially a problem when a token is stolen. For this reason, in high-security applications token systems are frequently combined with some other means of identification: this is often referred to as *two-factor authentication*. For instance, to gain access to a room or a computer, you might need to both present a token and type an authorization code. This is the technique used by automatic teller machines (ATMs) to identify bank account holders.

Biometrics: something that you are

A third technique becoming more commonly used by computers to determine a person's identity is to make a physical measurement of the person and compare the measurement with a profile that has been previously recorded. This technique is called a *biometric*, because it is based on measuring something about a living person. (Figure 6-4 shows an iris identification system.)

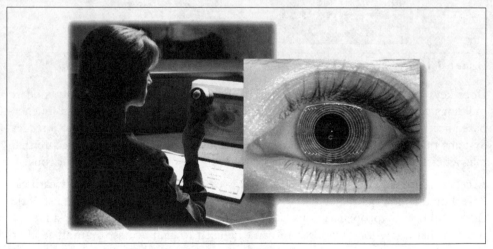

Figure 6-4. Using a biometric-based system to prove identity (reprinted with permission of Iridian)

Many kinds of biometrics are possible:

- Images of a person's face, retina, or iris
- Fingerprints
- Hand geometry

- Footprints and walking style
- Patterns of blood vessels in the retina
- DNA patterns
- Voice prints
- Handwriting characteristics
- Typing characteristics

Biometric techniques can be used for both ongoing identification and absolute identification. Using these techniques for ongoing identification is the simplest approach: the first time the user accesses the system, his biometric information is recorded. On subsequent accesses, the new biometric is compared with the stored record.

To use biometrics for absolute identification, it is necessary to construct a large database matching names with biometrics. The Federal Bureau of Investigation has such a database matching fingerprints to names, and another that matches DNA material.

Compared with passwords and access tokens, biometrics have two clear advantages:

- Under normal circumstances, you can't lose or forget your biometric.
- Biometrics can't readily be shared, copied, or stolen.

But biometric technology has been difficult to bring from the laboratory to the market. All biometric systems exhibit a certain level of *false positives,* in which the system erroneously declares a match when it shouldn't, and *false negatives,* in which the system erroneously declares that two biometrics are from different people, when in fact they are from the same person. To reduce the possibility of false matches, some biometric systems combine the biometric with a password or token. In the case of passwords, a user is typically asked to type a secret identification code, such as a PIN, and then give a biometric sample, such as a voice print. The system uses that PIN to retrieve a specific stored profile, which is then compared with the sample from the profile. In this manner, the system only needs to compare the provided biometric with a single stored measurement, rather than with the entire database.

Biometrics involve complicated technologies, but after nearly three decades of research, they are finally making their way into mainstream computing and access control systems. Voice prints, iris prints, and hand geometry systems for access control are increasingly being installed to safeguard high-security areas such as computer rooms. Low-cost fingerprint readers can now be purchased on PCMCIA cards for use with laptops; some laptops even have fingerprint readers built into them.

It's important to remember, however, that biometrics are not perfect:

- A person's biometric "print" must be on file in the computer's database before that person can be identified.
- If the database of biometric records is compromised, then the biometric identification is worthless.

- Unless the measuring equipment is specially protected, the equipment is vulnerable to sabotage and fraud. For example, a clever thief could defeat a voice-recognition system by recording a person speaking his passphrase and then playing it back.

Location: someplace where you are

With the development of computer systems that can readily determine the location of their users, it is now possible to deploy position-based authentication systems. For example, such a system might allow people in New Jersey to access a New Jersey bank but might deny access to others unless special arrangements have been previously made.

Although the Global Positioning System (GPS) can be readily used for obtaining location information, there are two serious hindrances for GPS in this application: the fact that GPS doesn't usually work indoors, and the fact that there is no way to securely get the positional information from the GPS receiver to the remote service that needs to do the verification. A better choice for position-based authentication is the positional services offered by some mobile telephone networks. With these systems, the network can determine the user's location and then directly report this information to the service, without risking that the information may be compromised while the user is authenticated.

A simple form of location-based authentication is to have a particular terminal or computer that is authorized to perform a special function. People who are in other locations are prohibited from exercising privilege. To date, location has not been used as a general system for authentication.

Using Public Keys for Identification

The identification and authentication techniques mentioned in the first part of this chapter all share a common flaw: to reliably identify an individual, that person must be in the presence of the person or computer that is performing the identification. If the person is not present—if the identification is being performed by telephone, by fax, or over the Internet—then there is high potential for fraud or abuse because of replay attacks.

Replay Attacks

To understand replay attacks, consider the case of a computer that verifies its user's identity with a fingerprint scanner. Under ideal conditions, a person sits down at the computer, presses his thumb to the scanner, and the computer verifies his identity. But consider the case shown in Figure 6-5, in which one computer acquires the fingerprint and another performs the verification. In this case, it is possible for an attacker to intercept the code for the digitized fingerprint as it moves over the network. Once the attacker has the fingerprint transmission, the attacker can use it to impersonate the victim.

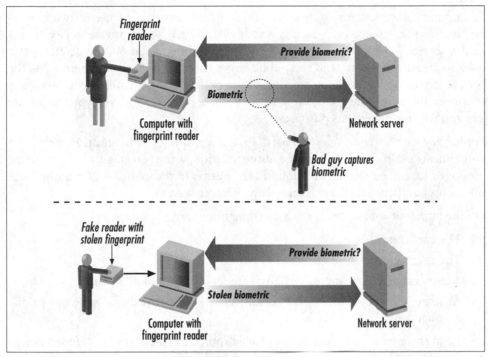

Figure 6-5. When a biometric verification is performed remotely over a computer network, the identification can be compromised by replay attacks (by tampering with the computer or software that measures the biometric).

Replay attacks aren't a problem for biometrics alone: they represent a fundamental attack against all of the digital identification systems mentioned in this chapter. For example, passwords can be eavesdropped and re-used by an attacker. Even position-based systems can be attacked with replay attacks.

Simple encryption provides a measure of protection against replay attacks because encryption makes it more difficult for an attacker to intercept passwords, digitized fingerprints, and other kinds of information used to prove identity. But straightforward encryption has an important limitation: although encryption protects the identification information while it is in transit, if the information is ever revealed to a hostile party, then the information is forever compromised!

This is why the practice of banks and credit card companies of using a person's Social Security number and his "mother's maiden name" is so problematic: there is no way for this information to be verified while at the same time keeping it secret, and once the information is no longer secret, it has no value for identification.

Stopping Replay Attacks with Public Key Cryptography

Properly implemented, public key cryptography can eliminate the risk of replay attacks.

In Chapter 3, we saw that public key cryptosystems involve the use of two cryptographic keys: a public key, which is widely distributed, and a private key, which is kept a secret. When public key systems are used for identification, the private key is used to create a signature and the public key is used to verify that signature. As the private key never leaves the possession of the person being identified—it never gets sent over the wire—there is no opportunity for an attacker to intercept the private key and use it for malicious purposes.

Public key cryptography can be used for either offline authentication or online authentication. In the case of offline authentication, a user creates a digitally-signed message that can be verified at a point in the future. In the case of online authentication, a user authenticates in real time with a remote server.

Offline authentication systems are fairly straightforward:

1. The user creates a message.
2. The user signs the message with his private key.
3. The message and the digital signature are sent to the remote server.
4. At some point in the future, the remote server verifies the digital signature on the message with the user's public key.

Online authentication systems are somewhat more complicated than offline authentication systems because they have more back-and-forth steps:

1. The user's computer makes a connection with a remote server.
2. The remote server sends the user a randomly-generated challenge.
3. The user's computer digitally signs the challenge with the user's private key.
4. The digitally signed challenge is sent back to the remote server.
5. The server verifies the signature with the user's public key.

Because of the challenge-response protocol, online systems are also generally more secure than offline systems.

PGP public keys

PGP is a sophisticated cryptographic system for performing public key encryption. Although the original PGP system was designed primarily for encrypting and digitally signing email, today it is used for all kinds of electronic documents. PGP also has facilities for creating and managing cryptographic keys.

You can think of a PGP public key as a kind of identity card. In the original version of PGP, a PGP public key included a person's name and the actual numbers used by the RSA encryption algorithm used for encrypting or signature verification. Newer versions of PGP allow you to add photographs and additional information to your public key. Simson's PGP public key is shown in text form in Figure 6-6, and in graphical form, as displayed in the Windows PGPkeys program, in Figure 6-7.* Using the private key that corresponds with the PGP public key shown, he can digitally sign his name so that anyone with his public key can verify his identity.

```
-----BEGIN PGP PUBLIC KEY BLOCK-----
Version: PGP 6.5.8

mQGiBDPT4LYRBAD/sUgzCctn4KqHoK3ZoK/RKX4x5Lh88PaLdFUWNJiur/HWhNN/
F5yBppqgziFSB6DWZ/Wmrz+NcMjFroiXdtY96eEeRNVW/d4PiooJ+mx5EMoykbB+
YyEhNY7RmTPWDFSmfEZLjVCL17RzUsmXEqBx8LSYGyvS+UArzDsfamPHiQCg/xlE
NTw5r6+2hjpIokYoWFbc8ocEANtEoQOHGx9PG8XHXikpd1PNodkD68ubPz2DlWyO
RNqg6ZYlUtbsSLAhG+fidaJ+bm3+6JaN7F18nBBTnaLYqX8Vyc1NbWbFmr0Cx0Ed
ma4DDp8bxueqHuec1vdEoRqEbsA+2RXU3Qcr9CwhKHRTfg+IV/3Ml4ZOsFlBOZoc
SAFhA/43R2ziDS+sxrLmFY9jvRKlquLfT6kIPCZUKB+tA/VVLG3uHsruXuumRgUS
ZolbD05zvVOY5AP5/SZhT5GRiiNXpaWSDLBKPz/EJVsZ9Pg1QDq9KcrGzZX+ZDAh
ArMC8qIZniHE1mVwOjrTgszOx9khCBGvY0xO7CdEcdaidKPnpLQlU2ltc29uIEwu
IEdhcmZpbmtlbCA8c2ltc29uZ0BhY20ub3JnPokATGQQEQIADgUCOodQ+wQLAwEC
AhkBAAoJEPKaG0LR8e7U+OsAoLgjooBAtrnYdVyjFIDED8vMvTPtAJ469yOR+kff
n/lSwV3Uu+xjaqha/rQwU2ltc29uIEwuIEdhcmZpbmtlbCA8c2xnQHdhbGRlbi5j
YW1icmlkZ2UubWVudXM+iQBLBBARAgALBQI6KP+sBAsDAQIACgkQ8pobQtHx7tQp
zQCfauoGugUM6vcnaMUUC5dcATFiDWkAniBbMC32NBWYPh+dBpZiVnjiv3W8uQQN
BDPT4LgQEAD5GKB+WgZhekOQldwFbIeG7GHszUUfDtjgo3nGydx6C6zkP+NGlLYw
SlPXfAIWSIC1FeUpmamfB3TT/+OhxZYgTphluNgN7hBdq7YXHFHYUMoiV0MpvpXo
Vis4eFwL2/hMTdXjqkbM+84X6CqdFGHjhKlP0YOEqHm274+nQ0YIxswdd1ckOEri
xPDojhNnl06SE2H22+slDhf99pj3yHx5sHIdOHX79sFzxIMRJitDYMPj6NYK/aEo
Jguuqa6zZQ+iAFMBoHzWq6MSHvoPKs4fdIRPyvMX86RA6dfSd7ZCLQI2wSbLaF6d
fJgJCo1+Le3kXXn11JJPmxiO/CqnS3wy9kJXtwh/CBdyorrWqULzBej5UxE5T7bx
brlLOCDaAadWoxTpj0BV89AHxstDqZSt90xkhkn4DIO9ZekX1KHTUPj1WV/cdlJP
PT2N286Z4VeSWc38uK50T8X8dryDxUcwYc58yWb/Ffm7/ZFexwGq01uejaClcjrU
GvC/RgBYK+X0iP1YTknbzSC0neSRBzZrM2w4DUUdD3yIsxx8Wy2O9vPJI8BD8KVb
GI2Ou1WMuF040zT9fBdXQ6MdGGzeMyEstSr/POGxKUAYEY18hKcKctaGxAMZyAcp
esqVDNmWn6vQClCbAkbTCD1mpF1Bn5x8vYlLIhkmuquiXsNV6z3WFwACAhAAhjai
F3K0JVEIias6jAgLaVYmG4Omk61aI6cNdrgk/J6nqCwoGRJx0vpj6GOHkfHD+d64
b6Q5R6quhzHfRcs2OoCcSamGAK7kg9jtDDJ+zM/q+EH2N9/tLLX8nAG7qMuJN/IK
Jb7e438tnQjOjVaC4hW9Ju945vzlMWcJqeri9DffcnMIvLqC/aV7erJqy/A8aj5O
au29ud7Y9wQcF4XrEC3nRv5PTW4U2xmYRdqTajqjg8qtkTQCpp9SIGUGx4AVbnik
5qLM/awjiIKp+n0LN1VCp2IGsNJKAn0bFuheuQBNTRKfW7KwO6fRC76518rAalyv
/0HkFS/pBe6JcXTVRAGZ8lRMqyrpvNjeBKHEsyUlecq5Xra9KIN7cEDjWZyaTU4C
EElnfFOTQtSbDzydT4dxmgLUG+HMRFE/g+Ax2I7lQCLUYEDB/saSXgAkFU18OVK9
niUANwdjRL60sZZTTrVQia+QStUIjVo/Ds691Iy0cZ4Zvjt9SFmRAvtPsZ0WfgOx
Df5TNI77nqWwoZHOEhLDMn+Wp+it4CDVJTzw98p7iE2IDXpoJElsuAl4VHdnCBsE
nmR9k7j5FnODBMKOvpp535az1PJwyV0fXQuO32snyrljb2nBV3dMkG2b4H85NT46
SUVZE/+UIwr6kKGe6rYTTrPUjQVkmq93TOoEmHKJAD8DBRgz0+C48pobQtHx7tQR
AvYTAJ9ATioJ1voy9+jLnQ8rrPDzxmAlnQCffTVnGNmzMxt8hO93MGXBwbf1lbw=
=VW4i
-----END PGP PUBLIC KEY BLOCK-----
```

Figure 6-6. Simson Garfinkels's PGP public key, in text form

---

* We won't reproduce Spaf's two keys here, but if you want to increase your confidence in using them, here are the key fingerprints: ID 0xF7AB8D54 is B28E 6E51 7BBF 80CD 0B7A 9074 1ECF E570 F7AB 8D54, and ID 0xFC0C02D5 is 9F30 B7C5 8B52 358A 424B 73EE 55EE C541. See *PGP: Pretty Good Privacy* (O'Reilly) to understand how to use these values.

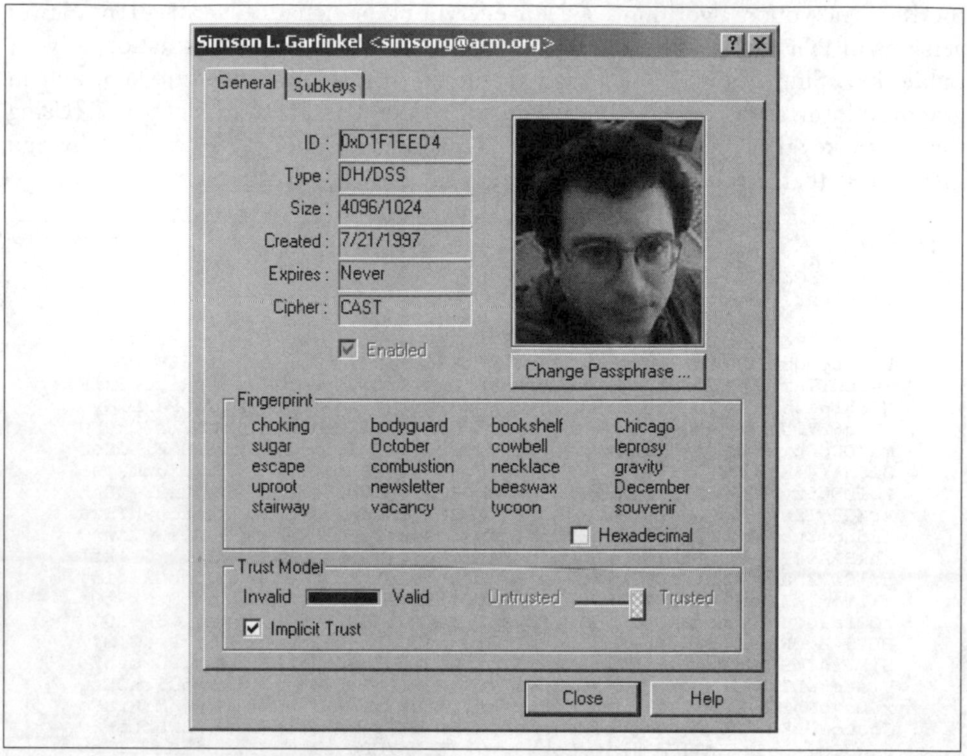

Figure 6-7. Simson Garfinkel's PGP public key, as shown by the Windows PGPkeys program

Of course, the fact that Simson Garfinkel's can to create a digital signature that matches a given public key doesn't really prove his identity. When a digital signature is used to "prove someone's identity," identity proving is not precisely what is taking place. Being able to create a valid digital signature doesn't prove you are a particular person: it proves you have possession of a particular private key. That's why it's possible to find keys on the public keyrings purporting to be for Hillary Clinton and Batman.

Creating and Storing the Private Key

For *digital signature validation* to become *identity authentication*, several preconditions need to be met:

1. Each private key/public key pair must be used by only one person.

2. The private key must be kept secure, lest it be compromised, captured, and used fraudulently by others.

3. There needs to be some sort of trust mechanism in place, so that the person verifying the identity can trust or believe that the name on the key is in fact the correct name.

If keys are carelessly generated, then it may be possible for an attacker to take a public key and determine the corresponding private key. If keys are not stored properly, then the attacker may simply be able to steal the private key.

While these rules look simple on the surface, in practice they can be exceedingly difficult to implement properly. Even worse, frequently it is difficult to evaluate a company's public key system and decide if it is more secure or less secure than a competing system.

There are a number of different alternatives for creating and storing keys. Roughly in order of decreasing security, they are:

1. Probably the most secure way to create and use a set of keys is to employ a cryptographic coprocessor such as a smart card.* A typical public key-compatible smart card has a small microprocessor with a hardware random number generator for creating keys and performing the basic public key algorithms; it also has a region of memory that can hold the keys and public key "certificates" (see Figure 6-8). In theory, the private key never actually leaves the card. Instead, if you want to sign or decrypt a piece of information, that piece of information has to be transmitted into the card, and the signed or decrypted answer transmitted off the card. Thus, attackers cannot use the private key unless they have possession of the smart card. Smart cards can be augmented with fingerprint readers or other biometric devices, so that the card will not create a signature unless the biometric is presented (see the discussion in the "Smart cards" section later in this chapter).

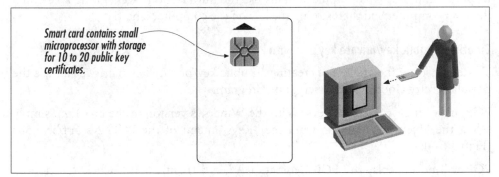

Smart card contains small microprocessor with storage for 10 to 20 public key certificates.

Figure 6-8. Using a smart card to store a private key/public key pair.

2. For those who do not wish to invest in special smart cards and smart card readers, another technique to manage private keys is to generate them on a desktop computer and then store the encrypted keys on a floppy disk or flash disk. When

---

* The discussion in this section pertains only to smart cards that contain a microprocessor capable of performing public key cryptography and storing the resultant keys. Most smart cards in use today cannot perform public key cryptography.

the key is needed, the user inserts the floppy disk into the computer's drive; the computer reads the encrypted private key into memory, decrypts the key, and finally uses the key to sign the requested information. This technique is less secure than the smart card because it requires that the private key be transferred into the computer's memory, where it could be attacked and compromised by a computer virus, Trojan horse, or other rogue program.

3. The simplest way to create and store a public key/private key pair is to generate the key inside the computer, then to encrypt the key using a passphrase and store the key in a file on the computer's hard disk. This is the technique that programs such as PGP and Netscape Navigator use to protect private keys. This technique is convenient. The disadvantage is that if somebody gains access to your computer and knows your passphrase, he or she can access your private key. And because the key must be decrypted by the computer to be used, it is vulnerable to attack inside the computer's memory by a rogue program or a Trojan horse.

4. The least secure way to generate a public key/private key pair is to let somebody else do it for you, and then to download the private and public keys. The fundamental problem with this approach is that the private key is by definition compromised: somebody else has a copy of it. Nevertheless, some organizations (and some governments) require that people use third-party key generation for this very reason: so that the organization will have a copy of each user's key, allowing the organization to decrypt all email sent to the individual.

In practice, most cryptographic systems use the third option—generating a key on a desktop computer and then storing the key on the computer's hard disk.

Creating a public key/private key pair with PGP

To demonstrate the process of creating a public key/private key pair, we can use the popular Pretty Good Privacy encryption program.

PGP makes it easy to create keys. With the Windows version of the program, simply select the "New Key" option from the "Keys" menu of the PGPkeys applications (Figure 6-9).

PGP will now display the PGP Generation Wizard (Figure 6-10). Click "Next" and the program will prompt you to enter the name and email address that will be associated with the key.

The PGP encryption system supports two kinds of public keys: keys based on the RSA encryption algorithm and keys based on the DSA algorithm. On the next window of the wizard, PGP allows you to choose which kind of key you wish to create, and then the number of bits you wish to have in the encryption key (Figure 6-11). More bits in the key makes the key more secure, but increases the amount of time that it takes to both encrypt and decrypt.

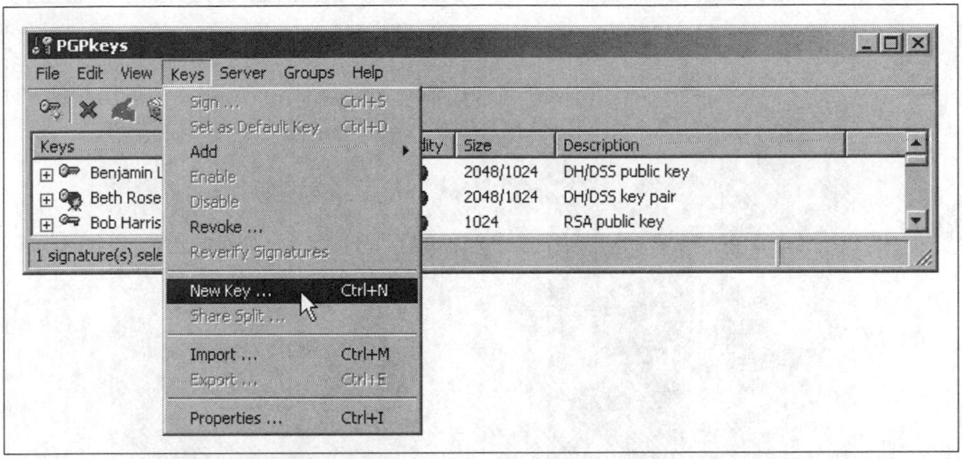

Figure 6-9. To create a new PGP key, select the "New Key..." option from the "Keys" menu of the PGPkeys application program

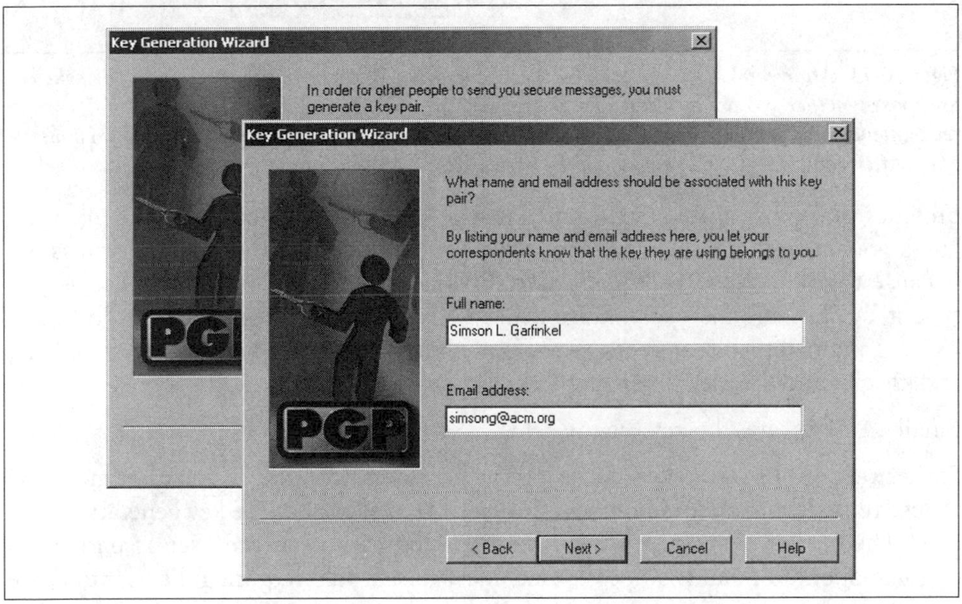

Figure 6-10. When you run the PGP Key Generation Wizard, you will be prompted to enter your full name and email address. This information is recorded on the key. You can change the full name or email address at a later time, but if you do, you will need to have your key reassigned.

After you have picked the algorithm and the key size, versions of PGP after 6.0 will allow you to pick when the key will expire. Many users choose to have their keys never expire, but some organizations choose to create new keys every year or every few years. After you set the key expiration, PGP asks you to type a passphrase that will be used to encrypt the key once it is created. This is the only protection that PGP

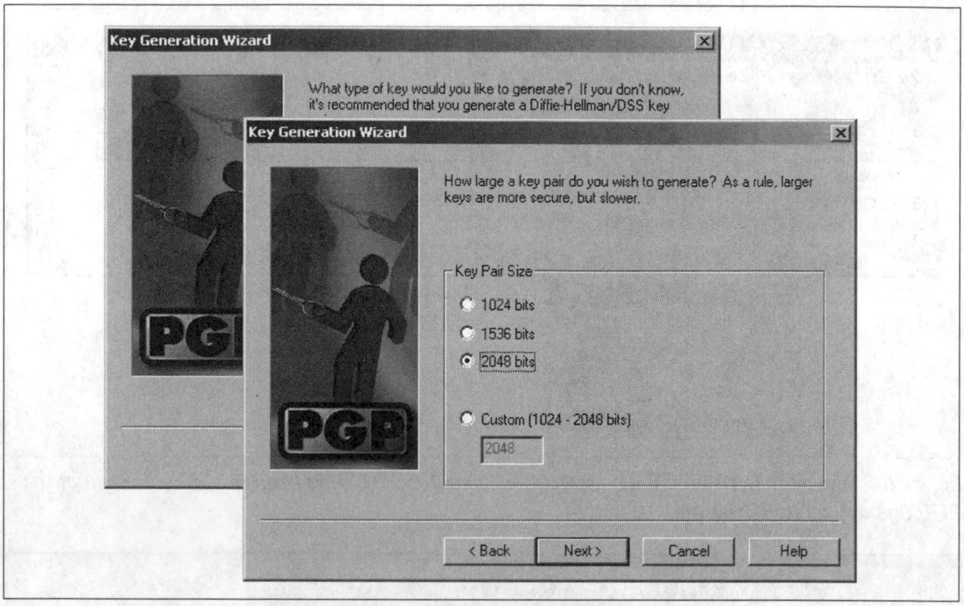

Figure 6-11. After you have given the PGP Key Generation Wizard your name, you will be asked to choose whether you are creating a Diffie-Helman/DSS key or an RSA key. Although PGP recommends that you use a Diffie-Helman key, such keys are not compatible with older versions of PGP. After you choose which algorithm the key will use, you can choose the key's size.

provides for your private key: if someone who has access to your encrypted key can guess your passphrase, he can decrypt the key and use it without your permission. Because the passphrase is so important, PGP actually rates your passphrase as you type it by showing the "passphrase quality" (Figure 6-12). Keys with a high "quality" are more difficult to guess. Good passphrases are long, have letters, numbers, and spaces, and are easy to remember.

Finally, PGP creates the key (Figure 6-13).

Earlier versions of PGP asked the user to type randomly on the keyboard or move the mouse to generate random numbers that were used as part of the key generation process. The current version of PGP gathers randomness from the user as part of its ongoing operations, and so does not include a special step requiring the user to move the mouse or type on the keyboard.

Smart cards

Smart cards are promising pieces of security technology. Take the card out of your computer, and you know that nobody else has access to your private key. Smart cards can also be programmed to require a PIN or passphrase before they will perform a cryptographic function; this helps protect your key in the event that the card is stolen. They can be programmed so that if many PINs are tried in succession, the

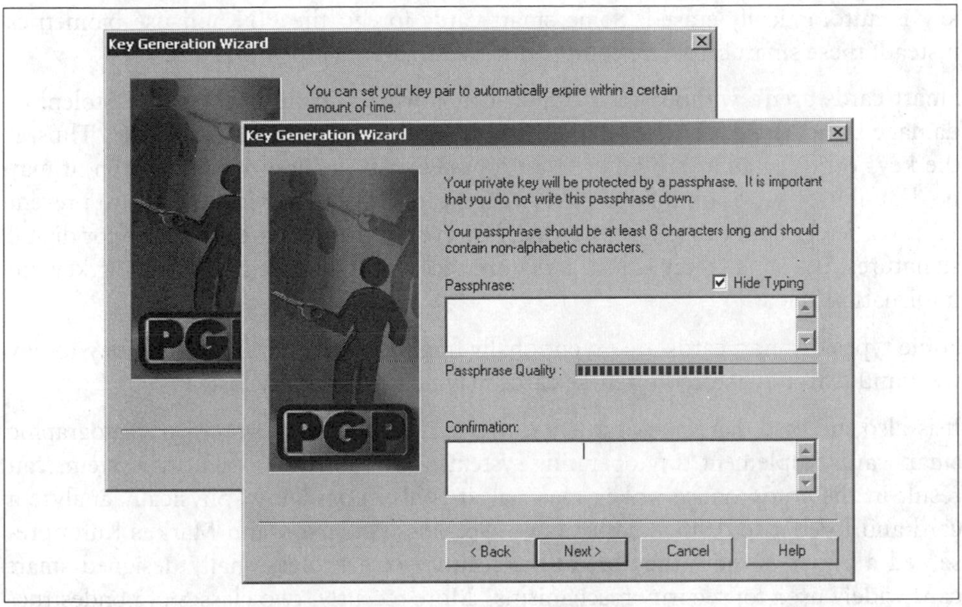

Figure 6-12. The PGP Key Generation Wizard allows you to specify when your key automatically expires. Although this is useful in high-security applications, most users won't use this feature. After you choose an expiration time, you are prompted for a passphrase. PGP shows a passphrase rating.

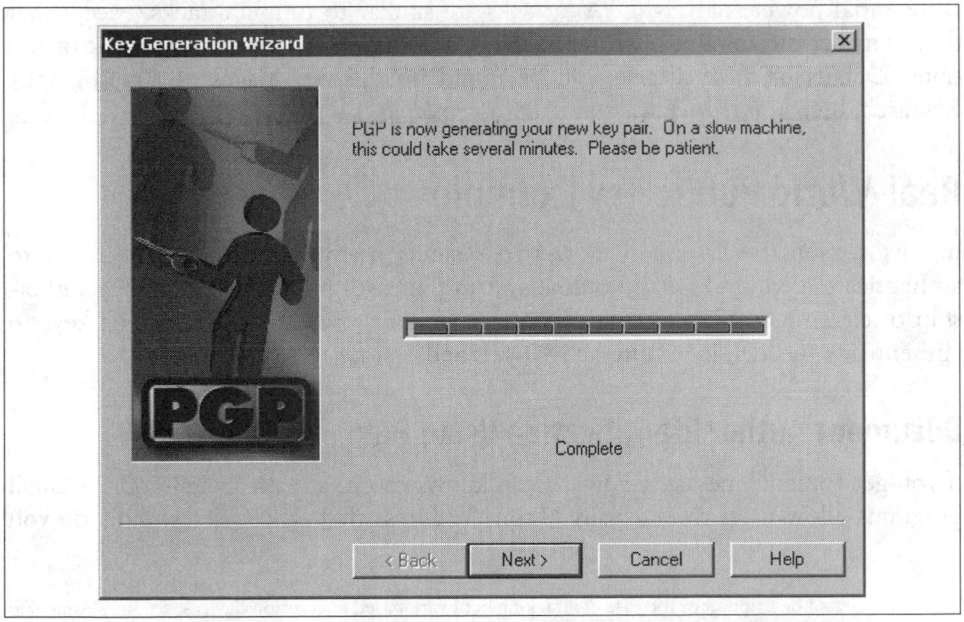

Figure 6-13. Once all of the parameters of the key have been entered, the PGP Key Generation Wizard creates a key pair.

key is automatically erased. Some smart cards forego the PIN and use biometrics instead: these smart cards are equipped with a small fingerprint reader.

Smart cards aren't without their drawbacks, however. If the card is lost, stolen, or damaged, the keys it contains are gone and no longer available to the user. Thus, if the keys on the card are to be used for long-term encryption of information, it may be desirable to have some form of card duplication system or key escrow to prevent key loss. Such measures are not needed, however, if the keys are only used for digital signatures. If a signing key is lost, it is only necessary to create a new signing key: no information is lost.

Some types of smart cards are exceptionally fragile and cannot hold up to day-to-day wear and tear. Keys stored on these cards may be inadvertently lost.

It is also the case that smart cards are not completely tamper-proof. Cryptographic smart cards implement tiny operating systems: flaws in these operating systems can result in the compromise of key material. It is also possible to physically analyze a card and force it to divulge its key. In 1996, Ross Anderson and Markus Kuhn presented a paper on how they broke the security of a professionally designed smart card widely used for security mechanisms.* More recently, two classes of nondestructive attacks have been identified on smart cards. Timing attacks are based on the observation that smart cards require slightly different amounts of time to perform encryption operations depending on the 1s and 0s in the keys that are being used. Differential power analysis (DPA) attacks are similar to timing attacks, except that they consider the amount of current used by the smart card for cryptographic operations. Details of these attacks can be found on the web pages of Cryptography Research, Inc., at *http://www.cryptography.com/dpa/*.

Real-World Public Key Examples

In this section, we'll explore how two systems use public key cryptography to authenticate identity: PGP, an offline system that uses public keys to prove authorship of electronic documents; and SSH, an online system that uses public keys to authenticate the identity of interactive users and remote systems.

Document Author Identification Using PGP

If you get an email message, how do you know who it is really from? Today's email programs allow users to enter any "From:" address that they wish, so how do you

---

* For an excellent description of the ease of attacking hardware-based encryption devices, see Ross Anderson and Markus Kuhn, "Tamper Resistance—a Cautionary Note," in *The Second USENIX Workshop on Electronic Commerce Proceedings*, Oakland, California, November 18–21, 1996, pp. 1–11, ISBN 1-880446-83-9. *http://www.usenix.org/publications/library/proceedings/ec96/full_papers/kuhn/*.

know that a message is really from the person listed in the message header? Email messages can travel through many different computers and be repeatedly forwarded, so how do you know that the message you are reading hasn't been altered since it was originally sent?

The underlying infrastructure of the Internet doesn't provide any mechanism for verifying the authorship of email messages. It's all too easy to claim you are somebody—or something—you aren't. It's this reality that was behind Peter Steiner's cartoon in the July 5, 1993 issue of *The New Yorker*, which portrayed two dogs in front of a computer; one says to the other, "On the Internet, nobody knows you're a dog."

But while it is possible to anonymously post messages and claim to be something that you aren't in the online world, it is also possible to establish your identity, and authenticate your authorship of documents and email messages that you create. One of the best ways to do this is using PGP.

Although PGP was originally written and released for the purpose of securing the contents of electronic communications from prying eyes, as we described earlier, one of the most popular current uses of the program is for digitally signing security advisories and security-related source code.

CERT/CC's PGP signatures

One of the best examples of an organization that uses PGP to sign its documents is the CERT/CC (Computer Emergency Response Team Coordination Center) at Carnegie Mellon University. The CERT/CC sends out many advisories by email of current computer security problems. Many of these advisories recommend specific actions, such as services that need to be reconfigured or patches that need to be downloaded. Because these documents are direct calls to action, it's important for system administrators to be able to verify the authenticity and integrity of the CERT messages before they act upon them—otherwise, a malicious attacker could issue a phony message that might recommend actions that would end up decreasing security.

To prevent this sort of abuse, CERT/CC sends its email advisories with a digital signature at the bottom. At the top of each advisory is a line that says "----BEGIN PGP SIGNED MESSAGE---". Here is an example:

```
-----BEGIN PGP SIGNED MESSAGE-----
Hash: SHA1 ======================================================================
CERT* Vendor-Initiated Bulletin VB-98.02
Jan. 20, 1998

Topic: Apache Security Advisory
Source: Marc Slemko, Apache Team Member
```

At the bottom each message is the PGP signature itself:

```
* Registered U.S. Patent and Trademark Office.
```

The CERT Coordination Center is part of the Software Engineering
Institute (SEI). The SEI is sponsored by the U. S. Department of Defense.

This file: ftp://ftp.cert.org/pub/cert_bulletins/VB-98.02.apache


```
-----BEGIN PGP SIGNATURE-----
Version: PGP for Personal Privacy 5.0
Charset: noconv

iQA/AwUBOBTEF1r9kb5qlZHQEQJDFgCgojyMi4lZX+O4nOM3Q2nZAuVDU5YAnjjm
CW9TXRG1uvYOeHFidVKSAsLL
=AE1/
-----END PGP SIGNATURE-----
```

The PGP signature at the bottom of the email message looks quite complicated and
somewhat official. But unlike signatures that are written with a pen and ink, you
can't verify a PGP signature by looking at it or by comparing it to another PGP signature that you might have on file. Instead, the signature can only be verified by using
the PGP encryption program, as described in the following sections.

Obtaining CERT/CC's PGP key

To verify the signature, the entire signed email message and the digital signature at
the bottom need to be saved in a file. You then process this file with a copy of PGP.

To verify the signature, PGP needs to have a copy of the public key that CERT/CC
used to sign this message. If you do not have the CERT/CC key on file, PGP will
complain that it cannot check the signature:

```
% pgp advisory.pgp
Pretty Good Privacy(tm) Version 6.5.1i
(c) 1999 Network Associates Inc.

Export of this software may be restricted by the U.S. government.

File is signed.  signature not checked.
Signature made 1999/10/25 20:57 GMT
key does not meet validity threshold.

WARNING:  Because this public key is not certified with a trusted
signature, it is not known with high confidence that this public key
actually belongs to: "(KeyID: 0x6A9591D0)".

Plaintext filename: advisory
%
```

There are two ways to get a copy of the CERT/CC PGP key. The easiest is to download the key directly from CERT/CC's web server. The advantage of this approach is

that you can be reasonably sure that the key is coming from CERT/CC. A copy of CERT/CC's PGP key is at the address *https://www.cert.org/pgp/cert_pgp_key.asc*. If you type this URL into Internet Explorer, for example, IE will attempt to download the file and give you the option of opening the file (with PGP) or saving the file on your disk, as shown in Figure 6-14.

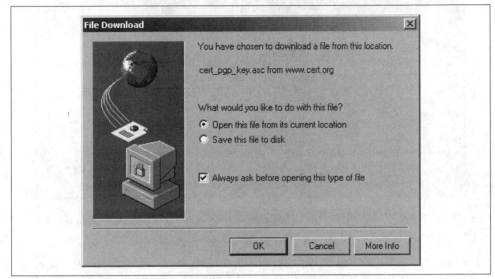

Figure 6-14. When you download the file, Internet Explorer allows you to open the file directly or save it to your disk. Choose "Open" to view the file with the PGPkeys application.

If you choose to open the file with PGP, the PGP program will then display information about the key and allow you to import it to your PGP key ring (Figure 6-15).

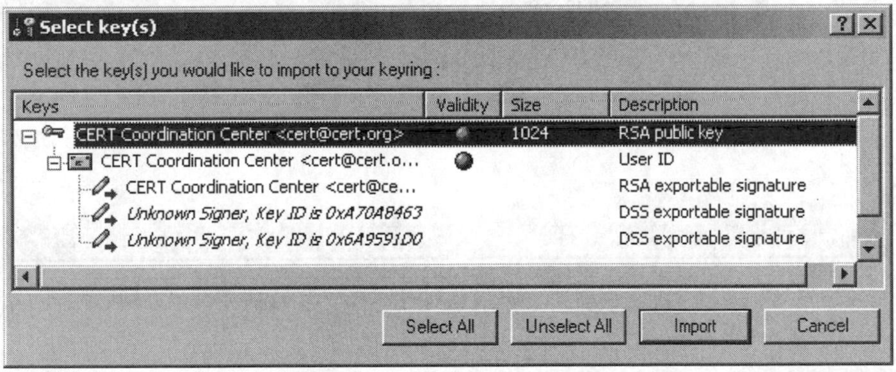

Figure 6-15. The PGPkeys application allows you to view the contents of any key on your hard disk. Once you view the key, you can decide whether or not to "import" the key—that is, to add it to your key chain.

The second way to download a copy of the CERT/CC's key is to use one of the PGP key servers. Current versions of the PGP from Network Associates have the ability to search the key server automatically. To conduct a search, choose the "Search" option from the "Server" menu, as shown in Figure 6-16.

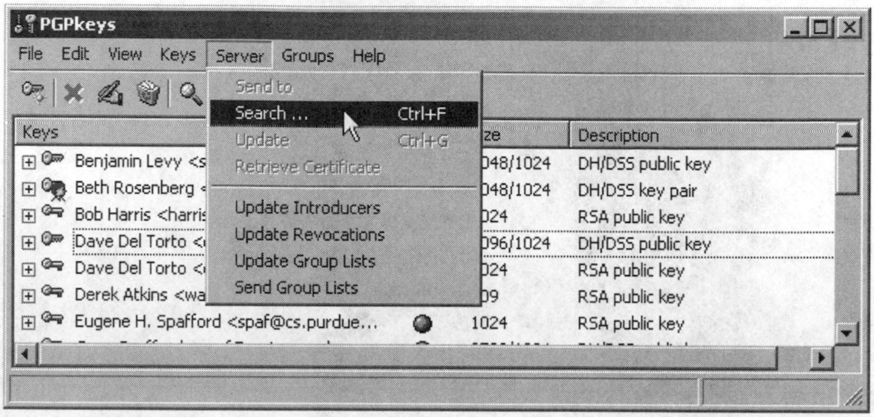

Figure 6-16. To search for a key on the PGP public key server, choose "Search..." from the "Server" menu

Then search for the key with the key that you wish to download. In this case, we search for KeyID 0X6A9591D0 because that is the one that signed the message we wish to verify (see Figure 6-17).

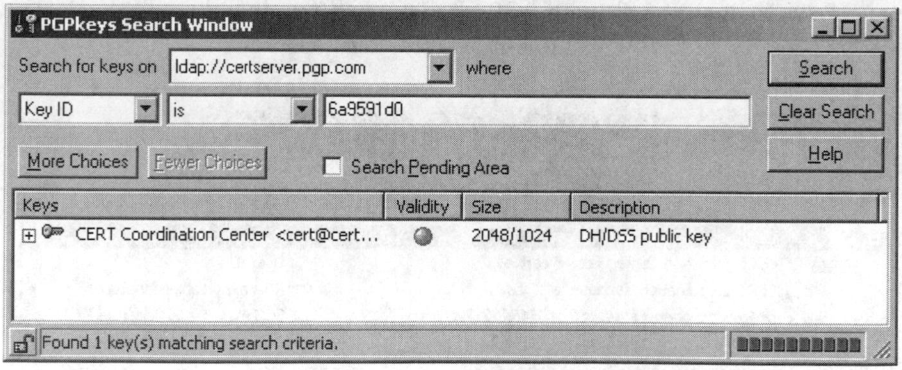

Figure 6-17. Searching for Key0x6A9591D0 on the PGP public key server finds the PGP key for the CERT Coordination Center

You can then import this key to your local key ring by right-clicking on the key and selecting "Import to local keyring" (Figure 6-18).

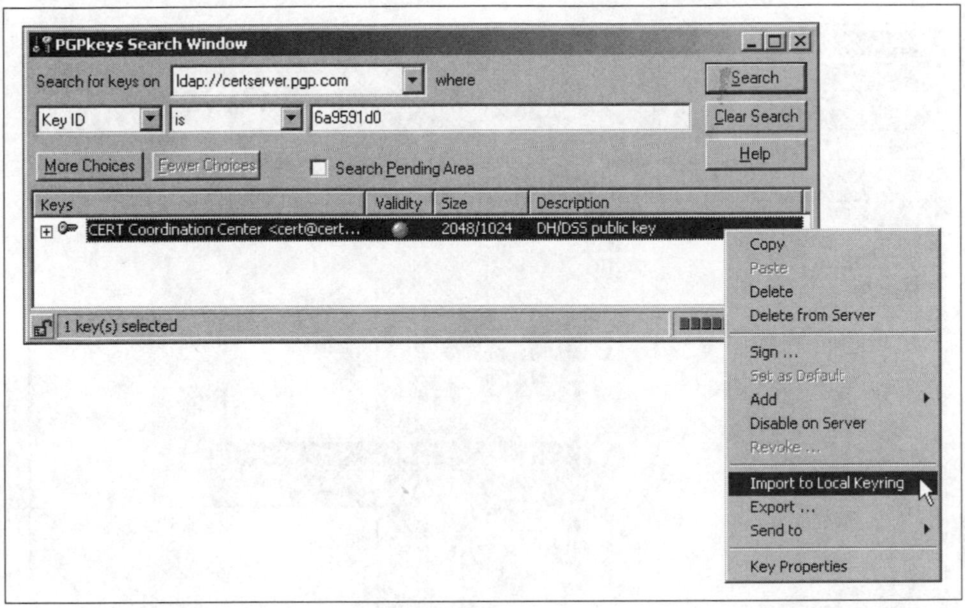

Figure 6-18. After you find a key on the public key server, you can import it by right-clicking on the key and choosing "Import to Local Keyring."

Verifying the PGP-signed file

Once you have a copy of a PGP key, you can use PGP to verify a signature. You can do so using either one of the command-line versions of PGP or the graphical version. The command-line version would give you a result that looks like this:

```
% pgp advisory.pgp
Pretty Good Privacy(tm) Version 6.5.1i
(c) 1999 Network Associates Inc.

Export of this software may be restricted by the U.S. government.

File is signed.  Good signature from user "CERT Coordination Center <cert@cert.org>".
Signature made 1999/10/25 20:57 GMT

Plaintext filename: advisory.pgp
%
```

Many people found PGP's original user interface somewhat difficult to use, so PGP, Inc. created an easier-to-use graphical user interface for Windows and Macintosh systems. With the Windows version, you can select the file that you wish to verify by right-clicking on the file's icon, as shown in Figure 6-19. With the Macintosh version you can use contextual menus, or the PGP menu to verify the file.

PGP will then verify the signature on the file (Figure 6-20).

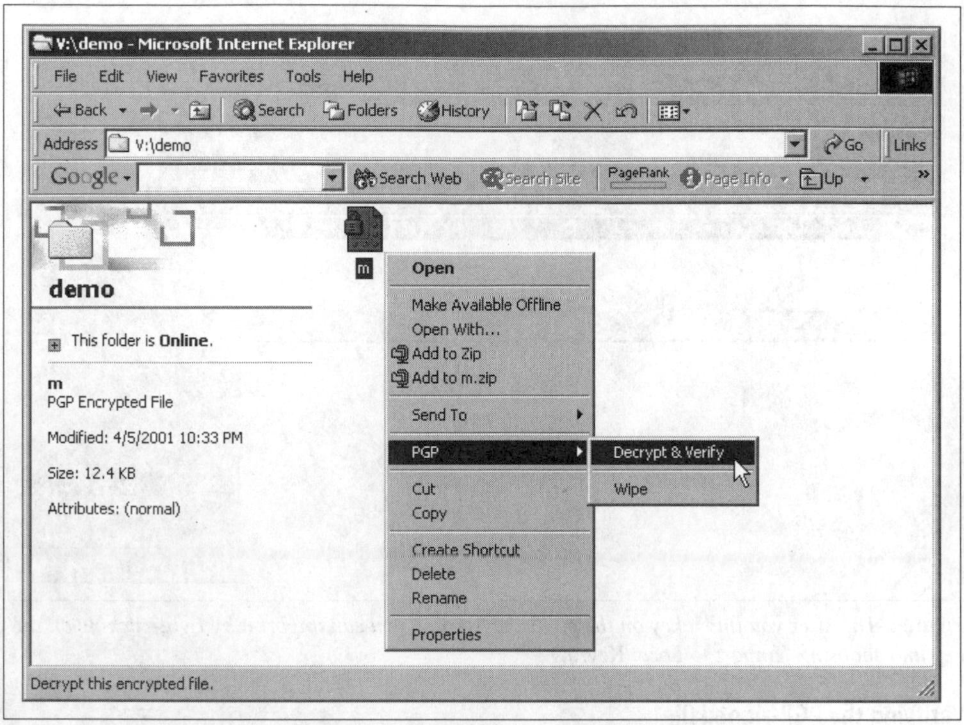

Figure 6-19. You can decrypt a PGP-encrypted file directly from Explorer by right-clicking on the file and choosing "Decrypt & Verify" from the PGP menu.

Figure 6-20. PGP displays the "Decrypting File(s)..." pop-up while it is decrypting a file. You can cancel this operation by clicking on the Cancel button.

And finally, the program will display a window indicating if the signature is valid or not (Figure 6-21).

PGP certification

Unfortunately, there is a security problem with the basic PGP signature scheme that we've presented here. The public key cryptography built into PGP allows you to be reasonably certain that the person who digitally signed the document is the same

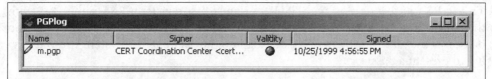

Figure 6-21. The PGPlog window will tell you whether a signature on a file is valid. In this case, the dot under "Validity" is green, and the signature is valid.

person who created the original PGP public key. But, there is no way to be sure that the person or organization whose name is on the PGP key is really who they claim to be. That is, there is no obvious way to certify the validity of the keys themselves.

CERT/CC sidesteps this problem by putting its PGP key on its web server. Many other people take this same approach. For instance, Gene Spafford puts links to his PGP public keys together with his contact information on his home page, at *http://www.cerias.purdue.edu/homes/spaf/*.

Another approach to certifying keys is to digitally sign them with other keys. This approach is discussed in detail in Chapter 7.

Public Key Authentication Using SSH

A good example of a program that can use public keys for identification and authorization is the Secure Shell (SSH), a virtual terminal program that uses encryption to protect information sent over the Internet from eavesdropping.[*]

Most people who use SSH simply use it as a secure "telnet" program. You can use SSH to log on to a remote system by typing *ssh hostname* from the Unix command line. The SSH program will contact the remote system; it will then ask for your password, and send the encrypted password over the network to the remote system. If the password matches the password for the account, the remote system allows you to log in. In this example, the SSH program is used to log into the computer called *queen*:

```
joker% ssh queen
simsong@queen's password: apas334
Last login: Sat Feb 24 22:55:08 2001 from king
Copyright (c) 1980, 1983, 1986, 1988, 1990, 1991, 1993, 1994
        The Regents of the University of California.  All rights reserved.
FreeBSD 4.1-RELEASE (GENERIC) #0: Fri Jul 28 14:30:31 GMT 2000

Welcome to FreeBSD!

queen%
```

As an alternative to passwords, SSH has an authentication system that is based on public key cryptography. SSH uses *RSA authentication*.

---

[*] SSH can actually use a variety of schemes for authentication, including passwords and Kerberos.

To use RSA authentication with SSH, you must first register a RSA public key with the SSH server as an "authorized key." Once a public key is registered, any user who possesses the matching private key can log into the SSH-enabled system without having to present a password.

You create a pair of SSH RSA keys with a program that is called *ssh-keygen*. This program creates two files:

$HOME/.ssh/identity.pub
> A public key.

$HOME/.ssh/identity
> The private key. The private key may optionally be encrypted with a passphrase.

In the next example, the *ssh-keygen* program is used to create a public key and the corresponding private key. Because no passphrase is provided, the private key is not encrypted:

```
joker% ssh-keygen
Generating RSA keys:  Key generation complete.
Enter file in which to save the key (/home/simsong/.ssh/identity):
Enter passphrase (empty for no passphrase):
Enter same passphrase again:
Your identification has been saved in /home/simsong/.ssh/identity.
Your public key has been saved in /home/simsong/.ssh/identity.pub.
The key fingerprint is:
84:eb:d7:fa:65:8d:96:92:1f:bf:d3:42:98:78:ed:6f simsong@joker
joker%
```

The file *identity.pub* contains the public key in an easy-to-read ASCII format. The format is ASCII so that it is easy to move the key to other systems using the Copy and Paste commands of most windowing systems:

```
1024 35
1153658856334728053800732002995091802768030672920855101567696799593546217442339589189
5696787703409046566143648578658507491069283044996527617870937935932744778012158701502
9036534589217371615742904736898660434209966667011326203219393036710140322082107451925
975857100476657321081074068664124438800483005581427153 simsong@joker
```

The file *identity*, meanwhile, contains the private key. Because this file is not designed to be readily moved, it is in a more compact binary representation:

```
SSH PRIVATE KEY FILE FORMAT 1.1
gIVcG«MOKñ...Ïá„>kû˘  ºòàòÛä˘#ï•º¿ú°h É  ‚f
/Ç 46ù>ª - ™˘À „... EJıâÈP OÏ´G‹]7‰}'êxüT´=˛Ñ#simsong@r2.nitroba.com** =Kø \â'á zØ/
1á"·fôû Z4jÕV}bŸÿ/K?`˘5ìœTpfJôÒ'qä"T{[ß™ï)˚]u[ (´<]xYw „Gk ƒChâ·Î‡·^E™,gÍcl}t  êlI¥E
9¨¡‰öÈ·15Ã–œç,»˜ñd ‚‡` ¿Nx[ï®ewÇ Q.Úv¬_¸Y
Søé êMd cQpdÚJÆ"{ˆ  x¢`§+Ø&- =Êy|Xî!‚"¡Ú`ÔUù¥Â¿5/£[Àû\õ
@¡ËÀ :ÚÑ w.e KPÔÛp^Ísu˘¸ ÇÏäÊzŸDÄÏ·vØÑ‰tõ®ùÛÂ£´m‹œ˘ ·I  +ƒäR ø k...
                         Ûr2: {323}
```

In order to use this public key, we will need to manually place it in the *.ssh* directory on the remote system in a file called *authorized_keys*. As its name implies, the *ssh/authorized_keys* file contains a list of keys that are authorized to log into the system without providing a password. The file can be created with the Unix *cat* command:

```
queen% cat >> .ssh/authorized_keys
1024 35
115365885633472805380073200299509180276803067292085510156769679959354621744233958 9189
569678770340904656614364857865850749106928304499652761787093793593274477801215870 1502
903653458921737161574290473689866043420996666701132620321939303671014032208210745 1925
975857100476657321081074068664124438800483005581427153 simsong@joker
queen%
```

Once the public key is present on the remote machine, the user (Simson) can log from *joker* into *queen* without providing a password:

```
joker% ssh queen
Last login: Sat Feb 24 22:55:08 2001 from king
Copyright (c) 1980, 1983, 1986, 1988, 1990, 1991, 1993, 1994
        The Regents of the University of California.  All rights reserved.
FreeBSD 4.1-RELEASE (GENERIC) #0: Fri Jul 28 14:30:31 GMT 2000

Welcome to FreeBSD!

queen%
```

An interesting feature of the *ssh* command is the "-v" (verbose) option, which causes the *ssh* program to print a log of each cryptographic step as the *ssh* client logs into the remote system:

```
joker% ssh -v queen
SSH Version OpenSSH_2.2.0, protocol versions 1.5/2.0.
Compiled with SSL (0x0090581f).
debug: Reading configuration data /etc/ssh/ssh_config
debug: ssh_connect: getuid 0 geteuid 0 anon 0
debug: Connecting to queen [199.174.100.189] port 22.
debug: Allocated local port 1017.
debug: Connection established.
debug: Remote protocol version 1.99, remote software version OpenSSH-2.1
debug: Local version string SSH-1.5-OpenSSH_2.2.0
debug: Waiting for server public key.
debug: Received server public key (768 bits) and host key (1024 bits).
debug: Host 'queen' is known and matches the RSA host key.
debug: Encryption type: 3des
debug: Sent encrypted session key.
debug: Installing crc compensation attack detector.
debug: Received encrypted confirmation.
debug: Trying RSA authentication with key 'simsong@joker'
debug: Received RSA challenge from server.
debug: Sending response to host key RSA challenge.
debug: Remote: RSA authentication accepted.
debug: RSA authentication accepted by server.
debug: Requesting pty.
debug: Requesting shell.
debug: Entering interactive session.
```

```
Last login: Sun Feb 25 17:20:40 2001 from sdsl-64-7-15-234
Copyright (c) 1980, 1983, 1986, 1988, 1990, 1991, 1993, 1994
        The Regents of the University of California.  All rights reserved.
FreeBSD 4.1-RELEASE (GENERIC) #0: Fri Jul 28 14:30:31 GMT 2000

Welcome to FreeBSD!

queen%
```

Viewing Your Key in Binary

If you are curious, you can use the Unix *cat -v* command to see the control characters in the *identity* file:

```
% cat -v identity
SSH PRIVATE KEY FILE FORMAT 1.1
^@^@^@^@^@^@^@^@^@^D^@^D^@M-$IVcGM-+MOKM-qM-^EM-OM-aM-^D>kM-{M-^M^NM-2M-2M-:M-rM-
`M-qM-[M-dM-^M#M-oM-^UM-:M-?M-zM-BM-:h M-I  M-8M-^Of^[
M-8M-CM-q.M-OM-h%^^M-oM-j!XM-^EM-iM-(M-^SM-C:=M-^T>M-:TM-@M-^LM-^@M-z^M/M-$^HM-
GM-^J4^GM-^P6M-y^Z>M-*M-=-M-=M-^YM-^MM-@M-2M-^DM-^EM-}EJM-^@M-bM-HPM--OM-OM-
^NG^DM-^K]7^DM-^I}M-^QM-jB^HxM-|T^EM-4=_^C^AM-Q^@^F#^@^@^@^Vsimsong@r2.nitroba.
com^R*^R*^CM-~=^EKM-xM-}\M-b'M-aM-1zM-X/1^^^?M-a^W"M-7fM-tM-{ Z4jM-UV}M-^ObM-^_
^SM-^?/K?`M-^]5M-l^^M-^\TpM-^CJM-t^UM-RM-^QqM-d^U"T^T{[M-_^\M- M-^YM-o)M-
0]u[^AM-<(M-4<]xY^SwM-}M-^DGkM-<M-^CChM-bM-7M-NM-^GM-/^^_EM-^Y^TM-^Bg^SM-
M^Bcl}tM-1M-3M-jlIM-%E      9M-(M-!%^CM-vM-JM-7^D15M-CM-^W^B^@M-^\M-g^DM-^BM-
;M-^XM-qdM-9M-8M-^G`M-wM-?NxM-^P[M-o^AM-.^PewM-GM-]Q.M-ZvM-,_M-^^Y
iM-y    #Y!M-.^VM-^@>qM-^KM-\M-pE[M-8M-9^TM-s^UOj+M-X&-M-5f^B^@M-Jy|XM-n!M-8M-
^SM-!M-Z`M-TUM-yM-%M-BM-?5/M-#[M-@M-{\M-u^MSM-xM-iM-wM-jMdM-3cQM-^OpdM-ZJM-FM-
^T{M-^H  xM-"^R^F`M-'^LM-GM-OM-d^BM-J2M-^_D^NM-C^B^@M-OM-7vM-XM-QM-^ItM-uM-.M-
yM-[M-BM-#M-4mM-^KM-^\M-^]M-&M-7IM-W ^E+^SM-^CM-dRM-]M-xM-9kM-V^M@M-!^ZM-KM-@M-
~:M-ZM-QM-ww.^TeM-^JKPM-TM-{^RpM-^HM-MsuM-^]M-8^KM-[^@^@^@^@r2: {325} %
%
```

Look at the lines that are underlined. The authentication with the public key takes place on these lines. First, the SSH client running on *joker* tells the remote SSH server that the client wishes to try RSA authentication with the key "simsong@joker". The remote machine sends an "RSA challenge." The RSA challenge is simply a number that the remote machine has randomly chosen; this random value is sometimes referred to as a *nonce*. Next, the SSH client on joker signs the RSA challenge and sends it back to the remote SSH server on *queen*. The server on *queen* verifies the signature[*] using the public key that it has on file. Finally, the remote machine allows the login. This process is shown schematically in Figure 6-22.

---

[*] Because the example uses RSA encryption, the remote system verifies the signature by decrypting the signature with the public key that is on file. If the decrypted signature is the same number as the original challenge, then the client must have possession of the matching RSA private key.

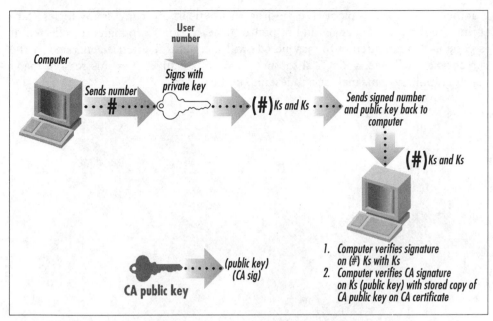

Figure 6-22. In a public key challenge-response process, a computer can provide a person with a number (the challenge) which must be signed. If the person can sign the number and return it to the computer, and if the digital signature can then be verified by the computer using the public key on file for the individual, the person must possess the private key that matches the given public key.

This process of exchanging a number, having the number signed, and then returning the signature is commonly called a public key *challenge-response*. It is the basis of many cryptographic protocols.

Notice that this technique cannot be readily compromised by an attacker who is eavesdropping on the communications link. Even if the attacker could see the number that is passed from the computer and see the signature that is sent back from the person to the computer, the attacker could not see the private key; the attacker thus will be unable to forge the person's signature in the future. The attacker could see that a valid signature was provided, and that's all.

The system can be compromised, however, if the attacker has access to the computer on which the private key resides. All the attacker has to do is copy the key, and the attacker can impersonate Simson. For this reason, the SSH system allows the user to further protect the private key by encrypting it. In practice, however, many people do not encrypt their SSH private keys.[*]

---

[*] Most SSH users do not encrypt their private keys because encrypting private keys on a Unix computer actually adds little security. If an attacker has the ability to overcome Unix permissions and read your private key file, the attacker can capture your keystrokes as you type your password to decrypt your private key.

Another attack is possible if an eavesdropper listens in on many, many logins, capturing the random challenges and responses for each one. If enough are collected, it is possible that an attempt to masquerade will succeed if the nonce generated by the server as a challenge is identical to one of saved exchanges. For this reason, many cryptographic systems include a timestamp in the nonce.

In this chapter:
- Understanding Digital Certificates with PGP
- Certification Authorities: Third-Party Registrars
- Public Key Infrastructure
- Open Policy Issues

## CHAPTER 7

Digital Identification II: Digital Certificates, CAs, and PKI

In the previous chapter, we explored three techniques for establishing and authenticating a person's identity: the use of paper documents, biometrics, and digital signatures. We saw in that chapter that digital signatures had a significant security advantage over the first two systems for e-commerce: because the private key used to "sign" a digital signature is not used by the recipient to verify the signature, digital signatures are not easily subverted by replay attacks. Identity-proving signatures cannot be reused (if the nonces are created with care), but must be created new each time that a person's identity needs to be proven. But as we also saw, digital signatures had a problem as well; for you to prove your identity to someone using a digital signature, that person needs to have your public key already on file. That is, being able to create a digital signature doesn't actually authenticate your identity, it simply proves that you have possession of a private key.

The use of digital certificates and a public key infrastructure (PKI) are attempts to tie absolute identity to digital signatures. A digital certificate is a special kind of digital signature—it is a digital signature that comes with an identity, which is designed to be interpreted by computers in an automated way. A public key infrastructure is a collection of technologies and policies for creating and using digital certificates. The effectiveness of these systems comes from a marriage of public key cryptography, carefully created and maintained policies, and the legal system.

Understanding Digital Certificates with PGP

Digital certificates (shown in Figure 7-1) allow public key cryptography to be used as a kind of general-purpose identification system. A digital certificate is a signed block of data that contains a public key and other information, such as a person's name, email address, or affiliation. For example, a university might issue digital certificates to its students that state that the students are enrolled at the university. The students could then get access to the university's web server by presenting their digital certificates along with their public keys.

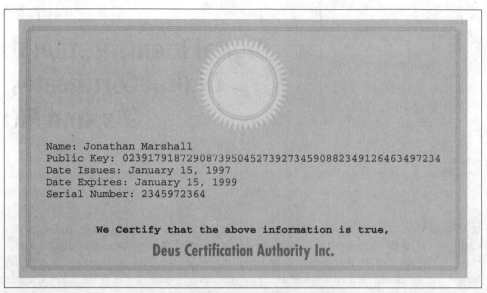

Figure 7-1. A digital certificate consists of a public key, additional information such as a person's name or affiliation, and a digital signature from a certification authority (CA).

In the remainder of this section, we'll use PGP's built-in key management facilities to demonstrate how digital certificates work. Although PGP certificates are not commonly used for identity-proving, the program's clear interface makes it particularly well-suited for this introduction. In the following section, "Certification Authorities: Third-Party Registrars," we'll show how these principles are used in more mainstream applications.

In the previous chapter, we showed how to use a PGP public key to verify the signer of a digital signature. In fact, PGP's "public keys" consist of much more than a simple RSA or DSA public key: PGP public keys are actually full-blown digital certificates. In addition to the public key, PGP's "public keys" contain the key holder author's name, email address, and digital signatures of their own. It's these secondary digital signatures that are crucial for using digital signatures as a system for identification.

Think back to the last chapter. In the section "Document Author Identification Using PGP," we used the CERT/CC public key to verify the Apache vendor bulletin that was distributed on January 20, 1998. Getting the public key for CERT/CC was relatively easy; we could download it either from their web page or from the PGP key server. And indeed, once we downloaded the key, the bulletin from CERT/CC verified perfectly. There was only one nagging question: how did we know that the public key we had downloaded really belonged to CERT/CC?

This question isn't simply an off-the-cuff interrogatory—it is a question with profoundly deep philosophical implications. How can you ever know if a PGP key really belongs to the individual or an organization whose name is on the key? How can we ever really know anything?

As it turns out, we can know quite a bit about the identity of key holders and the authenticity of digital certificates, as long as certain rules and procedures are followed in the creation and protection of these instruments.

Certifying Your Own Key

When we created the PGP key in the last chapter, PGP prompted us to enter our name and email address. This information was then attached to the key that we created. With this key, we certified our own information.

The ability for people to create and certify their own keys is one of the reasons that PGP became so popular in the 1990s. People could download a copy of PGP, create their own keys, and instantly start using it.

Alas, PGP's ease of key creation had its own problem: if you looked up a person's key on the key server, or if somebody emailed you a message that was signed with a key, there was really no way that you could be sure that the key really belonged to that person. There are a lot of pranksters out there, and by 1995 the PGP key servers were filled with fraudulent keys purporting to belong to U.S. President Bill Clinton, his cat Socks, Microsoft Chairman Bill Gates, and even PGP author Phil Zimmermann (see Figure 7-2). The CERT/CC even issued a warning about a fraudulent PGP key with the CERT/CC's name that had been put on the PGP key server (see Figure 7-3). None of these keys really belonged to the individual whose name was on them.

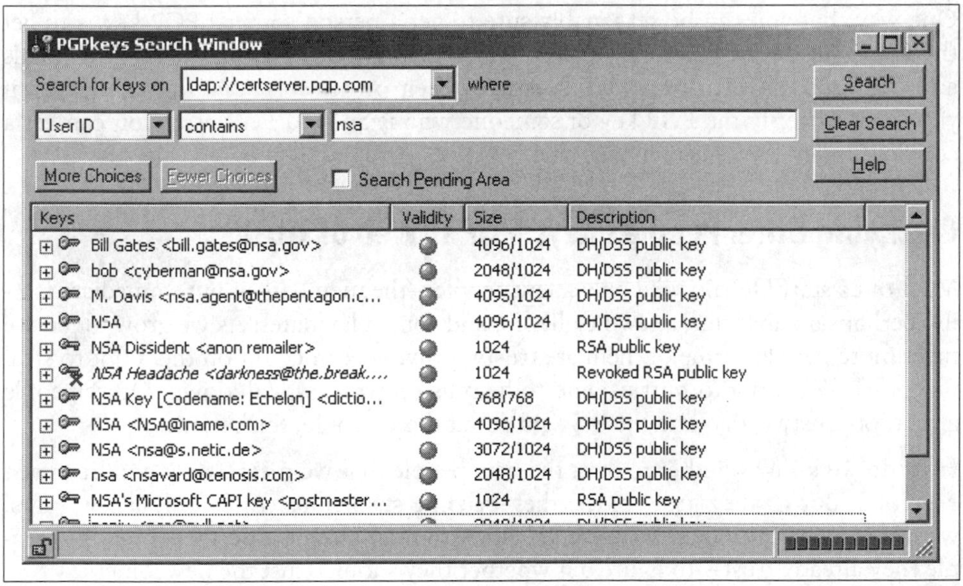

Figure 7-2. Many keys put on the PGP key server don't really belong to the person whose name is listed on them

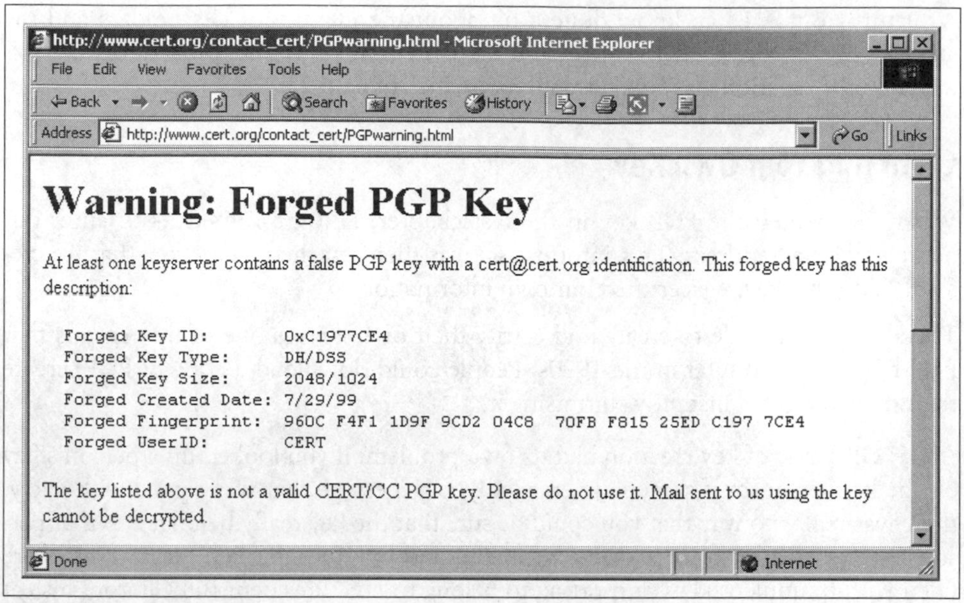

Figure 7-3. CERT/CC issued a warning about a fraudulent PGP key with CERT/CC's name that was put on the PGP key server.

The freedom that was a hallmark of PGP came with a cost: if you were given a person's PGP key, there was no way you could be sure that it belonged to that person.

One way that you can be reasonably sure to get a person's actual PGP key is to get the key from the person himself. In the last chapter, we saw that many individuals and organizations distribute PGP keys from their own web pages. In many cases, if you want to verify the PGP key of someone who is an avid PGP user, you can get a copy of his key from his own web site.

Certifying Other People's Keys: PGP's "Web of Trust"

Most of us start life knowing only a few people—the members of our immediate family, perhaps a babysitter, a few neighbors, and some playmates. As we grow older, we meet more people. Some of them are trustworthy; we can count on them not to steal our possessions, not to hurt us, and to help us up when we fall down. Other people aren't too trustworthy (and the less said about these people, the better).

How do we know whether to trust the new people that we meet? Most children trust everyone. But as they grow older, they become suspicious. After only a few years, when kids meet new people, those kids look to their parents and their friends—people they already trust—to figure out whether they should trust the newcomers.

Trust and validity

One of the strengths of PGP is that it has a system that mimics this community-based approach to trust for helping users to decide if they should trust keys. With PGP, users are able to sign the key certificates of other users. A signature on a key certificate is a promise made by the signer that the key really does belong to the person whose name and email address are listed on the key. If you believe a person's promises, then you are said to *trust* the key. If you have a key that has a signature (a promise) on it that you believe, then the key is said to be *valid*.

When you display your key ring with the PGPkeys application, each key appears with an indication of validity and trust:

Validity

An indication of whether you believe that the key you have in your possession actually belongs to the person to whom it says it belongs. Keys are valid if you created them or if they are signed with a key that you trust.

Trust

A measure of how much you believe the honesty and judgment of the person who holds the key. The more you trust a key, the more you trust the person who created the key to certify other people's keys.

Figure 7-4 shows a window from the PGPkeys application. In this case, the keys for Mr. Test Key, Niche Software, and Philip R. Zimmerman are listed as both valid and trusted. This means that this PGP key ring has signatures on the keys for these individuals who the user (Simson) trusts, and that he trusts other keys signed by these keys. The key from Niche Software is listed as valid but only half trusted; if Simson finds a signature from Niche Software on a key, he will not consider that key to be valid unless there is a second signature on the key that he also trusts. The key from Peter Gutmann is valid but not trusted, which means that Simson thinks the key belongs to Peter Gutmann, but he doesn't trust him to sign other people's keys. There are also five keys that are implicitly trusted: Mr. Test Key, two keys for Simson, and two keys for Vineyard.NET. These keys are implicitly trusted because Simson created them and their private keys are on the private key ring.

When he created PGP, Phil Zimmermann hoped that these casual relationships between key holders would build upon each other to create an ad hoc system for global key certification. Zimmermann then called this system the "Web of Trust" (see Figure 7-5).[*]

---

[*] More information on the Web of Trust can be found at *http://world.std.com/~cme/html/web.html*.

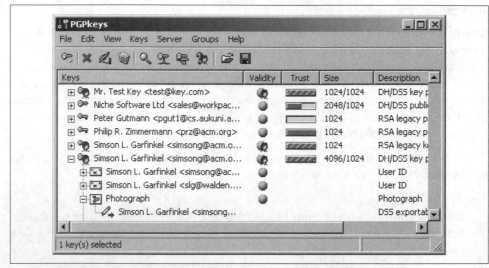

Figure 7-4. The PGPkeys application

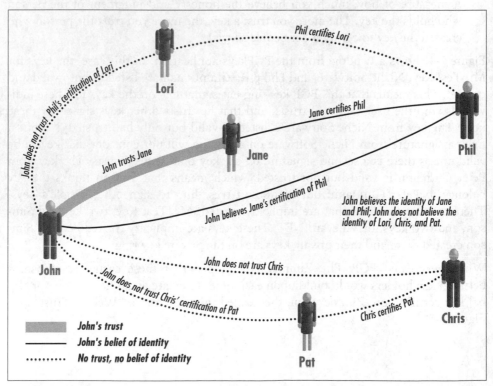

Figure 7-5. The PGP Web of Trust

The Web of Trust and the key servers

Today the Web of Trust is most visible on the PGP key servers. In April 2001, Simson looked his own key on the PGP public key server. He discovered that the key had five signatures on it: two from his own keys, one by Dave Del Torto, one by Eugene H. Spafford, and one by an "Unknown Signer" (see Figure 7-6) If you look up Simson's key and you trust signatures by Dave Del Torto, Eugene H. Spafford, or the "Unknown Signer,"* then you will know that the key is valid.

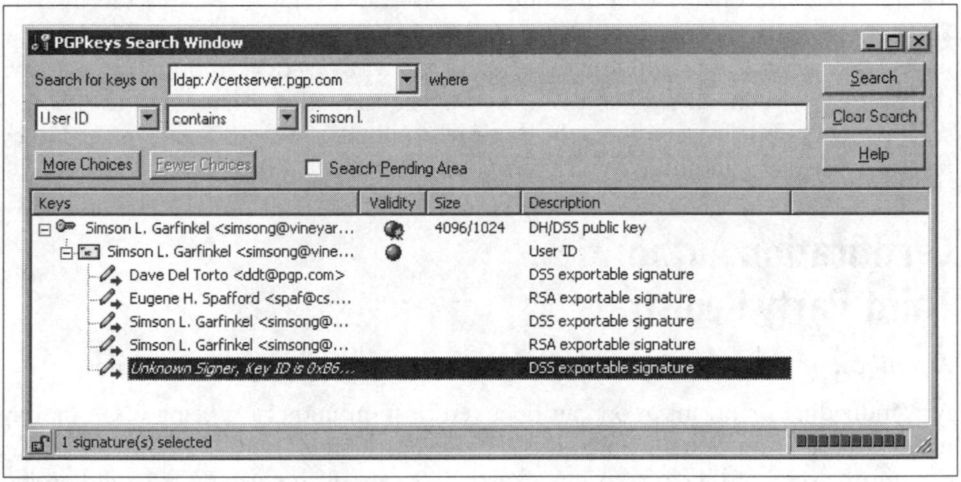

Figure 7-6. Simson's key on the PGP key server has five signatures on it.

Suppose you want to find our keys, but when you connect to the PGP key server you find several keys with our names on them. You might not know which key is the real key for each of us. However, if one of the keys on the key server is signed by someone whose key you trust, then you can differentiate between the actual key and the keys that are possibly fraudulent.†

Key signing parties

One way that PGP users work to extend the Web of Trust is by holding *key signing parties*. PGP users will gather, exchange floppy disks or business cards containing their keys, and then show each other their driver's licenses or passports. Having

---

* If you look up the KeyID of the unknown signer, you will find that it is Randy Antler (*randy@pilot.com*). We're not really sure who this is and Simson didn't ever meet him. He signed Simson's key when he downloaded the key to send Simson an email in August 2000. Because this person never met Simson face to face and did not have any real way to attest that the key really belonged to Simson, this signature may be considered suspect. It illustrates why you need to be cautious about trusting arbitrary signatures on a key without knowing something about the signer.

† Actually, if you consult the servers, you will find two valid keys for each of us: we each have an old-style RSA key and a newer DSS/DH key.

obtained a copy of someone's key and seen an apparently unimpeachable form of identification, people at the key signing party will then sign each other's keys and (usually) upload the signed keys to the key server.

Key signing parties are a lot of fun, especially in mixed company—and particularly when they are followed by trips to establishments involving the consumption of large quantities of alcohol, pizza, and/or chocolate. But while key signing parties are a great way to meet people, experience has shown that they are not a practical way to create a national database of cross-certified public keys—the coverage is simply too uneven. Some people have the time to go to key signing parties, but most don't. What's worse, having somebody's signature on your key gives away personal information—it says that you know each other, or at least that you met each other. That's why most large-scale uses of public key cryptography don't rely on PGP's Web of Trust. Instead, they rely on a tree of certifications, with a *certification authority* at the root.

Certification Authorities: Third-Party Registrars

A *certification authority* (CA) is any organization that issues digital certificates.

Any individual or organization can be a certification authority: being a CA simply means that the individual or organization signs certificates with a public key. A CA can impose standards before it signs a key; in the case of a university, it would probably verify that the key that it was about to sign really belonged to a bona fide student. Another CA might not have any standards at all. The world's largest CA, VeriSign, issues several different kinds of certificates. VeriSign signs certificates under its VeriSign Trust Network (VTN) for public use; the company also issues certificates for use within corporations. The lowest level of certificates issued by VTN have no assurance; the highest levels come with the promise that VTN attempted to establish the identity of the key holder before the certificate was issued.

Conceptually, a CA's certificate looks like a cryptographically signed index card. The certificates, signed by the certification authority's own private key, contain the name of the CA, that CA's public key, a serial number, and other information, as shown in Figure 7-7. To date, most certificates are a promise by the CA that a particular public key belongs to a particular individual or organization. But certificates can also be used for assertions. For example, the Commonwealth of Massachusetts could issue certificates saying that an individual is a licensed attorney in the Commonwealth. There are many different ways that a certification authority can offer service:

Internal CA
> An organization can operate a CA to certify its own employees. Certificates issued by an internal CA might certify an individual's name, position, and level of authority. These certificates could be used within the organization to control

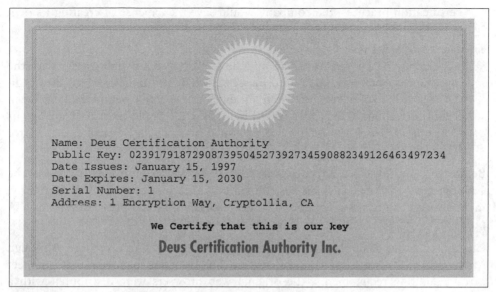

Name: Deus Certification Authority
Public Key: 023917918729087395045273927345908823491 26463497234
Date Issues: January 15, 1997
Date Expires: January 15, 2030
Serial Number: 1
Address: 1 Encryption Way, Cryptollia, CA

We Certify that this is our key

Deus Certification Authority Inc.

Figure 7-7. A schematic certification authority certificate.

access to internal resources or the flow of information. Such an internal CA would be the basis of the organization's public key infrastructure. (See the "Public Key Infrastructure" section later in this chapter.)

For example, a computer system used for purchasing could be set up so that any employee presenting a valid certificate saying that the employee was in the Purchasing Department would be given access. Internal CAs allow organizations to centralize access control to a large number of systems without having to distribute usernames, passwords, and access control lists throughout the enterprise. These systems can also implement so-called *single sign-on*, so that an employee needs to log into his or her computer only once, and then have access to the entire enterprise.

Companies can also operate internal CAs that issue certificates to customers. For example, some brokerages have required that their customers obtain certificates before they are allowed to execute high value trades over the Internet.

Outsourced employee CA

An organization might want to partake in the benefits of using digital certificates, but not have the technical ability to run its own certificate servers. Such an organization could contract with an outside firm to provide certification services for its own employees, exactly as a company might contract with a photo lab to create identification cards.

Outsourced customer CA

A company might contract with an outside firm to operate a certification authority to be operated for the company's customers. By trusting in the outside firm's certification practices, the company would save the expense of creating its own procedures.

Trusted third-party CA

A company or a government can operate a CA that binds public keys with the legal names of individuals and businesses. Such a CA can be used to allow individuals with no prior relationship to establish each other's identity and engage in legal transactions. Certificates issued by such a CA would be exactly analogous to driver's licenses and identity cards issued by a state's Department of Motor Vehicles.

Before you can use the certificates issued by a CA, you need to have a copy of the CA's public key. Public keys are distributed on certificates of their own. Currently, most of these certificates are prebundled in web browsers and operating systems. CA public keys can be added manually by the end user.

Clearly, CAs that do not have their keys prebundled are at a disadvantage. Although Microsoft and Netscape have now opened up their browsers to any CA that can meet certain auditing requirements, the original web browsers were distributed with a small number of carefully selected CA keys. The bundling of these keys was a tremendous advantage to these CAs and a barrier to others.

On December 19, 1999, VeriSign, the world's largest CA, bought Thawte Holdings, a South African corporation, for $575 million dollars of VeriSign stock.[*] In completing this transaction, VeriSign purchased its only significant competitor in the lucrative market of server certificates—the only other corporation in the world that was both offering CA services for SSL servers and that had succeeded in getting its certificates bundled with popular web browsers.[†]

Certification Practices Statement (CPS)

What does it mean to have a certified key? The answer to this question depends on who is doing the certification and what policies they are following. An internal CA that's run by a Fortune 500 company might certify that the person whose key is signed is an active employee. The hypothetical Cypherpunk Anonymous Key Signer, on the other hand, might sign any key that is sent to a particular electronic mail address.

The *certification practices statement* (CPS) is a legal document CAs publish that describes their policies and procedures for issuing and revoking digital certificates. It answers the question, "What does it mean when this organization signs a key?"

---

[*] *http://techdeals.lp.findlaw.com/agreements/verisign/exchange.html*

[†] Other corporations had succeeded in having their certificates bundled with early versions of Netscape Navigator or Internet Explorer, but never offered service to the general public. Even today, the Microsoft and Netscape browsers are distributed with a large number of CA keys belonging to apparently defunct projects.

CPS documents are designed to be read by humans, not by machines. It's possible that in the future the terms and conditions of CAs will become standardized enough that it will be possible for programs to automatically process CPS documents. A business might be willing to accept certification from a CA that guarantees minimum certification policies and a willingness to assume a certain amount of liability in the event that its certification policies are not followed—and provided that the CA is bonded by an appropriate bonding agency. Alternatively, laws or the market may encourage CAs to adopt standard policies throughout the industry, the same as credit card issuers have adopted more-or-less standard policies, choosing to distinguish themselves with different interest rates, service charges, and ancillary services.

The X.509 v3 Certificate

Although certification authorities can issue any kind of certificate, in practice the vast majority of CAs issue certificates that follow the X.509 v3 standard. Likewise, most cryptographic programs and protocols, including SSL, are only designed to use X.509 v3 certificates. The only notable exception to this is PGP, which uses its own certificate format, although recent versions support reading some X.509 certificates. (The Secure Shell (*ssh*) program does not actually use certificates, but instead relies on the registration of public keys.)

Each X.509 certificate contains a version number, a serial number, identity information, algorithm-related information, and the signature of the issuing authority. Figure 7-8 shows the structure of an X.509 certificate.

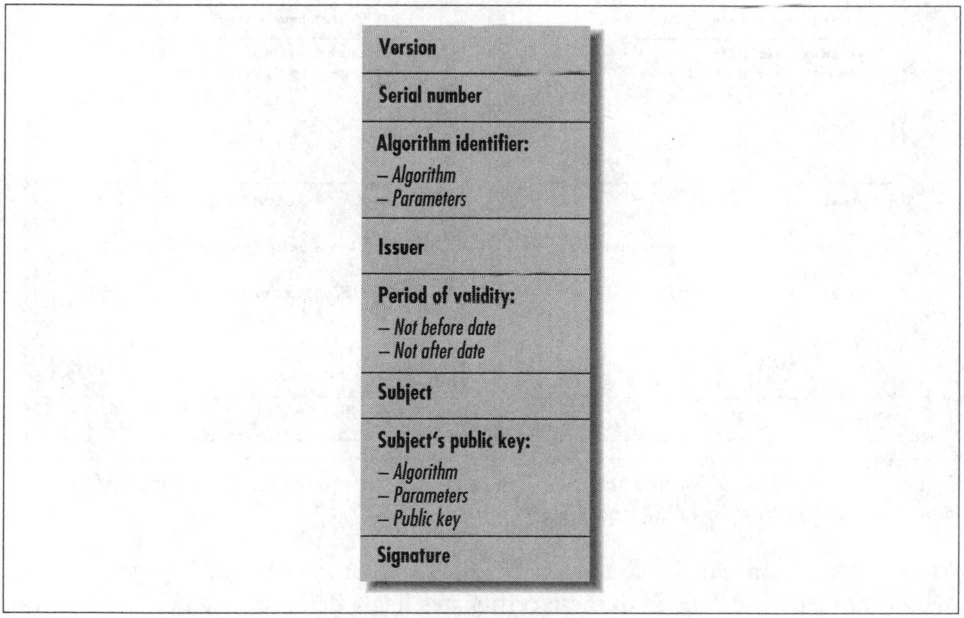

Figure 7-8. The schematic structure of a typical X.509 certificate

The industry adopted X.509 v3 certificates, rather than the original X.509 certificates, because the X.509 v3 standard allows arbitrary name/value pairs to be included in the standard certificate. These pairs can be used for many purposes and allow the uses of certificates to be expanded without changing the underlying protocol.

Exploring the X.509 v3 certificate

You can use Microsoft's Internet Explorer to display information about an X.509 v3 certificate. For example, if you are viewing a web page that was downloaded using the "https:" protocol, you can use Internet Explorer to show you the server's certificate. To view the certificates, choose the "Properties" option from the File menu while looking at a document that was downloaded using "https:" and click on the "Certificate" button.

Figure 7-9 shows the "General" certificate properties for two certificates downloaded from the web. The first is for the web site *https://www.vineyard.net/*, which belongs to Vineyard.NET, Inc. The second is for the web site *https://wfbdirect. wellsfargo.com/*, which is for Wells Fargo's Wells Fargo Bank Direct service. Overall, the "General" properties page is not terribly useful. Instead of listing the name of the organization that was issued the certificate, it merely shows the DNS address. The page doesn't even show the name of the organization that issued the certificate!

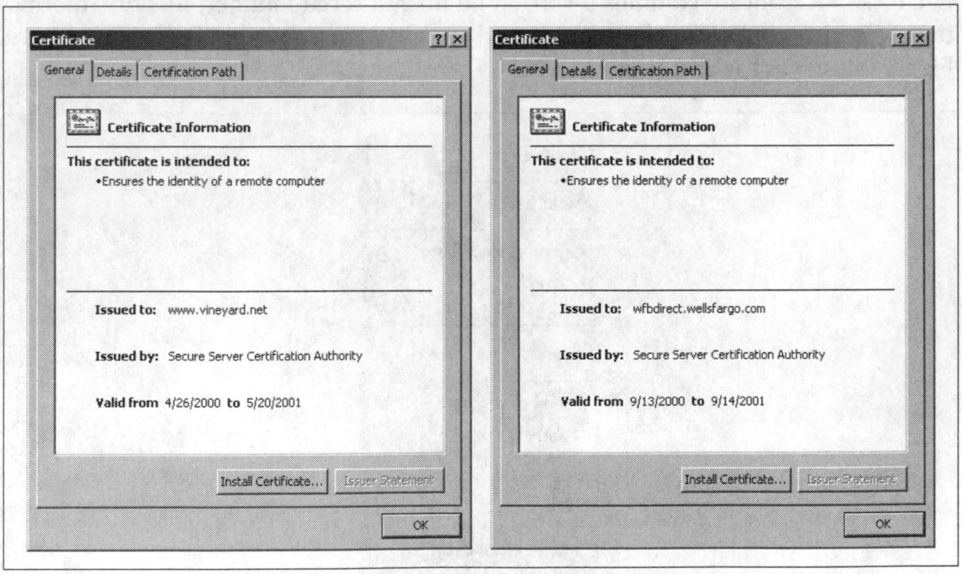

Figure 7-9. The "General" certificate properties, as viewed by Internet Explorer, for certificates downloaded from Vineyard.NET and Wells Fargo.

More information can be found on Internet Explorer's "Details" page, which is shown in Figure 7-10. Each of these certificates has a definite time period when it is valid, a "Subject," the certificate's public key, the "Thumbprint algorithm," and the "Thumbprint." Here, the word *thumbprint* is used as a synonym for *message digest*.

The Subject field is further divided into other fields:

Field Code	Meaning
CN	Common Name (for SSL certificates, the Common Name should be the DNS address of the server)
OU	Organizational Unit
O	Organization
L	Location
S	State
C	Country

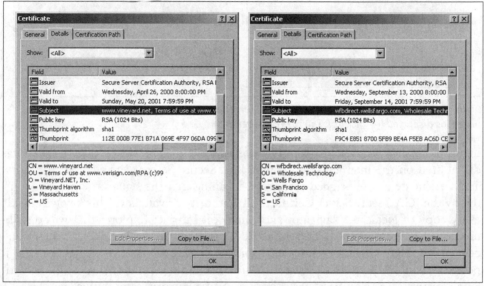

Figure 7-10. Some of the additional fields in the X.509 v3 certificates belonging to Vineyard.NET and Wells Fargo, as displayed by Microsoft Internet Explorer.

If you look carefully at the OU field of the Vineyard.NET certificate, you will notice that instead of indicating the organizational unit of Vineyard.NET, the OU field contains the URL of VeriSign's Relaying Party Agreement (RPA). VeriSign places the URL of the RPA in this field because not all client programs can display the certificate policies extension fields where this information would normally be placed.

Every browser can determine that these certificates are valid because each certificate is signed with a private key that matches a public key certificate that it trusts. The steps from a downloaded certificate to a certificate that is trusted is called the *certification path*. You can view the path using Internet Explorer's "Certificate Path" panel, as shown in Figure 7-11. The Certificate Path is similar to PGP's Web of Trust model, except that trust starts at the top and works its way down: if you trust a CA, then you automatically trust any keys that the CA signs. If that CA signs a key that is used to sign a third key, then you automatically trust that third key as well. This is called a *certificate chain*.

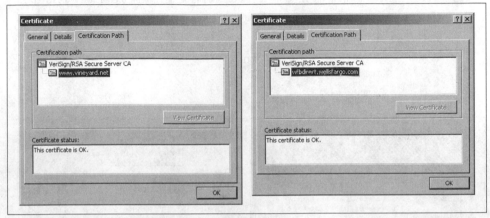

Figure 7-11. The Certificate Path panel for the certificates belonging to Vineyard.NET and Wells Fargo, as displayed by Microsoft Internet Explorer.

Figure 7-12 shows the fields from one of the earliest X.509 v3 certificates that was distributed on the Internet—the original RSA Secure Server Certification Authority. This certificate is a self-signed certificate, meaning that the signature on it was written by the RSA Secure Server Certification Authority private key. This key was inside every copy of Netscape Navigator and Microsoft Internet Explorer that was distributed until January 1, 2000. This single key was a critical factor in the financial success of VeriSign's digital certificate business, because it was this key that made it possible for VeriSign to issue site certificates. For a more detailed discussion of VeriSign's history, see "Certification Authorities: Some History" later in this chapter.

One of the interesting things about this certificate is that it is signed by the very organization (and public key) that it purports to identify. This is called a *self-signed certificate*. What it's saying, in effect, is this: "Here is my public key. It's mine. Trust me."

What makes it possible to trust this certificate is the social structure itself. The certificate comes inside programs such as Internet Explorer and Netscape Navigator. The people who created that software decided that the certificate was trustworthy; if you can't trust their judgment, then you really shouldn't trust Explorer or Navigator, and you've got to be able to trust those programs because they are the programs that you are using for verifying the other digital certificates. If you wanted further verification you could go to VeriSign's web site and verify the certificate or, if you are even more

```
     Data:
             Version: 0 (0x0)
             Serial Number:
                 02:41:00:00:01
             Signature Algorithm: MD2 digest with RSA Encryption
             Issuer: C=US, O=RSA Data Security, Inc.,
                         OU=Secure Server Certification Authority
             Validity:
                 Not Before: Wed Nov  9 15:54:17 1994
                 Not After: Fri Dec 31 15:54:17 1999
             Subject: C=US, O=RSA Data Security, Inc.,
                         OU=Secure Server Certification Authority
             Subject Public Key Info:
                 Public Key Algorithm: RSA Encryption
                 Public Key:
                     Modulus:
                         00:92:ce:7a:c1:ae:83:3e:5a:aa:89:83:57:ac:25:
                         01:76:0c:ad:ae:8e:2c:37:ce:eb:35:78:64:54:03:
                         e5:84:40:51:c9:bf:8f:08:e2:8a:82:08:d2:16:86:
                         37:55:e9:b1:21:02:ad:76:68:81:9a:05:a2:4b:c9:
                         4b:25:66:22:56:6c:88:07:8f:f7:81:59:6d:84:07:
                         65:70:13:71:76:3e:9b:77:4c:e3:50:89:56:98:48:
                         b9:1d:a7:29:1a:13:2e:4a:11:59:9c:1e:15:d5:49:
                         54:2c:73:3a:69:82:b1:97:39:9c:6d:70:67:48:e5:
                         dd:2d:d6:c8:1e:7b
                     Exponent: 65537 (0x10001)
     Signature Algorithm: MD2 digest with RSA Encryption
     Signature:
             88:d1:d1:79:21:ce:e2:8b:e8:f8:c1:7d:34:53:3f:61:83:d9:
             b6:0b:38:17:b6:e8:be:21:8d:8f:00:b8:8b:53:7e:44:67:1e:
             22:bd:97:27:e0:9c:85:cc:4a:f6:85:3b:b2:e2:be:92:d3:e5:
             0d:e9:af:5c:0e:0c:46:95:ff:a1:1c:5e:3e:e8:36:58:7a:73:
             a6:0a:f8:22:11:6b:c3:09:38:7e:26:bb:73:ef:00:bd:02:a4:
             f3:14:0d:30:3f:61:70:7b:20:fe:32:a3:9f:b3:f4:67:52:dc:
             b4:ee:84:8c:96:36:20:de:81:08:83:71:21:8a:0f:9e:a9
```

Figure 7-12. The original RSA Secure Server Certification Authority certificate

untrusting, you could call up VeriSign's technical support department, read them the public key, and ask the person if the key is really VeriSign's. Of course, you might not believe that the person who answered the phone really worked for Verisign and knew what they were talking about, but if you want to use computers, at some point you've got to trust somebody. (Trust us on this!)* Computers are so complicated that you simply cannot create your own microchips, circuit boards, operating systems, and application software necessary for a secure computing environment.

In point of fact, however, most Internet users are unaware of the trust that they are placing in their software and the certificates they contain. All they know is that the software works (or at least seems to work). In fact, the security provided by public

---

* For more information about the trust problem, see Chapter 27, "Who Do You Trust?" of *Practical Unix & Internet Security* (O'Reilly).

key cryptography is significantly greater than the security of the underlying operating systems.

Types of Certificates

There are four primary types of digital certificates in use on the Internet today:

Certification authority certificates
> These certificates contain the public keys of CAs and either the name of the CA or the name of the particular service being certified. These certificates are typically self-signed—that is, signed with the CA's own private key. CAs can also *cross-certify*, or sign each other's master keys. What such cross-certification actually means is an open question. Microsoft Windows, Microsoft Internet Explorer, and Netscape Navigator are all shipped with more than a dozen different CA certificates.

Server certificates
> These certificates contain the public key of an SSL server, the name of the organization that runs the server, the DNS name of the server, and the server's public key. Every cryptographically-enabled web server on the Internet must be equipped with a server certificate for the SSL encryption protocol to function properly. Although the originally stated purpose of these certificates was to allow consumers to determine the identity of web servers and to prevent man-in-the-middle attacks, in practice server certificates are not used for this purpose.

Personal certificates
> These certificates contain an individual's name and the individual's public key. They can have other information as well, such as the individual's email address, postal address, birth date, and other identifying information.
>
> Some banks and investment houses issue digital certificates to their depositors. The certificates are typically kept on the depositor's home computer and provide an extra level of assurance when the subscriber attempts to access his or her accounts.
>
> Many corporations issue digital certificates to their employees. Each web server that belongs to the organization can then simply grant access to anyone who has a valid certificate, without having to be equipped with an entire employee roster. This also frees employees from having to remember many individual usernames and passwords. Personal certificates are also required for users of the S/MIME email encryption protocol (described in Chapter 4).
>
> Personal certificates are a substantially more secure way of having people identify themselves on the Internet than the alternative: usernames and passwords. Personal certificates are described in detail in Chapter 6 and Chapter 22.

Software publisher certificates

These certificates are used to verify the signatures on software that is distributed, such as ActiveX components and downloadable executables. Every copy of recent Windows operating systems is distributed with a number of software publisher certificates that can be used to validate the signatures on Windows applications (see Figure 7-13).

Publisher certificates and code signing are described in Chapter 22.

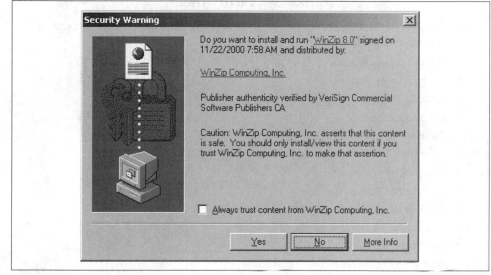

Figure 7-13. Digital signatures and software publisher certificates are used to verify the integrity and authorship of software that is downloaded over the Internet.

And this is only the beginning! Many security professionals believe that digital certificates will eventually be widely used throughout the Internet, computing, and society as a whole. Some proposed uses of digital certificates include the following:

- For consumers, digital certificates could be used to prove membership in an organization or the right to a legal privilege without revealing the consumer's name. For example, college-aged consumers could have digital certificates stating that they are over the age of 21. Students could then use these certificates to purchase alcohol without being forced to reveal their names.

- Age-proving digital certificates could also be used to control access to pornography and other information on the Internet that is legally restricted from minors.

- You might use digital certificates to eliminate junk mail from your email inbox. To do this, you would program your email system to reject all mail that is not digitally signed.

- Public keys and digital certificates will increasingly be used for signing contracts over the Internet.

- Digital certificates might be used as the authentication infrastructure for a national identity card.

But remember: the fact that people can authenticate themselves using certificates does not alone prove that they are who they claim to be. It only proves that they possess a secret key that has been signed by an appropriate certification authority.

How May I Certify Thee?

The Windows operating system allows you to specify for what purposes a certificate can be used. Allowable uses include:

- Server Authentication
- Client Authentication
- Code Signing
- Secure Email
- Time Stamping
- Microsoft Trust List Signing
- Microsoft Time Stamping
- IP security end system
- IP security tunnel termination
- IP security user
- Encrypting File System
- Windows Hardware Driver Verification
- Windows System Component Verification
- OEM Windows System Component Verification
- Embedded Windows System Component Verification
- Key Pack Licenses
- License Server Verification
- Smart Card Logon
- Digital Rights
- File Recovery

Additional purposes can be added on a certificate-by-certificate basis using the "Edit Properties..." button in the Certificate/Details panel (see Figure 7-10).

Netscape Navigator 6.0 also allows you to specify the so-called *trust settings* of what a certificate can be used for (see Figure 7-14). Perhaps because Navigator is not integrated with the operating system, Netscape allows only three uses for each certificate:

- "This certificate can identify web sites."
- "This certificate can identify mail users."
- "This certificate can identify software makers."

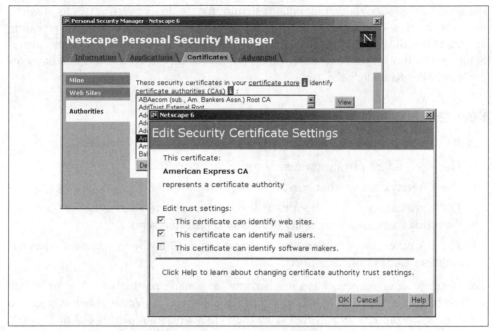

Figure 7-14. *Netscape Navigator 6.0's Security Manager allows you to specify for what purpose a certificate will be used.*

Minimal disclosure certificates

Digital certificates represent a threat to the privacy of their users. When you flash a driver's license at a bar to prove your age, the bartender doesn't copy down your name, address, birthday, height, weight, and whether you need glasses. But if you present a "driver's license digital certificate" to a web site to download some information, the web site would get all of the information and more. In many jurisdictions, an organization that obtained this information in the course of business would be free to do whatever it wished with the data. For example, the web site could use the height and weight information to compile a list of overweight individuals and then sell this list to an online merchant that marketed dieting aids.

One way to minimize the privacy threat is to have a lot of private/public key pairs and a lot of digital certificates. This approach doesn't work in practice, however: no reputable certification authority would issue a certificate saying "This person is over 21" without tying that certificate to the individual's name. Otherwise, the individual could give the certificate and the corresponding private key away without any repercussions.

A better way to minimize the privacy threat is by using *minimal disclosure certificates*. These certificates allow the holder to selectively reveal specific facts that are on a certificate without revealing others. A woman who wanted to gain access to a web site for a cancer survivors group might use minimal disclosure certificates to prove to the web site that she was a woman over 21 who had breast cancer without revealing her name or address. Minimal disclosure certificates were invented by the mathematician Stefan Brands and exclusively licensed in February 2000 to the Canadian corporation Zero Knowledge Systems.[*]

Revocation

Besides issuing certificates, CAs need a way of revoking them as well, because:

- The key holder's private key may become compromised.
- The CA may discover that it issued the certificate to the wrong person or entity.
- The certificate may have been issued to grant access to a particular service, and the individual may have lost his authorization for that service.
- The CA may have its systems compromised in such a way that someone has the ability to issue falsified certificates.

The need for effective revocation mechanisms was made particularly clear in March 2001, when Microsoft announced in a security advisory that VeriSign had issued two certificates, on January 29 and 30, "to an individual who fraudulently claimed to be a Microsoft employee. The common name assigned to both certificates is "Microsoft Corporation." Microsoft went on to note that "the ability to sign executable content using keys that purport to belong to Microsoft would clearly be advantageous to an attacker who wished to convince users to allow the content to run."[†]

Certificate revocation lists

One way that has been proposed for handling revocations is the *certificate revocation list* (CRL). A CRL is a list of every certificate that has been revoked by the CA that has not yet expired for other reasons. Ideally, a CA issues a CRL at regular intervals. Besides listing certificates that have been revoked, the CRL states how long it will be valid and where to get the next CRL.

Current practice is that X.509 v3 certificates should contain a field called the *CRL distribution point* (CDP). In theory, a program that wishes to verify if a certificate has been revoked should be able to download a CRL from the CDP to determine if the certificate has been revoked. As most certificates will be issued by a small number of CAs, it is reasonable to assume that a program might download a new CRL every day or every hour, and then cache this list for successive lookups.

[*] *http://www.wired.com/news/technology/0,1282,34496,00.html*
[†] *http://www.microsoft.com/technet/security/bulletin/MS01-017.asp*

CRLs and CDPs are interesting technology; they allow computers that are not connected to a network to determine if a certificate is valid or if it has been revoked. In practice, though, this technology has a variety of problems:

- If a CA is very popular, it is likely that the CRLs will grow very large. VeriSign's 900K CRL for its SSL server certificates can take more than 20 minutes to download over a dialup connection.
- There is a period between the time that a certificate is revoked and the time that the new CRL is distributed when a certificate appears to be valid but is not.
- The information contained in CRLs can be used for traffic analysis.
- Many programs do not properly implement CRLs and CDPs.

In the case of the fraudulently-issued Microsoft certificate, the bogus certificate was revoked and listed in VeriSign's CRL. Unfortunately, the certificates that VeriSign issued did not contain valid CDPs. (According to VeriSign, CDPs are not present in Authenticode certificates because of a bug in the implementation of Authenticode distributed with Internet Explorer 3.02.) Without the CDP, a program that attempted to verify the authenticity of the fraudulently-issued certificates does not know where to find the CRL on which the certificates were listed.

After the fraudulently-issued certificates were discovered, Microsoft attempted to resolve the problem by issuing operating system patch 28888. This patch contained:

- A CRL that listed the two certificates VeriSign had mistakenly issued.
- An additional revocation handler that causes Internet Explorer to consider the local CRL when evaluating the authenticity of certificates.

As the Microsoft experience shows, when you choose to trust a certification authority, you really do make yourself vulnerable to poor decisions that the CA may make or operating practices that it may have.

Real-time certificate validation

An alternative to CRLs is to use real-time validation of certificates. These systems consult an online database operated by the certification authority every time the authenticity of a certificate needs to be validated. Two technologies actively under development to aid real-time validation are the XML Key Management Specification and the Security Assertions Markup Language (SAML).

Real-time certification validation systems neatly dispense with the CRL problem, although they do require a network that is reliable and available. The primary problem with real-time validation is one of scale. As there are more and more users of certificates, the validation servers need to be faster and faster to serve the larger user community.

Furthermore real-time systems are vulnerable to denial of service (DoS) attacks. If it is not possible for a business to connect to the revocation server, what should be done with a certificate—trust it or discard it? If the default is to trust it, fraud can be committed by flooding the revocation server so as to make it unresponsive while a revoked certificate is used. If the default is to reject requests when the revocation server is unreachable, then it is possible to cause all transactions to be rejected using a DoS attack, thus damaging the reputation of the business.

Short-lived certificates

An alternative is simply to use certificates with very short expiration times—perhaps as short as one to two minutes. In effect, this requires the person using the certificate to communicate with the CA before every transaction to get a new certificate. In many cases, this method may be more efficient than having the recipient of the certificate verify it with the CA.

Public Key Infrastructure

Public key infrastructure (PKI) is the system of digital certificates, certification authorities, tools, systems, and hardware that are used to deploy public key technology.

The word "public" in PKI has had an ambiguous history. Many of the early proponents of PKI envisioned a single PKI, operated by or for the government, which would provide state-certified certificates. In one vision, each person in the United States would be issued a certificate. These certificates could be used for digitally signing tax returns, for conducting online business, and for other official purposes. As acceptance increased, it was envisioned that PKI certificates would become the electronic equivalent of driver's licenses.

The public PKI was a grand vision, but so far it hasn't happened. Companies such as VeriSign have issued millions of certificates to verify the identity of individuals and organizations, and the keys to sign these certificates have been widely distributed. Some of these so-called *trust hierarchies*, such as the trust hierarchy used to certify web server certificates, are used by more than a hundred million people. But they are run by *private* businesses, and not by governments. The word "public" in PKI refers to *public keys*, rather than to the public at large.

To understand the issues involved in PKI today, it's helpful to look back at how we got where we are today.

Certification Authorities: Some History

When Netscape Communications started business in 1995, the World Wide Web was then beginning to take off. The most popular web browser was Mosaic, a free web browser distributed by the National Center for Supercomputing Applications (NCSA). There were a plethora of web servers, none of them tremendously popular, from CERN, NCSA, and others.

Netscape's grand business strategy was to make money by selling software that brought commerce to the Internet. Netscape's plan was to let people buy and sell things using credit cards. At the time, many banks and security experts argued that the Internet wasn't ready for credit card commerce because there was no way to protect credit card numbers as they traveled over the network. Fundamentally, there were two basic objections:

1. There was no readily apparent way to protect credit card numbers as they traveled over the network. Without suitable protection, a person at an Internet service provider would be able to eavesdrop on customers and learn their credit card numbers. This information could then be used for fraudulent purposes. Likewise, it was assumed that online banking, investing, and other activities would never blossom unless consumers could be assured that their transactions and personal information would not be revealed to third parties.

2. Consumers had no way to verify the identity of a shop on the network. A consumer might try to buy something from a web site, only to discover that the web site was actually run by credit card thieves!

To solve these problems, Netscape's engineers invented the Secure Sockets Layer protocol (SSL), which we described in Chapter 5. This protocol provided for a cryptographically secure communications channel between a web server and a web browser. To prevent site-spoofing, the SSL protocol included a digital certificate verification system. The SSL protocol would not operate unless the web browser was in communication with a site that had a digital certificate that was signed by an appropriate key.

Netscape put the icon of a little broken key at the bottom of its web browser. When the Netscape Navigator program reached a web site that used the SSL protocol, the key would be whole. If Navigator reached a web site that did not use the SSL protocol, the key would be broken. Consumers were told that sites that used SSL were "secure" and safe to use. Consumers were advised not to type credit card numbers or other personal information into sites that were not secure.

Thus, the original Navigator program had two ingenious systems for revenue protection and wealth creation:

1. Consumers were basically told not to do business with web sites that did not support the SSL protocol, and the only web server that supported SSL was the Netscape Commerce Server sold by Netscape.

2. Once a company purchased the Netscape Commerce Server, that company had to purchase signed digital certificates that were signed by the certification authority whose key was built into the Netscape browser.

Rather than set up its own certification authority, which could have been seen by some companies as anticompetitive, Netscape turned to RSA Data Security, which had supplied the public key technology software on which Navigator was based. For several years RSA had been running its own CA called RSA Certification Services. This CA existed to support other protocols that require CAs, such as Privacy Enhanced Mail (PEM). RSA was more than happy to issue certificates for Netscape servers as well.

Microsoft broke Netscape's monopoly on cryptographically-enabled web servers when it released the Microsoft Internet Information Server (IIS). The monopoly was further broken when Eric Young created an open source implementation of the SSL protocol called SSLeay. Suddenly, there were many alternatives for organizations seeking to offer cryptographically-enabled web servers, and Netscape's products quickly lost market share.[*]

By all indications, the same sort of competition should have taken hold in the field of certification authorities, but it did not, in part because RSA Data Security aggressively enforced its patent rights. Without RSA's approval, CAs could only do business outside the U.S.

In 1995, RSA spun out its certificate services division to a new company called VeriSign. Many people complained that they did not want to be forced to purchase certificates from a single vendor, so Netscape, and later Microsoft, made provisions for supporting multiple CAs in its web browser:

- Netscape Navigator Version 1.0 contained a CA certificate for a single authority, the Secure Server Certification Authority, operated by RSA Data Security, Inc.

- Netscape Navigator Version 2.0 still came with support for only a single CA, but it allowed other CAs to be loaded with the user's permission.

- Netscape Navigator Version 3.0 came preloaded with certificates for 16 CAs at 11 companies (AT&T, BBN, Canada Post Corporation, CommerceNet, GTE Cyber-Trust, Keywitness, MCI Mail, RSA, Thawte, U.S. Postal Service, and VeriSign.) The program also contained a user interface for viewing the currently loaded certificates, deleting certificates that were already resident, or adding more.

- Internet Explorer 3.0 shipped with a subset of the Navigator 3.0 certificates (AT&T, Keywitness, MCI Mail, RSA, and VeriSign).

Although all of the seeds were in place for a competitive market, in practice that market never materialized. VeriSign quickly grew to be the primary source for SSL digital certificates on the Internet. Despite having their keys bundled in Navigator, AT&T, BBN, Canada Post, and others never offered commercial CA services. VeriSign's primary competitor for server certificates was the South African company called Thwate Holdings, which (as noted earlier) was eventually purchased by VeriSign.

---

[*] We don't mean to imply that this was the reason that Netscape lost market share.

Today, Internet Explorer and Netscape Navigator are shipped with a large number of built-in CA certificates. Nevertheless, VeriSign remains the dominant source of server certificates on the Internet today.

Internet Explorer Preinstalled Certificates

Both Netscape Navigator and Microsoft Internet Explorer come with a set of preinstalled certificates. Current versions of these programs allow you to view and modify these lists.

You can view the certificates that are preinstalled in Internet Explorer by following these steps:

1. Open the "Internet Options" control panel.
2. Select the "Content" tab.
3. Click on the button that says "Certificates..."

Internet Explorer will now display the "Certificates" panel (see Figure 7-15). The program supports a wide number of certificate types, including:

Personal
> Certificates issued to a user of the computer. These certificates are used to identify the user and to facilitate the exchange of encrypted electronic mail.
>
> No personal certificates are provided with Internet Explorer by default.

Other People
> Certificates issued to other people that the computer's user corresponds with. These certificates are used to verify signatures on electronic mail and to encrypt email that is destined for the other people.
>
> No "Other People" certificates are provided with Internet Explorer by default.

Intermediate Certification Authorities
> Intermediate Certification Authorities certificates are CA certificates that are bundled with Internet Explorer, but that are not trusted.
>
> Internet Explorer 5.0 provides for a number of Intermediate Certification Authorities, including:
> - MS SGC Authority
> - Root Agency
> - SecureNET CA SGC Root
> - Thawte Premium Server CA
> - Thawte Server CA
> - UTN-DATAC
> - VeriSign Class 1 Public Primary Certification Authority

- VeriSign Class 2 Public Primary Certification Authority
- VeriSign Class 3 Public Primary Certification Authority

Trusted Root Certification Authorities

These self-signed certificates are the roots of trust hierarchies. Trusted Root Certification Authorities are trusted, although Internet Explorer's interface allows you to control which certificates are trusted for which purposes.

Certificates are provided for a large number of Trusted Root Certification Authorities, as shown in Table 7-1.

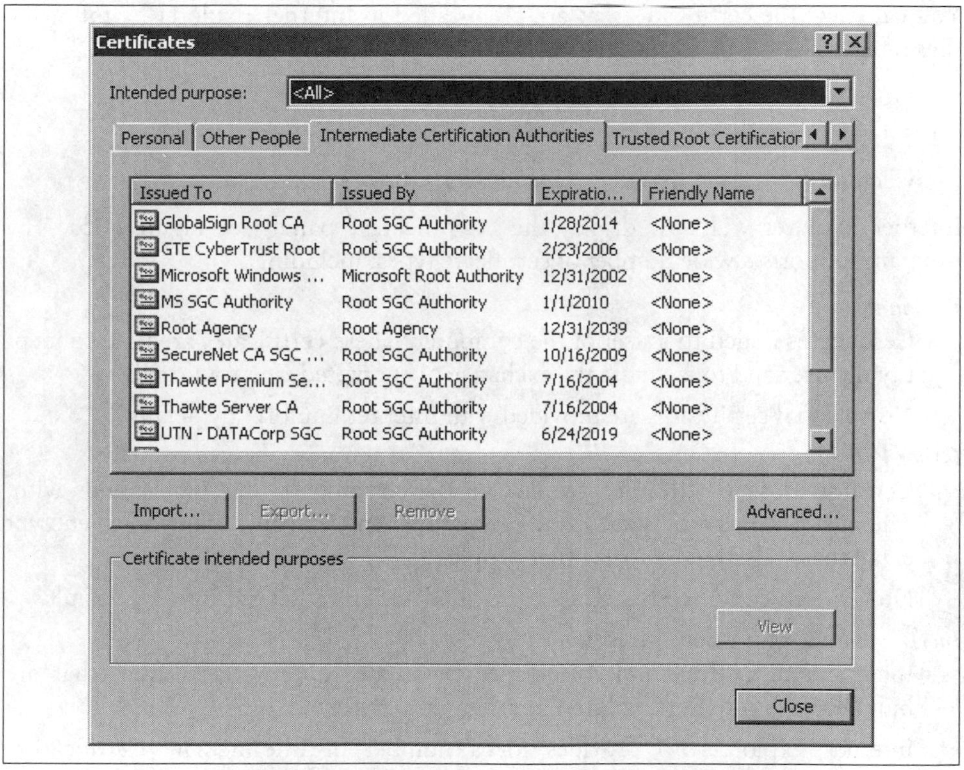

Figure 7-15. Internet Explorer comes with a set of built-in CA certificates.

Table 7-1. Certification authority keys bundled with Internet Explorer 5.0

Certification authority	Country	# of certificates
ABA.ECOM, Inc.	U.S.	1
Autoridad Certificadora de la Asociacion Nacional del Notariado Mexicano	Mexico	1
Autoridad Certificadora del Colegio Nacional de Correduria Publica Mexicana	Mexico	1
Baltimore EZ (Digital Signature Trust)	U.S.	1

Table 7-1. Certification authority keys bundled with Internet Explorer 5.0 (continued)

Certification authority	Country	# of certificates
Belgacom E-Trust	Belgium	1
C&W HKT SecureNet	Hong Kong	4
CA 1 (ViaCode)	Great Britain	1
Certiposte	France	2
Certisign Certificadora Digital Ltda.	Brazil	4
Certplus	France	4
Deutsche Telekom	Germany	2
Digital Signature Trust	U.S.	6
Entrust.net	U.S.	1
Equifax Secure Certification Authority	U.S.	4
EUnet International	N/A	1
FESTE	Spain	2
First Data Digital Certificates	U.S.	1
FNMT	Spain	1
GlobalSign	Belgium	1
GTE CyberTrust	U.S.	3
IPS Seguridad	Spain	1
Microsoft	U.S.	3
National Retail Federation (Digital Signature Trust)	U.S.	1
NetLock Tanusitvanykiado	Hungary	3
PTT Post	Netherlands	1
Saunalahden Serveri Oy	Finland	2
Secure Server Certification Authority, RSA Data Security	U.S.	1
SecureNet	Australia	4
SecureSign, Japan Certification Services, Inc.	Japan	3
Servicios de Certificacion, Servicios Electronicos, Administracion Nacional de Correos	Uruguay	1
SIA S.p.A.	Italy	2
Swisskey AG	Switzerland	1
TC TrustCenter for Security in Data Networks GmbH	Germany	5
Thawte Consulting	South Africa	6
United Parcel Service (Digital Secure Trust)	U.S.	1
UserTrust	U.S.	5
ValiCert Validation Authority	U.S.	3

Certification authority	Country	# of certificates
VeriSign	U.S.	21
Xcert EZ (Digital Secure Trust)	U.S.	1

That's 107 certificates that are distributed with Internet Explorer, the vast majority of which are used to certify email messages and web sites. Each of these certificates is given equal standing by IE—and that means users in the United States end up putting the same amount of trust into certificates issued by the billion-dollar corporation VeriSign and by the Servicios de Certificacion, Servicios Electronicos, Administracion Nacional de Correos in Uruguay.

According to Microsoft, the process for organizations to get their certificates bundled with Internet Explorer has changed over the years. In a personal communication that we received in April 2001, the process was described to us as follows:

> A CA submits its request to the alias *casubmit@microsoft.com*. They should include two contacts (name, email, telephone) from the company, the company address information, and how many roots they would like to submit. Somebody at Microsoft follows up with them from there. We look at several factors before accepting a root:
>
> 1. What is the root used for? Obviously privately used roots are not interesting to include in Microsoft products.
>
> 2. Has the CA been audited? We look to see if an appropriate third party has audited the CA. This audit would look at their root key generation, CPS, and operational controls.
>
> 3. Are the roots long lived? Roots only valid for a few years are not suitable for our program.

Netscape Navigator Preinstalled Certificates

Like Internet Explorer, Netscape Navigator is delivered with a large number of preinstalled certificates.

To view or edit the certificates that are built into Netscape Navigator 6.0, display the Netscape Security Manager using these steps under Windows:

1. Select the "Tasks" menu.
2. Select "Privacy and Security".
3. Select "Security Manager".
4. Click on the "Certificates" tab.
5. Select "Authorities".

This will display the Netscape Personal Security Manager (Figure 7-14).

On a Macintosh:

1. Select the "Edit" menu.
2. Select "Preferences".

3. Select "Privacy and Security" and expand its sublist.

4. Select "Certificates".

5. Select "Manage Certificates".

This will display the Netscape Certificate manager.

All of the certificates that are bundled into Netscape Navigator 6.0 are shown in Table 7-2.

Table 7-2. Certification authority keys bundled with Netscape Navigator 6.0

Certification authority	Country	# of certificates
ABA.ECOM, Inc	U.S.	1
AddTrust	Sweden	4
American Express	U.S.	2
Baltimore CyberTrust	U.S.	3
BankEngine	Canada	1
BelSign Object Publishing CA (Since renamed GlobalSign)	Brussels,	4
beTRUSTed	"WW"[a]	1
CertEngine	Canada	1
Deutsche Telekom	Germany	1
Digital Signature Trust	U.S.	4
E-Certify	Canada	2
Entrust.net	U.S.	3
Equifax Secure Certification Authority	U.S.	5
FortEngine	Canada	1
GlobalSign	Belgium	5
GTE CyberTrust	U.S.	5
MailEngine	Canada	1
TC TrustCenter	Germany	5
Thawte Consulting	South Africa	6
TraderEngine	Canada	1
United States Postal Service	U.S.	1
UserTrust	U.S.	5
ValiCert Validation Authority	U.S.	4
VeriSign (and RSA)	U.S.	18
Visa International	U.S.	5
Xcert (Digital Secure Trust)	U.S.	5

[a] This is what the key says; it does not correspond to any particular country code.

Multiple Certificates for a Single CA

Several companies have more than one CA certificate in the CA list. VeriSign has the most: 21 different certificates (22 if you count the RSA Secure Server Certification Authority.) The idea is to use signatures by different private keys to denote different levels of trust and authentication.

The evolution of VeriSign's practices is shown in Table 7-3 (for 1996) and Table 7-4 (for 2001). In 1996, VeriSign offered only four kinds of certificates—three for individuals, and one for "Secure Servers" (Table 7-3).

Table 7-3. VeriSign certificates in 1996

Certificate name	Certificate type	Certification practice	Cost	Liability protection
Class 1	Client[a]	VeriSign assures that the user can receive email at the given address and that no other certificate for the email address has been issued.	Free (nominally $9.95/year)	$100
Class 2	Client	VeriSign assures the identity of a digital ID holder through online identity verification against a consumer database.	$19.95/year	$5,000
Class 3	Client	VeriSign validates the entity applying for the certificate using background checks and investigative services.	$290/first year; $75/renewal	$100K
Secure Server	Server	VeriSign validates the entity applying for the certificate using background checks and investigative services.	$290/first year; $75/renewal	$100K

[a] See Chapter 21 for a description of this type of certificate.

VeriSign certificates come with liability protection in the form of VeriSign's "NetSure Protection." Backed by Lloyd's of London, NetSure is not an insurance policy. Instead, it is "an extended warranty program that protects VeriSign Server ID customers against economic loss resulting from the theft, corruption, impersonation, or loss of use of a certificate." VeriSign was the first company to offer this kind of protection on its certificates. But the warranty is somewhat limited, because the NetSure program has a per-certificate limit, rather than a per-transaction limit. Presented with a Netscape Secure Site Pro certificate, a merchant might reasonably assume that the certificate has $250,000 of insurance and feel comfortable engaging in a $1000 transaction. But if that same certificate were used to commit 1000 fraudulent transactions on the same day, then each merchant might ultimately be able to recover only $250 in compensation. Although the warranty program is commendable, the problem is that, unlike liability insurance policies, an insured certificate can be used in thousands of transactions within the space of a few seconds. When a car is insured, it can only be involved in one accident at a time.

As of September 2001, no claims had been presented to VeriSign under the program.

Table 7-4. VeriSign certificates in 2001

Certificate name	Certificate type	Strength[a]	Certification practice	Cost	NetSure protection
Class 1 Digital ID	Client[b]	N/A	VeriSign assures that the user can receive email at the given address.	$14.95 per year	$1000
Secure Site	Server	40-bit	VeriSign validates the entity applying for the certificate by verifying the organization's address using Dunn & Bradstreet.	$349 per year	$100K
Secure Site Pro	Server	128-bit	VeriSign validates the entity applying for the certificate by verifying the organization's address using Dunn & Bradstreet.	$895	$250K
Commerce Site	Server	40-bit	VeriSign validates the entity applying for the certificate by verifying the organization's address using Dunn & Bradstreet. Price includes a performance audit of the web site from two cities.	$995	$100K
Commerce Site Pro	Server	128-bit	VeriSign validates the entity applying for the certificate by verifying the organization's address using Dunn & Bradstreet. Price includes a performance audit of the web site from ten cities.	$1495	$250K
OnSite for ServerIDs	Intermediate CA	40-bit or 128-bit	After validating an organization and negotiating a fee, VeriSign issues a certificate that allows the organization to issue its own certificates for SSL servers throughout its own enterprise.	Negotiated	

[a] SSL certificates can specify the maximum allowable cryptographic strength to be used by the server. This provision was originally created to assist with the enforcement of U.S. export regulations. Today, this provision is used by VeriSign to extract higher revenue from organizations that are willing to pay for stronger encryption.
[b] See Chapter 22 for a description of this type of certificate.

Shortcomings of Today's CAs

It's unfortunate, but if you look closely into the root certificates that are bundled with Internet Explorer and Netscape Navigator, you'll see that there are significant inconsistencies and quality control problems with today's CAs.

Lack of permanence for Certificate Policies field

Internet Explorer's Certificate panel allows you to automatically open the web page that is associated with the certification practices statement for each of the certificates that is registered. This field is indicated as a URL in a field called "Certificate Policies" in the X.509 v3 certificate.

Here is the Certificate Policies field from the Autoridad Certificadora de la Asociacion Nacional del Notariado Mexicano, A.C. certificate that is bundled with Internet Explorer 5.0:

```
[1]Certificate Policy:
    PolicyIdentifier=2.16.840.1.113733.1.7.1.1
    [1,1]Policy Qualifier Info:
        Policy Qualifier Id=CPS
        Qualifier:
            www.NotariadoMexicano.org.mx/RCD/dpc
```

To view the CPS referenced in this certificate, follow these steps:

1. Select the certificate in the Certificate panel.

2. Click the "View" button.

3. Click the button that says "Issuer Statement." As Figure 7-16 shows, the General panel of the Certificate window on Netscape Navigator displays general information about a certificate. In this figure, the panel is displaying information for the self-signed certificate issued by the Autoridad Certificadora del Colegio Nacional de Corredurla Publica Mexicana Certification Authority. Because this certificate comes preloaded in Internet Explorer, Microsoft's operating system affords the same level of trust to these certificates as to those issued by all the other CAs, such as VeriSign. This may or may not be a problem; see Figure 7-17.

It is very important for a CA to maintain a web page at every URL that is listed in every certificate that it has ever issued. If these URLs move, links should be left in their place. If a CA changes its CPS, then it must archive each CPS at a unique URL. These links must remain accessible for the lifetime of any signed certificate that references the CPS. This is because the legal meaning of the certificate cannot be determined without reading the certificate practices statement. Furthermore, because it is possible that the meaning of a signature might be questioned many years after the signature is created, the URLs should probably remain active for a period of at least 20 years.

Unfortunately, as Figure 7-17 shows, many of the CA certificates point to CPSs that are no longer accessible. Here, the self-signed certificate distributed with Internet Explorer 5.0 for the Autoridad Certificadora del Colegio Nacional de Correduria Publica Mexicana, A.C. is valid from June 29, 1999 until June 29, 2009. The certificate claims that the certificate practices statement for this key is located at *http://www.correduriapublica.org.mx/RCD/dpc*. Nevertheless, by April 2001 the URL for that CPS was not accessible.

Inconsistencies for "Subject" and "Issuer" fields

The CA certificates that are bundled into Netscape Navigator and Internet Explorer are supposed to be the basis for the world's e-commerce infrastructure and legally binding agreements. Complicating this goal is the fact that there is a huge variation in the ways that the certificate fields are being used by different organizations.

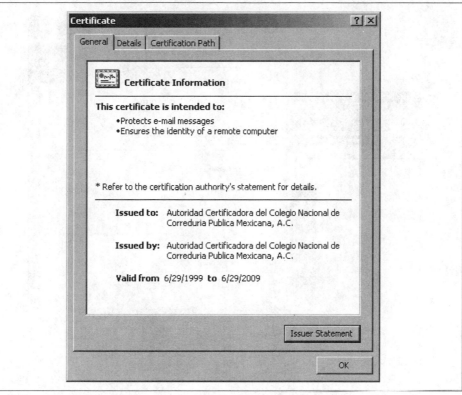

Figure 7-16. The General panel of Internet Explorer's Certificate window shows general information abut a certificate

For example, the Subject field of the ValiCert CA certificate has these qualifiers:

```
E = info@valicert.com
CN = http://www.valicert.com/
OU = ValiCert Class 1 Policy Validation Authority
O = ValiCert, Inc.
L = ValiCert Validation Network
```

In the same version of Internet Explorer, there is a VeriSign certificate for providing digitally-signed time that has a completely different set of qualifiers in the Subject field:

```
OU = NO LIABILITY ACCEPTED, (c)97 VeriSign, Inc.
OU = VeriSign Time Stamping Service Root
OU = VeriSign, Inc.
O = VeriSign Trust Network
```

There's a certificate for PTT Post in the Netherlands with an even stranger Subject field:

```
0.9.2342.19200300.100.1.3 = ca@ptt-post.nl
CN = PTT Post Root CA
OU = KeyMail
O = PTT Post
C = NL
```

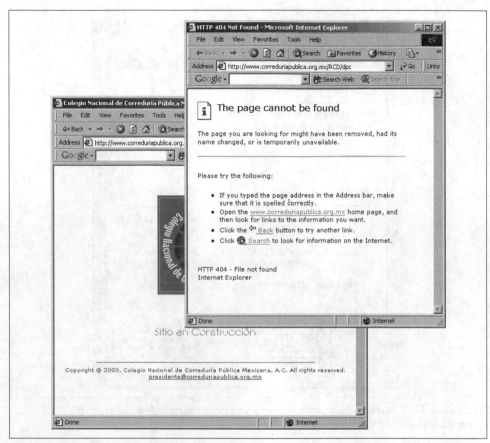

Figure 7-17. All CAs are not created equal. The home page of the web server for the Colegio Nacional de Correduria Publica Mexicana, A.C. reveals that the site is "en construcción"—and has been, apparently, for more than a year. The URL for the CA's certification practies statement does not exist. Yet this CA's key is fully trusted by Internet Explorer.

One of the better examples of Subject qualifiers can be found in the VeriSign Class 4 certificate that is distributed with Internet Explorer:

```
OU = VeriSign Trust Network
OU = (c) 1998 VeriSign, Inc. - For authorized use only
OU = Class 4 Public Primary Certification Authority - G2
O = VeriSign, Inc.
C = US
```

At the other end of the spectrum is SecureNet in Australia, which distributes four certificates with Internet Explorer. The company's "CA Class A" certificate is extraordinarily simple. It is used for certifying email and web server SSL connections. The certificate is valid June 30, 1999 until October 16, 2009. There is no CPS that is referenced in the certificate's fields. And the Subject field has only two values:

```
O = SecureNet CA Class B
C = au
```

Consistency in the use of the Distinguished Name and other fields is vital if certificates are to be processed in a programmatic way with software. Without this consistency, certificates would need to be visually inspected by individuals who are trained to understand all of the different styles and formats that legitimate names can have, so that valid certificates can be distinguished from rogue ones.

Unrealistic expiration dates

Early versions of the Netscape Navigator web browser were distributed with CA certificates that had expiration dates between December 25, 1999 and December 31, 1999. These products were in use far longer than anybody anticipated. When the end of 1999 rolled around, many of the products with these old CA certificates inside them simply stopped working. Although it should have been possible to simply download new certificates, users were advised to upgrade their entire applications because of other security problems with these early products. Many users were not happy that the software they had been depending on suddenly stopped working.

As a result of this experience, many CAs have decided to err in the other direction. They have started distributing CA certificates with unrealistically long expiration times. All of the certificates distributed with Internet Explorer 5.0 are 1024-bit RSA certificates, yet more than half of these certificates have expiration dates after January 1, 2019! As Figure 7-18 shows, VeriSign distributes eight certificates with Internet Explorer 5.5 that have expiration dates in the year 2028! Many cryptographers believe that 1024-bit RSA will not be a secure encryption system at that point in the future.

Open Policy Issues

When the first edition of this book was published in 1996, many people believed that a working public key infrastructure was a prerequisite for commerce on the World Wide Web. We disagreed. At that time, there was already substantial commerce occurring on the Internet based on old-style, easily forged credit cards, rather than high-tech digital signatures. We argued that the additional security offered by digital signatures might not be necessary if there was money to be made.

Today, the need for a widespread PKI is even more compelling, yet it seems more remote than ever. There are growing incidents of fraud on the Internet, and there is an increasing need to use digital signatures to do business. Yet despite the passage of digital signature legislation in the United States that makes a digital signature as legally binding as a written signature, widespread PKI seems further away today than it was in 1996.

It is not clear that the current vision of a public key infrastructure can even be built. Today's vision calls for a system with multiple CAs and with thousands or millions of different users, each obtaining, invalidating, and discarding certificates and public

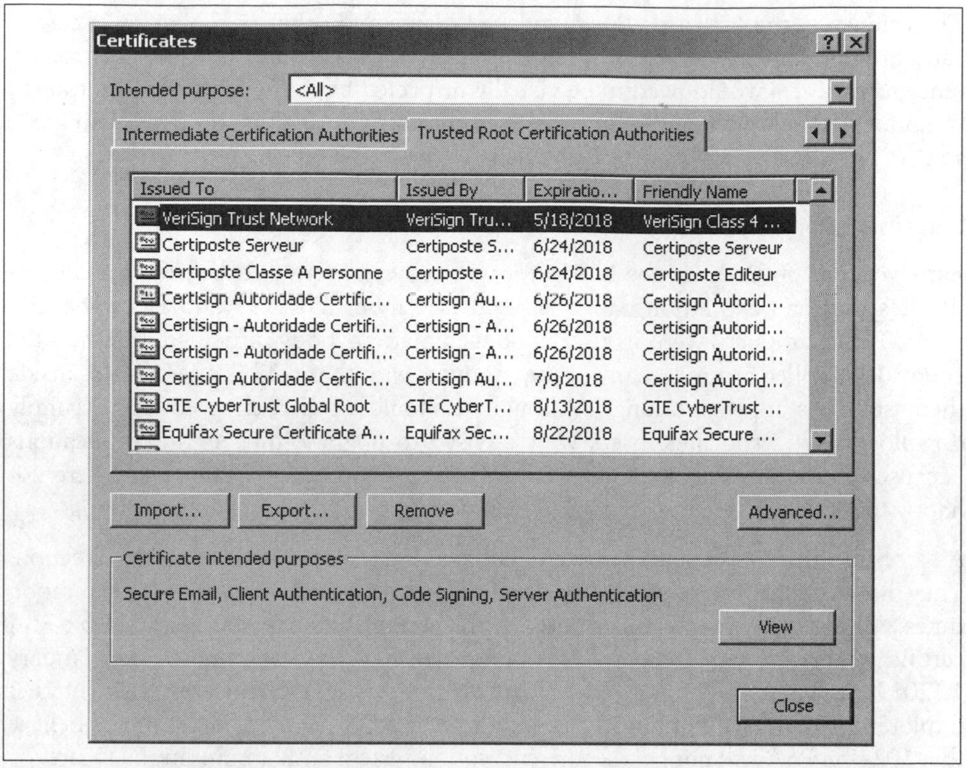

Figure 7-18. VeriSign distributes many keys with Internet Explorer 5.5 that have unrealistically late expiration dates

keys as needed. For the past 30 years, this type of technology has really not been tested outside the lab except in very controlled environments.[*]

In the following sections, we'll look at a few of the problems that must be faced in building a true PKI.

Private Keys Are Not People

Digital signatures facilitate proofs of identity, but they are not proofs of identity by themselves. All they prove is that a person (or a program) signing the digital signature has access to a particular private key that happens to match a particular public key that happens to be signed by a particular CA. Unless the private key is randomly generated and stored in such a way that it can only be used by one individual, the entire process may be suspect.

---

[*] Although smart cards have been used widely in Europe and are beginning to be used in the United States, these cards contain anonymous certificates that are not bound to individual identities and do not need to be invalidated if the cards are lost.

Unfortunately, both key generation and storage depend on the security of the end user's computer. But the majority of the computers used to run Netscape Navigator or Internet Explorer are unsecure. Many of these computers run software that is downloaded from the Internet without knowledge of its source. Some of these computers are infected by viruses. Some of the programs downloaded have Trojan horses pre-installed. And the most common operating system and browser are terribly buggy, with hundreds of security patches issued over the past few years, so it is possible that any arbitrary system in use on the network has been compromised in the recent past by parties unknown.

The companies issuing digital certificates don't have a solution to this problem yet. The closest that VeriSign comes to addressing the issue is a phrase in its certification practices statement that says:

> [E]ach certificate applicant shall securely generate his, her, or its own private key, using a trustworthy system, and take necessary precautions to prevent its compromise, loss, disclosure, modification, or unauthorized use.

But this is system engineering by license agreement! It simply doesn't solve the underlying computer security problems inherent in today's computer systems. Computers aren't trustworthy, because they can't prevent the intentional modification of programs by other programs or intruders. A computer virus or other rogue program could search its victim's computer for a copy of Netscape Navigator and modify the random number generator so that it always returned one of a million possible values. Public keys would still *appear* uncrackable, but anybody who knew about the virus would be able to forge your digital signature in no time.

Today's PCs are no better at storing private keys once they have been generated. Even though both Netscape Navigator and Internet Explorer can store keys encrypted, they have to be decrypted to be used. All an attacker has to do is write a program that manages to get itself run on the user's computer,* wait for the key to be decrypted, and then sends the key out over the network.

VeriSign knows this is a problem. "We do not, and cannot, control or monitor the end users' computer systems," says VeriSign's president Stratton Sclavos. "In the absence of implementing high-end PC cards for all subscribers, or controlling or participating in key generation, the storage of end user keys is fully within the control of end users."

Unfortunately, this means that users, and not VeriSign, are ultimately responsible for the fraudulent uses of keys, which leaves one wondering about the ultimate worth of VeriSign's per-key liability policies.

The advent of new technology may solve this problem. The widespread use of smart cards and smart card readers, for example, may make it much more difficult to steal somebody's private key. But it won't be impossible to do so.

---

* For example, by using Netscape's plug-in or Microsoft's ActiveX technology.

Distinguished Names Are Not People

Protecting private keys is not enough to establish the trustworthiness of the public key infrastructure. Merely possessing a private key and an X.509 v3 certificate for the matching public key signed by a CA doesn't prove that you are the person whose name appears in the Distinguished Name field of the certificate. All it proves is that somebody managed to get the CA to sign the corresponding public key.

Ideally, a distinguished name means what a CA says it means. Ideally, a CA has established a regimen of practices and assurances, and that CA is consistent in the application of its own policies. But how do you determine if the name in the Distinguished Name field is *really* correct? How do you evaluate the trustworthiness of a CA? Should private companies be CAs, or should that task be reserved for nations? Would a CA ever break its rules and issue fraudulent digital identification documents? After all, governments, including the United States, have been known to issue fraudulent passports when their interests have demanded that they do so.

How do you compare one CA with another CA? Some CAs voluntarily subscribe to audit methodologies such as SAS 70 or Web Trust for CAs; others do not. The American Bar Association Information Security Committee has published a book, *PKI Assessment Guidelines*, but few users have the skill or the access to be able to access the CAs that they might employ. Each CA promises that it will follow its own certification rules when it signs its digital signature. How do you know that a CA's rules will assure that a distinguished name on the certificate really belongs to the person they think it does?

If a CA offers several different products, then how do you tell them apart? A CA might offer several different signature products—some with rules like "We sign whatever key we see,"* and others with more involved certification regimens. How can you recognize which is which in an automated way? Once you've taken the time to understand the CA's rules, how do you know that the CA has really followed them? The case of VeriSign issuing keys with Microsoft's name on them is an example of the fact that accidents can happen.

In theory, many of these questions can be resolved through the creation of standards, audits, and formal systems of accreditation. Legislation can also be used to create standards. But in practice, efforts to date are not encouraging.

There Are Too Many Robert Smiths

For now, let's ignore the inherent difficulties in running a certification authority—ignore the difficulty of guarding keys and fighting fraud, and let's say that CAs are upstanding and honest corporate citizens and that they never make mistakes.

---

* This is currently the case for VeriSign's Class 1 digital IDs.

There are still some inherent problems with certificates themselves. If you get a certificate from a CA with the distinguished name "Simson L. Garfinkel", then there's an excellent chance that certificate belongs to him. That's because there is only one Simson L. Garfinkel in the United States and probably only one in the world as well.*

At least, we think that there is only one Simson L. Garfinkel. We've certainly never met another one. And Simson has searched the nation's credit data banks and checked with Internet search services, and so far it seems there is only one Simson L. Garfinkel in evidence. So it's probably Simson's certificate you've got there.

But what do you do with a certificate that says "Robert Smith" on it? How do you tell which Robert Smith it belongs to? The answer is that a certificate must contain more information than simply a person's name: it must contain enough information to uniquely and legally identify an individual. Unfortunately, you (somebody trying to use Robert Smith's certificate) might not know this additional information—so there are still too many Robert Smiths for you.

For large communities, identifying a person by name alone is of little value—there are simply too many chances for a name collision.

Today's Digital Certificates Don't Tell Enough

Another problem with the digital certificates currently being distributed on the Internet is that they don't have enough information in them to be truly useful. Sites that distribute pornography might want to use digital IDs to see if their customers are over 21, but they can't because, unlike driver's licenses, the digital certificates being issued by companies like VeriSign, Thawte, and GTE don't specify age. Sites that would like to have "women-only space" on the Net can't, because VeriSign's digital IDs don't specify gender. They don't even have your photograph or fingerprint, which makes it almost impossible to do business with somebody over the Internet, then have them show up at your office and prove that they are the same person.

Of course, if these digital certificates did have fields for a person's age, gender, or photograph, users on the Internet would say that these IDs violated their privacy if they disclosed that information without the user's consent. And they would be right. That's the whole point of an identification card: to remove privacy and anonymity, producing identity and accountability as a result.

Clearly, there is nothing fundamentally wrong with CAs disclosing information about subscribers, as long as they do so with the subscriber's consent. However, if all certificates disclose personal information, this choice may be illusory: it may be a choice between disclosing information and not using the system.

---

* This is either a tragedy or blessing. Many things, including really knowing who someone is, are relative to the observer—but that's the point of this section.

Are There Better Alternatives to Public Key Digital Signatures?

Should a technology that requires the use of private keys be used in cases where there is a high incentive to commit fraud and a history of fraud, as well as illegal activities by the intended keyholder?

While there is wide agreement that some form of digital timestamping or digital notary service is necessary, it is not clear that this is an ideal application for public key technology. The reason is that the signed timestamp is completely under the control of the service that is signing the timestamp. If the service's private key were compromised, either accidentally or intentionally, the service could issue fraudulent timestamps with different dates.

Bogus signatures and certificates might be issued because of a bribe, by a particular clerk acting on a grudge, or for political purposes.

Other technologies for timestamping exist that do not require the use of private keys. These technologies have the advantage that there is no way to compromise the system because there is no secret to be divulged. One such system is the *digital notary* marketed by Surety Technologies, Inc. Instead of treating each signature process as a distinct operation, the Surety system builds a hash-tree based, in part, on the contents of every document that is presented for digital timestamping. The root of the tree can be published once a week in *The New York Times* so that anyone may verify any signature. Tampering with Surety signatures is extremely difficult: the only way to do it is either to find a document with the same message digest (Surety uses a combination of MD5 and SHA-1, which are described in Chapter 3), or to change the root of the tree after it has been published. For more information about Surety and its digital notary system, consult its web site at *http://www.surety.com*.

X.509 v3 Does Not Allow Selective Disclosure

When a student from Stanford University flashes her state-issued California driver's license to gain entrance to a bar on Townsen Street, she is forced to show her true name, her address, and even her Social Security number to the person who is standing guard. The student trusts that the guard will not copy down or memorize any information that is not relevant to the task at hand—verifying that she is over 21.

As we discussed in the earlier section, "Minimal disclosure certificates," Stefan Brands has developed a system of certificates that allow selective disclosure. Although cryptography is promised, because the certificates are not compatible with X.509, the system is not currently being deployed.

Today, the only workable way to allow selective disclosure of personal information using X.509 digital certificates is to use multiple certificates, each one with a different digitally signed piece of personal information. If you want to prove that you are a woman, you provide the organization with your "XX" digital certificate. If you want to prove that you're over 21, you provide an organization with your "XXX" digital certificate. These certificates wouldn't even need to have your legal name on them. The certification authority would probably keep your name on file, however, should some problem arise with the certificate's use.

The IETF's Selective Public Key Infrastructure (SPKI) project is experimenting with small digital certificates that carry a single assertion. For more information on SPKI, see *http://world.std.com/~cme/html/spki.html*.

Digital Certificates Allow for Easy Data Aggregation

Over the past two decades, universal identifiers such as the U.S. Social Security number have become tools for systematically violating people's privacy. Universal identifiers can be used to aggregate information from many different sources to create comprehensive data profiles of individuals.

Digital certificates issued from a central location have the potential to become a far better tool for aggregating information than the Social Security number ever was. That's because digital signatures overcome the biggest problem that's been seen by people using Social Security numbers: poor data. People sometimes lie about their Social Security numbers; other times, these numbers are mistyped.

Today, when two businesses attempt to match individually identified records, the process is often difficult because the numbers don't match. By design, digital certificates will simplify this process by providing for verified electronic entry of the numbers. As a result, the practice of building large data banks of personal information aggregated from multiple sources is likely to increase.

How Many CAs Does Society Need?

Would the world be a better place if there were only one CA, and everybody trusted it? How about if there were two? What about two thousand? Is it better to have many CAs or a few? If you have only one or two, then everybody sort of knows the rules, but it puts that CA in a tremendous position of power. If the world has just one CA, then that CA can deny your existence in cyberspace by simply withholding its signature from your public key.

Do we really need CAs for certifying identity in all cases? Carl Ellison doesn't think so. In his paper on generalized certificates, Ellison writes:

> When I communicate with my lover, I don't need to know what city she's in and I certainly don't need to know that she's prosecutable. We aren't signing a contract. All I need is assurance that it's her key, and for that I use my own signature on her key. No CA ever needs to know she has a key, even though this is clearly an identity certificate case.

How Do You Loan a Key?

Here's another question asked, but not answered, by Carl Ellison: How do you handle people loaning out their private keys?

Suppose Carl is sick in the hospital and he wants you to go into his office and bring back his mail. To do this, he needs to give you his private key. Should he be able to do that? Should he revoke his key after you bring it back?

Suppose he's having a problem with a piece of software. It crashes when he uses private key A, but not when he uses private key B. Should he be legally allowed to give a copy of private key A to the software developer so she can figure out what's wrong with the program? Or is he jeopardizing the integrity of the entire public key infrastructure by doing this?

Suppose a private key isn't associated with a person, but is instead associated with a role that person plays within a company. Say it's the private key that's used for signing purchase orders. Is it okay for two people to have that private key? Or should the company create two private keys, one for each person who needs to sign purchase orders?

Why Do These Questions Matter?

People who are talking today about using a public key infrastructure seem to want a system that grants mathematical certainty to the establishment of identity. They want to be able to sign digital contracts and pass cryptographic tokens and know for sure that the person at the other end of the wire is who that person says he is. And they want to be able to seek legal recourse in the event that they are cheated.

The people who are actually setting up these systems seem to be a little wiser. They don't want a system that is perfect, simply one that is better than today's paper-based identification systems.

Unfortunately, it's not clear whether public key technology even gives that kind of assurance about identity. It's an unproven matter of faith among computer security specialists that private keys and digital certificates can be used to establish identity. But these same specialists will pick up the phone and call one another when the digital signature signed at the bottom of an email message doesn't verify. That's because it is very, very easy for the technology to screw up.

Probably the biggest single problem with digital signatures is the fact that they are so brittle. Change one bit in a document and the digital signature at the bottom becomes invalid. Computer security specialists make this out to be an impressive feature of the technology, but the fact is that paper, for all of its problems, is a superior medium for detecting alteration. That's because paper doesn't simply reveal that a change has been made to a document: it reveals *where* the change was made as well. And while the digital technologies will detect a single period changed to a comma, the technologies will also frequently detect changes that simply don't matter (e.g., a space being changed to two spaces) which causes people to expect signatures not to verify. Meanwhile, although it is possible to create better and better copies of documents, advances in watermarking, holography, and microprinting are allowing us to create new kinds of paper that cannot be readily copied or changed without leaving a detectable trace.

Society does need the ability to create unforgeable electronic documents and records. But while illegal aliens, underage high school students, and escaped convicts may be interested in creating forged credentials, few other people are. Society will have to discover ways of working with the problems inherent in these new digital identification technologies so that they can be used in a fair and equitable manner.

Brad Biddle on Digital Signatures and E-SIGN

This section was contributed by attorney Brad Biddle. In the first edition of this book, we reprinted Mr. Biddle's, "Ten Questions on Digital Signatures." Since the time of that book's publication, many states and the federal govenrment have adopted legislation giving legal status to digital signatures. In response to that legislation, Mr. Biddle has written this "short history of digital signature and electronic signature legislation," which we include, with his permission.

Beginning in 1995 there was a flurry of legislative attention related to digital signatures. The state of Utah enacted its Digital Signature Act, which was based on work done by the Information Security Committee of the American Bar Association's Section of Science and Technology. The Utah legislation, which became a model for other legislative bodies, envisioned a public key infrastructure supported by state-licensed certification authorities.

Through 1996 and 1997, the Utah model increasingly came under fire. Critics levied a number of arguments against the Utah approach:

- Its premise was based in part on an assumption that certification authorities faced an uncertain and potentially huge liability risk, and therefore wouldn't enter the marketplace. Critics argued that this assumption was wrong, and that any "excessive" CA liability risk was due to flawed CA business models, not a flawed legal environment.

- It provided one particular technology (PKI) and business model (the authentication model championed at the time primarily by VeriSign) with legal advantages over other authentication technologies and business models; this would potentially stifle innovation.

- It enshrined a speculative vision for how authentication would work in the commercial marketplace, rather than building on and then clarifying a market-developed model.

- It didn't solve the immediate, pressing problem facing online businesses: could contracts be formed electronically (e.g., via "clickthrough" agreements or via email)?

- It contained draconian liability rules for consumers. This became known as the "Grandma loses her house" problem: under the Utah Act, if a consumer lost control of her private key, she could face unlimited liability for resulting damages—that is, Grandma could fail to secure her computer from a malicious hacker and end up losing everything she owned.

- Under this approach, government-licensed CAs would collect vast amounts of sensitive transactional data, but the privacy issues associated weren't addressed in the legislation (leaving the question to privacy-unfriendly default rules).

States began considering alternative approaches to digital and "electronic" (non-public key) signatures. Massachusetts emerged at the opposite end of the spectrum from Utah, with a spare, minimalist approach designed to remove barriers to e-commerce posed by existing law (e.g., unnecessary "writing" requirements) but otherwise letting the marketplace evolve unfettered.

Other states tried to occupy ground between the Utah and Massachusetts extremes. California, for example, enacted a law that permitted electronic signatures in transactions involving state government, if certain security criteria were met. The California Secretary of State was tasked to determine which technologies met this criteria, and enacted regulations that permitted use of public key digital signatures and "signature dynamics," a biometric technology pushed by a company called PenOp.

E-SIGN and UETA

In 1998, in response to the wide variety of state laws, the National Conference of Commissioners on Uniform State Laws (NCCUSL) commissioned the drafting of the Uniform Electronic Transactions Act (UETA). After significant debate, the drafters adopted a "technology neutral" approach—that is, the law does not endorse PKI in any way, and largely follows the Massachusetts model. NCCUSL adopted UETA in July 1999. A number of different states subsequently enacted UETA, although some enacted it with significant variances from the "official" NCCUSL version.

Also in response to chaos at the state level, in 2000 Congress enacted E-SIGN, the Electronic Signatures in Global and National Commerce Act. E-SIGN is substantively very similar to UETA, although it added some consumer protection elements not found in UETA. Importantly, E-SIGN preempted (superseded) all state laws except state laws that conform to the official text of UETA. So, Utah-style digital signature laws, which had been enacted in several U.S. states, are now dead and completely replaced by E-SIGN (or a state enactment of UETA, if applicable). In the U.S., the law that applies to all e-signatures, including PKI digital signatures, is either E-SIGN (in states that have not enacted UETA), or UETA (in states that have enacted conforming versions of UETA).

The basic rules of both E-SIGN and UETA are quite simple: if a law requires a signature, an "electronic signature" will suffice—with "electronic signature" defined very broadly to include things like a plaintext typed name in an email or an electronic click on an "I agree" button (importantly, an electronic signature must be applied by a user with the intent to be bound to a contract). Similarly, if a law requires a "writing," an "electronic record" (a digital copy that meets certain very minimal security criteria) will do. This approach solves the "signed writing" problem discussed in more detail later, but avoids the pitfalls associated with the Utah model.

The debate that has occurred in the U.S. has been echoed at the international level. The Utah approach initially found favor in many countries. More recently, however, it appears that the tide may have turned. After much debate, the European Union enacted an "Electronic Signature Directive" that requires E.U. member states to enact legislation that is substantively similar to the E-SIGN/UETA approach (although the directive also contains some special rules applicable to certification authorities). Some Asian countries have enacted Utah-style laws, but because this has proven challenging for global businesses that want to engage in e-contracting in those regions, these countries have recently begun considering alternatives. Latin America, the Middle East, and Africa have largely been silent on the issue of electronic signatures.

Electronic contracting—it's more than just "signatures"!

Because the issues associated with digital and electronic signatures have received so much attention from the legal community, it is easy to miss the fact that signatures are only a small—and often irrelevant—element of electronic contracting.

It may be helpful to first make one point perfectly clear: under U.S. law (and under the law of most countries worldwide, although we won't attempt a detailed international analysis here), it is absolutely possible to form a contract electronically. E-SIGN and UETA have helped cement this conclusion, but really this wasn't a hard question even before these enactments.

Electronic contracting is, fundamentally, contracting. Contract law fundamentals apply. Any contract, electronic or not, requires (a) an "offer," (b) "acceptance," and (c) "consideration"—some promised exchange of value. A contract, electronic or not, will not be enforced if a successful defense can be raised: for example, if an element of the contract is "unconscionable" (violates public policy), if one of the contracting parties was too young to create a contract, and so on.

Two recent cases where courts declined to enforce electronic contracts provide interesting demonstrations of these principles. In one case, a judge refused to enforce a license agreement that was presented as a link on a page where users could download Netscape's SmartDownload software. Users were not forced—or even asked—to read the terms prior to downloading the software, nor was any sort of "I agree" button presented to users. The judge, focusing on what he called "the timeless issue of assent," found that there was no contract, not because of the electronic nature of the circumstances, but because there simply was no "acceptance" of the license terms by users.

In another case, a California judge refused to enforce a "forum selection" clause in AOL's electronic user agreement, because doing so would deprive a California litigant of consumer protection rules available under California law that would not be available under Virginia law. To the court, the question wasn't whether the contract was valid due to its electronic nature, but rather whether the forum selection clause violated public policy.

For the record, many U.S. courts have enforced electronic contracts. All this being said, there are two areas where electronic contracting raises some unique issues: (1) "signed writing" requirements, and (2) proof—that is, proving contract formation, proving what the substantive terms of a contract are, and proving party identity.

"Signed writing" requirements

"Signed writing" requirements have caused a great deal of confusion in connection with electronic contracting—probably unnecessarily.

Most contracts require neither a "signature" nor a "writing" to be valid. There are a small number of exceptions to this general rule, usually based on a policy of requiring more proof in connection with contracts where there is a higher degree of fraud risk or of high-stakes misunderstanding. Some examples of contracts that require a "signed writing" are contracts for:

- Sales of goods priced over $500
- Transfers of land
- Obligations that cannot be performed in less than one year
- Assignments (but not licenses) of some intellectual property

Courts have tended to construe the signed writing requirement very broadly, allowing, for example, fax headers or preprinted letterhead to serve as a "signature." It is likely that the courts would have treated email headers or plaintext email signatures in a similar manner. E-SIGN and UETA have made this question moot, however: as described earlier, under E-SIGN and UETA "signature" and "writing" requirements are very easily met electronically.

The bottom line is that despite the conventional wisdom to the contrary, when doing electronic contracting under U.S. law, meeting legal "signature" or "writing" requirements is not a significant issue, particularly in light of E-SIGN and UETA. (One caveat: E-SIGN has some special rules about "written notice" requirements in connection with certain legally-required consumer disclosures, applicable, for example, to the insurance and banking industries.)

Proof

"Proof" issues associated with electronic contracting present some challenging questions. Imagine the following scenario:

> Alice sends Bob a plaintext email that says "Bob, would you like to buy my car for $5000? Your friend, Alice." Bob replies with a plaintext email: "Yes. Regards, Bob."

Alice and Bob have formed a contract. There is an offer (Alice's email), acceptance (Bob's email), and consideration (the promised exchange of car and money). This is a sale of goods valued over $500, so a signed writing is required; per E-SIGN and UETA. Alice's plaintext "Alice" and Bob's plaintext "Bob"—or even their email headers—will meet the signature requirement, and the email will serve as a writing. Let's assume that there are no applicable defenses (both of the parties were capable of contracting, etc.). The contract law analysis is easy: there is a valid, enforceable contract.

But what if Bob claimed that he never sent the message at all? Once Bob denies that he sent the message, Alice will have the burden of proving to a court that, in fact, it was Bob who contracted with her and what the substance of their agreement was. In this scenario, such a burden would be difficult, but not necessarily impossible, to meet. Alice could, for example, subpoena server logs and determine that the message in fact came from Bob's computer; she could get testimony from, say, Bob's coworkers that he was sitting at his desk at the time that the message was sent. As a practical matter, under this scenario Alice would probably not be inclined to go to such lengths to enforce the agreement.

If Alice thought the risk of being unable to enforce the contract was too high, she could demand a more robust form of authentication from Bob. For example, she could require that Bob sign his email with a digital signature created with a key pair certified by a commercial CA. Note that use of a digital signature would not change the contract law analysis: digital signature or not, Alice and Bob have a contract. But use of a digital signature may make Alice's job of proving the contract easier, and make Bob's denial less credible.

Anyone engaging in electronic contracting will need to make a careful risk/benefit determination around questions of proof. A party to an electronic contract may have to go before a judge and show (a) that there was, in fact, a contract formed—that is, there was an offer, an acceptance, and consideration; (b) what the substance of the contract was; and (c) who the contracting parties are. Some methods of electronic contracting, such as the use of CA-authenticated digital signatures, may make proving these points relatively easy. In some cases, however, the cost and hassle of employing robust authentication techniques simply won't be worthwhile. For example, plenty of online businesses rely on "clickthrough" contracts where users self-report their identity. These businesses can still make good proof arguments: by keeping careful records, they can show how they formed contracts with users and show the substance of the contracts; they will have some evidence of user identity. But these businesses presumably have made a decision to forgo the proof benefits accorded by more robust authentication techniques after weighing these benefits, the associated costs, and the risks and consequences associated with potential unenforceability of their electronic contracts.

The bottom line is that it is easy to form a contract electronically, and electronic contracts may be formed in a variety of ways. But it may be difficult to prove an electronic contract in the event of a dispute. It is important to take this fact into account when engaging in electronic contracting, and to scale authentication techniques in accordance with the risk of unenforceability and the consequences if the contract were to be unenforceable.

## PART II

Privacy and Security for Users

This part of the book looks at the concerns of people using the Web to access information—that is, anybody who runs a web browser.

Chapter 8, *The Web's War on Your Privacy*, discusses the technical means by which personal information can be compromised on the Web.

Chapter 9, *Privacy-Protecting Techniques*, explores techniques that you can follow to increase your privacy while using the Web.

Chapter 10, *Privacy-Protecting Technologies*, continues the discussion of privacy self-help, by exploring programs and services that can further enhance your privacy.

Chapter 11, *Backups and Antitheft*, shows you how to protect against data loss and theft.

Chapter 12, *Mobile Code I: Plug-Ins, ActiveX, and Visual Basic*, explores how programs that travel over the Web can threaten your computer system and your personal information. This chapter focuses on the most dangerous programs that can be downloaded with email or through web pages.

Chapter 13, *Mobile Code II: Java, JavaScript, Flash, and Shockwave*, continues the discussion of mobile programs that can threaten computer users. This chapter focuses on the "safer" technologies that, it turns out, still have security implications.

In this chapter:
- Understanding Privacy
- User-Provided Information
- Log Files
- Understanding Cookies
- Web Bugs

CHAPTER 8

The Web's War on Your Privacy

You watch the Web, and the Web watches you. With a few notable exceptions, every time you look at a page on the World Wide Web, somewhere there is a computer that makes note of this fact. Visit a web site designed for parents of small children, then visit another site that is devoted to consumer electronics, and somewhere a computer slowly builds a profile of your interests. Take a few minutes to "register" for an account with your email address, and you'll soon start receiving a stream of emails in your inbox hawking "special offers."

As the Web has created unprecedented opportunities for consumers, it has also created heretofore unimaginable possibilities for marketers, sales organizations, hucksters, tricksters, and outright criminals. A marketing company that puts a billboard up by a highway is content knowing how many cars per day drive by its sign. That same company putting a banner advertisement up on a popular web site would like to know far more information about the people seeing its message—where they live, whether they get their Internet access from a business or through a university, what other web sites the person has visited, and sometimes, even their email addresses. It can be exceedingly difficult to determine the effectiveness of billboards and magazine advertisements. Web advertisements, by contrast, can be metered, examined, and analyzed. All of this power comes at a price to individual privacy, because detailed statistics require more detailed data collection.

The underlying technology of the Internet and the Web was designed to transfer information, not protect the privacy of people who use that information. There are now a whole host of web technologies that make it possible for web sites and third-party services to collect information on web users.

This chapter introduces the broad issue of privacy on the Web and the growing privacy threats. In Chapter 9 we'll describe some straightforward approaches that you can use to protect your privacy. Then in Chapter 10 we'll take a look at some additional software that you can run on your computer to further protect your privacy while enjoying the benefits of the Internet and the Web.

Understanding Privacy

As with most big concepts, people have different definitions for the word *privacy*. The Merriam-Webster dictionary dates the word privacy back to the 15th century and defines it as "the quality or state of being apart from company or observation" and "freedom from unauthorized intrusion."*

The Tort of Privacy

In a famous 1890 article in the *Harvard Law Review*,† Samuel Warren and Louis Brandeis argued that there should be a right to privacy, and that right should "protect those persons with whose affairs the community has no legitimate concern, from being dragged into an undesirable and undesired publicity" and "protect all persons, whatsoever; their position or station, from having matters which they may properly prefer to keep private, made public against their will."

Interestingly, Warren and Brandeis wrote that "truth of the matter published does not afford a defense." They held that a person's privacy is violated by a portrayal of that person's private life whether the portrayal is accurate or inaccurate. Finally, they wrote that: "The absence of 'malice' in the publisher does not afford a defense. Personal ill-will is not an ingredient of the offense, any more than in an ordinary case of trespass to person or to property." Over the past 110 years, the privacy violations described in the Warren/Brandeis paper have been reduced to four torts in American law:

Privacy intrusion
> For example, intruding into a person's private sphere.

Disclosure of private facts
> For example, the publication of private information about an individual for which the public has no compelling interest to have this information known.

Portrayal of information in false light
> For example, publishing lurid details of a person's private life that aren't actually true, or information that is strictly true but easily misinterpreted. This tort is similar to defamation, but it is not the same: works that do not defame can nevertheless portray a subject in false light. The false light tort is most common in works that fictionalize real people.

Appropriation
> For example, using a person's name or likeness for a commercial purpose without that person's permission.

---

* *http://members.eb.com/cgi-bin/dictionary?va=privacy*

† Samuel Warren and Louis Brandeis, "The Right of Privacy," *Harvard Law Review* 4 (1890), 193. It's at *http://www.lawrence.edu/fac/boardmaw/Privacy_brand_warr2.html*. The right to privacy is not without limit. Warren and Brandeis made clear exceptions for the distribution and publication of court records. They also wrote that the right to privacy ceases once facts about an individual are published by that person or with his consent.

The *Harvard Law Review* article was the basis for much legislation and litigation in the following years. But despite their vision, Warren and Brandeis didn't create a framework that extended to the computer age, where personal information for millions is now routinely collected, tabulated, indexed, used, and sold. Although similar to the tort of appropriation, the intrusions we face in the computer age have a distinctly different flavor.

In 1967, Columbia University professor Alan Westin created a new definition for privacy that seemed more appropriate to the computer age. Westin defined the term *informational privacy* as "the claim of individuals, groups, or institutions to determine for themselves when, how, and to what extent information about them is communicated to others."*

All of these types of privacy come into play on the Web today. Stalkers, spammers, and nosy family members routinely intrude into our mailboxes. Gossips and buggy programs alike distribute private facts beyond their intended audience. Some web sites will appropriate the names of their subscribers and use this information in marketing. Distributing information about a demographic, and then saying that a particular user is a member of that demographic may constitute false light. But the largest number of violations of personal privacy on the Web today fall into Westin's characterization of informational privacy—that is, many individuals have lost the ability to control how and to what extent information about them is communicated to marketing firms, government agencies, and nosy neighbors in the world's electronic village.

Personal, Private, and Personally Identifiable Information

The first thing that's apparent when you start to pick apart Westin's definition of information privacy is that there are many different kinds of "information" the definition can be applied to. The word "information" in Westin's definition could apply to a person's name, and it would certainly apply to a piece of paper that had a person's name, his Social Security number, and the list of web sites that the person had visited over the past month. But what if that piece of paper showed only the list of web sites and the first three digits of the person's Social Security number—would that piece of paper be considered personal information?

To deal with questions like this, academics have subdivided the term "information" into many different subcategories. A few of them are:

Personal information
> Information about a person. Your name, your date of birth, the school you attended, and the names of your parents are all personal information.

Private information
> Personal information that is not generally known. Some kinds of private information are protected by law. For example, in the United States education

---

* Westin, Alan. *Privacy and Freedom*, Atheneum Press, Boston, 1967.

records are considered private and cannot be released without the permission of the individual (or the individual's parent or guardian, in the case of a minor). Bank records are protected by law, although banks are allowed to sell the names and addresses of their customers for marketing purposes.

Most people have a large amount of information that they consider private but that is not protected under the law. For example, you might consider the name of the first person that you kissed to be private. Other information should be treated as private, even though it is widely available. For example, most people regard their Social Security numbers as private, even though they are available in many databases. This ambiguity arises in part because *private* is not a synonym for *secret* or *confidential*.

Whether or not a particular piece of information is private frequently depends on the context. For example, if your name is in a telephone directory, that information is not private. But if that directory is on the computer of an individual who is engaged in illegal activity, you might wish to keep the fact that your name is in his address book extremely private.

Personally identifiable information

Information from which a person's name or identity can be derived. Some personally identifiable information is obvious, such as a person's name or an account number. Some personal information, such as your shoe size, is not generally identifiable.

Anonymized information

The reverse of personally identifiable information. This is personal or private information that has been modified in some way so that identities of the individuals from whom the information was collected can no longer be discerned.

Aggregate information

Statistical information combined from many individuals to form a single record. One of the best examples of aggregate information is the statistics on census tracts that are released by the U.S. Census Bureau. According to the Bureau, "Census tracts usually have between 2,500 and 8,000 persons and, when first delineated, are designed to be homogeneous with respect to population characteristics, economic status, and living conditions. Census tracts do not cross county boundaries. The spatial size of census tracts varies widely depending on the density of settlement. Census tract boundaries are delineated with the intention of being maintained over a long time so that statistical comparisons can be made from census to census."[*]

In practice, these categories of personal information are far more fluid than it may seem at first. Often, aggregate information and anonymized information can be combined to identify and reveal particular characteristics of an individual. This process is

---

[*] *http://www.census.gov/geo/www/cen_tract.html*

called *triangulation*. For example, if you have a class with ten students, and you know that nine of the students are men and one of the students is pregnant, you know with some certainty which student in the class is pregnant. If you have a list of the names of the individuals in the class, you probably know the name of the woman who is pregnant, because most names are strongly identified with a particular gender.

Many Internet users are surprised how easy it is to determine identity from the seemingly anonymous information they provide to web sites. For example, some web sites require a person register with a name and address, while other web sites require only a Zip code and birthday. Yet for many people in the United States, there are only ten or so people who live in the same Zip code and share the same birthday. Consider:

> Number of individuals in the U.S. = approximately 284,000,000 (as of April 2001)
> Number of birthdays in the U.S. = 365.25
> Number of individuals in the U.S. with each birthday = 284,000,000 / 365.25
>   = approximately 777,549[*]
> Number of Zip codes in the U.S. = approximately 100,000
> Number of individuals in each zip code with the same birthday
>   = 777,549 / 100,000 = approximately 8 people

Thus, a web site that asks a visitor for a birthday, a Zip code, and an age is actually asking its visitors for personally identifiable information, even though it appears to be only asking for aggregate information. If that web site is hooked into the credit files of a company such as Equifax or Experian, the web site might, in turn, have access to information that the visitor considers personal and private, but that is, in fact, quite public and frequently shared among business partners.

User-Provided Information

Some of the most detailed, revealing, and damaging sources of personal information on the Internet are Internet users themselves. If you want to buy a t-shirt or a compact disc on the Web, you need to give that web merchant a name and address where the merchandise will be shipped. As the vast majority of the purchases made on the Web are made with credit cards, you'll probably also need to give a credit card number. And because there is a lot of fraud on the Internet, you probably won't get your merchandise without a lot of hassle unless you provide the name and the billing address for the credit card used to pay for the order.

Most web merchants go beyond the minimal information needed to satisfy online orders. For example, a merchant might ask for your email address and a few phone numbers, to allow the merchant to contact you in the event of a mishap. Many merchants set up *accounts* for their customers so that this information doesn't need to be entered time and again. These accounts require usernames and passwords. These

---

[*] This example assumes an even distribution of birthdays throughout the year and people throughout Zip codes, which is a simplification, but not a very big one.

accounts can be used to track a person's purchases over time. Some merchants go further, and ask their customers to provide the city of their birth, or their mother's maiden names, so that if a consumer forgets his password, another question can be asked (see Figures 8-1 and 8-2).

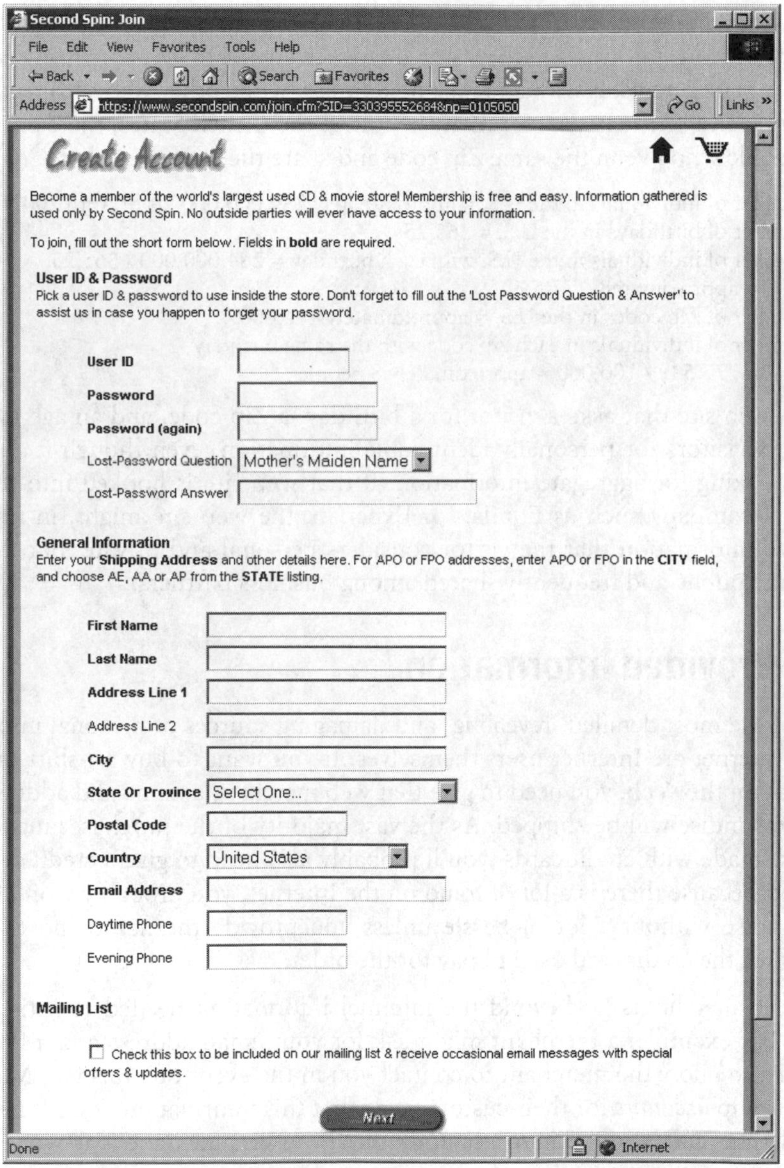

Figure 8-1. By far, the greatest kind of personal information on the Web today is the information provided by consumers when they register at web sites.

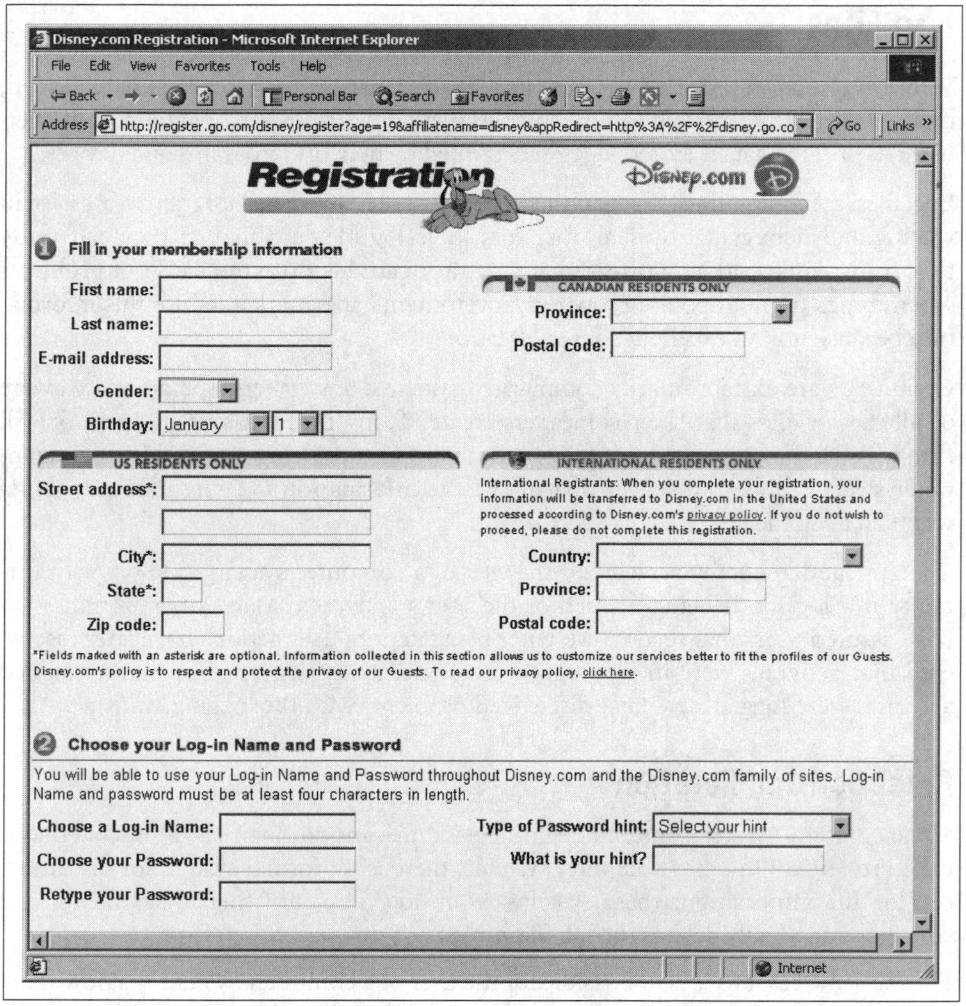

Figure 8-2. Disney's registration page for adults asks for name, email address, gender, and birthday, in addition to mailing address. Many people are surprised how identifying even simple demographic information can be. For example, in many cases a person can be uniquely identified by day of birth (without the year) and Zip code.

At the present time in the United States, there are few restrictions on what web sites can do with personal information once it is collected. While some merchants have posted so-called *privacy policies*, which may outline some of their rules and restrictions on personal information, posting of privacy policies is voluntary. (For more information on privacy policies, see Chapter 24.) Many other countries have more restrictive rules about what can and cannot be done with personal information, although these countries have, for the most part, been slow to extend their legal regimes to the world of the Internet.

Log Files

While information provided by users may be the most detailed information collected, by far the most pervasive information collection comes from the operation of the network itself. This data is stored in log files created by network programs and devices.

Log files are ubiquitous. Programmers add log files to their programs to assist in writing and debugging. System operators leave log files enabled so they can verify that software is working correctly, and so they can diagnose the cause of problems when things do not operate properly. Governments and marketers use this information because it is an excellent source of data.

Computers are extraordinarily complicated systems; few system operators are aware of all the log files that their computers create. Many times, a system operator will firmly assert that a particular piece of information is not being retained by their computer system, only to discover that in fact the information *is* being retained, somewhere in a log file.

There is fundamentally no way for the user of a computer system to know with certainty if a log file is being created of the user's activities. Many organizations that have assured users that records were not being kept of user actions have later discovered that activities were in fact logged. Likewise, many organizations that assumed activities were logged have later discovered problems with the logging system.

Retention and Rotation

Some computer systems automatically age and discard old log files, a process that is called *rotation*. On other computer systems, there is no formal system for discarding old log file information: these systems retain log files until their disks fill up and somebody manually deletes the log file entries.

For the same reasons it is impossible for the user of a computer system to know if her actions are being logged, it is also impossible to know how long log files are actually retained. Here is an example of a few log files from a moderately busy web server:

```
% ls -l access*
-rw-r----- 1 root      www     312714072 Apr 19 13:42 access_log
-rw-r----- 1 root      www     401536508 Apr 15 00:00 access_log.1
-rw-r----- 1 root      www      32408676 Apr  8 00:00 access_log.2.gz
-rw-r----- 1 root      www      31062796 Apr  1 00:00 access_log.3.gz
%
```

This computer appears to retain log files for one month. The file *access_log* contains a record for each web page downloaded since the beginning of April 15. The file *access_log.1* contains a list of all web pages downloaded from the start of April 8 to the end of April 14. The files *access_log.2.gz* and *access_log.3.gz* are for the two preceding weeks. These files are smaller than the first two files because they were compressed.

Despite appearances, the organization that operates this web server actually maintains log files for a significantly longer period of time. This is because the organization backs up the directory that contains the log files to magnetic tape. These tapes are stored off-site in a safe deposit box. Although there are no specific records of which log files are backed up and which are not, in an emergency (or under a court order), it might be possible for this organization to retrieve log file records that are a year old or even older.

Web Logs

Practically every time a web browser downloads a page on the Web, a record of this event is routinely recorded in the log files of the remote web server. If the web page is assembled using a database server, the database server may create log files of its own. Finally, web logs are also routinely kept on network firewalls, web proxies, and web caches. As a result, simple web browsing can result in a plethora of records being created on machines in locations that are controlled by multiple organizations.

Log files are under the control of the person or organization that controls the web server. Log files are frequently subpoenaed and used in lawsuits or criminal investigations. Log files can be used by employers to determine what employees are doing when they are at work. Log files can be used by a nosy system administrator to spy on others. But in the vast majority of cases, the information in log files is never looked at by anybody. Because most log files are never consulted, and because the contents of most log files are never revealed, most users of the Internet do not know the full extent of their activities are recorded.

What's in a web log?

The following information is either stored directly in most web log files or can be readily inferred from other information in web logs:

- The name and IP address of the computer that downloaded the web page.
- The time of the request.
- The URL that was requested.
- The time it took to download the file (this is an indication of the user's Internet connection).
- If HTTP authentication was used, the log file contains the username of the person who downloaded the file.
- Any errors that occurred.
- The previous web page that was downloaded by the web browser (called the *refer link*).
- The kind of web browser that was used.

This information can be combined with other log files—such as login/logout information from Internet service providers, or logs from mail servers—to discover the actual identity of the person who was doing the downloading. Normally this kind of cross-correlation requires the assistance of another organization, but that is not always the case.

For example, many ISPs dynamically assign IP addresses to computers each time they call up. A web server may know that a user accessed a page from the host *free-dial-77.freeport.mwci.net*; someone would then have to go to *mwci.net*'s log files to find out who the actual user was. On the other hand, sometimes computers are assigned permanent IP addresses; for several years, Simson used a computer named *pc-slg.vineyard.net* and Spaf would routinely check his email while on the road dialed in from *shire-ppp.cs.purdue.edu*.

A typical web server log is shown in Example 8-1.

Example 8-1. A sample web server log

```
free-dial-77.freeport.mwci.net - - [09/Mar/1997:00:04:11 -0500] "GET /awa/issue2/
    Woodstock.gif HTTP/1.0" 200 26385
"http://www.vineyard.net/awa/issue2/Wood.html" "Mozilla/2.0 (compatible; MSIE 3.01;
    Windows 95)" ""
free-dial-77.freeport.mwci.net - - [09/Mar/1997:00:04:27 -0500] "GET /awa/issue2/
    WoodstockWoodcut.gif HTTP/1.0" 200 54467
"http://www.vineyard.net/awa/issue2/Wood.html" "Mozilla/2.0 (compatible; MSIE 3.01;
    Windows 95)" ""
crawl4.atext.com - - [09/Mar/1997:00:04:30 -0500] "GET /org/mvcc/ HTTP/1.0" 200 10768 "-"
    "ArchitextSpider" ""
www-as6.proxy.aol.com - - [09/Mar/1997:00:04:34 -0500] "GET /cgi-bin/imagemap/mvol/cat2.
    map?31,39 HTTP/1.0" 302 - "http://www.mvol.com/" "Mozilla/2.0 (Compatible; AOL-IWENG
    3.0; Win16)" ""
www-as6.proxy.aol.com - - [09/Mar/1997:00:04:40 -0500] "GET /mvol/photo.html HTTP/1.0" 200
    6801
"http://www.mvol.com/" "Mozilla/2.0 (Compatible; AOL-IWENG 3.0; Win16)" ""
www-as6.proxy.aol.com - - [09/Mar/1997:00:04:48 -0500] "GET /mvol/photo2.gif HTTP/1.0" 200
    12748
"http://www.mvol.com/" "Mozilla/2.0 (Compatible; AOL-IWENG 3.0; Win16)" ""
free-dial-77.freeport.mwci.net - - [09/Mar/1997:00:05:07 -0500] "GET /awa/issue2/Wood.html
    HTTP/1.0" 200 37016
"http://www.altavista.digital.com/cgi-bin/query?pg=q&what=web&fmt=.&q=woodstock" "Mozilla/
    2.0 (compatible; MSIE 3.01; Windows 95)" ""
free-dial-77.freeport.mwci.net - - [09/Mar/1997:00:05:07 -0500] "GET /awa/issue2/
    Sprocket1.gif HTTP/1.0" 200 4648
"http://www.vineyard.net/awa/issue2/Wood.html" "Mozilla/2.0 (compatible; MSIE 3.01;
    Windows 95)" ""
free-dial-77.freeport.mwci.net - - [09/Mar/1997:00:05:08 -0500] "GET /awa/issue2/
    Sprocket2.gif HTTP/1.0" 200 5506
"http://www.vineyard.net/awa/issue2/Wood.html" "Mozilla/2.0 (compatible; MSIE 3.01;
    Windows 95)" ""
www-as6.proxy.aol.com - - [09/Mar/1997:00:05:09 -0500] "GET /mvol/peter/index.html HTTP/1.
    0" 200 891 "http://www.vineyard.net/mvol/photo.html" "Mozilla/2.0 (Compatible; AOL-
    IWENG 3.0; Win16)" ""
```

The refer link field

The refer link field is another source of privacy violations. It works like this: whenever you, as a web surfer, look for a new page, one of the pieces of information that is sent along is the URL of the page that you are currently looking at. (The HTTP specification says that sending this information should be an option left up to the user to decide, but we have never seen a web browser where sending the refer information is optional.)

One of the main uses that companies have found for the refer link is to gauge the effectiveness of advertisements they purchase on other web sites. Another use is charting how customers move through a site. The refer link field can also reveal personal information—namely, the URL of the page that a user was looking at before he or she clicked into your site.

Refer links frequently reveal unintended information. When you click the link of a web search engine, for instance, the refer link that is sent to the remote web server encodes the search that you were performing. Consider this entry from the log file of the *www.simson.net* web server:

```
pc109240.stofanet.dk - - [21/Mar/2001:16:27:25 -0500] "GET /clips/95.SJMN.
AltKeyboards.txt HTTP/1.1" 200 9988 "http://www.google.com/
search?hl=da&safe=off&q=%22Building+a+better+keyboard+%22&lr=" "Mozilla/4.0
(compatible; MSIE 5.5; Windows 98; Win 9x 4.90)"
```

This log file entry indicates that the user of the computer *pc109240.stofanet.dk* was searching on the web search engine Google for the phrase "Building a better keyboard" on March 21, 2001. Sometimes, the results of a refer field can give away far more information than the web user might wish.

As is the case with Google, the largest number of privacy violations involving refer fields occur with HTML forms that use the GET method (as opposed to the POST method). This is because the GET method encodes the contents of each field in the URL itself. The big advantage of using the GET method is that it allows people to bookmark filled-in-forms, such as searches. For example, opening the URL *http:// www.google.com/search?q=simson* will automatically perform a Google search for the name "Simson." But if the previous web page posted contained a credit card number or other personal information that was provided to a GET form, information leakage from one web site to another web site is inevitable.*

Obscuring web logs

Proxy servers can render web logs less useful. When a user accesses a web server through a proxy, the web server records the proxy's address, rather than the address

---

* The risk of transferring credit card numbers to third-party sites was reduced somewhat in 1997, when Netscape and Microsoft modified their browsers so that the refer link would no longer be passed from an SSL-enabled site to a non-SSL site.

of the user's machine. For example, most users who access the Internet through America Online do so through the company's proxy server.

Web proxies do not necessarily give web users anonymity: the user's identity can still be learned by referring to the proxy's logs. Proxies simply make the task more difficult.

RADIUS Logs

RADIUS (Remote Authentication Dial-In User Service) is widely used on the Internet by ISPs and large organizations to validate usernames/passwords for dialup users and to provide for proper accounting. Originally designed by Livingston, RADIUS is now widely implemented by Cisco, Nortel, Lucent, Redback, and most other vendors. Although RADIUS provides functionality that is similar to Cisco's proprietary TACACS and TACACS+ protocols, RADIUS became the dominant protocol because clients and servers were distributed in source-code form, because it was extensible, and because it provided for encryption of passwords sent over the wire (unlike TACACS).

RADIUS log files contain an astonishing amount of information, including usernames, times, IP addresses, and even CALLER-ID information. Here are two example RADIUS records that were created with a Livingston Portmaster 3:

```
Thu Apr 19 13:54:09 2001
        Acct-Session-Id = "0E027BE9"
        User-Name = "beth"
        NAS-IP-Address = 199.232.91.8
        NAS-Port = 43
        NAS-Port-Type = Async
        Acct-Status-Type = Start
        Acct-Authentic = RADIUS
        Connect-Info = "50666 LAPM/V42BIS"
        Called-Station-Id = "5086292329"
        Calling-Station-Id = "5086962222"
        Service-Type = Framed
        Framed-Protocol = PPP
        Framed-IP-Address = 199.232.91.50
        Acct-Delay-Time = 0

Thu Apr 19 13:54:52 2001
        Acct-Session-Id = "0E027BD6"
        User-Name = "simson"
        NAS-IP-Address = 199.232.91.8
        NAS-Port = 34
        NAS-Port-Type = Async
        Acct-Status-Type = Stop
        Acct-Session-Time = 2350
        Acct-Authentic = RADIUS
        Connect-Info = "14400 LAPM/V42BIS"
        Acct-Input-Octets = 18321
        Acct-Output-Octets = 108087
        Called-Station-Id = "6173442329"
```

```
Calling-Station-Id = "6178761111"
Acct-Terminate-Cause = Idle-Timeout
Vendor-Specific = vLivingston-020e49646c652054696d656f7574
Service-Type = Framed
Framed-Protocol = PPP
Framed-IP-Address = 199.232.91.38
Acct-Delay-Time = 0
```

The CALLER-ID information in RADIUS logs was instrumental in determining the identity of the author of the Melissa computer worm.

Mail Logs

Every time an email message is sent, received, or transported through a mail server, there is a good chance that some program somewhere is making note of that fact in a mail log file. Mail logs usually contain the from: and to: email addresses, the time that the message was sent, and the message-id. Subject: lines and content are usually not logged, although they certainly could be.

Here is an example of a mail log:

```
Apr 20 11:43:42 <mail.info> r2 sendmail[50422]: f3KGhg150422: from=<owner-
    august96@groucho.ctel.net>, size=2468, class=-60, nrcpts=1,
msgid=<l03130300b706172b0593@[192.168.1.55]>, proto=ESMTP, daemon=Daemon0,
    relay=groucho.ctel.net [209.222.72.2]
Apr 20 11:43:42 <mail.info> r2 sendmail[50423]: f3KGhg150422: to=<beth@walden.
    cambridge.ma.us>, delay=00:00:00, xdelay=00:00:00, mailer=local, pri=139359,
    relay=local, dsn=2.0.0, stat=Sent
Apr 20 11:43:54 <mail.info> r2 sendmail[50426]: f3KGhs150426: from=<elbows-
    request@mc.lcs.mit.edu>, size=1138, class=0, nrcpts=1, msgid=<Pine.GSO.4.21.
0104201114300.2335-100000@server.genericdomain.net>, proto=ESMTP, daemon=Daemon0,
    relay=mc.lcs.mit.edu [18.24.10.26]
Apr 20 11:43:58 <mail.info> r2 sendmail[50427]: f3KGhs150426: to=<beth@walden.
    cambridge.ma.us>, delay=00:00:04, xdelay=00:00:04, mailer=local, pri=30456,
    relay=local, dsn=2.0.0, stat=Sent
Apr 20 11:44:13 <mail.info> r2 sendmail[50432]: f3KGiC150432: from=<owner-
    august96@groucho.ctel.net>, size=4303, class=-60, nrcpts=1, msgid=<200104201642.
    NAA18970@kiln.isn.net>, proto=ESMTP, daemon=Daemon0, relay=groucho.ctel.net [209.
    222.72.2]
Apr 20 11:44:13 <mail.info> r2 sendmail[50433]: f3KGiC150432: to=<beth@walden.
    cambridge.ma.us>, delay=00:00:01, xdelay=00:00:00, mailer=local, pri=141458,
    relay=local, dsn=2.0.0, stat=Sent
```

Mail logs are useful for determining people who exchange email and users on mailing lists. (In the example above, the user "beth" is evidently on the mailing list *august96@groucho.ctel.net*.)

DNS Logs

The bind DNS nameserver produced by the Internet Software Consortium can be configured to log every DNS query that it receives. The bind log file contains the name of the host from which each query was made, the IP address from which the query was made, and the query itself. An example of such a log file is shown here:

```
Apr 20 13:18:17 <local2.info> r2 named[50916]: XX /206.196.128.1/queen.simson.net/A/IN
Apr 20 13:18:20 <local2.info> r2 named[50916]: XX+/64.7.15.234/2.72.222.209.in-addr.
   arpa/PTR/IN
Apr 20 13:18:20 <local2.info> r2 named[50916]: XX+/64.7.15.234/234.15.7.64.in-addr.
arpa/PTR/IN
Apr 20 13:18:20 <local2.info> r2 named[50916]: XX+/64.7.15.234/groucho.ctel.net/A/IN
Apr 20 13:18:20 <local2.info> r2 named[50916]: XX+/64.7.15.234/groucho.ctel.net/ANY/IN
Apr 20 13:18:20 <local2.info> r2 named[50916]: XX+/64.7.15.234/walden.cambridge.ma.us/
   ANY/IN
Apr 20 13:18:21 <local2.info> r2 named[50916]: XX+/64.7.15.234/ctel.net/ANY/IN
Apr 20 13:18:21 <local2.info> r2 named[50916]: XX+/64.7.15.234/earthlink.net/ANY/IN
Apr 20 13:18:36 <local2.info> r2 named[50916]: XX /209.20.178.33/queen.simson.net/A/IN
Apr 20 13:18:36 <local2.info> r2 named[50916]: XX /200.186.94.1/www.dbz.ex.com/A/IN
```

Logging DNS queries can be useful for system maintenance and forensic work. It is also a great way to silently monitor the activities of customers or other individuals. Because a computer must resolve a DNS address before a URL that contains a host-name can be resolved, monitoring a user's DNS usage provides an ISP with a detailed report of each web site that the user accesses. Monitoring DNS queries can also give pointers to attackers, as even attackers who launch their attacks from third-party machines frequently perform DNS queries from their home machines first.

Understanding Cookies

A *cookie* is a block of ASCII text that a web server can pass into a user's instance of Netscape Navigator (and many other web browsers). Once received, the web browser sends the cookie every time a new document is requested from the web server. Cookies are transmitted by the underlying HTTP protocol, which means that they can be sent with HTML files, images (GIFs, JPEGs, and PNGs), sounds, or any other data type.

Netscape introduced "cookies" with Navigator Version 2.0. The original purpose of cookies was to make it possible for a web server to track a client through multiple HTTP requests. This sort of tracking is needed for complex web-based applications that need to maintain state between web pages.

Typical applications for cookies include the following:

- A catalog site might use a cookie to implement an electronic "shopping cart."
- A news site might use cookies so that subscribers see local news and weather.
- A subscription-only site might use cookies to store subscription information, so that a username/password combination does not need to be presented each time the user visits the site.

The preliminary cookie specification can be found at *http://www.netscape.com/ newsref/std/cookie_spec.html*. RFC 2965, dated October 2000, outlines a proposed codification of the cookie specification, but as of August 2001 this standard had still not been adopted by the IETF.

The Cookie Protocol

A web server sends a cookie to your browser by transmitting a Set-Cookie message in the header of an HTTP transaction, before the HTML document itself is actually sent. Cookies can also be set using JavaScript.

Here is a sample Set-Cookie header:

```
Set-Cookie: comics=broomhilda+foxtrot+garfield; path=/comics; domain=.comics.net;
[secure]
```

The Set-Cookie header contains a series of name=value pairs that are encoded according to the HTTP specification for encoding URLs. The previous example contains a single name=value field that sets the name comics to be the value "broomhilda foxtrot garfield."* There are some special values:

expires=time

Specifies the time when the cookie will expire. If no expiration time is provided, then the cookie is not written to the computer's hard disk, and it lasts only as long as the current session.

domain=

Specifies which computers will be sent the cookie. Normally, cookies will only be sent back to the computer that first sent the cookie to the user. In this example, the cookie will be sent to any host in the *comics.net* domain. If the domain is left blank, the domain is assumed to be the same as the domain for the web server that provided the cookie.

path=

Controls which of the references will trigger the sending of the cookie. If path is not specified, the cookie will be sent for all HTTP transmissions to the web site. If *path=/directory*, then the cookie will only be sent when the pages underneath */directory* are referenced. In this example, the cookies will be sent to any URL that is underneath the */comics/* directory.

secure

If the word secure is provided as part of the Set-Cookie header, then the cookie can only be transmitted via SSL. (Don't depend on this facility to keep the contents of your cookies private, as they are still stored unencrypted on the hard disk.)

---

* Remember, the HTTP URL encoding mechanism converts spaces to plus signs (+).

Once a browser has a cookie, that cookie is transmitted by the browser with every successive request to the remote web site. For example, if the previous cookie was loaded into a browser and the browser attempted to fetch the URL *http://www.comics.net/index.html*, the following HTTP headers could be sent to the remote site:

```
GET /index.html HTTP/1.0
Cookie: comics=broomhilda+foxtrot+garfield
```

An example

Here is an actual HTTP header sent by the site *www.hotbot.com* at 8:10 a.m. on April 21, 2001:

```
HTTP/1.1 200 OK
Server: Microsoft-IIS/5.0
Date: Sat, 21 Apr 2001 12:05:56 GMT
Set-Cookie: lubid=01000008C73351C5086C3AE177A40000351200000000; expires=Mon, 18-Jan-
2038 08:00:00 GMT; domain=.lycos.com; path=/
Set-Cookie: p_uniqid=aD3QMJX/K93Z; expires=Fri, 21-Dec-2012 08:00:00 GMT; domain=;
path=/
Connection: Keep-Alive
Content-Length: 22592
Content-Type: text/html
Set-Cookie: remotehost=secondary=chi%2Emegapath&top=net; expires=Mon, 21-May-2001 07:
00:00 GMT; path=/
Set-Cookie: HB%5FSESSION=BT=lowend&BA=false&VE=&PL=Unknown&MI=u&BR=
Unknown&MA=0&BC=1; path=/
Cache-control: private
```

The HotBot site sends four cookies, shown in Table 8-1.

Table 8-1. Cookies sent by www.hotbot.com at 8:10 a.m. EST on April 21, 2001

Cookie #	Content	Domain	Expires	Path
1	lubid=01000008C73351C5086C3AE177A40000351200000000	.lycos.com	18-Jan-2038 08:00:00 GMT	/
2	p_uniqid=aD3QMJX/K93Z		21-Dec-2012 08:00:00 GMT	/
3	remotehost=secondary=chi%2Emegapath&top=net		21-May-2001 07:00:00	/
4	HB%5FSESSION=BT=lowend&BA=false&VE=&PL=Unknown&MI=u&BR=Unknown&MA=0&BC=1			/

Cookie #1 assigns a user tracking identifier to the web browser. Many web sites use such cookies to determine the number of unique visitors that they recover every month. Notice that although this cookie was downloaded from the site *www.hotbot.com*, its domain is set to *.lycos.com*. This cookie is what is called a *third-party cookie*. HotBot is a business unit of Lycos; this cookie allows Lycos to identify which Lycos users are also HotBot users. This type of cross-site cookie is permitted by some browsers but prohibited by others.

Cookie #2 is another user tracking cookie, but this one is solely for the HotBot site.

The purposes of Cookie #3 and Cookie #4 cannot immediately be determined from inspection. We contacted Lycos, Hotbot's owner, to find out the purpose of these cookies. We were pointed at FAQs about how to disable cookies, but after several months of trying, we were unable to discover their actual purpose.

Cookie Uses

Broadly speaking, there are two ways that a web site can implement cookies:

- The web site can use the cookie to contain the user's actual data.
- The cookie can simply contain a number of codes that key into a database that resides at the web provider.

Examples of these two approaches are shown in Table 8-2.

Table 8-2. Schematic views of cookies that contain customer data versus those that merely point to a database

Purpose of cookie	Possible contents for an implementation that keeps data on the user's computer	Possible contents for an implementation that keeps data on the provider's computer
Provide customized weather reports and local news for a web site.	ZIP=20568	UID=aaeff33413
Implement a shopping cart	PROD1=32 QUAN1=1 PROD2=34 QUAN2=1 PROD3=842 QUAN3=2	USER=342234
Provide sign-on to a web site	USER=gene PASS=gandalf	USER=gene

Cookies were originally envisioned as a place on the client where web servers could store user preferences and personal information. This way, no personal information would need to be stored on the client. But as the cookies from the HotBot web site show, today one of the most popular uses of cookies is to give a permanent identification number to each user so that the number of "unique visitors" to a web site can be measured. These numbers can be very important when a company is attempting to sell advertising space on its web site.

Many advertisers themselves use cookies to build comprehensive profiles of web users. These cookies are served with banner advertisements. Each time a web user views a banner advertisement, the database server at the advertising company notes the content of the web site that the customer was viewing. This information is then combined to create a web *profile*. A typical profile might say how much a person is interested in sports or in consumer electronics, or how much he follows current events and the news. Web advertisers say that these profiles are "anonymous" because they do not contain names, addresses, or other kinds of personally-identifiable information. However, it is possible to unmask this anonymous data if the profiles are combined with other information, such as IP addresses or registration information provided at web sites.

Cookies and Privacy

Cookies can be used to improve privacy or to weaken it. Unfortunately, it is very difficult to tell when a cookie is being used for one purpose and when it is used for another.

Cookies can significantly weaken personal privacy when they are used to tie together a whole set of seemingly unconnected facts and pieces of information from different web sites to create an electronic fingerprint of a person's online activities. Cookies like this usually contain a single identifier. This identifier is a key into a database. The cookie for Doubleclick in Example 8-2 is typical of such a cookie.

Cookies can also be used to improve privacy by eliminating the consolidation of personal information. Instead of storing the information in a central location, these cookies store a person's preferences in the cookie itself. For example, a web site might download a cookie into a person's web browser that records whether the person prefers to see web pages with a red background or with a blue background. A web site that offers news, sports, and financial information could use a cookie to store the user's preferred front page.

The cookie from the DigiCrime web site is this sort of privacy-protecting cookie:

```
www.digicrime.com    FALSE   FALSE   942189160   DigiCrime virus=1
```

This cookie tracks the number of times that the user has visited the DigiCrime web site without necessitating the creation of a large user tracking database on the DigiCrime site itself. Each time you visit the DigiCrime web site, the virus cookie is incremented. The web site has different behavior when the "virus" counter reaches different ordinals.

Keeping information about a user in a cookie, rather than in a database on the web server, means that it is not necessary to track sessions: the server can become essentially stateless. And there is no need to worry about expiring the database entries for people who clicked into the web site six months ago and haven't been heard from since. Perhaps most importantly, there is no database of personal information that needs to be protected.

Unfortunately, using cookies this way takes a lot of work and thoughtful programming. It's much simpler to hurl a cookie with a unique ID at somebody's browser and then index that number to a relational database on the server. For one thing, this makes it simpler to update the information contained in the database because there is no requirement to be able to read and decode the format of old cookies.

Cookies allow advertisers to have a great deal of control over the advertisements that each user sees, regardless of the actual web site that a person is visiting. For example, using cookies, an advertiser can assure that each person will only see a particular Internet advertisement once (unless the advertiser pays for repeat exposure, of course). Cookies can be used to display a sequence of advertisements to a single user, even if they are jumping around among different pages on different web sites. Cookies allow users to be targeted by area of interest. Advertisers can further tailor advertisements to take into account the query terms that web surfers use.

All cookies are open to examination. Unfortunately, it can be very difficult to determine what cookies are used for by merely examining them, as the cookies in Table 8-1 demonstrate.

Cookie Jars

Cookies are kept in the web browser's memory. If a cookie is persistent (that is, it has an expiration date), the cookie is also saved by the web browser on the computer's hard drive.

Netscape Navigator and Internet Explorer store cookies in different way. Navigator stores cookies in a single file called *cookies.txt*, which can be found in the user's preference directory. (On Unix systems, Navigator stores cookies in the *~/.netscape/cookies* file.)

A sample Netscape cookies file is shown in Example 8-2.

Example 8-2. A sample Netscape cookies file

```
# Netscape HTTP Cookie File
# http://www.netscape.com/newsref/std/cookie_spec.html
# This is a generated file!  Do not edit.
.techweb.com     TRUE  /wire/news FALSE 942169160 TechWeb 204.31.228.79.852255600 path=/
.hotwired.com    TRUE  /    FALSE 946684799 p_uniqid  yQ63oN3ALxO1a73pNR
.talk.com        TRUE  /    FALSE 946684799 p_uniqid  y46RXMoBwFwD16ZFTA
.packet.com      TRUE  /    FALSE 946684799 p_uniqid  y86ijMoA9MhsGhluvB
.boston.com      TRUE  /    FALSE 946684799 INTERSE   stl-mo8-10.ix.netcom.
com20748850376179639
.netscape.com    TRUE  /    FALSE 1609372800 MOZILLA  MOZ-ID=DFJAKGLKKJRPMNX[-]MOZ_VERS=1.
    2[-]MOZ_FLAG=2[-]MOZ_TYPE=5[-]MOZ_CK=AJpzO85+60jN_Ao1[-]
.netscape.com    TRUE  /    FALSE 1609372800 NS_IBD   IBD_
    SUBSCRIPTIONS=INC005|INC010|INC017|INC018|INC020|INC021|INC022|INC034|INC046
www.xmission.com   FALSE  /  FALSE  946511999  RoxenUserID  0x7398
ad.doubleclick.net FALSE  /  FALSE  942191940  IAF   22348bb
.focalink.com      TRUE   /  FALSE  946641600  SB_ID  adsO1.28425853273216764786
gtplacer.globaltrack.com  FALSE  /  FALSE 942105660 gtzopyid  85317245
.netscape.com      TRUE   /  FALSE  1585744496  REG_DATA  C_DATE_REG=13:06:51.304128 01/
    17/97[-]C_ATP=1[-]C_NUM=0[-]
www.digicrime.com  FALSE  FALSE  942189160  DigiCrime  virus=1
```

Internet Explorer saves each cookie in an individual file. The files are stored in the directory referenced by the Registry name *Cookies*, in the key *\HKEY_CURRENT_USER\ Software\Microsoft\Windows\CurrentVersion\Explorer\User Shell Folders*. This directory is *C:\Windows\Cookies* on Windows 95/98/ME systems configured for a single user, or in the directory *C:\Windows\Profiles\username\Cookies* on Windows 95/98/ME systems configured for multiple users (see Figure 8-3). A sample Internet Explorer *Cookies* file is shown in Example 8-3.

RFC 2109 on Cookies

RFC 2109 describes the HTTP state management system (i.e., cookies). According to the RFC, any web browser that implements cookies should provide users with at least the following controls:

- The ability to completely disable the sending and saving of cookies.
- An (preferably visual) indication as to whether cookies are in use.
- A means of specifying a set of domains for which cookies should or should not be saved.

Name	Internet Address	Type	Size	Expires	Last Modified	Last Accessed	Last Checked
simsong@switchboard	Cookie:simsong@switchboard.co...	Text Document	1 KB	4/28/09 9:35 AM	2/9/01 9:35 AM	2/9/01 9:35 AM	2/9/01 9:35 AM
simsong@mapsonus	Cookie:simsong@mapsonus.com/	Text Document	1 KB	4/28/09 9:35 AM	2/9/01 9:35 AM	2/9/01 9:35 AM	2/9/01 9:35 AM
gx	Cookie:simsong@trading.etrade.c...	Text Document	1 KB	2/9/02 5:48 PM	2/9/01 5:48 PM	2/9/01 5:48 PM	2/9/01 5:48 PM
simsong@www.mygeek	Cookie:simsong@www.mygeek.c...	Text Document	1 KB	2/9/03 5:50 PM	2/9/01 5:50 PM	2/9/01 5:50 PM	2/9/01 5:50 PM
simsong@amazon	Cookie:simsong@amazon.com/	Text Document	1 KB	1/1/36 4:00 AM	2/10/01 7:55 PM	2/10/01 7:55 PM	2/10/01 7:55 PM
simsong@aish	Cookie:simsong@aish.com/	Text Document	1 KB	1/18/38 2:00 AM	2/11/01 9:33 AM	2/11/01 9:33 AM	2/11/01 9:33 AM
simsong@avantgo	Cookie:simsong@avantgo.com/	Text Document	1 KB	2/20/11 12:26 PM	2/20/01 12:26 AM	2/20/01 12:26 AM	2/20/01 12:26 AM
simsong@www.bigfoot	Cookie:simsong@www.bigfoot.co...	Text Document	1 KB	2/25/11 5:01 PM	3/9/01 4:57 PM	3/9/01 4:57 PM	3/9/01 4:57 PM

Figure 8-3. Internet Explorer stores cookies in files in the Cookies directory. You can delete a cookie by clicking on the cookie with the mouse and hitting the "Delete" key.

Example 8-3. The contents of an Internet Explorer Cookies file.

```
SITESERVER
ID=94e349397f0ba875c43fac4e1497ed69
caregroup.org/
0
642859008
31887777
514252192
29395648
*
```

Cookie Security

Users can modify the contents of their cookies. For this reason, a web site should always regard a cookie's contents as potentially suspect. If the cookie is used to gain

---

access to information that might be considered private, confidential, or sensitive, then measures should be built into the cookie so that a modified cookie will not be accepted by the web application.

Consider the following two hypothetical cookies. Both of these cookies belong to a hypothetical web site that allows a consumer to view stored transactions. The cookies give the consumer access by providing the consumer's identification number to the web application server. The first cookie is not a secure cookie. The second cookie may be secure, as we will explain.

Cookie #1
    id=4531

Cookie #2
    id=34343339336

In the first cookie, the consumer's identification number is simply "4531." Presumably, these identification numbers are being assigned in a sequential order. If the consumer were to edit his or her cookie file and change the number from "4531" to another number, like "4533," it is quite probable that the consumer would then have access to another consumer's order information. Essentially, the first consumer can easily create counterfeit cookies!

A consumer visiting a web site that uses the second cookie can change his identification number as well. However, a consumer changing "34343339336" to another number is likely to be less successful than a consumer changing the number "4531." This second web site almost certainly does not assign its identification numbers sequentially; there are not 34,343,339,336 Internet users (yet)! So a consumer making a change to this second cookie is unlikely to accidentally hit upon a valid identification number belonging to another consumer.

To create the most secure cookies, some web sites use digital signatures or cryptographic MAC codes. Such techniques make it exceedingly unlikely that a consumer will be able to create a counterfeit cookie, provided that the MAC actually covers all of the information in the cookie, rather than the data in the fields after they are decoded. More information on creating cookies that are really secure can be found in Chapter 16.

Some web sites are set up so that if you have a cookie, you are given unrestricted access to your account information. Other web sites are set up so that even if you have a cookie, you must still type a password to gain access to your confidential information. In general, web sites that require a password to be typed are more secure. This is because your cookie can easily end up on somebody else's machine—for example, if you check your account information using a friend's computer. If you are a web developer, you should never make the mistake of thinking that cookies are secure.

Disabling Cookies

Both Netscape Navigator and Internet Explorer have options that will allow you to be notified when a cookie is received. Current versions of these programs allow you to accept all cookies, reject all cookies, or be prompted for each cookie whether you wish to accept it or not. Newer versions of these browsers allow you to control cookie acceptance on a site-by-site basis. Netscape 6.0 allows you to delete cookies on a case-by-case basis, as shown in Figure 8-4.

Unfortunately, neither browser will let you disable the sending of cookies that have already been accepted. To do that, you must toss your cookies.

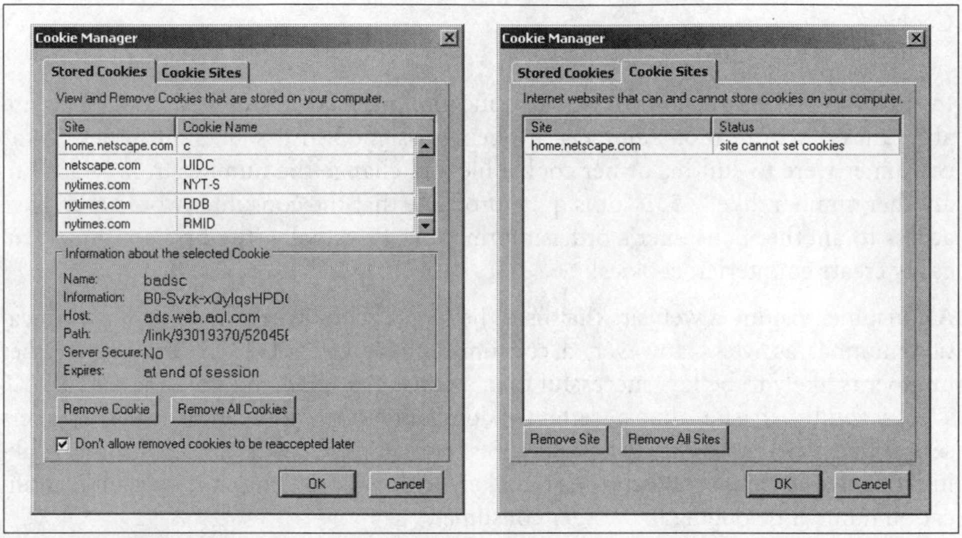

Figure 8-4. Netscape 6.0's Cookie Manager allows cookies to be controlled on a site-by-site basis

There are additional techniques that you can use to block cookies. These techniques work with all browsers, whether they have cookie control or not.

- Under Unix-based systems, users can delete the cookies file and replace it with a link to */dev/null*. On Windows systems, the file can be replaced with a zero-length file with permissions set to prevent reading and writing. On a Macintosh you can replace the file with a locked, zero-length file or folder.

- Alternatively, you can simply accept the cookies you wish and then make the cookies file read-only. This will prevent more cookies from being stored inside.

- You can disable cookies entirely by patching the binary executable for your copy of Netscape Navigator or Internet Explorer. Search for the string Set-Cookie and change it to Set-Fookie. It's unlikely that anyone will be sending you any Fookies, so that should be sufficient.

Filter programs, such as AdSubtract, can also give users control over cookies. For further information, see Chapter 10.

Web Bugs

In September 2000, the Colorado-based Privacy Foundation[*] released a report on a new technology for monitoring Internet users, which the foundation called *web bugs*. Although the use of this technology had been widely known in advertising circles, it had not previously been publicized to the larger community of Internet users.

Web bugs are small graphic images placed on web pages or in email messages to facilitate third-party tracking of users and collection of statistics. A typical web bug consists of a 1-pixel-by-1-pixel transparent GIF, making it invisible to the unassisted eye. To see a web bug, you must view the source of an HTML page or email message.

According to the foundation's Web Bug FAQ:[†]

> The word bug is being used to denote a small, eavesdropping device. It is not a euphemism for a programming error.... Rather than the term 'Web bugs,' the Internet advertising community prefers the more sanitized term 'clear GIF.' Web bugs are also known as '1-by-1 GIFs,' 'invisible GIFs,' and 'beacon GIFs.'

Web Bugs on Web Pages

Here are two web bugs that the Privacy Foundation found on the Intuit's home page for Quicken.COM:

```
<img src="http://ad.doubleclick.net/ad/pixel.quicken/NEW"
width=1 height=1 border=0>

<IMG WIDTH=1 HEIGHT=1 border=0
SRC="http://media.preferences.com/ping?ML_SD=IntuitTE_Intuit_1x1_RunOfSite_Any&db_
afcr=4B31-C2FB-10E2C&event=reghome&group=register&time=1999.10.27.20.5 6.37">
```

The first web bug causes a single 1×1 image to be fetched from the Doubleclick advertising server *ad.doubleclick.net*. This bug alerts Doubleclick to each individual that views the Quicken.COM home page. Doubleclick has built a sophisticated system for monitoring individuals who view Doubleclick's advertisements; this web bug allows Intuit to use Doubleclick's monitoring system without the need to first show a banner advertisement.

The second web bug fetches a 1×1 image from the MatchLogic *media.preferences.com* server. This bug is slightly more interesting in that it apparently sends to MatchLogic a unique user identification, similar to what might be found in a cookie. This web bug might allow Intuit and MatchLogic to knit together their two disparate user databases.

---

[*] *http://www.privacyfoundation.org/*

[†] *http://www.privacyfoundation.org/resources/webbug.asp*

Using two web bugs allows Intuit to compare Doubleclick's tracking and monitoring results with those of MatchLogic. Both, of course, can also be compared with the results that Intuit gets from analyzing its own log files.

Web bugs do not need to be 1×1 pixel graphics. Any image or other content that is pulled from a third-party web server can be used by a web site to monitor its users. Mainly, web bugs are a form of outsourced web site monitoring. They impact privacy by introducing a third party into a consumer web site relationship. Potentially, web bugs also allow movements between multiple web sites to be correlated, although the same can be done through banner advertisements or by the sharing of log files.

Web bugs can be placed on any piece of HTML. For example, the Privacy Foundation created a Yahoo user called webbug2000 and placed a web bug in the fictitious user's Yahoo Profile (see Figure 8-5).

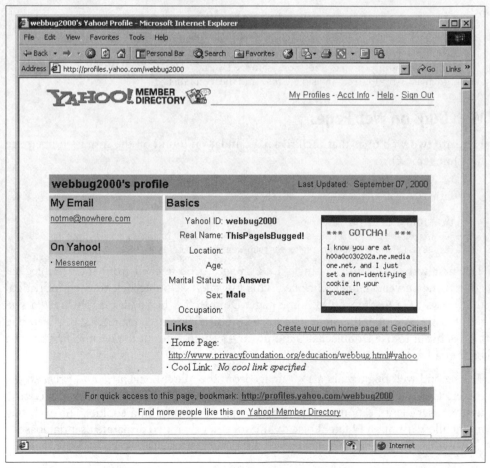

Figure 8-5. A Yahoo profile that was bugged with a web bug by the Privacy Foundation

Web Bugs in Email Messages and Word Files

Web bugs can be used in HTML email messages to determine whether a person reads an email. When the email message is viewed, the web bug is fetched from the remote server. If each web bug is given a unique identifier and causes a cookie to be downloaded, then an email-based web bug can also be used to determine if an email message is forwarded from one person to another.

Email-based web bugs are only active if the email message is read with a mail client that can display HTML messages, and even then, only if that computer is connected to the Internet.

Here's an example of two email-based web bugs the Privacy Foundation discovered:

```
<img width='1' height='1'
src="http://www.m0.net/m/logopen02.asp?vid=3&catid=370153037&email=SMITHS%40tiac.net"
alt=" ">
```

```
<IMG SRC="http://email.bn.com/cgi-bin/flosensing?x=ABYoAEhouX">
```

Web bugs can be placed in HTML Usenet messages to determine how many times a Usenet message is viewed.

Web bugs can also be placed in Microsoft Word files. This is possible because Microsoft Word allows images downloaded from web pages to be pasted directly into Word documents. Each time the Word document is opened, the image is downloaded anew. This in turn allows the web bug to track the usage and the movement of the Word document.

Uses of Web Bugs

According to the Privacy Foundation, companies use web bugs to accomplish the following tasks:

- Gather viewing and usage statistics for a particular page.
- Correlate usage statistics between multiple web sites.
- Profile users of a web site by gender, age, Zip code, and other demographics.
- Transfer personally identifiable information from the web site directly to an Internet marketing company. This transfer would be accomplished with a web bug URL that contains the personal information that the company wishes to transfer.
- Transfer search strings from a search engine to a marketing company.
- Verify the statistics reported by a banner advertising company, to gauge the effectiveness of different banner advertisements.
- Have third-party providers prepare web usage statistics for web sites that do not have the technical capability to prepare their own statistics.
- "Cookie sync," which is for synchronizing personal information in two different databases.
- See if users have enabled JavaScript, Java, ActiveX, and other technologies.
- Check if email messages are actually read and, if they are read, to see if they are forwarded.
- Detect copyright infringement.

Conclusion

In this chapter, we explored a number of techniques and technologies that have been developed for tracking users on the Internet. In the next chapter, we will examine techniques that you can use for protecting your privacy. Then in Chapter 10, we'll look at technologies you can use for fighting back.

## CHAPTER 9

Privacy-Protecting Techniques

In this chapter:
- Choosing a Good Service Provider
- Picking a Great Password
- Cleaning Up After Yourself
- Avoiding Spam and Junk Email
- Identity Theft

In the last chapter, we saw that there are many ways to collect personal information on the Internet. In this chapter, we'll look at some proven techniques to protect your privacy when you use the Internet. Most of these techniques are simple, common-sense rules that you can put into effect immediately—choosing a good service provider, using good passwords, cleaning up after yourself online, avoiding spam and junk email, and protecting yourself from identity theft. Then, in Chapter 10, we'll see how to extend these techniques using a variety of free and commercial programs and services. Finally, if you are interested in understanding the legal framework regarding personal information, see Chapter 24.

Choosing a Good Service Provider

The first and most important technique for protecting your privacy is to pick service providers who respect your privacy.

Here are some things to consider when you choose an ISP:

- Unless you take special measures to obscure the content and destinations of your Internet usage, your ISP can monitor every single web page that you visit, every email message that you send, every email message that you receive, and many other things about your Internet usage.

- If you have a dialup ISP, your ISP can also infer when you are at home, when you go on vacation, and other aspects of your schedule.

- If you check your email from work, your ISP can learn where you work.

- Many ISPs routinely monitor the actions of their subscribers for the purposes of testing equipment, learning about their user population, or collecting per-user demographics.

- Some ISPs will monitor the web sites that you visit and sell this information for the purpose of increasing their revenue. In some cases, the ISPs clearly state this policy and, in fact, use the sale of the data as a way of subsidizing the cost of Internet access. Other ISPs silently engage in this practice.

- Equipment is now on the market that allows ISPs to monitor the advertisements that are downloaded to your computer and, in some cases, replace the advertisements with different ones. This equipment is also capable of generating detailed user-level statistics.

- Some ISPs have strict policies regarding which employees have access to user data and how that data must be protected. Other ISPs have no policies at all.

- Many policies that are in use basically say "we can monitor anything that we want." However, not all ISPs that have these policies actually monitor their users.

ISPs are in a tremendous position of power with respect to their users, and there are few, if any, legal restrictions on what ISPs are allowed to do. Nevertheless, many ISPs have made a good faith attempt to protect the privacy of their users.

Within recent years most ISPs have written "privacy policies" that broadly outline the ISP's commitment (or lack thereof) to protecting their users' privacy. Unfortunately, the ISPs that lack a strong commitment can frequently obscure what they are doing by using carefully-drafted language. For example, an ISP can say that it will protect your personal information "to the full extent mandated under the law," safe in the knowledge that the law mandates no real protection. Other ISPs simply write no privacy policy at all. For further information about privacy policies, see Chapter 24.

Picking a Great Password

As we saw in Chapter 6, passwords are the simplest form of authentication. Passwords are a secret that you share with the computer. When you log in, you type your password to prove to the computer that you are who you claim to be. The computer ensures that the password you type matches the account that you have specified. If they match, you are allowed to proceed.

Using good passwords for your Internet services is a first line of defense for your privacy. If you pick a password that is easy to guess, then somebody who is targeting you will find it easier to gain access to your personal information. If you use the same password on a variety of different services, then a person who is able to discover the password for one of your services will be able to access other services.

Why Use Passwords?

Historically, most desktop personal computers did not use passwords. PCs were designed for use by a single person; in this environment, passwords were seen as an unwanted hassle.

If you are like most computer users, you probably got your first password when you got your first Internet email account: your password prevented other people from logging in to your Internet account and downloading your email. As your use of the Web grew, you were probably asked to create accounts on various web sites. For example, if you buy a book from Amazon, the Amazon web site will ask you for a password so that other users will not be able to view the books you have ordered.

Over the years, passwords have become a staple of desktop computers. Most versions of Microsoft Windows ask you to enter a username and a password before they will allow you to run a program. Windows uses the username and password in a limited fashion to control access to some personal information on your system. Likewise, the Macintosh and Unix operating systems can be programmed to use passwords as well.

Although passwords are currently one of the most important elements of computer security, users often receive only cursory instructions about selecting them.

As a user, you should be aware that by picking a bad password—or by revealing your password to an untrustworthy individual—you are potentially compromising your computer's security completely. If you are a system administrator, you should be sure that all of your users are familiar with the issues raised in this section.

Bad Passwords: Open Doors

A bad password is any password that can be guessed.

In the movie *Real Genius*, a computer recluse named Laszlo Hollyfeld breaks into a top-secret military computer over the telephone by guessing passwords. Laszlo starts by typing the password *AAAAAA*, then trying *AAAAAB*, then *AAAAAC*, and so on, until he finally finds the password that matches.

Real-life computer crackers are far more sophisticated. Instead of typing each password by hand, crackers use computer programs that automate this process. Instead of trying every combination of letters, starting with *AAAAAA* (or whatever), crackers use hit lists of common passwords such as *wizard* or *demo*. Even a modest home computer with a good password guessing program can try thousands of passwords in less than a day's time. Some hit lists used by crackers are several hundred thousand words in length.* Therefore, a password that *anybody* on the planet might use for a password is probably a password that you should avoid.

What are the passwords that you should avoid? Some examples are your name, your partner's name, or your pets' names. Other bad passwords are these names backwards

---

* In contrast, if you were to program a home computer to try all 6-letter combinations from *AAAAAA* to *ZZZZZZ*, it would have to try 308,915,776 different passwords. Guessing one password per second, that would require nearly ten years.

or followed by a single digit. Short passwords are also bad, because there are fewer of them; they are, therefore, more easily guessed. Especially bad are "magic words" from computer games, such as *xyzzy*. These magic words look secret and unguessable, but in fact they are widely known. Other bad choices for passwords include phone numbers, characters from your favorite movies or books, local landmark names, favorite drinks, or famous computer scientists (e.g., "Simson" or "Spaf"). See the sidebar later in this chapter for more bad choices. These words backwards or capitalized are also weak. Replacing the letter "l" (lowercase "L") with "1" (numeral one), or "E" with "3," adding a digit to either end, or other simple modifications of common words are also weak. Words in foreign languages are no better. Dictionaries for dozens of languages are available for download on the Internet and dozens of bulletin board systems.

In general, you need to be more careful when selecting and using passwords used for web-based services than when selecting and using passwords used to secure dialup services. This is because high-speed networks make it possible for attackers to guess literally hundreds or even thousands of passwords per second. By contrast, it is difficult to guess more than two or three dialup passwords per minute, because a new phone call usually needs to be placed for every two or three attempts.

Many web services will make a minimal attempt to prevent users from picking bad passwords. For example, some services will reject a password that contains your username. Other services will require that you pick a password that has both letters and numbers, or a password that contains a symbol such as a "$" or a "*". Unfortunately, there is no consistency among online services—some services require that you have symbols or special characters in your passwords, while other services reject passwords with these characters.

Smoking Joes

Surprisingly, experts believe that a significant percentage of all computers without password content controls contain at least one account where the username and the password are the same. Such accounts are often called "Joes." Joe accounts are easy for crackers to find and trivial to penetrate. Most computer crackers can find an entry point into almost any system simply by checking every account to see whether it is a Joe account. This is one reason why it is dangerous for a computer system or a service provider to make a list of valid usernames available to other users or outsiders.

Good Passwords: Locked Doors

Good passwords are passwords that are difficult to guess. The best passwords are difficult to guess because they:

• Have both uppercase and lowercase letters
• Have digits and/or punctuation characters as well as letters

- May include some control characters and/or spaces
- Are easy to remember, so they do not have to be written down
- Are at least seven or eight characters long
- Can be typed quickly, so somebody cannot determine what you type by watching over your shoulder

It's easy to pick a good password. Here are some suggestions:

- Take two short words and combine them with a special character or a number, like *robot4my* or *eye-con*.
- Put together an acronym that's special to you, like *Notfsw* (None Of This Fancy Stuff Works), *auPEGC* (All Unix programmers eat green cheese), or *Ttl*Hiww* (Twinkle, twinkle, little star. How I wonder what. . .).

Of course, *robot4my*, *eye-con*, *Notfsw*, *Ttl*Hiww*, and *auPEGC* are now all bad passwords because they've been printed here.

Bad Passwords

When picking passwords, avoid the following:

- Your name, spouse's name, or partner's name
- Your pet's name or your child's name
- Names of close friends or coworkers
- Names of your favorite fantasy characters
- Your boss's name
- Anybody else's name
- The name of the operating system you're using
- The hostname of your computer
- Your phone number or your license plate number
- Any part of your Social Security or employee ID number
- Anybody's birth date
- Other information easily obtained about you (e.g., address, alma mater)
- Words such as *wizard, guru, gandalf,* and so on
- Any username on the computer in any form (as is, capitalized, doubled, etc.)
- A word in the English dictionary or in a foreign dictionary
- Place names or any proper nouns
- Passwords of all the same letter
- Simple patterns of letters on the keyboard, like *qwerty*
- Any of these spelled backwards
- Any of these followed or prepended by a single digit

Although some people like to pick passwords that are significantly longer than eight characters, these passwords rarely improve security over well-chosen passwords with seven or eight characters. If a password is chosen from eight random letters and numbers, then there is virtually no chance that the password will be guessed by a brute-force attack. This is because there are 36^8 or 2,821,109,907,456 possible 8-character passwords using simply lowercase letters and numbers; even if you could guess 1000 passwords each second, it would take 89 years to try all possible combinations. But a second reason that passwords longer than eight characters frequently do not improve security is that many computer systems truncate passwords at eight characters and ignore the additional characters that are entered.

Picking a good password is only half the battle. Once you have a good password, your next job is to keep your password a secret, so that you are the only person who has control of it.

Writing Down Passwords

There is a tired story about a high school student who gets a password to his school's computer, logs in after hours, and changes his grades. How does the student get the password? By walking into the school's office, looking at an academic officer's terminal, and writing down the username and password handwritten on a sticky note.

Unfortunately, the story is true—thousands of times over.

Users are admonished: "Never write down your password." The reason is simple—if you write down your password, somebody else can find it and use it to break into your computer. A memorized password is more secure than the same password written down, simply because there is less opportunity for other people to learn it.

On the other hand, a password that *must* be written down to be remembered is quite likely a password that is not going to be guessed easily. If you write your password on something kept in your wallet, the chances of somebody who steals your wallet using the password to break into your computer account are remote indeed.*

If you must write down your password, then at least follow a few precautions:

* When you write it down, don't identify your password as being a password.
* Don't include the name of the account, network name, or phone number of the computer on the same piece of paper as your password.
* Don't attach the password to the terminal, keyboard, or any part of your computer.

---

* Unless, of course, you happen to be an important person, and your wallet is stolen or rifled as part of an elaborate plot. In their book *Cyberpunks*, authors John Markoff and Katie Hafner describe a woman named "Susan Thunder" who broke into military computers by doing just that: she would pick up officers at bars and go home with them. Later that night, while the officer was sleeping, Thunder would get up, go through the man's wallet, and look for telephone numbers, usernames, and passwords.

- Don't write your actual password. Instead, disguise it, by mixing in other characters or by scrambling the written version of the password in a way that you can remember. For example, if your password is *Iluvfred*, you might write "fredIluv" or "vfredxyIu" or perhaps "Last week, I lost Uncle Vernon's 'fried rice & eggplant delight' recipe—remember to call him after 3 p.m."—to throw off a potential wallet-snatcher.[*]

- Consider using an encrypting password-keeping program on a handheld computer (see Table 9-1).

Here are some other things to avoid:

- Don't record a password online (in a file, in a database, or in an email message), unless the password is encrypted.

- Likewise, *never send a password to another user via electronic mail*. Many attackers scan email files for the word "password," hoping to find an email message where one person is telling another person a password for another computer.

Strategies for Managing Multiple Usernames and Passwords

In today's world we are forced to memorize literally hundreds of public and private identifiers and authenticators. There are telephone numbers, birthdates, bank account numbers, usernames, passwords, and more.

The simplest way to manage this sea of information is to simplify it. For example, you might use the same username for your office computer, your home computer, and all of the web sites where you need to register. And to simplify things further, you might use the same password at all of these locations as well.

Unfortunately, there are many problems that arise when you use the same usernames and passwords at multiple locations:

- If a password is compromised, an attacker can use the compromised password to gain access to multiple systems.

- The management of a computer system usually has the ability to access the usernames and passwords of its users.[†] If you use the same username and password on multiple computers, the management of one of these computers will inevitably be able to access passwords that are stored unencrypted. One computer

---

[*] We hope that last one required some thought. The 3 p.m. means to start with the third word and take the first letter of every word. With some thought, you can come up with something equally obscure that you will remember.

[†] Many computer systems store passwords unencrypted in a database, making it easy for management to access the usernames and passwords of their users. But even on computer systems where passwords are stored encrypted, it is possible for management to access the passwords of users: management simply modifies the computer's software so that passwords are saved when they are typed.

system operator might use your username and password to gain access to another system.

- Many computer systems place incompatible restrictions on the passwords that you can pick. For example, some web sites require that you enter a password that contains a special symbol, such as a "%" or a "&". Other web sites specifically do not allow passwords to be typed with these characters.

- If you decide to change the password for some of the systems, you now need to remember which systems use the old password and which use the new password.

As a result, even if you try to use the same password on every computer, you'll soon find that you have multiple passwords that you need to remember. Here are some strategies for dealing with all of that data.

Password classes

One strategy for managing passwords is to divide them into different classes—for example, your standard password, your standard banking password, your standard email passwords, your online gaming password, and then a "low security" password that you use for everything else.

Password bases

Another strategy for managing passwords is to have a base password that can be modified for each different service. For example, your base password might be *kxyzzy* followed by the first letter of the name of the computer you're using. For the web site Amazon.com, your password might be *kxyzzya*, while on Hotmail your password might be *kxyzzyh*. However, you shouldn't be quite this obvious in your modifications as the pattern will be apparent to an observer.

Password rotation

Many people rotate their passwords. That is, all of the accounts that they create in the fall of one year use a particular password, then when winter comes, they switch to a second password, and when spring comes, they switch to a third password. This kind of password rotation is marginally more secure than using the same password on every computer. However, password rotation requires that you remember which sites have the new password and which have the old one. Eventually, password rotation is just as difficult as having a different password for each site.

Password keepers

Finally, you can use a radically different password for each of your accounts, but track each of your passwords in a special-purpose, password-keeping program. These programs remember all of your accounts, each account's password, the date that the password was created, and any other pertinent information. This information is then encrypted using a single password.

Password keeper functionality is built into the most recent versions of Netscape Navigator and Microsoft Internet Explorer. They are available in third-party "wallet" programs, such as Gator, that interoperate with these browers. Password keepers are also available as stand-alone programs for computers running the Windows, Macintosh, and PalmOS operating systems (see Table 9-1).

Table 9-1. Recommended password keeper programs

Platform	Program	Location
PalmOS	GNU keyring	*http://gnukeyring.sourceforge.net/*
PalmOS	Strip	*http://www.zetetic.net*
Windows	Password Keeper 2000	*http://www.gregorybraun.com/PassKeep.html*
Windows	Password Safe	*http://www.counterpane.com/passsafe.html*
Macintosh 8.x, 9.x	Mac OS Keychain	Built in; see the Keychain Access control panel

It is also possible to build your own password safe with PGP. Simply encrypt a text file of accounts and passwords with your PGP key, and decrypt it when you want to read or edit the list. Remember to use the "wipe" option when deleting the decrypted file, and don't leave the file decrypted on disk any longer than strictly necessary.

Sharing Passwords

There are many good reasons to restrict who has access to your password. Because your password is the primary lock for your personal information, if you share your password, you are implicitly giving other people access to your data. In many circumstances, you are also giving that person the ability to impersonate you—either by sending out email with your name, or by purchasing things on your behalf.

Of course, we all share our house and office keys from time to time. Likewise, we all need to share the occasional password. The strategies in this section are designed to help you make intelligent choices to minimize the potential damage of this risky behavior.

Be careful when you share your password with others!

Giving somebody your password is very similar to giving that person a key to your house or office: you need to trust that person well, because that person could enter your house when you are not there and take whatever he wants.

When you share a password with somebody, make sure the person understands the trust that you are placing in him. Don't treat your password lightly—otherwise, he might follow your example and do the same. For example, don't shout your password across the room. If you write the password down on a piece of paper, fold the paper in half when you hand it to the person as a way of indicating that the information should be guarded. And *never* email a plaintext password—email can be accidentally misdirected, misdelivered, and unintentionally forwarded to third parties.

Change your password when the person no longer needs it

If you share your house key, you run the risk that the key might be copied. One way to protect against this is by using keys that are hard to duplicate. But a better approach is to change your locks when your friend no longer needs access. Changing locks can be an expensive and time-consuming operation, but it's quite easy to change passwords. Therefore, after you have finished sharing a password, you should change it.

Resist social engineering attacks

One of the most common ways for attackers to steal passwords is to use social engineering attacks—that is, to ask a lot of people for their passwords, and see who responds. Crooks know that if they ask a few hundred people for their password, it's likely that somebody will answer.

Here are some common social engineering techniques:

- An email message arrives that claims to be from your Internet service provider. The message informs you that you have been asked to "beta test" a new service. There is a link given at the bottom of the email message. When you click the link, you are taken to a web page where you are asked to sign in with your username and password. After you sign in, you are told that your account is not yet authorized; try again later. In fact, the web server where you typed your username and password belongs to an attacker, who immediately logs into your ISP account and changes your password, locking you out in the process.

- A person claiming to be a new employee calls the company's computer support group and says that he cannot access his account. The support group tells the employee the password. The caller thanks the support person profusely, then hangs up. In fact, the person who called up is not the new employee, but an outsider who saw a press release on the company's web site welcoming the new employee to the company. That outsider now has access to the employee's email and files.

- You get a phone call at your desk from a person who claims to be in your company's IT group. The person tells you that there is a problem with the company's backup system and it hasn't been able to record your information for several weeks. They think that the problem is your password, and ask that you change your password to "pass1234" so that they can diagnose the problem. You comply—giving the outsider access to your account in the process.

Social engineering attacks succeed because people want to be helpful and many computer users lack sufficient understanding of proper security rules and procedures.

Beware of Password Sniffers and Stealers

Even if you pick a good password and don't tell it to another human, your password might still be stolen by hostile software.

Password sniffers

Passwords can be intercepted as they move through the Internet. This interception is performed by programs known as *password sniffers*. These programs work by monitoring all of the Internet traffic that moves across a particular connection and recording the packets belonging to protocols that send passwords without using encryption.

Every Internet protocol that uses unencrypted passwords can be vulnerable to password sniffers. Specific protocols targeted by password sniffers include:

- FTP (File Transfer Protocol)
- HTTP (Hypertext Transfer Protocol)*
- POP (Post Office Protocol)
- TELNET (Remote Terminal Protocol)
- RLOGIN (Remote login for UNIX machines)

Password sniffers have been an ongoing problem on the Internet since the late-1980s. Sniffers have been found on local area networks at universities, corporations, and government agencies. Sniffers have been found on the backbones of Internet service providers, giving them access to thousands of new passwords every minute. Sniffers have even been found on classified military networks.

There is no way to know if your password is being captured by a password sniffer. Nevertheless, you can protect yourself from sniffers by avoiding protocols that send passwords in cleartext. For every protocol that is susceptible to password sniffing, there is an alternate protocol that uses encryption to protect passwords as they are sent. For example:

Instead of using this protocol	Use these cryptographic protocols
FTP	scp (secure shell)
	FTPS (FTP over SSL)
HTTP	HTTPS (HTTP over SSL)

---

* HTTP 1.1 has a challenge-response protocol that does not require the user's password be sent in the clear over the network, but to use this system both the web server and the web client must support HTTP 1.1, and the challenge-response protocol must be specifically enabled on the web server. To date, few web services use this feature.

Instead of using this protocol	Use these cryptographic protocols
POP	POPS (POP over SSL)
	KPOP (POP with Kerberos authentication)
	APOP (POP with encrypted nonces)
TELNET	SSH (Secure Shell)

Because the cryptographic protocols require higher computational overhead and are frequently more difficult to set up, many online services simply do not make these services available to their customers. Other online services make the cryptographic protocols available but do not advertise them. But there are always choices on the Internet. For example, as of this writing, the web-based email providers HotMail, Yahoo, and AOL do not allow users to download their email using HTTPS, but instead require that the users send usernames and passwords using HTTP. But other web-based email providers, including Hushmail, do provide a higher level of security.

Keystroke recorders and keyboard sniffers

Instead of compromising your Internet connection, an attacker can compromise your very computer system with a program or a physical device that records your keystrokes. These devices can record everything you type, including your username, your password, the credit card numbers that you type, and your correspondence. Some devices store the information until it is retrieved at a later point in time, while other devices attempt to covertly transmit the information to somewhere else on the Internet.

Keystroke recorders can be exceedingly difficult to detect. For example, the KeyKatch manufactured by Codex Data Systems (shown in Figure 9-1) is a device the size of a spool of thread that attaches between a keyboard and a desktop computer. The device records every keystroke typed and cannot be detected except by physical inspection. Such devices can be used for industrial espionage, for spying on household members, or for satisfying prurient interests. On the other hand, the KeyKatch can also be used as a backup device, because it will keep a copy of everything you type and be able to recreate any document or email message should the information be accidentally lost as the result of a computer failure.

Figure 9-1. The KeyKatch is a small device that attaches between a keyboard and a desktop computer and can record more than two million keystrokes (reprinted with permission)

Some programs can be set up to record the information stored on a computer's screen at regular intervals. These screen recorders provide another way to covertly monitor a computer user.

Some keystroke recording programs are sold on the open market for investigation and surveillance work. These programs are also distributed by the computer underground. For example, Back Orifice 2000 is a complex espionage program that allows remote monitoring, screen scraping, file transfer, and encrypted communications; it also supports a plug-in architecture for additional exploits.

Beware of public terminals

Whereas it is relatively unlikely that your home or office computer would be compromised with a keyboard sniffer or screen recorder program, this is not the case with public Internet terminals at trade shows, libraries, and many Internet kiosks. Although it is dangerous to generalize, public Internet terminals have a significantly higher chance of being infected with hostile programs because these terminals are often poorly monitored and because some programs (such as Back Orifice) are so easily installed.

To protect yourself from the hostile programs running on public terminals, you may wish to follow these precautions:

- Do not use public terminals for the purpose of accessing confidential information sources.
- If you must use a public terminals while traveling on an extended trip, get a disposable web mail account for the occasion. Do not forward your email to the web mail account. Instead, tell your correspondents of the new address and have them use the new address only for the duration of the trip.

Cleaning Up After Yourself

When you use the Internet, you leave traces of the web sites that you visit and the information that you see on your computer. Another person can learn a lot about the web sites that you have visited by examining your computer for these electronic footprints. This process of computer examination is called *computer forensics*, and it has become a hot area of research in recent years. Special-purpose programs can also examine your computer and either prepare a report, or transmit the report over the Internet to someone else.

Although it can be very hard to remove all traces of a web site that you have seen or an email message that you have downloaded, you can do a good job of cleaning up your computer with only a small amount of work. There are also a growing number of programs that can automatically clean up your computer at regular intervals, as we'll see in the next chapter.

Downloaded Software and Web Browser Extensions

In recent years, a large number of companies have developed companion software designed to be downloaded and installed by Internet users.

Examples of such software include the Real Audio player, the Macromind Shockwave player, and Google's "Google Bar." Almost always, this software is distributed for free and Internet users are strongly encouraged to install it.

In many cases, these software downloads are benign. But in a significant number of instances, these programs have been found to leak considerable information back to the companies that are distributing them. For example:

- In October 1999, computer security expert Richard Smith discovered that the RealJukeBox music player monitored the music that its users were listening to and sent this information back to Real.com's servers. Included in the information sent back was an identification number, allowing the company to identify each of its users: "To make matters worse, it even collected this data when the computer was not connected to the Internet and arranged to transmit it later. This behavior arguably had little to do with the functionality originally offered to consumers."[a]

- Likewise, Richard Smith discovered that a program called CometCursor, which changed the cursor of a browser to match the "theme" of the visited web site, was silently tracking and transmitting browser records when users browsed member web sites.

In a follow-up survey of 16 browser extension programs, Smith and four other researchers found that half of the browser programs transmitted significant amounts of personal information from the user's web browser to the company that had created the browser add-in program.

They wrote:

> We believe that the number of unreported but significant privacy problems in Internet software far exceeds the number of reported privacy-related cases. We also think that most of these unreported problems are best explained by oversight on the part of developers and entrepreneurs unfamiliar with common privacy pitfalls. The Internet is still a relatively new deployment environment, and little guidance is available to those who want to do the right thing. By showing some privacy consequences of early decisions, we hope to help minimize future lapses.[b]

a. "The Privacy Practices of Web Browser Extensions," by David M. Martin, Jr., Richard M. Smith, Michael Brittain, Ivan Fetch, and Hailin Wu. December 6, 2000, The Privacy Foundation, p. 14.

b. Ibid, p. 25.

Browser Cache

Each time your web browser attempts to fetch a URL from the Internet, it first checks a special directory called the *browser cache* to see if it has a copy of the information that it is about to download. The browser cache can dramatically speed up the process of web browsing. For example, if you are clicking through a web site that has lots of little buttons, each of the buttons only needs to be downloaded once, even though the same buttons might appear on every page. But if another person can gain access to your computer, the browser cache will provide that person with copies of the web pages that you have visited. There are several ways to minimize the privacy impact of your browser's cache:

- You can usually configure your browser so that HTML pages and images downloaded by SSL are not cached on your hard disk. This way, confidential information such as bank statements and credit card numbers will not be locally stored. This is the default for many web browsers.

- You can configure your browser so that no HTML pages or images are cached. Although this approach will give you the maximum amount of privacy, it will also significantly decrease your browsing performance.

- You can manually delete the information in your browser's cache when you leave a particularly sensitive site. Alternatively, you can inspect the browser's cache and delete the specific material that you believe to be sensitive.

Managing your cache with Internet Explorer

You can manage Internet Explorer's cache with the Microsoft "Internet Properties" control panel. Clicking the "Delete Files..." button will cause Internet Explorer to delete all of the files in its cache. Alternatively, you can click the "Settings..." button and then the View Files . . . buttons (see Figure 9-2) to open the directory that contains IE's cache. From here, you can delete the files as you see fit (see Figure 9-3). Beyond temporary files, Internet Explorer can also download executable code in the form of ActiveX components from web sites. You can view these ActiveX components by clicking the "View Objects..." button on Internet Explorer's "Settings" panel (see Figure 9-4). If you wish, you can then delete applets that you no longer wish to have resident on your computer. Should you ever visit a web site that requires one of these applets, you can always reinstall it.

Managing your cache with Netscape Navigator

To clear the web page cache with Netscape Navigator, select "Preferences" from the "Edit" menu. Click on the "Advanced" category, and then select "Cache." Press the button labeled "Clear Disk Cache" to clear Netscape's disk cache. Then press "Clear Memory Cache" to clear Netscape's memory cache (see Figure 9-5).

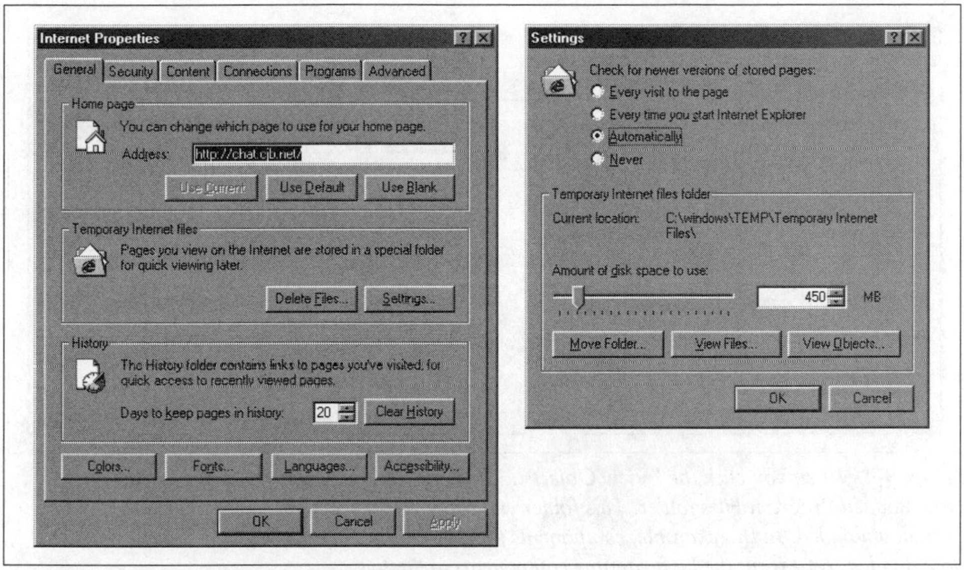

Figure 9-2. With the Internet Explorer "Internet Properties" control panel, you can control the browser's cache by clicking on the "Delete Files . . . " and "Settings . . . " buttons. If you click the "Settings . . . " button, the Settings panel will appear. Click the "View Files . . . " button to display the directory containing cookies and browser cache.

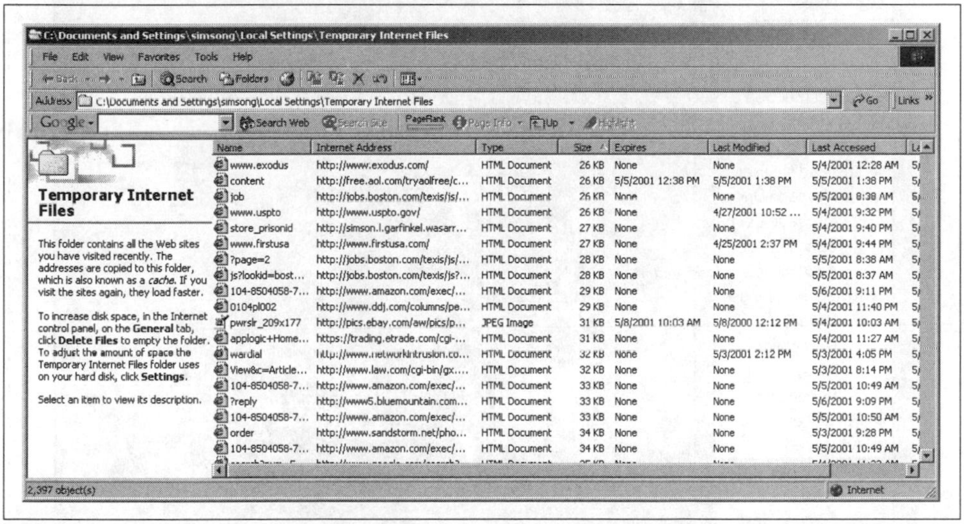

Figure 9-3. When you click on the View Files button, Internet Explorer opens up the Temporary Internet Files folder. This folder can contain cookies, JPEG files, and HTML documents. You can delete them as you wish without damaging your computer.

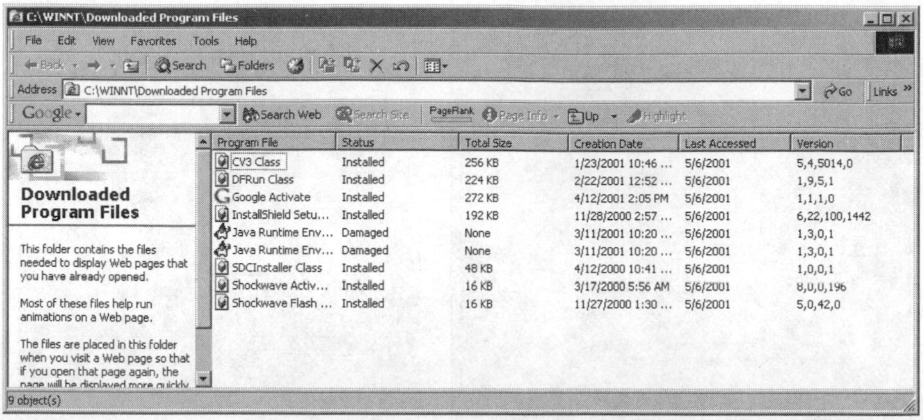

Figure 9-4. When you click the "View Objects..." button, Internet Explorer opens up the Downloaded Program Files folder. This folder will show you the ActiveX components that have been downloaded. In this example, components for several third-party programs have been downloaded. All except the Java runtime components are active.

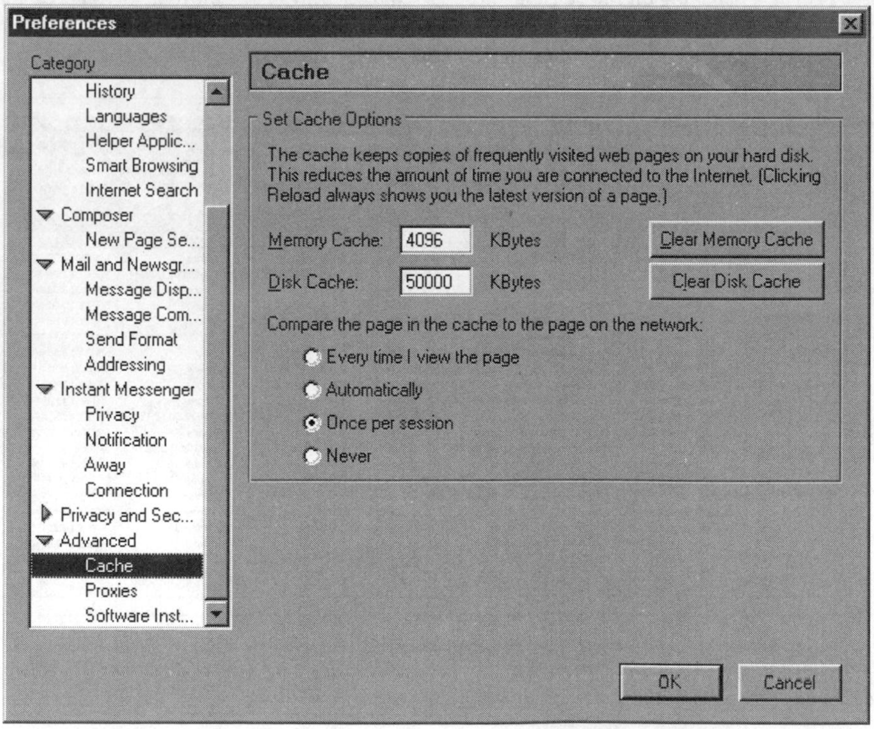

Figure 9-5. Buttons on Netscape Preferences panel allow you to clear the cache

Cookies

As we saw in the previous chapter, cookies are used for many purposes on the Internet, including implementing shopping carts, providing personalized experiences, and tracking your movement from web site to web site. Cookies can be very powerful—so powerful, in fact, that if somebody can access your cookies, they might be able to steal your identity or at least learn information about you that you would like to remain private.

Crushing Internet Explorer's cookies

Internet Explorer stores cookies in a folder in the *History* directory. The directory is pointed to by the Registry value name "Cookies," in the key *HKEY_CURRENT_USER\ Software\Microsoft\Windows\CurrentVersion\Explorer\User Shell Folders*. In practice, this folder can be located in many places, including:

```
C:\Documents and Settings\simsong\Local Settings\Temp\Cookies
C:\Windows\Cookies
C:\Windows\Temp\Cookies
```

The *Cookies* folder may be the same folder as your browser's cache directory, or it may be its own directory. No matter where it is, you can delete the cookies by selecting them with your cursor and then pressing the Backspace or Delete key.

Crushing Netscape's cookies

Netscape Navigator stores its cookies in a single file that is called *cookies.txt* and is stored in the user's profile directory. Although you can manage your Netscape cookies by shutting down the program and editing this file by hand, an easier way is to use the Netscape Cookie Manager (see Figure 9-6).

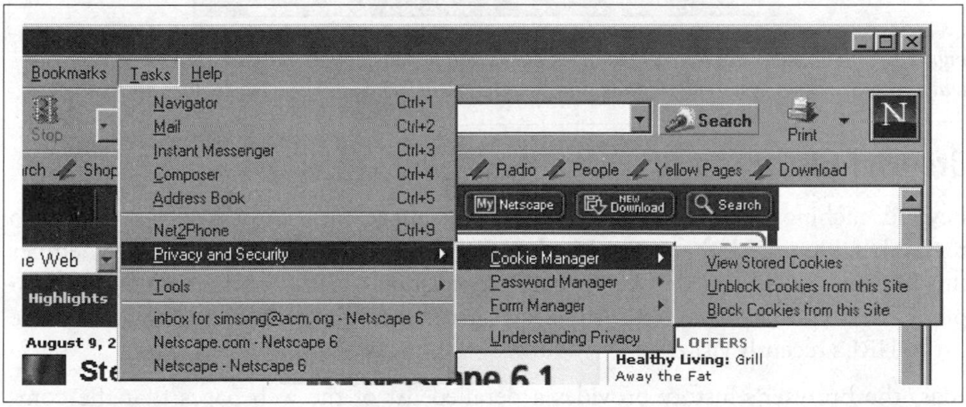

Figure 9-6. *Netscape's Cookie Manager is accessed through the "Privacy and Security" submenu of the Tasks menu.*

Selecting "View Stored Cookies" causes Netscape to display the Cookie Manager (see Figure 9-7). With this interface you can remove an individual cookie or all of your cookies. You can also block cookies from individual sites using the "Block Cookies from this Site" menu option of the Cookie Manager submenu (see Figure 9-6).

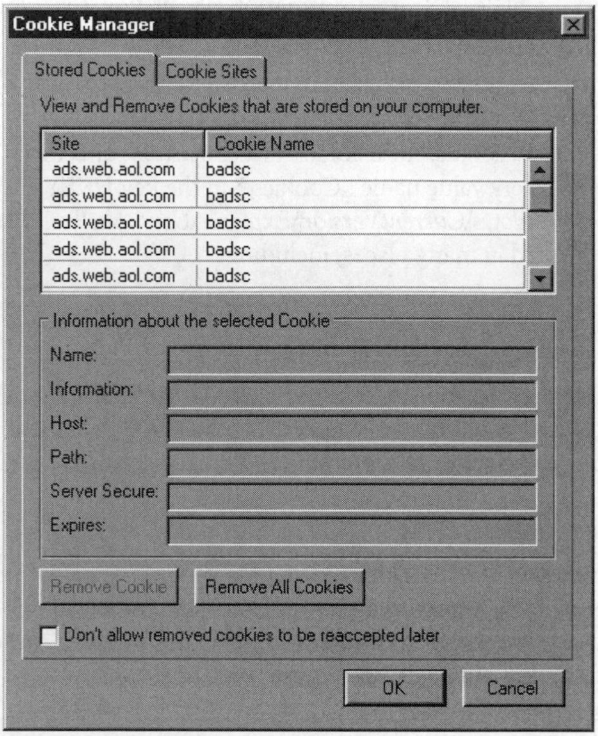

Figure 9-7. The Netscape Cookie Manager shows you which cookies have been accepted from which site. It allows you to block individual cookies, to delete a cookie, or to remove all cookies.

Browser History

Beyond caching the downloaded HTML and image files, most browsers will also remember every URL that they visited within the past few days. Browsers remember this information so that they can provide *completion*—that is, so that when the computer user types a partial URL, the browser can automatically complete it from the list of URLs recently visited.

Alas, the browser's history provides a detailed list of the web pages that the computer user has visited—potentially sensitive information. This information is even more sensitive when the URLs contain search strings and account names. So you may wish to clear your browser's history after you visit a particularly sensitive site.

Clearing Internet Explorer's browser history

Internet Explorer stores its browser history in a compound file stored in the History directory. This directory is pointed to by the Registry value name "History" located at the key *HKEY_CURRENT_USER\Software\Microsoft\Windows\CurrentVersion\ Explorer\User Shell Folders.*[*] In practice, this folder can be located in many places, including:

```
c:\Windows\History
c:\windows\temp\history
c:\windows\profiles\username\History
```

If you view this directory with Windows' *COMMAND.COM* window, you will see only one file:

```
C:\WINDOWS\Profiles\simsong\History\History.IE5>dir

Volume in drive C has no label
Volume Serial Number is 1E5B-0EFD
Directory of C:\WINDOWS\Profiles\simsong\History\History.IE5

.            <DIR>        06-19-00  9:35p .
..           <DIR>        06-19-00  9:35p ..
INDEX   DAT      606,208  01-30-01  9:35p index.dat
        1 file(s)         606,208 bytes
        2 dir(s)      221,679,616 bytes free

C:\WINDOWS\Profiles\simsong\History\History.IE5>
```

There is also a hidden file called *DESKTOP.INI*, which you can see with the *ATTRIB* command:

```
C:\WINDOWS\Profiles\simsong\History\History.IE5>attrib *.*
    SH      DESKTOP.INI
            INDEX.DAT
C:\WINDOWS\Profiles\simsong\History\History.IE5>attrib -s -h *.ini

C:\WINDOWS\Profiles\simsong\History\History.IE5>dir

Volume in drive C has no label
Volume Serial Number is 1E5B-0EFD
Directory of C:\WINDOWS\Profiles\simsong\History\History.IE5
```

---

[*] When we refer to registry keys, we mean under Windows. If you are a Macintosh user, all of the information is in files that are likely to be in one place in the *Preferences* folder in your *System Folder* (for Mac OS 8.x and 9.x). Simply find your preference folder and look inside—like most things on the Mac, it should be obvious what is what.

```
    .               <DIR>           06-19-00   9:35p .
    ..              <DIR>           06-19-00   9:35p ..
DESKTOP INI              113        08-23-99   3:05p desktop.ini
INDEX   DAT          606,208        01-30-01   9:35p index.dat
        2 file(s)         606,321 bytes
        2 dir(s)      221,679,616 bytes free

C:\WINDOWS\Profiles\simsong\History\History.IE5>
```

If you view this directory through Internet Explorer, an Explorer extension will make the *index.dat* file appear as a set of databases, as shown in Figure 9-8.

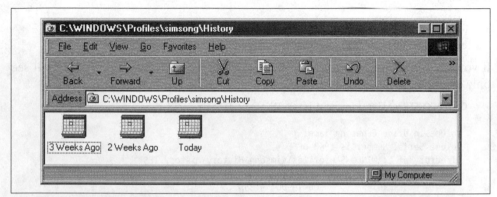

Figure 9-8. Internet Explorer has a shell extension that makes the file index.dat in the History folder appear as a set of tiny calendars. If you double-click on one of the little calendar icons, you will see the individual history records that it contains.

You can use the Internet Explorer Internet Properties control panel (Figure 9-2) to control the history that your browser keeps. You can erase the history by clicking the button labeled "Clear History."

In addition to history, Internet Explorer remembers the names of the URLs that you recently typed. These URLs are stored in the Registry Key *HKEY_CURRENT_USER\ Software\Microsoft\Internet Explorer\TypedURLs*. You can delete these keys one by one or all at once. (See Figure 9-9.)

Clearing Netscape Navigator's browser history

To clear Navigator's history list, select "Preferences," choose the "Navigator" item, and then select the "History" subitem. Click the button to clear the history list.

Passwords, Form-Filling, and AutoComplete Settings

Internet Explorer and Netscape Navigator both have the ability to remember what you type on web forms and the username/password combinations that you provide

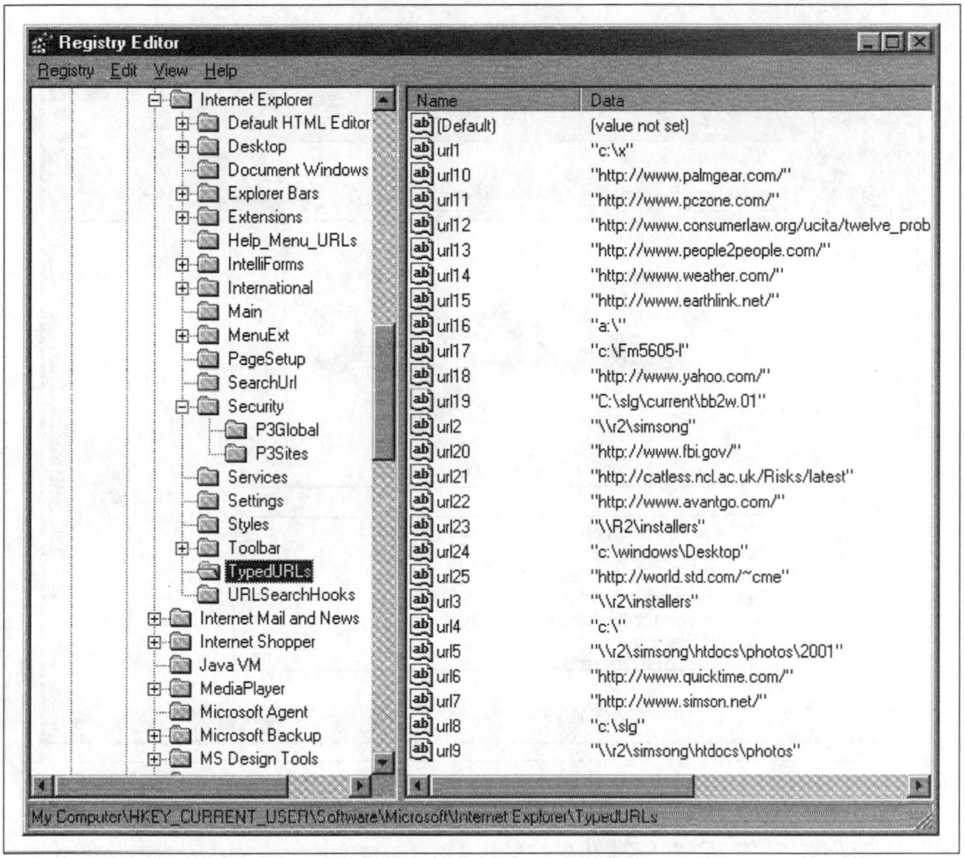

Figure 9-9. Internet Explorer stores the last typed URLs at the Registry Key HKEY_CURRENT_ USER\Software\Microsoft\Internet Explorer\TypedURLs.

to web sites. By default, the programs will automatically provide this information (when prompted) to save you from typing (Figure 9-10). Although this is a very handy feature, it can also reveal considerable information about your web usage habits to other people who have access to your computer.

Clearing AutoComplete with Internet Explorer

You can control Internet Explorer's AutoComplete feature by clicking on the "Content" tab of the Internet Properties Control Panel and then clicking on the "Auto-Complete..." button. This will bring up the "AutoComplete Settings" panel (see Figure 9-11). Click "Clear Forms" to clear all of the AutoComplete information for web forms. You can click "Clear Passwords" to have Internet Explorer forget all of the username/password combinations for the web sites that you have visited.

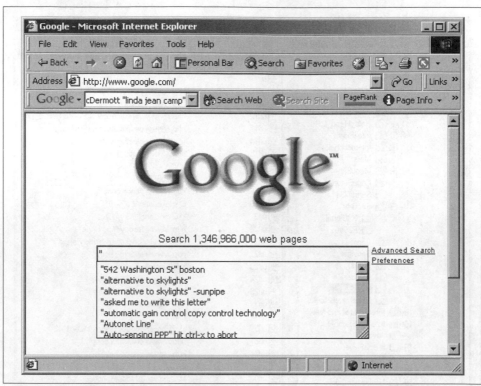

Figure 9-10. Internet Explorer's AutoComplete system will remember fields that you recently entered into web forms. This feature can be very handy, but it can also reveal information to other people who have access to your computer.

Clearing sensitive information with Netscape Navigator

Netscape allows you to remove other "sensitive information," such as stored passwords, using the Password Manager. To access the Password Manager, select the "Tasks" menu, the "Privacy and Security" submenu, the "Password Manager," then "Clear sensitive information" (see Figure 9-12).

Avoiding Spam and Junk Email

Unwanted electronic mail is the number one consumer complaint on the Internet today. A 1999 study by BrightMail, a company that develops antispam technology, found that 84 percent of Internet users had received spam; 42 percent loathed the time it takes to handle spam; 30 percent found it to be a "significant invasion of privacy;" 15 percent found it offensive; and ISPs suffered account churn rates as high as 7.2 percent as a direct result of spam.

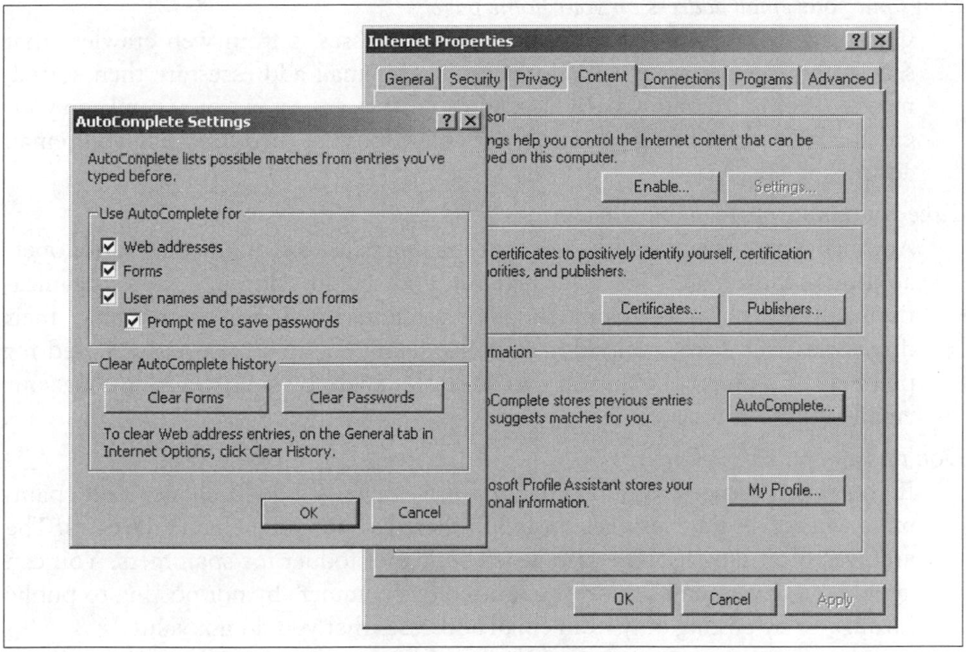

Figure 9-11. Internet Explorer's AutoComplete Settings panel allows you to control where AutoComplete is used. You can also clear AutoComplete information for forms and/or passwords.

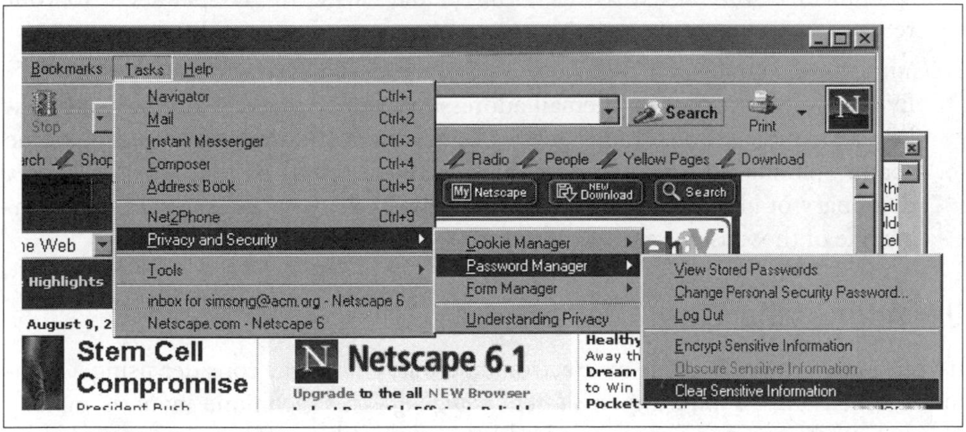

Figure 9-12. Netscape's Password Manager has an option that allows you to clear sensitive information that is stored on your computer.

Protect Your Email Address

To send you junk mail, a spammer must have your email address. By understanding how spammers get email addresses, you can keep your mailbox relatively spam-free:

Don't put your email address on your home page

One place that spammers get their email addresses is from web crawlers that search the Internet for email addresses. These email addresses are then sorted, indexed, compiled onto CD-ROMs, and sold. The easiest way you can keep your email address from being put into these collections is to avoid putting your email address on a web page.

Take your name out of online directories

Another source of email addresses that spammers use are online directories operated by organizations like AOL, BigFoot, and Yahoo. Although these organizations all try to fight spammers and prohibit spammers from using their directories to collect email addresses, invariably online directories are used for precisely this purpose. You can avoid a lot of spam by simply asking that your email address be unlisted.

Don't post to public mailing lists

If you post messages to public mailing lists, there is a good chance that spammers will scrape the messages posted to these lists for valid email addresses. The archives of mailing lists are also a rich source of fodder for spammers. You can avoid having your email address captured by spammers by not posting to public forums, or by posting only from email addresses that you do not value.

Don't post to Usenet

Likewise, Netnews postings on Usenet are another source of email addresses for spammers. If you post to Usenet, you should expect to get spam sent to your return address.

Pick an unusual username

Even if you never post your email address in a public place, if you have a popular username like *bob*, *kathy*, or even *bob7*, you should expect to receive some spam. Spammers frequently engage in *dictionary attacks*—that is, they have a dictionary of likely usernames, and they send their spam messages to every single one of those usernames at the top 1000 Internet service providers.

Use Address Munging

If you don't want to become an electronic hermit, you might consider using a technique called *address munging* or *address mangling*. This technique involves making obvious modifications to your email address so that the web crawlers operated by spammers will not be able to harvest your actual email address. For example:

Instead of using this email address	Use this munged address
bob@aol.com	bob@remove-me.aol.com
jason@vineyard.net	jason@nospam.vineyard.net

Instead of using this email address	Use this munged address
barbara@microsoft.com	barbara@microsoft.com.remove
nosmis@acm.org	nosmis@acm.org.nospam

In general, it is considered better form to mangle the domain name. If you mangle the username (e.g., "bob-nospam@aol.com," rather than "bob@remove-me.aol.com"), the spammer will still deliver your email message to your ISP, and then your ISP will need to figure out what to do with it.

When you mangle the domain name, the spammer is unable to deliver the spam message to your ISP.

Use an Antispam Service or Software

Yet another alternative in the war against spam is to employ an antispam service or antispam software.

Antispam services are organizations that analyze your incoming email and determine whether or not it is spam. Some services attempt to match the incoming email against known spam. Other services keep track of a *whitelist* of addresses from which you are willing to accept email; other people who attempt to send you a message get a note back asking them to click on a link or reply to an email message to be added to your whitelist. The theory here is that spammers, who mostly use bogus return-addresses, won't ever see the email messages with instructions on how to get added to your whitelist.

Two popular antispam services are:

- BrightMail personal edition (*http://www.brightmail.com/*)
- SpamCop (*http://www.spamcop.net/*)

Antispam software is software that performs much the same function as the antispam services, except that the software runs on your mail server or on your desktop computer. The big advantage of these programs over antispam services is that your mail never leaves your computer. The disadvantage is that you need to maintain the software.

Two popular antispam programs are:

- SpammerSlammer (*http://www.nowtools.com/*)
- Spam Exterminator (*http://www.unisyn.com/*)

A great deal of useful information about stopping spammers, and links to antispam services, may be found at *http://www.junkbusters.com/*. This site also has information on stopping junk paper mail, web banner ads, as well as those annoying telemarketing calls.

Identity Theft

In 1991, a car salesman from Orlando, Florida named Steven Shaw obtained the credit report for a journalist in Washington named, coincidently enough, Stephen Shaw. For Steven Shaw, getting Stephen Shaw's credit report was easier than you might think: for years, the consumer reporting firm Equifax had aggressively marketed its credit reporting service to car dealers. The service lets salespeople weed out the Sunday window-shoppers from the serious prospects by asking for a customer's name and then surreptitiously disappearing into the back room and running a quick credit check. In all likelihood, the Shaw in Florida had simply gone fishing for someone with a similar-sounding name and a good credit history.

Once Steven Shaw in Florida had Stephen Shaw's Social Security number and credit report, he had everything he needed to steal the journalist's identity. Besides stating that Stephen Shaw had excellent credit, the report listed his current and previous addresses, his mother's maiden name, and the account numbers of all of his major credit cards. Jackpot!

"He used my information to open 35 accounts and racked up $100,000 worth of charges," says Stephen Shaw. "He tagged me for everything under the sun—car loans, personal loans, bank accounts, stereos, furniture, appliances, clothes, airline tickets."

Because all the accounts were opened using Stephen Shaw's name and Social Security number, all of the businesses held the Washington-based Stephen Shaw liable for the money that the other Shaw spent. And when the bills weren't paid, the companies told Equifax and the other credit bureaus that Stephen Shaw, the man who once had stellar credit, was now a deadbeat.

Stories of consumer fraud similar to what happened to Stephen Shaw have become epidemic in recent years. Called *identity theft*, this crime was relatively rare in the 1980s and early 1990s. In recent years, however, cases of identity theft have skyrocketed. It's now estimated that there have been more than a million victims of identity theft throughout the United States. Chances are that you know somebody who has been directly affected by this crime.

Sometimes the crook gets the personal information from inside sources. In April 1996, federal prosecutors charged a group of Social Security Administration employees with stealing personal information on more than 11,000 people and selling the data to credit fraud rings, who used the information to activate stolen credit cards and ring up huge bills. Other times, crooks pose as homeless people and rummage through urban trash cans, looking for bank and credit card statements.

Not all cases of identity theft start with a stolen credit report or a misappropriated bank statement. Some cases begin with a fraudulently filed change of address form, directing the victim's mail to an abandoned building. And no paper trail need be created at all. In May 1997, the *Seattle Times* reported that hundreds of people in the Seattle area had received suspicious crank phone calls. The caller claimed to be from a radio station that was giving away money; the check would be in the mail as soon as the people picking up the phone provided their Social Security numbers.

Some people found the calls suspicious and telephoned the station or the police. Others presumably handed over the information that the callers requested. Similar scams are epidemic on America Online, the world's largest online service, where they have been given the evocative name *phishing*.

Stephen Shaw says it took him more than four years to resolve his problems—a period that appears to be typical for most identity theft victims. That's four years of harassing calls from bill collectors, of getting more and more angry letters in the mail, of not knowing what else is being done in your name. Four years of having your creditors think of you as a deadbeat. During this period, it's virtually impossible for the victim to obtain a new credit card or a mortgage. One of the cruelest results of identity theft is that many victims find themselves unemployable; in addition to job references, many businesses routinely check the credit reports of their job applicants.

Protecting Yourself From Identity Theft

Identity theft is made possible because companies that grant credit—especially credit card companies—are always on the lookout for new customers, and they don't have a good way to verify the identity of a person who mails in an application or places an order over the telephone. So the credit-granting companies make a dangerous assumption: they take it for granted that if you know a person's name, address, telephone number, Social Security number, and mother's maiden name, *you must be that person*. And when the merchandise is bought and the bills aren't paid, that person is the one held responsible.

Of course, it's relatively easy to learn a person's name, address, telephone number, Social Security number, and mother's maiden name. Credit bureaus hand this data out to their customers. Lookup services make this information available, at minimal cost, over the Internet. And many consumers, unaware of the risk, will readily divulge this information to people who call on the phone and claim to be from a bank or credit card agency.

There are lots of technical changes that could be made to lower the incidence of identity theft. One change, for example, would be to require a person applying for a credit card to show up in person and have a photograph taken, recorded, and put on the back of the credit card. This would act as a deterrent, because most identity thieves don't want to have records created that could be used to trace back to their actual identity. But few credit card issuers would ever mandate the use of photographs, as it would effectively end the industry's marketing strategy of sending credit cards to new customers through the mail, without the need to have local branch offices.

Fortunately, you aren't powerless. There are a number of strategies that you can use right now to help protect yourself from identity theft:

Shred your trash

One of the most common ways for crooks to get hold of your Social Security number and credit card accounts is to go rummaging around through your trash. Fortunately, there's an easy way to put an end to this problem: buy a personal shredder. In recent years, the prices of shredders have dropped from hundreds of dollars to less than $25. For $50, you can buy a fairly good strip shredder that sits on top of a trash can and will shred five pieces of paper at a time into long strips that present more trouble than most crooks are willing to handle. Remember, the goal of a shredder is not to make your trash illegible; it's just to make your trash harder to read than somebody else's.

Of course, strip shredders are not perfect. If you demand higher security, you can buy a cross-cut shredder that will make it virtually impossible for somebody going through your trash to reassemble anything. Expect to spend between $100 and $400 on a good cross-cut shredder.

Simply buying a shredder is not enough: *you must use it*. It's good procedure to shred every piece of paper that has your name or an account number on it. Some people believe in shredding everything—on the grounds that this makes their trash even harder for a crook to reassemble. But if you are using a decent shredder, there is no need to shred everything—just shredding the important stuff will do.

Monitor your credit report

The longer identity theft goes on, the harder it is to put your life back together. For this reason, you should monitor your credit report on a regular basis. There are three major credit reporting firms in the United States (see Table 9-2), and any one of them will send you your credit report for free if you have been denied credit, insurance, or a job within the past 90 days. Some states have also passed laws that require the credit reporting agencies to give you one free report each year. If you don't live in one of these states, you can still get a report by paying between $5 and $15 to the credit reporting firms.

As of this writing, both Experian and Equifax made it possible to view your credit report on the Internet after answering a few questions designed to prove your identity; TransUnion will allow you to order your report on-line, but they send it to you via surface mail. Equifax also offers a CreditWatch service that will tell you when there is unusual or suspicious activity in your credit history.

Table 9-2. *The United States' major credit reporting agencies*

Name	Contact information	Online access
Equifax	Equifax Consumer Direct P.O. Box 105496 Atlanta, GA 30348-5496 Attn: Customer Care customer.care@equifax.com	*http://www.equifax.com/*
Experian	Experian Consumer Services 901 West Bond Street Lincoln, NE 68521 1-888 EXPERIAN (1-888-397-3742) Does not accept email queries	*http://www.experian.com/*
TransUnion	TransUnion P.O. Box 2000 Chester, PA 19022 1-800-888-4213 Does not accept email queries	*http://www.transunion.com/*

Be careful of what you carry in your wallet or purse

What would happen if you lost your wallet right now? Chances are, you would be in trouble. You wouldn't simply have lost needed plastic—somebody who found your wallet would have a virtual "identity theft kit" with your name on it.

To protect yourself from lost wallets, try to carry only what you absolutely need. Don't carry your Social Security card or a birth certificate—you don't need them. Ideally, make sure that your Social Security number doesn't appear in your wallet at all.

Once you have minimized the number of cards that are in your wallet, take them all out and photocopy their fronts and backs. This way, if your wallet is lost, you'll have a record of what was lost and you'll be in a position to quickly cancel them all.

Cancel unnecessary credit card accounts

Don't apply for every credit card available. If you have a lot of plastic, see if you can get rid of all but the essential ones.

Ask organizations to use numbers other than your Social Security number as your account number

The bad news is that many organizations use Social Security numbers as account numbers. The good news is that many organizations will give you a different number if you ask. In Massachusetts, for example, most drivers' license numbers are the drivers' SSN, but the Registry of Motor Vehicles will issue an "S-Number" if the driver requests it. Likewise, Blue Cross of Massachusetts doesn't use SSNs as their account numbers, but numbers that are slightly different.

If possible, confine all of your online purchases to a single credit card, and use another credit card for your offline purchases

There has been considerably more fraud associated with credit cards that are used for online purchases than with those that are not used for online transactions.

In particular, if you have an American Express card, consider using the "Private Payments" service associated with the cards. This is a service that will generate a one-time number to use in online shopping. There is no need to actually send your real account number to any merchant on the Web. See the AmEx page at *http://www.americanexpress.com/privatepayments/*.

Don't give out personal information to people who call you claiming to represent credit card companies, banks, or companies giving away prizes

If your credit card company calls you telling you that there is suspicious activity on your account, make the operator prove that he or she really works for the company before you cooperate with them.

Use passwords

A growing number of companies are allowing their customers to put a "password" on an account, rather than relying on the customer's "mother's maiden name." See if your bank, credit card company, and utilities allow you to put passwords on your accounts. If they do, take advantage of this service.

If you are the victim of identity theft, follow these steps:

- Report the crime to your local police department, to the Secret Service, and to the postal inspector at your local post office.

- Call the Federal Trade Commission's Identity Theft Hotline 1-877-ID THEFT (1-877-438-4338). The FTC is keeping statistics at the Identity Theft Data Clearinghouse to gauge the severity of the identity theft problem. They will also give you advice and counseling.

- Contact your bank and credit card companies to alert them to the problem.

- Contact the banks and credit card companies where the fraudulent accounts have been opened and advise them of what has happened. Be aware: these companies may not believe you, especially if they think you owe them thousands of dollars. Nevertheless, you must persevere if you wish to clear your name.

- Get a copy of your credit report from Equifax, Experian, and TransUnion. Yes, you must get a copy of the report from *each* of these credit reporting agencies! Go through the report line by line, and challenge every single piece of information that appears incorrect, even if the incorrect information isn't obviously part of the identity theft incident. You may also wish to speak to the fraud departments at these organizations, although you may find them less than helpful.

- Consider obtaining the assistance of an attorney to aid you in clearing your record. This may not be inexpensive, but legal advice and assistance can be very helpful, especially in getting financial institutions to pay attention.

Ultimately, identity theft is flourishing because credit-granting companies are not being forced to cover the costs of their lax security procedures. The eagerness with which credit companies send out preapproved credit card applications and the ease with which stores will open a revolving charge account for a new customer creates the risk of fraud. When the fraud takes place, the credit grantor simply notes that payment was not made in the consumer's credit file and moves on; the consumer is left to pick up the pieces and otherwise deal with the cost of a stolen identity.

It stands to reason, then, that the easiest way to reduce fraud would be to force the companies that are creating the risk to suffer the consequences. One way to do that would be by penalizing companies that add provably false information to a consumer credit report in the same way we penalize individuals who file false police reports. Such penalties would force credit grantors to do a better job of identifying the individuals to whom they grant credit, and this, in turn, would help limit the crime of identity theft. However, it may be a while before this happens—financial institutions have well-paid lobbyists who help quash legislation on topics such as this.

## CHAPTER 10

Privacy-Protecting Technologies

In this chapter:
- Blocking Ads and Crushing Cookies
- Anonymous Browsing
- Secure Email

In this chapter, we'll look at a few classes of programs that you can use to safeguard your privacy while using the Web. Collectively, these technologies are frequently referred to as *privacy-protecting technologies*.

For each major section in this chapter, we have attempted to introduce the broad program category (blocking ads, crushing cookies, anonymous browsing, and secure email), give a few examples of programs in the category, and then finally show one or two of these programs in action. Because the Internet is a fast-changing place, it's quite possible that some or all of the programs discussed here will no longer be available by the time this book appears in print. It's also possible that new programs will be introduced that are not mentioned here. That's why you should use this chapter as a survey of the kinds of tools that are available for enhancing web privacy, rather than as an actual buyer's guide.

Blocking Ads and Crushing Cookies

If you are interested in protecting your privacy from web advertisers—or if you simply want to see fewer advertisements when you browse the Internet—then you will find yourself in something of a quandary. That's because the companies that are developing web browsers—Microsoft, Netscape, and Opera Software—have all developed business units that make money by showing advertisements to consumers.[*] Browsers have become programs for delivering ads (see Figure 10-1).

A web that is filled with advertisements doesn't pose a problem for many consumers. After all, advertisements are everywhere: they are on our highways, in our newspapers and magazines, on television, and even on so-called "public radio" stations. Why should the Internet be any different?

---

[*] Mozilla, the open source browser based on Netscape's code, has no such profit motive, and contains per-site image filtering that can be used to block advertisements.

Figure 10-1. On today's Internet, companies that develop web browsers have also created large web sites that are funded by advertising dollars. Browsers have become, in effect, programs for delivering advertisements to consumers.

But as we saw in the previous chapter, the Web *is* different from other advertising venues. For starters, it's simply not possible for a company buying a billboard along a busy highway to get a list of the names, addresses, and phone numbers of all the people who glance up to read their advertisement. A company that sells magazine advertisement space can't correlate the advertisements in five different publications that you've responded to, and then sell your name as a "premium customer." Yet these kinds of invasive practices are possible on the Internet. Fortunately, the design of the Internet also makes it possible to mount a significant defense against the primary privacy-invading tools of advertisers—their cookies—as well as against the advertisements themselves.

Local HTTP Proxies

To allow browsing from behind a corporate firewall, web browsers often use services called *proxy servers*. A proxy server is a program that receives a request from a web browser and forwards the request to the remote web server. The proxy then waits for the response from the remote server and, when it is received, sends the request back to the original browser client that made the request. Most proxy servers are located on corporate firewalls. They allow organizations to carefully control the information that passes between the corporate LAN and the rest of the Internet.

A *local HTTP proxy* is a program designed to proxy HTTP (web) traffic. It runs on your local computer (see Figure 10-2). The local HTTP proxy's position between your computer and the rest of the Web gives the proxy the opportunity to monitor what you are doing, preview the pages, and, optionally, modify the content that you see.

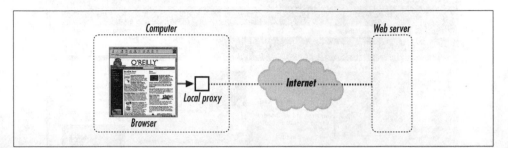

Figure 10-2. A local HTTP proxy sits between the browser on your computer and the rest of the Internet. Because of its position, a local proxy can change the way that you view the Web.

A local HTTP proxy can do many things, including:

- Record every web page that is viewed.
- Selectively grant or block access to specific web sites or pages within those sites.
- Introduce new cookies into your browser.
- Remove cookies sent from remote web sites to your computer, or vice versa.
- Edit the HTML your computer receives, changing the content of web pages.
- Modify the images that are downloaded via HTTP before they are displayed on your computer's screen.

Many of these functions sound quite nefarious and they can be—if somebody else is running the HTTP proxy. But if you have control of the HTTP proxy, then the proxy gives you the ability to control your web browser in ways that were not envisioned (or are simply not allowed) by the browser's creator.

 One thing that most local HTTP proxies won't do is intercept encrypted traffic between your web browser and a remote web site. The traffic isn't intercepted because such an interception would trigger a warning message from your web browser saying that the certificate on the web site did not match the web site's domain name. This type of interception is precisely what the SSL protocol was designed to prevent, so it's a good thing SSL prevents it. There are some HTTP proxies that can intercept SSL-encrypted traffic, however. One way to do so is by creating SSL certificates on the fly using a public key/private key combination that is embedded into the HTTP proxy. Another way to do it is by intercepting the TCP/IP traffic as it moves through the computer's operating system, tapping into the data flow after the data has been decrypted but before it has been given to the application program. This type of interception is easy on Windows for people using Internet Explorer, but it's difficult on other operating systems.

Using Ad Blockers

One of the most obvious things to do with a local HTTP proxy is to prevent web advertisements. There are two ways a local proxy can block advertisements. Assuming the proxy can identify an advertisement (a tricky task), the proxy could block the URLs associated with the ads or could edit out the HTML that causes the advertisement to be displayed. These techniques are demonstrated in Figures 10-3, 10-4, and 10-5.

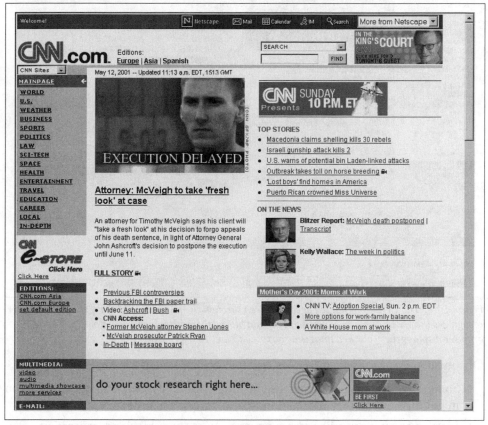

Figure 10-3. The CCN.com home page on May 12, 2001. This page contains four advertisements.

There are many reasons you might want to block an advertisement on a web site:

- Advertisements are annoying and distracting.

- Advertisements take up space on web pages that is better spent on content.

- It takes time to download advertisements. By blocking them, you can make web pages download 5 to 10 seconds faster than they would download with the advertisements. Over a day of browsing, this time savings adds up.

- Many advertisements contain built-in tracking technology, such as cookies. By blocking the advertisements, you limit the amount by which you are tracked.

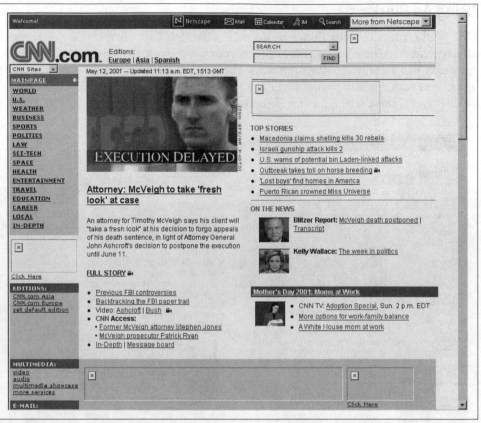

Figure 10-4. The CNN.com home page, as viewed through the Junkbuster HTTP proxy. Junkbuster recognizes the URLs of many advertisements and blocks them from being downloaded. The web browser displays these blocked images as boxes with an "X."

Of course, there are disadvantages as well to blocking advertisements:

- Some advertisements contain useful information. By blocking these ads, you might miss out on this information, special offers, and other distractions.

- Many web sites are advertiser-supported. When you block advertisements, you deny these web sites needed revenue. If everybody blocked advertisements, these web sites would be forced to close or find another way to support themselves, such as by inserting advertising content directly into their editorial product.

Many programs that block advertisements also *crush cookies*; that is, they can selectively allow or deny the transfer of cookies between remote sites and your computer.

One of the big advantages of selective cookie blocking is that you can block cookies from some companies, such as Internet advertising firms, while still allowing cookies from companies that you do business with, such as banks and online brokerage firms.

Figure 10-5. The CNN.com home page, as viewed through the AdSubtract HTTP proxy. AdSubtract edits the HTML as it travels from the web site to the browser and automatically removes the tags that cause some advertisements to be displayed. Notice how the page is automatically reformatted so that more content appears on the screen.

Ad blockers can perform many other useful functions beyond blocking advertisements and crushing cookies, including:

- Removing background music from web pages
- Removing background images from web pages
- Removing JavaScript, Java, and ActiveX from web pages
- Modifying animated GIFs so that they don't move around
- Blocking pop-up windows
- Preventing web sites from reprogramming your "Back" button and web browser's history
- Disabling web pages that automatically refresh themselves
- Blocking refer links from being transmitted from one web site to another

It is simply astonishing how effective ad blockers can be—and how many advertisements are present on today's Web. Spend a few minutes browsing on the Web with an ad blocker, and you might discover that upwards of 50 advertisements have been blocked after viewing only a handful of pages.

Many companies have incorporated ad blocker technology into their products. Some of the products are free; others have a small charge. Most of the programs run only on Windows. In some cases, a Windows-based proxy can provide an ad blocking service to other computers on your local area network. Table 10-1 provides a summary of some ad-blocking programs currently available.

Table 10-1. A survey of ad blocking programs

Program	Features	Comments
AdSubtract[a] *http://www.adsubtract.com*	Ad blocking Cookie management Sophisticated filtering	Windows only. Several different versions (some free) with different features available.
Internet Junkbuster Proxy *http://www.junkbuster.com*	Ad blocking Cookie management	Free. Windows and a variety of Unix systems.
Freedom Internet Privacy Suite *http://www.freedom.net*	Ad blocking Cookie management Form-filling Many other privacy features	Free. Windows and Linux. Optional subscription service provides for anonymous web browsing and email.
Norton Internet Security *http://www.symantec.com/sabu/nis/nis_pe/*	Ad blocking Cookie management Personal firewall Many other security features	Windows only.
WebWasher *http://www.webwasher.com*	Ad blocking Cookie management Sophisticated filtering	Windows only.

[a] Simson Garfinkel is on the advisory board of AdSubtract's publisher, InterMute.

Anonymous Browsing

Although they're great for blocking advertisements and crushing cookies, there's one thing that HTTP proxies can't do, and that's hide your IP address. Fundamentally, there is no way for a proxy to change your IP address, because if it did, the remote web server wouldn't be able to send you back the web pages that you request!

But despite the apparent difficulty of doing so, there are good reasons for wanting to protect your IP address from other computers on the Internet: IP addresses and hostnames can contain personal information and, like cookies, they can be used for correlating browsing activities across different web sites. Finally, your IP address can be used to track back seemingly "anonymous" web transactions to uncover your true identity—something that you may wish to prevent from happening.

Consider these hostnames and IP addresses that were recovered from log files:

daily-bugle.media.mit.edu 18.85.13.120

This hostname and its matching IP address belonged to a desktop computer at the MIT Media Lab in the early 1990s. Because this computer was only used by one person, wherever this person went on the Internet, he left tracks in log files that could be traced directly back to him. As the computer *daily-bugle* was also used to send mail and post to the Usenet, it was relatively simple to determine the identity of the person using this computer.

h00a0c030202a.ne.mediaone.net 108.21.147.24

This hostname was assigned by Media One to a cable modem subscriber in Cambridge, Massachusetts. Wherever that user goes on the Internet, he leaves his hostname and IP address in the log files. Media One assigns hostnames based on the MAC address of their users' Ethernet cards (e.g., *h00a0c030202a*). As most Media One users do not run their own mail servers or news servers, it's somewhat harder to map this address to a person's name. However, if you served Media One with a court order, the information would surely be forthcoming.

proxy-1558.public.svc.webtv.net 209.240.221.130

This hostname and its matching IP address belong to a proxy server at WebTV Networks in Palo Alto, California. This hostname and IP address can't be traced back to a specific user, because the proxy server is used by many different users over the course of time. However, the proxy server also keeps log files. Given a court order, WebTV would be forced to reveal this information.

asy5.vineyard.net 199.232.93.24

This hostname and matching IP address belong to a dialup server at Vineyard.NET in Martha's Vineyard, Massachusetts. As with the WebTV proxy, this hostname and IP address is reassigned to different users over time. But as with WebTV, records of who uses the IP address are kept, and when needed, these records can and will be turned over to authorities.

Many web-based email services transmit the IP address of the web browser with every email message that is sent in the mail headers of each message. For example, here are some headers from an email message sent using the Hotmail service:

```
Received: (from mail@localhost)
        by apache.vineyard.net (8.9.0/8.9.0) id BAA18526
        for <simsong@vineyard.net>; Mon, 20 Mar 2000 01:28:39 -0500 (EST)
Received: from f254.law3.hotmail.com(209.185.240.27) by apache.vineyard.net via smap/
slg (V2.0)
        id sma018473; Mon Mar 20 01:28:20 2000
Received: (qmail 36458 invoked by uid 0); 20 Mar 2000 06:28:18 -0000
Message-ID: <20000320062818.36457.qmail@hotmail.com>
Received: from 24.1.20.191 by www.hotmail.com with HTTP;
        Sun, 19 Mar 2000 22:28:18 PST
X-Originating-IP: [24.1.20.191]
To: simsong@vineyard.net
```

```
Date: Sun, 19 Mar 2000 22:28:18 PST
Mime-Version: 1.0
Content-Type: text/plain; format=flowed
Status: RO
```

For many people, the small leakage of personal information that comes from IP addresses is tolerable and no cause of real concern. But other people are quite concerned. For example, you may be working at one company and interested in viewing the web site of one of your competitors. Although there's nothing wrong or illegal about viewing a competitor's web site, you might not want that company to know that you are downloading every single page of their web site every day. Or you might be monitoring the web pages of an ex-lover and you don't want to make the person feel anxious about your constant checking.* Or you might simply want to hide your tracks for other, personal reason. But whatever your motivation, if you want to protect your IP address, fear not: you have many alternatives.

Simple Approaches to Protecting Your IP Address

Here are some simple approaches that you can use to prevent the disclosure of your IP address:

Browse from a public terminal at a library

One of the best ways to assure anonymity when browsing online is to browse from a public terminal at an organization that is committed to the privacy of its patrons. Internet terminals at public libraries and many university libraries afford excellent opportunities for private web browsing.

Use America Online

When you browse the Internet using AOL's built-in web browser, you are actually viewing the Web through AOL's caching proxy servers. These proxy servers do a great job hiding your IP address. Instead of leaving a descriptive IP address and hostname, you will instead leave a series of caching proxy servers, such as this:

```
cache-rp03.proxy.aol.com
cache-dh03.proxy.aol.com
cache-df04.proxy.aol.com
cache-dg05.proxy.aol.com
cache-fra-aa03.proxy.aol.com
cache-fra-ac08.proxy.aol.com
cache-fra-aa03.proxy.aol.com
cache-mtc-al02.proxy.aol.com
cache-mtc-ak08.proxy.aol.com
cache-mtc-al04.proxy.aol.com
cache-mtc-al02.proxy.aol.com
```

---

* Yes, this could be considered stalking. Obviously, there are occasions where anonymity on the Internet may be a bad idea—it can hide stalking, fraud, harassment, libel, and other criminal activities. The community, as a whole, has yet to decide the right balance. But whatever that balance may be, that is beyond the charter of this book.

```
cache-mtc-am03.proxy.aol.com
cache-rr07.proxy.aol.com
cache-mtc-al02.proxy.aol.com
cache-fra-aa03.proxy.aol.com
cache-mtc-af06.proxy.aol.com
cache-dg02.proxy.aol.com
```

Although America Online's privacy policies in the past have been somewhat suspect, your privacy with AOL is likely to remain secure unless you are suspected of being involved in illegal activities or you anger a corporation or individual that is likely to bring legal action against AOL. Thus, for many individuals, simply using an AOL account can guarantee a large amount of practical privacy, even though this privacy is not as iron-clad as other available approaches.

Use your ISP's web cache or proxy server

Many ISPs make web caches or proxy servers available to their customers. When you view a web page through a cache, the remote web server frequently is given the IP address of the proxy server and not the end user. Thus, using an ISP's web cache or proxy server can be a good way to protect your IP address from remote servers.

 Unless your ISP has specifically made a claim to protect your privacy, using the ISP's web cache to protect your privacy can actually backfire. If you are using the ISP's web cache or proxy server, then every one of your web requests goes through the ISP's software before it goes to the Internet. This allows the ISP to monitor every web page that you view. This information can also be recorded in the ISP's log files. Further, some web caches can be configured to report to the remote system the IP address of the browser that is accessing the cache. Thus, unless there is a specific claim of privacy being made, using the ISP's web cache or proxy server may actually decrease your privacy.

Anonymous Web Browsing Services

While all of the simple approaches described in the previous section work, none of them are foolproof. If you are truly in need of secure, anonymous web browsing, then you should use an anonymous web browsing service.

Most anonymous web browsing services operate as proxy servers. That is, your web browser speaks to the anonymous web browsing service, and then the web browsing service speaks to other web sites on the Internet, as shown in Figure 10-6. As with the web proxies and caches, somebody looking at their log file sees a request coming in from the anonymous web browsing service, but they can't track the request back beyond that without asking the company operating the proxy for help. But unlike an ISP that might operate a proxy or a cache, the anonymous service guarantees that they will not keep any log files, so there's no way they can render assistance in the event of a lawsuit or a court order.

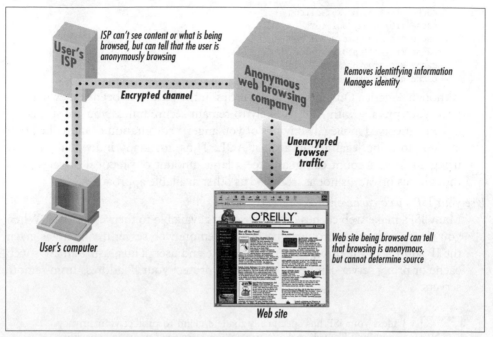

Figure 10-6. An anonymous web browsing service acts like a proxy server or a cache, except that no records are kept by the operator

There are several anonymous web browsing services available today, each with its own special twist.

Anonymizer.com

Anonymizer.com was one of the first anonymous web browsing services. Unlike other services, Anonymizer requires no special software to be installed on your computer and no configuration changes to be made. Instead, users click to the web site *http://www.anonymizer.com/* and enter the URL of the site that they wish to visit. The Anonymizer server fetches the web page and displays it within your browser. What's particularly clever about Anonymizer is that it rewrites the URLs for images and links that it finds in the downloaded HTML, so that when you click on a link, it continues to fetch subsequent web pages through the anonymous web browsing services.

For example, if the Anonymizer finds this HTML tag on a web page:

```
<a href="http://www.simson.net/">Simson's home page</a>
```

it might rewrite the URL to be this:

```
<a href="http://anon.free.anonymizer.com/http://www.simson.net/">Simson's home
page</a>
```

When we clicked on the link, the following entry showed up in our web server log:

```
anon-ascella.proxy.anonymizer.com - - [13/May/2001:16:01:58 -0400] "GET / HTTP/1.
0" 200 18581 "-" "Mozilla/4.0  (TuringOS; Turing Machine; 0.0)"
```

Figure 10-7 shows a web page viewed through the Anonymizer. Anonymizer.com operates both a free service and a commercial service. The free service is slow and subsidized by commercials (which are shown to you anonymously). As of May 2001, the commercial service was roughly $5/month. Anonymizer also offers a *secure tunneling* service, which gives you a cryptographic tunnel between your browser and the anonymizer server. This tunnel prevents your ISP or others from seeing the contents of the traffic between your computer and Anonymizer.

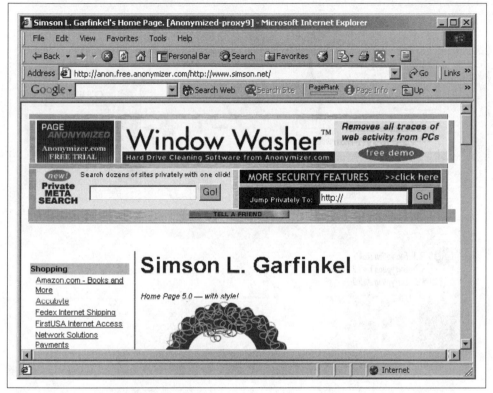

Figure 10-7. The Anonymizer web privacy service uses URL rewriting to provide anonymous web browsing

Freedom, by Zero Knowledge Systems

The ZKS Freedom system takes a more cautious, but also a more expensive, approach than Anonymizer to providing anonymous web browsing. Instead of running all web traffic through a single server, which might be compromised by its owner, the Freedom Network is designed so that each packet is sent through at least three separate servers, each one operated by a different organization (and in many cases, each one in a different country or political entity), as shown in Figure 10-8. When a person using the Freedom Network starts up his computer, the user's client identifies a path through the Freedom Network that encrypted communications will follow. Each packet sent over the Freedom Network is encrypted with three distinct layers of encryption. The packets are sent from the user's computer to the first computer in the path. The first computer decrypts the outer cryptographic shell and then passes the packet to the second server. The second server decrypts the middle cryptographic shell and passes the packet to the third server. The third server decrypts the innermost cryptographic shell and sends the packet to its ultimate destination.

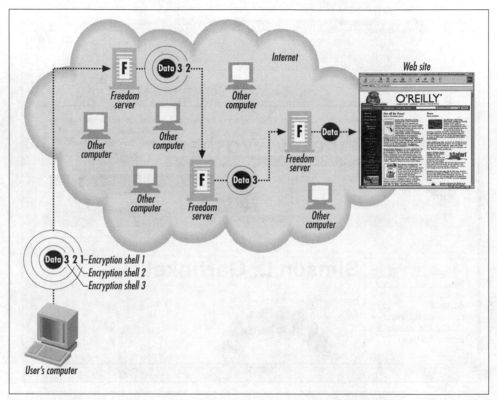

Figure 10-8. Each packet of data sent through the Freedom Network is encrypted with three distinct layers of encryption

In addition to anonymous browsing and chat, the Freedom Network offers "untraceable encrypted email." The Freedom Internet Privacy Suite control panel can keep track of multiple identities, which ZKS calls *nyms*, to the point of filling out different "names" and "addresses" on web-based forms when different nyms are being employed. Each nym can have its own set of cookies or, alternatively, have cookies blocked.

The system is quite comprehensive. The cost is currently $49.95 per year, which includes 5 nyms.

safeWeb

safeWeb is an anonymous web browsing service that is similar to Anonymizer. com. The key differences are that safeWeb is free (supported by non-tracking banner advertisements), it uses SSL encryption to prevent eavesdropping, and it has more customization capabilities (see Figure 10-9).

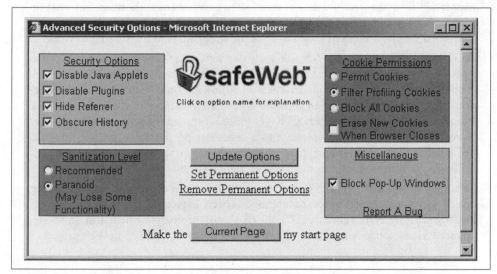

Figure 10-9. safeWeb's customization panel allows you to control how much information about your computer is revealed when you browse "anonymously"

Secure Email

Despite the attention that is now being paid to topics such as cookies, advertisements, and anonymous browsing, these are all relative newcomers to a privacy issue that dominated the field of internet security for much of the 1990s—the sending of encrypted email.

Today, email carries some of our most confidential information. Yet basic email, as a communications medium, is riddled with poor security. Consider these potential email threats:

- By sending an email message, you might reveal your name, your address, your location, or other personal information that you would rather keep confidential.

- Your email message might be monitored by your employer or your ISP without your permission.

- Your email message could be delivered to the wrong recipient, either because of an error with the mail system, or because you inadvertently selected the wrong recipient from your mail program's address book.

Triangle Boy

Anonymous web browsing services like Anonymizer.com and SafeWeb give users a great way to hide their identity from the web sites that they are viewing. And when you combine these services with SSL link encryption, they are a powerful system for hiding your tracks from the watchful gaze of your ISP or government authorities. But what do you do when you are a dissident in a country like China or Saudi Arabia where the state-controlled ISPs have blocked access to all of the anonymous web browsing services?

This is the problem that safeWeb's Triangle Boy service seeks to solve. Triangle Boy is a network of lightweight "packet reflectors" located around the Internet. The network is operated by companies and individuals who have reasonably fast network connections and who are committed to allowing unrestricted Internet access from less-than-free regimes. If you are in a region that is locked from accessing safeWeb's primary server, all you need to do is connect to a computer on the Triangle Boy network. Because the whole thing is encrypted with SSL, there's no way for your ISP or its controlling government to intercept and decode the message.

Triangle Boy is a great help to human rights workers and democracy advocates, but one of the project's chief sources of funding has been, in fact, the United States Central Intelligence Agency. In February 2001, the CIA's non-profit investment arm, In-Q-Tel, invested $1 million in SafeWeb to support Triangle Boy and other SafeWeb projects.[a]

a. http://www.technews.com/news/01/162113.html

- Your email message could "bounce" into a postmaster mailbox—possibly because a computer between your computer and the recipient's computer was unable to properly relay the message.

- Once your email message is delivered, it might be seen by someone other than the intended recipient. (For example, somebody could gain unauthorized access to your correspondent's computer, or the message might be turned over to an attorney as part of a discovery process.)

- The intended recipient might forward the email message to someone against your wishes.

- You might leave a job where you had been using your old email address for both business and personal email. Your former employer decides not to forward your old email to your new address, but to have it bounce—or, worse yet, to have it delivered to the mailbox of somebody else in the organization.

- Your email might be maliciously edited while it sits on your correspondent's mail server, before it is picked up by the intended recipient.

Some of these threats may seem improbable, but in fact every one of these threats has happened to the authors of this book over the past decade! These are not hypothetical threats—they are real risks that we are all living with today.

At the same time, none of these threats are insurmountable; all of them can be solved with the correct application of technology and procedure, as we will explain.

Hotmail, Yahoo Mail, and Other Web-Based Email Services

One of the simplest ways to improve your email privacy is to use a web-based email provider. These systems provide free or low-cost email accounts that you can check from anywhere on the Internet. Because they are not associated with a particular ISP or employer, they make good choices for semi-permanent email addresses.* When combined with anonymous browsing services, web-based email can provide private and virtually untraceable email.

Web-based email systems are not without their dangers. Some of the problems that you may encounter with these systems include:

- Using these services gives the email provider complete, unrestricted access to your email. For many people this isn't an issue, but for some it's a serious concern.
- Few of these services have provisions for encrypting email. As a result, there are no protections against mail that is accidentally delivered to the wrong address. There are also no protections against search warrants, subpoenas, and rogue employees at the email provider itself.
- As most of the email providers do not support SSL encryption, your mail is susceptible to interception by a network monitoring device located on your local area network or at your ISP.
- Some of the web-based providers will attach advertisements to the bottom of your outgoing email messages.

Despite these drawbacks, the careful and selective use of web-based email can dramatically improve email privacy for many individuals. And because it takes less than five minutes to set up a free email account, web-based systems make it practical to create an email address for a single purpose, use it, and then discard it.

Hushmail

Hushmail is a web-based email provider with a difference (see Figure 10-10). Unlike Hotmail, Yahoo Mail, and the others, Hushmail encrypts all email messages passing

---

* Other good choices for semi-permanent email addresses are professional organizations and university alumni organizations, many of which now offer "email forwarding for life." Instead of providing mailboxes, these organizations provide email addresses that you can set up to forward to a specific ISP or web-based email provider that you happen to be using at a particular time.

through the system so that the messages cannot be read by anybody, not even by Hushmail's staff. Unlike other web-based mail systems, even if Hushmail is served with a police warrant or sued in a civil court, the company cannot provide unencrypted email messages.

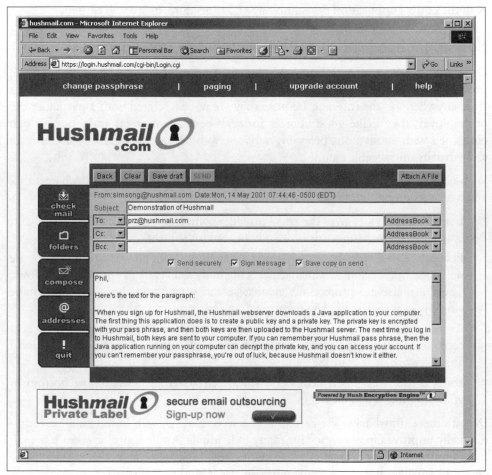

Figure 10-10. Hushmail looks like other web-based mail systems, but it is much more secure because all messages are encrypted and decrypted on the end user machines, rather than the server

Hushmail can provide this level of security because the unencrypted email messages are never present on the company's servers. That's because Hushmail's encryption doesn't take place on the Hushmail servers—it takes place instead on each user's computer (see Figure 10-11).

When you sign up for Hushmail, the Hushmail web server downloads a Java application to your computer. The first thing this application does is to create a public key

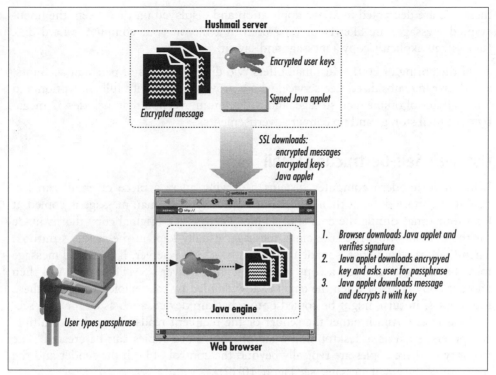

Figure 10-11. Encryption in the Hushmail system happens inside a browser on the end user's computer

and a private key. The private key is encrypted with your passphrase, and then both keys are uploaded to the Hushmail server. The next time you log in to Hushmail, both keys are sent to your computer. If you can remember your Hushmail pass-phrase, then the Java application running on your computer can decrypt the private key, and you can access your account. If you can't remember your passphrase, you're out of luck, because Hushmail doesn't know it either.

Hushmail is as easy to use as other web-based mail systems. The encryption is completely automatic. When you send email to another Hushmail user, the system automatically downloads the user's key from the Hushmail server and uses this key to encrypt the message that you are sending them. When you are sent encrypted mail, the system automatically decrypts the message before displaying it.[*]

While Hushmail is easy to use, the fact that the unencrypted messages never appear on Hushmail's servers makes the system very secure. And because the Hushmail

---

[*] You can also use Hushmail to exchange email with the wider Internet, but as of May 2001 the system does not encrypt these messages. Hushmail plans to adopt the OpenPGP standard for exchanging email messages with non-Hushmail users.

messages are decrypted in a Java application and displayed on the screen, the unencrypted messages are likewise never stored in a file on your computer's hard disk (unless you explicitly copy a message and save it).

As of the spring of 2001, Hushmail offers two different kinds of personal accounts: an advertising-subsidized free service, which provides users with full encryption and 5 megabytes of online mail storage, and a "Premium" version that includes 32 megabytes of mail storage and no banner advertisements.

Omniva's Self-Destructing Email

With many modern computer systems, throwing away a piece of email can frequently be more difficult than holding onto it. A typical email message is copied at least four times during the course of its life. There is the original copy that is made for the person who writes the email message, usually kept in the sender's outbox. Then there is a copy that is made by the sender's SMTP server. If the email message moves across the Internet, a copy is made at the receiver's SMTP server. And then another copy is made when the email is downloaded by the recipient. Each of these four copies, in turn, might be copied onto a backup device, such as a tape or a second hard disk. And if either the sender or the recipient reads the mail on multiple computers, such as a desktop and a laptop, still more copies can be created. The majority of these copies are typically beyond the control of both the sender and the recipient of the email message (see Figure 10-12).

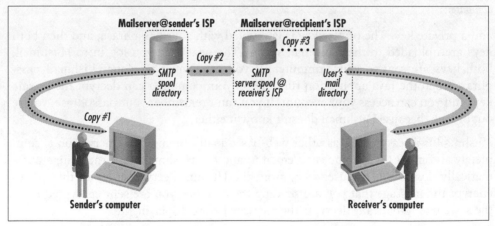

Figure 10-12. The typical email message is copied at least four times—and sometimes many more

These multiple copies of email messages on different computer systems can be a boon to investigators, attorneys in litigation, and nosy coworkers. In the 1980s, copies of Oliver North's email messages that were discovered by government investigators on backup tapes proved essential in unraveling the Iran-Contra affair, the

Reagan Administration's "arms-for-hostages" scandal. Email messages again proved invaluable to government investigators during the anti-trust investigation of Microsoft in the 1990s. And when Northwest Airlines and its workers were engaged in a labor dispute in February 1999, the airlines accused its workers of staging an illegal "sick-out." The airline got a court order to seize the home computers of more than 20 workers who were suspected of coordinating the job action.

Because of their candor, detail, and voluminousness, email messages are now routinely sought in divorce proceedings, civil litigation, and criminal trials. It's illegal to destroy email and other evidence after a lawsuit or court action has been initiated, but it's completely legal to proactively destroy documents if such destruction is part of routine business practices. For this reason, many companies and government offices have instituted mandatory *document retention* or *document destruction policies*. These policies specify what kinds of documents should be retained, how long they should be kept, and when documents should be destroyed. But many of these policies are openly ignored because they are, in practice, so difficult to implement.

In a free and open society, it feels somewhat odd to be advocating that documents should be routinely destroyed—indeed, the examples of Oliver North and Microsoft point out the dangers of a well-heeded document destruction policy. But the systematic destruction of documents may be one of the few ways to assure long-term privacy for routine communications. Email presents a particular challenge to document destruction policies because it is copied in so many places. Once an email message is copied onto a magnetic tape and that tape is put into a safe deposit box, there is no practical way to recover the message for routine deletion.

Omniva Policy Systems is an email destruction system that overcomes this seemingly impossible challenge with a seemingly counterintuitive solution. When a user creates a message using the Omniva system, the user chooses an expiration date for the email. The Omniva email system then creates a unique encryption key for the message, encrypts the message, and sends both the encryption key and the expiration date to Omniva's servers. The encrypted message is then sent to the recipients (see Figure 10-13). By relying on cryptography, the Omniva system doesn't try to destroy all of the copies of an email that have been made. Instead, the system grants conditional access to email messages only for a limited time (see Figure 10-14).

When the recipient of the message tries to read the message, his mail client contacts the Omniva server and downloads the key. The mail client decrypts the encrypted message and displays it. But the client doesn't save the decrypted message on the disk. If the recipient wants to read the message again in a few days, he needs to download another copy of the decryption key (see Figure 10-15). This whole process happens automatically whenever the mail message is viewed. Once a message has gone past an expiration time, the key is deleted so that the message can no longer be read.

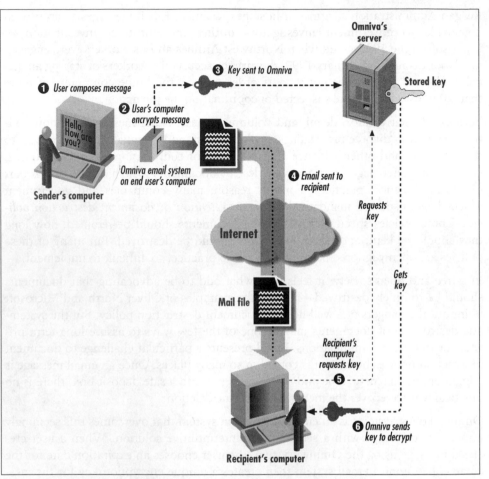

Figure 10-13. The Omniva email system relies on encryption and a central key server to assure that email messages will be unintelligible after their expiration date.

Omniva email is not perfect. Forwarded email messages retain the self-destruction capability, but if you manually copy a message out of a window and paste it into a second, the new message will not automatically self-destruct. You can always print an email message, and unless you then shred the paper, the printed copy will be around for a long time. But the Omniva email system does make it possible for mutually consenting parties to implement email destruction policies, with different expiration times, on a message-by-message basis.

Furthermore, the Omniva email system does significantly increase the privacy that is afforded to email users, because email messages that are accidentally bounced into postmaster's mail boxes or saved on magnetic backup tapes are unintelligible without the decryption key.

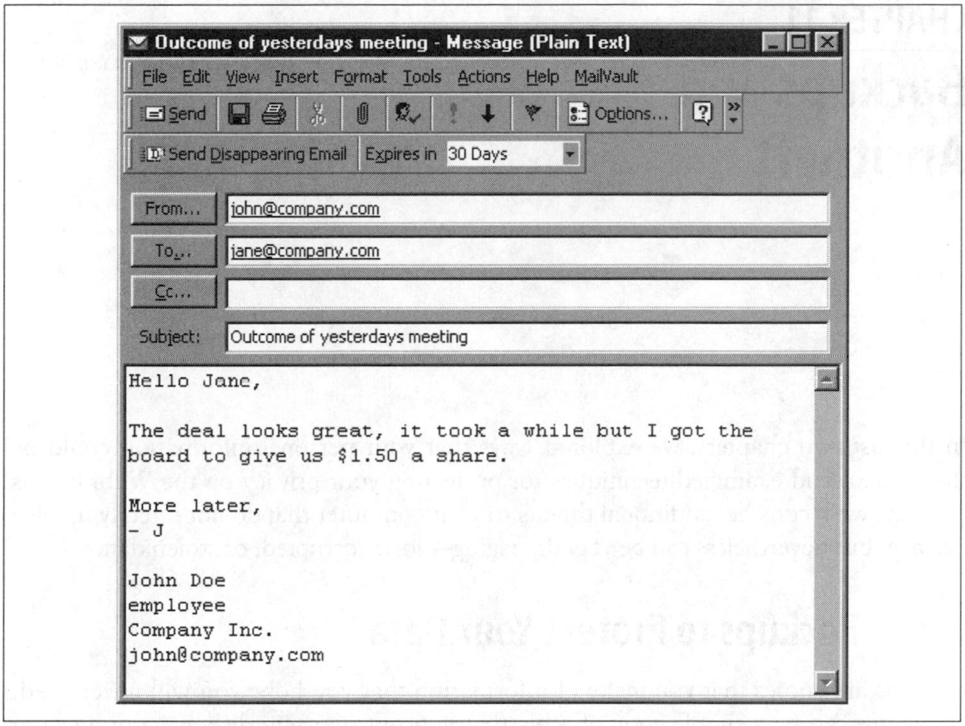

Figure 10-14. A message composed with the Omniva system message is given an expiration date

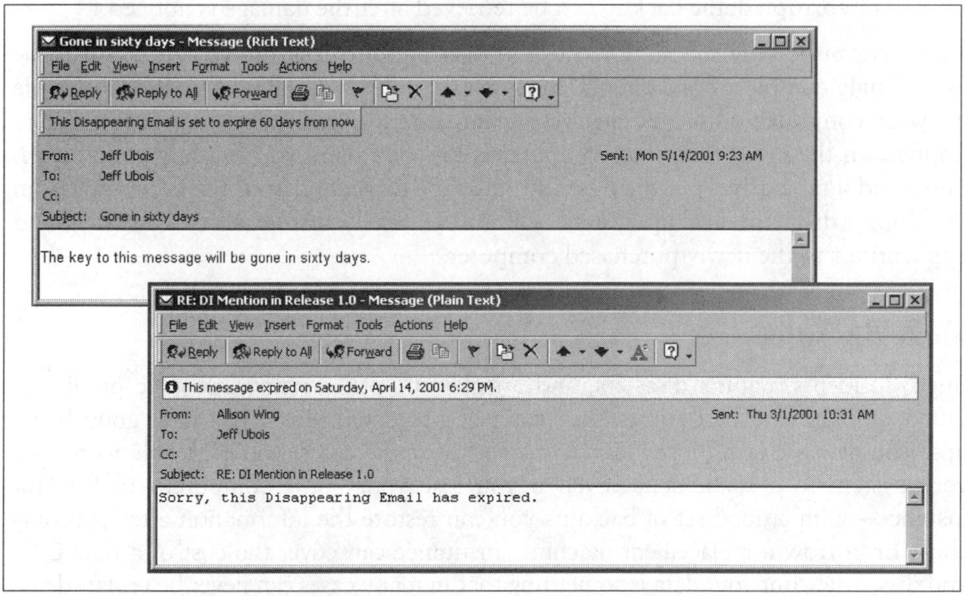

Figure 10-15. Viewing a message on Omniva Email depends on whether the message has expired. This example shows a message that hasn't expired (left) and another message that has (right).

CHAPTER 11

Backups and Antitheft

In this chapter:
- Using Backups to Protect Your Data
- Preventing Theft

In the last two chapters, we explored ways that your personal information could be threatened, and examined techniques for protecting your privacy on the Web. In this chapter, we'll consider additional threats to your computer that do not directly involve privacy, but nevertheless can be very damaging—lost, corrupted, or stolen data.

Using Backups to Protect Your Data

Backups are copies that you make of information that you hope you will never need. A backup can be a simple copy of a file that you put on a Zip disk and put away in the top drawer of your desk for safekeeping. If the original file is inadvertently deleted or corrupted, the backup can be retrieved after the damage is noticed.

Backups can be very simple, like the Zip disk in your desk drawer, or they can be exceedingly complex. For example, many backup systems will let you copy every file on your computer onto a 30-gigabyte magnetic tape and create a special "restore floppy." In the event that your computer is lost or stolen, you can buy a new computer and a tape drive, put the tape into the tape drive, and boot the computer from the floppy disk; the backup system will automatically restore all of your files and applications to the newly-purchased computer.

Make Backups!

Bugs, accidents, natural disasters, and attacks on your system cannot be predicted. Often, despite your best efforts, they can't be prevented. But if you have good backups, you at least won't lose your data—and in many cases, you'll be able to restore your system to a stable state. Even if you lose your entire computer—to fire, for instance—with a good set of backups you can restore the information after you purchase or borrow a replacement machine. Insurance can cover the cost of a new CPU and disk drive, but your data is something that in many cases can never be replaced.

Backups and RAID

One of the best ways to protect your data from the failure of a disk is to store all of your data on two or more drives. A few years ago, storing data on multiple spinning platters was a strategy that only well-funded data centers could pursue. But now, thanks to the ever-plummeting cost of storage combined with widespread adoption of "best practices" standards, RAID (Redundant Arrays of Inexpensive Disk) systems have become commonplace on servers and are becoming standard on workstations as well. Systems based on RAID were pioneered in the 1980s. Today, RAID systems are available in four common versions:

RAID 0 (striping)

These systems use two or more hard disks to simulate a single drive that has twice the capacity and twice the speed. The systems work by storing alternating blocks of data on the first drive and the second drive. RAID 0 systems actually decrease the reliability of the disk drive subsystem, because the data stored on the disk becomes unusable if either drive fails.

RAID 1 (mirroring)

These systems store the same data on both drives. Data is written to both drives simultaneously; read operations can be serviced by either drive. As a result, RAID 1 systems tend to have significantly improved performance when compared with a single-drive system.

RAID 5 (parity)

These systems store N drives worth of data on N+1 drives, using mathematical functions so that the data can be recovered in the event that any drive fails. That is, three drives can be used to store two drives worth of data, or six drives can be used to store five drives worth of data. RAID 5 offers a lower cost per byte than RAID 1, but it has significantly decreased performance.

RAID 0+1

These systems use four disks configured into two mirror sets of two striped drives. These systems thus use four drives to store two disks worth of data, providing the redundancy of RAID 1 with the speed improvement of RAID 0. This is the most expensive form of RAID.

If you have a RAID system, you may be tempted not to do backups at all: after all, the redundant drives protect against hardware failure. But RAID does not protect against accidental file deletion, theft, or fire. For this reason, even if you have a RAID system, you should still perform regular backups.

Why Make Backups?

Backups are important only if you value the work that you do on your computer. If you use your computer as a paperweight, then you don't need to make backups. Years ago, making daily backups was a common practice because computer hardware would often fail for no obvious reason. A backup was the only protection against data loss. Today, hardware failure is still a good reason to back up your system. Hard disk failures are a random process: even though a typical hard disk will now last for five years or more, an organization that has 20 or 30 hard disks can expect a significant drive failure every few months. Drives frequently fail without warning—sometimes only a few days after they have been put into service. It's prudent, therefore, to back up your computer after you install its operating system and your basic load of applications. Not only will this first backup allow you to analyze your system after an attack to see what has been modified, but it will also save the time of rebuilding your system from scratch in the event of a hardware failure.

Backups are important for a number of other reasons as well:

Archival information

Backups provide archival information that lets you compare current versions of software and databases with older ones. This capability lets you determine what you've changed—intentionally or by accident. It also provides an invaluable resource if you ever need to go back and reconstruct the history of a project, either as an academic exercise or to provide evidence in a court case. Being able to review multiple backups to determine how a document changed over time, when it changed, or who changed it, is probably the most important use of backups.

User error

Users—especially novice users—accidentally delete their files. With graphical user interfaces, it's all too easy to accidentally drag one folder on top of another with the same name. Making periodic backups makes it possible to restore files that are accidentally deleted, protecting users from their own mistakes. Mistakes aren't limited to novices, either. More than one expert has accidentally overwritten a file by issuing an incorrect editor or compiler command, or accidentally reformatting a Unix file system by typing *newfs/dev/ad0c* instead of *newfs/dev/da0c*.

System-staff error

Sometimes your system staff may make a mistake. For example, a system administrator deleting old accounts might accidentally delete an active one.

Hardware failure

Hardware breaks from time to time, often destroying data in the process: disk crashes are not unheard of. If you have a backup, you can restore the data on a different computer system.

Software failure

Many application programs, including Microsoft Word, Excel, and Access, have been known to occasionally corrupt their data files. If you have a backup and your application program suddenly deletes half of your 500 × 500-cell spreadsheet, you will be able to recover your data.

Electronic break-ins and vandalism

Computer attackers and malicious viruses frequently alter or delete data. Your backups may prove invaluable in recovering from a break-in or a virus incident.

Theft

Computers are easy to steal and all too easy to sell. Cash from your insurance company can buy you a new computer, but it can't bring back your data. Not only should you make a backup, but you should also take it out of your computer and store it in a safe place—there are all too many cases of tape drives whose backups were stolen along with the computer system.

Natural disaster

Sometimes rain falls and buildings are washed away. Sometimes the earth shakes and buildings are demolished. Fires are also very effective at destroying the places where we keep our computers. Mother Nature is inventive and not always kind. As with theft, your insurance company can buy you a new computer, but it can't bring back your data.

Other disasters

Sometimes Mother Nature isn't to blame: truck bombs explode; gas pipes leak and cause explosions; and coffee spills through ventilation holes. We even know of one instance in which EPA inspectors came into a building and found asbestos in the A/C ducts, so they forced everyone to leave within 10 minutes, and then sealed the building for several months!

With all of these different uses for backups, it's not surprising that there are so many different forms of backups in use today. Here are just a few:

- Copy your critical files to a floppy disk or a high-density removable magnetic or optical disk.
- Copy your disk to a spare or "mirror" disk.
- Make periodic Zip or "tar" archives of your important files. You can keep these backups on your primary system or you can copy them to another computer, possibly at a different location.
- Make backups onto magnetic or optical tape.
- Back up your files over a network or over the Internet to another computer that you own, or to an Internet backup service. Some of these services can be exceedingly sophisticated. For example, the services can examine the MD5 checksums of your files and only back up files that are "unique." Thus, if you have a thousand computers, each with a copy of Microsoft Office, none of those application files need to be copied over the network in order to add them to the backup.

What Should You Back Up?

There are two approaches to computer backup systems:

1. Back up everything that is unique to your system—user accounts, data files, and important system directories that have been customized for your computer. This approach saves tape and decreases the amount of time that a backup takes; in the

event of a system failure, you recover by reinstalling your computer's operating system, reloading all of the applications, and then restoring your backup tapes.

2. Back up everything, because restoring a complete system is easier than restoring an incomplete one, and tape/CD-ROM is cheap.

We recommend the second approach. While some of the information you back up is already "backed up" on the original distribution disks or tapes you used to load the system onto your hard disk, distribution disks or tapes sometimes get lost. Furthermore, as your system ages, programs get installed in the operating system's reserved directories as security holes get discovered and patched, and as other changes occur. If you've ever tried to restore your system after a disaster,* you know how much easier the process is when everything is in the same place.

For this reason, we recommend that you store *everything* from your system (and that means everything necessary to reinstall the system from scratch—every last file) onto backup media at regular, predefined intervals. How often you do this depends on the speed of your backup equipment and the amount of storage space allocated for backups. You might want to do a total backup once a week, or you might want to do it only twice a year. *But please do it!*

Types of Backups

There are three basic types of backups:

Level-zero backup
> Makes a copy of your original system. When your system is first installed, before people have started to use it, back up every file and program on the system. Such a backup can be invaluable after a break-in.†

Full backup
> Makes a copy to the backup device of every file on your computer. This method is similar to a day-zero backup, except that you do it on a regular basis.

Incremental backup
> Makes a copy to the backup device of only those items in a filesystem that have been modified after a particular event (such as the application of a vendor patch) or date (such as the date of the last full backup).

Full backups and incremental backups work together. A common backup strategy is:

- Make a full backup on the first day of every other week.

- Make an incremental backup every evening of everything that has been modified since the last full backup.

---

* Imagine having to reapply 75 vendor "jumbo patches" or "hot fixes" by hand, plus all the little security patches you got off the Net and derived from this book, plus all the tweaks to optimize performance—and imagine doing this for each system you manage. Ouch!

† We recommend that you also do such a backup immediately after you restore your system after recovering from a break-in. Even if you have left a hole open and the intruder returns, you'll save a lot of time if you are able to fix the hole in the backup, rather than starting from scratch again.

Most administrators of large systems plan and store their backups by disk drive or disk partition. Different partitions usually require different backup strategies. Some partitions, such as your system partition (if it is separate), should probably be backed up whenever you make a change to them, on the theory that every change that you make to them is too important to lose. You should use full backups with these systems, rather than incremental backups, because they are only usable in their entirety.

On the other hand, partitions that are used for keeping user files are more amenable to incremental backups. Partitions that are used solely for storing application programs really only need to be backed up when new programs are installed or when the configuration of existing programs is changed.

When you make incremental backups, use a rotating set of backup tapes.[*] The backup you do tonight shouldn't write over the tape you used for your backup last night. Otherwise, if your computer crashes in the middle of tonight's backup, you would lose the data on the disk, the data in tonight's backup (because it is incomplete), and the data in last night's backup (because you partially overwrote it with tonight's backup). Ideally, perform an incremental backup once a night, and have a different tape for every night of the week, as shown in Figure 11-1.

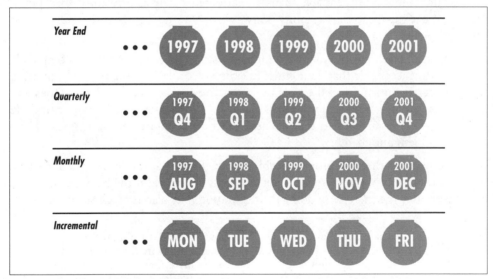

Figure 11-1. An incremental backup

Guarding Against Media Failure

You can use two distinct sets of backup tapes to create a *tandem backup*. With this backup strategy, you create two complete backups (call them A and B) on successive

---

[*] Of course, all types also rotate around a spindle. "Rotating" means that the tapes are rotated with each other according to a schedule.

backup occasions. Then, when you perform your first incremental backup, the "A incremental," you back up all of the files that were created or modified after the last A backup, even if they are on the B backup. The second time you perform an incremental backup, the "B incremental," you write out all of the files that were created or modified since the last B backup (even if they are on the A incremental backup.) This system protects you against media failure, because every file is backed up in two locations. It does, however, double the amount of time that you will spend performing backups.

Some kinds of tapes—in particular, 4mm or 8mm video tape and Digital Audio Tape (DAT)—cannot be reused repeatedly without degrading the quality of the backup. If you use the same tape cartridge for more than a fixed number of backups (usually, 50 or 100), you should get a new one. Be certain to see what the vendor recommends—and don't push that limit. The few pennies you may save by using a tape beyond its useful range will not offset the cost of a major loss.

Try to restore a few files chosen at random from your backups each time, to make sure that your equipment and software are functioning properly. Stories abound about computer centers that have lost disk drives and gone to their backup tapes, only to find them all unreadable. This scenario can occur as a result of bad tapes, improper backup procedures, faulty software, operator error (see the sidebar), or other problems.

At least once a year, you should attempt to restore your entire system completely from backups to ensure that your entire backup system is working properly. Starting with a different, unconfigured computer, see if you can restore all of your tapes and get the new computer operational. Sometimes you will discover that some critical file is missing from your backup tapes. These practice trials are the best times to discover a problem and fix it.

A related exercise that can prove valuable is to pick a file at random, once a week or once a month, and try to restore it. Not only will this reveal if the backups are comprehensive, but the exercise of doing the restoration may also provide some insight.

 We have heard many stories about how the tape drive used to make the backup tapes had a speed or alignment problem. Such a problem results in the tapes being readable by the drive that made them, but unreadable on every other tape drive in the world! Be sure that you try loading your tapes on other drives when you check them.

How Long Should You Keep a Backup?

It may take a week or a month to realize that a file has been deleted. Therefore, you should keep some backup tapes for a week, some for a month, and some for several months. Many organizations make yearly or quarterly backups that they archive indefinitely. After all, tape or CD-ROM is cheap, and *del* is forever. Keeping a yearly

A Classic Case of Backup Horror

Sometimes, the weakest link in the backup chain is the human responsible for making the backup. Even when everything is automated and requires little thought, things can go badly awry. The following was presented to one of the authors as a true story. The names and agency have been omitted for obvious reasons.

It seems that a government agency had hired a new night operator to do the backups of their Unix systems. The operator indicated that she had prior computer operations experience. Even if she hadn't, that was okay—little was needed in this job because the backup was largely the result of an automated script. All the operator had to do was log in at the terminal in the machine room located next to the tape cabinet, start up a command script, and follow the directions. The large disk array would then be backed up with the correct options.

All went fine for several months, until one morning, the system administrator met the operator leaving. She was asked how the job was going. "Fine," she replied. Then the system administrator asked if she needed some extra tapes to go with the tapes she was using every night—he noticed that the disks were getting nearer to full capacity as they approached the end of the fiscal year. He was met by a blank stare and the chilling reply, "What tapes?"

Further investigation revealed that the operator didn't know she was responsible for selecting tapes from the cabinet and mounting them. When she started the command file (using the Unix *dump* program), it would pause while mapping the sectors on disk that it needed to write to tape. She would wait a few minutes, see no message, and assume that the backup was proceeding. She would then retire to the lounge to read.

Meanwhile, the tape program would, after some time, begin prompting the operator to mount a tape and press the return key. No tape was forthcoming, however, and the mandatory security software installed on the system logged out the terminal and cleared the screen after 60 minutes of no typing. The operator would come back some hours later and see no error messages of any kind.

The panicked supervisor immediately started day-zero dumps of all the computer's disks. Fortunately, the system didn't crash during the process. Procedures were changed, and the operator was given more complete training.

How do you know if the people doing *your* backups are doing them correctly?

or a biannual backup "forever" is a small investment in the event that it should ever be needed again.

You may wish to keep on your system an index or listing of the names of the files on your backup tapes. This way, if you ever need to restore a file, you can find the right tape to use by scanning the index, rather than by reading in every single tape. Having a printed copy of these indexes is also a good idea, especially if you keep the online index on a system that may need to be restored!

If you keep your backups for a long period of time, you should be sure to migrate the data on your backups each time you purchase a new backup system. Otherwise, you might find yourself stuck with a lot of tapes that can't be read by anyone, anywhere. This happened in the late 1980s to the MIT Artificial Intelligence Laboratory, which had a collection of research reports and projects from the 1970s on seven-track tape. One day, the lab started a project to put all of the old work online once more. The only problem was that there didn't appear to be a working seven-track tape drive anywhere in the country that the lab could use to restore the data.

Security for Backups

Backups pose a double problem for computer security. On the one hand, your backup tape is your safety net; ideally, it should be kept far away from your computer system so that a local disaster cannot ruin both. On the other hand, the backup contains a complete copy of every file on your system, so the backup itself must be carefully protected.

Physical security for backups

If you use tape drives to make backups, be sure to take the tape out of the drive. One company in San Francisco that made backups every day never bothered removing the cartridge tape from their drive: when their computer was stolen over a long weekend by professional thieves who went through a false ceiling in their office building, they lost everything. "The lesson is that the removable storage media is much safer when you remove it from the drive," said an employee after the incident.

Do not store your backup tapes in the same room as your computer system. Any disaster that might damage or destroy your computers is likely to damage or destroy anything in the immediate vicinity of those computers as well. This rule applies to fire, flood, explosion, and building collapse.

You may wish to consider investing in a fireproof safe to protect your backup tapes. However, the safe should be placed *off site*, rather than right next to your computer system. While fireproof safes do protect against fire and theft, they don't protect your data against explosion, many kinds of water damage, and building collapse.

Be certain that any safe you use for storing backups is actually designed for storing your form of media. One of the fireproof lockboxes from the neighborhood discount store might not be magnetically safe for your tapes. It might be heat-resistant enough for storing paper, but not for storing magnetic tape, which cannot withstand the same high temperatures. Also, some of the generic fire-resistant boxes for paper are designed with a liquid in the walls that evaporates or foams when exposed to heat, to help protect paper inside. Unfortunately, these chemicals can damage the plastic in magnetic tape or CD-ROMs.

Write-protect your backups

After you have removed a backup tape from a drive, do yourself a favor and flip the write-protect switch. A write-protected tape cannot be accidentally erased.

If you are using the tape for incremental backups, you can flip the write-protect switch when you remove the tape, and then flip it again when you reinsert the tape later. If you forget to unprotect the tape, your software will probably give you an error and let you try again. On the other hand, having the tape write-protected will save your data if you accidentally put the wrong tape in the tape drive, or run a program on the wrong tape.

Data security for backups

File protections and passwords protect the information stored on your computer's hard disk, but anybody who has your backup tapes can restore your files (and read the information contained in them) on another computer. For this reason, keep your backup tapes under lock and key.

Several years ago, an employee at a computer magazine pocketed a 4mm cartridge backup tape that was on the desk of the system manager. When the employee got the tape home, he discovered that it contained hundreds of megabytes of personal files, articles in progress, customer and advertising lists, contracts, and detailed business plans for a new venture that the magazine's parent company was planning. The tape also included tens of thousands of dollars worth of computer application programs, many of which were branded with the magazine's name and license numbers. Quite a find for an insider who was setting up a competing publication!

When you transfer your backup tapes from your computer to the backup location, protect the tapes at least as well as you normally protect the computers themselves. Letting a messenger carry the tapes from building to building may not be appropriate if the material on the tapes is sensitive. Getting information from a tape by bribing an underpaid courier, or by knocking him unconscious and stealing it, is usually easier and cheaper than breaching a firewall, cracking some passwords, and avoiding detection online.

The use of encryption can dramatically improve security for backup tapes. However, if you do choose to encrypt your backup tapes, be sure that the encryption key is known by more than one person. You may wish to escrow your key. Otherwise, the backups may be worthless if the only person with the key forgets it, becomes incapacitated, or decides to hold your data for ransom.

Here are some recommendations for storing a backup tape's encryption key:

- Change your keys infrequently if you change them at all. If you do change your keys, you must remember the old ones as well as the new, which probably means writing them all down in the same place. So you don't really get any security from changing the keys in the first place. Physical security of your backup tape should be your first line of defense.

- Store copies of the key on pieces of paper in envelopes. Give the envelopes to each member of your organization's board of directors, or chief officers.

- If your organization uses an encryption system such as PGP that allows a message to be encrypted for multiple recipients, encrypt and distribute the backup encryption key so that it can be decrypted by anyone on the board.

- Alternately, you might consider a secret-sharing system, so that the key can be decrypted by any two or three board members working together, but not by any board member on his own.

Legal Issues

Finally, some firms should be careful about backing up too much information, or holding it for too long. Recently, backup tapes have become targets in lawsuits and criminal investigations. Backup tapes can be obtained by subpoena or during discovery in lawsuits. If your organization has a policy regarding the destruction of old paper files, you should extend this policy to backup tapes as well.

You may wish to segregate potentially sensitive data so that it is stored on separate backup tapes. For example, you can store applications on one tape, pending cases on another tape, and library files and archives on a third.

Back up your data, but back up with caution.

Deciding upon a Backup Strategy

The key to deciding upon a good strategy for backups is to understand the importance and time-sensitivity of your data. As a start, we suggest that the answers to the following questions will help you plan your backups:

- How quickly do you need to resume operations after a complete loss of the main system?

- How quickly do you need to resume operations after a partial loss?

- Can you perform restores while the system is "live"?

- Can you perform backups while the system is "live"?

- What data do you need restored first? Next? Last?

- Of the users you must listen to, who will complain the most if their data is not available?

- What will cause the biggest loss if it is not available?

- Who loses data most often from equipment or human failures?

- How many spare copies of the backups must you have to feel safe?

- How long do you need to keep each backup?
- How much are you willing or able to spend?

Preventing Theft

Computer theft—especially laptop theft—is a growing problem for businesses and individuals alike. The loss of a computer system can be merely annoying or can be an expensive ordeal. But if the computer contains information that is irreplaceable or extraordinarily sensitive, it can be devastating.

Fortunately, by following a small number of simple and inexpensive measures, you can dramatically reduce the chance that your laptop or desktop computer will be stolen.

Understanding Computer Theft

People steal computer systems for a wide variety of reasons. Many computer systems are stolen for resale—either the complete system or, in the case of sophisticated thieves, the individual components, which are harder to trace. Other computers are stolen by people who cannot afford to purchase their own computers. Still others are stolen for the information that they contain, usually by people who wish to obtain the information but sometimes by those who simply wish to deprive the computer's owner of the use of the information. No matter why a computer is stolen, most computer thefts have one common element: opportunity. In most cases, computers are stolen because they have been left unprotected.

Locks

Mobility is one of the great selling points of laptops. It is also the key feature that leads to laptop theft. One of the best ways to decrease the chance of having your laptop stolen is to lock it to a desk, a pipe, or another large object.

Most laptops sold today are equipped with a security slot (Figure 11-2). For less than $50 you can purchase a cable lock that attaches to a nearby object and locks into the security slot. Once set, the lock cannot be removed without either using the key or damaging the laptop case, which makes it very difficult to resell the laptop. These locks prevent most grab-and-run laptop thefts. One of the largest suppliers of laptop locks is Kensington, which holds several key patents, although Kryptonite now makes a line of laptop locks as well.

Tagging

Another way to decrease the chance of theft and increase the likelihood of return is to tag your computer equipment with permanent or semipermanent equipment tags.

Figure 11-2. Most laptops today are sold with a security slot (reprinted with permission of Kensington)

Tags work because it is illegal to knowingly buy or sell stolen property—the tags make it very difficult for potential buyer or seller to claim that they didn't know that the computer was stolen.

The best equipment tags are clearly visible and individually serial-numbered, so that an organization can track its property. A low-cost tagging system is manufactured by Secure Tracking of Office Property (*http://www.stoptheft.com*) (Figure 11-3). These tags are individually serial-numbered and come with a three-year tracking service. If a piece of equipment with a STOP tag is found, the company can arrange to have it sent by overnight delivery back to the original owner. An 800 number on the tag makes returning the property easy.

According to the company, many reports of laptop "theft" in airports are actually cases in which a harried traveler accidentally leaves a laptop at a chair or table when they are running for a flight. The STOP tag makes it easier for airport personnel to return the laptop than to keep it.

STOP tags are affixed to the laptop's case with a special adhesive that is rated for 800 pounds if properly applied. Underneath the tag is a tattoo that will embed itself in plastic cases. Should the tag be removed, the words "Stolen Property" and STOP's 800-number remain visible.

Figure 11-3. The Security Tracking of Office Property (STOP) tag is a simple and effective way to label your laptop (reprinted with permission)

STOP tags are used by many universities, businesses, and the U.S. government. No laptop should be without one.

Laptop Recovery Software and Services

Several companies now sell PC "tracing" programs. The tracing program hides in several locations on a laptop and places a call to the tracing service on a regular basis to reveal its location. The calls can be made using either a telephone line or an IP connection. Normally these "calls home" are ignored, but if the laptop is reported stolen to the tracing service, the police are notified about the location of the stolen property.

Laptop recovery software works quite well, but it typically cannot survive a complete reformat of the computer's hard disk. Of course, as few thieves actually reformat the hard disks of computers that they steal, this usually isn't a problem.

Absolute Software Corporation's Computrace (*http://www.computrace.com*) tracking system costs under $60 and requires a PC running DOS or Windows.

Of course, many of these systems work on desktop systems as well as laptops. Thus, you can protect systems that you believe are at a heightened risk of being stolen.

Awareness

Even if you decide not to invest in antitheft technology, you can still reduce your chances of theft by taking simple precautions:

- Don't leave your laptop unattended in a restaurant, bar, store, or other public place.
- Don't leave your laptop unattended in a hotel room. If you must leave your laptop in a hotel room, lock it in your luggage.
- If you are traveling by cab, don't put your laptop in the trunk of the taxi. Instead, take your laptop out of your luggage and carry it to your destination.
- Don't leave a laptop on a table that is next to a first-floor window, especially if the window is open.

## CHAPTER 12

Mobile Code I: Plug-Ins, ActiveX, and Visual Basic

In this chapter:
- When Good Browsers Go Bad
- Helper Applications and Plug-ins
- Microsoft's ActiveX
- The Risks of Downloaded Code
- Conclusion

Web browsers are amazing technology, but from the very birth of the World Wide Web, they have never provided enough functionality for web developers. Browsers, after all, are static programs: a browser can only display so many types of information in so many ways. For this reason, from the start, web developers have looked for ways to augment the functionality of browsers by asking users to download and run additional programs. Sun, Microsoft, and Netscape have further developed technologies for automatically downloading and running programs on demand. Programs that move in this fashion are frequently called *mobile code*.

Most mobile code behaves as expected. But it doesn't have to. Many programs have bugs in them: running them will occasionally cause your computer to crash. Some programs are downright malicious; they might erase all of the information on your computer's disk, plant a virus, or seek out confidential information stored on your computer and transmit it to a secret location on the Internet. And some companies have used active content to learn the email addresses or browsing history of people who thought that they were anonymously browsing a web site.

Thus, the purveyors of mobile code systems have had to walk a tightrope. They've had to design systems that have tangible benefits for both web publishers and users, while simultaneously limiting the malicious damage that these systems can create. This balance has been tremendously difficult to achieve. All of the mobile code schemes discussed in this chapter have suffered security lapses that would allow a malicious web operator to download programs that could then install viruses or reformat the hard disks of anyone who visited the hostile web site or received the hostile code by email.

Although the majority of mobile code security problems have been quickly fixed, other structural flaws remain. If you are working in a high-security environment, your safest bet is to disable active content technologies and avoid downloading new programs unless the new programs specifically correct a security problem with an application that you have already installed.

When Good Browsers Go Bad

A program that you download and run on your computer can fundamentally change how your computer behaves. After all, web browsers, email programs, and operating systems are nothing more than programs themselves. These programs can be subtly modified or changed by other programs that you download.

This plasticity of modern operating systems and the flexibility created by mobile code is one of the reasons for the great success of the Internet. At the start of the web revolution, early adopters were given copies of web browsers such as Mosaic and Netscape Navigator 0.9 on floppy disks. As newer, better browsers came out, users simply downloaded upgraded programs. Overall, this scheme worked pretty well.

Unfortunately, this plasticity is easy for an attacker to exploit. Code is opaque: it is frequently impossible to understand what a program will do without actually running the program. What's possibly even more frightening is the fact that it's frequently impossible to determine what a program has done *even after you have run it*. Many programs have many ways of hiding their operations, and few computer systems have sufficiently powerful auditing tools.

The goal of many attacks is to be able to run an arbitrary program on the target computer. Once the attacker can specify a program to run, the attacker can use that program to search through the target computer's files, to steal information, and to plant viruses or other programs that will effectively hide the attacker's tracks.

Surprisingly, it isn't hard to get at least a few victims to run a program. Traditionally, one of the easiest ways to get a victim to run a program is to simply email it to a few thousand victims; one of them will surely run it. Another approach is to post the program on a web page and email out the URLs. What's harder is to have a program be run by a specific target, or to arrange for millions of users to run a program, or to have a hostile program in circulation for a long time before someone notices the damage that the program is doing. But as time passes, even these challenges have been conquered.

History is on the side of the attackers. Internet users have been taught to download programs and run them without question. Web browsers, including Netscape Navigator and Internet Explorer, were initially distributed by downloads. And systems that extend the capabilities of these web browsers, such as the RealAudio player and the Adobe Acrobat Reader, are distributed by downloads as well.

As the examples in this section will show, there can be grave consequences to blindly trusting code that you download off the Internet.

Card Shark

In January 1996, a digital payments company called First Virtual Holdings demonstrated a program that was designed to show how easy it is to compromise a consumer's computer system. First Virtual's scientists had created the program to prove that home computers were not sufficiently secure to be trusted with credit card numbers. Instead, the program demonstrated the danger of running untrusted code.

Affectionately called "Card Shark," First Virtual's program was designed to look like a conventional screensaver. But screensavers are interesting programs: on Windows at the time, screensavers had the ability to monitor every keystroke that the user made.

The Card Shark program took advantage of the Windows built-in monitoring ability. Normally, Card Shark would run silently in the background of your computer. If you didn't type on your computer's keyboard for a while, the screen would blank. You could make the screen reappear by typing a few characters. But Card Shark's real purpose was to sniff and capture credit card numbers. While Card Shark was running, the program was silently scanning the computer's keyboard and waiting for a user to type a credit card number.* When the user typed one of these numbers, Card Shark played ominous music, displayed a window on the screen, and informed the user that he or she had been "sharked."

The program's designers at First Virtual said that while Card Shark made its intention clear, another program could be far more subtle. Instead of playing music, the hostile program could encrypt the captured credit card numbers and post them anonymously to a Usenet newsgroup. The program could then be bundled in a popular screensaver and distributed widely on the Internet. The result would be tens of thousands of compromised credit card numbers, with no readily apparent connection. Issuing banks could lose tens of millions of dollars over a weekend to credit card fraud. First Virtual wrote Card Shark to demonstrate the danger of typing credit card numbers into a web browser. Even if the web browser was using SSL to send the encrypted credit card numbers over the Internet, the company argued, the PC computing platform was fundamentally unsecure and unsecurable. A better alternative, claimed the company, was First Virtual's patented payment system that had users register their credit cards by dialing an 800 number with a touch-tone telephone and typing the card's number into a remote computer that was properly secured. Anything else was too risky.

Alas, despite the risks, neither banks nor consumers accepted the First Virtual Payment System, and First Virtual ended up morphing into an email marketing company. Consumers now routinely type credit card numbers into unsecured computers—safe with the knowledge that their liability in the event of fraud is limited to $50—without ever stopping to consider that they could be readily sharked.

David.exe

In January 1997, a scam surfaced involving long distance telephone calls, pornography, and the Internet. The scam involved a web site called *sexygirls.com* that promised

---

* Because of their structure, credit card numbers are exceedingly easy to recognize. For information about this structure, see ""The charge card check digit algorithm" in Chapter 25.

subscribers "free pornography." There was just one catch; to view the pornography, a user first had to download and run a special "viewer" program called *david.exe*.

When the viewer program was downloaded and run, the program disconnected the user's computer from its local dialup Internet service provider, turned off the modem's speaker, and placed an international telephone call to Moldova. Once connected overseas, the user's computer was then reconnected to the Internet and the pornography could be seen.

It turns out that the "free" pornography was actually paid for by the $2 per minute long distance telephone charges, charges that were split between the American telephone company, the Moldovan phone company, and the operators of the *sexygirls. com* web site. Some victims ran up phone bills totaling thousands of dollars—money that they needed to pay to their local phone company or else risk losing telephone service. (A spokesperson for AT&T insisted that the telephone charges would have to be paid, because the calls had in fact been placed. It was later revealed that the phone calls had actually been terminated in Canada, rather than Moldova.)*

The U.S. Federal Trade Commission opened an investigation. A month later, on February 13, 1997, the Federal Trade Commission filed suit against two companies—Audiotex Connection, Inc., Promo Line, Inc., and three individuals in connection with the scam.† The FTC charged the defendants with violating Section 5(a) of the FTC Act, 15 U.S.C. 45(a), which outlaws "unfair or deceptive acts or practices in or affecting commerce." That spring the FTC filed a second suit against a company called Beylen Telecom, Ltd., in conjunction with a similar web site called *erotical2000.com*.

The Sexygirls.com case was the FTC's first case of prosecuting online fraud against consumers, and it went extraordinarily well. That November the defendants in the Sexygirls.com case settled with the FTC. Among the terms of the settlements were these:

- The defendants were prohibited from further representing that consumers could use their software to view "computer images for free," and from offering calls "without posting specific disclosures."

- In all future dealings with phone companies, the defendants were required to receive written or contractual assurance from third parties that the consumers' calls would actually go through to the country indicated.

---

* Eric Greenberg notes that this kind of attack does not require the Internet. A fairly common telephone scam in 1996 was for companies operating phone sex services in the Caribbean to call 800 numbers associated with digital pagers, in an attempt to get the pagers' owners to return calls to the telephone number on the islands. These islands are part of the North American Numbering Plan, so they have regular area codes, similar to telephone numbers in the United States and Canada. But calling these numbers costs many dollars per minute—a charge that is shared between the telephone company and the phone sex operator.

† *http://www.ftc.gov/os/1997/9702/audiotex.htm*

- The defendants would pay approximately $760,000 to AT&T and MCI, which would then issue credits to their customers who had been victimized by the scam.
- The defendants would further pay the FTC $40,000, to refund losses of customers who did not use AT&T or MCI.

The Erotica2000.com case was settled a few months later. Ultimately, all of the 27,000 victims who were defrauded in the two cases received full restitution—a total of $2.14 million dollars.

The Chaos Quicken Checkout

In February 1997, Lutz Donnerhacke, a member of Germany's Chaos Computer Club, demonstrated an ActiveX control that could initiate wire transfers using the European version of the Quicken home banking program. The program worked by starting up a copy of Quicken on the user's computer and recording such a transfer in the user's checking account ledger.

Written in Visual Basic as a demonstration for a television station, the ActiveX control did not attempt to hide its actions. But Donnerhacke said if he had actually been interested in stealing money, he could have made the program much more stealthy.

Unlike credit card charges, there is no $50 liability limit on wire transfers.

ILOVEYOU

On May 4, 2000, a computer worm started spreading like wildfire in corporate and government email systems all over the world. Written in Visual Basic, the program arrived by email—usually sent by a friend—with the subject line "ILOVEYOU". The email consisted of a one-line message, "kindly check the attached LOVELETTER coming from me," and an attachment called *LOVE-LETTER-FOR-YOU.TXT.vbs* (see Figure 12-1). As most Windows systems are configured not to display file extensions, most of the recipients of this message saw only the *LOVE-LETTER-FOR-YOU.TXT* and they opened the attachment.

The attachment was a 292-line Visual Basic Script file (the first lines are shown in Example 12-1). When run, the worm installed itself in the system registry (so that it would rerun every time the computer was booted), sent a copy of itself to every address in the user's Microsoft Outlook address book, and then proceeded to delete every JPEG and MP3 file on the victim's disk drives.

It is difficult to calculate the damage done by the Love Bug. Organizations that had standardized on Microsoft Exchange and Outlook were particularly hard hit, with dozens or hundreds of copies of the worm being sent to every person in their organizations. Email systems were overloaded and crashed. Millions of computers had to be disinfected. And the program, widely distributed, was soon being used as the basis for many copycat worms and viruses.

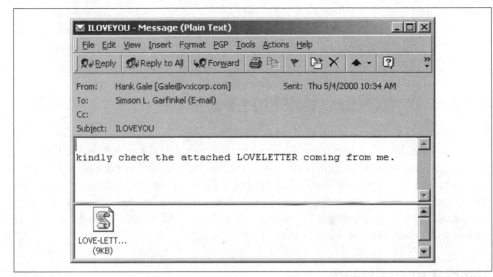

Figure 12-1. Falling in love was never easier than it was on May 4, 2000.

Example 12-1. The first 20 lines of the ILOVEYOU virus

```
rem barok -loveletter(vbe) <i hate go to school>
rem by: spyder / ispyder@mail.com / @GRAMMERSoft Group / = Manila,Philippines
On Error Resume Next
dim fso,dirsystem,dirwin,dirtemp,eq,ctr,file,vbscopy,dow
eq=3D""
ctr=3D0
Set fso =3D CreateObject("Scripting.FileSystemObject")
set file =3D fso.OpenTextFile(WScript.ScriptFullname,1)
vbscopy=3Dfile.ReadAll
main( )
sub main( )
On Error Resume Next
dim wscr,rr
set wscr=3DCreateObject("WScript.Shell")
rr=3Dwscr.RegRead("HKEY_CURRENT_USER\Software\Microsoft\Windows =
Scripting Host\Settings\Timeout")
if (rr>=3D1) then
wscr.RegWrite "HKEY_CURRENT_USER\Software\Microsoft\Windows Scripting =
Host\Settings\Timeout",0,"REG_DWORD"
```

It could have been much worse. After all, most of the computers could be disinfected without manually reinstalling the operating system. If the ILOVEYOU worm had deleted EXE files instead of MP3 files, the cost of recovery would have run into billions of dollars. And if the ILOVEYOU worm had initialized the erasable BIOS that is stored in the EEPROM on many computers, the worm could have caused thousands of companies to fail.

Perhaps most troubling about the ILOVEYOU worm and its copycats is that most of the people who ran the program had not made a conscious choice to run a program that they had downloaded from the Internet. Most of the victims thought that they were merely opening a letter that had been sent to them by a friend or officemate. For years, office workers had been warned about the danger of "opening attachments" from strangers. In the end, those warnings turned out to be worthless.

Helper Applications and Plug-ins

With all of these documented examples (and more) of the damage that downloaded programs can do, why do people continue to download and run programs? One reason is that the web sites that people visit frequently require the downloads. Many web sites are authored with so-called "rich media"—animations, interactive graphics, broadcast audio, streaming video clips—that can only be viewed by using a particular program called a *helper application* or a *plug-in*. Although these programs are widely used, they are not without their risks.

The History of Helpers

The original web browsers could only display a limited number of media types, such as HTML, ASCII text, GIFs, and XBM files. When a web server attempted to download files with an unrecognized MIME type, the web browsers would save the file to the computer's hard disk and launch a registered helper application to process the downloaded data.

Helper applications proved to be a simple and clean way to extend the functionality of web browsers. When you click on a link to hear a song using RealAudio, for instance, your web browser downloads a small file and then gives this file to the RealAudio player. The file contains a pointer to another URL on the Internet from which the RealAudio player should actually download the song. Without this level of indirection, it would be necessary to either have the web browser download the entire song before playing it (as was common practice before the introduction of RealAudio), or else it would have been necessary to modify the web browser itself to make the RealAudio program work.

But helper applications have an important limitation: if a helper application wants to display information on the computer's screen, it has to display that information in its own window—and not in the browser's window. Helper applications also can't ordinarily modify the way that a browser operates.

Plug-ins were introduced with Netscape Navigator as a simple way of overcoming the limitations of helper applications. A plug-in allows a third party to extend the functionality of a browser. One of the simplest uses for plug-ins is to replace helper applications used by web browsers. Instead of requiring that data be specially downloaded, saved in a file, and processed by a helper application, the data can be left in the browser's memory pool and processed directly by the plug-in. But plug-ins are not limited to the display of information. In the fall of 1996, Microsoft released a plug-in that replaced Netscape's Java virtual machine with its own. Network Associates distributes a plug-in that adds PGP email encryption to Netscape Communicator's email package. Macromedia's Flash and Shockwave technologies are implemented with plug-ins. Adobe has a plug-in that makes it possible to view Acrobat files directly in web browsers.

Getting the Plug-In

Traditionally, plug-ins have been manually downloaded by the web user. The plug-ins are then installed when the user runs a special installer or "setup" utility. The plug-in installer puts a copy of the plug-in into a special directory and registers the plug-in directly with the web browser. When new instances of the web browser are started, the program scans its list of registered plug-ins and the file types that each plug-in supports. If the browser downloads a file with a registered file type, the plug-in is automatically loaded into the browser's memory and started.

If the required plug-in is not present, Netscape can give the user the option of automatically downloading and installing the plug-in. In Navigator 2.0, the window that allowed people to install the plug-in had a button labeled "Plug-in Info." Clicking this button caused Navigator to switch to a web page describing the plug-ins currently available and linking to another web page containing Netscape's Plug-in Security warning:

Plug-in Security Implications

When running network applications such as Netscape Navigator, it is important to understand the security implications of actions you request the application to perform. If you choose to download a plug-in, you should know that:

* Plug-ins have full access to all the data on your machine.

* Plug-ins are written and supplied by third parties.

To protect your machine and its documents, you should make certain you trust both the third party and the site providing the plug-in.

If you download from a site with poor security, a plug-in from even a trusted company could potentially be replaced by an alternative plug-in containing a virus or other unwanted behavior.

...Copyright © 1996 Netscape Communications Corporation

Unfortunately, most users didn't have the necessary tools or training to act upon Netscape's message. Confronted with this message, most users simply clicked past the warning page and downloaded the plug-in. Few realized that a plug-in can do far more damage than simply crashing their computer.

Later versions of Netscape did away with the plug-in security warning and just displayed a window with a button labeled "Get the Plug-in" (see Figure 12-2).

Plug-ins for Internet Explorer are Windows dynamic linked libraries (DLLs) that are specially registered in the Windows registry. They are usually installed by small executable files that are downloaded using Internet Explorer. Thus, when you attempt

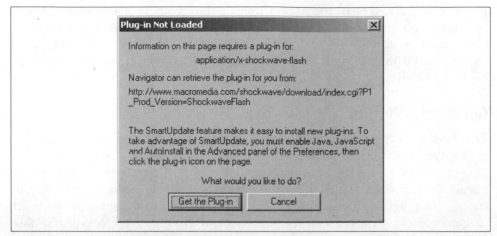

Figure 12-2. The Plug-in Not Loaded page for Netscape Navigator 6.0 suggests that the user enable Java, JavaScript, and AutoInstall, but it does not warn the user about the potential security risks of doing so—or of downloading the plug-in itself.

to install an Internet Explorer plug-in, Internet Explorer displays the standard window that is displayed whenever an executable program is downloaded.

For example, Figure 12-3 shows the panel that IE displays when the Google Toolbar for Internet Explorer is downloaded. This executable is digitally signed using Microsoft's Authenticode technology (see the section "Microsoft's ActiveX" later in this chapter), so Internet Explorer can display the program's given name as well as the distinguished name on the certificate of the public key that is used to verify the signature. Microsoft's warning makes a lot more sense than Netscape's.

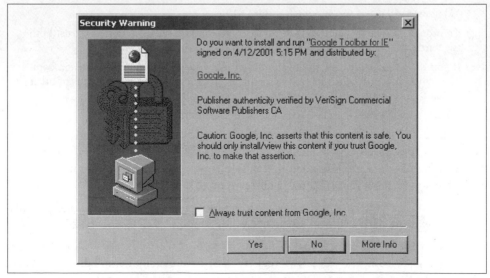

Figure 12-3. Internet Explorer displays this panel when the Google Toolbar for IE is downloaded

Evaluating Plug-In Security

Given the original warning from Netscape and the current warning from Microsoft, what is the proper procedure for evaluating a plug-in to determine if it is safe or not?

Fortunately, most plug-ins aren't hostile applications that will scan your hard drive and delete your files. Most well known plug-ins—such as the plug-in for Adobe Acrobat or Macromedia's Flash—are well behaved programs that do what they advertise and little more. Google, for instance, has two versions of its plug-in: one version that maintains your privacy, and another version that sends the URL of every web page you visit to Google's server so that it can display the "PageRank" of any web page you visit. The difference is clearly disclosed to users.

Security-conscious individuals should simply avoid downloading plug-ins that are not widely used on the Internet. Otherwise, you might end up like the victims in the Sexygirls.com case. But you also need to be sure that the copy of the Adobe Acrobat or Flash plug-in that you are downloading is actually being downloaded from the official Adobe or Macromedia site. Otherwise, you might think that you are down-loading the Flash plug-in, but actually be downloading *david.exe* from Sexygirls!

Even after you have made the decision to download a well known plug-in, you need to be sure that you are actually downloading the plug-in that you think you are downloading! You also may wish to verify that no vulnerabilities have been discovered with the plug-in itself. There have been cases of vulnerabilities being found in widely used plug-ins that would allow an attacker to use the plug-ins to compromise the security of the plug-in's users.

There are many ways your computer might be damaged by a plug-in. For example:

- The plug-in might be a truly malicious program, ready to damage your computer when you make the mistake of downloading it and running it. It might seek out credit card numbers, make your computer dial expensive phone numbers, or encrypt your hard disk and demand a ransom.

- The plug-in might be a legitimate plug-in, but a copy might have been modified in some way to exhibit new dangerous behaviors. For example, the plug-in might change your default security settings, or disable your browser's ability to validate digital signatures.

- There might not be a malicious byte of code in your plug-in's executable, but there might be a bug that can be misused by someone else against your best interests.

- The plug-in might implement a general-purpose programming language that can subsequently be misused by an attacker.

Once you have downloaded and run a plug-in, there's really no way to protect your computer against these attacks. (Some vendors have developed what they claim are "sandboxes" for mobile code, but experience with these programs is not consistent.)

It is nearly impossible to determine if a plug-in has hidden security problems. That's because plug-ins are provided precompiled and without source code. Unless you work for the company that creates the plug-in, it is usually not possible to inspect the actual plug-in's source code. Instead, you must trust the company that makes the plug-in and hope the people there have your best interests at heart. As the Sexygirls. com case shows, that's not always a valid assumption.

What's worse, there is no safety in numbers: simply because a plug-in works well for others, that doesn't mean that the plug-in will work safely for you. It is fairly trivial to create a program that behaves one way for most computer users but another way for a particular target. Such a program could also be programmed to cover its tracks. If you are the victim of a targeted plug-in attack and you do notice a problem, you might be more likely to ascribe it to a passing bug or strange interaction because no one else will ever report it.

Microsoft's ActiveX

ActiveX is a collection of technologies, protocols, and APIs developed by Microsoft that are used for automatically downloading executable machine code over the Internet. The code is bundled into a single file called an *ActiveX control* and the file has the extension OCX. You can think of an ActiveX control as a self-installing plug-in.

ActiveX controls are automatically downloaded when Internet Explorer encounters a web page containing an <OBJECT> tag that references an ActiveX control. Depending on the current setting for Internet Explorer, these tags either are ignored or cause software to be downloaded. If the control is downloaded (again depending on the security setting of Internet Explorer), the control may be run directly, or the user may be prompted as to whether the control should or should not be run. This process is shown in Figure 12-4.

ActiveX is an extraordinarily powerful technology. Because raw machine code is downloaded and run, the ActiveX controls can do anything—from displaying a new file type to upgrading your computer's operating system!

Despite the similarities between ActiveX controls and plug-ins, there are a few significant differences:

- ActiveX applets have been used for much more than plug-ins. Whereas plug-ins are primarily used to extend a web browser so that it can accommodate a new document type, ActiveX controls have also been used for:
  — Upgrading systems (e.g., Microsoft's Windows Update)
  — Performing flash upgrades to ROM BIOS chips
  — Providing conventional Windows applications within a "browser" interface (e.g., Siebel's ActiveX Data Control Interface)

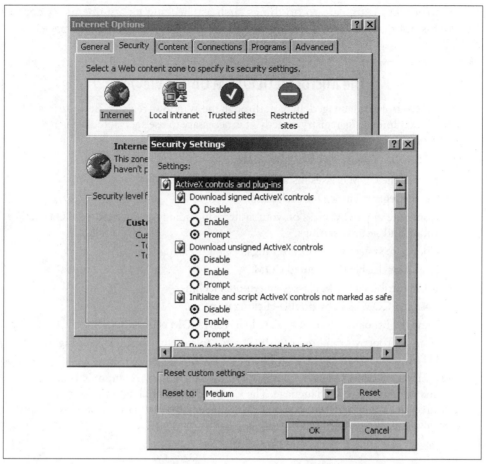

Figure 12-4. Internet Explorer's security settings determine whether ActiveX controls will be downloaded and how they will be run.

- Every ActiveX control is given a unique Class Identifier (CLSID). This key is assigned by the developer's computer when the control is first created. For example, the Microsoft Calendar control has the key {B196B288-BAB4-101A-B69C-00AA00341D07}.

- ActiveX controls are downloaded and run automatically, while plug-ins need to be manually installed, even when they are "automatically" downloaded.

- By default, Internet Explorer will not run an ActiveX control that is not digitally signed with a public key that has a matching "software publisher's certificate."

- For a control to be invokable from a web page, the ActiveX control must be marked "safe for scripting." Authors of controls that are marked "safe for scripting" promise that they have implemented a "sandbox" architecture in which the control takes extra care to do things such as checking its arguments. A control that is not marked "safe for scripting" cannot be invoked from a web page.

The Microsoft OLE/COM Object Viewer

ActiveX controls are managed, in part, through the Windows registry. Because it is difficult to manipulate the registry directly, it is necessary to use special tools, such as the Microsoft OLE/COM Object Viewer.

The OLE/COM Object Viewer allows you to:

- Browse the COM classes installed on your machine.
- See the registry entries for each class.
- Configure any COM class on your system, including the Distributed COM activation and security settings.
- Configure systemwide COM settings.
- Enable or disable Distributed COM.
- Run Distributed COM classes on remote machines.
- Test any COM class by double-clicking its name.
- View the list of interfaces associated with any COM class supports.
- Copy a properly formatted <OBJECT> tag to the clipboard for inserting into an HTML document.

The OLE/COM Object Viewer works with both WIN32 native components and components written in the Java language. The viewer is distributed with the Windows NT Resource Kit. The executable can also be downloaded from *http://www.microsoft.com/ Com/resources/oleview.asp*.

ActiveX's history has been somewhat colored by Microsoft's attempt to position it as an alternative to Java during the "browser wars" of the late 1990s. At the time, much of the developer and academic community's attention was focused on the alleged portability and security that was provided by the trendy Java language (see Chapter 13). These people attacked ActiveX, correctly pointing out that it was neither portable nor secure, nor could it be.

Today it is clear that ActiveX really isn't an alternative to Java, nor was it a weapon against Netscape. ActiveX is instead a tool for making the client-side applications written for the Windows API a more integral part of the World Wide Web—and in the process making the Web somewhat less useful for computers running other operating systems. And ActiveX certainly isn't a weapon against Navigator, as there are now plug-ins that allow ActiveX controls to be run directly on Navigator itself.[*]

---

[*] *http://www.esker.com/online/eskerplus_v3/eskerplus30plugin.htm*

Indeed, ActiveX controls can even be written in Java! Controls written in Java can have restricted access to your computer system, based on Java's access control model, or they can have the same unrestricted access to your computer as controls written in C++.

The <OBJECT> Tag

ActiveX controls are invoked by web pages that contain the <OBJECT> tag. The parameters to the tag specify where the ActiveX control is downloaded from and the class ID that is to be run. Following the <OBJECT> tag are named parameters that are passed to the ActiveX control once it starts executing.

For example, here is an <OBJECT> tag that displays a movie using the Macromedia's Flash ActiveX applet:

```
<OBJECT classid="clsid:D27CDB6E-AE6D-11cf-96B8-444553540000"
 codebase="http://active.macromedia.com/flash2/cabs/swflash.cab#version=4,0,0,0"
 ID=master_ie WIDTH=100% HEIGHT=100%>
<PARAM NAME=movie VALUE="master_ie.swf">
<PARAM NAME=loop VALUE=false>
<PARAM NAME=menu VALUE=false>
<PARAM NAME=quality VALUE=high>
<PARAM NAME=bgcolor VALUE=#000000>
<EMBED src="master_ie.swf" loop=false menu=false quality=high bgcolor=#000000
               WIDTH=100% HEIGHT=100% TYPE="application/x-shockwave-flash"
               PLUGINSPAGE="http://www.macromedia.com/shockwave/download/index.
cgi?P1_Prod_Version=ShockwaveFlash">
</EMBED>
</OBJECT>
```

When the <OBJECT> tag is encountered by a web browser that implements the ActiveX protocol, the browser first checks the class ID to determine if the control is already present on the system. If so, it is run with the given parameters. If not, the browser downloads the control, optionally verifies the control using a digital signature mechanism, loads it into the browser's address space, sets up the parameters provided by the HTML page, and finally executes the code. The process is depicted in Figure 12-5.

Netscape Navigator 4.0 and above use the same <OBJECT> tags for downloading plug-ins. With the exception of Authenticode validation, described in the next section, Netscape plug-ins are now essentially ActiveX controls.

Authenticode

The power and the danger of ActiveX is that downloaded applets basically have the run of your system. Microsoft's engineers didn't think that this was a problem, because consumers routinely run programs that arrive preinstalled with their computer or that are purchased in stores.

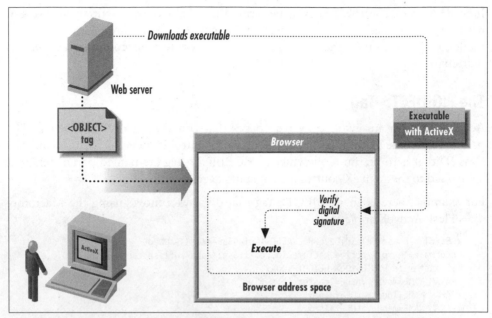

Figure 12-5. ActiveX controls are composed of executable code that is downloaded from a web server and run on a local computer

But there is a fundamental difference between a program that you buy in the store and ones that you download over the Internet. The key difference between such programs, the engineers reasoned, is that when you buy a program in the store, you know who sold it to you—and you know who made the program. If the program contains hostile code or a Trojan horse, you know who to sue. That's not the case with code downloaded over the Internet. A program represented as from Microsoft might actually come from some data thief or even a spy for a foreign government.

Instead of trying to develop a fundamentally new system for downloading code that would be "safe," *a la* Java, Microsoft decided that it would be easier to simply bring the assurances of the physical world to the online world. The obvious way to do this was to build a public key infrastructure (PKI) system for Windows executables. Microsoft calls the system *Authenticode*.

The Authenticode system defines a standard for digitally signing Windows executables and CAB files. The signature consists of a digitally signed cryptographic checksum for the signed objects and a public key certificate that contains a key that will validate the signature. The certificate itself is supposed to be signed by a certification authority that has a "software publisher's certificate" in the Microsoft Internet Explorer certificate store.

The Authenticode technology makes it possible to examine a signed ActiveX control and determine who signed it, and validate that the control has been unmodified since the time it was signed. The process of creating signed programs and verifying the signatures is described in Chapter 22.

Authenticode signatures can be used for different purposes depending on what precisely is being signed:

Windows executables

> Authenticode allows Windows users to see the name of the organization (or individual) that signed the executable. It also allows the user to verify that the executable hasn't been damaged, tampered with, or infected with a virus since the time it was signed. The Windows operating system allows programs to be run whether they have been signed or not, but it will issue a warning if the user attempts to run a downloaded program that does not contain a valid Authenticode signature.

ActiveX controls distributed in machine code

> Authenticode is the basis of the ActiveX security model. The standard security policy for Internet Explorer is that ActiveX applets that have valid Authenticode signatures can be run with the user's permission, while ActiveX applets that do not have valid signatures will simply be ignored. Users can also click a check box that tells Internet Explorer to "trust all content" from a particular signer—for example, to trust all content from Microsoft. This is not the default.

ActiveX controls distributed in Java bytecode

> Under Internet Explorer 4.0 and later, Authenticode signatures can also be used as the basis for determining what access permissions are granted to a particular Java program while the program is running. If a control mixes machine code and Java, or if both Java and machine code controls are resident on the same page, the capabilities-controlled access permitted by the Java system is rendered irrelevant.

Internet Explorer only checks Authenticode signatures when the control is downloaded from the network. Downloaded controls are installed in a special Internet Explorer directory. Any control placed in this directory is implicitly trusted, whether it is signed or not. In the past, security problems have been discovered with controls that were preloaded by computer vendors (see the sidebar "The Bogus Microsoft Certificates").

With Windows 2000, Microsoft introduced the use of Authenticode technology for signing critical components of the Windows operating system itself. This technology is also present in Windows ME. It is likely that the use of Authenticode technology in the operating system will make it easier to detect and diagnose computer viruses and other kinds of hostile code in the operating system.

Chapter 22 discusses how to digitally sign executables using Microsoft's Authenticode tools. The remainder of this chapter discusses Authenticode from the user's perspective.

Misconceptions About ActiveX

This information comes from the Results of the Security in ActiveX Workshop, Pittsburgh, Pennsylvania, U.S., August 22–23, 2000. It is published at the CERT Coordination Center, Software Engineering Institute, Carnegie Mellon University, Pittsburgh, PA, 15213 (*http://www.cert.org/reports/activeX_report.pdf*).

Misconception #1 All ActiveX controls are equally dangerous

The purposes and quality of ActiveX controls vary widely, the same as any type of software does. There is nothing inherent in an ActiveX control that necessarily presents a security risk, though (as we discuss later) it may be difficult for system administrators to evaluate the risk presented by a given ActiveX control.

Misconception #2 ActiveX controls are different from "regular" .EXE files

ActiveX controls are the same as "regular" .EXE files. ActiveX controls share many attributes with ordinary executable files. They run directly on your hardware, are generally opaque, written in a variety of high-level languages, and vary substantially in functionality, quality, and security characteristics. But unlike ordinary executable files, ActiveX controls can be mobile and can often be invoked remotely.

Misconception #3 The greatest security danger presented by ActiveX controls is intentionally hostile controls like Internet Exploder.

It is true that intentionally malicious ActiveX controls can potentially do a great deal of damage. However, in practice very few overtly malicious controls exist, and Microsoft's Authenticode technology provides some protection. Of significantly greater concern is the "repurposing" of legitimate controls by attackers through vulnerabilities in those controls.

Misconception #4 All signed controls are safe controls

Nothing could be further from the truth. Microsoft's digital signature technology, Authenticode, provides a high degree of verification that the control was produced by the signer and has not been modified by an interloper. A digital signature does not, however, provide any guarantee of benevolence or competence. It is up to the end user to decide if a given control from a given producer is trustworthy. And the decision about trustworthiness involves two parts: malevolence and competence.

Misconception #5 Avoiding Internet Explorer and Outlook makes you safe from ActiveX problems

Many third-party applications take advantage of ActiveX controls as part of their ordinary operation. Additionally, third-party tools can execute scripts. Indeed, the Windows Scripting Host can be used by any application. Thus, avoiding Internet Explorer and Outlook does not guard you from all attacks based on ActiveX controls. However, avoiding all Microsoft products does provide that protection.

Does Authenticode Work?

From its very introduction, Authenticode has been an extraordinarily controversial technology—not because of what it does, but because of what it does not do. When

Microsoft introduced Authenticode, it positioned it as a technology that could bring the safety of Java to downloaded ActiveX applets.

Of course, Authenticode doesn't provide safety for ActiveX. Authenticode provides limited accountability. Authenticode allows you to determine the key that was used to sign an ActiveX control—nothing more and nothing less. If an ActiveX control is signed, and if it is signed by the same organization that created the control, and if that organization took great pains to ensure that there would be no hostile functionality in the applet, then Authenticode really does provide an added measure of protection against downloaded mobile code. But there are many potential problems with the Authenticode security model:

- The ActiveX control might contain malicious code that was put there without the knowledge of the individual or organization responsible for signing the ActiveX control.

- The ActiveX control might not contain any intentionally malicious code, but there may be a way to make the ActiveX control do something malicious nevertheless, thanks to a buffer overflow or some other coding problem.

- The organization that codes and signs the ActiveX control might be malicious in nature and not care if you identify them after the fact. For instance, it could be a front company for a terrorist group or organized crime. By the time that the bad things have been traced back to them, the guilty parties have disappeared or moved to countries with no extradition treaties.

- A signed ActiveX control that is intentionally hostile might erase its digital signature after it starts execution, and there will be no record that a signed control was responsible for the damage.

- If a computer is damaged, it's likely that there will be many signed ActiveX controls resident on the system. It can be extremely difficult, and perhaps impossible, to determine which ActiveX control was responsible for the damage.

Fred McLain, the author of the Internet Exploder applet (see the next section, "Internet Exploder"), explains that the security Authenticode provides to computers is similar to the security provided to the users of valet parking. Imagine that you are a frequent user of valet parking at a variety of fine restaurants in the Seattle, Redmond, and Bothel areas. Now imagine that after a month of heavy restaurant binging, you notice that your car is driving strangely, so you take the car to a mechanic. The mechanic looks at the undercarriage for a few moments, then pulls out a big stick, some straw, and a fist-full of dirt. "Looks like somebody was driving off-road with your car," he says. "Your gas tank is punctured, and there are other problems as well. Who did this?" You shake your head. You know it was one of the valet parking attendants. But which one? There is no way to know for sure.

It's important to understand that critics of the Authenticode technology are not opposed to code signing on principle. Using digital signatures to authenticate executables is a great way to detect viruses and accidentally corrupted programs. The objections are to the promotion of Authenticode as a technology that could provide safety for downloaded programs.

The Bogus Microsoft Certificates

The Authenticode and ActiveX security model depends on the certification authorities doing a trustworthy job. Because ActiveX bases its security entirely on the reputation of the code's signer, all bets are off if an attacker is able to get a certificate that says "Microsoft Corporation" and then use this certificate to sign hostile ActiveX Controls.

The problem with the ActiveX security model is that certification authorities are not perfect. Indeed, on two occasions in January 2001, an individual or organization that fraudulently claimed to be "Microsoft Corporation" obtained two code-signing certificates from VeriSign, the world's largest and most prestigious certification authority.

As discussed in the "Revocation" section in Chapter 7, in January 2001, VeriSign apparently issued two certificates to someone fraudulently claiming to represent Microsoft Corporation. VeriSign's audit and validation procedures detected the fraud approximately one month after the certificates were issued.

But there was a problem: although the certificates were revoked and added to VeriSign's certificate revocation list (CRL), the techniques used by VeriSign to distribute CRLs and the techniques used by Authenticode to download CRLs were not compatible. VeriSign distributes CRLs from a so-called "well-known location," *http://crl. verisign.com/*. Microsoft's Authenticode implementation, meanwhile, requires that certificates contain a CRL Distribution Point (CDP) field, as specified by RFC 2459. But VeriSign's certificates, at least in January 2001, did not include a CDP. According to VeriSign, the company had refrained from including the CDP because it aggravated a bug in Internet Explorer 3.02's Authenticode implementation.

To help resolve the issue, Microsoft issued a security patch that allowed the Authenticode implementation to reference a local CRL, and that included a CRL that contained the two bogus certificates. Details can be found at *http://www.microsoft.com/technet/ security/bulletin/MS01-017.asp*.

Internet Exploder

To prove that Authenticode could not provide safety, in 1996 a Seattle area programmer named Fred McLain created a demonstration "hostile applet" called Internet Exploder. The control would run a 10-second countdown, after which time it would perform a clean shutdown of Windows 95 and power off the computer (if it was running on a system with advanced power management). McLain then obtained a VeriSign personal software publisher's digital certificate, signed his Exploder control, and placed the signed control on his web site.

McLain said that his demonstration was a very restrained one: his Exploder control could have done real damage to a user's computer. For example, it could have planted viruses, or reformatted a user's hard disk, or scrambled data. McLain said that ActiveX was a fundamentally unsafe technology, and that people should stay clear of the technology and instead use Netscape Navigator.

These statements made McLain the darling of executives at Microsoft's rivals Netscape and Sun. Executives at Microsoft and VeriSign, meanwhile, said that McLain had violated the license agreement, called the Software Publisher's Pledge, under which he had obtained his VeriSign certificate. He had violated the pledge, they said, by willfully signing a program that was certifiably hostile—a program that launched a denial-of-service attack against a user's own computer. After several weeks of back-and-forth arguments, VeriSign revoked McLain's software publisher's certificate. It was the first digital certificate ever revoked by VeriSign without the permission of the certificate holder.

For people using Internet Explorer 3.0, the revocation of McLain's digital ID didn't have much effect. That's because Explorer 3.0 didn't have the ability to query VeriSign's database and determine if a digital certificate was valid or had been revoked. For these people, clicking on McLain's web page still allowed them to enjoy the full effects of the Exploder.

Soon after McLain's digital ID was revoked, Microsoft released Internet Explorer Version 3.0.1. This version implemented real-time checking of revoked certificates. People using Explorer 3.0.1 who clicked on McLain's web page were told that the ActiveX control was invalid, because it was not signed with a valid digital ID (assuming that they had the security level of their browser set to check certificates and notify the user).

Proponents of ActiveX said the Exploder incident showed how Authenticode worked in practice: an individual had signed a hostile control and that individual's digital ID had been revoked. The damage was contained. But opponents of ActiveX said that McLain had shown. ActiveX is flawed. Exploder didn't have to be so obvious about what it was doing. It could have tried to attack other computers on the user's network, compromise critical system programs, or plant viruses. It was only because of McLain's openness and honesty that people didn't encounter something more malicious.

Risky Controls

Somewhat surprisingly, in the years since ActiveX was first introduced by Microsoft, there have been no other significant cases of a hostile ActiveX control that was digitally signed with an Authenticode certificate and then distributed.[*] As there have

---

[*] More accurately, there have been no significant cases widely reported. We don't know of any cases that have occurred, but we can't be sure that some haven't occurred and been kept quiet—or gone undetected.

been a large number of viruses and other Trojan horses distributed during the same time period, it seems somewhat surprising that Microsoft's position on the deterrent effect of digital signatures has apparently had some merit. On the whole, writers of viruses and Trojan horses have not been willing to digitally sign their wares. Of course, to date it has been so easy to spread hostile code via Outlook and Word documents that there has been little reason to go to the additional trouble of doing it via ActiveX controls.

This is not to say that ActiveX is a safe technology. On the contrary, a number of problems have been found with ActiveX controls that were created by legitimate software companies, digitally signed, and distributed. These problems include the following:

- Microsoft marked the "Microsoft Office UA Control" as "safe for scripting" in Office 2000. The control implemented the "show me" feature in Microsoft's interactive help system. Because the control was marked "safe for scripting," a hostile web site could use the control to activate and select any dialog box on a Windows-based computer that had both Internet Explorer and Office 2000 installed. This vulnerability was discovered in March 2000 by L0pht Research Labs and @Stake. The CERT/CC advisory can be found at *http://www.cert.org/advisories/CA-2000-07.html.*

- The ActiveX components associated with Microsoft Access contained a programming bug that caused Microsoft Access documents to be loaded and executed when referenced on any web page—without first prompting the user that the content was about to be executed. This bug allowed a web site operator to run any command on any computer that visited the web site, provided that the computer was running Internet Explorer and contained a copy of Microsoft Access. This vulnerability was discovered in July 2000 by Georgi Guninski and was published by Jesper Johansson, editor of the SANS Windows Security Digest, who called the vulnerability "probably the most dangerous programming error in Windows workstation that Microsoft has made." The SANS advisory can be found at *http://www.sans.org/newlook/resources/win_flaw.htm.*

More information about risky ActiveX controls can be found in CERT/CC's 53-page report, *Results of the Security in ActiveX Workshop,* which can be downloaded from *http://www.cert.org/reports/activeX_report.pdf.*

The Risks of Downloaded Code

Fred McLain's Internet Exploder showed that an ActiveX control can turn off your computer. But it could have done far worse damage. Indeed, it is hard to exaggerate the attacks that could be written and the subsequent risks of executing code downloaded from the Internet.

Programs That Spend Your Money

Increasingly, programs running computers can spend the money of their owners. What happens when money is spent by a program without the owner's permission? Who is liable for the funds spent? How can owners prevent these attacks? To answer these questions, it's necessary to first understand how the money is being spent.

Telephone billing records

One of the first recorded cases of a computer program that could spend money on behalf of somebody else was the pornography viewer distributed by the Sexygirls web site (described earlier in this chapter).

In this case, what made it possible for the money to be spent was the international long distance system, which already has provisions for billing individuals for long distance telephone calls placed on telephone lines. Because a program running on the computer could place a telephone call of its choosing, and because there is a system for charging people for these calls, the program could spend money.

Although the Sexygirls pornography viewer spent money by placing international telephone calls, it could just as easily have dialed telephone numbers in the 976 exchange or the 900 area code, both of which are used for teletext services. The international nature of the telephone calls simply makes it harder for authorities to refund the money spent, because the terms of these calls are subject to international agreements.

One way to protect against these calls would be to have some sort of trusted operating system that does not allow a modem to be dialed without informing the person sitting at the computer. Another approach would be to limit the telephone's ability to place international telephone calls, in the same way that telephones can be blocked from calling 976 and 900 numbers.* But ultimately, it might be more successful to use the threat of legal action as a deterrent against this form of attack.

Electronic funds transfers

If you use your computer for home banking, then a hostile program can initiate a funds transfer without your knowledge. Although it sounds difficult to do, in fact it has already been demonstrated. As we mentioned earlier, in February 1997, Germany's Chaos Computer Club demonstrated an ActiveX control that would hack into a copy of Quicken running on a Windows-based PC and initiate funds transfers, all without the user entering any passwords into the program. The control

---

* There is a perhaps apocryphal story of a New York City janitor who got his own 976 number in the 1980s and called it from the telephone of any office that he cleaned. Blocking calls to the 976 exchange and the 900 area code prevents such attacks.

worked by finding a communications buffer used by the European version of Quicken and preloading the buffer with transactions.

Programs That Violate Privacy and Steal Confidential Information

One of the easiest attacks for downloaded code to carry out against a networked environment is the systematic and targeted theft of private and confidential information. The reason for this ease is the network itself: besides being used to download programs to the host machine, the network can be used to upload confidential information. Unfortunately, this type of attack can also be one of the most difficult threats to detect and guard against.

A program that is downloaded to an end user's machine can scan that computer's hard disk or the network for important information. This scan can easily be masked to avoid detection. The program can then smuggle the data to the outside world using the computer's network connection.

A wealth of private data

Programs running on a modern computer can do far more than simply scan their own hard drives for confidential information; they can become eyes and ears for attackers:

- Any computer that has an Ethernet interface can run a packet sniffer—eavesdropping on network traffic, capturing passwords, and generally compromising a corporation's internal security.

- Once a program has gained a foothold on one computer, it can use the network to spread worm-like to other computers. Robert T. Morris' Internet Worm used this sort of technique to spread to thousands of computers on the Internet in 1988. Computers running Windows 95/98/ME are considerably less secure than the Unix computers that were penetrated by the Internet Worm, and usually much less well administered. And while Windows NT, 2000, and XP do offer more advanced security controls, the simple fact is that the overwhelming number of these systems are not properly managed or maintained. Even Windows systems operated by Microsoft have been broken into, potentially compromising personal data. The CodeRed worms of late 2001 are an abject realization of these risks.

- Programs that have access to audio or video devices can bug physical space. Few computers have small red lights to indicate when the microphone is on and listening or when the video camera is recording. A bugging capability can even be hidden in programs that legitimately have access to your computer's facilities: imagine a video conferencing ActiveX control that sends selected frames and an audio track to an anonymous computer somewhere in South America.

- Companies developing new hardware should have even deeper worries. Imagine a chip manufacturer that decides to test a new graphic accelerator using a multiuser video game downloaded from the Internet. What the chip manufacturer doesn't realize is that as part of the game's startup procedure it benchmarks the hardware on which it is running and reports the results back to a central facility. Is this market research on the part of the game publisher or industrial espionage on the part of its parent company? It's difficult to tell.

Firewalls Offer Little Protection

In recent years, many organizations have created firewalls to prevent break-ins from the outside network. But there are many ways that information can be smuggled through even the most sophisticated firewall. Consider:

- The information could be sent by electronic mail.
- The information could be encrypted and sent by electronic mail.
- The information could be sent via HTTP using GET or POST commands.
- The information could be encoded in domain name service queries.
- The information could be posted in a Usenet posting, masquerading as a binary file or image.
- The information could be placed in the data payload area of IP *ping* packets.
- An attacker program could scan for the presence of a modem and use it.

Confidential information can be hidden so that it appears innocuous. For example, it can be encrypted, compressed, and put in the message ID of mail messages. The spaces after periods can be modulated to contain information. Word choice itself can be altered to encode data. The timing of packets sent over the network can be modulated to hide still more information. Some data hiding schemes are ingenious; information that is compressed, encrypted, and hidden in this manner is mathematically indistinguishable from noise.

Computers that are left on 24 hours a day can transmit confidential information at night, when such actions are less likely to be observed. They can scan the keyboard for activity and only transmit when the screensaver is active (indicating that the computer has been left alone).

Signed Code Is Not Safe Code

Code signing does not provide users with a safe environment to run their programs. Instead, code signing is intended to provide users with an audit trail. If a signed program misbehaves, you should be able to interrogate the signed binary and decide who to sue. And as Fred McLain's Internet Exploder demonstrates, once the author of a malicious applet is identified, the associated software publisher's credentials can be revoked, preventing others from being harmed by the signed applet.

Unfortunately, security through code signing has many problems:

Audit trails are vulnerable

Once it is running, a signed ActiveX control might erase the audit trail that would allow you to identify the applet and its author. Or the applet might merely edit the audit trail, changing the name of the person who actually signed it to "Microsoft, Inc." The control might even erase itself, further complicating the task of finding and punishing the author. Current versions of Microsoft's Internet Explorer don't even have audit trails, although audit trails may be added to a later release.

The damage that an ActiveX control does may not be immediately visible

Audit trails are only useful if somebody looks at them. Unfortunately, there are many ways that a rogue piece of software can harm the user, each of which is virtually invisible to that person. For example, a rogue control could turn on the computer's microphone and transform it into a clandestine room bug. Or the applet could gather sensitive data from the user, for instance, by scanning the computer's hard disk for credit card numbers. All of this information could then be surreptitiously sent out over the Internet.

Authenticode does not protect the user against bugs and viruses

Signed, buggy code can do a great deal of damage. And signed controls by legitimate authors may be accidentally infected with viruses before signing and distribution.

Signed controls may be dangerous when improperly used

Consider an ActiveX control written for the express purpose of deleting files on the user's hard drive. This control might be written for a major computer company and signed with that company's key. The legitimate purpose of the control might be to delete temporary files that result from installing software. Since the name of the file that is deleted is not hardcoded into the control, but instead resides on the HTML page, an attacker could distribute the signed control as is and use it to delete files that were never intended to be deleted by the program's authors.

The Authenticode software is itself vulnerable

The validation routines used by the Authenticode system are themselves vulnerable to attack, either by signed applets with undocumented features or through other means, such as Trojan horses placed in other programs.

Ultimately, the force and power of code signing is that companies that create misbehaving applets can be challenged through the legal system. But will ActiveX audit trails hold up in a court of law? If the company that signed the control is located in another country, will it even be possible to get them into court?

Code signing does prove the integrity and authenticity of a piece of software purchased in a computer store or downloaded over the Internet. But code signing does not promote accountability because it is nearly impossible to tell if a piece of software is malicious.

Signed Code Can Be Hijacked

Signed ActiveX controls can be hijacked; they can be referenced by web sites that have no relationship with the site on which they reside, and can be used for purposes other than those intended by the individual or organization that signed the control.

There are several ways that an attacker could hijack another organization's ActiveX control. One way is to *inline* a control without the permission of the operators of the web site on which it resides, similar to the way that an image might be inlined.[*] Alternately, an ActiveX control could simply be downloaded and republished on another site, as with a stolen GIF or JPEG image.[†]

Once an attacker has developed a technique for running a signed ActiveX control from the web page of his or her choice, the attacker can then experiment with giving the ActiveX control different parameters from the ones with which it is normally invoked. For example, an attacker might be able to repurpose an ActiveX control that deletes a file in a temporary directory to make it delete a critical file in the *\WIN-DOWS* directory. Or the attacker might search for buffer or stack overflow errors, which could be exploited to let the attacker run arbitrary machine code.[‡]

Hijacking presents problems for both users and software publishers. It is a problem for users because there is no real way to evaluate its threat. Not only does a user need to "trust" that a particular software publisher will not harm his computer, but to be positive that there are no lurking bugs that can be exploited by evildoers, the user also needs to trust that the software publisher has followed the absolute highest standards in producing its ActiveX controls.[§] And hijacking poses a problem for software publishers, because a hijacked ActiveX control will still be signed by the original publisher: any audit trails or logs created by the computer will point to the publisher, and not to the individual or organization that is responsible for the attack!

---

[*] Inlined images are a growing problem on the Internet today. Inlining happens when an HTML file on one site references an image on another site through the use of a <IMG SRC=> tag that specifies the remote image's URL. Inlining is considered antisocial because it is used without the permission of the site that holds and downloads the image—and frequently to further the commercial interests of the first site with which it has no formal relation.

[†] Developers at Microsoft are trying to create a system for giving HTML pages digital signatures. Such a system would allow a developer to create ActiveX controls that could only be run from a specially signed page.

[‡] Anecdotal reports suggest that many ActiveX controls, including controls being commercially distributed, will crash if they are run from web pages with parameters that are unexpectedly long. Programs that crash under these conditions usually have bounds-checking errors. In recent years, bounds errors have become one of the primary sources of security-related bugs. Specially tailored, excessively long input frequently ends up on the program's stack, where it can be executed.

[§] Companies such as Microsoft, Sun, and other firms, as well as individual programmers working on free software, have consistently demonstrated that they are not capable of producing software that is free of these kinds of bugs.

Reconstructing an Attack

The transitory nature of downloaded code poses an additional problem for computer security professionals: it can be difficult, if not impossible, to reconstruct an attack after it happens.

Imagine that a person in a large corporation discovers that a rogue piece of software is running on his computer. The program may be a packet sniffer; it's scanning all of the TCP/IP traffic, looking for passwords, and posting a message to Usenet once a day that contains the passwords in an encrypted message. How does the computer security team at this corporation discover who planted the rogue program, so that they can determine the damage and prevent it from happening again?

The first thing that the company should do, of course, is to immediately change all user passwords. Then, they should force all users to call the security administrator, prove their identities, and be told their new passwords.

The second thing the company should do is to install software such as *ssh* or a cryptographically-enabled web server so that plaintext passwords are not sent over the internal network.

Determining the venue of attack will be more difficult. If the user has been browsing the Internet using a version of Microsoft's Internet Explorer that supports ActiveX, tracking down the problem may be difficult. Internet Explorer currently doesn't keep detailed logs of the Java and ActiveX components that it has downloaded and run. The company's security team might be able to reconstruct what happened based on the browser's cache. Then again, the hostile applet has probably erased it.

It's important to note that technologies such as code signing of ActiveX and Java applets don't help this problem. Suppose that a company only accepts signed applets from 1 of 30 other companies, 3 of which are competitors. How do you determine which of the signed applets that have been downloaded to the contaminated machine is the one that planted the malicious code? The attacker has probably replaced the malicious code on the source page with an innocuous version immediately after you downloaded the problem code.

It turns out the only way for the company to actually reconstruct what has happened is if that company has previously recorded all of the programs that have been downloaded to the compromised machine. This could be done with a web proxy server that records all *.class* files and ActiveX components.[*] At least then the company has a chance of reconstructing what has happened.

---

[*] Turning a web proxy server into a security server was proposed by the Princeton University Secure Internet Programming group.

Recovering from an Attack

While to date there is no case of a malicious ActiveX control that's been signed by an Authenticode certificate being surreptitiously released into the wild, it is unrealistic to think that there will be no such controls released at some point in the future. What is harder to imagine, though, is how the victims of such an attack could seek redress against the author of the program—even if that attack is commissioned with a signed control that has not been hijacked.

Consider a possible scenario for a malicious control. A group with an innocuous-sounding name but extreme political views obtains a commercial software publisher's certificate. (The group has no problem obtaining the certificate because it is, after all, a legally incorporated entity. Or perhaps it is only a single individual who has filed with his town and obtained a business license, which legally allows him to operate under a nonincorporated name.) The group creates an ActiveX control that displays a marquee animation when run on a web page and, covertly, installs a stealth virus at the same time. The group's chief hacker then signs the control and places it on several web pages that people may browse.

Afterwards, many people around the world download the control. They see the certificate notice, but they don't know how to tell whether it is safe, so they authorize the download. Or, quite possibly, many of the users have been annoyed by the alerts about signatures, so they have set the security level to "low" and the control is run without warning.

Three months later, on a day of some political significance, thousands or tens of thousands of computers are disabled.

Now, consider the obstacles to overcome in seeking redress:

- The users must somehow trace the virus back to the control.
- The users must trace the control back to the group that signed it.
- The users must find an appropriate venue in which to bring suit. If they are in a different state in the U.S., this may mean federal court where there is a multiple-year wait for trial time. If the group has disbanded, there may be no place to bring suit.
- The users will need to pay lawyer fees, court costs, filing fees, investigation costs, and other expenses.

In the end, after years of waiting, the users may not win the lawsuit. Even if they do, the group may not have any resources to pay for the losses, or it may declare bankruptcy. Thus, victims could lose several hundreds or thousands of dollars in time and lost data, and then spend hundreds of times that amount only to receive nothing.

Conclusion

Downloaded machine code can severely compromise the reliability and security of any computer's operating system. Although once there was a time when Internet users would routinely spend hours each month downloading new browsers, email clients, and plug-ins, that time is fortunately drawing to an end. The current generation of Internet software is more than adequate for most users, and today's new computers usually come with a wide variety of plug-ins and helper applications preinstalled. As a result, the joys of multimegabyte downloads over relatively slow dialup modems is quickly receding from memory.

On the other hand, few users understand the dangers that downloaded code can pose for their computer systems. With the advent of high-speed Internet connections provided by cable modems and DSL lines, more and more users are likely to surf and sample not only interesting web sites, but programs as well. Internet connections that are always on increase the opportunities for stealthily-crafted Trojan horse programs to do their damage without being detected.

In the next chapter, we'll explore a variety of technologies that are designed to mitigate the dangers of downloaded code: Java, JavaScript, Flash, and Shockwave.

In this chapter:
- Java
- JavaScript
- Flash and Shockwave
- Conclusion

CHAPTER 13

Mobile Code II: Java, JavaScript, Flash, and Shockwave

In the last chapter we examined the risks inherent in downloading and running plugins, ActiveX controls, and other kinds of machine code. We saw that while many of these programs are well behaved, they can occasionally be quite vicious. Once a downloaded program starts running, it inherits all of the privileges and access rights of the user who invoked it.

Java, JavaScript, Flash, and Shockwave are all attempts to allow web developers to realize many of the benefits of mobile code without assuming the corresponding dangers. Instead of downloading raw executable machine code, all of these systems download an intermediate language that is then interpreted on the user's computer. In theory, these interpreted languages can provide additional security by simply not implementing dangerous functionality. For example, JavaScript has no built-in mechanism to read files on the local computer's hard disk, so it should be impossible to write a JavaScript program that scans the user's hard disk for interesting files and then uploads these files to a hostile web server.

In practice, Java, JavaScript, Flash, and Shockwave do provide significantly more security than the mobile code techniques than were considered in the previous chapter. But because of implementation failings and occasional design flaws, none of these systems actually provide as much security as their inventors claim.

Java

Java is a complex object-oriented language that has a syntax resembling that of the C++ language. Invented by engineers at Sun Microsystems, Java was originally intended for writing small programs that would be downloaded over cable modems to television set-top boxes. Because the theory was that set-top boxes might change over time, Java programs were intended to run on a virtual computer that could be adapted, over time, to any particular combination of computer hardware and software. Because it was theoretically operating-system independent, Java was quickly championed by competitors of Microsoft, who saw the new language as a way of attacking the entrenched monopoly of the Windows/Intel desktop computing environment.

Alas, raising the performance of Java applications to the level of native desktop applications proved to be beyond the technical abilities of the entire computer industry. By the late 1990s, most of the "Java on the desktop" projects had failed. At the same time, Java became increasingly popular for server-side applications—particularly at large financial companies, who found that they could develop Java applications on relatively slow desktop computers and then simply move the programs to large-scale "enterprise" servers and have the programs run a hundred times faster and/or serve thousands of simultaneous users.

Today Java also lives on as an instructional language at many colleges and universities. A subset of the Java language is now used on some embedded devices, including smart cards and cellular telephones. Finally, many web sites continue to download small Java "applets" such as stock and news tickers to their visitors. Ironically, these applets finally deliver on Java's original vision—they are small, mobile programs that can be downloaded over a reasonably fast Internet connection and that provide a limited amount of local interactivity.

A Little Java Demonstration

Here is a simple Java program:

```
import java.awt.*;
import java.applet.*;
public class HelloWorld extends Applet {
  public void paint (Graphics g){
    g.drawString("Hello World!", 100, 25);
  }
}
```

This program creates a Java applet class called *HelloWorld*. The class has a single method called *paint*. When the class is loaded and run, the string "Hello World!" is displayed at location (100,25).

The Java program must be placed in a file called *HelloWorld.java*. It is then compiled with the *javac* Java compiler, creating a file called *HelloWorld.class*:

```
% javac HelloWorld.java
% ls -l Hello*
-rw-rw-r--  1 simsong  wheel  418 May 27 16:10 HelloWorld.class
-rw-rw-r--  1 simsong  wheel  167 May 27 16:05 HelloWorld.java
%
```

To display this applet, you need to have an HTML file that references the class file with an <APPLET> tag. Here is such an HTML file:

```
<html><head>
<title>Hello Java!</title>
</head>
<body>
<hr>
```

```
<APPLET code = "HelloWorld.class" width = 300 height = 50 ></applet>
<hr>
</body></html>
```

If the HTML file and the *HelloWorld.class* class file are placed in the same directory on the web server, you can run the Java applet by viewing the HTML file using a Java-enabled browser. Once the HTML file loads, the browser will automatically download the file *HelloWorld.class* and start executing the applet. You can also run the applet using the Java program Applet Viewer. Both are shown in Figure 13-1.

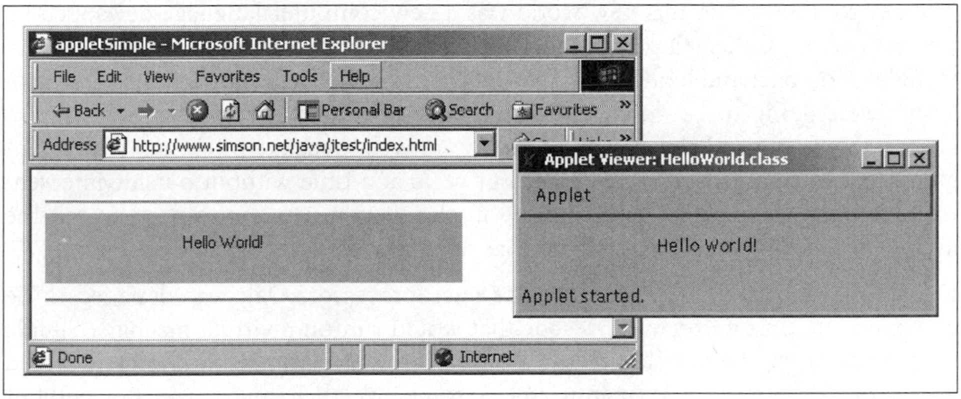

Figure 13-1. The HelloWorld Java applet running in a web browsers and in the Java Applet Viewer

The HTML 4.0 specification states that the <APPLET> tag has been deprecated in favor of the <OBJECT> tag. Using the <OBJECT> tag, the previous example could be rewritten:

```
<html><head>
<title>Hello Java!</title>
</head>
<body>
<hr>
<OBJECT code = "HelloWorld.class" width = 300 height = 50 ></OBJECT>
<hr>
</body></html>
```

For more information on the <OBJECT> tag, see *http://www.w3.org/TR/html4/ struct/objects.html*, and the many excellent Java books available today.

Java's History

Although today Java is widely thought of as a reasonably secure language for writing programs that are downloaded over the Internet to web browsers, it wasn't designed for this purpose. Indeed, Java's security model was added largely as an afterthought. To understand the security issues with Java today, it's important to understand something about the history of the language.

Java came into existence in April 1991 when a group of "refugee" engineers from Sun Microsystems were hard at work on a stealth project designed to catapult Sun into the world of consumer electronics. Sun envisioned a future in which toasters, remote control systems, stereos, and cable decoder boxes were all programmed using a common computer language with programs that would be downloaded on demand over a network. The stealth project was designed to leverage Sun's experience with computer languages, system design, and silicon manufacturing to turn the company into a major consumer electronics technology supplier.

The key to dominating this new world was a new computer language developed by James Gosling. Called Oak, the language was designed to produce programs that would be compact and highly reliable. Compactness was necessary because Oak programs were going to be downloaded over networks whenever it was necessary to change them. And reliability was necessary, as well, because programs in this language had to be able to run for months or years at a time without outside intervention: you can't expect to dominate the market if you sometimes need to tell the average American that his toaster oven has to be rebooted to continue operation.

Instead of being compiled for a specific microprocessor, Oak was designed to be compiled into an interpreted bytecode that would run on a virtual machine. Simple economics drove the decision to use a virtual machine: a portable bytecode would allow consumer electronics manufacturers to change their microprocessor without losing compatibility with existing programs. Unlike the desktop computers of the day, the microprocessor would truly become a commodity.*

The first test for Oak was an interactive cable TV decoder box that Sun was designing for Time Warner. In April 1993, Time Warner assured Sun that the workstation vendor would be awarded Time Warner's contract for the interactive cable TV trial because Sun had superior technology. But on June 14, 1993, Time Warner awarded the set-top box contract to Silicon Graphics, Inc. It was perhaps just as well for Sun that interactive cable TV was a failure.†

In the months that followed, the Oak team repositioned their language for the world of CD-ROMs and multimedia publishing. The goal was to use Oak to develop CD-ROM applications that could run on Windows, Macs, and Unix-based personal

---

* Sun was correct that desktop computers were destined to become a commodity, but it happened a different way than Sun anticipated. Instead of adopting a new architecture and architecture-based programming language, companies such as Advanced Micro Devices and TransMeta simply cloned the overly-complex Intel x86 instruction set. Meanwhile, Intel started releasing low-cost microprocessors such as its Celeron series, essentially competing with itself.

† Eric Greenberg, formerly a lead in Netscape's security group, writes, "Jim Clark, Netscape's founder, initially envisioned Mosaic as a product to be used within an interactive cable TV box for programming the programs you wanted to see. This was the first business model for Mosaic. Fortunately, the Mosaic team saw past this pipe dream and quickly focused on the Internet and the enterprise." (Eric Greenberg, personal communication, March 22, 1997)

---

computers. Right around this time, another multiplatform phenomenon was sweeping the computer industry: the World Wide Web. This was great news for the Oak team; they had a language that was designed to be small and portable. The team quickly realized that they could use the Web to download programs to an end user's computer and have the programs run instantly on the user's desktop.

In July 1994, Patrick Naughton, a member of the team, wrote a "throwaway" web browser named WebRunner to demonstrate the idea. Within a month, the browser was rewritten from scratch in Oak, and a system for running downloaded applets was designed and implemented. Realizing that "Oak" was a poor name for a computer language, Sun renamed the language "Java" after the coffee craze that was sweeping the country. Eight months later, Sun formally announced Java and its HotJava web browser at the 1995 SunWorld tradeshow.

That same day, Netscape announced its intention to license Java for use in the Netscape Navigator web browser.

Java, the Language

Java is a modern object-oriented language that has a syntax similar to C++, dynamic binding, garbage collection, and a simple inheritance model. Although Java was largely promoted as a language for the World Wide Web, Java is, in fact, a general-purpose computer language that can be used for writing anything from simple five-line toy programs to complicated applications. One of the largest users of Java today are investment houses, which have used Java to create large-scale web-based applications and financial models.

What initially distinguished the typical Java implementation from other computer languages was the runtime environment. Instead of being compiled for a particular microprocessor, Java programs are compiled into a processor-independent *bytecode*. This bytecode is loaded into a computer's memory by the *Java Class Loader*. Finally, the bytecode is run on a *Java virtual machine* (JVM).

The Java virtual machine can run Java programs directly on an operating system such as Windows or Mac OS; alternately, the JVM can be embedded inside a web browser, allowing programs to be executed as they are downloaded from the Web. The JVM can execute the Java bytecode directly using an interpreter. Or, it can use a "just-in-time" compiler to convert the bytecode into the native machine code of the particular computer on which it is running. This whole Java cycle is depicted in Figure 13-2.

Java can also be compiled directly into machine code and run on a target system. Used this way, Java loses its runtime advantage of being able to run on any computer and any operating system that has a Java virtual machine, but it retains many of its advantages over C++ (and similar languages), including that of generating code that has automatic memory management.

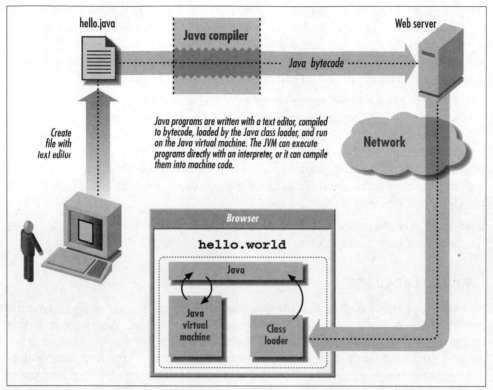

Figure 13-2. The Java cycle

Java Safety

From the beginning, the Oak team wanted to create a language that would encourage programmers to write code that was inherently reliable. Starting with C++, Gosling and his team removed many of the features from C++ that are confusing or commonly misused. In this way, they sought to increase the *safety* of the language and the reliability of programs written with it.

The main way that Java achieves this reliability is by providing automatic memory management. Specifically:

- Instead of forcing the programmer to manually manage memory with *malloc()* and *free()*, Java has a working garbage collection system. As a result, Java programmers don't need to worry about memory leaks, or about the possibility that they are using memory in one part of an application that is still in use by another.

- Java has built-in bounds checking on all strings and arrays. This eliminates buffer overruns, which are another major source of C and C++ programming errors and security flaws.

- The Java language doesn't have pointers that can be arithmetically manipulated and dereferenced. That's good, because many C/C++ programmers don't understand the difference between a pointer to an object and the object itself.* Contrary to the understanding of many non-Java programmers, however, Java does have "object references" that behave in a fashion similar to C pointers in many circumstances.

- Java has only single inheritance, making Java class hierarchies easier to understand. And because Java classes can implement multiple interfaces, the language supports many of the advantages of multiple-inheritance languages.

- Java is strongly typed, so you don't have problems where one part of a program thinks that an object has one type, and another part of a program thinks that an object has another type.

- Java has a sophisticated exception-handling system.

All of these features combine to make Java what's generally known as a *safe* programming language: Java programs rarely misbehave wildly when given data that is slightly unexpected. (Instead, they simply generate an exception, which usually causes the program to terminate with a runtime error.) Because most security problems are the result of bugs and programming errors, it is thought that programs written in the Java language will be more secure than programs written in traditional languages such as C and C++.

In fact, Java's claims of security-through-safety are largely true: network daemons and web server plug-ins written in Java simply do not have the buffer overflow problems that have plagued the same programs written in C and C++. But there have been some controversies around Java security; for example, Java's supporters claimed that Java's safe execution environment could also provide sufficient security for executing downloaded mobile code. As we'll see, that is an overstatement.

Java Security

Java was not designed to be a secure programming language. Under Java's original vision, programs would only be downloaded by an equipment manufacturer or an approved content provider. Java was designed for a closed programmer community and for a somewhat constrained set of target environments.

When Java was repositioned for the Web, security became an obvious concern. By design, the Web allows any user to download any page from anyone on the Internet, whether or not it is from an approved content provider. If web users can download and

---

* C lets you do some interesting things. For instance, if you define *char *p; int i;* in a program, you can then use the terms *p[i]* and *i[p]* almost interchangeably in your code. Few C programmers understand the language well enough to understand quirks such as this.

run a program by simply clicking on a web page, there needs to be some mechanism for protecting users from malicious and poorly constructed programs.

Safety is not security

Having a safe programming language protects users from many conventional security problems. That's because many security-related problems are actually the result of programming faults.* As we've stated, Java eliminates many traditional sources of bugs, such as buffer overflows.

But a safe programming language alone cannot protect users from programs that are intentionally malicious.† To provide protection against these underlying attacks (and countless others), it's necessary to place limits on what downloaded programs can do.

Java employs a variety of techniques to limit what a downloaded program can do. The main techniques are the Java sandbox, the SecurityManager class, the Class Loader, and the Bytecode Verifier. These processes are illustrated in Figure 13-3 and described in the following sections.

Sandbox

> Java programs are prohibited from directly manipulating a computer's hardware or making direct calls to the computer's operating system. Instead, Java programs run on a virtual computer inside a restricted virtual space. Sun terms this approach to security the Java "sandbox," likening the Java execution environment to a place where a child can build and break things, generally not get hurt, and not hurt the outside world.

SecurityManager class

> If all Java programs were restricted so that they couldn't send information over the network, couldn't read or write from the user's hard disk, and couldn't manipulate the computer's input/output devices, they would probably be nearly secure: after all, there would be little damage that the programs could do.‡ Of course, these limitations would also make Java a much less exciting programming environment. There wouldn't be much of anything interesting that Java programs could do either.

---

* In technical terminology, programmers make *errors* that result in *faults* being present in the code. When the faults cause the code to produce results different from the specifications, that is a *failure*. Most casual users simply refer to all of these as "bugs," and here in the book, we will too.

† Ironically, Java's safety is an aid to people writing Trojan horses and hostile applications. Safety helps minimize the chances that a Trojan horse program will crash while it is reformatting your hard disk. Safety also helps ensure that the applet scanning your computer for confidential documents and surreptitiously mailing them to a remote site on the Internet won't go into an infinite loop.

‡ But the code could replicate itself and tie up processing resources, resulting in a denial-of-service attack.

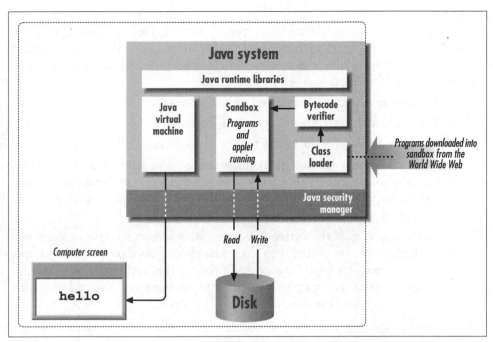

Figure 13-3. *The Java sandbox, SecurityManager class, Class Loader, and Bytecode Verifier*

Java uses a series of special classes that allow programs running inside the sandbox to communicate with the outside world. For example, the Java class *FileOutputStream* allows a Java program to open a file for writing to the user's hard disk.

The creators of Java believed that programs that are downloaded from an untrusted source, such as the Internet, should run with fewer privileges than programs that are run directly from the user's hard disk. They created a special class, called *SecurityManager*, which is designed to be called before any "dangerous" operation is executed. The *SecurityManager* class determines whether the operation should or should not be allowed.

Class Loader

Because most of the security checks in the Java programming environment are written in the Java language itself, it's important to ensure that a malicious piece of program code can't disable the checks. One way to launch such an attack would be to have a malicious program disable the standard *SecurityManager* class or replace it with a more permissive version.

Such an attack could be carried out by a downloaded piece of machine code or a Java applet that exploited a bug in the Java runtime system. To prevent this attack, the Class Loader examines classes to make sure that they do not violate the runtime system.

Bytecode Verifier

To further protect the Java runtime security system, Java employs a Bytecode Verifier. The verifier is supposed to ensure that the bytecode that is downloaded could only have been created by compiling a valid Java program. For example, the Bytecode Verifier is supposed to assure that:

- The downloaded program doesn't forge pointers.
- The program doesn't violate access restrictions.
- The program doesn't violate the type of any objects.

The Bytecode Verifier was originally implemented as a series of *ad hoc* checks, although there has been some academic work on developing bytecode verifiers that use theorem-proving and other formal systems for algorithmically asserting that the bytecode is "provably correct."

One of the purposes of the Bytecode Verifier was to allow the Java runtime system to replace runtime checks with load-time checks. As a program only needs to be loaded once, this would theoretically allow a Java application to run faster than might be expected in a purely interpretive environment. Verified programs could also be compiled into machine code without risk.

There are many problems with the Java security approach. These are described later in this chapter in the section "Java Security Problems."

Java Security Policy

Java security policy is complicated by the fact that the Java programming language is designed for two fundamentally different purposes:

- Java is a general-purpose computer language for creating word processors, electronic mail clients, web browsers, and other kinds of productivity software. These programs might be resident on a user's computer or downloaded from an organization's internal web server.
- Java is a language that is used to download applications from the Web that perform animations, create interactive chat systems, and perform complex calculations on the user's machine.

These different purposes require fundamentally different security policies: you want to be able to read files on your hard disk with your word processor, but it is probably inappropriate for an applet that implements a chat system to do the same. This dual nature leads to a much more complicated security model, which in turn leads to more potential bugs in the Java security enforcement mechanisms.

Java's original implementors envisioned three different security policies that could be enforced by web browsers that implemented the Java programming language:

1. Do not run Java programs.

2. Run Java programs with different privileges depending on the source of the program. Programs downloaded from web pages would run with severe restrictions. Programs loaded off the user's hard drive would have no restrictions. Table 13-1 summarizes a variety of restrictions.

3. No restrictions on Java programs. Allow the Java program to do anything at all with the computer's hard disk, network connectivity, and anything else.

Sun's HotJava browser implemented all three of these policies; the choice was left to the user. Most users chose policy #2.

Table 13-1. Some of the restrictions on downloaded Java applets present in most web browsers

Restriction	Reason
Cannot read the contents of files or directories on the client computer.	Protects the confidentiality of information on the user's computer.
Cannot write, rename, or delete files on the client computer.	Protects the user's data from unauthorized modification.
Cannot initiate a network connection to a computer other than the computer from which the Java applet was downloaded.	Prevents a downloaded applet from probing for security problems behind an organization's firewall.
Cannot receive network connections.	Prevents an applet from appearing to be a legitimate server on an organization's internal network.
Cannot display a window without a special "untrusted" border.	Prevents applets from creating windows that appear to be system windows.
Cannot create a ClassLoader or SecurityManager.	Prevents subverting the Java type checking system and disabling all Java security checks.
Cannot run system programs.	Prevents running arbitrary code.

As web developers have tried to do more with active content, Microsoft and Netscape have been forced to allow downloaded Java programs to execute more functions on the local computer. Rather than giving potentially hostile Java applets *carte blanche*, both companies have modified their Java runtime environments so that the user could decide on an applet-by-applet or program-by-program basis whether or not additional capabilities should be granted.

Internet Explorer's "security zones"

The Internet is an exceedingly complicated place; a security policy that makes sense for one web site might not make sense for another. You might work on a critical computer and normally want to have Java disabled; however, the HR department at your corporation might deploy an application that requires you to use Java to file employee evaluations and schedule vacation time.

Rather than force users to routinely open control panels as they move from one web site to another, Microsoft's Internet Explorer allows you to create multiple security policies for different categories of web sites, and then to assign web sites to these different categories. Microsoft calls these categories *security zones*. They were introduced with Internet Explorer 4 and are controlled with the "Security" tab of the Internet Options control panel (see Figure 13-4).

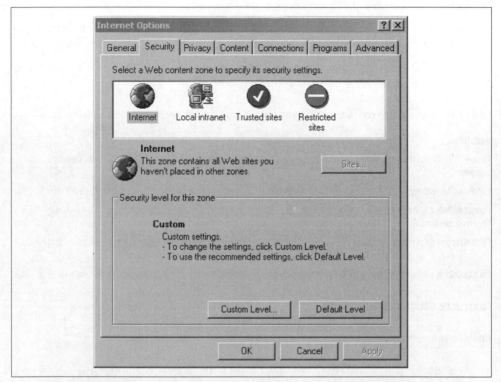

Figure 13-4. Microsoft's Internet Explorer allows you to assign different security policies to different categories of web sites. These categories are called security zones. Besides the four security zones that are shown in the window, there is a fifth security zone called the "My Computer zone."

Internet Explorer has five predefined security zones:

Local intranet zone

This zone is for all web sites that are located behind an organization's firewall, all sites that are accessed using Microsoft's networking protocols, and all sites that are accessed by unqualified domain names (e.g., *http://site/*). You can also add individual web sites to the Local intranet zone (see Figure 13-5). This is useful for organizations that have intranets accessed over the Internet using SSL. (If you need to access an intranet site without using SSL, you should uncheck the box that says "Require server verification (*https:*) for all sites in this zone." Using SSL is more secure because it encrypts the data, and because server certificates are used to verify the identity of the remote site, rather than relying on DNS.)

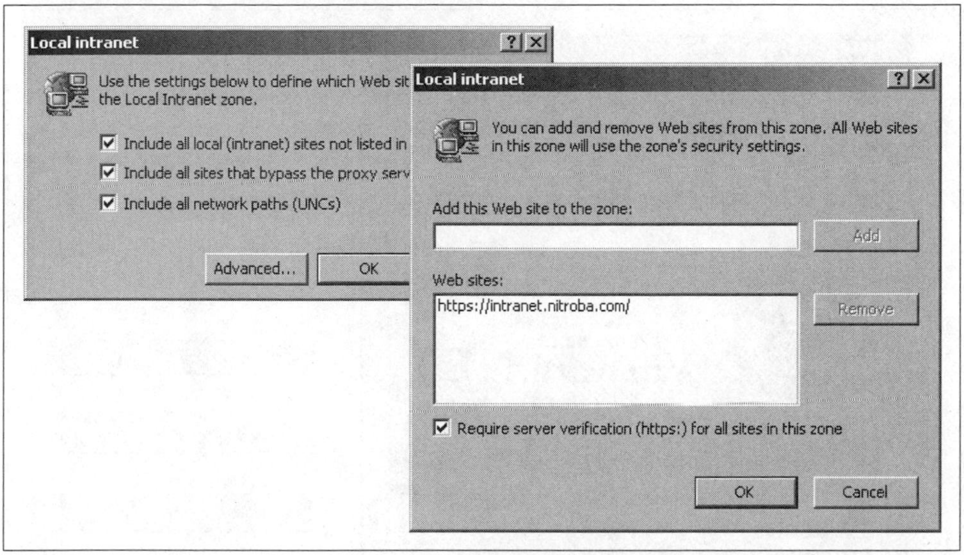

Figure 13-5. Internet Explorer allows you to control which web sites are included by default in the Local intranet zone. You can also explicitly add sites to the Local intranet zone.

Trusted sites zone

This zone is used for web sites that you specifically wish to trust. By default, this zone is assigned a "low" security level. This level allows all active content to be run without prompting the user or requiring that the content be digitally signed. By default, there are no sites in this zone.

Restricted sites zone

This zone is designed to be used for web sites that you do not wish to trust. By default, this zone is assigned a "high" security level.

Internet zone

This zone is for all web sites that are not in the Local intranet, Trusted sites, or Restricted sites zones. By default, this zone is assigned a "medium" security level.

My Computer zone

This security zone includes everything that is stored on the computer on which Internet Explorer is running—everything on your hard drive or removable media—but it excludes cached Java classes in the Temporary Internet Files folder.

Internet Explorer displays the current security zone in the lower right-hand corner of the status bar (see Figure 13-6).

There is an description of security zones in Chapter 7 of the Internet Explorer Resource Kit (*http://www.microsoft.com/technet/index/defaultHome.asp?url=/TechNet/IE/reskit/ie5/part1/ch07zone.asp*).

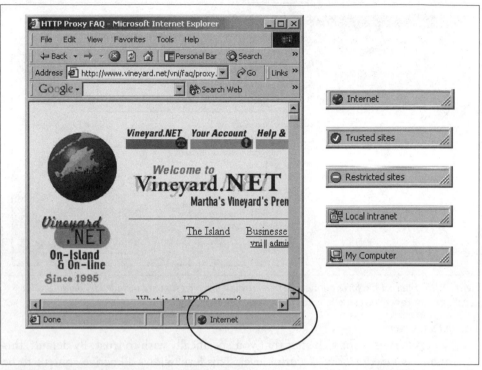

Figure 13-6. Internet Explorer displays the current security zone in the lower right-hand corner of the status bar.

Setting Java policy in Microsoft Internet Explorer

Microsoft Internet Explorer 4.0 and above establish four different policies for running Java programs. The policy that Internet Explorer uses depends on the current security zone for the web page that you are viewing. You can also create custom policies. These policies can be distributed to other users with the Internet Explorer Customization Wizard or the Internet Explorer's Administrator's Kit Profile Manager, both of which are included with the Internet Explorer Resource Kit.

To change the security policy for an Internet security zone, click on the Select the Security tab from the Internet Options panel, then select the Custom Level button. This will display the Security Settings panel (see Figure 13-7).

The default Java security policies are:

Disable Java
> This setting prevents Java programs and applets from executing.

High safety
> This setting allows applets to run in the Java sandbox. It is the default setting for security zones that have the "high," "medium," and "medium-low" security levels.

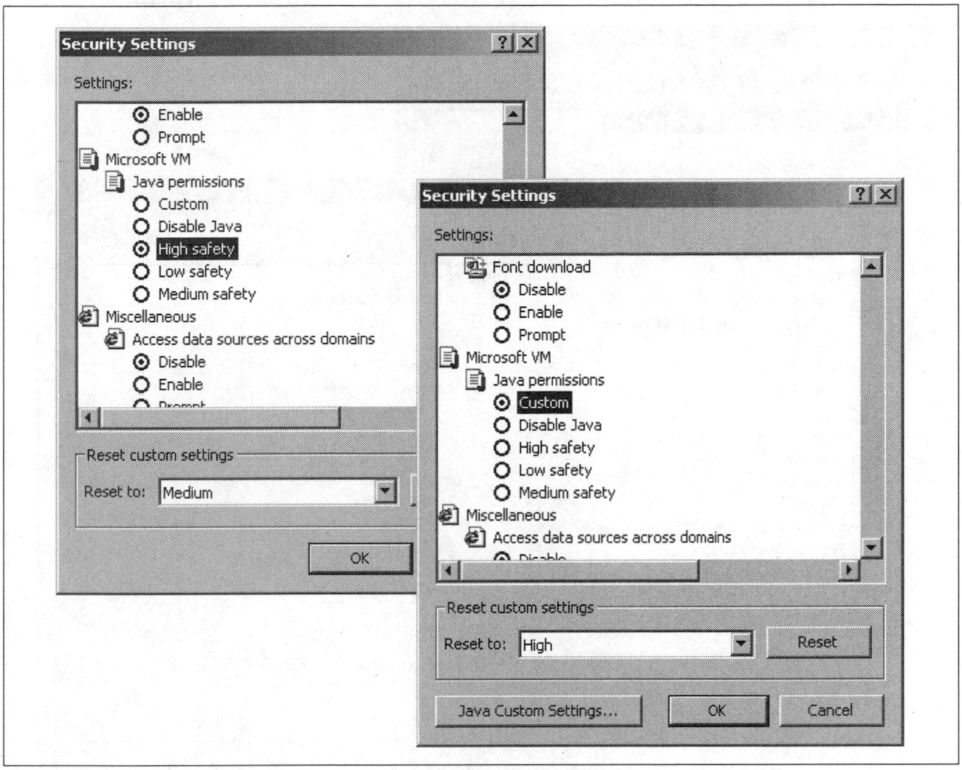

Figure 13-7. The Internet Explorer Security Settings panel allows you to change the security policy for the Microsoft Java virtual machine. If you select the Custom option, a button will appear allowing you to specify custom policy attributes.

Medium safety

> This setting allows applets to run in the Java sandbox, to access "scratch space," and to access files as allowed by the user.

Low safety

> This setting allows Java applets to run outside the Java sandbox, accessing all resources on your computer and making network connections to any other computer on the Internet. This is the default setting for security zones that have the "low" security level.

Custom

> This setting allows you to specify each individual permission. When you select Custom, the Java Custom Settings... button appears, providing you with fine-grained control over the Java custom settings. See Figure 13-8.

It is somewhat surprising that Microsoft decided to allow Java to be executed from sites that are in the Restricted security zone. You can increase the security of Internet

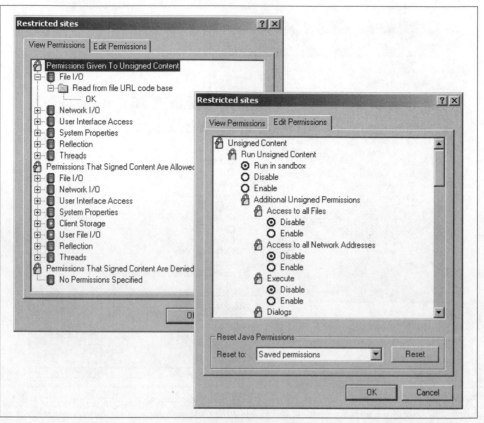

Figure 13-8. When you press the Java Custom Settings... button in Figure 13-7, Internet Explorer displays a panel that gives fine-grained control over the Java security settings. Most users will not need to adjust these settings.

Explorer by disabling Java for these sites. To disable Java for sites that are in the Restricted Sites security zone, follow these steps:

1. Select Internet Options from Internet Explorer's Tools menu.

2. Select the Security tab.

3. Select the Restricted Sites icon.

4. Click the Custom Level button.

5. Scroll down to the Microsoft VM section of the Security Settings window.

6. Underneath Java permissions, select Disable Java.

Setting Java policy in Netscape Navigator

Netscape Navigator 6.0's Java policy can be set using the Advanced selection option of Netscape's Preferences control panel. On this panel there is a check-box followed by the words "Enable Java."

If this check-box is selected, then Java applets will be run on downloaded web pages. If this check-box is not selected, Java applets will not run.

 If you would like to have more control over the Java security policy with Netscape Navigator, consider using an ad blocker such as AdSubtract or Web Washer. These programs allow you to selectively block or allow the execution of Java applets on a site-by-site basis. (Sophisticated users can also use the Java security policy file to obtain similar results.)

Java Security Problems

Since its initial release, the Java programming language has received almost as much attention in the newspapers for its security problems as for its actual uses. The majority of the Java security problems were found between 1996 and 1998 by a group of researchers at Princeton University's Secure Internet Programming (SIP) group. Most of the security problems discovered by the Princeton team were implementation errors: bugs in the Java runtime system that allowed specially-crafted Java applications to break out of the Java sandbox and execute arbitrary programs on the end user's machine. But a few of the problems discovered were design flaws in the Java language itself. The major errors found by the Princeton team included:

- Bugs with the Java virtual machine that let programs violate Java's type system. Once the type system is violated, it is possible to convince the JVM to execute arbitrary machine code.*

- Class library bugs, which allow hostile programs to learn "private" information about the user or, in the case of Sun's HotJava browser, edit the browser's settings.

- Fundamental design errors leading to web spoofing and other problems.

Most of the implementation errors discovered by the group were fixed shortly after they were reported. A complete list of the Princeton group's findings is on the Web at *http://www.cs.princeton.edu/sip/*.

Since then, more problems have been found in various implementations. For example, in August 2000, an error was found in the Java engine present in Netscape Navigator versions 4.04 through 4.74. The error, in a package called *netscape.net*, allowed Java applets to read any file on the host computer using the URL "file" protocol. For example, a Java applet could read the contents of the computer's *autoexec.bat* file by opening the URL *file:///c:/autoexec.bat*. The Java applet could then transmit the contents of files read in this manner to the web server from which the applet was downloaded. A programmer by the name of Dan Brumleve wrote a program called "Brown Orifice" to demonstrate the vulnerability. The Brown Orifice program ran a local web server on the victim's computer and allowed any machine on the Internet to view any file on the victim's computer. The vulnerability and the Brown Orifice program were publicized by CERT/CC in advisory CA-2000-15, which can be downloaded from *http://www.cert.org/advisories/CA-2000-15.html*. A similar problem was discovered in Microsoft's Java VM.†

Alas, the most serious problem with Java is a not bug or a typo, but a fundamental design flaw: Java's security model was not formally specified until years after it was

---

* Indeed, Java's entire security system depends on maintaining the integrity of the Java type system. Maintaining that integrity depends on the absolute proper functioning of the *SecurityManager* class and the Bytecode Verifier. While the *SecurityManager* class was 500 lines long in the first set of Java implementations that were commercialized, the Bytecode Verifier was 3500 lines of rather twisty code. To make things worse, there was no clear theory or reason as to what makes Java bytecode correct and what makes it incorrect, other than the operational definition that "valid bytecode is bytecode that passes the Bytecode Verifier." For further information, see McGraw, Gary, and Edward W. Felten, *Securing Java: Getting Down to Business with Mobile Code, 2nd Edition* (John Wiley & Sons).

† *http://www.microsoft.com/technet/security/bulletin/ms00-059.asp*

released! The Princeton group was forced to conclude that many of the apparent problems that they found in Java weren't necessarily security problems because no formal security model existed.

A formal security model would provide a sound theoretical and practical basis for the security policy decisions in the Java language. Such a model would start with policy goals—what sort of functionality is desired of Java applets? The model would then explore the sort of capabilities the Java language and environment needs to provide these functions. The model might consider how the Java type system is used to enforce security, and therefore how the type system needs to be protected to provide those features. Unfortunately, no such security model was ever created.

According to the book *Securing Java* by Gary McGraw and Ed Felton:

> Some progress was made toward this goal in a report commissioned by Sun back in 1996. The report, entitled Security Reference Model for JDK 1.0.2, explained (in informal English) Java's implicit security policy (at least for the base security sandbox). The SRM is available through *www.javasoft.com/security/SRM.html*. Creating the SRM was a useful exercise; unfortunately, any utility provided by the SRM was caught in the Internet-time cross fire. The SRM is completely out of date. Given the rigorous security demands of electronic commerce, documents like the SRM should be demanded by organizations using consumerware in their security-critical systems.

The good news for Java users and developers is that the vast majority of the security problems found were addressed shortly after they were discovered. Furthermore, there are no cases of Java flaws being used on a widespread basis to compromise end-user machines.

On the other hand, the fact that so many flaws were discovered so readily with Java implementations indicates that the technology was released prematurely into the marketplace and onto computer user's desktops. Ideally, outside security reviews should take place before products are released, rather than afterwards.[*]

While the basic implementation flaws were all fixed, their presence created a vulnerability that continues to this day, because many browsers are still running the old, buggy Java engines. In our opinion, software vendors such as Sun and Microsoft need to be more open with their internal reviews, and they need to slow down the pace of development so that code can be evaluated more rigorously before it is deployed to millions of users. (Netscape used to have problems with openness, but as a result of creating the Mozilla project, large amounts of the Navigator code base have been released for public inspection and use.)

Users and customers, meanwhile, need to demand higher levels of security and overall software quality. They must also be willing to allow vendors to properly test code,

---

[*] We say "ideally" because we realize this isn't how the marketplace has worked with most security-critical technology people use.

rather than demanding the right to download the earliest "alpha," "beta," or "prerelease" program.

We recommend that users in high security environments disable Java entirely.

Hostile Applets

Dr. Mark LaDue, a graduate of Georgia Tech, has spent a considerable amount of energy developing a series of Java applets that demonstrate flaws in various implementations of Java. Applets that he has developed will crash a computer running Java, take control of a workstation on which it is running, factor integers without your permission, and divulge your email address. He has also developed a "self-defending applet killer" that will stop any other applets that are running and will kill any applet that is downloaded afterwards.

These applets and more can be found at LaDue's web page entitled "A Collection of Increasingly Hostile Applets" currently at *http://www.cigital.com/hostile-applets/* and *http://metro.to/mladue/hostile-applets/index.html*. (The URL seems to change from time to time because of threatened legal action.)

JavaScript

Invented by Brendan Eich and originally called LiveScript, JavaScript is a programming language that Netscape developed to add forms validation, other local calculations, and some forms of interaction to web browsers. JavaScript programs reside in HTML files, usually surrounded by <script> tags (so that they will be recognized by JavaScript-enabled browsers) and HTML comment tags (so that they will be ignored by browsers that do not understand JavaScript).

Full JavaScript allows HTML files to command the browser. JavaScript programs create new windows, fill out fields in forms, jump to new URLs, process image maps locally, change the HTML content of the page itself, compute mathematical results, and perform many other functions. JavaScript can also modify the appearance of web browsers, making visual elements of the web browser appear or disappear dynamically. JavaScript makes messages appear in the status line of web browsers—some of the earliest JavaScript applications displayed moving banners across the web browser's status line. Early versions of JavaScript could even reprogram a browser's history, although this feature has now been disabled. (It was abused by pornographic web sites.)

A web page can contain multiple JavaScript sections, called *scripts*. The scripts are programmed to run when the web page loads, when a button or link on the page is touched or clicked with the mouse, or after a certain amount of time has passed.

Scripts can also access elements on the page using the Document Object Model (DOM).

Unlike Java, JavaScript code is interpreted directly by the web browser. This fact has made it difficult to filter JavaScript out of web pages—in many cases, it is possible to send HTML to a web browser that appears to be free of JavaScript, but that actually contains JavaScript programs.

A Touch of JavaScript

Here is a simple HTML file that contains an embedded JavaScript program. The HTML comment characters (<!-- and -->) are largely anachronistic. They are present so that a browser that does not understand the <script> and </script> tags will simply treat the JavaScript as a comment and not display the program. These days, many JavaScript developers are dropping the comment characters, as the vast majority of browsers in use understand the <script> tag (although they may ignore the embedded JavaScript):

```
<html>
<head>
<title>Hello World!</title>
<body>
This is a JavaScript Demo
</body>
<script language="JavaScript">
<!--
alert("Hello World!");
-->
</script>
</html>
```

When this program runs, it displays a little window that says "Hello World!", as shown in Figure 13-9.

JavaScript programs can interact with forms, frames, and other objects on a web page using the browser's Document Object Model. Briefly, DOM exposes specific objects and functionality of the browser to a running JavaScript program. JavaScript can also be used to control a browser—for example, JavaScript can be used to open new windows, click the browser's Back button, and even access the browser's history (but only the history of the current site).

JavaScript is an amazing language; the more you study it, the more things you find.* For example, if you wish to draw a graph in your HTML file, you can do so with a very simple piece of JavaScript in your program and the JavaScript Graph Builder library

---

* Much of Netscape Navigator 6.0 is written in JavaScript!

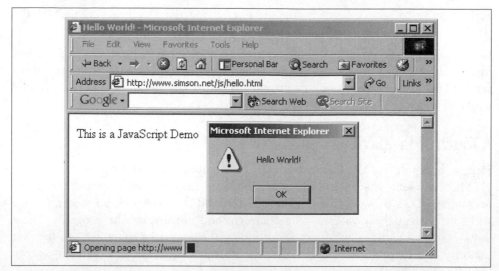

Figure 13-9. The JavaScript Hello World program.

created by Netscape Engineer Michael Bostock. Here is an example of the JavaScript needed to create a simple graph of coin flipping results:

```
<html><head>
<title>Coin Flipping Results</title>
<body><CENTER>
<SCRIPT LANGUAGE="JavaScript1.2" SRC="graph.js"></SCRIPT>
<SCRIPT LANGUAGE="JavaScript">
if(parseInt(navigator.appVersion) >= 4) {
    var g = new Graph(300,200);
    g.addRow(100,90,110,101,102,103);
    g.addRow(100,90,85,93,98,102);
    g.scale = 50;
    g.setDate(7,11,2001);
g.title = "Daily Coin Flipping Results";
g.xLabel = "Date";
g.yLabel = "Heads";
g.setLegend("Penny","Quarter");
g.build();
} else {
  document.writeln("<b>This graph requires a Netscape version 4 or higher browser to
display</b>");
}
</center></script></body></html>
```

When this HTML file is loaded, it produces a graph similar to the one shown in Figure 13-10.

JavaScript's ultimate utility is somewhat muted by incompatibilities among the JavaScript implementations in different web browsers. With each new version of Netscape Navigator, Netscape has made significant and occasionally incompatible

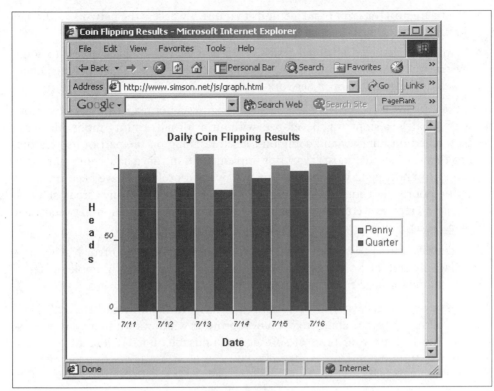

Figure 13-10. Michael Bostock's Graph Builder Library can create impressive graphics using JavaScript.

changes to the JavaScript language. Microsoft did not license JavaScript from Netscape, but instead created its own clone named JScript. These versions were theoretically merged into a scripting language, specification ECMA-262, also known as ECMAScript, in June 1997.[*] Unfortunately, continuing differences in the Document Object Model between Netscape Navigator and Microsoft Internet Explorer mean that most web pages that use complicated JavaScript require "client-sniffing" code that detects the browser that the user has, and adjusts the JavaScript appropriately.

JavaScript Security Overview

JavaScript programs should be inherently more secure than programs written in Java or other programming languages for a number of reasons:

- There are no JavaScript methods that directly access the files on the client computer.

---

[*] For information on ECMA see *http://www.ecma.ch/*. The ECMA-262 specification can be downloaded from *http://www.ecma.ch/ecma1/stand/ecma-262.htm*.

- There are no JavaScript basic methods that directly access the network, although JavaScript programs can load URLs and submit HTML forms.*

- With code signing, individual JavaScript programs can be given access to some system functionality (such as the ability to read files) without opening others (such as the ability to open network connections).

Alas, the anticipated security of JavaScript's design was not realized in its execution. As with Java, JavaScript was developed without a formal security model. Instead, security relied on hunches and common-sense reasoning on the part of its creators. Add to this the fact that most JavaScript implementations have had significant bugs, and you can understand why many security flaws and problems have been traced to buggy or poorly thought out JavaScript implementations. In many circumstances, JavaScript's creators were simply unable to anticipate the interaction between their language and the other aspects of various web browsers.

All of the discovered flaws were fixed shortly after they were reported. Navigator 3 was relatively free of JavaScript problems, and Navigator 4 finally implemented a security model for JavaScript code running on browsers.

But alas, even when JavaScript is running properly, normal, "well behaved" JavaScript programs have the ability to open new browser windows without your permission, and to lock up your browser so that it is unusable. For versions of Netscape prior to 6.1 running on Unix computers, you can even use JavaScript to crash the user's window system.

We recommend that users in high security environments disable JavaScript.

JavaScript Security Flaws

Because a piece of downloaded JavaScript runs inside the browser itself, it potentially has access to any information that the browser has. Early JavaScript implementations featured a variety of problems that could lead to loss of confidentiality or privacy, including the following:

- JavaScript could be used to create forms that automatically submitted themselves by email. This allowed a malicious HTML page to forge email in the name of the person viewing the page. ("Viewing this page automatically sends the President and his cat an electronic death threat from your web browser.") This feature could also be used to collect the email addresses of people visiting a web page. ("Thank you for visiting our web page; your name and email address have automatically been added to the Flat Earth Society mailing list.")

---

* Netscape Navigator Version 6 supports "signed JavaScript" code, which is allowed to access the full API of the browser through the XPConnect System. This provides access to the network and files.

- JavaScript programs had access to the user's browser "history" mechanism. This allowed a web site to discover the URLs of all of the other web pages that you had visited during your session. This feature could be combined with the previous feature to perform a form of automated eavesdropping.
- A remote site could use JavaScript to upload arbitrary files from the user's disk drives to the hostile server.
- A JavaScript program running in one window could monitor the URLs of pages visited in other windows.

All known bugs that could compromise the privacy or the security of the user's computer were corrected by Microsoft and Netscape shortly after the bugs were discovered. Unfortunately, users are not quick to upload patches—especially as many of these "patches" have required users to download a new multimegabyte program and reinstall the browser, and have sometimes broken needed functions.

JavaScript Denial-of-Service Attacks

JavaScript can be used to mount effective denial-of-service attacks against the users of web browsers. A *denial-of-service attack* is an attack in which a user (or a program) takes up so much of a shared resource that none of the resource is left for other users or uses. These attacks can be resident on web pages or they can be sent to users with JavaScript-enabled mail readers in electronic mail. Most of these attacks result in the crashing of the computer on which the web page is running. This can represent an annoyance or a loss of productivity for most users and corporations, and it can be a serious problem for web browsers that are used in safety-critical applications or in network monitoring systems.

Of course, any programming language or environment that allows systemwide resources to be allocated and then places no limitations on the allocation of such resources is subject to denial-of-service attacks. But JavaScript is especially sensitive to such attacks because of the power that it gives active content over the computer's web browser.

Can't break a running script

Both Navigator and Explorer's Java and JavaScript implementations suffer from the fact that you can't break out of a running Java or JavaScript program (easily or at all, depending on version). If you want to terminate a program, your only real choice is to exit the browser itself.

Unfortunately, exiting the browser can be complicated by the fact that the browser itself may have stopped listening to menu commands as a result of an ongoing denial-of-service attack. In this case, it will be necessary to find some other way to terminate the browser, such as typing Control-Alt-Del under Windows or Command-Option-Escape under Mac OS.

Many users do not know about these "tricks" for forcing a running program to quit. Therefore, your typical Macintosh or Windows users, faced with this JavaScript-based HTML attack, may find themselves with no choice other than turning off their machines:

```
<html>
<head><title>Denial-of-service Demonstration</title>
</head>
<body>
<script>
while(1){
        alert("This is a JavaScript alert.");
}
</script>
</body>
```

To further complicate matters, it turns out that the JavaScript *alert()* method has had different semantics when running under some versions of Windows and Mac OS from those used when running on Unix. For web browsers running on Windows and Mac OS clients, the JavaScript *alert()* method is blocking: it waits for you to click the OK button before going on. But under Netscape's Unix clients prior to Navigator 6.1, the *alert()* method does not block. Instead, Netscape brings up hundreds (or even thousands) of little alert windows. This will actually cause most Unix window managers to crash, making this an effective denial-of-service attack not only against the browser, but against the user's entire workspace.

Window system attacks

Both Java and JavaScript allow downloaded code to create and manage windows on the user's machine. Graphical User Interface (GUI) operations consume a tremendous amount of system resources on most computers. By creating many windows, the user's entire computer can be rendered inoperable.

One of the more annoying features of JavaScript is the ability to register a JavaScript function that will be executed when the current JavaScript page is unloaded—that is, if the Back button is hit or if the window is closed. Many porn sites on the Internet use this feature to bring up new windows when you attempt to close an existing window. A particularly amusing exploit that uses this feature was first introduced by Kevin McCurley on his "DigiCrime" web site (*http://www.digicrime.com/*). The exploit consists of an HTML file with an embedded JavaScript attack that causes two new windows to be opened every time you attempt to close the window on which the HTML page resides. A message displayed on the screen says "Your only way out now is to kill the browser."

Here is an example of such a script:

```
<html>
<script language="JavaScript">
```

```
function again( ) {
    var n1 = Math.floor(Math.random( )*1000000);
    var n2 = Math.floor(Math.random( )*1000000);

    window.open('js-close-attack.html', n1, 'width=300,height=200');
    window.open('js-close-attack.html', n2 , 'width=300,height=200');
}
</script>

<head>
<title>JavaScript onUnload Demonstration</title>
</head>
<body  onUnload="again( )">
<center><h1>Thanks to Digicrime!</h1>
<hr>
Your only option now is to turn off your computer.

<a href="javascript:again( )">attack</a>

<hr>
</center>
</html>
```

The real culprit here is not JavaScript's ability to hook onto the unLoad event, of course, but its ability to make new windows. Change the onUnload tag to an onLoad tag in this script for even more highjinks!

 Netscape 6 gives the user the option of preventing a script from opening new windows. For details, see: *http://www.mozilla.org/projects/security/components/ConfigPolicy.html.*

CPU and stack attacks

Not everything is doom and gloom in the denial-of-service attack department, however. Early versions of Internet Explorer and Netscape Navigator were both susceptible to CPU and stack-space attacks written in JavaScript. But these vulnerabilities have now largely been repaired.

Consider this HTML file that uses JavaScript to display the first 100,000 Fibonacci numbers:

```
<html>
<head><title>Fibonacci Test Page</title>
</head>
<body>
<h1>The Fibonacci Series</h1>
<script>
function fibonacci(n)
{
 if(n>1) return fibonacci(n-1)+fibonacci(n-2);
 if(n>=0) return 0;
```

```
  return 1;
}
for(i=0;i<100000;i++){
  document.write("Fibonacci number "+i+" is "+fibonacci(i)+"<br>");
}

</script>
</body>
</html>
```

When this page is loaded into either browser, the browser becomes unresponsive. After a pause of approximately 30 seconds, both Internet Explorer and Netscape Navigator will display a warning that allows you to abort the execution of the running script (see Figure 13-11).

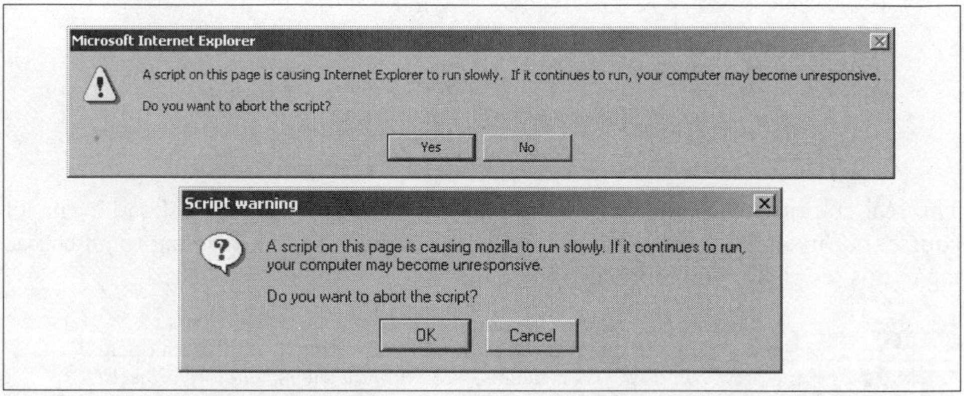

Figure 13-11. Although early versions of Internet Explorer and Netscape Navigator (a.k.a. Mozilla) did not properly handle JavaScript-based denial-of-service attacks, the current versions will display these warnings if they are asked to execute a script that takes too much time.

JavaScript Spoofing Attacks

Ed Felten at Princeton University notes that people are constantly making security-related decisions. To make these decisions, people use contextual information provided by their computer. For example, when a user dials in to a computer, the user knows to type her dialup username and password. At the same time, most users know to avoid typing their dialup username and password into a chat room on America Online.

Java and JavaScript can be used to confuse the user. This can result in a user's making a mistake and providing security-related information to the wrong party.

Spoofing username/password pop-ups with Java

When an untrusted Java applet creates a window, most web browsers label the window in some manner so that the user knows that it is unsecure. Netscape Navigator, for instance, will display the window with the message "untrusted applet." The intention of this labeling is to alert the user: users may not wish to type their login usernames and passwords into a window that's not "trusted."

When an applet runs inside a browser window itself, no such labeling takes place. A rogue HTML page can easily display an innocuous background and then use a Java applet to create a traditional web browser username/password panel. The applet can even detect an attempt to drag the spoofed "window" and make it move on the page appropriately. The user can't determine the difference unless she tries to drag the window outside the browser's window.

Applets aren't limited to spoofing web username/password panels. An applet could easily display other username/password panels. For example, a web server could check to see if a user has accessed a web page using a Windows personal computer dialed up with the Microsoft PPP dialer. If this is detected, the applet could display a window that told the user that the connection had been disconnected, followed by a request to reconnect (see Figures 13-12 and 13-13).

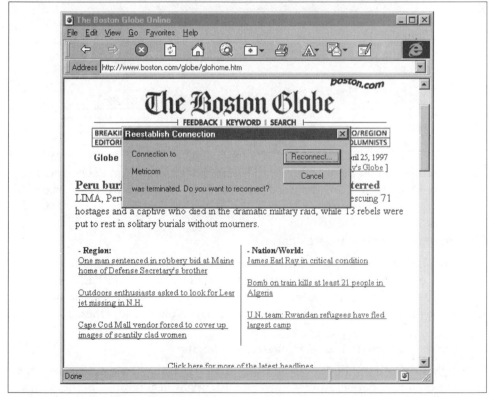

Figure 13-12. Your connection has been terminated; is this window real or Java?

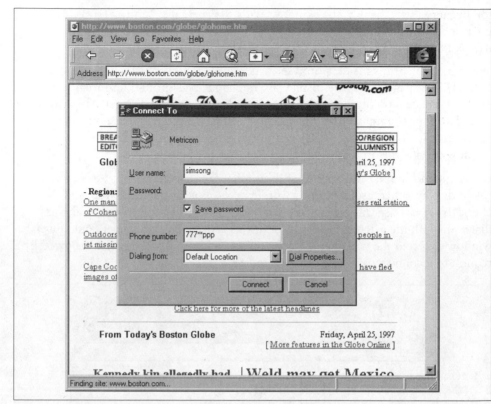

Figure 13-13. The reconnection request.

The applet could even play the sound of a modem dialing and connecting. An astute user might realize that the modem is still connected, but many probably would not. Send such an applet to a few thousand users, and you'll probably get dozens of dial-up usernames and passwords.

Spoofing browser status with JavaScript

Felten notes that many users' security decisions are based on URLs and filenames. A Windows user might know that downloading a file called *HAPPY.EXE* might be more dangerous than downloading a file called *HAPPY.GIF* because the first is an executable program, whereas the second is an image. Now consider these two URLs:

```
https://www.mall.com/order.html
https://www.university.edu/users/guest/open/order.html
```

Although the naming of both of these URLs implies that they are secure order pages, either or both may not be. At that, the first URL might inspire trust, but fewer users might feel comfortable typing a credit card number into the second.

JavaScript has several tools that can be used for spoofing user context. These include the following:

- JavaScript can display boxes containing arbitrary text.
- JavaScript can change the content of the browser's status line.
- On some browsers, JavaScript can be used to hide the browser's "Goto:" field and replace it with a constructed field built from a frame.

For example, the status line of the browser normally displays the URL that will be accessed if the user clicks on a link. But using JavaScript, you can make a user believe that one URL actually points someplace else. For example, this HTML link will display the URL *http://www.shopping.com/order-entry.html* when the mouse is moved over the link, but clicking on the link will jump to the web page *http://www.attacker.org/trapped.html*.

```
<a href="http://www.attacker.org/trapped.html" onMouseover="window.status='http://
www.shopping.com/order-entry.html';return true">Click Here to enter your credit card
number</a>
```

Many users might be willing to run any program that they downloaded from a trusted domain. However, there are many ways to trick a user's web browser into downloading a program from one domain but displaying visual cues that indicate the program is in fact being downloaded from another. Consider these issues when downloading a file *SETUP.EXE*, apparently from a host at Microsoft Corporation:

- The user may think that the file is being downloaded from the domain *MICROSOFT.COM*, when the file is in fact being downloaded from *MICROS0FT.COM* (a domain in which the letter "O" has been changed to the digit "0").
- The user may see that the file is being downloaded from *MICROSOFT.CO.FI*, and not know whether or not that is a domain associated with Microsoft.
- The web browser may display the beginning and the end but truncate the characters in the middle of a large URL. For example, the browser may display that a file is being downloaded from the address *http://www.microsoft.co.../setup.exe*. But the user might not realize that the file being downloaded actually has the URL *http://www.microsoft.com.attacker.org/guests/users/hacker/setup.exe*.

One way to minimize spoofing risks is by producing "unspoofable" areas—status displays on the browser's window that cannot be rewritten by JavaScript or Java. For example, Netscape Navigator may display part of the web server's DNS name in an area that cannot be overwritten by a program running in the web browser. This may help solve some problems. A better approach would be to have the web browser display, in a prominent area, the distinguished name that is on a web server's public key certificate. (See Chapter 17 for more information on server certificates.)

Mirror worlds

Felten *et al.* have demonstrated that it is possible to use the techniques mentioned in the preceding sections to create a mirror World Wide Web site. The site uses a combination of URL rewriting, JavaScript substituting techniques, long hostnames, and caching to replicate the content of one web site on another.

A mirror world constructed in this fashion can essentially trap users, monitoring all of the pages that they request, capturing passwords, and even conducting man-in-the-middle attacks (described in Chapter 5) on SSL connections. A suspicious user could detect such a mirror world attack by looking at the distinguished name on an SSL certificate, and he could break out of the mirror world by using the web browser's Open Location function or using a bookmark. However, it is conjectured that most users would not discover the attack, and would divulge significant information to the attacker.

There are many ways to lure a user into a mirror world. The URL could be put in a public area where it is likely to be tried. For example, it could be sent to a mailing list or posted on a web-based bulletin board. The URL could be added to a search engine. Once inside the mirror world, the only way out would be by using a bookmarked web site or using the browser's Back button.

Although a mirror world attack is easily traced back to the web site that is conducting it, this information may not in itself be useful. The attacking site may be in a foreign country. Alternatively, it may be a web site that has itself been compromised.

Flash and Shockwave

Macromedia's Flash and Shockwave plug-ins offer yet another form of rich media for many web designers. Both of these systems are designed to allow web designers to create complex animations that can interact with the user. Programs written in Flash and Shockwave can display graphics, read the mouse, have the user fill out forms, and control the web browser.

Conceptually, Flash and Shockwave are similar to Java in that these systems use bytecode that is downloaded from the web site to the computer and run with a special plug-in or "player." Their security is supposed to come from the fact that there is a limited repertoire of commands available to Flash and Shockwave programs. Unfortunately, the security is somewhat compromised by the lack of peer review for these proprietary products.

Consider the Macromedia Shockwave plug-in. In January 1997, Simson learned that the Shockwave plug-in contained instructions for reading and writing directly to the filesystems of the computer on which the web browser is running. This would seem to be a security problem. So Simson contacted Macromedia, spoke with an engineer, and was told that the Shockwave plug-in could only read and write to files stored in a particular directory in the Shockwave folder. The engineer said that Macromedia had been very careful to ensure that the plug-in could read and write to no other files on the system. The engineer further said that there was no way to use the system to store executable files.

Then on March 10, 1997, David de Vitry posted a message to the Bugtraq mailing lists that said the Shockwave plug-in could be used to read email messages stored in the Netscape mail folders. Apparently, the Shockwave GETNETTEXT command can read from many different folders located within the Netscape directory, rather than only from Shockwave "preference" files. Reportedly, this Shockwave bug also affected Macromedia's plug-in with Internet Explorer.

Macromedia said that it would be issuing a bug fix. Unfortunately, there's no way to know whether or not other security problems are lurking and misunderstood by the company's own engineers. This is true for *every* plug-in, not simply Macromedia's. However, because the Macromedia plug-ins are exceedingly widespread, a flaw that is found with them can directly compromise the security of millions of individual computers.

Conclusion

Java, JavaScript, Flash, and Shockwave are here to stay. Although Java will probably never live up to its initial hype, Java-based stock tickers, mortgage calculators, and graphing agents provide web developers with convenient and reasonably secure systems for moving computation from the web server to the end user's computer. Likewise JavaScript, despite some initial bumps, has shaped up to be a reasonably secure system for implementing shopping carts and providing client-side form validation.

Because of the risks that arise from buggy implementation and the poor track records of Java and JavaScript to date, we recommend that none of the mobile code systems described in the chapter be used in high security environments. However, most Internet users can probably use these technologies without much fear—provided that they are careful to download browser updates when security problems are discovered.

## PART III

Web Server Security

This part of the book is addressed to people and organizations that are operating their own servers that are attached to the Internet. The chapters in this part focus on the mechanics of web server operation. They are particularly relevant to corporations that operate their own web servers, administrators at Internet service providers (ISPs), and home users who run their own servers at the end of cable modems or DSL lines.

Chapter 14, *Physical Security for Servers*, addresses one of the most important but frequently overlooked topics—how to protect your computer's physical well-being.

Chapter 15, *Host Security for Servers*, explores security having to do with your computer's operating system.

Chapter 16, *Securing Web Applications*, discusses the added security issues that arise when running web servers that can execute programs or scripts.

Chapter 17, *Deploying SSL Server Certificates*, gives step-by-step instructions for enabling SSL on the Apache and IIS web servers.

Chapter 18, *Securing Your Web Service*, broadens the security discussion to show how to defend your service against problems resulting from your ISP or the Internet's Domain Name Service (DNS).

Chapter 19, *Computer Crime*, explores the specific legal options available to you after your computer system has been broken into, as well as other legal issues of concern to administrators.

In this chapter:
- Planning for the Forgotten Threats
- Protecting Computer Hardware
- Protecting Your Data
- Personnel
- Story: A Failed Site Inspection

## CHAPTER 14

Physical Security
for Servers

"Physical security" is almost everything that happens before you start typing commands on the keyboard. It's the alarm system that calls the police department when a late-night thief tries to break into your building. It's the key lock on your computer's power supply that makes it harder for unauthorized people to turn off the machine. It's the locked computer room with the closed-circuit camera that prevents unauthorized physical access to your servers and communications infrastructure. And it's the uninteruptable power supply and power conditioners that help to isolate your computers from the vagaries of the power grid.

This chapter discusses basic approaches to physical security. It is written for people who think that this type of security is of little or no concern—unfortunately, the majority of system administrators. Despite the fact that physical security is often overlooked, it is extraordinarily important. You may have the best encryption and security tools in place, and your systems may be safely hidden behind a firewall. However, if a janitor working late at night for your cleaning service decides to steal a laptop or server that's been left out on a table in somebody's cubicle, those other fancy defenses aren't going to be much help.

Planning for the Forgotten Threats

Surprisingly, many organizations do not consider physical security to be of the utmost concern. As an example, one New York investment house was spending tens of thousands of dollars on computer security measures to prevent break-ins during the day, only to discover that its cleaning staff was propping open the doors to the computer room at night while the floor was being mopped. A magazine in San Francisco had more than $100,000 worth of computers stolen over a holiday: an employee had used his electronic key card to unlock the building and disarm the alarm system; after getting inside, the person went to the supply closet where the alarm system was located and removed the paper log from the alarm system's printer.

Other organizations feel that physical security is simply too complicated or too difficut to handle properly. No amount of physical security on the part of the tenants of the World Trade Center could have protected them from the collapse of their office buildings after the terrorist attack of September 11, 2001. Likewise, few organizations have the ability to protect their servers from a nuclear attack. But it is important not to let these catastrophic possiblities paralyze and prevent an organization from doing careful disaster planning: those organizations that did the best job of restoring operations after September 11 were the ones that had spent the money to build and maintain redundant off-site mirror facilities.

Physical security is one of the most frequently forgotten forms of security because the issues that physical security encompasses—the threats, practices, and protections—are different for practically every different site and organization. Physical security resists simple treatment in books on computer security, as different organizations running the identical system software might have dramatically different physical security needs. To make matters worse, many popular books on computer system security do not even mention physical security! Because physical security must be installed on-site, it cannot be preinstalled by the operating system vendor, sold by telemarketers, or downloaded over the Internet as part of a free set of security tools.

Anything that we write about physical security must therefore be broadly stated and general. Because every site is different, this chapter can't give you a set of specific recommendations. It can only give you a starting point, a list of issues to consider, and a suggested procedure for formulating your actual plan.

The Physical Security Plan

The first step to physically securing your installation is to formulate a written plan addressing your current physical security needs and your intended future direction. Ideally, your physical plan should be part of your site's written security policy. This plan should be reviewed by others for completeness, and it should be approved by your organization's senior management. Thus, the purpose of the plan is both planning and political buy-in.

Your security plan should include:

- Descriptions of the physical assets that you are protecting
- Descriptions of the physical areas where the assets are located
- A description of your *security perimeter*—the boundary between the rest of the world and your secured area—and the holes in the perimeter
- The threats (e.g., attacks, accidents, or natural disasters) that you are protecting against and their likelihood
- Your security defenses, and ways of improving them

- The estimated cost of specific improvements
- The value of the information that you are protecting

If you are managing a particularly critical installation, take great care in formulating this plan. Have it reviewed by an outside firm that specializes in disaster recovery planning and risk assessment. Consider your security plan a sensitive document: by its very nature, it contains detailed information on your defenses' weakest points.

A detailed security plan may seem like overkill for smaller businesses, some educational institutions, and most home systems. Nevertheless, simply enumerating the threats and the measures that you are using to protect against them will serve you well in understanding how to protect your informational assets. Is fire a possibility? If so, you may wish to invest in a fireproof safe for backups (cost: as little as $200), or you may wish to contract with an off-site backup provider (cost: approximately $20/month per PC). Is theft a possibility? If so, you may wish to purchase a lock for your computer (cost: approximately $30). Do you back up your server but not your desktop PCs? If so, you may wish to make sure that people in your organization know this, so that they store files on the file server, and not on their computer's "desktop."

If the very idea of planning is repulsive to you, then this aspect should be delegated to someone in your organization who is more suited to the task. At the very least, you should ask yourself these five questions:

1. Does anybody other than you ever have physical access to your computers?
2. What would happen if that person had a breakdown or an angry outburst and tried to smash your system with a hammer?
3. What would happen if someone in the employ of your biggest competitor were to come into the building unnoticed?
4. If there were a fire in your building and the computers were rendered unusable, would the inability to access these systems cripple or destroy your organization?
5. If some disaster were to befall your system, how would you face your angry users?

The Disaster Recovery Plan

You should have a plan for immediately securing temporary computer equipment and for loading your backups onto new systems in case your computer is ever stolen or damaged. This plan is known as a *disaster recovery plan*.

We recommend that you do the following:

- Establish a plan for rapidly acquiring new equipment in the event of theft, fire, or equipment failure.
- Test this plan by renting (or borrowing) a computer system and trying to restore your backups.

If you ask, you may discover that your computer dealer is willing to lend you a system that is faster than the original system for the purpose of evaluation. There is probably no better way to evaluate a system than to load your backup tapes onto the system and see if they work. (Be sure to delete and purge the computer's disk drives before returning them to your vendor!)

Other Contingencies

Beyond the items mentioned earlier, you may also wish to consider the impact on your computer operations of the following:

Loss of phone service or network connections
> How will the loss of service impact your regular operations?

Vendor continuity
> How important is support? Can you move to another hardware or software system if your vendor goes out of business or makes changes you don't wish to adopt?

Significant absenteeism of staff
> Will this impact your ability to operate?

Death or incapacitation of key personnel
> Can every member of your computer organization be replaced? What are the contingency plans?

Protecting Computer Hardware

Physically protecting a computer presents many of the same problems that arise when protecting typewriters, jewelry, and file cabinets. As with a typewriter, an office computer is something that many people inside the office need to access on an ongoing basis. As with jewelry, computers are valuable and generally easy for a thief to sell. But the real danger in having a computer stolen isn't the loss of the system's hardware but the loss of the data that was stored on the computer's disks. As with legal files and financial records, if you don't have a backup—or if the backup is stolen or destroyed along with the computer—the data you have lost may well be irreplaceable. Even if you do have a backup, you will still need to spend valuable time setting up a replacement system. Finally, there is always the chance that the stolen information itself, or even the mere fact that information was stolen, will be used against you.

Your computers are among the most expensive possessions in your home or office; they are also the pieces of equipment that you can least afford to lose.[*]

---

[*] We know of some computer professionals who say, "I don't care if the thief steals my computer; I only wish that he would first take out the hard drive!" Unfortunately, you can rarely reason in this manner with would-be thieves.

To make matters worse, computers and computer media are by far the most temperamental objects in today's homes and offices. Few people worry that their television sets will be damaged if they're turned on during a lightning storm, but a computer's power supply can be blown out simply by leaving the machine *plugged into the wall* if lightning strikes nearby. Even if the power surge doesn't destroy the information on your hard disk, it still may make the information inaccessible until the computer system is repaired.

Power surges don't come only during storms: one of the authors once had a workstation ruined because a vacuum cleaner was plugged into the same outlet as the running workstation. When the vacuum was switched on, the power surge fatally shorted out the workstation's power supply. Because the computer was an aging Digital Pro 350 workstation with a proprietary disk interface and filesystem, it proved to be cheaper to throw out the machine and lose the data, rather than attempt to salvage the hardware and information stored on the machine's disk. This proved to be an expensive form of spring cleaning!

There are several measures that you can take to protect your computer system against physical threats. Many of them will simultaneously protect the system from dangers posed by nature, outsiders, and inside saboteurs.

The Environment

Computers often require exactly the right balance of physical and environmental conditions to operate properly. Altering this balance can cause your computer to fail in unexpected and often undesirable ways. Even worse, your computer might continue to operate erratically, producing incorrect results and corrupting valuable data.

In this respect, computers are a lot like people: they don't work well if they're too hot, too cold, or submerged in water without special protection.

Fire

Computers are notoriously bad at surviving fires. If the flames don't cause your system's case and circuit boards to ignite, the heat might melt your hard drive and all the solder holding the electronic components in place. Your computer might even survive the fire, only to be destroyed by the water used to fight the flames.

You can increase the chances that your computer will survive a fire by making sure that there is good fire-extinguishing equipment nearby.

Gas-charged fire extinguishers are popular for large corporate computer rooms. These work by physically blocking oxygen from coming into contact with the burning materials. Unfortunately, gases may also asphyxiate humans in the area. For this reason, all automatic gas discharge systems have loud alarms that sound before the gas is discharged. Commonly used gases include nitrogen, argon, and less frequently, carbon dioxide.[*]

Here are some guidelines for fire control:

- Make sure that you have a hand-held fire extinguisher near the doorway of your computer room. Train your computer operators in the proper use of the fire extinguisher. This training should ideally include the actual use of a fire extinguisher—surprisingly, few people have ever discharged a fire extinguisher! One good way to do this is to have your employees practice outdoors with extinguishers that need to be recharged (usually once every year or two). Repeat the training at least once a year.

- Check the recharge state of each fire extinguisher every month. Extinguishers with gauges will show if they need recharging. All extinguishers should be recharged and examined by a professional on a periodic basis (sometimes those gauges stick in the "full" position!).

- If you have a gas-discharge system, make sure everyone who enters the computer room knows what to do when the alarm sounds. Post warning signs in appropriate places.

- If you have an automatic fire-alarm system, make sure you can override it in the event of a false alarm.

- Ensure that there is telephone access for your operators and users who may discover a fire. If you have a PBX, make sure that there is at least one backup telephone that goes directly to the phone company.

Many modern computers will not be damaged by automatic sprinkler systems, provided that the computer's power is turned off before the water starts to flow (although disks, tapes, and printouts in the open may suffer). Consequently, you should have your computer's power automatically cut if the water sprinkler triggers.[†]

Getting sensitive electronics wet is never a good idea. But if your computer has been soaked after the power was cut, you can possibly recover the system by completely drying the system and then carefully reapplying the power. If your water has a very high mineral content, you may find it necessary to have the computer's circuit boards professionally cleaned before attempting to power up. In some cases, you may find it easier to simply remove your computer's disk drives and put them into a new computer. You should immediately copy the data onto new disks, rather than attempting to run with the salvaged equipment.

---

[*] Older systems used a gas called Halon. Halon is currently banned from general use because of its effects on ozone in the environment. One of the replacements for Halon is marketed under the name HF200.

[†] If you have an uninteruptable power supply, be sure that it automatically disconnects, as well.

Because many computers can now survive exposure to water, many fire-protection experts now suggest that a water sprinkler system may be as good as (or better than) a gas discharge system. In particular, a water system will continue to run long after a gas system is exhausted, so it's more likely to work against major fires. Such a system is also less expensive to maintain, and less hazardous to humans.

If you choose to have a water-based sprinkler system installed, be sure it is a "dry-pipe" system. These systems keep water out of the pipes until an alarm is actually triggered, rather than having the sprinkler heads pressurized all the time. Because they are not continuously pressurized, dry-pipe systems tend to be resistant to leaks.[*]

Be sure that your wiring is protected, in addition to your computers. Be certain that smoke detectors and sprinkler heads are appropriately positioned to cover wires in wiring trays (often above your suspended ceilings) and in wiring closets.

Smoke

Smoke is very damaging to computer equipment. Smoke is a potent abrasive and collects on the heads of magnetic disks, optical disks, and tape drives. A single smoke particle can cause a severe disk crash on some kinds of older disk drives that lack a sealed drive compartment.

Sometimes smoke is generated by computers themselves. Electrical fires—particularly those caused by the transformers in video monitors—can produce a pungent, acrid smoke that may damage other equipment and may also be poisonous or a carcinogen. Several years ago, an entire laboratory at Stanford had to be evacuated because of the toxic smoke caused by a fire in a single video monitor.

Another signifcant danger is the smoke that comes from cigarettes and pipes. Such smoke is a hazard to people and computers alike. Besides the known cancer risk, tobacco smoke can cause premature failure of keyboards and require that they be cleaned more often. Nonsmokers in a smoky environment will not perform as well as they might otherwise, both in the short and long term. In many locales, smoking in public or semi-public places is now illegal.

Here are some guidelines for smoke control:

- Do not permit smoking in your computer room or around the people who use the computers.
- Install smoke detectors in every room with computer or terminal equipment.
- If you have a raised floor, mount smoke detectors *underneath* the floor as well.
- If you have suspended ceilings, mount smoke detectors *above* the ceiling tiles.

[*] We know of one instance where a maintenance man accidentally knocked the sprinkler head off with a stepladder. The water came out in such quantity that the panels for the raised floor were floating before the water was shut off. The mess took more than a week to clean up.

Get a Carbon Monoxide Detector!

Carbon monoxide (CO) won't harm your computer, but it might silently kill any humans in the vicinity. One of the authors of this book became quite sick in February 1994 when his home chimney was inadvertently plugged and the furnace exhaust started venting into his house. Low-cost carbon monoxide detectors are readily available. You should install them wherever coal, oil, or gas-fired appliances are used.

If you think this warning doesn't apply to your computer environment, think again. Closed office buildings can build up strong concentrations of CO from faulty heater venting, problems with generator exhaust (as from a UPS), or even trucks idling outside with their exhaust near the building air intake.

Dust

Dust destroys data. As with smoke, dust can collect on the heads of magnetic disks, tape drives, and optical drives. Dust is abrasive and will slowly destroy both the recording head and the media.

Many kinds of dust are somewhat conductive. The design of many computers sucks large amounts of air and dust through the computer's insides for cooling. Invariably, a layer of dust will accumulate on a computer's circuit boards, covering every surface, exposed and otherwise. Eventually, the dust may cause circuits to short, fail, or at least behave erratically.

Here are some guidelines for dust control:

- Keep your computer room as dust-free as possible.
- If your computer has air filters, clean or replace them on a regular basis.
- Get a special vacuum for your computers and use it on a regular basis. Be sure to vacuum behind your computers. You may also wish to vacuum your keyboards. Ideally, your vacuum cleaner should have a microfilter (HEPA or ULPA) so that dust removed from the computers is not simply blown back into your computer room.
- In environments with dust that you can't control, consider getting keyboard dust covers to use when the keyboards are idle for long periods of time. However, don't simply throw homemade covers over your computers—doing so can cause computers to overheat, and some covers can build up significant static charges.

Earthquake

While some parts of the world are subject to frequent and severe earthquakes, nearly every part of the planet experiences the occasional temblor. In the United States, for example, the San Francisco Bay Area experiences several earthquakes every year; a major earthquake is expected within the next 20 years that may be equal in force to the great San Francisco earthquake of 1906. Scientists also say there is an 80% chance that the Eastern half of the United States may experience a similar earthquake within the next 30 years: the only truly unknown factor is where it will occur. One of the most powerful U.S. earthquakes in the last 200 years didn't occur in California, but along the New Madrid fault—the quake actually changed the course of the Mississippi River! As a result, several Eastern cities have enacted stringent anti-earthquake building codes modeled on California's. These days, many new buildings in Boston are built with diagonal cross-braces, using the type of construction that one might expect to see in San Francisco.

While some buildings collapse in an earthquake, most remain standing. Careful attention to the placement of shelves and bookcases in your office can increase the chances that you and your computers will survive all but the worst disasters.

Here are some guidelines for earthquake control:

- Avoid placing computers on any high surfaces; for example, on top of file cabinets.
- Do not place heavy objects on bookcases or shelves near computers in such a way that they might fall on the computer during an earthquake.
- To protect your computers from falling debris, place them underneath strong tables when an earthquake is possible.
- Do not place computers on desks next to windows—especially on higher floors. In an earthquake, the computer could be thrown through the window, destroying the computer and creating a hazard for people on the ground below.
- Consider physically attaching the computer to the surface on which it is resting. You can use bolts, tie-downs, straps, or other implements. (This practice also helps deter theft.)

Explosion

Although computers are not prone to explosion, buildings can be—especially if the building is equipped with natural gas or is used to store inflammable solvents.

If you need to operate a computer in an area where there is a risk of explosion, you might consider purchasing a system with a ruggedized case. Disk drives can be shock-mounted within a computer; if explosion is a constant hazard, consider using a ruggedized laptop with an easily removed, shock-resistant hard drive.

Here are some guidelines for explosion control:

- Consider the real possibility of explosion on your premises. Make sure that solvents, if present, are stored in appropriate containers in clean, uncluttered areas.
- Keep your backups in blast-proof vaults or off-site.
- Keep computers away from windows.

Temperature extremes

Computers, like people, operate best within certain temperature ranges. Most computer systems should be kept between 50 and 90 degrees Fahrenheit (10 to 32 degrees Celsius). If the ambient temperature around your computer gets too high, the computer cannot adequately cool itself, and internal components can be damaged. If the temperature gets too cold, the system can undergo thermal shock when it is turned on, causing circuit boards or integrated circuits to crack.

Here are some basic guidelines for temperature control:

- Check your computer's documentation to see what temperature ranges it can tolerate.

- Install a temperature alarm in your computer room that is triggered by a temperature that is too low or too high. Set the alarm to go off when the temperature gets within 15–20 degrees (F) of the limits your system can take. Some alarms can even be connected to a phone line and programmed to dial predefined phone numbers and tell you, with a synthesized voice, "Your computer room is too hot."

- Be careful about placing computers too close to walls, which can interfere with air circulation. Most manufacturers recommend that their systems have 6 to 12 inches of open space on every side. If you cannot afford the necessary space, lower the computer's upper-level temperature by 10 degrees Fahrenheit or more.

- If you are transporting a computer (such as a laptop) outside in very cold or hot weather, give it a chance to reach room temperature before starting it.

Bugs (biological)

Sometimes insects and other kinds of bugs find their way into computers. Indeed, the very term *bug*, used to describe something wrong with a computer program, dates back to the 1950s, when Grace Murray Hopper found a moth trapped between a pair of relay contacts on Harvard University's Mark 1 computer.

Insects have a strange predilection for getting trapped between the high-voltage contacts of switching power supplies. Others have insatiable cravings for the insulation that covers wires carrying line current, and the high-pitched whine that switching power supplies emit. Spider webs inside computers collect dust like a magnet. For all these reasons, you should take active measures to limit the amount of insect life in your machine room.

Electrical noise

\Motors, fans, heavy equipment, and even other computers generate electrical noise that can cause intermittent problems with the computer you are using. This noise can be transmitted through space or nearby power lines.

Electrical surges are a special kind of electrical noise that consists of one (or a few) high-voltage spikes. As we've mentioned, an ordinary vacuum cleaner plugged into the same electrical outlet as a workstation can generate a spike capable of destroying the workstation's power supply.

Here are some guidelines for electrical noise control:

- Make sure that there is no heavy equipment on the electrical circuit that powers your computer system.
- If possible, have a special electrical circuit with an isolated ground installed for each computer system.
- Install a line filter on your computer's power supply. Some UPS systems are built to act as power filters. UPSs are affordable for even home systems, and some include integrated signalling that can (with appropriate software) shut your computer down gracefully after a prolonged power outage.
- If you have problems with static, you may wish to install a static (grounding) mat around the computer's area, or to apply antistatic sprays to your carpet.
- Walkie-talkies, cellular telephones, and other kinds of radio transmitters can cause computers to malfunction when they are transmitting. Powerful transmitters can even cause permanent damage to systems. Transmitters have also been known to trigger the explosive charges in some sealed fire-extinguisher systems (e.g., Halon). All radio transmitters should be kept at least five feet from the computer, cables, and peripherals. If many people in your organization use portable transmitters, consider posting signs instructing them not to transmit in the computer's vicinity.

Lightning

Lightning generates large power surges that can damage even computers with otherwise protected electrical supplies. If lightning strikes your building's metal frame (or hits your building's lightning rod), the resulting current can generate an intense magnetic field on its way to the ground.

Here are some guidelines for lightning control:

- If possible, turn off and unplug computer systems during lightning storms.
- Make sure that your backup tapes, if they are kept on magnetic media, are stored as far as possible from the building's structural steel members.
- Surge suppressor outlet strips will not protect your system from a direct strike, but may help if the storm is distant. Some surge suppressors include additional protection for sensitive telephone equipment; however, this extra protection may be of questionable value in most areas, because by law, telephone circuits must be equipped with lightning arresters.

- In some remote areas, modems can still be damaged by lightning, even though they are on lines equipped with lightning arresters. In these areas, modems may benefit from additional lightning protection.

- Do not run copper network cables (e.g., Ethernet or Category 5 cables) outdoors unless the cables are in a metal conduit. Specifically, do not run a network cable out an office window, across the wall or roof of a building, and into another office. If you run a cable outdoors and lightning hits within a few thousand feet of your location, there is an excellent chance that the lightning will induce a surge in the network cable, and this surge will then be transmitted directly into your computer system—or worse, channel a direct lightning strike to the system and users.

Vibration

Vibration can put an early end to your computer system by literally shaking it apart. Even gentle vibration, over time, can work printed circuit boards out of their connectors and integrated circuits out of their sockets. Vibration can cause hard disk drives to come out of alignment and increase the chance for catastrophic failure and resulting data loss. Here are some guidelines for vibration control:

- Isolate your computer from vibration as much as possible.

- If you are in a high-vibration environment, place your computer on a rubber or foam mat to dampen vibrations, but make sure the mat does not block ventilation openings.

- Laptop computers are frequently equipped with hard disks that are better at resisting vibration than are desktop machines.

- Don't put your printer on top of a computer. Printers are mechanical devices; they generate vibrations. Desktop space may be a problem, but the unexpected failure of your computer's disk drive or system board is a bigger problem.

Humidity

Humidity is your computer's friend—but as with all friends, you can get too much of a good thing. Humidity prevents the buildup of static charge. If your computer room is too dry, static discharge between operators and your computer (or between the computer's moving parts) may destroy information or damage your computer itself. If the computer room is too humid, you may experience condensation on chilled surfaces. Collecting condensate can short out and damage the electrical circuits.

Here are some guidelines for humidity control:

- For optimal performance, keep the relative humidity of your computer room above 20%, but keep it well below the dew point (which depends on the ambient room temperature).

- In environments that require high reliability, you may wish to have a humidity alarm that will ring when the humidity is out of your acceptable range.
- Some equipment has special humidity restrictions. Check your manuals.

Water

Water can destroy your computer. The primary danger is an electrical short, which can happen if water bridges between a circuit-board trace carrying voltage and a trace carrying ground. A short will cause too much current to be pulled through a trace, heat up the trace, and possibly melt it. Shorts can also destroy electronic components by pulling too much current through them.

Water usually comes from rain or flooding. Sometimes it comes from an errant sprinkler system. Water also may come from strange places, such as a toilet overflowing on a higher floor, vandalism, or the fire department.

Here are some guidelines for water control:

- Mount a water sensor on the floor near the computer system.
- If you have a raised floor in your computer room, mount water detectors underneath the floor and above it.
- Do not keep your computer in the basement of your building if your area is prone to flooding, or if your building has a sprinkler system.
- Because water rises, you may wish to have two alarms, located at different heights. The first water sensor should ring an alarm; the second should automatically cut off power to your computer equipment. Automatic power cutoffs can save a lot of money if the flood happens off-hours, or if the flood occurs when the person who is supposed to attend to the alarm is otherwise occupied. More importantly, cutoffs can save lives: electricity, water, and people shouldn't mix.

Environmental monitoring

To detect spurious problems, continuously monitor and record your computer room's temperature and relative humidity. As a general rule of thumb, every 1,000 square feet of office space should have its own recording equipment. Log and check recordings on a regular basis.

Preventing Accidents

In addition to environmental problems, your computer system is vulnerable to a multitude of accidents. While it is impossible to prevent all accidents, careful planning can minimize the impact of accidents that will inevitably occur.

Food and drink

People need food and drink to stay alive. Computers, on the other hand, need to stay away from food and drink. One of the fastest ways of putting a desktop keyboard out of commission is to pour a soft drink or cup of coffee between the keys. If this keyboard is your system console (as is the case with most PCs), you may be unable to reboot the computer until the console is replaced (we know this from experience).

Food—especially oily food—collects on people's fingers and from there gets on anything that a person touches. Often this includes dirt-sensitive surfaces such as magnetic tapes and optical disks. Sometimes food can be cleaned away; other times it cannot. Oils from foods also tend to get onto screens, increasing glare and decreasing readability. Some screens are equipped with special quarter-wavelength antiglare coatings: when touched with oily hands, the fingerprints will glow with an annoying iridescence. Generally, the simplest rule is the safest: keep all food and drink away from your computer systems.*

Physical Access

Simple common sense will tell you to keep your computer in a locked room. But how safe is that room? Sometimes a room that appears to be safe is actually wide open.

Raised floors and dropped ceilings

In many modern office buildings, internal walls do not extend above dropped ceilings or beneath raised floors. This type of construction makes it easy for people in adjoining rooms, and sometimes adjoining offices, to gain access.

Here are some guidelines for dealing with raised floors and dropped ceilings:

- Make sure that your building's internal walls extend above your dropped ceilings so intruders cannot enter locked offices simply by climbing over the walls.
- Likewise, if you have raised floors, make sure that the building's walls extend down to the real floor.

Entrance through air ducts

If the air ducts that serve your computer room are large enough, intruders can use them to gain entrance to an otherwise secured area.

Here are some guidelines for dealing with air ducts:

- Areas that need large amounts of ventilation should be served by several small ducts, none of which is large enough for a person to traverse.

---

* Perhaps more than any other rule in this chapter, this rule is honored most often in the breach.

- As an alternative, screens can be welded over air vents, or even within air ducts, to prevent unauthorized entry. (This approach is not as good as using small ventilation ducts because screens can be cut; think about all the various adventure movies you've seen.)
- The truly paranoid administrator may wish to place motion detectors inside air ducts.

Glass walls

Although glass walls and large windows frequently add architectural panache, they can be severe security risks. Glass walls are easy to break; a brick and a bottle of gasoline thrown through a window can cause an incredible amount of damage. An attacker can also gain critical knowledge, such as passwords or information about system operations, simply by watching people on the other side of a glass wall or window.

Here are some guidelines for dealing with glass walls:

- Avoid glass walls and large windows for security-sensitive areas.
- If you must have some amount of natural light, consider walls made of translucent glass blocks.
- Glass walls are good for rooms which must be guarded but which the guard is not allowed to enter. For these situations, glass walls are preferable to closed-circuit TV, because glass walls are harder to spoof.

Vandalism

Computer systems are good targets for vandalism. Reasons for vandalism include:

- Intentional disruption of services (e.g., a student who has homework due)
- Revenge (e.g., a fired employee)
- Riots
- Strike-related violence
- Political or ideologic statement
- Entertainment for the feebleminded

Computer vandalism is often fast, easy, and tremendously damaging. Sometimes, vandalism is actually sabotage presented as random mischief.

In principle, any part of a computer system—or the building that houses it—may be a target for vandalism. In practice, some targets are more vulnerable than others.

Ventilation holes

Several years ago, 60 workstations at the Massachusetts Institute of Technology were destroyed in a single evening by a student who poured Coca-Cola into each computer's ventilation holes. Authorities surmised that the vandal was a student who had not completed a problem set due the next day.

Computers that have ventilation holes need them. Don't seal up the holes to prevent this sort of vandalism. However, a rigidly enforced policy against food and drink in the computer room—or a 24-hour guard, in person or via closed-circuit TV—can help prevent this kind of incident from happening at your site.

Network cables

Local and wide area networks are exceedingly vulnerable to vandalism. In many cases, a vandal can disable an entire subnet of workstations by cutting a single wire with a pair of wire cutters. Compared with Ethernet, fiber optic cables are at the same time more vulnerable (they can be more easily damaged), more difficult to repair (they are difficult to splice), and more attractive targets (they often carry more information).

One simple method for protecting a network cable is to run it through physically secure locations. For example, Ethernet cable is often placed in cable trays or suspended from ceilings with plastic loops. But Ethernet can also be run through steel conduits. Besides protecting against vandalism, this practice protects against some forms of network eavesdropping, and may help protect your cables in the event of a small fire.

Some high-security installations use double-walled, shielded conduits with a pressurized gas between the layers. Pressure sensors on the conduit break off all traffic or sound a warning bell if the pressure ever drops, as might occur if someone breached the walls of the pipe.

Many universities have networks that rely on Ethernet or fiber optic cables strung through the basements. A single frustrated student with a pair of scissors or a pocket-knife can halt the work of thousands of students and professors.

Some organizations believe that an alternative to physically protecting their network cables is to have redundant connections between various locations on their campus. While it is true that redundant connections will protect an organization from a single failure, if redundancy is the only protection against cable cuts, all an aggressive attacker needs to do is to cut the cable in several locations.

We also have heard stories about a fiber optic cable suffering small fractures because someone stepped on it. A fracture of this type is difficult to locate because there is no break in the coating. Once again, it pays to be careful where you place your cables.

"Temporary" cable runs often turn into permanent or semipermanent installations, so take the extra time and effort to install cable correctly the first time.

Network connectors

In addition to cutting a cable, a vandal who has access to a network's endpoint—a network connector—can electronically disable or damage the network. All networks based on wire are vulnerable to attacks with high voltage. At one university in the late 1980s, a student destroyed a cluster of workstations by plugging the thin-wire Ethernet cable into a 110VAC wall outlet. (The student wanted to simulate a lightning strike because he realized that he wasn't going to complete his assignment by the time it was due the next morning.)

Defending Against Acts of War and Terrorism

The successful attack on New York's World Trade Center demonstrated that even computers that are not used by the military and are not operated in a war zone may be the object of terrorist attacks. Because computers are attractive targets, you may wish to consider additional structural protection for your computer room. If your computers are in any way involved in support of something that might inspire violent protest—university research with animal subjects, oil exploration, fashion design using furs, lumber production—you should definitely consider extra protection for them.

Although protection is important, it is simply impossible to defend against many attacks. In many cases, you should devise a system of hot backups and mirrored disks and servers. With a reasonably fast network link, you can arrange for files stored on one computer to be simultaneously copied to another system on the other side of town—or the other side of the world. Sites that cannot afford simultaneous backup can have hourly or nightly incremental dumps made across the network link. Although a tank or suicide bomber may destroy your computer center, your data can be safely protected someplace else.

Preventing Theft

Because many computers are relatively small and valuable, they are easily stolen and easily sold. Even computers that are relatively difficult to fence have been stolen by thieves who thought that they were actually stealing something fungible. As with any expensive piece of equipment, you should attempt to protect your computer investment with physical measures such as locks and bolts.

Physically secure your computer

A variety of physical tie-down devices are available to bolt computers to tables or cabinets. Although they cannot prevent theft, they make it more difficult.

RAM theft

In past years, businesses and universities have suffered a rash of RAM thefts. Thieves enter offices, open computers, and remove some or all of the computer's RAM (see Figure 14-1). Many computer businesses and universities have also had major thefts of advanced processor chips. RAM and late-model CPU chips are easily sold on the open market. They are virtually untraceable. And, when thieves steal only some of the RAM inside a computer, weeks or months may pass before the theft is noticed.

High-density RAM modules and processor cards can be worth their weight in gold. If a user complains that a computer is suddenly running more slowly than it did the day before, check its RAM, and then check to see that its case is physically secured.

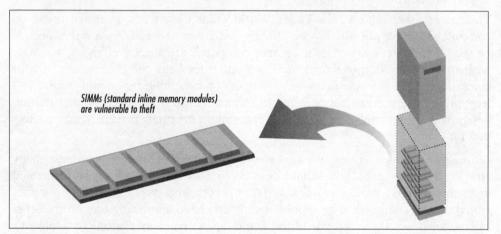

Figure 14-1. There are many recent cases of theft of all or part of computer RAM. RAM is easy to resell and all but untraceable.

Encryption

If your computer is stolen, the information it contains will be at the mercy of the equipment's new "owners." They may erase it or they may read it. Sensitive information can be sold, used for blackmail, or used to compromise other computer systems.

You can never make something impossible to steal. But you can make stolen information virtually useless—provided that it is encrypted and the thief does not know the encryption key. For this reason, even with the best computer-security mechanisms and physical deterrents, sensitive information should be encrypted using an encryption system that is difficult to break. We recommend you acquire and use a strong encryption system so that even if your computer is stolen, the sensitive information it contains will not be compromised.

Laptops and portable computers

Laptops and other kinds of portable computers present a special hazard. They are easily stolen, difficult to tie down (they then cease to be portable!), and easily resold. Personnel with laptops should be trained to be especially vigilant in protecting their computers. In particular, theft of laptops in airports has been reported to be a major problem.*

One way to minimize laptop theft is to make the laptops harder to resell. You may do this by engraving a laptop with your name and telephone number. (Do not engrave the laptop with your Social Security number, as this will enable a thief to cause you other problems!) Alternatively, you may equip your laptop with a property tag, such as those sold by Secure Tracking of Office Property (see Figure 11-3).

Laptop theft may not be motivated by resale potential. Often, competitive intelligence is more easily obtained by stealing a laptop with critical information than by hacking into a protected network. Thus, good encryption on a portable computer is critical. This can be accomplished using built-in software, such as the Windows 2000 Encrypted File System, or using an add-on product, such as PGP Disk by Network Associates.

Protecting Your Data

There is a strong overlap between the physical security of your computer systems and the privacy and integrity of your data. After all, if somebody steals your computer, they probably have your data. Unfortunately, there are many attacks on your data that may circumvent the physical measures mentioned in earlier sections.

This section explores several different types of attacks on data and discusses approaches for protecting against these attacks. It recapitulates some advice given elsewhere in the book in a slightly different manner.

Eavesdropping

Electronic *eavesdropping* is perhaps the most sinister type of data piracy. Even with modest equipment, an eavesdropper can make a complete transcript of a victim's actions—every keystroke and every piece of information viewed on a screen or sent

---

* Note that there is some evidence that many "thefts" inside airports are actually instances of people forgetting to take their computers with them when they leave. It is easier to report to management that your laptop was stolen rather than admit you forgot it at the airport bar!

to a printer. The victim, meanwhile, usually knows nothing of the attacker's presence and blithely goes about his or her work, revealing not only sensitive information, but the passwords and procedures necessary for obtaining even more information.

In many cases, you cannot possibly know if you're being monitored. Sometimes you will learn of an eavesdropper's presence when the attacker attempts to make use of the information obtained: often you cannot prevent significant damage at that point. With care and vigilance, however, you can significantly decrease the risk of being monitored.

Encryption provides significant protection against eavesdropping. Thus, in many cases, it makes sense to assume that your communications are being monitored and to encrypt all communications as a matter of course.

Wiretapping

By their very nature, electrical wires are prime candidates for eavesdropping (hence the name *wiretapping*). An attacker can follow an entire conversation over a pair of wires with a simple splice—sometimes without even touching the wires physically: a simple induction loop coiled around a terminal wire is enough to pick up most voice and RS-232 communications. Similar measures are effective for monitoring local area networks. Reportedly, national-level intelligence agencies have been able to wiretap underwater optical cables by analyzing the electrical emissions of amplifiers and repeaters.

Here are some guidelines for preventing wiretapping:

- Routinely inspect all wires that carry data (especially terminal wires and telephone lines used for modems) for physical damage.
- Protect your wires from monitoring by using shielded cable. Armored cable provides additional protection.
- If you are very security conscious, place your cables in steel conduit. In high-security applications, the conduit can be pressurized with gas; gas pressure monitors can be used to trip an alarm system in the event of tampering. However, these approaches are expensive to install and maintain.

Eavesdropping over local area networks (Ethernet and twisted pair)

Local area networks that are based on Ethernet or twisted pair are susceptible to eavesdropping; simply plugging a packet monitor into an unused network connection can often allow an attacker to intercept the entire contents of the local area network traffic. For this reason, unused offices should not have *live* Ethernet or twisted-pair ports inside them: disable these ports at your wiring closet.

Many organizations have used Ethernet switches to increase the capacity of their networks. A switch does not rebroadcast all traffic to all ports, as if they were on a shared Ethernet; instead, it determines the hardware address of each machine on each line, and only sends a computer the packets that it should receive. Switches can significantly improve the security of these networks by minimizing the potential for eavesdropping. Nevertheless, you should not rely on switches for your security: a sufficiently skilled attacker can even monitor a switched LAN.

You may wish to periodically scan all of the Internet numbers that have been allocated to your subnet to make sure that no unauthorized Internet hosts are operating on your network. You can also run LAN monitoring software and have alarms sound each time a packet is detected with a previously unknown Ethernet address.

 The freely available Unix program *arpwatch* will monitor your local area network for new Ethernet cards and alert you when they are detected; *arpwatch* also reports when an Ethernet MAC address starts using a different IP address.

Some Ethernet hubs and switches can be set to monitor the IP numbers of incoming packets. If a packet comes in from a computer connected to the hub that doesn't match what the hub has been told is correct, it can raise an alarm or shut down the link. This capability helps prevent various forms of Ethernet spoofing. Some hubs can also be configured with *MAC address filtering* or *lock-down*, so that if an unauthorized MAC address is used on a port, that port will be automatically disabled.

Eavesdropping on 802.11 wireless LANs

In recent years, high-speed wireless LANs have become increasingly popular at many universities and corporations. Presently, these systems are not secure. Even when the so-called WEP encryption system is in use, it is possible for an attacker to masquerade as an authorized user and gain access to the wireless LAN. The information moving through the air can also be trivially eavesdropped. Wireless LANs should not be used in security-conscious environments. If a wireless LAN must be used in your environment, locate the Wireless Access Point outside your organization's firewall and require that your users employ a second layer of encryption, such as a VPN or SSL.

Eavesdropping by radio and using TEMPEST

Every piece of electrical equipment emits radiation in the form of radio waves. Using specialized equipment, it is possible to analyze the emitted radiation generated by computer equipment and determine the calculations that caused the radiation to be emitted in the first place.

Radio eavesdropping is a special kind of tapping that security agencies (in the U.S. these agencies include the FBI, CIA, and NSA) are particularly concerned about. In the 1980s, a certification system called TEMPEST was developed in the U.S. to rate the susceptibility of computer equipment to such monitoring. Computers that are TEMPEST-certified are generally substantially less susceptible to radio monitoring than computers that are not, but they are usually more expensive and larger because of the extra shielding.

As an alternative to certifying individual computers, you can now TEMPEST-certify rooms or entire buildings. Several office buildings constructed in Maryland and northern Virginia are encased in a conductive skin that dampens radio emissions coming from within. As the majority of RF emissions that can be analyzed result from video monitors, it is possible to minimize these emissions by using different screen fonts. Professor Ross Anderson[*] at the University of Cambridge has developed such a set of fonts that he calls Soft Tempest.[†]

Although TEMPEST is not a concern for most computer users, the possibility of electronic eavesdropping by radio should not be discounted. Performing such eavesdropping is much easier than you might expect. It is possible to find plans published on the Internet that will allow you to build low-cost eavesdropping devices that work against common PCs.

Fiber optic cable

A good type of physical protection is to use fiber optic media for a network. It is more difficult to tap into a fiber optic cable than it is to connect into an insulated coaxial cable (although an optical "vampire" tap exists that can tap a fiber optic network simply by clamping down on the cable). Successful taps often require cutting the fiber optic cable first, thus giving a clear indication that something is amiss. Fiber optic cabling is also less susceptible to signal interference and grounding. However, fiber is sometimes easier to break or damage, and more difficult to repair than standard coaxial cable.

Keyboard monitors

As we described in Chapter 9, several companies sell small keyboard monitors that can be physically connected between a keyboard and a computer. These monitors capture every keystroke as it is typed. They are impossible to detect with software. To dump the contents of the memory, the eavesdropper must have physical access to the computer and type a password on the keyboard. The keyboard monitor then displays a menu that allows the operator to dump or clear its memory. A typical device costs $200 and has two megabytes of memory.

---

[*] *http://www.cl.cam.ac.uk/users/rja14/*

† The fonts can be downloaded from *http://www.cl.cam.ac.uk/~mgk25/st-fonts.zip*.

Protecting Backups

Backups should be a prerequisite of any computer operation—secure or otherwise—but the information stored on backup tapes is extremely vulnerable. When the information is stored on a computer, the operating system's mechanisms of checks and protections prevent unauthorized people from viewing the data (and can possibly log failed attempts). After information is written onto a backup tape, anybody who has physical possession of the tape can read its contents.

For this reason, protect your backups at least as well as you normally protect your computers themselves.

Here are some guidelines for protecting your backups:

- Don't leave backups unattended in a computer room that is generally accessible. Somebody could take a backup and then have access to all of the files on your system.

- Don't entrust backups to a messenger who is not bonded.

- Sanitize backup tapes before you sell them, use them as scratch tapes, or otherwise dispose of them. (See the section called "Sanitizing Media Before Disposal" later in this chapter.)

- Most backup programs allow you to encrypt the data before it is written to a backup. Encrypted backups dramatically reduce the chances that a backup tape or CD-ROM, if stolen, will be usable by an adversary. If you use a cryptographic backup system, it is important that you protect your key—both so that an attacker will not learn the key, and so that your key will not be lost in the event that you have a change of staff.

Verify your backups

You should periodically verify your backups to make sure they contain valid data. (See Chapter 11 for details.)

You need to verify backups that are months or years old in addition to backups that were made yesterday or the week before. Sometimes, backups in archives are slowly erased by environmental conditions. Magnetic tape is also susceptible to a process called *print through*, in which the magnetic domains on one piece of tape wound on a spool affect the next layer.

The only way to find out if this process is harming your backups is to test them periodically. You can also minimize print through by spinning your tapes to the end and then rewinding them, because the tape will not align in the same way when the tape is rewound. We recommend that at least once a year, you check a sample of your backup tapes to make sure that they contain valid data.

Protect your backups

Many of the hazards to computers mentioned in the first part of this chapter are equally hazardous to backups. To maximize the chances of your data's surviving in the event of an accident or malicious incident, keep your computer system and your backups in different locations.

Sanitizing Media Before Disposal

When you discard disk drives, CD-ROMs, or tapes, make sure that the data on the media has been completely erased. This process is called *sanitizing*.

Simply deleting a file that is on your hard disk doesn't delete the data associated with the file. Parts of the original data—and sometimes entire files—can usually be easily recovered. When you are disposing of old media, be sure to destroy the data itself, in addition to the directory entries.

Modern hard disks pose a unique problem for media sanitizing because of the large amount of hidden and reserved storage. A typical 1-gigabyte hard disk may have as much as 400 megabytes of additional storage; some of this storage is used for media testing and bad-block remapping, but much of it is unused during normal operations. With special software, you can access this reserved storage area; you could even install "hard disk viruses" that can reprogram a hard disk controller, take over the computer's peripheral bus and transfer data between two devices, or feed faulty data to the host computer. For these reasons, hard disks must be sanitized with special software that is specially written for each particular disk drive's model number and revision level.

If you are a system administrator, you have an additional responsibility to sanitize your backup tapes before you dispose of them. Although you may not think that any sensitive or confidential information is stored on the tapes, your users may have been storing such information without your knowledge.

For tapes, you can use a bulk eraser—a hand-held electromagnet that has a hefty field. Experiment with reading back the information stored on tapes that you have "bulk erased" until you know how much erasing is necessary to eliminate your data. You can sometimes use these same erasers on disks, but modern disks use such high densities of information, and require specially recorded "timing tracks," that use of a bulk eraser may keep you from using the disk but not really eliminate the information on it.

 Do not locate your bulk eraser near your disks or good tapes! Also beware of placing the eraser in another room, on the other side of a wall from your disks or tapes. People who have pacemakers should be warned not to approach the eraser.

Some software exists to overwrite optical media, thus erasing the contents of even write-once items. However, the effectiveness of these methods varies from media type to media type, and the overwriting may still leave some residues. For this reason, physical destruction may be preferable.

Unfortunately, physical destruction is getting harder and harder to do. While incinerators do a remarkably good job of destroying tapes, stringent environmental regulations have forced many organizations to abandon this practice. Organizations have likewise had to give up acid baths. Until recently, crushing was preferred for hard disk drives and disk packs. But as disk densities get higher and higher, disk drives must be crushed into smaller and smaller pieces to frustrate laboratory analysis of the resulting material. As a result, physical destruction is losing popularity when compared with software-based techniques for declassifying or sanitizing computer media.

One common sanitizing method involves overwriting the entire tape. If you are dealing with highly confidential or security-related materials, you may wish to overwrite the disk or tape several times, because data can be recovered from tapes that have been overwritten only once. Commonly, tapes are overwritten three times—once with blocks of 0s, then with blocks of 1s, and then with random numbers. Finally, the tape may be degaussed—or run through a bandsaw several times to reduce it to thousands of tiny pieces of plastic.

We recommend that you thoroughly sanitize all media before disposal by choosing a method that is best suited to your level of risk and need.

Sanitizing Printed Media

In the last section, we discussed the importance of erasing magnetic media before disposing of it. However, that media is not the only material that should be carefully "sanitized" before disposal. Other material that may find its way into the trash may contain information that is useful to crackers or competitors. This includes printouts of software (including incomplete versions), memos, design documents, preliminary code, planning documents, internal newsletters, company phone books, manuals, and other material.

Obviously, some program printouts might be used against you, especially if enough printouts are collected over time to derive a complete picture of your software development and web organization. If the code is commented well enough, it may also give away clues as to the identity of beta testers and customers, testing strategies, and marketing plans.

Other material may be used to derive information about company personnel and operations. With a company phone book, someone could masquerade as an employee over the telephone and obtain sensitive information, including dialup numbers, account names, and passwords. Sound far-fetched? Think again—there are numerous stories of such social engineering. The more internal information an outsider has, the more easily he can obtain sensitive information. By knowing the names, office numbers, and extensions of company officials and their staff, he can easily convince an overworked and undertrained operator that he needs to violate the written policy—or incur the wrath of the "vice president" on the phone.

Other information that may find its way into your dumpster includes the types and versions of your operating systems and computers, serial numbers, patch levels, and so on. It may include hostnames, IP numbers, account names, and other information critical to an attacker. We have heard of some firms disposing of listings of their complete firewall configuration and filter rules—a gold mine for someone seeking to infiltrate the computers.

How will this information find its way into the wrong hands? Well, *dumpster diving* or *trashing* is one such way. After hours, someone intent on breaking your security could be rummaging through your dumpster, looking for useful information. In one case we heard recounted, a "diver" dressed up as a street person (letting his beard grow a bit and not bathing for a few days), splashed a little cheap booze on himself, half-filled a mesh bag with empty soda cans, and went to work. As he went from dumpster to dumpster in an industrial office park, he was effectively invisible: busy and well-paid executives seem to see through the homeless and unfortunate. If someone began to approach him, he would pluck invisible bugs from his shirt and talk loudly to himself. In the one case where he was accosted by a security guard, he was able to the convince the guard to let him continue looking for "cans" for spare change. He even panhandled the guard to give him $5 for a meal!

Perhaps you have your dumpster inside a guarded fence. But what happens after it is picked up by the trash hauler? Is it dumped where someone can go though the information off your premises?

Consider carefully the value of the information you throw away. Consider investing in shredders for each location where information of value might be thrown away. Educate your users not to dispose of sensitive material in their refuse at home, but to bring it in to the office to be shredded. If your organization is large enough and local ordinances allow, you may also wish to incinerate some sensitive paper waste on-site.

Home users are also vulnerable to this kind of scavenging. Unsanitized disposal of papers with passwords or system information, credit card receipts and bills, and personal documents may lead to unwanted intrusions (into privacy as well as web pages). A personal shredder can be purchased for a small amount of money at any large discount store or office supply outlet. This should be routinely used on documents that may contain any sensitive information.

Protecting Local Storage

In addition to computers and mass-storage systems, many other pieces of electrical data-processing equipment store information. For example, terminals, modems, and laser printers often contain pieces of memory that may be downloaded and uploaded with appropriate control sequences.

Naturally, any piece of memory that is used to hold sensitive information presents a security problem, especially if that piece of memory is not protected with a password, encryption, or other similar mechanism. However, the local storage in many devices presents an additional security problem, because sensitive information is frequently copied into such local storage without the knowledge of the computer user.

Printer buffers

Computers can transmit information many times faster than most printers can print it. For this reason, printers are sometimes equipped with *printer spoolers*—boxes with semiconductor memory that receive information quickly from the computer and transmit it to the printer at a slower rate.

Many printer spoolers have the ability to make multiple copies of a document. Sometimes, this function is accomplished with a COPY button on the front of the printer spooler. Whenever the COPY button is pressed, a copy of everything that has been printed is sent to the printer for a second time. The security risk is obvious: if sensitive information is still in the printer's buffer, an attacker can use the COPY button to make a copy for himself.

Today, many high-speed laser printers are programmable and contain significant amounts of local storage. (Some laser printers have internal hard disks that can be used to store hundreds of megabytes of information.) Some of these printers can be programmed to store a copy of any document printed for later use. Other printers use the local storage as a buffer; unless the buffer is appropriately sanitized after printing, an attacker with sufficient skill can retrieve some or all of the contained data. The same is true of some networked fax machines.

Printer output

One form of local storage you may not think of is the output of your workgroup printer. If the printer is located in a semipublic location, the output may be vulnerable to theft or copying before it is claimed. You should ensure that printers, plotters, and other output devices are in a secured location. Fax machines face similar vulnerabilities.

X terminals

Many X Windows terminals have substantial amounts of local storage. Some X terminals even have hard disks that can be accessed from over the network. Few support any cryptographic protocols.

Here are some guidelines for using X terminals securely:

- If your users work with sensitive information, they should turn off their X terminals at the end of the day to clear the terminals' RAM memory.

- If your X terminals have hard disks, you should be sure that the terminals are password-protected so that they cannot be easily reprogrammed over the network. Do not allow service personnel to remove the X terminals for repair unless the disks are first removed and erased.

Function keys

Many smart terminals are equipped with function keys that can be programmed to send an arbitrary sequence of keystrokes to the computer whenever a function key is pressed. If a function key is used to store a password, then any person who has physical access to the terminal can impersonate the terminal's primary user. If a terminal is stolen, then the passwords are compromised. Therefore, we recommend that you never use function keys to store passwords or other kinds of sensitive information (such as cryptographic keys).

Unattended Terminals

Unattended terminals where users have left themselves logged in present a special attraction for vandals (as well as for computer crackers). A vandal can access the person's files with impunity. Alternatively, the vandal can use the person's account as a starting point for launching an attack against the computer system or the entire network: any tracing of the attack will *usually* point fingers back toward the account's owner, not to the vandal. Not only does this scenario allow someone to create a "back door" into the account of the user involved, and thus gain longer-term access, but also an untrained attacker could commit some email mayhem. Imagine someone sending email, as you, to the CEO or the Dean, making some lunatic and obscene suggestions? Or perhaps email to *whitehouse.gov* with a threat against the President?* Hence, you should never leave terminals unattended for more than short periods of time.

---

* Don't even *think* about doing this yourself! The Secret Service investigates each and every threat against the President, the President's family, and certain other officials. They take such threats very seriously, and they are not known for their senses of humor. They are also *very* skilled at tracing down the real culprit in such incidents—we know from observing their work on a number of occasions. These threats simply aren't funny, especially if you end up facing federal criminal charges as a result.

Some systems have the ability to log a user off automatically—or at least to blank his screen and lock his keyboard—when the user's terminal has been idle for more than a few minutes.

Built-in shell autologout

If you use the C shell under Unix, you can use the *autologout* shell variable to log you out automatically after you have been idle for a specified number of minutes. Normally, this variable is set in your *~/.cshrc* file. (Note that the *autologout* variable is not available under all versions of the C shell.)

For example, if you wish to be logged out automatically after you have been idle for 10 minutes, place this line in your *~/.cshrc* file:

```
set autologout=10
```

Note that the C shell will log you out only if you idle at the C shell's command prompt. If you are idle within an application, such as a word processor, you will remain logged in.

ksh (the Korn shell) has a TMOUT variable that performs a similar function. TMOUT is specified in seconds:

```
TMOUT=600
```

Screensavers

You may wish to use a screen saver that automatically locks your workstation after the keyboard and mouse have been inactive for more than a predetermined number of minutes. There are many screensavers to chose from on a variety of platforms, including Unix, Mac OS, and Windows NT.

Many vendor-supplied screensavers respond to built-in passwords in addition to the user's passwords. The Unix *lock* program, for example, once had a back door that would allow any user's terminal to be unlocked with the password *hasta la vista*—and this fact was undocumented in the manual. Unless you have the source code for a program, there is no way to determine whether it has a back door of any kind. You would be better off using a vendor-supplied locking tool than leaving your terminal unattended and unlocked while you go for coffee. But be attentive, and beware.

Key Switches

Some kinds of computers have key switches that can be used to prevent the system from being rebooted in single-user mode. Some computers also have ROM monitors that prevent the system from being rebooted in single-user mode without a password. For instance, all new Macintosh systems have support in their Open Firmware for a password to control boot configuration access.

Key switches and ROM monitor passwords provide additional security and should be used when possible. However, you should also remember that any computer can be unplugged. The most important way to protect a computer is to restrict physical access to that computer.

Personnel

The people who have access to your system may not all have your best interests in mind. We've heard stories in home environments where playmates of children have introduced viruses into home office systems, and where spouses have scoured disks for evidence of marital infidelity—and then trashed systems where they have found it. In business environments, there are stories of cleaning staff and office temps who have been caught sabotaging or snooping on company computers.

You may not be able to choose your family, but you can have some impact on who accesses the computers at your company location. You can do this with background checks (it is amazing how many people don't adequately check references) and periodic rechecks. Depending on the nature of your business and the laws in place governing employment law, you may also be able to execute credit checks, lie detector tests, and criminal background checks. You may even be able to execute a security clearance requirement. You can also require that personnel be *bonded*—special assurance from a third party that the individual is trusted, in which the third party performs the background investigation.

Examples of people whose backgrounds should be examined include:

- System operators and administrators
- Temporary workers and contractors who have access to the system
- Cleaning and maintenance personnel
- Security guards
- Delivery personnel who have regular or unsupervised access
- Consultants

The personnel who do have access should be trained about security and loss prevention and periodically retrained. Personnel should also be briefed on incident response procedures and on the penalties for security violations.

Story: A Failed Site Inspection

> If you can't be a good example, then you'll just have to be a horrible warning.
> —Catherine Aird

Several years ago, a consumer-products firm with worldwide operations invited one of the authors to a casual tour of one of the company's main sites. The site, located in an office park with several large buildings, included computers for product design and testing, and nationwide management of inventory, sales, and customer support. It included a sophisticated, automated voice-response system costing thousands of dollars a month to operate, hundreds of users, and dozens of T1 (1.44 Mbits/sec) communications lines for the corporate network, carrying both voice and data communications.

The company thought that it had reasonable security, given the fact that it didn't have anything serious to lose. After all, the firm was in the consumer-products business—no government secrets or high-stakes stock and bond trading here.

What We Found

After a brief, three-hour inspection, the company had some second thoughts about its security. Even without a formal site audit, the following items were discovered during our short visit.

Fire hazards

- All of the company's terminal and network cables were suspended from hangers above false ceilings throughout the buildings. Although smoke detectors and sprinklers were located below the false ceiling, none were located above, where the cables were located. If there were a short or an electrical fire, it could spread throughout a substantial portion of the wiring plant and be very difficult, if not impossible, to control. No internal firestops had been built for the wiring channels, either.

- Several of the fire extinguishers scattered throughout the building had no inspection tags or were shown as being overdue for an inspection.

Potential for eavesdropping and data theft

- Network taps throughout the buildings were live and unprotected. An attacker with a laptop computer could easily penetrate and monitor the network; alternatively, with a pair of scissors or wirecutters, an attacker could disable portions of the corporate network.

- An attacker could get above the false ceiling through conference rooms, bathrooms, janitor's closets, and many other locations throughout the building, thereby gaining direct access to the company's network cables. A monitoring station (possibly equipped with a small radio transmitter) could be left in such a location for an extended period of time.

- Many of the unused cubicles had machines that were not assigned to a particular user, but were nevertheless live on the network. An attacker could sit down at a machine, gain system privileges, and use that machine as a point for further attacks against the information infrastructure.

- The company had no controls or policies on modems, thus allowing any user to set up a private SLIP or PPP connection to bypass the firewall.
- Several important systems had unprotected backup tapes on a nearby table or shelf.

Easy pickings

- None of the equipment had any inventory-control stickers or permanent markings. If the equipment were stolen, it would not be recoverable.
- There was no central inventory of equipment. If items were lost, stolen, or damaged, there was no way to determine the extent and nature of the loss.
- Only one door to the building had an actual guard in place. People could enter and leave with equipment through other doors.
- When we arrived outside a back door with our hands full, a helpful employee opened the door and held it for us without requesting ID or proof that we should be allowed inside.
- Strangers walking about the building were not challenged. Employees did not wear tags and apparently made the assumption that anybody on the premises was authorized to be there.

Physical access to critical computers

- Internal rooms with particularly sensitive equipment did not have locks on the doors.
- Although the main computer room was protected with a card key entry system, entry could be gained from an adjacent conference room or hallway under the raised floor.
- Many special-purpose systems were located in workrooms without locks on the doors. When users were not present, the machines were unmonitored and unprotected.

Possibilities for sabotage

- The network between two buildings consisted of a bidirectional, fault-tolerant ring network. But the fault tolerance was compromised because both fibers were routed through the same unprotected conduit.
- The conduit between two buildings could be accessed through an unlocked manhole in the parking lot. An attacker located outside the buildings could easily shut down the entire network with heavy cable cutters or a small incendiary device.

Nothing to Lose?

Simply by walking through this company's base of operations, we discovered that this company would be an easy target for many attacks, both complicated and primitive. The attacker might be a corporate spy for a competing firm, or might simply be a disgruntled employee. Given the ease of stealing computer equipment, the company also had reason to fear less-than-honest employees. Without adequate inventory or other controls, the company might not be able to discover and prove any wide-scale fraud, nor would they be able to recover insurance in the event of any loss.

Furthermore, despite the fact that the company thought that it had "nothing to lose," an internal estimate had put the cost of computer downtime at several million dollars per hour because of its use in customer-service management, order processing, and parts management. An employee out for revenge or personal gain could easily put a serious dent into this company's bottom line with a small expenditure of effort, and with little chance of being caught.

Indeed, the company had a lot to lose.

What about *your* site?

## CHAPTER 15

Host Security for Servers

In this chapter:
- Current Host Security Problems
- Securing the Host Computer
- Minimizing Risk by Minimizing Services
- Operating Securely
- Secure Remote Access and Content Updating
- Firewalls and the Web
- Conclusion

Host security is the security of the computer on which your web server is running. Traditionally, host security has been a computer security topic unto itself. Whole books (including a couple of our own) have been written on it.

Host security was in its heyday in the 1980s and early 1990s, when dozens or even hundreds of people shared the same computer. Many of these systems were at universities, where one of the goals of the system operators was to prevent students from seeing each other's coursework. Other systems were at government installations, where the systems needed to store and segregate "Secret" from "Top Secret" information. As a result, host security was traditionally concerned with questions of protecting the operating system from users, protecting users from each other, and performing auditing measures.

The 1990s saw a dramatic shift in the emphasis and importance of host security. It seems that many organizations place less emphasis on host security when each person had exclusive use of a computer. This perspective is misguided because, as we have seen, distributed systems can be as vulnerable (if not more so) to the security problems that can affect large time-sharing systems. One explanation for the decreased attention to host security is that assuring host security in a distributed environment is significantly more complicated and more expensive, and in fact has proven to be beyond the capabilities of many organizations. Another explanation is that too many people are more concerned with cost and ease of deploying systems that are impossible to secure.*

The Web has reignited interest in host security. The measures that were developed in the 1980s and 1990s for protecting a computer system against its users and protecting the users against each other work equally well for protecting a computer system

---

* This is especially true of government systems. Sadly, cost-containment pressures have led even the military to build safety-critical systems—systems absolutely vital for national and theater defense—on commercial platforms with defective or weak security features and horrendous records of exploitable flaws in released products.

against an external attacker—especially if that attacker is able to gain some sort of foothold in your computer system to start running his own programs. After all, the computer on which your web server is running has access to all of the web server's files; it can monitor all of the web server's communications and it can even modify the web server itself. If an attacker has control of your computer's operating system, it is impossible to use that computer to provide secure services.

Because of size and time constraints, this book cannot provide you with a step-by-step guide to building a secure Internet host. Instead, this chapter discusses some of the most common security problems that affect computers being used to offer web services and then describes how to build a web server that minimizes these problems. Appendix E includes references to other books that provide more detailed host security information.

Current Host Security Problems

Most of the problems that Robert Metcalfe identified in RFC 602 back in 1973 (see the sidebar "RFC 602" in Chapter 4) remain today. Many organizations that run servers on the Internet simply do not secure their servers against external attack. Other problems have gotten worse: people still pick easy-to-guess passwords, and many passwords are simply "sniffed" out of the Internet using a variety of readily available packet sniffers. And people still break into computers for the thrill, except that now many of them also steal information for financial gain or to make some ideologic point.

Perhaps the only problem that Metcalfe identified in 1973 that has been solved is the problem of unauthorized people accessing the Internet through unrestricted dial-ups—that is, dialup lines that do not require entering a username and password. But this problem has been solved in a strange way. Thanks to the commercialization of the Internet, the number of unrestricted dialups is quite small. On the other hand, today it is so easy to procure a "trial" account from an Internet service provider (frequently without providing anything in the way of real identification) that the real threat is no longer unauthorized users; it's the "authorized" ones.

A Taxonomy of Attacks

Back in 1973, two of the biggest vulnerabilities Metcalfe had to confront were dialup servers that didn't require passwords and username/password combinations that were freely shared among users. These are both problems nearly thirty years later: a study by computer consultant Peter Shipley found more than 50,000 dialup modems in the San Francisco Bay Area, of which more than 2%—more than 1000—allowed unrestricted access to any caller, without the need to enter a username and password. Among the vulnerable systems were the dispatch system for the Oakland Fire Department, the order-entry system for a popular bookstore, and records systems belonging to several medical practices. Shipley found these dialups by dialing every single phone number in the San Francisco Bay Area; it is reasonable to suspect that others are engaged in a similar vulnerability assessment project (perhaps with a less academic goal).

But while unsecured dialups remain a significant problem, they are now simply one of many venues for an attacker to gain access and control over a target computer system. Many of these techniques give the attacker the ability to run code on the target machine. These techniques include:

Remote exploits

Vulnerabilities exist in many computers that make it possible for an attacker to compromise, penetrate, or simply disable the system over the network without actually logging into the system. For example, Microsoft Windows NT 4.0 was vulnerable to the *ping of death*, which allowed anybody on the Internet to crash a Windows NT 4.0 system by simply sending the computer a specially crafted "ping" packet. As another example, version 8.2 through 8.2.2 of the Internet Software Consortium's BIND Domain Name Service were vulnerable to the *DNS remote root exploit*. This exploit allowed a remote user to gain "root" (superuser administrative) privileges on any computer running the vulnerable versions of BIND.

Many remote exploits are based on the *buffer overflow* technique. This technique relies on the way that the C programming language lays out information inside the computer's memory. The remote system might try to store 100 bytes into a buffer that is only set up to hold 30 or 40 bytes. The resulting information overwrites the C program's stack frame and causes machine code specified by the attacker to be executed.*

Malicious programs

Another way for an attacker to compromise a system is to provide the system's users with a hostile program and wait for them to run the program. Some programs when run will install hidden services that give attackers remote access capabilities to the compromised machine; these programs are called *back doors* because they offer attackers a way into the system that bypasses conventional security measures. *Trojan horses* are programs that appear to have one function but actually have another purpose that is malicious, similar to the great wooden horse that the Greeks allegedly used to trick the Trojans and end the siege of Troy.

Viruses and *worms* are self-replicating programs that can travel between computers as attachments on email or independently over a network. *Viruses* modify programs on your computer, adding to them their viral *payload*. *Worms* don't

---

* This form of attack is at least 35 years old and well known. It is astonishing that vendors are still building software that can be exploited this way.

modify existing programs, but they can install back doors or drop viruses on the systems they visit.

Stolen usernames and passwords and social engineering

On many computer systems it is possible to exploit bugs or other vulnerabilities to parlay ordinary access granted to normal users into "superuser" or "administrative" access that is granted to system operators. Thus, with ordinary usernames and passwords, a moderately skilled attacker can gain full run of many systems. Because these exploits can frequently be traced to the particular username, attackers commonly use a stolen username and password.

One of the most common ways for an attacker to get a username and password is *social engineering*. Social engineering is one of the simplest and most effective means of gaining unauthorized access to a computer system. For a social engineering attack, an attacker basically telephones the target organization and tries to socially extract information. For example, the attacker might pretend to be a new employee who has forgotten the password for his or her account and needs to have the password "reset." Or the attacker might pretend to be a service representative, claiming that the Administrator account needs to have its password changed so that routine maintenance can be performed. Social engineering attacks are effective because people generally want to be helpful.

Phishing

Social engineering can also be automated. There are many so-called *phishing* programs that will send social engineering emails to thousands or tens of thousands of users at a time. Some programs solicit usernames and passwords. Others try for valid credit cards. For example, one scam is to send email to users of an online service telling them that their credit cards have expired and that they need to enter a new one at the URL that is provided. Of course, the URL goes to the attacker's web server, not to the ISP's.

Frequency of Attack

Scale is another important difference between the security landscape that Bob Metcalfe faced in 1973 and the one we are facing today. In 1981, there were only 231 computers on the Arpanet, and those computers were mostly used for research purposes. Today there are millions of computers in constant connection to the Internet—with tens of millions more that are connected at some point during the day. These computers are being used for all manner of communications, commerce, and government activities.

As businesses, governments, and individuals have used the Internet to communicate faster and more efficiently than ever before, so too have the bad guys. Exactly as the Internet has made it possible to archive and easily distribute a wealth of information about science, technology, business, and art, it has also made it possible for attackers to discover, exchange, distribute, and archive more information about computer vulnerabilities. Back in the 1970s it was relatively rare for attackers outside of national agencies to work in groups of more than a few people. There were some people who were very good at gaining unauthorized access, to be sure, but on the whole, the knowledge of how to compromise computer systems was confined to small groups of relatively few people. Today there are literally thousands of organized and semi-organized groups of attackers—all exchanging information regarding computer vulnerabilities and exploits. Techniques, and in many cases complete programs for penetrating system security, are now widely distributed by email, through newsgroups, on web pages, and over Internet Relay Chat (IRC). Tools for compromising security—password sniffers, denial-of-service exploits, and prepackaged Trojan horses—are distributed as well.

Attackers now use automated tools to search out vulnerable computers and, in some cases, to automatically break in, plant back doors, and hide the damage. High-speed Internet connections have made it possible for attackers to rapidly scan and attack millions of computers within a very short period of time.

This increased scale has profound implications for anyone attempting to maintain a secure computer. In years past, many computers with known vulnerabilities could stay on the network for months or even years without somebody breaking into them. This is no longer the case. These days, if your computer has a known vulnerability, there is a very good chance that somebody will find that vulnerability and exploit it.

In fact, the widespread use of automated tools has resulted in many documented cases of systems being placed into service and hooked to the Internet, but before the owners could download and install all the needed vendor patches, the systems were discovered, probed, and attacked, and back doors installed.

The Honeynet Project (*http://project.honeynet.org/*) is an open Internet research project that is attempting to gauge the scale of the attacker community by setting up vulnerable computers on the Internet and seeing how long it takes before the computers are compromised. The results are not encouraging. In June 2001, for instance, the Honeynet Project announced that it took only 72 hours, on average, before somebody breaks into a newly installed Red Hat 6.2 system using one of the well-known exploits. A typical system on the Internet is scanned dozens of times a day. Windows 98 computers with file sharing enabled—a typical configuration for many home users—are scanned almost once an hour and typically broken into in less than a day. In one case, a server was hacked only 15 minutes after it was put on the network.

Understanding Your Adversaries

Who is breaking into networked computers with the most sophisticated of attacks? It almost doesn't matter—no matter who the attackers may be, they all need to be guarded against.

Script kiddies

As clichéd as it may sound, in many cases the attackers are children and teenagers—people who sadly have not (yet) developed the morals or sense of responsibility that is sufficient to keep their technical skills in check.

It is common to refer to young people who use sophisticated attack tools as *script kiddies*.* The term is quite derisive. The word "script" implies that the attackers use readily available attack scripts that can be downloaded from the Internet to do their bidding, rather than creating their own attacks. And, of course, the attackers are called "kiddies" because so many of them turn out to be underage when they are apprehended.

Script kiddies should be considered a serious threat and feared for the same reason that teenagers with guns should be respected and feared.† We don't call gang-bangers *gun kiddies* simply because youthful gang members don't have the technical acumen to design a Colt 45 revolver or cast the steel. Instead, most people realize that teenagers with handguns should be feared even more than adults, because a teenager is less likely to understand the consequences of his actions should he pull the trigger and thus more likely to pull it.

The same is true of script kiddies. In May 2001, for instance, the web site of Gibson Research Corporation was the subject of a devastating distributed denial-of-service attack that shut down its web site for more than 17 hours. The attack was orchestrated by more than 400 Windows computers around the Internet that had been compromised by an automated attack. As it turns out, Steve Gibson was able to get a copy of the attack program, reverse-engineer it, and trace it back. It turned out that his attacker was a 13-year-old girl.

Likewise, when authorities in Canada arrested "Mafiaboy" on April 19, 2000, for the February 2000 attacks on Yahoo, E*TRADE, CNN, and many other high-profile sites—attacks that caused more than $1.7 billion in damages—they couldn't release the suspect's name to the public because the 16-year-old was shielded by Canada's laws protecting the privacy of minors.‡

Script kiddies may not have the technical skills necessary to write their own attack scripts and Trojan horses, but it hardly matters. They have the tools and increasingly they show few reservations about using them. Either they do not understand the grave damage they cause, or they do not care.

What does a script kiddie do when he grows up? Nobody is really sure—to date, there are no reliable studies.

---

* We have also heard them referred to as ankle-biters.

† In this sentence,, we use the word "respected" to mean "taken seriously," and not "treated with honor because of skill or accomplishment."

‡ *http://news.cnet.com/news/0-1005-200-4523277.html*

Anecdotal reports suggest that many script kiddies go straight. Some lose interest in computers; some become system operators and network administrators; and some even go into the field of computer security. (The wisdom of hiring one of these individuals to watch over your network is a matter of debate within the computer security community.) But it is unquestionably clear that some individuals continue their lives of crime past their 18th birthdays. (Most stop at 18 because they are no longer "shielded" by laws that provide more lenient sentencing for juveniles.)

Industrial spies

There appears to be a growing black market for information stolen from computer systems. Some individuals have tried to ransom or extort the information from its rightful owners—for example, by offering to help a company close its vulnerabilities in exchange for a large cash payment. There have also been reports of attackers who have tried to sell industrial secrets to competitors of the companies that they have penetrated. Such transactions are illegal in the United States and in many other countries, but not in all.

Ideologues and national agents

There is a small but growing population of "hacktivists" who break into sites for ideologic or political reasons. Often, the intent of these people is to deface web pages to make a statement of some kind. We have seen cases of defacement of law enforcement agencies, destruction of web sites by environmental groups, and destruction of research computing sites involving animal studies. Sometimes, the protesters are making a political statement; they may be advancing an ideologic cause, or they may merely be anarchists striking a blow against technology or business.

Sometimes, these incidents may be carried out against national interests. For instance, a guerilla movement may deface sites belonging to a government opponent. In other cases, you see individuals in one jurisdiction attempting to make some point by attacking sites in another, such as in the Israeli-Palestinian conflict, the ongoing tension between Pakistan and India, and the aftermath of the accidental bombing of the Chinese embassy by U.S. forces. Many of these attacks may be spontaneous, but some may be coordinated or financed by the governments themselves.

These incidents can also affect third parties. For instance, during a Chinese crackdown, many ISPs around the world hosting web pages of adherents of Falun Gong found their servers under attack from sites inside China. Because of the coordination and replication of the attacks, authorities believed they were actually state-sponsored. ISPs have been attacked by vigilantes because they sell service to spammers, provide web service for hate groups, or seem to be associated with child pornographers—even if the ISP owners and operators were unaware of these activities!

Organized crime

The apocryphal quote by Willie Sutton about why he robbed banks, "Because that's where the money is," also applies on the Net. Vast amounts of valuable information and financial data flow through the Internet. It would be naive to believe that the criminal element is unaware of this, or is uninterested in expanding into the networked world. There have been incidents of fraud, information piracy, and money laundering conducted online that officials believe are related to organized crime. Communications on the Net have been used to advance and coordinate prostitution and pornography, gambling, trafficking in illegal substances, gun running, and other activities commonly involving organized crime. Furthermore, law enforcement sites may be targeted by criminals to discover what is known about them, or to discover identities of informants and witnesses.

With network globalization, the threats have a longer reach. The Russian mob, Sicilian Mafia, Japanese Yakuza, South American drug families, and Los Angeles gangs (to name a few) are all a few mouse clicks away on the network. Many law enforcement officials worry as a result that the Internet is a "growth" area for crime in the coming decade.

Rogue employees and insurance fraud

Finally, there are many cases of tactically skilled employees who have turned against their employers out of revenge, malice, or boredom. In some cases, terminated employees have planted Trojan horses or logic bombs in their employer's computers. In other cases, computer systems have been destroyed by employees as part of insurance scams.

What the Attacker Wants

Compromising a computer system is usually not an end in itself. Instead, most attackers seek to use compromised systems as a stepping stone for further attacks and vandalism. After an attacker compromises a system, the system can be used for many nefarious purposes, including:

- Launching probes or exploits against other systems
- Participating in *distributed denial-of-service* (DDOS) attacks
- Running covert servers (e.g., the attacker might set up an Internet Relay Chat server that will act as a rendezvous point for Trojan horses and viruses that are sending back captured data)
- Covertly monitoring the network of the organization that owns the compromised system, with the goal of compromising more systems
- Becoming a repository for attack tools, stolen information, pornography, or other kinds of contraband information

There are many reasons that compromised systems make excellent platforms for these kinds of illegal activities. If a compromised system is connected to a high-speed Internet connection, the system may be able to do much more damage and mayhem than other systems that the attacker controls. Compromised systems can also be used to make it more difficult for authorities to trace an attacker's actions back to the person behind the keyboard. If an attacker hops through many computers in different jurisdictions—for example, from a compromised Unix account in France to a Windows proxy server in South Korea to an academic computer center in Mexico to a backbone router in New York—it may be effectively impossible to trace the attacker backward to the source.

Tools of the Attacker's Trade

Tools that are commonly used by attackers include:

nc (a.k.a. netcat)
> Originally written by "Hobbit," *netcat* is the Swiss Army knife for IP-based networks. As such, it is a valuable diagnostic and administrative tool as well as useful to attackers. You can use *netcat* to send arbitrary data to arbitrary TCP/IP ports on remote computers, to set up local TCP/IP servers, and to perform rudimentary port scans.

trinoo (a.k.a. trin00)
> *trinoo* is the attack server that was originally written by the DoS Project. *trinoo* waits for a message from a remote system and, upon receiving the message, launches a denial-of-service attack against a third party. Versions of *trinoo* are available for most Unix operating systems, including Solaris and Red Hat Linux. The presence of *trinoo* is usually hidden. A detailed analysis of *trinoo* can be found at *http://staff.washington.edu/dittrich/misc/trinoo.analysis*.

Back Orifice and Netbus
> These Windows-based programs are Trojan horses that allow an attacker to remotely monitor keystrokes, access files, upload and download programs, and run programs on compromised systems.

bots
> Short for robots, *bots* are small programs that are typically planted by an attacker on a collection of computers scattered around the Internet. Bots are one of the primary tools for conducting distributed denial-of-service attacks and for maintaining control on Internet Relay Chat channels. Bots can be distributed by viruses or Trojan horses. They can remain dormant for days, weeks, or years until they are activated. Bots can even engage in autonomous actions.

root kits
> A *root kit* is a program or collection of programs that simultaneously gives the attacker superuser privileges on a computer, plants back doors on the computer, and erases any trace that the attacker has been present. Originally, root

kits were designed for Unix systems (hence the name "root"), but root kits have been developed for Windows systems as well. A typical root kit might attempt a dozen or so different exploits to obtain superuser privileges. Once superuser privileges are achieved, the root kit might patch the *login* program to add a back door, then modify the computer's kernel so that any attempt to read the *login* program returns the original, unmodified program, rather than the modified one. The *netstat* command might be modified so that network connections from the attacker's machine are not displayed. Finally, the root kit might then erase the last five minutes of the computer's log files.

Securing the Host Computer

Here are some of the ways you might go about defending your computer system from these individuals.

Security Through Policy

It's tempting to approach host security as a checklist of *do's* and *don't's* for computers and networks. After all, to damage a computer, an attacker must have access. So in theory, to operate a secure system, all you need to do is to block all of the venues by which an attacker can get access, and the resulting system will be secure.

In practice, however, it has proved nearly impossible to have a computer that offers services over the network and yet still denies all access to attackers. Often access comes through unintended holes, such as a carelessly coded CGI script (see Chapter 16), or a buffer overflow attack that is known to the attacker but not the computer's operators.

Instead of approaching host security as a laundry list of specific technical action items, it's better to look at the kinds of practices that make computers less secure, and then explore the specific policy initiatives that you can implement to improve your security outlook.

For more than a decade, there have been nine widespread practices on the Internet that make host security far worse than it needs to be. These practices are:

- Failure to think about security as a fundamental aspect of system setup and design (establishing policy)
- Purchase and configuration of computing systems based on issues of cost or compatibility rather than on the desired functionality and security needs
- Transmitting of plaintext, reusable passwords over networks
- Failure to use security tools properly, if they are used at all
- Failure to obtain and maintain software that's free of all known bugs and security holes

- Failure to track security developments and take preventative action
- Lack of adequate logging
- Lack of adequate backup procedures
- Lack of adequate system and network monitoring

Security is defined by policy. In some environments, every user is allowed to install or modify the organization's web pages. In others, only a few users are allowed to even read the pages. In some environments, any user can shut down or reboot the system. In others, it requires signed authorization from the CIO to so much as replace a file.

Policy helps users understand what is allowed. Policy guides administrators and managers in making choices about system configuration and use. Policy helps designers create systems that realize the organization's goals. The most basic security is a clear statement of what actions are allowed and disallowed, and by whom. Standards and guidelines should include the answers to these questions:

- Who is allowed access, what is the nature of that access, and who authorizes such access?
- Who is responsible for security, for upgrades, for backups, and for maintenance?
- What kinds of material are allowed on served pages?
- Which sites and external users are to be allowed access to pages and data served?
- What kinds of testing and evaluation must be performed on software and pages before they are installed?
- How will complaints and requests about the server and page content be handled?
- How should the organization react to security incidents?
- How and when should the policy itself be updated?
- Who is allowed to speak to members of the press, law enforcement, and other entities outside the organization in the event of questions or an incident?

We recommend that your policy documents be written and made available to everyone associated with your organization. Care given to the development of the policy can head off lots of potential problems.

Keeping Abreast of Bugs and Flaws

The Internet is a powerful tool for transmitting information. In a matter of minutes, news of the latest security flaw can be sent around the world and read by thousands or hundreds of thousands of individuals who may be eager to exploit it. Some of these individuals may attempt to break into your computer with their new knowledge. Sometimes they may be successful.

Thus, if you administer a computer that is connected to the Internet, it is important that you monitor bulletins issued by your vendor and that you install security-related patches as soon as they are made available. Most vendors have mailing lists that are specifically for security-related information.

Another source of information are FIRST* teams such as the CERT/CC (Computer Emergency Response Team, Coordination Center) at the Software Engineering Institute. The CERT/CC collects reports of computer crime, provides the information to vendors, and distributes information from vendors regarding vulnerabilities of their systems. Experience over time, however, has shown that CERT/CC and many other response teams do not make information available in a timely fashion. We suggest that you monitor announcements from the response teams, but that you don't depend on them as your primary information source.

Most software vendors maintain their own mailing lists of patches and announcements. You would be well-advised to subscribe to the lists of all your component vendors, including those of your routers and switches. If your ISP has a list, be sure to be on that one, too.

As a backup, you might also subscribe to one or two of the security-related mailing lists, such as *nt-security, bugtraq,* and *firewalls.*

Before you install any patch, be sure it is an authentic patch provided by your vendor. You can often check a file's digital signatures and cryptographic checksum to determine the authenticity and integrity of a patch before you install it. Also, be very wary of applying patches found in mailing lists and on bulletin boards: at worst, they may be planted to trick people into installing a new vulnerability. At best, they are often produced by inexperienced programmers whose systems are unlike yours, so their solutions may cause more damage than they fix. Caveat emptor!

Choosing Your Vendor

Today there are many choices for organizations setting up web-based services. Should your computer run Windows, Mac OS, Unix, or a "free" Unix-like operating system? Should your computer system use an "industry-standard" Intel-compatible microprocessor, or a SPARC, PowerPC, or another processor? Should you purchase the computer with or without support? What level of support is appropriate?

Many purchase decisions are based on factors such as the cost of the system, the reputation of the vendor, and the experience of the person making the purchase. Few organizations base their purchase decisions on the security of the underlying system.

Some vendors and platforms have better security pedigrees than the others, because different manufacturers value code quality and security differently. But the size of the user base also affects the security that a system will provide—even relatively secure

---

* Forum of Incident Response and Security Teams, the worldwide consortium of major computer incident response groups. Visit *http://www.first.org* for more information.

systems can become "unsecure" in the face of a large number of well-funded adversaries who widely publicize their findings.

Considering the importance of a reliable computing platform, it is amazing how many organizations will continue to purchase software from vendors whose products have suffered repeated security vulnerabilities. One of the biggest threats to the security of your system is the presence of software *faults* or *bugs*. These can cause your web server or client to crash, corrupt your information, or, worst of all, allow outsiders unauthorized access. It is stunning to see how many organizations are willing to operate mission-critical systems on "beta" or "pre-beta" software releases. It is difficult to understand Chief Information Officers who say that they know the product that they are purchasing is buggy, filled with vulnerabilities, and likely to increase the costs of their operations, but they feel that they have no choice but to purchase the software because "everybody else" is buying the same software.

As a large number of web sites are based on Windows NT running on Intel-compatible microprocessors, there is an incredibly high incentive for attackers to find vulnerabilities with this configuration.* For this reason, some organizations have decided to deploy uncommon configurations—such as OpenBSD running on Solaris SPARC computers—simply because fewer attackers have experience with these systems.

While the underlying operating system is important, equally important are the applications and the customized software that are layered on top of this base. A secure underlying system can be made vulnerable by a single vulnerable script that was written by a consultant to provide additional functionality.

Some steps that you should follow before specifying and deploying a new system include:

- Determine which vendors have the best reputation for producing bug-free, well-documented software. Vendors place different levels of emphasis on code quality and security. Find out what specific measures your vendors use to assure high security—such as the security criteria that they employ, data flow analysis, code audits, and/or penetration testing. Ask the vendors for copies of their metrics and test evaluations from reviews. You might also check the historical trends associated with the discovery and reporting of security flaws in software by that vendor. One source may be found at *http://www.securityfocus.com/vdb/stats.html*. (Because of the evolution in generally accepted methods of flaw discovery and reporting, we suggest that you don't use figures before 1997 or so in your evaluation, as they may not be reliable.)

---

* There are other reasons why Microsoft products seem to be a favorite of attackers. These include the large numbers of vulnerabilities that keep being discovered, the complexity of the software which makes the software difficult for administrators to secure, and the simple fact that Microsoft is disliked by many people.

- Investigate how your proposed vendors respond to reports of security or performance-relevant faults in their products. Is your proposed vendor timely and open in dealing with problems? Some vendors have a history of ignoring users unless there is significant bad press from complaints or incidents. These vendors should be avoided.

- Explore the importance your vendor attributes to good design, with issues of security, safety, and user interfaces. Systems resistant to attacks and user mistakes are much better to use in situations where you need dependable operation.

- Determine whether your organization would be better off using "old-generation" software for which the problems are presumably well-known, or "leading-edge" software that offers new features.

- Choose the system with the least number of features that does what you want well. Hardware is relatively inexpensive: buying a system to devote to a reduced configuration for a web server (for example) may be a better purchase than a clone of one of your standard systems that results in a massive break-in.

Here are some things to request or require when shopping for software and systems:

- Proof that good software engineering practices were followed in the design, coding, and testing of the software.

- Documentation showing the results of testing the software and system in environments similar to yours. Ideally, testing should include both operational testing and stress testing.

- A written statement of the vendor's policy for accepting, documenting, and responding to reports of faults in the product.

- A written statement of how the vendor notifies customers of newly fixed security flaws. (The most responsible vendors release notices through FIRST teams and through customer mailing lists; the least responsible vendors never announce fixes, or bury them in lists of other bug fixes in obscure locations.)

- Examples of previous notifications and bug fixes.

Although the computer industry is beginning to take computer security seriously, more change is needed. It is still the case that no software vendor will warrant its products against losses related to unsecured code—not even the vendors of security products. Typically, losses are limited to the cost of the media upon which the product was distributed.

A few insurance companies are now issuing policies to cover losses from break-ins and defacements of web sites. You should investigate these policies to see if there are different rates for different systems. As time goes on, rates should adjust to reflect the configurations that present less risk (and thus warrant smaller premiums).[*]

---

[*] As of late 2001, at least one insurance company charges higher premiums to customers using Windows and/or IIS as platforms.

To date, the major force for change appears to be public humiliation in the news media. One approach that still needs to be attempted is product liability lawsuits. In the meantime, if you add your voice to those of others requiring better security, you not only help raise awareness, but you should be able to protect yourself somewhat by making a better platform choice.

Installation I: Inventory Your System

Once you have decided upon a vendor, hardware platform, and software, you need to install everything. Installation is an extremely important process. Frequently, mistakes made during installation can come back to haunt you after you have brought your system online and gone on to other projects. So take your time and be certain of what you are doing.

First, it's important to inventory all of your systems. Write down the serial numbers, the amount of RAM, the kinds of processors, option cards, and other hardware configuration options. Make sure that you have copies of this information in at least two locations—one easy way to do so is to type the information into a spreadsheet and email a copy to yourself at home. This information will be useful for diagnosing performance issues. If you suffer a theft or loss, it will be useful for insurance purposes, too.

You should also inventory your software. For each product, note the vendor, the distribution, and the release. If you have software that comes with activation codes, it may be useful to record these as well. However, if you record the activation codes, you should attempt to secure them, because the distribution of activation codes could be considered software piracy by some vendors. (Distribution of more than ten activation codes with intent to defraud may be a felony under U.S. law.)

Be sure that you save all of the original packing material, documentation, blow-in inserts, and other information that comes with your computers and software. This can be critical if you are returning the equipment or need to relocate it. It is also surprising how many companies put vital information on seemingly innocuous printouts. Frequently, last minute inserts can be security or safety warnings, so be sure to at least glance at every piece of paper that you receive with your hardware and software.

Installation II: Installing the Software and Patches

Before you start to install the software for your computer, check the web site of each vendor to make sure you have all of the security patches and bug fixes for the version of the software that you intend to install. It is a good idea to read the release notes for both the base operating system and the patches. Some vendors distribute patches that must be installed in a particular order—installing the patches out of order can sometimes result in security vulnerabilities being reintroduced!

Next it is time to start installing your software. If at all possible, you should disconnect your computer from the Internet at the start of the installation procedure and not connect it until you are finished. There are many recorded cases of computers connected to the Internet being compromised between the time that the computer's base operating system was installed and the time that the patches were going to be installed. Unfortunately, it is increasingly difficult to install updates and register without software being connected to the Internet.

Once you have made sure that your computer is not connected to the Internet, install the computer's base operating system, any operating system patches, then the application programs and the application patches. Keep a notebook and record every specific action that you take. Such a log can be immensely useful if you are going to be installing several computers and hope to delegate the activity to others.

At this point, before any further work is done, you should make a complete backup of the computer system. This backup will be invaluable if your computer is compromised by an attacker or a hardware failure.

After your first backup is finished, you can make any local customizations that are required. You should then make a second backup of your computer system onto a different tape, CD, or disk.

Finally, make sure that all of the distribution software and the backups are stored in a place that is safe and will not be forgotten. Make sure that physical access to the computer is restricted. You may also wish to remove the floppy disk drive or CDs to make it more difficult for a person who has physical access for a brief period of time to compromise your server.

Minimizing Risk by Minimizing Services

An important way to minimize the threats to your web server is by minimizing the other services that are offered by the computer on which the web server is running. This technique works because each network service carries its own risks. By eliminating all nonessential services, you eliminate potential avenues through which an attacker could break into your system.

Table 15-1 lists some of the services that you should disable or restrict if you wish to run a secure server. Many of these services are widely considered "safe" today, but that doesn't mean that a serious flaw won't be discovered in one of these services sometime in the future. For example, in the spring of 2001 a vulnerability was found with the Berkeley Internet Name Daemon (BIND) that allowed anyone on the Internet to obtain superuser privileges on any Unix computer running the most common version of the software package. Sites that had nameservers running on their web servers were vulnerable. Sites that had turned off their nameservers were not.

If you don't need a service, disable it.

Making a Pre-Mac OS X Your Web Server

If security is your primary concern in running a web server, then you may wish to consider running your web server on a Macintosh computer running the OS 7, OS 8, or OS 9 operating systems. Because these versions of the Macintosh operating system were not delivered with a command-line interpreter, it is extremely difficult for attackers to break into the system and run programs of their own choosing. The Mac OS also doesn't come with dozens of network services enabled that can be compromised. And Apple has a very good history of providing carefully written, apparently bug-free code.

At least four web servers are available for the Macintosh:

- MacHTTP is a freely available web server that is easy to administer.
- WebStar, a commercial version of MacHTTP, is sold by StarNine Technologies, a subsidiary of Quarterdeck.
- WebStar Pro is an SSL-enabled version of WebStar, also sold by StarNine Technologies.
- Apple's personal web server is shipped with Mac OS 9 and possibly some releases of Mac OS 8.

Apple's Mac OS X operating system is based on FreeBSD. As such, its security is expected to be roughly similar to other Unix-based operating systems.

Table 15-1. Services to restrict on a secure server

Service to restrict	Reason
Domain Name Service (DNS)	Bugs in DNS implementations can be used to compromise your web server. Ideally, you should deploy computers that are only used for nameservice and nothing else. If you cannot run your own secure nameservers, you may wish to obtain nameservice from an upstream provider.
Mail (SMTP, POP, IMAP, etc.)	Bugs in *sendmail* and other mailers can be used to break into a computer system. Ideally, you should run mail services on computers other than your web server.
finger	*finger* can be used to learn information about a computer system that can then be used to launch other attacks. Bugs in the *finger* program can be used to compromise your site. *finger* was a very popular protocol in the 1980s and early 1990s, but its need today is questionable. Do not run *finger* in secure environments.
netstat, systat	*snetstat* and *systat* can reveal your system's configuration and usage patterns. Do not provide these services on secure machines.
chargen, echo	These services can be used to launch data-driven attacks and denial-of-service attacks. Disable them.
FTP	Do not run FTP if you can avoid it. The standard FTP sends usernames and passwords without encryption, opening up accounts accessed by FTP to attack. Although it is possible to use FTP with nonreusable password systems such as S/Key or SecureID, a better alternative is to use *scp* (Secure Copy, part of the *ssh* package) or WEB-DAV over SSL. If you must use FTP, use it only for updating the web server. If you need to run an anonymous FTP server, it should be run on a separate computer, and at the very least with a separate filesystem different from your web server.

Table 15-1. Services to restrict on a secure server (continued)

Service to restrict	Reason
Telnet	Do not allow interactive logins to your web server for anyone other than the site administrator (webmaster). If possible, use only a cryptographically enabled remote access systems, such as *ssh* or Kerberized Telnet. If you must Telnet without encryption, use a one-time password system, such as S/Key or SecureID.
Berkeley "r" commands (*rlogin*, *rsh*, *rdist*, etc.)	These commands use IP addresses for authentication that can be (and have been) spoofed. Use *ssh* and *scp* instead.

 On a Unix server, you can easily restrict unneeded services by commenting out appropriate lines in *inetd.conf*. Another small handful of services that run as standalone daemons (portmapper is an example) can be eliminated in the "rc" files, found in the files */etc/rc* and */etc/rc.local*, and the subdirectories below */etc/rc.d* and */usr/local/etc/rc.d*. Many Unix servers now include support for the TCP wrappers file *hosts.allow*. By modifying this file, you can effectively control which hosts are allowed to access which services on your computer. You can also use IP filtering tools, such as *ipfw*, to provide host-based access control for outbound services.

Disabling IP services with an NT or Windows 2000 system is a little trickier, because settings are sprinkled throughout the registry, and some services have to be functioning for the sake of NT. Many NT services can be audited and disabled using the Services control panel.

The good news is that NT servers come with built-in access list capability. You can use this to prohibit all traffic to certain ports, and thereby achieve the same results as you would by shutting down services. (You can set IP filtering under the control panel's advanced TCP/IP settings.)

Operating Securely

In general, the longer a computer is used, the less secure it becomes. New software gets installed, increasing the complexity of the system and increasing the chance that a vulnerability will be introduced. Sometimes a security measure might be disabled by an administrator who is looking to get something done quickly. Meanwhile, vulnerabilities with the existing system are more likely to be discovered. Operating systems that were believed to be absolutely secure one day can be fatally vulnerable the next.

Thus, if you spend the time and money to deploy a secure system, but you do not maintain the system, you are wasting your resources. Organizations that hire security consultants are often the most guilty offenders: these organizations frequently bring in some high-powered consultants for a brief engagement. The consultants write a report and leave. Even if the consultants actually succeeded in making the systems more secure, the beneficial results are only temporary.

Keep Abreast of New Vulnerabilities

In today's environment, you must stay abreast of newly discovered vulnerabilities if you wish to maintain a secure computer that is connected to the Internet. The day has long passed when security vulnerabilities were kept quiet. These days vulnerabilities are usually publicized with breathtaking speed once they are discovered. What's more, once a vulnerability is known, exploits are quickly developed and distributed across the Internet. In many cases, system administrators only have a few hours between the time that a vulnerability is first publicized and the time when they will start to be attacked with it.

One way that you can minimize the impact of newly discovered vulnerabilities is by isolating your web server from the Internet using a firewall or IP filtering (see the section "Firewalls and the Web" later in this chapter). But this isolation is not a cure-all, because vulnerabilities have also been discovered in the hardware or software that you use for the isolation. Also, some flaws exploit protocols you need to allow through your firewall. There is no substitute for vigilance.

Logging

Many of the services on networked computers can be configured to keep a log of their activities. Computers that run the Unix and NT operating systems can have their logging systems customized so that events are written into a single file, written to multiple files, or sent over the network to another computer, a printer, or another device.

Logs are invaluable when recovering from a security-related incident. Often they will tell you how an attacker broke in and even give you clues to track down who the attacker is. Log files may be submitted as evidence to a court of law if they are kept on a regular basis as part of normal business practice.

You should have logging enabled for all of your servers and you should be sure that these logs are examined on a regular basis. You may wish to write a small script that scans through the log file on a daily basis and filters out well-known events that you are expecting, or use a log analyzer, as mentioned earlier. The events that are left will be, by definition, the events that you are not expecting. Once you have a list of these events, you can either go back to modify your scripts to suppress them, or you can make phone calls to figure out why they have occurred.

Although some programs maintain their own log files, most programs on both Unix and Windows now use the system-wide logging facilities that these operating systems provide. A notable exception to this rule is web servers.

Log files are also useful for gauging the capacity of your system. For example, you might consider logging all of the following parameters on a regular basis. They will not only help you spot security violations, but also help you determine when your systems need to be upgraded:

- Utilization of your external network connection
- Utilization of your internal network
- CPU load of your servers
- Disk utilization

See the discussion of the privacy implications of log files in Chapter 8.

Setting up a log server

If a person breaks into your computer, the first thing that they will do is to cover their tracks by either erasing or subtly modifying your log files. As logs are normally kept on the computer that has been compromised, they are vulnerable. The only way to protect your logs is to set up a secured log server that will collect log entries from other computers on your network.

A log server is a single, secure computer that you set up to receive log messages from other computers on your network. This log server can be either inside or outside your firewall; you may even wish to set up two log servers, one on each side.

Your log server should be a computer system that offers no services to the network and does not have any user accounts. The idea is to make the log server the most secure computer on your network—even if an attacker breaks into all of the other computers on your network, you want the log server to remain secure.* Log servers should be used in addition to local logging, not as a substitute.

Logging on Unix

The modern Unix logging system assigns a facility and a priority to each log message. The facility specifies which part of the Unix system generated the logging message. Typical facilities are *kern* for the kernel, *news* for the Netnews system, *auth* for the authentication system, etc. Priorities indicate the level of the message's severity—*info* for an informative message, *alert* for alerts, *crit* for critical messages, and so on.

The Unix file */etc/syslog.conf* specifies what the operating system should do with logging messages. Messages can be appended to a file, sent using interactive messages to users who are currently logged on, transmitted to another machine, sent to a program of your own design, or some combination of all of these.

---

* The previous edition of this book noted that an alternative to setting up a single-purpose log server would be to have a form of write-only log storage such as an obsolete PC connected to your log host using a serial cable. This computer could simply record the log entries in a disk file and display them on a console. In the event that the log server was broken into, you would still have a record of log events on the PC. Alas, these kinds of home-brew logging systems are now simply too complex for most organizations to manage, although they still work well.

Unix log files need to be pruned on a regular basis, or else they will overwhelm your computer's disk. One way to prune log files is to *rotate* them. Typical rotation procedures involve copying existing log files to new locations, compressing the files, and storing a few copies. The Unix command *newsyslog* automates this process. It is controlled by the configuration file */etc/newsyslog.conf*.

Logging on Windows 2000

Logging on Microsoft Windows 2000 systems is controlled by the logging service. Auditing is disabled by default on Windows 2000 Professional and on some versions of Windows 2000 Server. You should enable auditing to catch bad login attempts and to watch the IP services you are offering. Be careful, though: you can generate a lot of information very quickly. Logs are kept locally, and should be reviewed on a regular basis. Windows log files are automatically pruned on a regular basis by the logging service. To enable auditing, run the Local Security Policy application in the Administrative Tools folder of the system control panel. Click on Local Policies Audit Policy; then double-click on the policy that you wish to change (see Figure 15-1).

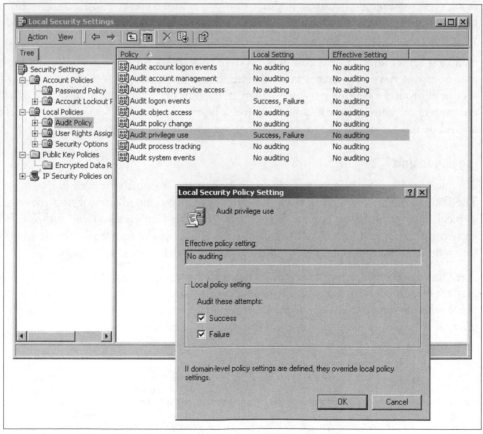

Figure 15-1. Enable auditing from the Local Secure Policy Setting application.

To view the contents of the log, run the Event Viewer application. You can change the retention time of log events by selecting the Properties item from the Action menu (see Figure 15-2).

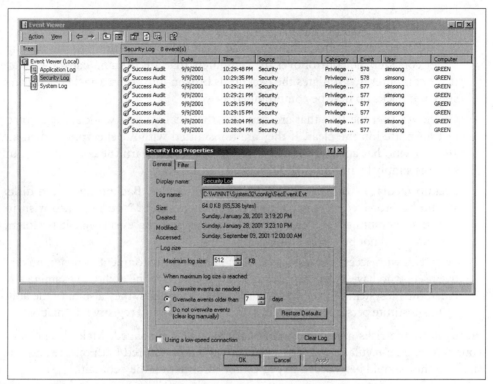

Figure 15-2. Run the Event Viewer application to view the contents of the log.

Backups

A backup is simply a copy of data that is written to tape or other long-term storage media. Computer users are routinely admonished to back up their work on a regular basis. Site administrators can be responsible for backups of dozens or hundreds of machines. Chapter 11 discusses backups in some detail.

Backups serve many important roles in web security:

- They protect you from equipment failures.
- They protect you from accidental file deletions.
- They protect you from break-ins, because files that are deleted or modified by an attacker can be restored from a backup.
- They allow you to determine the extent of an attacker's damage, because you can detect changes in your system by comparing its files with the files stored on your backup tapes.

Backups systems are not without their problems, however:

- You must verify that the data on the backup tape is intact and can actually be used to restore a working system. Otherwise, your backup may lull you into a false sense of security.

- Look closely at systems that back up several computers across a local area network. These systems frequently give the computer that is running the backup server considerable control over the computers that are running backup clients. If the computer that initiates the backups is broken into by an attacker, then any system it backs up may be compromised as well.

- Check whether the files that are sent over the local area network are encrypted or transmitted in the clear. If they are transmitted without encryption, then an attacker who has access to your network traffic could learn the contents of your systems simply by monitoring the backup.

- Backup media, by definition, contain all of your files. Backup tapes and disks should be protected at least as well as your computers. You may also wish to consider encrypting your backup media, so that in the event that it is stolen, your data will not be compromised.

- Be careful with access control lists (ACLs) in an NT environment. Nonadministrative users who have rights to perform backups also have the ability to examine any file in the filesystem. Furthermore, if they can restore files, they also have the ability to substitute personalized versions of user database and registry information.

Fortunately, the risks associated with backups can be managed. Make backups of your system on a regular basis. These backups should be stored both on-site and off-site, and they should be guarded to protect the information they contain.

Using Security Tools

A *security tool* is a special program that you can run to evaluate or enhance the security of your site. Many security tools that are available today were developed at universities or by independent specialists and are freely distributed over the Internet. There are also several good tools that are marketed commercially.

There are five kinds of tools that you should consider using:

- Tools that take a snapshot of your system and look for potential weaknesses
- Tools that monitor your system over time, looking for unauthorized changes
- Tools that scan your network, looking for network-based weaknesses
- Tools that monitor your system and network to identify attacks in progress, including attacks by malware
- Tools that record all network activity for later analysis

Automated tools are (usually) a low-cost, highly effective way to monitor and improve your system's security. Some of these tools are also routinely employed by attackers to find weaknesses in sites around the Internet. Therefore, it behooves you to obtain your own tools and use them on a regular basis.

Snapshot tools

A *snapshot* or *static audit tool* will scan your system for weaknesses and report them to you. For example, on your Unix system a tool might look at the */etc/passwd* file to ensure that it is not writeable by anyone other than the superuser. Snapshot tools perform many (perhaps hundreds) of checks in a short amount of time. One of the best-known programs and the first generally available was developed for Unix: COPS, written by Dan Farmer with assistance and supervision by Gene Spafford. Unfortunately, COPS is now several years out of date and has not been updated in a long time.

A more up-to-date Unix snapshot tool is Tiger, from Texas A&M University. Tiger runs on a wider variety of operating systems and is easy to install. Tiger performs nearly all of the checks that are in COPS, plus many more. Unfortunately, it produces a report that can be very difficult to interpret because of its length. It also is unclear if the tool is being maintained. You can find the most recent version at *http:// www.net.tamu.edu/ftp/security/TAMU/*.

Several packages are available in the Windows world. The Kane Security Analyst (KSA) from Intrusion Detection, Inc. (*http://www.intrusion.com/*) will check passwords and permissions (ACL), and monitor data integrity. NAT is a free tool for assessing NetBIOS and NT password security made available by Security Advisors (*http://www.secnet.com*). Two tools for checking NT passwords are ScanNT, written by Andy Baron (*http://www.ntsecurity.com/Products/ScanNT/index.htm*), and L0phft Crack, by the "computer security researchers" at L0phft Heavy Industries (now part of @Stake).

A snapshot program should be run on a regular basis—no less than once a month and probably at least once a week. Carefully evaluate the output of these programs, and follow up if possible.

Finally, be careful that you do not leave the output from a snapshot security tool in a place that is accessible to others: by definition, the holes that they can find can easily be exploited by attackers.

Change-detecting tools

It's also important to monitor your system on a regular basis for unauthorized changes. That's because one of the first things that an attacker usually does once he breaks in is to modify your system to make it easier to regain access in the future, and/or to hide evidence of the break-in. Scanning for changes won't prevent a break-in—but it may alert you to the fact that your system has been compromised. As most break-ins go unnoticed for some time, change-detecting tools may be the only way that you can be alerted to an intruder's presence and take appropriate action.

When more than one person is administering a system, change reports also give users an easy way to keep track of each other's actions.

Some vendors have started to include automated checking systems as part of their base operating system. The BSD/OS operating system, for example, includes an automated tool that runs every night and looks for any changes that have occurred in the system configuration files that are in the */etc* directory. To perform this change, the BSD/OS scripts use comparison copies; that is, they make a copy of every */etc* file every night and use the *diff* command to compare the actual file in */etc* with the copy. Called the "daily insecurity report," these reports are automatically mailed to the system manager account. Unfortunately, this system is easy for an experienced attacker to subvert, because the comparison files are included on the same computer as the original files. For this reason, more sophisticated systems are run from removable media. The media is also used to keep either the copies of the comparison copies of each file or their cryptographic checksums.

Tripwire is another tool that can automatically scan for changes. Originally developed by Gene Kim and Gene Spafford at Purdue University, Tripwire is now commercially maintained and sold by Tripwire Inc. for both Unix and Windows systems; see *http://www.tripwire.com/* for details.* The program can store the results of a Tripwire scan on removable media or report the results to a central Tripwire management console. An open source version of Tripwire is available for Linux systems. At one time (and perhaps still), various versions of Tripwire constituted the most commonly used intrusion and change detection system in use in the world.

Network scanning programs

You should use automated tools to scan your network. These tools check for well-known security-related bugs in network programs such as *sendmail* and *ftpd*. Your computers are certainly being scanned by crackers interested in breaking into your systems, so you might as well run these programs yourselves. Here are several we recommend:

- One of the most widely publicized scanning programs of all time was SATAN, written by Dan Farmer and Wietse Venema. Before its release in April 1995, SATAN was the subject of many front page stories in both the trade and general press. SATAN derives its power from the fact that it can scan a group of machines on a local or remote network. You can use it to check the security policy for a group of machines that you are responsible for, or you can point it beyond your firewall and see how well your counterpart at a competing business

---

* The Tripwire for Web Pages offering is worth mentioning; it notes any changes to pages served by an Apache web server and alerts the administrator. This protects against unauthorized alterations or defacements.

is doing. SATAN has an easy-to-use interface* and a modular architecture that makes it possible to add new features to the program. Nevertheless, SATAN is not that powerful: the program scans only for very well-known vulnerabilities, many of which have been fixed in recent years. It is no longer maintained, and we're listing it here mainly for historical purposes.

- Several companies sell commercial scanners. One of the most widely known of these companies is Internet Security Systems, Inc., which commercialized the freeware scanner by the same name. Scanners are also sold by Axent, Network Associates, and others. You can learn more about these programs from their vendors' respective web sites.

- SomarSoft (*http://www.somarsoft.com*) offers several tools for analyzing information culled from Windows NT logs and databases. KSA, mentioned under "Snapshot tools," also provides analysis and integrity checking for NT environments. Likewise, some commercial virus scanning products can provide signature-based integrity checks for NT binaries and data files.

Intrusion detection systems

Intrusion detection system (IDS) programs are the operating system equivalent of burglar alarms. As their name implies, these tools scan a computer as it runs, watching for the tell-tale signs of a break-in.

When computer crackers break into a system, they normally make changes to the computer to make it easier for them to break in again in the future. They frequently use the compromised computer as a jumping-off point for further attacks against the organization or against other computers on the Internet. The simplest intrusion detection tools look for these changes by scanning system programs to see if they have been modified.

Intrusion detection systems can either be host based or network based. A host-based system looks for intrusions on that particular host. Most of these programs rely on secure auditing systems built into the operating system. Network-based systems monitor a network for the tell-tale signs of a break-in on another computer. Most of these systems are essentially sophisticated network monitoring systems that use Ethernet interfaces as packet sniffers.

Most working intrusion detection tools are commercial. Some representative systems currently available are:

- Tripwire, described earlier in this chapter in the section "Change-detecting tools."
- Dragon, marketed by Enterasys, is a highly-rated and powerful intrusion detection system for hosts and networks (*http://www.enterasys.com/ids/*).

---

* SATAN was actually one of the first programs to be administered from a web browser.

- Cisco Secure IDS (Formerly NetRanger), which uses network monitoring to scan for intrusions (*http://www.cisco.com/*).

- Realsecure Manager and Realsecure Network Sensor, by Internet Security Systems (*http://www.iss.net/*).

- Shadow, a freeware network monitoring and IDS system created and maintained by the Naval Surface Warfare Center (*http://www.nswc.navy.mil/ISSEC/CID/*).

Virus scanners

There is a huge market for antivirus tools. Several major vendors market a variety of tools to be used on individual hosts, networks, mail servers, and more. Network Associates and Symantec appear to be the major vendors of these tools in North America. The product features and coverage change frequently, so it is difficult to say with certainty what is current and recommended. However, most antivirus tools detect roughly the same viruses in approximately the same manner, so we can almost say that any current version of products by these two companies will work.

Note that antivirus tools are not needed for Unix or Linux systems—there are only three or four reported viruses for these platforms, and they do not spread well. An integrity monitor (such as Tripwire) will also perform any antivirus function needed on these platforms as a side-effect of the way it works.

Mac OS systems do not generally need an antivirus tool unless you are in the habit of using old media that may be contaminated, or you use a Microsoft product with macros enabled (e.g., Word, Excel, or Outlook). Historically, there have only been about 60 viruses discovered for the Mac in the last dozen years. None of these seem to be still in general circulation, although there are undoubtedly reservoirs on old, infected diskettes.

The majority of discovered viruses (more than 72,000 by some counts in late 2001) are for Microsoft software—DOS, Windows, NT, and Visual Basic Scripting. Luckily, many of these are no longer in general circulation or work on currently platforms; perhaps only 300–400 are in common circulation. However, some vendors report new virus reports are at the level of 12–15 per day, the majority in macro languages. Thus, if you run any of these platforms, you need to have antivirus software in place and updated regularly.

Network recording and logging tools

Intrusion detection systems are like sophisticated alarm systems: they have sensors and alarms, and if an intruder happens to trip over one of them, the IDS will record this fact. But the fundamental problem with intrusion detection systems is that they can only record what they have been programmed to notice.

Network recording and logging tools take a different approach. Instead of having well-placed alarms, these systems record all of the traffic that passes over a network,

---

allowing retrospective analysis. These systems are typically run on computers with large disks. (An 80-gigabyte hard disk, for example, can store nearly two weeks of typical traffic sent over a T1 line.) In the event of a break-in or other incident, the recorded traffic can be analyzed.

A variety of recording systems are now available, including:

- NFR, by NFR Security (*http://www.nfr.com/*)
- NetVCR, by NIKSU (*http://www.niksun.com/*)
- Silent Runner, by Raytheon (*http://www.silentrunner.com/*)
- NetIntercept, by Sandstorm Enterprises (*http://www.sandstorm.net/*)[*]

Secure Remote Access and Content Updating

Once you have your web server up and running, securely logged and monitored, you will next be faced with a troubling real-world question: how will your users update the web server's content?

In the early days of the World Wide Web, most content was created live on web servers by programmers and developers using Unix text editors such as *emacs* and *vi*. These days most content is created on desktop PCs and Macs and then uploaded to the web server. This upload is fundamentally a file transfer operation. Unfortunately, a holdover of the U.S. government's two-decade war on cryptography is that the Internet's most common file transfer protocol, FTP, sends usernames and passwords without first encrypting them. This makes the protocol vulnerable to password sniffing.

The Risk of Password Sniffing

Password sniffing is a significant security risk on the Internet today. Passwords sent without encryption can be intercepted by a network monitor program and conveyed to attackers. Stolen passwords can be used to rewrite web pages and break into other Internet accounts. When the stolen passwords belong to system administrators with additional security privileges, even more serious mayhem can be wrought.

Unfortunately, usernames and passwords sent unencrypted over the Internet remain one of the most common ways of authenticating users on the network today. Plaintext passwords are widely used by many Internet protocols, including remote login (Telnet/*rlogin*), file transfer (FTP), remote email reading (POP3/IMAP), and web access (HTTP).

---

[*] Simson Garfinkel and Gene Spafford are both founders of Sandstorm.

Using Encryption to Protect Against Sniffing

The only general way to defeat password sniffing is to avoid using plaintext usernames and reusable passwords, or employ encryption. There are three likely alternatives:

Use a token-based authentication system
> Examples are the SecurID system from Security Dynamics (see Figure 15-3) or the SecureNet Key from Digital Pathways. These tokens are actually small hand-held computers that allow you to use a different password every time you log into the remote site. As the eavesdroppers do not posses the token, they cannot access your account at a later time.

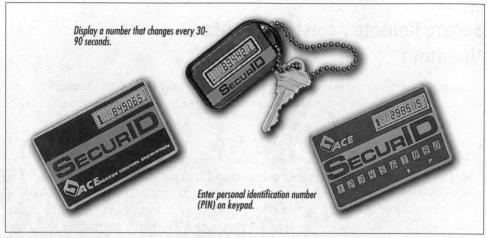

Display a number that changes every 30-90 seconds.

Enter personal identification number (PIN) on keypad.

Figure 15-3. Security Dynamics' SecurID card (reprinted with permission)

Use a nonreusable password system
> An example is S/Key. With S/Key, users are given printouts with a list of hundreds of passwords. Each time they use a password, they cross it out, and use the next one (see Figure 15-4).

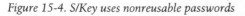

```
xy3221      seeme4
screen42!   421mefoo
apss42      Jo4!me
foobedobe
sometix4
Abrac!42
ohmy000
asyucan
```

Figure 15-4. S/Key uses nonreusable passwords

Use a system that relies on encryption

Doing so prevents the sending of your password in the clear over the network. These systems include Kerberos, Secure Shell (*ssh*), Secure Copy (*scp*), and Secure Sockets Layer (SSL)/Transport Layer Security (TLS). Encryption schemes can be used with conventional reusable passwords, with nonreusable passwords such as S/Key for additional protection, or with a public key digital signature certificate system.

> Windows NT file sharing uses a one-way hash for sending encrypted passwords over a local area network, but these passwords can be "cracked" using a suitable program. Be careful; by default, Windows NT and 2000 operate in a "compatibility" mode which allows legacy Windows for Workgroups and Windows 95 systems to connect without using encryption. And even when "encryption" is enabled on a Windows system, the Microsoft file sharing protocol only encrypts passwords: usernames and the contents of files are still sent in the clear. What's more, since authentication only takes place at the beginning of the TCP/IP session, NT file share connections can be hijacked once a session has been authenticated. Overall, Windows NT file sharing offers more security than plaintext protocols such as FTP, but less security than protocols such as *scp*.

Cryptographic techniques have the advantage of encrypting all information transmitted between the two network computers. They also protect ongoing connections from *session hijacking*, which occurs when an attacker seizes control of a network session after a legitimate user has authenticated. Unfortunately, encryption schemes require that you have specially modified versions of both the Internet servers and clients for each protocol that you wish to protect. There are also interoperability concerns because of encryption restrictions by various governments and proprietary incompatibilities.

Encryption can be staged at one or more levels:

Application level

In the most specific cases, applications can be written or retrofitted for secured transfer. Because the encryption and authentication are typically negotiated in the application's client/server handshake, sessions are limited to individual protocols or services.

Transport/network level

Encryption at the transport layer (e.g., TCP/IP) or network layer (e.g., IP), on the other hand, can often be applied to a variety of services. Potentially, the encryption will be transparent to the application; system network services can substitute encrypted transport for nonencrypted transport without affecting the application. SSL and TLS are examples of transport-level encryption standards.

Network level

> Virtual private networks (VPNs) are typically built upon standards for network-level encryption and authentication. The IPSec proposal is quickly becoming the de facto VPN standard (see RFCs 1825 through 1829). Note that the degree of encryption available to you depends on where the secured session is conducted; government restrictions limit the extent of cryptographic methods.

We *strongly* recommend the use of encryption to protect all administrative Telnet and file transfer sessions between a web server and an administrative workstation. If possible, encryption should be used to protect *all* Telnet and file transfer sessions.

Secure Content Updating

Most organizations create their web documents on a different computer from their web server and then transfer those documents to the server when they are completed. It is therefore important for these organizations to have a technique for securely gaining access to their web servers to update these files.

In the best circumstances, the web server will be secured behind its own network interface on the company firewall. This will place the server logically "outside," yet still afford it protection from the firewall. You can then cut an outbound channel extending from the internal LAN through the firewall and out to the server for updates. (We show this configuration in Chapter 2.)

Secure update access is a little trickier when the web server is situated remotely. A few of the tools mentioned here have built-in security features. These should be supplemented with address-based filtering or challenge/response mechanisms, if possible. However, the safest way to provide unfettered remote update access is through an encrypted, authenticated VPN connection; access will be secured, and traffic will be protected from packet sniffing.

Here are a few possible server update methods:

1. Copy the files using the *scp* cryptographic protocol or a file synchronization system over *ssh*.
2. Manually copy the files one at a time or directory-by-directory using FTP.
3. Copy them using a Unix-specific protocol, such as *rcp* or *rdist*.
4. Have the web server access the files from a file server using a network file transfer protocol such as Network File System (NFS).
5. For NT-based web servers, allow SMB (NetBIOS) file sharing across the firewall or even (with great care) across the Internet.
6. Perform a physical transfer using tape or removable disk.

All of these techniques have advantages and disadvantages.

scp/ssh

The *scp* (secure copy) program is one of the most secure ways that you can use to update files on a remote server. The *scp* program is a part of the Secure Shell (*ssh*) distribution. It encrypts all file transfers and can optionally use public key certificates for authentication. Using encryption eliminates the possibility of password sniffing. The program is available for Windows, Mac OS, and Unix. *scp* can even recursively copy whole directories.

One problem with *scp* is that it will transfer files from your desktop to the remote server, but it will not delete files from the remote server when they are no longer needed. If you want synchronization, rather than replication, you may wish to consider one of the file synchronization programs that are now available for Unix shown in Table 15-2. All of these programs can use *ssh* as their underlying transport, which provides for encryption and reliable authentication

Table 15-2. Synchronization programs for Unix and Windows that use ssh as the transport layer

Program	Platforms	Comments
rdist, rdist6	Unix	Allows for "distfiles" that will copy the same content to multiple machines at the same time. A fast approach.
rsync	Unix	Offers more control than *rdist*. Has a clever update system for transferring log files.
unison	Unix, Windows	Allows for two-way synchronization between multiple computers. File deletion is handled through the use of metainformation stored with each ynchronization set.
Interarchy	Mac OS	A full-fledged FTP client that can transfer files to or from the Mac using FTP or HTTP. It has commands to transfer whole hierarchies and to mirror hierarchies. At Version 5, Interarchy has an "ftp disk" option that will create a local mirror of a remote FTP hierarchy: you update the local copy, and Interarchy mirrors the copy on the remote site.

FTP

The advantage of the FTP protocol is that there are a wide number of FTP clients available for computers running nearly every operating system including OS/2, Windows, Mac OS, and Unix. Thus, if you rely on FTP to update files, many people will be able to update them. On the other hand, most FTP servers have provision only for simple username and password authentication. As previously noted, passwords sent in the clear over the Internet can easily be sniffed. It is possible, however, to employ stronger authentication systems with FTP, such as S/Key or the SecureID card. The FTP control channel can also be tunneled over *ssh* (see the sidebar).

Unix rcp or rdist

Using a Unix-specific protocol such as *rcp* or *rdist* has the advantage that many of these protocols have already been modified to allow for increased security. If you are going to use *rcp* or *rdist*, you might wish to use a version that uses the

Using SSH and FTP Together

The FTP protocol uses two ports on the server: port 21 for the control connection and (usually) port 20 for the data connection. The portion of the connection that you need to be concerned with is what flows to port 21, because that is the stream that includes your password.

One way to configure *ssh* to support FTP is to set the local *ssh* client to relay local connections to port 21 on to your web server machine's port 21. Then configure your local FTP client to use "passive" FTP mode when transferring files, and open your FTP connection to host *localhost* (IP 127.0.0.1) (*not* to the actual web server host!).

What will happen is that your FTP control communication will flow directly to your local port 21 without going across the net. *ssh* will encrypt the traffic and pass it to the remote web server. The web server will open a data port (not port 20), and return the number and IP address of the port over the encrypted link. Your client then connects directly to the web server host to perform the transfer. This approach protects your password and username, but does not incur the overhead of encrypting all the data flowing back and forth.

Kerberos protocol for authentication. The *rdist* program can also be run over *ssh*, as described previously. Using encryption eliminates the possibility of password sniffing. Unfortunately, you will need to use specially adapted clients with these servers.

Another advantage of *rcp* is that you can use a *.rhost* file, which allows you to perform authentication based on IP addresses. Although this approach makes your computer vulnerable to IP spoofing—an attack that happens when one computer sends out IP packets that claim to be from another—the risk of password sniffing is considerably greater. There is only one widely publicized case in which IP spoofing was used to break into a computer, while there are literally thousands of recorded instances in which password sniffers were used by crackers to break into systems. Furthermore, you can configure your network's routers to automatically reject incoming IP packets that claim to be from your internal network, greatly improving your site's resistance to IP spoofing attacks. (Of course, this doesn't help you if the web server is out on the Internet.)

NFS

Using a distributed filesystem such as NFS to provide content to your web server is an intriguing idea. You can have the web server mount the NFS filesystem read-only. The NFS server should likewise export the filesystem read-only, and it should only export the filesystem that contains web server files. An advantage of this system is that it gives you an easy way to update the web server's content without actually logging in to the web server. Another advantage is that you can have multiple web servers access the same NFS filesystem.

The primary disadvantage of using a read-only NFS filesystem to provide files to your web server is that there can be significant performance penalties using NFS. You can minimize this impact by using a web cache between the web server and the rest of the Internet, or by using an ultra-high-performance NFS appliance server. The speed of NFS is also not a factor for web pages that are programmatically generated: the overhead of the CGI scripts far outweighs the overhead of NFS.

SMB

Providing for Windows file sharing (SMB) traffic to NT-based web servers will let you take advantage of web tools that depend on shares. The trick is to make sure that necessary ports (137/TCP, 138/UDP, and 139/TCP) are invisible to anyone else on the Internet. You can ensure that this is the case with address filtering and appropriate spoof-checking, or by conducting traffic within a VPN tunnel. The danger with this approach is that you expose more than you intended: printing, access to default shares, and other logon and system registry information become visible, too.

Whether or not you plan to connect to a remote NT-based web server with Windows file sharing, there are a few precautions you should take before wheeling the web server out past the moat:

- Disable guest logins altogether. Guest logins are enabled by default on NT Workstation and may be enabled by an administrator on the Server version. Likewise, toss out any extra logins that you don't absolutely need.

- Disable administrative logins from the network, if possible. If you must administer the server remotely, then change the name of the "Administrator" account to something else, so that it will be more difficult for an attacker to guess. You can use IP filters to further reduce the chance that an attacker will gain access to your remote administration system.[*]

Physical transfer

Transferring the files using physical media is very attractive for some installations. No network-capable services are required, and thus none are vulnerable. On the down side, such transfers require physical access to both the server and the development system for each installed change.

Dialup Modems

In this age of Internet access, it's easy to forget that modems still offer attackers a back door. Many organizations have modems that allow relatively unrestricted access to their networks, servers, and workstations. Modems can be installed to allow remote access and power-cycling of equipment in the event that a primary

---

[*] Because the remote machine may not be available to participate in WINS (and it certainly won't be answering broadcasts), you may need to make an entry in *lmhosts* on local clients or on local WINS servers.

Internet connection fails. Given the opportunity, many employees will set up modems on their desktop computers with programs like Carbon Copy or pcANY-WHERE, so that they can access their computers while working at home. Finally, many building and environmental systems, including elevators, HVAC equipment, and even pay phones are equipped with dialup modems for remote control.

There is nothing inherently secure about a dialup modem that requires callers to enter a username and a password before access is granted. The problem is that many dialup modems do not require even this most basic of remote authentication protocols. As we noted earlier about Pete Shipley's survey of modems, approximately 2% of the ones he found did not have passwords in place.

Organizations should establish policies as to whether or not employees and system operators can set up their own dialup modems. The policy should state who has the authority to set up dialup modems, how they should be secured, and whether or not the phone numbers need to be centrally reported.

Once a policy is in place, organizations should perform routine telephone scans to verify compliance with their policy. Several telephone scanners are now available, including:

PhoneSweep by Sandstorm Enterprises
> The first commercial telephone scanner. Developed in part by Simson Garfinkel, PhoneSweep is a high-speed scanner that can dial with up to 16 phone lines at a time. It has an expert system that can recognize more than 300 kinds of remote access systems. Information is available at *http://www.sandstorm.net/*.

TeleSweep by Securelogix
> A telephone scanner that has a feature set that is similar to PhoneSweep's. Information can be found at *http://www.securelogix.com/*.

THL-SCAN
> A DOS-based scanner developed primarily for the computer underground.

Toneloc
> Another DOS-based program that can scan up to an entire telephone exchange with a single modem. Toneloc's features were designed for the computer underground, but it is widely used by computer consultants and organizations.

For organizations that require the highest degree of security, several companies now sell telephone firewalls. (Firewalls are described in the next section.) These systems sit between an organization's PBX and the outside world and monitor both incoming and outgoing telephone calls for the telltale signs of fax or modem communications. If a fax or modem tone is detected originating or terminating at an unauthorized line, the telephone firewall automatically terminates the call. One of the most widely used telephone firewalls is TeleWall by Securelogix.

Firewalls and the Web

In the world of fire prevention and control, a *firewall* is a barrier that is designed to prevent the spread of fire from one area to another. Firewalls in buildings are typically thick brick affairs, with only a few openings for doors that automatically close when the fire alarm gets set off. In a car, firewalls are designed to protect the occupants from engine fires. Overall, the fundamental guiding principle is that a firewall does not prevent fires, but instead merely contains the fire and gives people time to escape.

In the world of the Internet, the term *firewall* is taken to mean some kind of filter or barrier that affects the Internet traffic passed between two networks. Firewalls are often used as a perimeter defense, making it possible for an organization to decide which protocols it will exchange with the outside world. Firewalls can also be used to block access to particular sites on the Internet—for example, to prevent employees from downloading information from servers that are on a blacklist of pornographic sites.

One problem with firewalls is that organizations tend to adopt laxer internal security controls once a firewall is deployed. After all, the thinking goes, if a firewall is deployed and is keeping out the bad guys, why bother with internal controls such as encryption and passwords? The problem with this thinking is that it overlooks the fact that many attacks come from trusted insiders—according to the FBI, organizations should assume that 1% of their employees are malicious and acting against the organization's interests. Another problem with lax internal controls is that occasionally firewalls are bypassed; without strong internal controls, a failed or bypassed firewall will leave the organization wide open.

This section describes only the basics of firewalls. For a very complete discussion, see *Building Internet Firewalls*, by Elizabeth Zwicky, Simon Cooper, and Brent Chapman (O'Reilly).

Types of Firewalls

There are several kinds of firewalls in use on the Internet today.

Packet filtering
> A *packet filtering firewall* is basically a router with a special set of filters that determines whether each packet is allowed to cross over a network boundary. Packet filtering firewalls can be easily implemented with most routers today, although they can also be purchased as standalone appliances. Packet filtering firewalls can be easily programmed to block all incoming connections from the Internet except for requests to a web server, and to allow outgoing connections of only particular types.

Packet filtering firewalls are fast and cheap—they are easy to purchase, quick to implement, and relatively straightforward to keep operating. The main problem with a packet filtering firewall is that packets that are allowed to pass through the firewall travel unimpeded from the source to the destination. Thus, if your packet filtering firewall allows SMTP connections from the outside to your mail server, and if an exploit is discovered for the version of *sendmail* that you are running, then your packet filtering firewall will not protect your *sendmail* server from the exploit.

Proxy

A *proxy firewall* overcomes some of the limitations of packet filtering firewalls by breaking the direct connection between the inside network and the outside network. Instead of allowing through the packets that correspond with SMTP, HTTP, SNMP and other protocols, a proxy firewall has a matched pair of servers and clients for each protocol that act as intermediaries between the two worlds. The problem with a proxy firewall is that the proxies themselves can also represent a vulnerability, allowing an attacker to break into your firewall! In theory, this shouldn't happen because the firewall vendors, being security companies, are supposed to do a better job writing their servers than the operating system vendors. But you can never be sure.

Network Address Translation

These days, most firewalls support *Network Address Translation* (NAT), a technology that transparently rewrites the IP addresses of Internet connections as they move across the firewall boundary. NAT is a handy technology; many organizations use NAT and IP addresses in Net 10 (e.g., 10.0.0.0 through 10.255.255.255) to allow for hundreds or thousands of desktop computers to hide behind a single IP address on the Internet. NAT also lets an organization change its upstream Internet provider without having to reconfigure every computer on its internal network.

Virtual Private Networks

Many firewalls also support *Virtual Private Networks* (VPN), a technique that allows computers outside the firewall to tunnel their traffic through the firewall and then appear as if they are behind it. The primary purpose of VPN technology is to allow customers working at home or on the road to access Microsoft Windows file shares, Microsoft Exchange servers, and many corporate intranets that are not sufficiently secured to allow them to be placed on the external Internet. The problem with VPNs is that they can also allow attackers to tunnel seamlessly through a firewall. In December 2000, Microsoft revealed that its corporate network had been penetrated by attackers who had broken in using a VPN client running on an employee's home computer.

Protecting LANs with Firewalls

As discussed earlier, the primary use of firewalls is to protect LANs that are simply not secure enough to be placed on the Internet. Rather than patching every Windows desktop workstation and server to make sure that they will not crash if they receive the ping of death, it's easier and cheaper to simply program the organization's firewall to block all ICMP Echo packets from the outside world. This policy is sound until somebody inside your company starts sending out pings of death from your local network.

Protecting Web Servers with Firewalls

Firewalls can also be used to protect web servers. As with a LAN, the big advantage to protecting a web server with a firewall is that you can control the protocols the web server will see and the ones it will be shielded from. If your web server only offers HTTP services to the outside world, you can configure your firewall so that it will not pass traffic on anything other than port 80. If your web server also needs to support HTTP over SSL, you can open port 443.

In the event that a vulnerability is found with your web server, a firewall may prevent the attacker from using your web server as a base for attacking other computers on the Internet. For maximum protection, the firewall should also isolate the firewall from your own internal network (see Figure 15-5). This should prevent an attacker who compromises your web server from using it as a base for attacking your own organization.

One of the nice advantages of using a firewall to protect your web server is that you can then use the firewall's VPN capabilities to allow you to securely update the web server's content.

Conclusion

In this chapter we looked at a range of issues affecting host and network security for organizations operating web servers. We saw that practically every business decision that you make for your computers can have significant security impacts. Many businesses treat security as an afterthought, something that can be added after other decisions have already been made—such as the choice of vendor, the decision whether or not to use consultants, and the allocated budget for personnel.

A chapter such as this one cannot convey all the knowledge necessary to securely operate a computer on the Internet today. This is just an introduction to this important topic. For specific details of securing a Unix computer on the Internet, we recommend

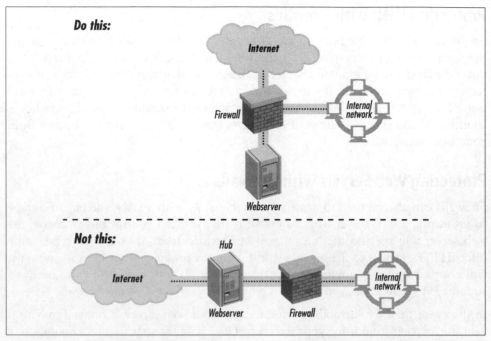

Figure 15-5. For high security, use a firewall to protect your web server from attackers on the Internet. Position the firewall so that it also protects your own organization from the web server.

our book *Practical Unix & Internet Security*. Even though the book was published back in 1996, much of the information that it contains is still current. That book, combined with this one and updates from your vendor, will provide you with the information that you need to operate a Unix computer securely on the Internet today.

If you are running a computer with a Microsoft operating system on the Internet, we recommend the book *Securing Windows NT/2000 Servers for the Internet* by Stefan Norberg (O'Reilly).

In this chapter:
- A Legacy of Extensibility and Risk
- Rules to Code By
- Securely Using Fields, Hidden Fields, and Cookies
- Rules for Programming Languages
- Using PHP Securely
- Writing Scripts That Run with Additional Privileges
- Connecting to Databases
- Conclusion

## CHAPTER 16

Securing Web Applications

Web servers are fine programs for displaying static information such as brochures, FAQs, and product catalogs. But applications that are customized for the user or that implement business logic (such as shopping carts) require that servers be extended with specialized code that executes each time the web page is fetched. This code most often takes the form of *scripts* or *programs* that are run when a particular URL is accessed. There is no limit to what a good programming team can do with a web server, a programming language, and enough time. Unfortunately, programs that provide additional functionality over the Web can have flaws that allow attackers to compromise the system on which the web server is running. These flaws are rarely evident when the program is run as intended.

This chapter focuses on programming techniques that you can use to make web programs more secure.

A Legacy of Extensibility and Risk

There are four primary techniques that web developers can use to create web-based applications:

CGI

The Common Gateway Interface (CGI) was the first means of extending web servers. When a URL referencing a CGI program is requested from the web server, the web server runs the CGI program in a separate process, captures the program's output, and sends the results to the requesting web browser. Parameters to the CGI programs are encoded as environment variables and also provided to the program on standard input.

CGI programs can perform database queries and display the results, allow people to perform complex financial calculations, and allow web users to "chat" with others on the Internet. Indeed, practically every innovative use of the World Wide Web, from web search engines to web pages that let you track the status of overnight packages, was originally written using the CGI interface.

Plug-ins, loadable modules, and Application Programmer Interfaces (APIs)
> The second technique developed to extend web servers involved modifying the web server with extension modules, usually written in C or C++. The extension module was then loaded into the web server at runtime. Plug-ins, modules, and APIs are a faster way to interface custom programs to web servers because they do not require that a new process be started for each web interaction. Instead, the web server process itself runs application code within its own address space that is invoked through a documented interface. But these techniques have a distinct disadvantage: the plug-in code can be very difficult to write, and a single bug can cause the entire web server to crash.

Embedded scripting languages
> Web-based scripting languages were the third technique developed for adding programmatic functionality to web pages. These systems allow developers to place small programs, usually called scripts, directly into the web page. An interpreter embedded in the web server runs the program contained on the web page before the resulting code is sent to the web browser. Embedded scripts tend to be quite fast. Microsoft's ASP, PHP, server-side JavaScript, and *mod_perl* are all examples of embedded scripting languages.

Embedded web server
> Finally, some systems do away with the web server completely and embed their own HTTP server into the web application itself.

Largely as a result of their power, the extension techniques enumerated here can completely compromise the security of your web server and the host on which it is running. That's because potentially *any* program can be run through these interfaces. This includes programs that have security problems, programs that give outsiders access to your computer, and even programs that change or erase critical files on your system.

Two techniques can limit the damage that can be caused by web applications:

- The programs themselves should be designed and inspected to ensure that they can perform only the desired functions.

- The programs should be run in a restricted environment. If these programs can be subverted by an attacker to do something unexpected, the damage that they could do will be limited.

On operating systems that allow for multiple users running at multiple authorization levels, web servers are normally run under a restricted account, usually the *nobody* or the *httpd* user. Programs that are spawned from the web server through either CGI or API interfaces are then run as the same restricted user.[*]

---

[*] In a multiuser environment, such as a web server at an ISP or a university, it is common practice to use the *cgiwrap* script so that CGI programs are run with the subscriber's permissions, rather than with the web server's.

Unfortunately, other operating systems do not have the same notion of restricted users. On Windows 3.1, Windows 95/98/ME, and the Mac OS 7–9 operating systems prior to Mac OS X, there is no easy way for the operating system to restrict the reach of a CGI program.

Programs That Should Not Be CGIs

Interpreters, shells, scripting engines, and other extensible programs should never appear in a *cgi-bin* directory, nor should they be located elsewhere on a computer where they might be invoked by a request to the web server process. Programs that are installed in this way allow attackers to run any program they wish on your computer.

For example, on Windows-based systems the Perl executable *PERL.EXE* should never appear in the *cgi-bin* directory. It is easy to probe a computer to see if it has been improperly configured. To make matters worse, some search engines can be used to find vulnerable machines automatically. Unfortunately, many Windows-based web servers have been configured this way because it makes it easier to set up Perl scripts on these servers.

Another source of concern are programs or scripts that are distributed with web servers and later found to have security flaws. Because webmasters rarely delete programs that are part of the default installation—it can be quite difficult to find out if a script is in use or not—these dangerous programs and scripts may persist for months or even years, even if new versions of the web server are installed that do not contain the bug.

An example of such a vulnerable script is a script named *phf* that was distributed with the NCSA web server and many early versions of the Apache web server. Although the script was designed to give web developers another tool, attackers discovered a way to use the script to retrieve files from the computer on which the script was running. This is an example of an unintended side effect, as explained in the next section.

 To protect yourself from programs, scripts, and CGIs in which security faults may be later discovered, you may wish to move *all* of the programs that are installed by default with your web sever into a directory where they cannot be accessed, and only restore the programs when they are specifically needed.

Unintended Side Effects

To understand the potential problems with server-side programming, consider the CGI script in Example 16-1.[*]

---

[*] The ReadForm functions are based on Steven E. Brenner's *cgi-lib.pl*. It is used here so that the reader can see the entire program. The serious Perl programmer should use the *CGI.pm* Perl module, which is available from the CPAN archives.

Example 16-1. A CGI script with a problem

```perl
#!/usr/local/bin/perl
#
# bad_finger
#

sub ReadForm {
  my (*in) = @_ if @_;
  my ($i, $key, $val, $input);

  # Read in text if we were called in a query
  if($ENV('REQUEST_METHOD') eq "GET"){
    $input = $ENV('QUERY_STRING');
  }
  if($ENV('REQUEST_METHOD') eq "POST"){
    read(STDIN,$input,$ENV{'CONTENT_LENGTH'});
  }

  @in = split(/[&;]/,$input);

  for($i = 0; $i<scalar(@in); $i++){
    $in[$i] =~ s/\+/ /g;              # plus to space
    ($key, $val) = split(/=/,$in[$i],2);# get key and value

    # Convert %XX from hex numbers to alphanumeric
    $key =~ s/%(..)/pack("c",hex($1))/ge;
    $val =~ s/%(..)/pack("c",hex($1))/ge;

    # Add to array
    $in{$key} .= "\0" if (defined($in{$key})); # \0 is the mult. separator
    $in{$key} .= $val;

  }
  return length($in);
}
#########################################################################
#
# The real action (and the security problems) follow

print "Content-type: text/html\n\n<html>";

if(&ReadForm(*input)){
    print "<pre>\n";
    print `/usr/bin/finger $input{'command'}`;
    print "</pre>\n";
}

print <<XX;
<hr>
<form method="post" action="bad_finger">
Finger command: <input type="text" size="40" name="command">
</form>
XX
```

The first half of this script defines a Perl function, ReadForm, which will be used throughout this chapter for CGI form handling. There are no problems with this function—all it does is take input from a CGI GET or POST operation and stuff the variables into an associative array provided by the programmer.

The second half of this script defines a *finger* gateway. If called by the result of a normal HTTP GET command, it simply generates the HTML for a CGI form:

```
Content-type: text/html

<html><hr>
<form method="post" action="bad_finger">
Finger command: <input type="text" size="40" name="command">
</form>
```

This produces the expected display in a web browser, as shown in Figure 16-1.

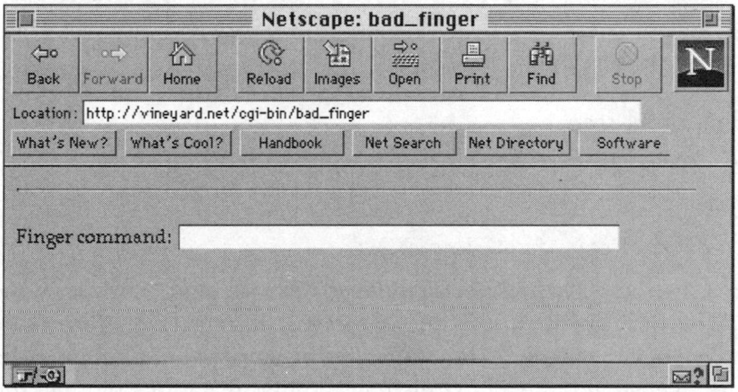

Figure 16-1. The finger gateway

Type a typical user ID such as spaf@cs.purdue.edu, into the field, hit Return, and you'll get the expected result (see Figure 16-2).

Despite the fact that this script works as expected, it has a serious problem: an attacker can use this script to seriously compromise the security of your computer.

You might have security problems similar to this one in the CGI scripts on your server. Security problems in scripts can remain dormant for years before they are exploited.

Sometimes, obscure security holes may even be inserted by the programmer who first wrote the scripts—a sort of "back door" that allows the programmer to gain access in the future, should the programmer's legitimate means of access be lost. These back doors can be much harder to find than a simple undocumented account or password. We discuss this problem in the next section.

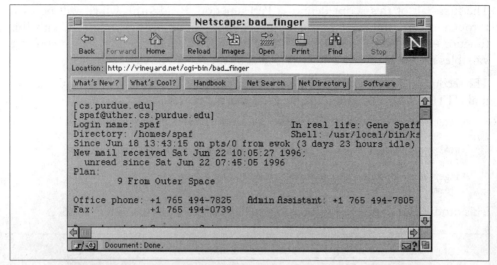

Figure 16-2. The form displayed by the finger script

The problem with the script

The problem with the script shown previously is the single line that executes the *finger* command:

```
print `/usr/bin/finger $input{'command'}`;
```

This line executes the program */usr/bin/finger* with the input provided and displays the result. The problem with this line is the way in which the *finger* command is invoked—from Perl's backquote function. The backquote function provides its input to the Unix shell—and the Unix shell may interpret some of that input in an unwanted manner!

Thus, when we sent the value spaf@cs.purdue.edu to this CGI script, it ran the Unix command:

```
print `/usr/bin/finger spaf@cs.purdue.edu`;
```

and that evaluated to:

```
/usr/bin/finger spaf@cs.purdue.edu
```

and that then produced the expected result.

The Unix shell is known and admired for its power and flexibility by programmers and malicious hackers alike. One of the interesting abilities of the Unix shell is the ability to put multiple commands on a single line. For example, if we wanted to run the *finger* command in the background and, while we are waiting, do an *ls* command on the current directory, we might execute this command:

```
/usr/bin/finger spaf@cs.purdue.edu & /bin/ls -l
```

And indeed, if we type in the name spaf@cs.purdue.edu & /bin/ls -l as our *finger* request (see Figure 16-3), the *bad_finger* script will happily execute it, which produces the output (see Figure 16-4).

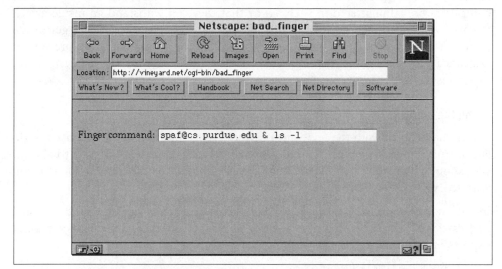

Figure 16-3. Attacking the bad_finger script

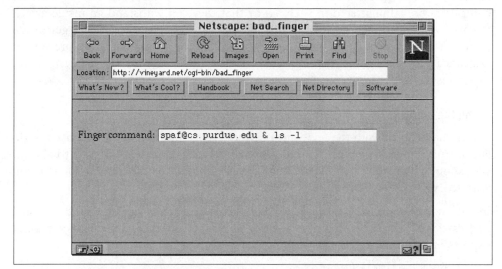

Figure 16-4. Output from the bad_finger script under attack

What's the harm in allowing a user to list the files? By looking at the files, an attacker might learn about other confidential information stored on the web server. Also, the */bin/ls* command is simply one of many commands that the attacker might run. The attacker could easily run commands to delete files, send an "xterm" back to his own computer, initiate denial-of-service attacks to other computers, or even crash your machine.

Although most operating systems are not fundamentally unsecure, few operational computers are administered in such a way that they can withstand an inside attack from a determined attacker. Thus, you must ensure that attackers never get inside your system: deny the attacker the ability to run arbitrary commands. To prevent an attacker from gaining this foothold, you must be sure that your server's scripts and programs cannot be turned against you.

Fixing the problem

Fixing the problem with the *bad_finger* script is remarkably easy. All you need to do is not trust the user's input. Instead of merely sending $input{'command'} to a shell, you should filter the input, extracting legal characters for the command that you wish to execute.

In the case of *finger*, there is a very small set of characters that are valid in email addresses or hostnames. The next script selects those characters with a regular expression pattern match:

```
if(&ReadForm(*input)){
    $input{'command'} =~ m/([\w+@\.\-]*)/i;        # Match alphanumerics, @ and -
    print "<pre>\n";
    print `/usr/bin/finger $1`;
    print "<pre>\n";
}
```

This command works as before, except that now it won't pass on characters such as "&", ";", or "'" to the subshell.

Notice that this example *matches legal characters*, rather than *filters out disallowed ones*. This is an important distinction! Many publications recommend filtering out special characters—and then they don't tell you all of the characters that you need to remove. Indeed, it's sometimes difficult to know, because the list of characters to remove depends on how you employ the user input as well as which shells and programs are invoked. For example, if you write a script that accepts a number or a date, you might wish to allow the characters "." and "/". If you are writing a script that accepts a filename, you may wish to filter out these characters to prevent an attacker from specifying a pathname that is in a different directory—for example, *../.. /../../../etc/passwd*. This is why best practice recommends selecting which characters to let through, rather than guessing which characters should be filtered out.[*]

---

[*] Another reason that you should select the characters that are matched rather than choose which characters to filter out is that different programs called by your script may treat 8-bit and multibyte characters in different ways. You may not filter out the 8-bit or multibyte versions of a special character, but when they reach the underlying system they may be interpreted as single-byte, 7-bit characters—much to your dismay.

The script can be made more secure (and somewhat faster) by using Perl's *system* function to run the *finger* command directly. This entirely avoids calling the shell:

```
if(&ReadForm(*input)){
    $input{'command'} =~ m/([\w+@\-]*)/i;          # Match alphanumerics, @ and -
    print "<pre>\n";
    system '/usr/bin/finger', $1;
    print "<pre>\n";
}
```

The next section gives many rules of thumb to help you avoid these kinds of problems in your CGI and API programs.

Rules to Code By

Most security-related bugs in computer programs are simply that: bugs. For whatever reason, these faults keep your program from operating properly.

General Principles for Writing Secure Scripts

Over the years, we have developed a list of general principles by which to code. What follows is an excerpt from that list, edited for its particular relevance to CGI and API programs:

1. Carefully design the program before you start. Be certain that you understand what you are trying to build. Carefully consider the environment in which it will run, the input and output behavior, files used, arguments recognized, signals caught, and other aspects of behavior. List all of the errors that might occur, and how your program will deal with them. Write a code specification in English (or your native language) before writing the code in the computer language of your choice.

2. Show the specification to another person. Before you start writing code, show the specification that you have written to another programmer. Make sure they can understand the specification and that they think it will work. If you can't convince another programmer that your paper design will work, you should go back to the design phase and make your specification clearer. The time you spend now will be repaid many times over in the future.

3. Write and test small sections at a time. As you start to write your program, start small and test frequently. When you test your sections, test them with both expected data and unexpected data. Where practical, functions should validate their arguments and perform reasonable actions (such as exiting with an error message or returning an error code) when presented with unreasonable data. A large number of security-related programs are simply bugs that have exploitable consequences. By writing code that is more reliable, you will also be writing code that is more secure.

4. Check all values provided by the user. An astonishing number of security-related bugs arise because an attacker sends an unexpected value or an unanticipated format to a program or a function within a program. A simple way to avoid these types of problems is by having your scripts always check and validate all of their arguments. Argument checking will not noticeably slow your scripts, but it will make them less susceptible to hostile users. As an added benefit, argument checking and error reporting will make the process of catching nonsecurity-related bugs easier.

For further information on this topic, see "Securely Using Fields, Hidden Fields, and Cookies," later in this chapter.

The Seven Design Principles of Computer Security

In 1975, Jerome Saltzer and M. D. Schroeder described seven criteria for building secure computing systems.[a] These criteria are still noteworthy today. They are:

Least privilege
> Every user and process should have the least set of access rights necessary. Least privilege limits the damage that can be done by malicious attackers and errors alike. Access rights should be explicitly required, rather than given to users by default.

Economy of mechanism
> The design of the system should be small and simple so that it can be verified and correctly implemented.

Complete mediation
> Every access should be checked for proper authorization.

Open design
> Security should not depend upon the ignorance of the attacker. This criterion precludes back doors in the system, which give access to users who know about them.

Separation of privilege
> Where possible, access to system resources should depend on more than one condition being satisfied.

Least common mechanism
> Users should be isolated from one another by the system. This limits both covert monitoring and cooperative efforts to override system security mechanisms.

Psychological acceptability
> The security controls must be easy to use so that they will be used and not bypassed.

a. Saltzer, J. H. and Schroeder, M. D., "The Protection of Information in Computer Systems," *Proceedings of the IEEE*, September 1975. As reported in Denning, Dorothy, *Cryptography and Data Security* (Addison-Wesley).

---

5. Check arguments that you pass to operating system functions. Even though your program is calling the system function, you should check the arguments to be sure that they are what you expect them to be. For example, if you think that your program is opening a file in the current directory, you might want to use the *index()* function in C or Perl to see if the filename contains a slash character (/). If the file contains a slash, and it shouldn't, the program shouldn't open the file.

6. Check all return codes from system calls. The POSIX programming specification (which is followed by both C and Perl) requires that every system call provide a return code. Even system calls that you think cannot fail, such as *write()*, *chdir()*, or *chown()* can fail under exceptional circumstances and return appropriate return codes. When a call fails, check the *errno* variable to determine why it failed. Have your program log the unexpected value and then cleanly terminate if the system call fails for any unexpected reason. This approach will be a great help in tracking down both programming bugs and security problems later on.

   If you think that a system call should not fail and it does, react appropriately. If you can't think of anything appropriate to do, have your program delete all of its temporary files and exit.

7. Have internal consistency-checking code. If you think that a variable inside your program can only have the values 1, 2, or 3, check to ensure that it does, and generate an error condition if it does not. (You can do this easily using the *assert* macro if you are programming in C.)

8. Include lots of logging. You are almost always better off having too much logging rather than too little. Rather than simply writing the results to standard error, and relying on your web server's log file, report your log information to a dedicated log file. It will make it easier for you to find the problems. Alternatively, consider using the *syslog* facility (under Unix), so that logs can be redirected to users or files, piped to programs, and/or sent to other machines. (Remember to do bounds checking on arguments passed to *syslog()* to avoid buffer overflows.)

   Here is specific information that you might wish to log:
   - The name of the program being run
   - The time that the program was run
   - The process number (PID)
   - Values provided to the program
   - Invalid arguments or failures in consistency checking
   - The host from which the request came, both hostname and IP address

9. Some information should not be logged. Other information should only be logged in specially restricted or encrypted log files. Be especially careful with passwords, both those that are valid and those that are not valid. Logging valid usernames and passwords makes it possible for anybody who accesses the log

file to compromise your user's accounts. Logging failed username/password attempts may give a person who has access to the log file enough information to break in, because many failed password attempts are simply one- or two-character typos.

10. Make the critical portion of your program as small and as simple as possible.

11. Read through your code. Think of how you might attack it yourself. What happens if the program gets unexpected input? What happens if you are able to delay the program between two system calls?

12. Always use full pathnames for any filename argument, for both commands and data files.

13. Rather than depending on the current directory, set it yourself.

14. Test your completed program thoroughly. Be sure to test it with both expected data and unexpected data.

15. Be aware of race conditions. These can be manifest as a deadlock or as failure of two calls to execute in close sequence:

Deadlock conditions

Remember that more than one copy of your program may be running at the same time. Use file locking for any files that you modify. Provide a way to recover the locks in the event that the program crashes while a lock is held. Avoid deadlocks or "deadly embraces," which can occur when one program attempts to lock file A and then file B, while another program already holds a lock for file B and then attempts to lock file A.

Sequence conditions

Be aware that your program does not execute *atomically*. That is, the program can be interrupted between any two operations to let another program run for a while—including one that is trying to abuse yours. Thus, check your code carefully for any pair of operations that might fail if arbitrary code is executed between them.

In particular, when you are performing a series of operations on a file such as changing its owner, *stat*ing the file, or changing its mode, first open the file and then use the *fchown(), fstat(),* or *fchmod()* system calls. Doing so will prevent the file from being replaced while your program is running (a possible race condition). Also avoid the use of the *access()* function to determine your ability to access a file: using the *access()* function followed by an *open()* is a race condition, and almost always a bug.

16. Don't have your program dump core except during your testing. Core files can fill up a filesystem. Core files can contain confidential information. In some cases, an attacker can actually use the fact that a program dumps core to break into a system. Instead of dumping core, have your program log the appropriate problem and exit. Use the *setrlimit()* function to limit the size of the core file to 0.

17. Do not create files in world-writable directories. If your script needs to run as the *nobody* user, then have the directory in which it needs to create files owned by the *nobody* user. Give each script, or at the very least each subsystem, its own namespace for temporary files. (You can do this by giving each script its own directory for temporary files, or else by having each script prepend its temporary files with its own name.) Do not store temporary files in the */tmp* directory if the web server is also used as a general host for Unix shell activities.

18. Don't place undue reliance on the source IP address in the packets of connections you receive. Such items may be forged, altered, or hijacked with proxy servers.

19. Include some form of load shedding or load limiting in your server to handle cases of excessive load. For example, you can have the script check the load and exit with a polite error message if the load is over 5. This will make it harder for an attacker to launch a denial-of-service attack against your server by repeatedly calling the same script. It will also protect your server from a particular failure mode in which hundreds of users all hit the "reload" button on a slow-running script in an effort to make it run faster.

20. Put reasonable time-outs on the clock time used by your script while it is running. Your program may become blocked for any number of reasons; for example, a read request from a remote server may hang or the user's web browser may not accept information that you send to it. An easy technique to solve both of these problems is to put hard limits on the amount of real time that your CGI script can use. Once it uses more than its allotted amount of real time, it should clean up and exit. Most modern systems support some call to set such a limit.

21. Put reasonable limits on the CPU time used by your CGI script while it is running. A bug in your CGI script may put it in an infinite loop. To protect your users and your server against this possibility, you should place a hard limit on the total amount of CPU time that the CGI script can consume.

22. Do not require the user to send a reusable password in plaintext over the network connection to authenticate herself. If you use usernames and passwords, use a cryptographically enabled web server so that the password is not sent in plaintext. Alternatively, use client-side certificates to provide authentication. If your users access an Internet Information Server web server through Internet Explorer, then you can use the NT challenge/response (NTLM), a Microsoft proprietary modification to the HTTP protocol. Finally, you can use HTTP Digest Authentication, which has an MD5 MAC to verify a shared password between the web server and the web browser. Apache 2.0 and above support Digest-based authentication with the *mod_auth_digest* module; support in many browsers is increasing. The primary disadvantage of digest authentication is that it requires the web server to maintain an essentially unencrypted copy of each user's password. For details on digest authentication, search for the AuthDigestFile directive

in the Apache documentation, or look at *http://www.apache.org/docs-2.0/mod/mod_auth_digest.html*.

23. Have your code reviewed by another competent programmer (or two, or more). After they have reviewed it, "walk through" the code with them and explain what each part does. We have found that such reviews are a surefire way to discover logic errors. Trying to explain why something is done a certain way often results in an exclamation of "Wait a moment . . . why did I do *that?*"

24. Whenever possible, reuse code. Don't write your own CGI library when you can use one that's already been debugged. But beware of reusing code that contains Trojan horses.

Remember, most security flaws are actually programming faults. In a way, this is good news for programmers. When you make your program more secure, you'll simultaneously be making it more reliable.

Securely Using Fields, Hidden Fields, and Cookies

One of the reasons that it can be difficult to develop secure web applications has to do with the very architecture of web applications. When you develop an application, you generally write a body of code that runs locally on the web server and a much smaller body of code that is downloaded and run remotely on the user's web browser. You might spend a lot of time making sure that these two code bases work properly together. For example, it's very important to make sure that the field names downloaded in web forms exactly match the field names that server-side scripts are expecting. And you will probably spend time making sure that the HTML forms, JavaScript, and other codes that are downloaded to the browser work properly on a wide range of different browser programs.

Even in the best of times, it can be difficult to get software on the web browser and the web server to properly synchronize and interoperate. What makes this whole process difficult from the security perspective is that attackers, by definition, don't play by the rules. Sure, they can run your HTML forms and JavaScript in well-behaved browsers, but they can also pick apart the code, analyze it, and send completely made-up responses back to your web server. These sorts of attacks are difficult to detect because they are very hard for normal web developers to test against—after all, most web developers don't have a stable of CGI-script attack tools.

There is nothing inherently wrong with storing this information on the web browser instead of the web server; indeed, storing this information on the browser eliminates the need for a backend database, user tracking, and a lot of other technology. But if you store information on the user's web browser, you must validate this information when it is passed back to the web server to make sure that it has not been modified.

Many programmers do not realize the need to validate information returned from the web browser to the server. For example, in December 1999 engineers at Internet Security Systems (ISS) discovered that many e-commerce scripts *from different vendors* all shared a common vulnerability: they maintained the shopping cart, complete with the price for each item, on the user's web browser without using any form of validation.* When an invoice was prepared and a credit card charged, they blindly trusted the prices provided by the shopping carts. Thus, any attacker who wanted to give himself a discount could simply go shopping, save the server's HTML onto his hard drive, edit the prices, and then click on the "Buy" button.

In a Spring 2001 study,† four MIT graduate students discovered that many e-commerce sites did not properly validate the information in cookies. As a result, Sit and Fu were able to make subtle modifications in the cookies at e-commerce sites and gain access to unauthorized information.

Using Fields Securely

When checking arguments in your program, pay special attention to the following:

- Filter the contents of every field, selecting the characters that are appropriate for each response. For example, if a field is supposed to be a credit card number, select out the characters 0–9 and leave all other characters behind. This will also allow people to enter their credit card numbers with spaces or dashes.

- After you filter, check the length of every argument. If the length is incorrect, do not proceed, but instead generate an error.

- If you use a selection list, make certain that the value provided by the user was one of the legal values. Attackers can provide any value that they wish: they are not constrained by the allowable values in the selection list.

- Even if your forms use JavaScript to validate the contents of a form before it is submitted, be sure that you revalidate the contents on the server. An attacker can easily turn off JavaScript or bypass it entirely.

Hidden Fields and Compound URLs

A *hidden field* is a field that the web server sends to the web browser that is not displayed on the user's web page. Instead, the field merely sits in the browser's memory. When the form on the page is sent back to the server, the field and its contents are sent back.

---

* ISS reported the security problem to the 11 vendors in December 1999, then released the information about the vulnerability to the press in February 2000. For further information, see *http://www.cnn.com/2000/TECH/computing/02/04/shop.glitch.idg/*.

† See "Dos and Don'ts of Client Authentication on the Web," *USENIX and MIT Technical Report 818*, by Kevin Fu, Emil Sit, Kendra Smith, and Nick Feamster.

Some web developers use hidden fields to store information that is used for session tracking on e-commerce systems. For example, instead of using HTTP Basic Authentication, developers sometimes embed the username and password provided by the user as hidden fields in all future form entries:

```
<INPUT TYPE="hidden" NAME="username" VALUE="simsong">
<INPUT TYPE="hidden" NAME="password" VALUE="myauth11">
```

Hidden fields can also be used to implement a shopping cart:

```
<INPUT TYPE="hidden" NAME="items" VALUE="3">
<INPUT TYPE="hidden" NAME="item1" VALUE="Book of Secrets:$4.99">
<INPUT TYPE="hidden" NAME="item2" VALUE="Nasty Software:$45.32">
<INPUT TYPE="hidden" NAME="item3" VALUE="Helping Hand:$32.23">
```

Instead of embedding this information in hidden fields, it can be placed directly in the URL. These URLs will then be interpreted as if they were forms that were posted using the HTTP GET protocol. For example, this URL embeds a username and password:

```
http://www.vineyard.net/cgi-bin/password_tester?username=simsong&password=myauth11
```

It's quite easy to use hidden fields. Little or no information needs to be stored on the server. And unlike cookies, which are limited to 4096 bytes, hidden fields can be practically any length whatsoever.

There are problems with using hidden fields in this way, however:

- If the user presses the "Back" button, items may be removed from the shopping cart. Sometimes this is the desired behavior, but usually it is not.

- HTML pages used by one person might be viewed by other people, possibly because the computer is shared. In this circumstance, the first user's username, password, or shopping cart contents might be disclosed.

- If you use URLs to embed information, the complete URL—*including the embedded information*—will be stored in the web server's log files. The full URL may also be passed by the user's browser in the referrer [sic] header when the user accesses another web server. This may compromise the user's privacy and/or security.

- In the vast majority of cases, the contents of the hidden field received by the web server are identical to what was originally provided. But there is no guarantee. An attacker can save your HTML to a file, analyze the form, and issue his own HTTP GET or POST command with whatever contents he desires. An attacker can also submit the same web page over and over, with slight modifications, probing for vulnerabilities. There is no way to stop this sort of behavior, so you must defend against it.

There's no way to correct the problem with the "Back" button, but the second and third problems can be handled using cryptography, as described in the section, "Using Cryptography to Strengthen Hidden Fields, Compound URLs, and Cookies."

Using Cookies

One attractive alternative to using hidden fields or URLs is to store information such as usernames, passwords, shopping cart contents, and so on, in HTTP cookies.

Users can modify their cookies, so cookies used for user tracking, shopping carts, and other types of e-commerce applications have all of the same problems described for hidden fields or compound URLs. But cookies also have problems all their own, including:

- Old cookies may continue to be used, even after they have "expired."
- Users may make long-term copies of cookies that are supposed to remain ephemeral and not ever be copied onto a hard drive.
- Some users are suspicious of cookies and simply turn off the feature.

Please see the section "Understanding Cookies" in Chapter 8 for a further discussion of cookies.

Using Cryptography to Strengthen Hidden Fields, Compound URLs, and Cookies

Many of the problems discussed in this section can be solved by using cryptography to protect the information in hidden fields, compound URLs, and cookies. Cryptography can:

- Prevent users from understanding the information stored on their computer.
- Allow web server applications to detect unauthorized or accidental changes to this information.

Here are the three examples from the previous sections, recoded to use cryptography.

Username and password authentication:

```
<INPUT TYPE="hidden" NAME="auth"
VALUE="p6e6J6FwQOkOtqLFTFYq5EXRO3GQ1wYWGOZsVnkO9yv7ItIHG17ymls4UM%2F1bwHygRhp7ECawzUm
%0AKl3Q%2BKRYhlmGILFtbde8%0A:">
```

A secure shopping cart:

```
<INPUT TYPE="hidden" NAME="cart"
VALUE="fLkrNxpQ9GKv9%2FrAvnLhuLnNDAV5OKhNPjPhqG6fMJoJ5kCQ5u1ghOij8JBqphBxdGVNOdja41XJ
%0APLsT%2Bt1kydWN4Q%2BO9pWOyR9eIPLrzaDsZxauNPEe7cymPmXwd%2B6c1L49uTwdNTKoSOXAThDzow%3
D%3D%0A:">
```

A compound URL:

```
http://www.vineyard.net/cgi-bin/password_
tester?p6e6J6FwQOkOtqLFTFYq5EXRO3GQ1wYWGOZsVnkO9yv7ItIHG17ymls4UM%2F1bwHygRhp7ECawzUm
%0AKl3Q%2BKRYhlmGILFtbde8%0A:
```

In each of these cases, the individual human-readable variables have been replaced with a cryptographic block of information. This block is created with the following procedure:[*]

1. Take the individual variables that need to be preserved and encode them as a string. (This is called *marshalling*.)

2. Prepend a 4-byte timestamp to these variables. (The timestamp protects against replay attacks.)

3. Compress the data. (This saves space.)

4. Prepend to the data the length of the string. (Required for decryption with block cipher.)

5. Encrypt the string using a symmetric encryption function with a secret key.

6. Calculate an HMAC function of this encrypted string and prepend it to the encrypted string. (HMAC protects all encrypted, compressed, and marshalled data.)

7. Encode the resulting string with Base64, then escape the non-URL characters and return the resulting string.

8. Use this escaped, Base64-encoded, encrypted, compressed string for hidden fields, compound URLs, and cookies.

To decode and validate this encrypted string, simply follow these steps in reverse:

1. Isolate the escaped, Base64-encoded, encrypted, compressed string from the hidden field, compound URL, or cookie.

2. Unescape the Base64 representation.

3. Remove the Base64 coding.

4. Verify the HMAC. If it doesn't verify, then the string has been tampered with. Report an error and return.

5. Unencrypt the data.

6. Recover the length and use this to truncate the unencrypted data to the original length. (This step is needed because block encryption functions will append null bytes to data to pad it out to an even block.)

7. Decompress the compressed data.

8. Recover the timestamp from the beginning of the uncompressed data. If the timestamp is too old, disregard.

9. Return the remaining data to the caller, which will decode all of the original variables from the string.

---

[*] This implementation is not designed to protect against the cookie shifting attack. For more information, see slide #29 of *http://cookies.ks.mit.edu/pubs/webauth:sec10-slides.pdf*.

This must all look tremendously complicated and computationally intensive. In fact, it is quite easy to code up and can run very quickly, as MD5 and symmetric encryption functions are quite fast. When we ran the code in Example 16-2 on a very slow 233Mhz K6 computer, for instance, we were able to do 1000 *secure_encode()* operations in just 90 seconds of CPU time, including the time to start up one copy of the Perl 5.05 interpreter—that's roughly 90 msec for each *secure_encode()* operation.

Example 16-2. Secure cookie generation and decoding

```perl
#
# Program to demonstrate secure_encode and secure_decode, two functions
# that securely encode and decode timestamped, encrypted strings.
#
# Makes extensive use of Perl libraries

use Digest::HMAC_MD5 qw(hmac_md5);
use CGI;
use Crypt::TripleDES;
use MIME::Base64;
use Compress::Zlib;
use strict;

my $des3 = new Crypt::TripleDES;


#
# Configuration parameters

my $passphrase = "Now is the encryption time";
my $digest_key  = "some nasty key";
my $timeout = 7*24*60*60;  # maximum age of tokens, in seconds (this is one week)

# secure_encode:
# Takes a string and securely encodes it.  Because we use a block cipher
# that will pad out the data to the next block, we need to record the
# length of the data. It is put in the first four bytes of the data
# before encryption.

sub secure_encode {
    my $tdata  = pack('I',time) . $_[0];            # Prepend the time (packed)
    my $cdata  = compress($tdata); # Compress
    my $lcdata = pack('I',length($cdata)) . $cdata;  # prepend the length
    my $edata  = $des3->encrypt3($lcdata,$passphrase);  # encrypt
    my $hmac   = hmac_md5($edata,$digest_key);       # compute hmac
    my $hedata = $hmac . $edata;
    return CGI::escape(encode_base64($hedata));      # return hmac . edata
}


#
# Secure decode. Return undef if decryption fails, -1 if timestamp is out of date
# and the value otherwise
```

Example 16-2. Secure cookie generation and decoding (continued)

```perl
sub secure_decode {
    my $hedata = decode_base64(CGI::unescape($_[0])); # get mac & encrypted data

    my $hmac  = substr($hedata,0,16); # hmac from data
    my $edata = substr($hedata,16);

    # Now verify the HMAC
    if( hmac_md5($edata, $digest_key) ne $hmac){
        print STDERR "DIGEST doesn't verify. \n";
        return undef;
    }

    my $lcdata = $des3->decrypt3($edata,$passphrase);

    my $datalen = unpack('I',substr($lcdata,0,4)); # recover the length
    my $cdata   = substr($lcdata,4,$datalen);       # recover the compressed data

    my $tdata = uncompress($cdata); # get the uncompressed data

    # check the timestamp
    my $otime = unpack('I',substr($tdata,0,4));
    if($otime + $timeout < time){
        print STDERR "timeout\n";
        return -1;
    }

    # Return the data that is after the timestamp
    return substr($tdata,4);
}

my $enc = secure_encode("username=simsong&password=myauth11");

print "encode $enc:\n";
print secure_decode($enc),"\n";
```

Rules for Programming Languages

This section provides rules for making programs written in specific programming languages more secure.

Rules for Perl

Here are some rules to follow to make your Perl scripts more secure:

1. Use Perl's tainting features for all CGI programs. These features are invoked by placing the "-T" option at the beginning of your Perl script. Perl's tainting features make it more suited than C to CGI programming. When enabled, tainting

marks all variables that are supplied by users as "tainted." Variables whose values are dependent on tainted variables are themselves tainted as well. Tainted values cannot be used to open files or for system calls. Untainted information can only be extracted from a tainted variable by the use of Perl's string match operations.

2. The tainting feature also requires that you set the PATH environment variable to a known "safe value" before allowing your program to invoke the *system()* call.

3. Remember that Perl ignores tainting for filenames that are opened read-only. Nevertheless, be sure that you untaint all filenames, and not simply filenames that are used for writing.

4. Consider using Perl's emulation mode for handling SUID scripts safely if you are running an older version of Unix.

5. Always set your program's PATH environment variable, even if you are not running SUID or under Unix.

6. Be sure that the Perl interpreter and all of its libraries are installed so that they cannot be modified by anyone other than the administrator. Otherwise, a person who can modify your Perl libraries can affect the behavior of any Perl program that calls them.

Security-Related CGI/API Variables

Web servers usually set environment variables that are made available to CGI and API programs. Some of these variables directly pertain to the user authorization process. They are:

HTTPS_RANDOM
> A 256-bit random value that changes with each CGI invocation (Netscape).

REMOTE_HOST
> The hostname of the computer on which the web browser is running; for example, *dialup10.vineyard.net*.

REMOTE_USER
> The authenticated username of the person using the web browser; for example, *simsong*.

REMOTE_ADDR
> The address of the computer on which the web browser is running; for example, *204.17.195.47*. Although it should be logged in your server's log files, you may wish to have your scripts log it separately.

AUTH_TYPE
> The type of authentication being employed; for example, *Basic*.

Rules for C

It is substantially harder to write secure programs in C than it is in the Perl programming language; Perl has automatic memory management whereas C does not. Furthermore, because of the lack of facilities for dealing with large programs, Perl program sources tend to be smaller and more modular than their C counterparts. Nevertheless, one very important reason to write CGI programs in C remains: speed. Each time a CGI program is run, the program must be loaded into memory and executed. If your CGI program is written in Perl, the entire Perl interpreter must be loaded and the Perl program compiled before the CGI program can run. The overhead from these two operations dwarfs the time required by the CGI program itself. The overhead of loading Perl can be eliminated by using the Apache Perl module or Microsoft's Internet Information Server *perl* script. Nevertheless, if you insist on using C, here are some suggestions:

1. Use routines that check buffer boundaries when manipulating strings of arbitrary length; in particular, note the following:

Avoid	Use instead
gets ( )	*fget ( )*
strcpy ( )	*strncpy ( )*
strcat ( )	*strncat ( )*

2. Use the following library calls with great care—they can overflow either a destination buffer or an internal, static buffer on some systems: *sprintf( ), fscanf( ), scanf( ), sscanf( ), vsprintf( ), realpath( ), getopt( ), getpass( ), streadd( ), strecpy( ),* and *strtrns( )*. Check to make sure that you have the version of the *syslog( )* library that checks the length of its arguments.

3. There may be other routines in libraries on your system of which you should be somewhat cautious. Note carefully if a copy or transformation is performed into a string argument without benefit of a length parameter to delimit it. Also note if the documentation for a function says that the routine returns a pointer to a result in static storage. If an attacker can provide the necessary input to overflow these buffers, you may have a major problem.

4. Make good use of available tools. If you have an ANSI C compiler available, use it, and use prototypes for calls. Consider investing in analysis tools such as Purify (*http://www.rational.com/*).

5. Instruct your compiler to generate as many warnings as possible. If you are using the GNU C compiler, you can do this easily by specifying the *-Wall* option.[*]

---

[*] Microsoft #*include* files generate errors when compiled with /W4. Use the #*pragma* function to disable particular warnings for particular #*include* files. It is a sad comment on Microsoft's quality assurance that the company's own #*include* files generate warnings. Microsoft's programmers must not compile their code with /W4.

With Microsoft VC++, use the /W4 warning level. If your compiler cannot generate warnings, use the *lint* program to check for common mistakes.

6. If you are expecting to create a new file with the open call, then you should use the O_EXCL | O_CREAT flags to cause the routine to fail if the file exists.

7. If you expect the file to exist, be sure to omit the O_CREAT flag so that the routine will fail if the file is not there.[*]

8. If you need to create a temporary file, use the *tmpfile()* or *mkstemp()* function. This step will create a temporary file, open the file, delete the file, and return a file handle. The open file can be passed to a subprocess created with *fork()* and *exec()*, but the contents of the file cannot be read by any other program on the system. The space associated with the file will automatically be returned to the operating system when your program exits. If possible, create the temporary file in a closed directory, such as */tmp/root/*.

 The *mktemp()* library call is not safe to use in a program that is running with extra privilege. Using *mktemp()* results in a race condition between a file test and a file open. This condition is a well known problem and relatively easy to exploit. Avoid the standard *mktemp()* call.

Rules for the Unix Shell

Don't write CGI scripts with the Unix shells (*sh*, *csh*, *ksh*, *bash*, or *tcsh*) for anything but the most trivial script. It's too easy to make a mistake, and there are many lurking security problems with these languages.

Using PHP Securely

PHP is a widely used and loved server-side scripting language for building web pages. Originally called Personal Home Page, and then PHP3, PHP now stands for PHP Hypertext Preprocessor. The web site for PHP development is *http://www.php.org/*. PHP is an official project of The Apache Foundation.[†]

---

[*] Note that on some systems, if the pathname in the open call refers to a symbolic link that names a file that does not exist, the call may not behave as you expect. This scenario should be tested on your system so you know what to expect.

[†] Some of the information presented in this section is based on Shaun Clowes' presentation at the Blackhat Briefings Asia 2001. Clowes' paper on PHP security, "A Study in Scarlet," can be downloaded from *http://www.securereality.com.au/archives/studyinscarlet.txt*.

Introduction to PHP

Although originally developed under Unix with the Apache web server, PHP now runs on Unix and Windows and with both Apache and Microsoft's IIS. Some of the key advantages of PHP include:

- It is easy to use and very fast. Even though PHP scripts are interpreted at run-time, the interpreter is built into the web server. As a result, PHP pages can run significantly faster (more than 10 times faster is not uncommon) than the equivalent Perl/CGI web pages.*

- Unlike CGI scripts, PHP pages do not need to be made "executable" or placed in special directories to run: if PHP is enabled in the web server, all you need to do is to give an HTML file a *.php* or *.php3* extension and the PHP system will automatically run.

- The PHP interpreter shows errors directly on the web page, not in a log file.

- PHP can cache connections to the MySQL database system. As a result, PHP pages that are fed from information in a database can display dramatically faster than database-driven pages using other systems.

- PHP is extremely powerful. Scripts written in PHP can open files, open network connections, and execute other programs.

All of these factors combine to make PHP very popular.

Here is a simple PHP script:

```
<html><head><title>PHP Test</title></head>
<body>
<?php
    echo "Hello World!<p>";
?>
</body></html>
```

Place this script in a file called *demo.php* and read the page from your web server, and you'll see:

```
Hello World!
```

The key mechanism here involves the tags *<?php* and *?>*. When the PHP interpreter starts up, it scans the *.php* page and looks for these tags. Any text that is not between these tags is sent to the web browser. Any code between these tags is executed in place. This process continues until the entire file is read, at which point the PHP interpreter returns to the Apache web server.

PHP variables look and act a lot like Perl variables. That is, variables begin with dollar signs and are untyped; they switch between being numbers or strings as needed.

---

* Perl/CGI web pages are slow because a new copy of the Perl interpreter is started each time a page is downloaded. Perl pages that are served using the *mod_perl* interface can be as fast or faster than PHP pages.

If a variable occurs within a double-quoted string, the variable is automatically sub-stituted. To see how this works, let's modify the PHP script so that it counts to 5:

```
<html><head><title>PHP Test</title></head>
<body>
<?php
    for($i=0;$i<5;$i++){
       echo "This is line $i<br>";
    }
?>
</body></html>
```

Here is the result:

```
This is line 0
This is line 1
This is line 2
This is line 3
This is line 4
```

And here is the HTML file that the script actually generated:

```
<title>PHP Test</title></head>
<body>
This is line 0<br>This is line 1<br>This is line 2<br>This is line 3<br>This is line
4<br></body></html>
```

The two key points about this second demonstration are that PHP doesn't require you to declare your variables, and the PHP interpreter really doesn't know much about the HTML that it produces—it just shoots it out and lets the browser display it.

Controlling PHP

PHP's behavior is controlled by the PHP initialization file, *php.ini*. PHP directives can also be placed in the Apache *httpd.conf* file.

Using the Apache configuration file, many PHP features can be controlled on a directory-by-directory basis. For example, the section shown here, taken from an *httpd.conf* file, enables the PHP3 safe mode (described later in the chapter in the section "PHP Safe Mode") by default in the directory */htdocs* but not in the directory */staffdocs*:

```
<IfModule mod_php3.c>
  AddType application/x-httpd-php .php
  AddType application/x-httpd-php3 .php3

  <Directory /htdocs/>
    php3_safe_mode on
  </Directory>
  <Directory /htdocs/>
    php3_safe_mode off
  </Directory>
</IfModule>
```

Understanding PHP Security Issues

PHP is an incredibly powerful system. Unfortunately, it is also a very lax system: many of the protections available in other scripting environments do not exist in PHP. This can be a great advantage when you are trying to get something out quickly, but it can also create problems for security-sensitive environments.

PHP is also a widely used system. PHP is used on shared web servers run by ISPs. It is also part of the default installation for many single-user Linux installations. As is typically the case with complicated systems, the environment in which you run PHP will determine many of the security concerns that you may need to address. PHP presents a number of challenges because of its vast power:

- If you have a shared computer that uses PHP for many different users (for example, an ISP that uses PHP on its customer web server), some users may be able to use PHP to access private files belonging to other users.

- If you have PHP installed on a computer where users are not allowed to run their own programs, your users may be able to use PHP to bypass this restriction.

Many of the potential security problems with PHP arise because it is possible to make changes to the PHP script's runtime environment in ways that may not have been anticipated by the original script programmer—or ways that may not be evident to people who review the script after the original programmer leaves. Thus:

- Programmers can use some relatively obscure PHP behaviors to hide back doors into your system. These back doors might even be hidden from other programmers working on the same project.

- If you download and run PHP scripts that are commonly available on the Internet, attackers may discover flaws in these scripts and use those flaws to break into your system.

In the following sections, we look at specific security issues that arise when using PHP and explore techniques for handling them.

PHP Installation Issues

Although PHP is designed to be installed as an Apache module, it can also be installed as a standalone binary in the web server's *cgi-bin* directory. Although CERT advisory CA 96-11 specifically recommends against installing interpreters in a web server's *cgi-bin* directory, PHP is designed to try to make such an installation as secure as possible. Nevertheless, we do not recommend this method of installation— mostly because PHP runs much faster when it is installed as an Apache module.

If you must install PHP as a separate executable, the PHP manual recommends placing the PHP interpreter outside of the web server's hierarchy. That is, instead of installing the PHP interpreter in *cgi-bin*, install it as */usr/local/bin/php*. To use the

PHP interpreter, you need to place *#!/usr/local/bin/php* at the beginning of each file that uses PHP. Thus, the demo script at the beginning of this section becomes:

```
#!/usr/local/bin/php
<html><head><title>PHP Test</title></head>
<body><?php echo "Hello World!<p>"; ?>
</body></html>
```

PHP Variables

One of the features of PHP that makes it very easy to use is the lax way that PHP variables are managed. By default, the following all appear as global variables in the PHP namespace whenever a PHP script is run:

- Web server environment variables that are typically set for CGI connections, such as HTTP_USER_AGENT and DOCUMENT_ROOT
- Environment variables that were present when the web server was started up
- Variables that were provided as part of an HTTP GET
- Variables that were provided as part of an HTTP POST
- Variables that were present in a cookie
- Global variables that are set in subroutine libraries

The danger here is that if a variable is specified in more than one location, one variable will shadow another. What's more, it is not possible for a running PHP script to determine why a global variable was set.

Attacks with global variables

For example, you may have a PHP script that depends on an environment variable MAILDIR being set with the location of the mail directory. This environment variable might be set by a library or might be set in the web server's environment space before the web server is started up. Here is such a script:

```
<html><head><title>PHP Test</title></head>
<body>
<?php
   echo "The value of MAILDIR is $MAILDIR\n";
   ?>
</body></html>
```

Under normal circumstances, the value of MAILDIR is */var/spool/mail,* and this script displays:

```
The value of MAILDIR is /var/spool/mail
```

However, if the script is fetched with a URL such as *http://www.simson.net/demo. php?MAILDIR=/etc/passwd,* then the script will display:

```
The value of MAILDIR is /etc/passwd
```

Many PHP scripts will use the value of global variables to determine their behavior. For example, a script might validate a username and a password, and set an authorized variable if the user is authorized:

```php
<?php
if( validate_user($user,$pass)) {
  $authorized=1;
}
?>
```

At some point later in the script, your program checks to see if the user is authorized:

```php
<? php
if($authorized){
  display_secret_data( );
}
```

The problem with this approach is that the user can set the *$authorized* variable in the URL, simply by appending *&authorized=1*. The script has no way of knowing that the *$authorized* variable was set by the user and not by the script itself. The solution to this problem is to not rely on the default value of any variable. Instead, manually set each variable before it is used:

```php
<?php
$authorized=0;
if( validate_user($user,$pass)) {
  $authorized=1;
}
?>
```

You can catch many of these errors by calling the function *error_reporting(E_ALL)* at the beginning of all of your PHP scripts. This function will cause PHP to generate a warning if you use a variable before it is first assigned—that is, if you are depending on the default value.

 Some programmers recommend checking the PHP arrays HTTP_ GET_VARS, HTTP_POST_VARS, HTTP_COOKIE_VARS, and HTTP_POST_FILES to see if a variable was passed in by the user. You can do this, but it is easy to make a mistake, and if the PHP maintainers decide to add a fifth way that the user can specify variables, you'll need to update all of your scripts. It's much simpler and safer to assign the value of "0" or "" to every variable before you use it.

register_globals = off

The best solution to the problem of global variables is to prevent environment, GET, POST, Cookie, and Server variables from becoming global variables by setting *register_globals = off* in the PHP configuration file.

If you turn off *register_globals*, you will need to manually interrogate the HTTP_ARS, HTTP_POST_VARS, HTTP_COOKIE_VARS, and HTTP_POST_FILES variables, rather than relying on their being globally registered. As a result, this code:

```
<html><head><title>PHP Test</title></head>
<body>
<?php print "Hello, $username!<p>"; ?>

</body></html>
```

becomes:

```
<html><head><title>PHP Test</title></head>
<body>
<?php
    print "Hello, ";
    print $HTTP_GET_VARS['username'];
    print "!<p>";

?>
</body></html>
```

Unfortunately, this will also break most PHP programs that you might download from the Internet.

Database Authentication Credentials

Most database systems require that the client provide a username and a password when the connection is made. It is common practice for PHP programmers to embed the usernames and passwords for their database servers directly in their scripts, as shown here:

```
<?php
mysql_pconnect("dbase","user","password");
...
```

The problem with this approach is that anybody who can view the raw source of the PHP file can learn the username and password for the database server. If you are on a shared web server, it may be impossible for one group of users to keep another group from viewing the contents of their scripts. In a Unix environment, for example, other users can simply hard link your password-containing scripts to a file in their web server directory with the *.txt* extension. Even if the other user does not have permission to read your file, the web server will, and thus the user will be able to read the contents of your script—and your password.

A better approach to protecting the contents of your scripts is to keep your database passwords in a file and read this out when it is needed. For example:

```
<?php
#
```

```
# Create the connection
#

$fp = fopen("/usr/local/adm/dbpasswords/http", "r");
$pass = fgets($fp,14);
fclose($fp);
mysql_pconnect("mysql.vineyard.net","http",$pass);
?>
```

The security of this system can be enhanced by using PHP's safe mode and giving each user a different *open_basedir*. Ultimately, however, the best security comes from giving each user his or her own copy of the Apache web server.

URL fopen( )

A curious feature of PHP is that the *fopen()* function can open URLs in addition to files. The following PHP page will actually display MIT's home page:

```
<html><head><title>PHP Test</title></head>
<body>
<?php
        $f = fopen("http://www.mit.edu","r");
        while($j = fgets($f,65536)){
                print $j;
        }
?>
</body></html>
```

When a web browser pulls down this page, it causes the PHP interpreter to open up a connection to *www.mit.edu*, download the page, and then send the page, one line at a time, back to the web browser.

The problem with PHP's URL *fopen()* feature is that the URL interpretation is done by all PHP functions that open files—including the *include()* function. This can be a problem with cascading include files that rely on global variables to specify the directory from which the code is included.

Shaun Clowes' demonstration of this problem involves two files, *main.php* and *loadlanguage.php*, which might be used for loading a particular language-specific include file.

In *main.php*:

```
<?php
 $libDir = "/libdir";
 $langDir = "$libdir/languages";

 ...

 include("$libdir/loadlanguage.php":
?>
```

In *libdir/loadlanguage.php*:

```php
<?php
...

include("$langDir/$userLang");
?>
```

The attack is quite straightforward. The attacker simply sends the web server an HTTP GET command that references *libdir/loadlanguage.php* with the PHP global variable *$langDir* to be *http:* and sets the global variable *$userLang* to be */www. attacker.com/somefile.php3*. This causes the web server to download the file *http:// www.attacker.com/somefile.php* and execute the PHP code that it contains. The attack is possible because the file *libdir/loadlanguage.php* expects that the calling file will set two particular global variables, but it is possible to shortcircuit the calling file and call the library file directly.

Granted, these sorts of attacks are hard to carry out: if you write all of your own scripts and keep them secret, even if you have these vulnerabilities, they probably won't be used against you. But it can be difficult for a site to keep its scripts secret, and many sites make use of scripts downloaded from public sources.

Hide Your Scripts

Because many problems may be lurking in your PHP scripts, we recommend that you not make your scripts publicly available. This can be harder than you imagine. For example, you need to be sure that your PHP scripts are *always* processed by the PHP interpreter. For example, they should not be accessible by FTP.

The PHP documentation recommends that you make it impossible for an attacker to turn on debugging code that you may have placed in your own scripts. For example, many programmers typically use variables such as *debug* or *showerrors* to put their scripts into debugging mode. But an attacker can do the same thing using PHP's powerful global variable facility. For example, this code snippet, placed anywhere on the Internet, could be used to probe the URL *http://www.ex.com/index.php* for debugging code:

```
<form method="post" action="http://www.ex.com/index.
php?errors=Y&showerrors=1"&debug=1">
<input type="hidden" name="errors" value="Y">
<input type="hidden" name="showerrors" value="1">
<input type="hidden" name="debug" value="1">
<input type="submit" name="probe">
</form>
```

Finally, you can hide the fact that you are using PHP entirely, by configuring your web server so that an extension other than *.php* is used, as follows:

```
# Make PHP code look like unknown type
AddType application/x-httpd-php .bop .foo .l33t
```

Alternatively, configure your web server so that the PHP parser is used to parse all HTML files, rather than simply those ending with *.php*. This is shown here:

```
# Make all PHP code look like html
AddType application/x-httpd-php .htm .html
```

PHP Safe Mode

PHP *safe mode* can be used to disable certain functions in the PHP interpreter based on where the particular PHP script resides. Safe mode is particularly useful for ISPs, where different individuals or organizations are using a shared resource.

The PHP manual states: "It is architecturally incorrect to try to solve this problem at the PHP level, but since the alternatives at the web server and OS levels aren't very realistic, many people, especially ISPs, use safe mode for now."

In fact, some ISPs do set up their web servers with a separate Apache process for each customer. Unfortunately, this can be exceedingly resource-intensive and is not necessary for many applications. Thus, safe mode is widely used.

Controlling safe mode

The configuration flags that control safe mode are shown in Table 16-1.

Table 16-1. PHP configuration flags that control safe mode

Configuration value	Default	Effect
safe_mode	Off	Turns safe mode on or off.
open_basedir		If this value is set, then all file operations (e.g., *fopen, fread, fclose,* etc.), must take place underneath this directory. Setting *open_basedir* can be used as an alternative to safe mode or in conjunction with it.
safe_mode_exec_dir		PHP will only run executables that are contained within this directory.
safe_mode_allowed_env_vars	PHP_	Users can only modify environment variables that begin with PHP_.
safe_mode_protected_env_vars	LD_LIBRARY_PATH	Users cannot modify these variables at all.
disable_functions		Allows individual functions to be disabled.

Safe mode restrictions

When safe mode is on, the following restrictions are in place:

- Most commands that result in files being opened, renamed, linked, or otherwise modified (e.g., *fopen(), dmbopen(), dbase_open(),* etc.) will only allow files to be opened that have the same UID as the owner of the script that is being executed.
- The *system()* function can only execute scripts that are in the *safe_mode_exec_dir*.
- The *dl()*, backtick (e.g., `command`), and *shell_exec()* functions are disabled.

For more information about safe mode, see *http://www.php.net/manual/en/features.safe-mode.php*.

PHP Configuration File Settings

In his paper "A Study In Scarlet: Exploiting Common Vulnerabilities in PHP Applications," Shaun Clowes recommends this checklist for securing PHP environments:

set register_globals=off
> This will prevent users from setting variables in your PHP scripts.

set safe_mode=on
> This will enable safe mode, which significantly improves the security of PHP scripts. "This is a great option for ISP environments (for which it is designed), but it can also greatly improve the security of normal PHP environments given proper configuration," Clowes writes. "It can also be a complete pain in the neck."

set open_basedir
> This restricts the PHP system to a particular directory hierarchy that you specify.

set display_errors=off, log_errors=on
> This causes PHP to write its errors to a log file, rather than displaying them in the web browser. This makes debugging scripts harder, but it also makes it more difficult for an attacker to reverse-engineer your scripts. A good compromise is to set *display_errors=on* for development systems but set it off for production environments.

set allow_url_fopen=off
> This will prevent PHP from opening URLs when you think it is opening files.

Writing Scripts That Run with Additional Privileges

Many scripts need to run with user permissions different from those of the web server itself. On a Unix computer, the easiest way to do this is to make the script SUID or SGID. By doing this, the script runs with the permissions of the owner of the file, rather than those of the web server itself. On Macintosh, DOS, and Windows 95 systems, there is no such choice—scripts run with the same privileges and can access everything on the system.

Unfortunately, programs that run with additional privileges traditionally have been a source of security problems. This list of suggestions is based on those problems and specially tailored for the problems faced by the web developer:

1. Avoid using the superuser (SUID root or SGID *wheel*) unless it is vital that your program perform actions that can only be performed by the superuser. For

example, you will need to use SUID root if you want your program to modify system databases such as */etc/passwd*. But if you merely wish to have the program access a restricted database of your own creation, create a special Unix user for that application and have your scripts SUID to that user.

2. If your program needs to perform some functions as superuser but generally does not require SUID permissions, consider putting the SUID part in a different program and constructing a carefully controlled and monitored interface between the two.

3. If you need SUID or SGID permissions, use them for their intended purpose as early in the program as possible and then revoke them by returning the effective and real UIDs and GIDs to those of the process that invoked the program.

4. Avoid writing SUID scripts in shell languages, especially in *csh* or its derivatives.

5. Consider creating a different username or group for each application to prevent unexpected interactions and amplification of abuse.

6. In general, use the *setuid( )* and *setgid( )* functions to bracket the sections of your code that require superuser privileges. For example:

```
setuid(0);                    /* Become superuser to open the master file */
fd = open("/etc/masterfile",O_RDONLY);
setuid(-1);                   /* Give up superuser for now */
if(fd<0) error_open( );       /* Handle errors */
```

7. Use the full pathnames for all files that you open.

8. For scripts, use the *chroot()* call for further restricting your script to a particular directory. The *chroot()* call changes the *root* directory of a process to a specified subdirectory within your filesystem. This change essentially gives the calling process a private world from which it cannot escape. For example, if you have a program that only needs to listen to the network and write into a log file that is stored in the directory */usr/local/logs*, then you could execute the following system call to restrict the program to that directory:

```
chroot("/usr/local/logs");
```

Use the *chroot()* call only with CGI programs, never with modules that are called by an API. Because of the difficulties with shared libraries on some systems, you may find it easier to use *chroot()* with Perl than with C.

Connecting to Databases

It is common for a CGI program or script to connect to databases that are external to the web server. External databases can be used for many purposes, such as storing user preferences, implementing shopping carts, and even order processing. When the script runs, it opens a connection to the database, issues a query, gets the result, and then uses the result to formulate a response to the user. On some systems, a new database connection is created each time a new script is run. Other systems maintain a small number of persistent connections which are cached.

Database-backed web sites give a tremendous amount of power and flexibility to the web designer. Unfortunately, this approach can also reduce the overall security of the system: many of the security incidents mentioned earlier in this book happened because an attacker was able to execute arbitrary SQL commands on the database server and view the results. (For example, recall the story of the attacker who was able to obtain tens of thousands of credit card numbers from an e-commerce site.) If you decide to deploy a database server to supplement your web site, it is important to be sure that the server will be deployed and used securely.

Protect Account Information

Before the database server provides results to the script running on the web server, the server needs to authenticate the script to make sure it is authorized to access the information. Most databases use a simple username/password for account authentication, which means the script needs to have a valid username/password and present this information to the database server each time a request is issued.

Among many developers it is common practice to simply code the username and password into the scripts that require access to the database server. Unfortunately, this practice has several problems:

- If an attacker is able to view the script, the attacker will learn the username and password.
- If many scripts require access to the username and password, then it must be stored in several scripts.
- Changing the username and password requires modifying the script. When the script is modified, other changes may be made inadvertently.

Instead of storing the database username and password in the script, a better approach is to store this information in a file on the web server. This approach isolates the authentication information from the script that is performing the database request, which improves both maintainability and security. The server script then opens this file and reads the username and password prior to issuing a database request.

Use Filtering and Quoting to Screen Out Raw SQL

As we mentioned earlier in this chapter, it is extremely important to filter all data from the user to make sure that it contains only allowable characters. When working with SQL servers, it is further important to properly quote data provided by the user before sending the data to the server. These procedures are used to prevent users from constructing their own SQL commands and sending that data to the SQL server.

For example, if you have a web form that asks a person for his name and then stores this information into a database, it might be tempting to simply take the person's name from a field, put that field into a variable called *$name*, and then construct a SQL command using this variable. Consider:

```
$name = param('name');
sql_send("insert into names (name) value ('$name');");
```

Unfortunately, this is not safe: an attacker who has knowledge of your application can provide a specially crafted name that results in arbitrary SQL commands being executed. Consider this name:

```
Simson Garfinkel')"; delete from names;
```

When this name is used to build the SQL command, the resultant string will actually be interpreted as three commands—one that makes an insertion into the database, a second that deletes all of the data in the names table, and a third that contains a syntax error:

```
insert into names (name) value ('Simson Garfinkel')"; delete from names; ');
```

Given this text, most SQL servers will insert a record into the *names* table, delete all of the data, and then report a SQL error.

The way to protect scripts from these kinds of attacks is to make sure that you first carefully filter incoming data, and that you next quote all of the remaining data properly before sending it to the SQL server.

Quoting is best done with a separate function that is always called whenever any string is sent to the SQL server. If you are using the Perl language, a nifty approach is to have the quote function automatically add the SQL quotes as well. Here is such a function:

```
sub squote {
    my $ret = $_[0];

    $ret =~ s/\'\\\'/g;
    return '.' . $ret . '.';
}
```

You could then use this function in the previous example, like this:

```
$qname = squote(param('name'));
sql_send("insert into names (name) value ($qname);");
```

Another approach is to precompile your SQL queries using variable binding. Variable binding allows you to precompile SQL queries with placeholders instead of actual variables. To return to our original example, you might compile the system using a hypothetical SQL interface that uses the @ sign as a placeholder for variables:

```
$func = sql_compile("insert into name (name) value (@)");
```

You might then execute this function with some other hypothetical function:

```
$name = param('name');
sql_bind($func,1,$name);        # bind the variable name to the first variable
sql_exec($func);                # execute the bound function
```

Different systems will have different syntaxes and APIs for compiling, binding, and executing SQL queries. Some SQL client libraries, such as the MySQL client library, don't support variable binding at all, so it's important to understand the approaches mentioned earlier.

Protect the Database Itself

Finally, it is important that you protect the database server itself:

- Configure your firewall or network topology so that it is impossible for people outside your organization to access your database server. For example, you may wish to set up your web server with two Ethernet adapters—one that connects to the Internet, and one that connects to a small firewall appliance that, in turn, connects to your database server. The firewall should be set up so that only database queries can pass between the web server and the database server. This setup is shown in Figure 16-5.

- Make sure logins on the database server are limited. The individuals with login capabilities should be the system administrator and the database administrator.

- Make sure that the database server is backed up, physically protected, and maintained in the same way as your other secure servers.

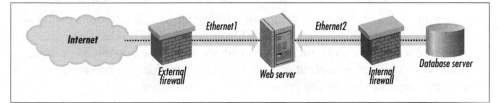

Figure 16-5. Connecting a database server and a web server to the Internet and your internal network with multiple firewalls.

Conclusion

Writing secure web applications is a difficult task. Any program that runs on your web server can potentially compromise the security of the entire system. To make things worse, no amount of testing will tell you if your programs are error-free. The solution to this apparent dilemma is to follow strict rules when writing your own programs and then to have those scripts carefully evaluated by someone you trust. Good luck!

CHAPTER 17

Deploying SSL Server Certificates

In this chapter:

- Creating SSL Servers with FreeSBD
- Installing an SSL Certificate on Microsoft IIS
- Obtaining a Certificate from a Commercial CA
- When things Go Wrong

This chapter describes how to create and install SSL (Secure Sockets Layer) certificates using the Open SSL implementation and the Apache *mod_ssl* module on the FreeBSD operating system. (See Chapter 5 for basic information on SSL. See Chapters 6 and 7 for information about digital certificates.) We will also show you how to get a certificate that is signed by the VeriSign certification authority. The process is decribed in detail to give you a feel for how the mechanics of the process work. However, as it is likely you will be performing this process with different software than described here, refer to your own documentation before beginning the procedure.

Planning for Your SSL Server

To set up a cryptographically enabled web server, you must complete these steps:

1. Plan your SSL installation. Why do you want to use SSL? What protocols do you want to use with SSL? Which server will you be using? Where will you be keeping your web server's private key? Do you want it to be possible for people to connect to your server *without* using SSL? Make sure that you know the answers to these questions before you proceed to avoid any false starts.

2. Obtain a web server that supports SSL. Most likely, you will either download your web server over the Internet or install it from a CD-ROM.

3. Install the web server.

4. Create a private/public key pair for your web server.

5. Create your own self-signed certificate so you can test your installation and get your secure web server running immediately.

Once your system is up and running, you may wish to get a signed certificate from a third-party certification authority (CA). If so, you must:

1. Send the public key to the CA.

2. Send other, supporting documents to the certification authority.

3. Receive your signed X.509 v3 public certificate from the certification authority.

4. Install the certificate on your web server.

We'll describe each of these steps in detail in the following sections.

Choosing a Server

To deploy SSL within your organization, you will first need to decide what you want to do with the protocol. Some of your choices for SSL include:

- Using SSL to encrypt HTTP traffic. By deploying a web server that understands the SSL protocol and changing your *http://* URLs to *https://*, you can get protection from eavesdropping. This is the most common way that SSL is deployed within organizations.

- Using SSL to encrypt POP, SMTP, IMAP, and other mail protocols. Many popular email clients (e.g., Microsoft Outlook, Outlook Express, and Netscape Communicator) allow email to be received and sent using SSL encryption. The advantage of SSL is that it prevents an attacker from sniffing your password or eavesdropping on the content of your email.

- Using SSL to encrypt LDAP authentication traffic.

- Using SSL to encrypt your own proprietary protocols.

A few years ago, obtaining, compiling, and installing an SSL-equipped web server could be quite a challenge. U.S. corporations had the option of purchasing an SSL-enabled web server from Microsoft or Netscape. But for organizations outside the U.S., or for U.S. organizations and individuals that wished to use open source software, patent and export restrictions made simply getting the software a real challenge.

Those days are long over. Both commercial and free SSL implementations are now readily available. Today there are many software packages that support SSL. A sampling of such programs is shown in Table 17-1.

Table 17-1. A few popular servers that support the SSL protocol

Package	Creator	Obtain from
OpenSSL	OpenSSL Development Team	*www.openssl.org*
Apache mod_ssl (requires OpenSSL)	Apache Software Foundation	*www.apache.org*
Microsoft Internet Information Server	Microsoft Corporation	Bundled with Windows NT, 2000, and XP
Netscape Enterprise and Suitespot	Netscape Communications	*www.netscape.com*
Covalent SSL (SSL accelerator)	Covalent Technologies, Inc.	*www.covalent.net*
Apache Stronghold (commercial Apache)	C2Net	*www.c2.net*

If you are running a web server on Microsoft Windows NT, 2000, or XP, then you have an SSL-enabled web server bundled into your operating system. Furthermore, Microsoft's CryptoAPI makes SSL/TLS services available to any program that sets a flag when opening or accepting a TCP/IP connection.

If you are using Linux, there's a good chance that an SSL-enabled web server was bundled along with your operating system; if not, you can download the RPM installation packages from many different locations on the Internet. Versions of the Apache web server with either the Apache-SSL or *mod_ssl* SSL packages can be downloaded and automatically installed with NetBSD, FreeBSD, and OpenBSD.

Deciding on the Private Key Store

SSL derives its security from public key cryptography. To use SSL, you need to have a public/private key pair and a certificate that is signed by an appropriate certification authority. The security of your web server's SSL communications depends, in part, on the security of your private key. With the private key, any attacker who has access to the data stream can in theory decode the contents of your SSL communications. Thus, it behooves you to make sure that the key is properly protected.

There are three widely accepted practices for maintaining server private keys. In decreasing order of security, they are:

Keep the key in special-purpose hardware

Several corporations have created special-purpose hardware that generates your SSL key pair, securely holds the SSL private key, and performs SSL cryptographic operations at high speed. Using special-purpose hardware, especially hardware that implements the FIPS 140-1 specification, is the most secure way that you can implement SSL within an organization. Even if an attacker breaks into your computer, that attacker will be unable to copy or otherwise compromise your private key.

If you opt for special-purpose hardware, your web server needs to have special drivers to interoperate with the hardware. Each time an SSL request comes in, the web server will hand the encrypted data to the special-purpose hardware to be decrypted. The decrypted data will then be returned to your web server. Special-purpose hardware can also significantly improve the speed of your SSL server.

Keep the key encrypted on your web server

Keeping your keys encrypted in a file on your web server is a compromise between security and cost. With this configuration, your key is protected with a passphrase. When the web server starts up, a person needs to manually type the passphrase on the computer's console so that the web server can decrypt the key and start offering encrypted service. Although this approach seems secure, it is actually quite easy to find the decrypted key in the web server's memory space. A second problem with this approach is that you need to have a person who knows the passphrase present whenever the web server is rebooted.

Keep the key unencrypted in a file on the web server

Keeping keys unencrypted on the web server is the most common way for cryptographically enabled web sites to maintain their private keys. This approach allows you to reboot the web server at will without having to worry about having somebody around who knows the passphrase. On the other hand, if somebody breaks into your web server, they will be able to make a copy of the key for themselves and decrypt any communications between your web server and your users that are intercepted. In practice, this is not a significant risk.

In the early days of e-commerce there was much concern and consternation about the security of web server keys. In practice, much of this concern seems to have been overblown. Most attackers do not try to steal server keys and then use those keys to decrypt intercepted communications. Instead, most attackers simply break into the web server and either compromise its operating system or download information from back-end databases, neatly circumventing the cryptography. This is possible because web server keys are only used to encrypt communications, not stored data.

In practice, the minor security improvement that comes from storing keys encrypted is not worth the increased difficulty of operations. For the overwhelming majority of SSL applications, keeping SSL keys unencrypted on the web server and using traditional host security to protect the web server and the computer's operating system offers sufficient security.

Although we do not recommend encrypting SSL private keys, we do recommend that certification authority private keys be protected, either through encryption, special hardware, or by having them reside on computers that are not physically connected to the Internet. The reason for this added security is that a compromised CA key can be used to compromise an entire PKI system, rather than simply a single web server.

Server Certificates

Every SSL server must have an SSL server certificate. When a browser connects to a web server using the SSL protocol, the server sends the browser its public key in an X.509 v3 certificate. The certificate is used to authenticate the identity of the server and to distribute the server's public key, which is used to encrypt the initial information that is sent to the server by the client.

The SSL certificate format

Netscape defined the SSL 2.0 certificate format in the document *http://home. netscape.com/eng/security/ssl_2.0_certificate.html*.

SSL certificates must contain the following fields:

- Key length of signature.
- Certificate serial number (must be unique within a certification authority).
- Distinguished name.
- Signature algorithm (specifies which algorithm is used).
- Subject common name. This is the DNS name of the server. Netscape Navigator Version 3.0 allows wildcard patterns, such as *.netscape.com to sign all hosts with Netscape's domain. Specifically, Navigator Version 3.0 allows the following wildcards in the *subject.commonName* field:

Pattern	Meaning
*	Matches anything
?	Matches one character
\	Escapes a special character (e.g., * matches "*")
$	Matches the end of a string
[abc]	Matches a, b, or c
[a-z]	Matches the characters a through z
[^az]	Matches any character except a or z
~	This character, followed by another pattern, causes any host whose name matches that following pattern to *not* match the *subject.commonName* field
(abc|def)	Matches abc or def

These pattern-matching operators are similar, but not identical, to the Unix regular expression matching functions. If you decide to use them, you should be careful: some clients do not properly implement these wildcards. Also, some CAs will not sign certificates that contain wildcards; others will sign them only on a case-by-case basis.

The reliance on DNS in the SSL specification is surprising, considering the DNS system itself is not secure, and considering DNS names are frequently different from the name of the organization that is offering web service. Instead of having a web browser attempt to validate that the DNS name in the certificate is the same as the DNS name of the machine it has connected to, web browsers would probably do better by displaying the server's distinguished name prominently in the browser's window. For reasons that are unclear, no browser vendor has ever taken this step.

Certificates for certification authorities are nearly identical to the certificates for SSL servers, except that instead of a distinguished name, the certification authority's name is located in the Common Name field. According to Netscape's documentation:

> The common name will be displayed when the user chooses to view the list of trusted certification authorities in the Security Preferences dialog box (under the Options menu). Examples include *Netscape Test CA* or *Certs-R-Us Level 42 CA*. Examples of names that are not recommended are *Certification authority* and *CA Root*.

Creating SSL Servers with FreeBSD

In this section, we demonstrate how to install and configure the Apache web server with *mod_ssl* on the FreeBSD operating system.

History

The history of the Apache web server is well documented and will only briefly be recounted here. Basically, Tim Berners-Lee wrote the original web server while on staff at CERN. Rob McCool at the National Center for Supercomputing Applications wrote a web server that implemented the same HTTP protocol; the server was called NCSA *httpd*. By the time that McCool left NCSA in 1994, that server had become the most popular web server on the Internet, and at that point the project stalled. A group of webmasters got together and decided to resurrect the project. They took a number of patches and improvements and created the first release of the Apache ("a patchy") web server in April 1995.

When the first Apache web server was released, it did not implement Netscape's Secure Sockets Layer encryption system. This technical restriction came about because of two legal restrictions—intellectual property law and export control law. From an intellectual property perspective, the SSL protocol required the use of the RSA public key algorithm, which was protected by patent, and the RC2 or RC4 algorithms, which RSA claimed were protected by trade secret, even though the two algorithms had been reverse-engineered and posted to the Internet.

And even if an implementation of SSL was created that did not infringe upon the RSA property rights, U.S. export control law at the time would have prohibited the cryptographic source code from being exported outside the U.S.

The obvious way around these legal problems was for someone outside of the U.S. to reimplement SSL. And that's exactly what happened. In 1995 two Australian programmers, Eric Young and Tim Hudson, created an independent SSL implementation and posted it to the Internet. Called SSLeay, the Young/Hudson program was reasonably complete, quite primitive, and somewhat buggy. But SSLeay was distributed in source-code form and with a license that allowed it to be incorporated into any other program, provided that credit was given to Young and Hudson.

In 1999, RSA Data Security hired Young and Hudson to set up an RSA Australian subsidiary. This move was largely designed to get around U.S. export controls of the time. Because the SSLeay code had been developed and was maintained outside the U.S., RSA was free to sell the product anywhere in the world it wished (with the exception of several "outlaw" countries to which export was blocked by Australia). RSA began selling the product as RSA BSafe SSL-C and continued development on its own.

Meanwhile, as Young and Hudson began concentrating on commercial software, a new group of programmers from around the world started working on refining the SSLeay program. The software was renamed OpenSSL. Work on OpenSSL has continued more or less continuously ever since.

Initially, there was a large set of patches that needed to be applied to the Apache source code to make it handle SSL connections. The Apache-SSL project integrated Apache with SSLeay, creating an easy to install system. Apache-SSL was commercialized under the trademark Stronghold by Community Connexion, a.k.a. C2Net, an Internet service provider turned software developer that was eventually purchased by RedHat Software. Meanwhile, in April 1998 Ralf S. Engelschall created an SSL Apache module called *mod_ssl*.

The differences among all of these various Apache and SSL combinations are rather subtle. The Apache-SSL project says that it emphasizes reliability, performance, and security while dismissively stating that the *mod_ssl* project emphasizes features. On the other hand, *mod_ssl* integrates more cleanly with the Apache code base and is somewhat easier to administer. Although many people think that this sort of competition between various open source projects is a needless and wasteful duplication of effort, the competition driven by this "capitalism of ideas" does seem to be more efficient at motivating individuals.

Obtaining the Programs

You can download each of the open source SSL programs from their respective web sites, as shown in Table 17-2. If you are not up to building your own web server, you can download RPM archives or packages for your particular operating system.

Table 17-2. URLs for popular open source SSL programs

Program	Purpose	Location
Apache	Base web server	*www.apache.org*
OpenSSL	SSL implementation	*www.openssl.org*
Apache-SSL	Original integration of Apache and SSLeay	*www.apache-ssl.org*
mod_ssl	Builds SSL system directly into Apache	*www.modssl.org*

Installing Apache and mod_ssl on FreeBSD

FreeBSD Version 4.3 has two different Apache and SSL combinations in the *ports* directory: */usr/ports/www/apache13-modssl* for *mod_ssl*, and */usr/ports/www/apache13-ssl* for Apache-SSL. These systems rely on the copy of OpenSSL that is pre-installed with FreeBSD 4.3, which makes installation considerably easier than with previous releases of FreeBSD or other free Unix operating systems.

To install a basic HTTP server with SSL, you can simply *cd* into one of these directories and type *make install*. The FreeBSD ports system will search the source code on a variety of FTP servers, download the code, apply any FreeBSD-specific patches, compile it, and install it.

Before you use the *ports* system, you should use the *cvsup* command to make sure that you have a current copy of the */usr/ports* directory—some ports change almost weekly. Also, most security problems are addressed in the *ports* collections soon after they are reported. Once you have verified that your *ports* collection is up-to-date, simply *cd* and type *make:*[*]

```
unix# cd /usr/ports/www/apache13-modssl
unix# make
>> apache_1.3.20.tar.gz doesn't seem to exist in /usr/ports/distfiles/.
>> Attempting to fetch from http://www.apache.org/dist/httpd/.

Receiving apache_1.3.20.tar.gz (1973138 bytes): 100%
1973138 bytes transferred in 15.0 seconds (128.87 kBps)
>> mod_ssl-2.8.4-1.3.20.tar.gz doesn't seem to exist in /usr/ports/distfiles/.
>> Attempting to fetch from http://www.apache.org/dist/httpd/.
fetch: mod_ssl-2.8.4-1.3.20.tar.gz: Not Found
>> Attempting to fetch from http://www.modssl.org/source/.

Receiving mod_ssl-2.8.4-1.3.20.tar.gz (751936 bytes): 0%
...
```

And so it goes for another hour or so. From a "full" installation of FreeBSD 4.3, the install of *apache13-modssl* performs the following steps:[†]

1. Downloads Apache 1.3.20.
2. Downloads *mod_ssl-2.8.4*.
3. Downloads, compiles, and installs mm-1.1.3 (shared memory library).
4. Compiles and installs *mod_ssl*.
5. Compiles and installs Apache.

When all of the downloads and compiles are finished, you will see the following:

```
<=== src/support
+---------------------------------------------------------------------+
| Before you install the package you now should prepare the SSL       |
| certificate system by running the 'make certificate' command.       |
```

---

[*] Note that it is necessary to type *make install* as root. This is because various packages in the */usr/ports* directory require other packages to be compiled and installed before you can use them. Using the ports system means that you need to implicitly trust the FreeBSD project for the code that you run on your computer. Of course, by running FreeBSD, you are implicitly trusting the project, so the additional risk of using the ports system is probably negligible.

[†] The version numbers included in this list are for demonstration purposes only. As time goes on, these version numbers will certainly change.

```
| For different situations the following variants are provided:        |
|                                                                      |
| % make certificate TYPE=dummy     (dummy self-signed Snake Oil cert) |
| % make certificate TYPE=test      (test cert signed by Snake Oil CA) |
| % make certificate TYPE=custom    (custom cert signed by own CA)     |
| % make certificate TYPE=existing (existing cert)                     |
|         CRT=/path/to/your.crt [KEY=/path/to/your.key]                |
|                                                                      |
| Use TYPE=dummy     when you're a  vendor package maintainer,         |
| the TYPE=test      when you're an admin but want to do tests only,   |
| the TYPE=custom    when you're an admin willing to run a real server |
| and TYPE=existing when you're an admin who upgrades a server.        |
| (The default is TYPE=test)                                           |
|                                                                      |
| Additionally add ALGO=RSA (default) or ALGO=DSA to select           |
| the signature algorithm used for the generated certificate.          |
|                                                                      |
| Use 'make certificate VIEW=1' to display the generated data.         |
|                                                                      |
| Thanks for using Apache & mod_ssl.       Ralf S. Engelschall         |
|                                          rse@engelschall.com         |
|                                          www.engelschall.com         |
+----------------------------------------------------------------------+
<=== src
===>  Creating Dummy Certificate for Server (SnakeOil)
      [use 'make certificate' to create a real one]
unix#
```

Despite the instructions, you can go ahead and type *make install*. This will install a cryptographically enabled web server with the "Snake Oil" self-signed certificate:

```
unix# make install
===>  Installing for apache+mod_ssl-1.3.20+2.8.4
===>   `apache+mod_ssl-1.3.20+2.8.4 depends on shared library: mm.11 - found
===> [mktree: Creating Apache installation tree]
./src/helpers/mkdir.sh /usr/local/bin
./src/helpers/mkdir.sh /usr/local/sbin
./src/helpers/mkdir.sh /usr/local/libexec/apache

...

<=== [config]
===>   Generating temporary packing list
Installing /usr/local/etc/rc.d/apache.sh startup file.
===>   Compressing manual pages for apache+mod_ssl-1.3.20+2.8.4
===>   Registering installation for apache+mod_ssl-1.3.20+2.8.4
===>  SECURITY NOTE:
      This port has installed the following startup scripts which may cause
      network services to be started at boot time.
/usr/local/etc/rc.d/apache.sh
```

```
            If there are vulnerabilities in these programs there may be a security
            risk to the system. FreeBSD makes no guarantee about the security of
            ports included in the Ports Collection. Please type 'make deinstall'
            to deinstall the port if this is a concern.
    unix#
```

The default configuration built from the */usr/ports* uses the pathnames and directories described in Table 17-3. Although use of these pathnames cleanly integrates the Apache web server with the rest of the FreeBSD system, it does have the disadvantage of scattering the installation all over the operating system. You may wish to modify the installation so that all executables, log files, and configuration information are stored beneath */usr/local/apache*.

Table 17-3. Programs, log files, and directories used by Apache with mod_ssl on FreeBSD

Path	Purpose
/usr/local/sbin/apachectl	Apache control program; used for starting and stopping server
/usr/local/sbin/httpd	Apache executable program
/usr/local/etc/apache/	Apache configuration files, including *access.conf, httpd.conf, magic, mime.types,* and *srm.conf*
/usr/local/etc/apache/ssl.crl	*mod_ssl* certificate revocation list directory
/usr/local/etc/apache/ssl.crt	*mod_ssl* certificate directory
/usr/local/etc/apache/ssl.csr	*mod_ssl* certificate signing request directory
/usr/local/etc/apache/ssl.key	*mod_ssl* private key directory
/usr/local/etc/apache/ssl.prm	*mod_ssl* DSA parameter files
/usr/local/www/data	The actual web pages
/var/log/httpd-access.log	Apache access log file
/var/log/httpd-error.log	Apache error log file

Verifying the Initial Installation

Your cryptographically enabled server is now installed, a public/secret key pair has been created, and your server has been equipped with a "Snake Oil" test certificate. Now what?

The test certificate will allow you to begin immediately using your server's cryptographic features. However, because the certificate is not signed by a recognized certification authority, when users click into your web site they should be informed by their browser that the server has not been properly authenticated.

Before you go further, check your web server to make sure that it operates both without and with encryption. Then you will need to install a proper server certificate— either a self-signed certificate from your own certification authority, or a certificate signed by a well-known CA such as VeriSign.

To test the server, you can either set up a nameserver that points to your server, or you can test to the server's IP address. In this example we'll test with the IP address of our server, which happens to be 204.17.195.80.

1. First enter the URL of the server into a web browser using *http:* as the protocol. In this example, we entered the URL *http://204.17.195.80/* into a web browser. The resulting page is shown in Figure 17-1.

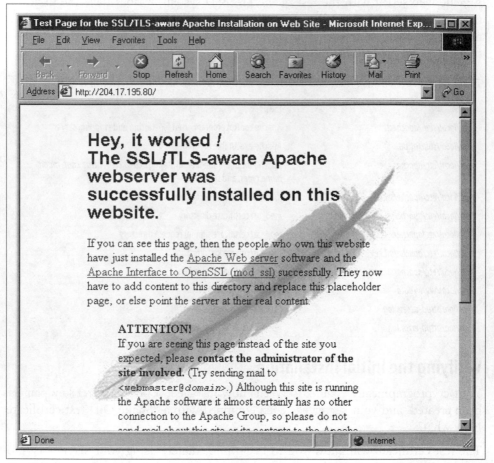

Figure 17-1. Verify that the web server you installed works to serve HTTP connections by going to the server's IP address with a web browser.

2. Next enter the same URL, but substitute *https:* for *http:*. Your web browser should generate a warning that the certificate is issued by an organization that you do not trust, and that the name on the certificate does not match the DNS address of the server. Internet Explorer's warning is shown in Figure 17-2, while Netscape's warning is shown in Figure 17-3.

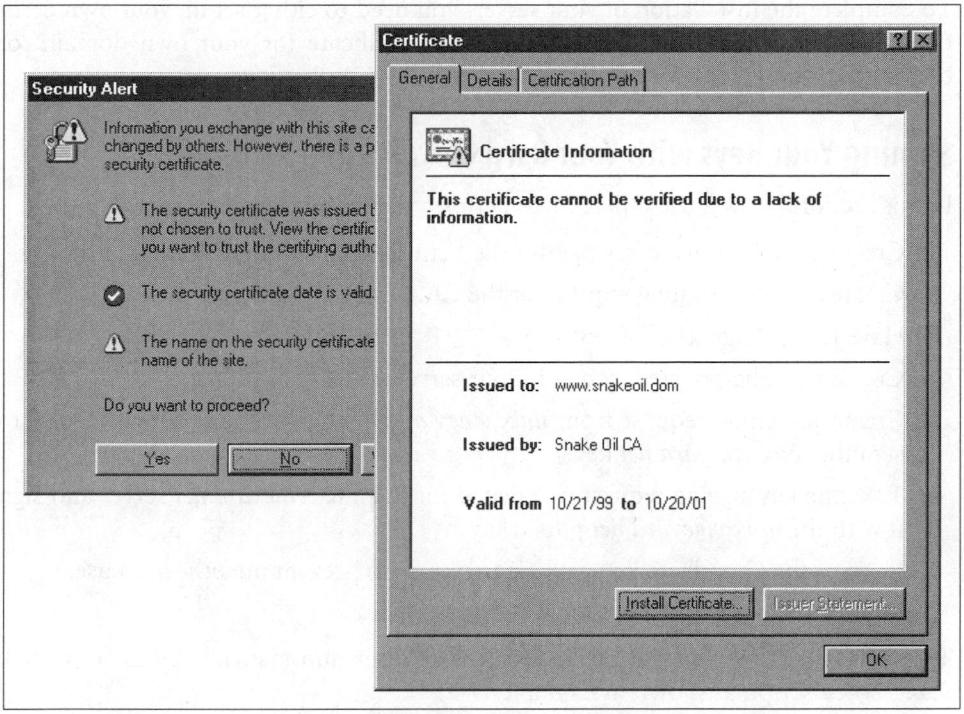

Figure 17-2. Internet Explorer warns that the "Snake Oil" certificate is not valid. If you choose to view the certificate, you'll see it is issued by the Snake Oil CA for the domain www.snakeoil.dom.

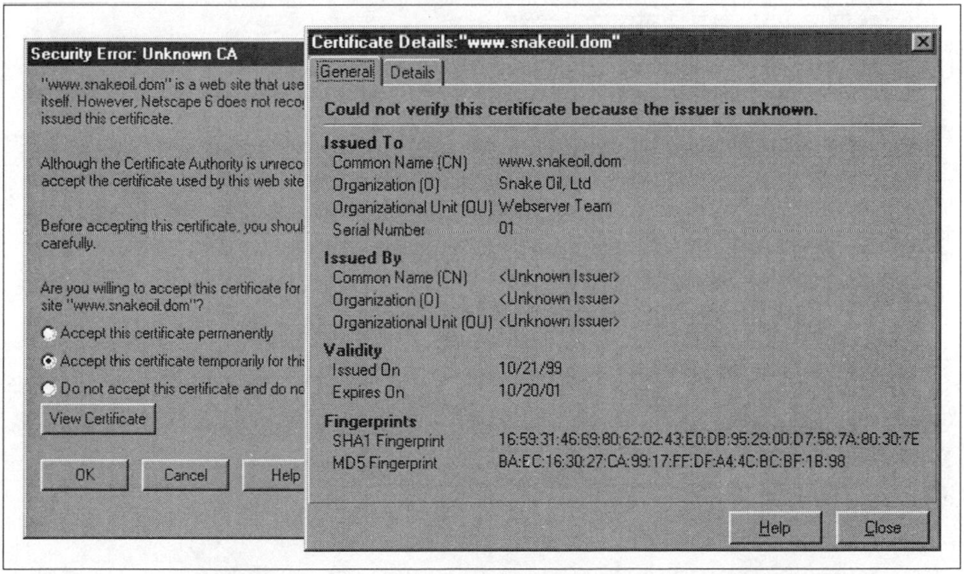

Figure 17-3. Netscape Navigator warns that the "Snake Oil" certificate is not valid. If you choose to view the certificate, you'll see it is issued by the Snake Oil CA for the domain www.snakeoil.dom.

To complete the installation of your server, you need to either set up your own certification authority and create a proper server certificate for your own domain, or obtain (that is, purchase) a certificate from another CA.

Signing Your Keys with Your Own Certification Authority

In this section, we will use OpenSSL to perform the following steps:

1. Create a public/private key pair for the fictitious Nitroba certification authority.
2. Create an X.509 signing request for the CA.
3. Have the CA sign its own key.
4. Create a public/private key pair for our server, *unix.vineyard.net*.
5. Create a signing request from *unix.vineyard.net* to Nitroba, asking Nitroba to sign the *unix.vineyard.net* key.
6. Take the key signing request we created for the *unix.vineyard.net* server and sign it with the *unix.vineyard.net* public key.
7. Encrypt the CA private key with a passphrase to prevent unauthorized use.
8. Decline to encrypt the server key with a passphrase.

This may seem complicated, but in fact it is all done automatically by the OpenSSL *makecert.ca* script, as shown in Example 17-1.

Example 17-1. Creating CA and server certificates using OpenSSL's makecert.ca script

```
unix# cd /usr/ports/www/apache13-modssl; make certificate TYPE=custom
===>  Creating Test Certificate for Server
SSL Certificate Generation Utility (mkcert.sh)
Copyright (c) 1998-2000 Ralf S. Engelschall, All Rights Reserved.

Generating custom certificate signed by own CA [CUSTOM]

_____

STEP 0: Decide the signature algorithm used for certificates
The generated X.509 certificates can contain either
RSA or DSA based ingredients. Select the one you want to use.
Signature Algorithm ((R)SA or (D)SA) [R]:R

_____

STEP 1: Generating RSA private key for CA (1024 bit) [ca.key]
3660275 semi-random bytes loaded
Generating RSA private key, 1024 bit long modulus
.....++++++
.......................++++++
e is 65537 (0x10001)

_____

STEP 2: Generating X.509 certificate signing request for CA [ca.csr]
Using configuration from .mkcert.cfg
You are about to be asked to enter information that will be incorporated
```

Example 17-1. Creating CA and server certificates using OpenSSL's makecert.ca script (continued)

```
into your certificate request.
What you are about to enter is what is called a Distinguished Name or a DN.
There are quite a few fields but you can leave some blank
For some fields there will be a default value,
If you enter '.', the field will be left blank.
-----
1. Country Name            (2 letter code) [XY]:US
2. State or Province Name   (full name)     [Snake Desert]:MA
3. Locality Name            (eg, city)      [Snake Town]:Nitroba Village
4. Organization Name        (eg, company)   [Snake Oil, Ltd]:Nitroba Networks
5. Organizational Unit Name (eg, section)   [Certificate Authority]:
6. Common Name              (eg, CA name)   [Snake Oil CA]:Nitroba CA
7. Email Address            (eg, name@FQDN) [ca@snakeoil.dom]:keys@nitroba.com
8. Certificate Validity     (days)          [365]:3650
```

```
STEP 3: Generating X.509 certificate for CA signed by itself [ca.crt]
Certificate Version (1 or 3) [3]:
Signature ok
subject=/C=US/ST=MA/L=Nitroba Village/O=Nitroba Networks/OU=Certificate Authority/
CN=Nitroba CA/Email=keys@nitroba.com
Getting Private key
Verify: matching certificate & key modulus
read RSA key
Verify: matching certificate signature
../conf/ssl.crt/ca.crt: /C=US/ST=MA/L=Nitroba Village/O=Nitroba Networks/OU=Certificate
Authority/CN=Nitroba CA/Email=keys@nitroba.com
error 18 at 0 depth lookup:self signed certificate
OK
```

```
STEP 4: Generating RSA private key for SERVER (1024 bit) [server.key]
3660275 semi-random bytes loaded
Generating RSA private key, 1024 bit long modulus
........++++++
.....................++++++
e is 65537 (0x10001)
```

```
STEP 5: Generating X.509 certificate signing request for SERVER [server.csr]
Using configuration from .mkcert.cfg
You are about to be asked to enter information that will be incorporated
into your certificate request.
What you are about to enter is what is called a Distinguished Name or a DN.
There are quite a few fields but you can leave some blank
For some fields there will be a default value,
If you enter '.', the field will be left blank.
-----
1. Country Name            (2 letter code) [XY]:US
2. State or Province Name   (full name)     [Snake Desert]:Massachusetts
3. Locality Name            (eg, city)      [Snake Town]:Vineyard Haven
```

Example 17-1. Creating CA and server certificates using OpenSSL's makecert.ca script (continued)

```
4. Organization Name       (eg, company)  [Snake Oil, Ltd]:Vineyard.NET, Inc.
5. Organizational Unit Name (eg, section)  [Webserver Team]:UNIX Division
6. Common Name             (eg, FQDN)     [www.snakeoil.dom]:unix.vineyard.net
7. Email Address           (eg, name@fqdn) [www@snakeoil.dom]:unix@vineyard.net
8. Certificate Validity    (days)         [365]:
```

```
STEP 6: Generating X.509 certificate signed by own CA [server.crt]
Certificate Version (1 or 3) [3]:
Signature ok
subject=/C=US/ST=MA/L=Vineyard Haven/O=Vineyard.NET, Inc./OU=UNIX Division/CN=unix.
vineyard.net/Email=unix@vineyard.net
Getting CA Private Key
Verify: matching certificate & key modulus
read RSA key
Verify: matching certificate signature
../conf/ssl.crt/server.crt: OK
```

```
STEP 7: Enrypting RSA private key of CA with a pass phrase for security [ca.key]
The contents of the ca.key file (the generated private key) has to be
kept secret. So we strongly recommend you to encrypt the server.key file
with a Triple-DES cipher and a Pass Phrase.
Encrypt the private key now? [Y/n]: y
read RSA key
writing RSA key
Enter PEM pass phrase:
Verifying password - Enter PEM pass phrase:
Fine, you're using an encrypted private key.
```

```
STEP 8: Encrypting RSA private key of SERVER with a pass phrase for security [server.key]
The contents of the server.key file (the generated private key) has to be
kept secret. So we strongly recommend you to encrypt the server.key file
with a Triple-DES cipher and a Pass Phrase.
Encrypt the private key now? [Y/n]: n
Warning, you're using an unencrypted RSA private key.
Please notice this fact and do this on your own risk.
```

```
RESULT: CA and Server Certification Files
```

o   conf/ssl.key/ca.key
    The PEM-encoded RSA private key file of the CA which you can
    use to sign other servers or clients. KEEP THIS FILE PRIVATE!

o   conf/ssl.crt/ca.crt
    The PEM-encoded X.509 certificate file of the CA which you use to
    sign other servers or clients. When you sign clients with it (for
    SSL client authentication) you can configure this file with the
    'SSLCACertificateFile' directive.

Example 17-1. Creating CA and server certificates using OpenSSL's makecert.ca script (continued)

o conf/ssl.key/server.key
   The PEM-encoded RSA private key file of the server which you configure
   with the 'SSLCertificateKeyFile' directive (automatically done
   when you install via APACI). KEEP THIS FILE PRIVATE!

o conf/ssl.crt/server.crt
   The PEM-encoded X.509 certificate file of the server which you configure
   with the 'SSLCertificateFile' directive (automatically done
   when you install via APACI).

o conf/ssl.csr/server.csr
   The PEM-encoded X.509 certificate signing request of the server file which
   you can send to an official Certificate Authority (CA) in order
   to request a real server certificate (signed by this CA instead
   of our own CA) which later can replace the conf/ssl.crt/server.crt
   file.

Congratulations that you establish your server with real certificates.

unix#

The certificate that is created is stored in an ASCII file encoded in the PEM certificate format. The Nitroba certificate is shown in Example 17-2.

Example 17-2. The Nitroba certificate, encoded using the PEM format

```
-----BEGIN CERTIFICATE-----
MIIDMjCCApugAwIBAgIBATANBgkqhkiG9w0BAQQFADCBpTELMAkGA1UEBhMCVVMx
CzAJBgNVBAgTAk1BMRgwFgYDVQQHEw9OaXRyb2JhIFZpbGxhZ2UxGTAXBgNVBAoT
EE5pdHJvYmEgTmV0d29ya3MxHjAcBgNVBAsTFUNlcnRpZmljYXRlIFF1dGhvcml0
eTETMBEGA1UEAxMKTml0cm9iYSBDQTEfMBOGCSqGSIb3DQEJARYQa2V5c0BuaXRy
b2JhLmNvbTAeFwOwMTA3MDgwMzAwMjRaFwOwMjA3MDgwMzAwMjRaMIGmMQswCQYD
VQQGEwJVUzELMAkGA1UECBMCTUExFzAVBgNVBAcTDlZpbmV5YXJkIEhhdmVuMRsw
GQYDVQQKExJWaW5leWFyZC5ORVQsIEluYy4xFjAUBgNVBAsTDVV0SVggRGl2aXNp
b24xGjAYBgNVBAMTEXVuaXgudmluZXlhcmQubmVOMSAwHgYJKoZIhvcNAQkBFhF1
bml4QHZpbmV5YXJkLm5ldDCBnzANBgkqhkiG9w0BAQEFAAOBjQAwgYkCgYEAp27A
cMnfnLhITAY4RZAmEoyl1gtODwj9Rj7cX3QniAs66fI+UtKEeAfOTPYgxUEk/NbY
JmxLyaMdJDoHoc4ZcOy4cFIXVbZUyYAoadPgCjJwOR8vE3sUlmzQO5ZLWZGWUUhW
1kpZPKusuAlEBjlzpsDscX/isdKxpvGOA23tpkECAwEAAaNvMGOwHAYDVRORBBUw
E4ERdW5peEB2aW5leWFyZC5uZXQwOgYJYIZIAYb4QgENBCOWK21vZF9zc2wgZ2Vu
ZXJhdGVkIGN1c3RvbSBzZXJ2ZXIgY2VydGlmaWNhdGUwEQYJYIZIAYb4QgEBBAQD
AgZAMAOGCSqGSIb3DQEBBAUAA4GBABatsM3U/LjtKlq4yrfFS9AOupQfS4AA6cgl
UMrxonYY41/gyUS6V20AWZZiUYyH3ym/vr7buWD2EOjTKsNYd1unCz3vOzsjhSfb
Z6Xg3qOPqlX/2SOvoemcV2iqc2fQ9wHdYAJIzWgV9dTIRsPoa1OIKaA/iivQBZq7
j+mehS9M
-----END CERTIFICATE-----
```

To use these certificates we must follow these steps:

1. View the web server's configuration file and determine the location where *mod_ssl* expects to find the web server's certificate and private key.

2. Install the certificate and the private key for the Unix server in the directory where they are expected by the web server.

3. Put a copy of the Nitroba CA key where it can be loaded into our web browser.

4. Load the Nitroba key into the web browser.

5. Verify that the web page is accessible without generating an error message.

OpenSSL Command Line

If you don't want to use the *mkcert.sh* command, run OpenSSL from the command line. First, use the *openssl* program to create an RSA key. Then use it to create a certificate signing request (CSR). Finally, either sign the request yourself, or provide the CSR to a third-party CA to sign for you. To use OpenSSL to create a server key, with */dev/random* as a source of random numbers, use:

```
# openssl genrsa -out server.key -rand /dev/random 1024
To do this you 0 semi-random bytes loaded
Generating RSA private key, 1024 bit long modulus
.........+++++++++++++
..........................................+++++++++++
e is 65537 (0x10001)
#
```

To create a signing request you will need an OpenSSL configuration file that tells OpenSSL which variables need to be filled in for the CSR. The command line is:

```
unix# openssl req -config openssl.cnf -new -key server.key -out server.csr
Using configuration from openssl.cnf
You are about to be asked to enter information that will be incorporated
into your certificate request.
What you are about to enter is what is called a Distinguished Name or a DN.
There are quite a few fields but you can leave some blank
For some fields there will be a default value,
If you enter '.', the field will be left blank.
-----
Country Name (2 letter code) [AU]:US
State or Province Name (full name) [Some-State]:Massachusetts
Locality Name (eg, city) []:Belmont
Organization Name (eg, company) [Internet Widgits Pty Ltd]:Unix Wizards
Organizational Unit Name (eg, section) []:
Common Name (eg, YOUR name) []:unix.vineyard.net
Email Address []:unix@vineyard.net

Please enter the following 'extra' attributes
to be sent with your certificate request
A challenge password []:my password
An optional company name []:
unix#
```

—continued—

You can use the OpenSSL *ciphers* command to decode this string:

```
unix# cat server.csr
-----BEGIN CERTIFICATE REQUEST-----
MIIB6TCCAVICAQAwgYwxCzAJBgNVBAYTAlVTMRYwFAYDVQQIEw1NYXNzYWNodXNl
dHRzMRAwDgYDVQQHEwdCZWxtb25OMRUwEwYDVQQKEwxVbml4IFdpemFyZHMxGjAY
BgNVBAMTEXVuaXgudmluZXlhcmQubmVOMSAwHgYJKoZIhvcNAQkBFhF1bml4QHZp
bmV5YXJkLm5ldDCBnzANBgkqhkiG9w0BAQEFAAOBjQAwgYkCgYEA4ap7x1pyG3qc
b4BD+AsEdJPLu+lVNgrjLCHPL1FcVIHoi/7Dkm+nP1o+Sm/w56g6ZZUo2fwBj+/f
LtofkoYq19yA1ja+dSntk65qcyFJRmEvgp9nx28vcIFFQR59UnvoA58ZmC7JZkbs
VPiiwOdOIInQmoV/mba28MRPTzjvvzMCAwEAAaAcMBoGCSqGSIb3DQEJBzENEwtt
eSBwYXNzd29yZDANBgkqhkiG9w0BAQQFAAOBgQAeZNpyY33INxsYBpupI+MmYng6
pZNYTZy1gCTOsU53jI4YldBDrI/OTLLaqaBc7Ohg8i55Ue7A6Zhb1eFaORZu6t1v
4wb7Dk+OgtX/J6WqRYee72niO/d7QCYdaTwMkDO8ktw8oUANaYjUrdZ1X6XJINpy
klvIk1a2fZozPsmZDQ==
-----END CERTIFICATE REQUEST-----
unix#
```

The Apache mod_ssl configuration file

The behavior of *mod_ssl* is controlled by the Apache *httpd.conf* configuration file. By default, this file is installed in */usr/local/etc/apache/httpd.conf*. General configuration information for *mod_ssl* is throughout the file. The configuration of the specific keys and certificates is done on a per-host basis in the VirtualHost section, which is usually at the end.

Near the beginning of the Apache 1.3 configuration file is a list of modules that should be loaded when the server starts up. At the end of this list is the <IfDefine SSL> conditional directive, and then an AddModule directive. This will add the *mod_ssl* module if SSL was defined when the web server was compiled:

```
...
AddModule mod_unique_id.c
AddModule mod_so.c
AddModule mod_setenvif.c
<IfDefine SSL>
AddModule mod_ssl.c
</IfDefine>
```

The next reference to SSL is to the port on which this copy of Apache is configured. If SSL support is included, the web server is commanded to listen on ports 80 and 443:

```
#
# Port: The port to which the standalone server listens. For
# ports < 1023, you will need httpd to be run as root initially.
#
Port 80
##
##   SSL Support
```

```
##
## When we also provide SSL we have to listen to the
## standard HTTP port (see above) and to the HTTPS port
##
<IfDefine SSL>
Listen 80
Listen 443
</IfDefine>
```

The next SSL reference adds the MIME types for SSL certificates and certificate revocation lists:

```
##
## SSL Global Context
##
## All SSL configuration in this context applies both to
## the main server and all SSL-enabled virtual hosts.
##


#
#  Some MIME-types for downloading Certificates and CRLs
#
<IfDefine SSL>
AddType application/x-x509-ca-cert .crt
AddType application/x-pkcs7-crl    .crl
</IfDefine>
```

The next section configures how the Apache server will ask for the SSL passphrase (if you encrypted your server key). It sets the SSLSessionCache, a shared memory file that allows SSL servers in different *httpd* processes to share the master secret for SSL sessions, specifies the random number generator that the SSL implementation will use, and sets where SSL-specific errors will be logged:

```
<IfModule mod_ssl.c>

#   Pass Phrase Dialog:
#   Configure the pass phrase gathering process.
#   The filtering dialog program (`builtin' is an internal
#   terminal dialog) has to provide the pass phrase on stdout.
SSLPassPhraseDialog  builtin

#   Inter-Process Session Cache:
#   Configure the SSL Session Cache: First the mechanism
#   to use and second the expiring timeout (in seconds).
#SSLSessionCache         none
#SSLSessionCache         shmht:/var/run/ssl_scache(512000)
#SSLSessionCache         shmcb:/var/run/ssl_scache(512000)
SSLSessionCache         dbm:/var/run/ssl_scache
SSLSessionCacheTimeout  300

#   Semaphore:
#   Configure the path to the mutual exclusion semaphore the
#   SSL engine uses internally for inter-process synchronization.
SSLMutex  file:/var/run/ssl_mutex
```

```
#   Pseudo Random Number Generator (PRNG):
#   Configure one or more sources to seed the PRNG of the
#   SSL library. The seed data should be of good random quality.
#   WARNING! On some platforms /dev/random blocks if not enough entropy
#   is available. This means you then cannot use the /dev/random device
#   because it would lead to very long connection times (as long as
#   it requires to make more entropy available). But usually those
#   platforms additionally provide a /dev/urandom device which doesn't
#   block. So, if available, use this one instead. Read the mod_ssl User
#   Manual for more details.
SSLRandomSeed startup builtin
SSLRandomSeed connect builtin
#SSLRandomSeed startup file:/dev/random  512
#SSLRandomSeed startup file:/dev/urandom 512
#SSLRandomSeed connect file:/dev/random  512
#SSLRandomSeed connect file:/dev/urandom 512
#   Logging:
#   The home of the dedicated SSL protocol logfile. Errors are
#   additionally duplicated in the general error log file.  Put
#   this somewhere where it cannot be used for symlink attacks on
#   a real server (i.e., somewhere where only root can write).
#   Log levels are (ascending order: higher ones include lower ones):
#   none, error, warn, info, trace, debug.
SSLLog      /var/log/ssl_engine_log
SSLLogLevel info

</IfModule>
```

At the bottom of the *httpd.conf* file is the VirtualHost section for the SSL server.

Unlike conventional HTTP, SSL 2.0 (but not 3.0) requires that you give a separate IP address to each domain hosted at your web server. This is because SSL encrypts the initial HTTP query sent from the client to the server, so it is not possible for the web server to determine the destination host before the certificate is sent. SSL 3.0 servers can send multiple certificates to an SSL 3.0 client when the client connects, so it is not necessary to have a separate IP address for each domain. But it is recommended for perfomance reasons.

The VirtualHost sets its own DocumentRoot, ServerName, ServerAdmin, ErrorLog, etc. Normally, they're the same as the unencrypted server defined at the top of the file.

```
<IfDefine SSL>

##
## SSL Virtual Host Context
##

<VirtualHost _default_:443>

#  General setup for the virtual host
DocumentRoot "/usr/local/www/data"
ServerName unix.vineyard.net
```

```
ServerAdmin unix@vineyard.net
ErrorLog /var/log/httpd-error.log
TransferLog /var/log/httpd-access.log
```

The next section configures SSL for the virtual host. If SSL is not turned on, the Apache server will speak traditional unencrypted HTTP on port 443—probably not what you want. After SSL is switched on, the set of ciphers to be used are selected:

```
#   SSL Engine Switch:
#   Enable/Disable SSL for this virtual host.
SSLEngine on

#   SSL Cipher Suite:
#   List the ciphers that the client is permitted to negotiate.
#   See the mod_ssl documentation for a complete list.
SSLCipherSuite ALL:!ADH:!EXPORT56:RC4+RSA:+HIGH:+MEDIUM:+LOW:+SSLv2:+EXP:+eNULL
```

You can use the OpenSSL ciphers command to decode this string:

```
% openssl ciphers -v "ALL:\!ADH:\!EXPORT56:RC4+RSA:+HIGH:+MEDIUM:+LOW:+SSLv2:+EXP:+eNULL"
DHE-DSS-RC4-SHA         SSLv3 Kx=DH       Au=DSS  Enc=RC4(128)  Mac=SHA1
EDH-RSA-DES-CBC3-SHA    SSLv3 Kx=DH       Au=RSA  Enc=3DES(168) Mac=SHA1
EDH-DSS-DES-CBC3-SHA    SSLv3 Kx=DH       Au=DSS  Enc=3DES(168) Mac=SHA1
DES-CBC3-SHA            SSLv3 Kx=RSA      Au=RSA  Enc=3DES(168) Mac=SHA1
RC4-SHA                 SSLv3 Kx=RSA      Au=RSA  Enc=RC4(128)  Mac=SHA1
RC4-MD5                 SSLv3 Kx=RSA      Au=RSA  Enc=RC4(128)  Mac=MD5
EDH-RSA-DES-CBC-SHA     SSLv3 Kx=DH       Au=RSA  Enc=DES(56)   Mac=SHA1
EDH-DSS-DES-CBC-SHA     SSLv3 Kx=DH       Au=DSS  Enc=DES(56)   Mac=SHA1
DES-CBC-SHA             SSLv3 Kx=RSA      Au=RSA  Enc=DES(56)   Mac=SHA1
DES-CBC3-MD5            SSLv2 Kx=RSA      Au=RSA  Enc=3DES(168) Mac=MD5
RC2-CBC-MD5            SSLv2 Kx=RSA      Au=RSA  Enc=RC2(128)  Mac=MD5
RC4-MD5                 SSLv2 Kx=RSA      Au=RSA  Enc=RC4(128)  Mac=MD5
RC4-64-MD5             SSLv2 Kx=RSA      Au=RSA  Enc=RC4(64)   Mac=MD5
DES-CBC-MD5            SSLv2 Kx=RSA      Au=RSA  Enc=DES(56)   Mac=MD5
EXP-EDH-RSA-DES-CBC-SHA SSLv3 Kx=DH(512)  Au=RSA  Enc=DES(40)   Mac=SHA1 export
EXP-EDH-DSS-DES-CBC-SHA SSLv3 Kx=DH(512)  Au=DSS  Enc=DES(40)   Mac=SHA1 export
EXP-DES-CBC-SHA         SSLv3 Kx=RSA(512) Au=RSA  Enc=DES(40)   Mac=SHA1 export
EXP-RC2-CBC-MD5        SSLv3 Kx=RSA(512) Au=RSA  Enc=RC2(40)   Mac=MD5  export
EXP-RC4-MD5            SSLv3 Kx=RSA(512) Au=RSA  Enc=RC4(40)   Mac=MD5  export
EXP-RC2-CBC-MD5        SSLv2 Kx=RSA(512) Au=RSA  Enc=RC2(40)   Mac=MD5  export
EXP-RC4-MD5            SSLv2 Kx=RSA(512) Au=RSA  Enc=RC4(40)   Mac=MD5  export
%
```

Now it is time to specify the path of the certificate and the keys. A DSA certificate is only required if you intend to use the DSA ciphers; you probably don't want to do that.

```
#   Server Certificate:
#   Point SSLCertificateFile at a PEM encoded certificate.  If
#   the certificate is encrypted, then you will be prompted for a
#   pass phrase.  Note that a kill -HUP will prompt again. A test
#   certificate can be generated with `make certificate' under
#   built time. Keep in mind that if you've both a RSA and a DSA
#   certificate you can configure both in parallel (to also allow
#   the use of DSA ciphers, etc.)
```

```
SSLCertificateFile /usr/local/etc/apache/ssl.crt/server.crt
#SSLCertificateFile /usr/local/etc/apache/ssl.crt/server-dsa.crt

#   Server Private Key:
#   If the key is not combined with the certificate, use this
#   directive to point at the key file.  Keep in mind that if
#   you've both a RSA and a DSA private key you can configure
#   both in parallel (to also allow the use of DSA ciphers, etc.)
SSLCertificateKeyFile /usr/local/etc/apache/ssl.key/server.key
#SSLCertificateKeyFile /usr/local/etc/apache/ssl.key/server-dsa.key
```

These options are used for client authentication using SSL; we'll discuss them in detail in Chapter 21. For now, let's leave them turned off:

```
#   Server Certificate Chain:
#   Point SSLCertificateChainFile at a file containing the
#   concatenation of PEM encoded CA certificates which form the
#   certificate chain for the server certificate. Alternatively
#   the referenced file can be the same as SSLCertificateFile
#   when the CA certificates are directly appended to the server
#   certificate for convenience.
#SSLCertificateChainFile /usr/local/etc/apache/ssl.crt/ca.crt

#   Certificate Authority (CA):
#   Set the CA certificate verification path where to find CA
#   certificates for client authentication or alternatively one
#   huge file containing all of them (file must be PEM encoded)
#   Note: Inside SSLCACertificatePath you need hash symlinks
#         to point to the certificate files. Use the provided
#         Makefile to update the hash symlinks after changes.
#SSLCACertificatePath /usr/local/etc/apache/ssl.crt
#SSLCACertificateFile /usr/local/etc/apache/ssl.crt/ca-bundle.crt

#   Certificate Revocation Lists (CRL):
#   Set the CA revocation path where to find CA CRLs for client
#   authentication or alternatively one huge file containing all
#   of them (file must be PEM encoded)
#   Note: Inside SSLCARevocationPath you need hash symlinks
#         to point to the certificate files. Use the provided
#         Makefile to update the hash symlinks after changes.
#SSLCARevocationPath /usr/local/etc/apache/ssl.crl
#SSLCARevocationFile /usr/local/etc/apache/ssl.crl/ca-bundle.crl

#   Client Authentication (Type):
#   Client certificate verification type and depth.  Types are
#   none, optional, require and optional_no_ca.  Depth is a
#   number which specifies how deeply to verify the certificate
#   issuer chain before deciding the certificate is not valid.
#SSLVerifyClient require
#SSLVerifyDepth  10

#   Access Control:
#   With SSLRequire you can do per-directory access control based
#   on arbitrary complex boolean expressions containing server
#   variable checks and other lookup directives.  The syntax is a
```

```
#   mixture between C and Perl.  See the mod_ssl documentation
#   for more details.
#<Location />
#SSLRequire (    %{SSL_CIPHER} !~ m/^(EXP|NULL)/ \
#              and %{SSL_CLIENT_S_DN_O} eq "Snake Oil, Ltd." \
#              and %{SSL_CLIENT_S_DN_OU} in {"Staff", "CA", "Dev"} \
#              and %{TIME_WDAY} >= 1 and %{TIME_WDAY} <= 5 \
#              and %{TIME_HOUR} >= 8 and %{TIME_HOUR} <= 20        ) \
#           or %{REMOTE_ADDR} =~ m/^192\.76\.162\.[0-9]+$/
#</Location>
```

This SSLOptions directive allows you to adjust the SSL implementation, as indicated by the comments. The default configuration uses the +StdEnvVars option for any URL that references a CGI, SHTML, Perl, or PHP3 script. This option causes *mod_ssl* to set variables allowing the script to determine whether or not SSL was used to invoke the script, which encryption algorithm was used, its strength, and other useful data. If you are using SSL client-side certificates, the certificate information will be passed in an environment variable as well:

```
#   SSL Engine Options:
#   Set various options for the SSL engine.
#   o FakeBasicAuth:
#     Translate the client X.509 into a Basic Authorization.  This means that
#     the standard Auth/DBMAuth methods can be used for access control.  The
#     user name is the `one line' version of the client's X.509 certificate.
#     Note that no password is obtained from the user. Every entry in the user
#     file needs this password: `xxj31ZMTZzkVA'.
#   o ExportCertData:
#     This exports two additional environment variables: SSL_CLIENT_CERT and
#     SSL_SERVER_CERT. These contain the PEM-encoded certificates of the
#     server (always existing) and the client (only existing when client
#     authentication is used). This can be used to import the certificates
#     into CGI scripts.
#   o StdEnvVars:
#     This exports the standard SSL/TLS related `SSL_*' environment variables.
#     Per default this exportation is switched off for performance reasons,
#     because the extraction step is an expensive operation and is usually
#     useless for serving static content. So one usually enables the
#     exportation for CGI and SSI requests only.
#   o CompatEnvVars:
#     This exports obsolete environment variables for backward compatibility
#     to Apache-SSL 1.x, mod_ssl 2.0.x, Sioux 1.0 and Stronghold 2.x. Use this
#     to provide compatibility to existing CGI scripts.
#   o StrictRequire:
#     This denies access when "SSLRequireSSL" or "SSLRequire" applied even
#     under a "Satisfy any" situation, i.e., when it applies, access is denied
#     and no other module can change it.
#   o OptRenegotiate:
#     This enables optimized SSL connection renegotiation handling when SSL
#     directives are used in per-directory context.
#SSLOptions +FakeBasicAuth +ExportCertData +CompatEnvVars +StrictRequire
<Files ~ "\.(cgi|shtml|phtml|php3?)$">
    SSLOptions +StdEnvVars
```

```
</Files>
<Directory "/usr/local/www/cgi-bin">
    SSLOptions +StdEnvVars
</Directory>
```

Some versions of Microsoft Internet Explorer generate errors when the SSL server uses the SSL keepalive facility. These errors result from a bug in the way that Internet Explorer handles SSL requests; they are tremendously annoying. The errors don't happen when Internet Explorer is used with Internet Information Server, since IIS has similar errors in its implementation. If you are using *mod_ssl*, you can instruct the module to not use keepalives if the HTTP User Agent contains the string "MSIE"—that is, if it is Microsoft Internet Explorer.

```
#   SSL Protocol Adjustments:
#   The safe and default but still SSL/TLS standard compliant shutdown
#   approach is that mod_ssl sends the close notify alert but doesn't wait for
#   the close notify alert from client. When you need a different shutdown
#   approach you can use one of the following variables:
#   o ssl-unclean-shutdown:
#     This forces an unclean shutdown when the connection is closed, i.e., no
#     SSL close notify alert is sent or allowed to received.  This violates
#     the SSL/TLS standard but is needed for some brain-dead browsers. Use
#     this when you receive I/O errors because of the standard approach where
#     mod_ssl sends the close notify alert.
#   o ssl-accurate-shutdown:
#     This forces an accurate shutdown when the connection is closed, i.e., a
#     SSL close notify alert is sent and mod_ssl waits for the close notify
#     alert of the client. This is 100% SSL/TLS standard compliant, but in
#     practice often causes hanging connections with brain-dead browsers. Use
#     this only for browsers where you know that their SSL implementation
#     works correctly.
#   Notice: Most problems of broken clients are also related to the HTTP
#   keep-alive facility, so you usually additionally want to disable
#   keep-alive for those clients, too. Use variable "nokeepalive" for this.
#   Similarly, one has to force some clients to use HTTP/1.0 to workaround
#   their broken HTTP/1.1 implementation. Use variables "downgrade-1.0" and
#   "force-response-1.0" for this.
SetEnvIf User-Agent ".*MSIE.*" \
         nokeepalive ssl-unclean-shutdown \
         downgrade-1.0 force-response-1.0
```

Finally, *mod_ssl* creates its own log file of the protocols and ciphers used for each HTTP request:

```
#   Per-Server Logging:
#   The home of a custom SSL log file. Use this when you want a
#   compact non-error SSL logfile on a virtual host basis.
CustomLog /var/log/ssl_request_log \
         "%t %h %{SSL_PROTOCOL}x %{SSL_CIPHER}x \"%r\" %b"

</VirtualHost>

</IfDefine>
```

Installing the key and certificate on the web server

Having read this log file, we now know where the files we created should be located:*

/usr/ports/www/apache13-modssl/work/apache_1.3.20/conf/ssl.key/server.key
> This is your SSL server private key. It should be installed at */usr/local/etc/apache/ssl.key/server.key*.

/usr/ports/www/apache13-modssl/work/apache_1.3.20/conf/ssl.crt/server.crt
> This is your SSL server certificate, signed by the Nitroba certification authority. It should be installed at */usr/local/etc/apache/ssl.crt/server.crt*.

/usr/ports/www/apache13-modssl/work/apache_1.3.20/conf/ssl.crt/ca.crt
> This is the certificate for the Nitroba certification authority that we created previously. It is not installed into the Apache hierarchy, because the web server does not need it. Instead, it should be placed somewhere underneath the Document-Root so that the server key can be downloaded to web browsers. We are going to install this file in */usr/local/www/data/nitroba.crt*.

After the files are updated, it is necessary to stop *httpd* and restart it:

```
unix# cd /usr/ports/www/apache13-modssl/work/apache_1.3.20/conf
unix# cp ssl.key/server.key /usr/local/etc/apache/ssl.key/server.key
unix# cp ssl.crt/server.crt /usr/local/etc/apache/ssl.crt/server.crt
unix# cp ssl.crt/ca.crt /usr/local/www/data/nitroba.crt.
unix# cp ssl.crt/ca.crt /usr/local/www/data/nitroba.crt
unix#
unix# apachectl stop
/usr/local/sbin/apachectl stop: httpd stopped
unix# apachectl startssl
/usr/local/sbin/apachectl startssl: httpd started
unix#
```

If we now go to *https://unix.vineyard.net/*, we get a different alert, as shown in Figure 17-4. This time we are told the certificate is valid but not trusted. If you click the "Install Certificate" button at this point you will bring up the Internet Explorer Certificate Installation Wizard. However, even if you install the *unix.vineyard.net* certificate, the certificate will not be trusted. This is because the you need to install the Nitroba CA certificate.

Installing the Nitroba CA certificate into Internet Explorer

For Internet Explorer to use the *unix.vineyard.net* server certificate, it is necessary to add the Nitroba CA certificate to Internet Explorer's Trusted CA Certificate Store. This is easy to do! Recall that the Nitroba CA certificate was placed in the Apache

---

* If you followed the installation script's instructions and typed *make certificate* before you typed *make install*, then you do not need to manually move the keys and certificates into their final locations, because this has already been done for you.

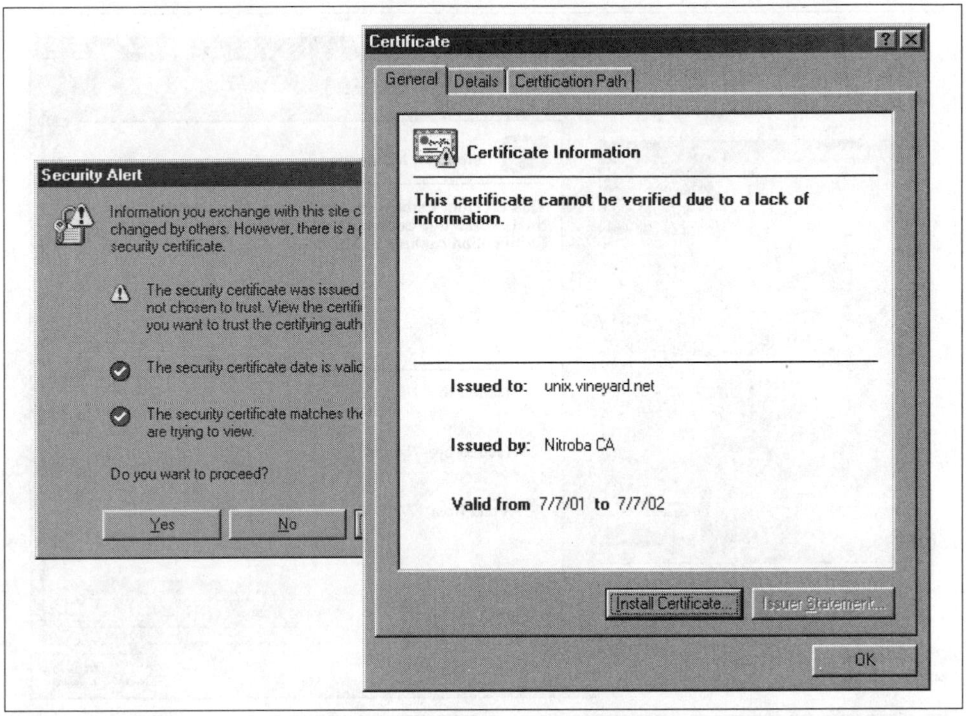

Figure 17-4. We get a different security alert after the unix.vineyard.net certificate is loaded onto the mod_ssl apache web server. If you click on the Certification Path tab, you'll be told "The issuer of this certificate was not able to be found," because no certificate for the Nitroba CA is on file.

DocumentRoot directory with the name *nitroba.crt*. To install the certificate, we simply follow these steps:

1. Visit *http://unix.vineyard.net/nitroba.crt*. This will cause Internet Explorer to download the certificate file. Tell IE that you wish to "Open" the certificate, rather than save it. Opening the certificate causes Internet Explorer to display the Certificate Information. (See Figure 17-5.)

2. Click the Install button on the Certificate Information window. This will bring up the Certificate Manager Import Wizard. Tell the Wizard to import the certificate automatically into the correct store based on the certificate type. (See Figure 17-6.)

3. Finally, Internet Explorer displays the relevant fields of the certificate and asks if you really want to import it. Click Yes. (See Figure 17-7.)

Once the certificate is imported, we can now visit *https://unix.vineyard.net/* without getting any errors at all! From within Internet Explorer, select File → Properties to display the properties of the HTML page, then select Certificates to learn about the certificate that was used to encrypt the page's SSL connection. The Certificate Path page indicates that the certificate *unix.vineyard.net* was signed by the Nitroba CA.

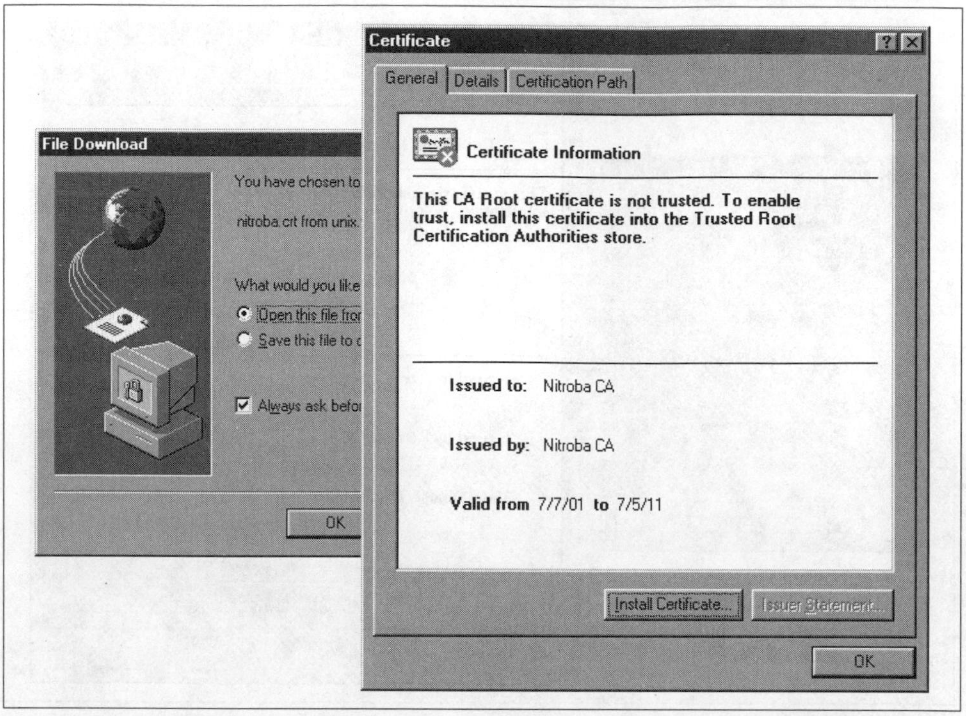

Figure 17-5. When you visit http://unix.vineyard.net/nitroba.crt, the Nitroba CA certificate is downloaded. Internet Explorer allows you to open the certificate or save it. If you open the certificate, IE will display the Certificate Information and allow you to install the certificate.

The General page says that the Nitroba CA certificate has been approved for many uses, including:

- Windows System Component Verification
- Windows Hardware Driver Verification
- Allowing data on disk to be encrypted
- Allowing secured communication on the Internet
- Allowing you to digitally sign a Certificate Trust List
- Allowing data to be signed with the current time
- Ensuring that email came from the sender
- Protecting email from tampering
- Ensuring that the content of email cannot be viewed by others
- Protecting software from tampering after publication
- Ensuring that software came from a software publisher
- Guaranteeing your identity to a remote computer
- Guaranteeing the identity of a remote computer

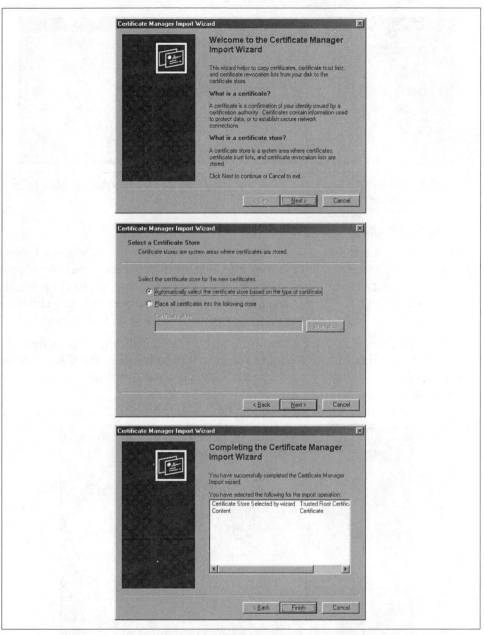

Figure 17-6. The Certificate Manager Import Wizard allows you to import a certificate into the certificate store of your choice. For most uses, just take the default choices.

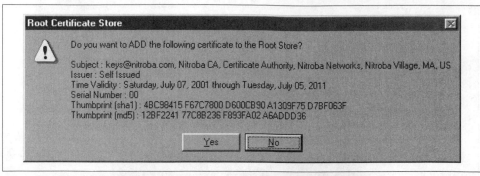

Figure 17-7. After the Certificate Manager Import Wizard runs, Internet Explorer displays the information about the certificate and allows you to import it or not.

Installing the Nitroba CA certificate into Netscape Navigator

Installing new CA certificates is somewhat easier using Netscape. When you browse to a web site that is signed with an unknown CA, both Netscape 4 and Netscape 6 allow you to reject the certificate, accept it for the current session, or accept it permanently (see Figure 17-3). This is somewhat simpler than Internet Explorer's approach of requiring you to download the CA key before the web site itself will be used.

The procedure for adding a CA certificate to Netscape is analogous to adding the certificate to Internet Explorer: simply visit a URL which causes the CA key to be downloaded. This brings up Navigator's Downloading Certificate window (see Figure 17-8).

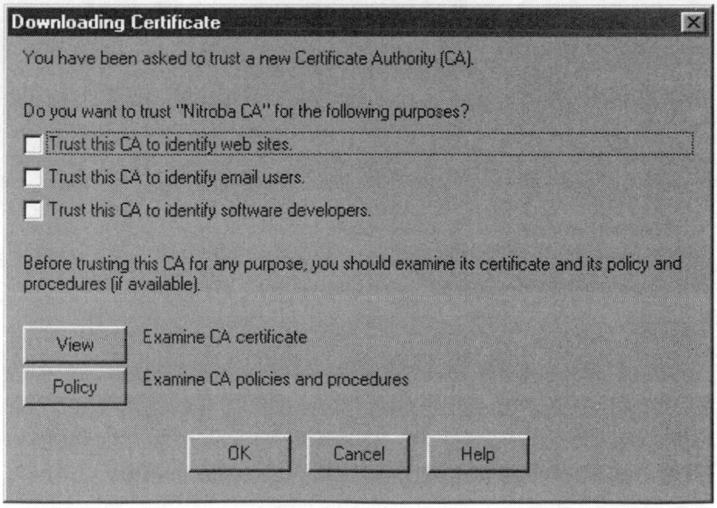

Figure 17-8. When you download a CA key with Netscape Navigator, you can choose what uses should be allowed to the CA key.

Netscape's interface also allows you to view the CA's certificate policy statement, if the location of a statement has been identified in the CA's certificate. No such policy was created for the Nitroba certificate—another reason that you should not trust it!

Securing Other Services

You can use OpenSSL to secure other services besides HTTP. Many sites, for instance, will want to use OpenSSL to secure POP, IMAP, and SMTP, as all of these services potentially send usernames and passwords over the Internet without encryption. Using SSL causes these services to be encrypted, dramatically reducing the chances of having passwords compromised.

SSL encryption can be added to any standard Unix daemon using *sslwrap*. The *sslwrap* program is started by */etc/inetd* according to a specification in the */etc/inetd. conf* file. The program's command-line options include the certificate that it should use and the address of the private key.

Here is a sample of a section from the */etc/inetd.conf* file on the Unix server that was created in the previous examples. It provides for POP, IMAP, and SMTP encryption using the *pop3s*, *imaps*, and *smtps* service names:

```
pop3s   stream  tcp    nowait  root    /usr/local/bin/sslwrap sslwrap
  -cert /usr/local/etc/apache/conf/ssl.crt/server.crt
  -key /usr/local/etc/apache/conf/ssl.key/server.key -port pop3
imaps stream  tcp    nowait  root    /usr/local/bin/sslwrap sslwrap
  -cert /usr/local/etc/apache/conf/ssl.crt/server.crt
  -key /usr/local/etc/apache/conf/ssl.key/server.key -port imap
smtps stream  tcp    nowait  root    /usr/local/bin/sslwrap sslwrap
  -cert /usr/local/etc/apache/conf/ssl.crt/server.crt
  -key /usr/local/etc/apache/conf/ssl.key/server.key -port smtp
```

The *sslwrap* program is not installed by default, but can be installed from */usr/ports/ security/sslwrap* on FreeBSD systems.

Installing an SSL Certificate on Microsoft IIS

Microsoft's Internet Information Services (IIS) is a web service that contains all of the tools necessary to create and deploy certificates for an SSL-enabled web server. For a discussion of how to install IIS and control access to IIS web pages and directories, see Chapter 20.

To create SSL certificates, follow these steps:

1. Run the Computer Management application from the Administrative Tools folder of the computer's Control Panel.

2. Select Services and Applications → Internet Informaton Services → Default Web Site from the tree.

3. Choose "Properties" from the Action menu.

4. Select the "Directory Security" tab.

5. Press the "Server Certificate…" button inside the "Secure communications" box. This will start the "Web Server Certificate Wizard" (see Figure 17-9).

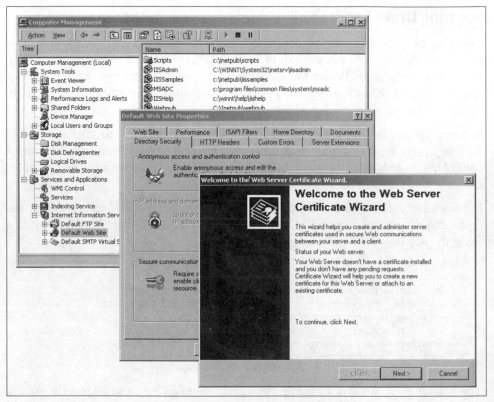

Figure 17-9. The Web Server Certificate Wizard

6. Select "Create a new certificate."

7. Select "Prepare the request now, but send it later."

8. Choose a name for the certificate and a bit length. Although the default is 512 bits, you should probably choose 1024 bits or more.

9. Specify an Organization and an Organizational unit.

10. Specify the domain of your server for the Common name (e.g., *www.company.com*).

11. Specify the geographical information.

12. You will now be prompted for a location in which to save the certificate. The default is *c:\certreq.txt*.

13. The certificate request will be created in the file that you specify.

After you create the certificate, you can send it to a certification authority. Alternatively, you can sign it yourself using OpenSSL. Here we sign the certificate request using OpenSSL:

```
# openssl ca -in /tmp/req.csr -out /tmp/out.cer -policy policy_anything
Using configuration from /etc/ssl/openssl.cnf
Check that the request matches the signature
Signature ok
The Subjects Distinguished Name is as follows
commonName            :PRINTABLE:'localhost'
organizationalUnitName:PRINTABLE:'Secure Server division'
organizationName      :PRINTABLE:'Servers Are Us'
localityName          :PRINTABLE:'Belmont'
stateOrProvinceName   :PRINTABLE:'Massachusetts'
countryName           :PRINTABLE:'AU'
Certificate is to be certified until Sep 17 04:47:53 2002 GMT (365 days)
Sign the certificate? [y/n]:y


1 out of 1 certificate requests certified, commit? [y/n]y
Write out database with 1 new entries
Data Base Updated
#
```

Once you have a signed certificate, you will use the Web Server Certificate Wizard to import the certificate into IIS:

1. Press the "Certificate..." button on the "Default Web Site Properties" window to start the Web Server Certificate Wizard.

2. You will be told that there is a pending certificate request and that the certification authority has not yet responded. You can either delete the pending request or process it; the latter installs the certificate. Select "Process the pending request and install the certificate."

3. You will be prompted for the path and filename of the certification authority's reponse.

4. You will be shown a summary of the fields on the certificate. Click "Next."

5. Click "Finish." The certificate is now imported.

6. IIS should automatically start up SSL services.

7. Once the certificate is loaded, you can manage SSL communications by clicking the "Edit..." button on the Default Web Site Properties window. This will bring up the "Secure Communications" window, as shown in Figure 17-10.

Obtaining a Certificate from a Commercial CA

The self-signed certificates created earlier in this chapter allow you to take advantage of the capabilities of any SSL-enabled client or server. These certificates are sufficient

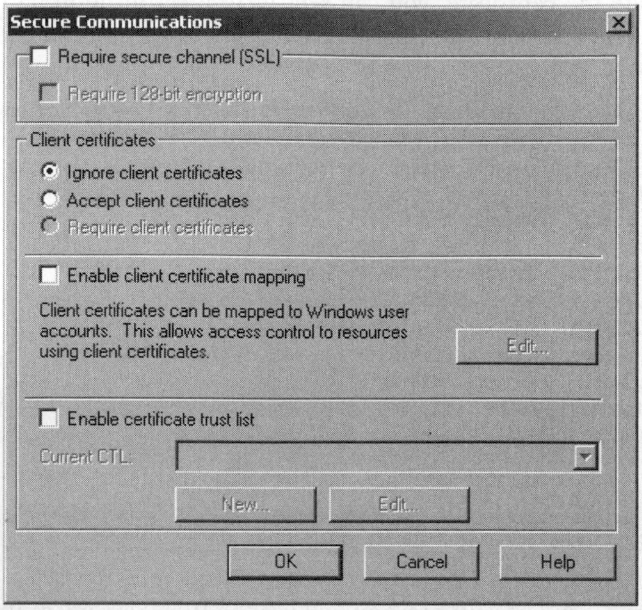

Figure 17-10. The Secure Communications window allows you to manage the SSL certificate installed on your copy of IIS

for the overwhelming majority of uses. However, many organizations choose to purchase a certificate from a certification authority such as VeriSign. There are several advantages to using a certificate that is signed by a commercial CA in preference to a key that is self-signed:

- Because VeriSign and other CAs have their keys distributed with Internet Explorer and Netscape, your users will not have to manually add your internal CA's key to their web browser.

- Because VeriSign and other CAs attempt to verify the identity of an organization before signing that organization's key, your users may have some assurance that your web server actually belongs to the organization whose name is on the certificate. This can be useful in e-commerce applications where you are asking users to divulge personal information such as their names, addresses, Social Security numbers, or credit card numbers.

If you wish to use a certificate from a commercial CA, you will need to create a certificate signing request, send the CSR to the organization, convince the CA to sign your key, and install the certificate that you get back from the CA. The process of convincing the CA to sign your key usually involves presenting the organization with some sort of tangible proof that you represent the organization whose key is being signed and then paying the CA some amount of money.

VeriSign now offers a 14-day "trial" certificate that companies can use to get up and running immediately. Like the certificates created earlier in this chapter, the VeriSign trial certificate is signed with a "test CA root" rather than the actual VeriSign production root. This test root allows VeriSign to hand out test certificates automatically from its web site, before the bona fides of an organization are verified. Once the bona fides are verified and VeriSign's fee is paid, VeriSign will send you a new certificate that can be installed on top of the trial certificate. No new CSR needs to be produced because both certificates handle the same key.

The steps to obtaining a trial certificate are:

1. Generate a certificate signing request (CSR). This request can be signed by any CA. In the previous pages, it was signed by the Nitroba CA. But it can also be signed by a commercial CA such as VeriSign (see Example 17-3).

2. Submit the CSR.

3. Complete VeriSign's application.

4. Install the test CA root.

5. Install the test server ID.

Generating a CSR with OpenSSL is quite easy: if you followed these steps, a CSR was automatically generated when you created your self-signed key. In fact, OpenSSL generated two CSRs: one for the Nitroba CA, and one for the Unix server. Both of these requests were then signed with the Nitroba CA's private key. If you want to have VeriSign sign your server's public key, all you need to do is to paste the server's CSR into the form on the VeriSign web site (see Figure 17-11). Be careful not to paste in the CSR for your private CA.

Example 17-3. The unix.vineyard.net server certificate signing request (CSR)

```
unix# cat server.csr
-----BEGIN CERTIFICATE REQUEST-----
MIIB5zCCAVACAQAwgaYxCzAJBgNVBAYTAlVTMQswCQYDVQQIEwJNQTEXMBUGA1UE
BxMOVmluZXlhcmQgSGF2ZW4xGzAZBgNVBAoTElZpbmV5YXJkLk5FVCwgSW5jLjEW
MBQGA1UECxMNVU5JWCBEaXZpc2lvbjEaMBgGA1UEAxMRdW5peC52aW5leWFyZC5u
ZXQxIDAeBgkqhkiG9w0BCQEWEXVuaXhAdmluZXlhcmQubmVOMIGfMA0GCSqGSIb3
DQEBAQUAA4GNADCBiQKBgQCnbsBwyd+cuEhMBjhFkCYSjKXWC3QPCP1GPtxfdCeI
Czrp8j5SOoR4B85M9iDFQST81tgmbEvJoxOkOgehzhlzTLhwUhdVtlTJgChp0+AK
MnA5Hy8TexSWbNA7lktZkZZRSFbWSlk8q6y4CUQGOXOmwOxxf+KxOrGm8bQDbe2m
QQIDAQABoAAwDQYJKoZIhvcNAQEEBQADgYEAOFvLUdhMkXEE61hNNnbimHgMCfve
tFFOjxJvJJd3S2ufDV4Gp5HQBNPRd4JXFoMVdaRzB9ysDLgX98IzwbktTn9W1dEd
1D8z3TtFttbB2pQ/FRg7Sst+Ix+zk1BOjhFGnCPubr/VZPfUGAYqiFRinRXIBe4j
1iCQDrLZyUxZJ3A=
-----END CERTIFICATE REQUEST-----
```

It is important to be sure that your CSR has the two-letter ISO abbreviation for your country and not the full, spelled-out name, and that the CSR has the full, spelled-out name of your state, and not a postal abbreviation. VeriSign will not process your

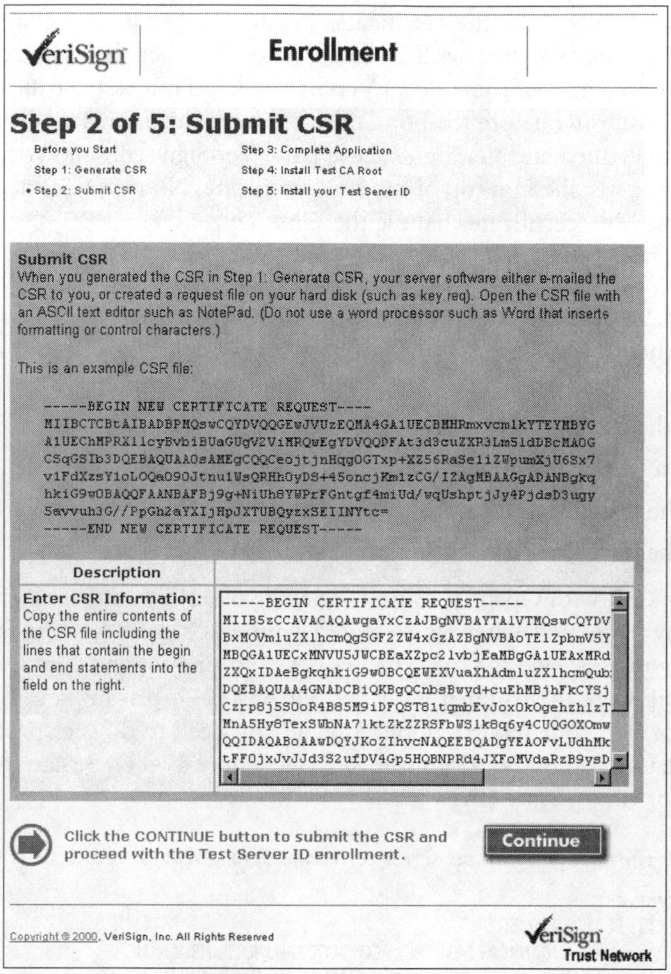

Figure 17-11. To get a VeriSign certificate, you must paste your CSR into VeriSign's web site.

request if there is a problem with your CSR. If there are no problems, VeriSign will send you the completed certificate by email. Copy this certificate into a file and place it in the location on your web server, as indicated by the Apache configuration file or by the IIS configuration.

When Things Go Wrong

When a web browser makes a connection to an SSL web server, it checks on a number of the fields in the server's X.509 v3 certificates. If the contents of a field don't match what the web browser expects, it can alert the user or disallow the connection.

This section summarizes some of the problems that can befall even the most well-intentioned site administrators.

Not Yet Valid and Expired Certificates

When a web browser opens an SSL connection to a server, it checks the dates on the certificates that the server presents to make sure that they are valid. If the certificate has expired (or if the client's clock and calendar are not properly set), it will alert the user. Some programs that use SSL simply inform the user that a certificate has expired (or is not yet valid) and give the user the option to continue. Other programs do not give the user the option.

If the date on the certificate looks valid, then it is possible the date on the user's computer is wrong—for example, the clocks of many desktop computers will reset to 1980 if their internal battery dies. If you can't figure out why a certificate is out of date, check your computer's clock.

Certificate Renewal

Like most other identification documents, X.509 v3 certificates expire. When they expire, you need to get new ones if you wish to continue to offer X.509 v3–based services. In many cases, you can simply request that a new certificate be issued for your existing public key.

The authority that issues the X.509 v3 certificate determines when the certificate will expire. These days, most third-party CAs seem to be issuing certificates that expire one year after the date on which they are signed. Why pick one year? Here are some practical reasons:

- The longer a certificate is used, the greater the chance that its associated private key will be compromised.

- The speed of computers and our knowledge of public key cryptography are both improving rapidly. A secure certificate that is signed today may be unsecure in two years because of advances in technology. Short expiration times therefore increase confidence in the public key infrastructure.

- Business licenses tend to be for a period of one or two years. If a business license is used in part to validate a certificate, it seems unreasonable to issue a certificate that outlives these master documents.

- Most third-party CAs are selling certification services. Selling a certificate that expires in one year means that you can count on a steady revenue stream from certificate renewals roughly a year after you first go into business.

- Having a certificate expire once a year assures that companies that fire their webmasters and don't hire anybody new will be suitably punished before long.

Be sure to obtain a new certificate for your organization well before your current certificate expires!

Remember, it is the SSL client that determines whether or not a server's certificate has expired when it connects to the server. Thus, clients that have their clocks set incorrectly frequently report that a server's certificate has expired, when in fact it has not.

When you apply for your new certificate, you may wish to request that it become valid before your current certificate expires. Otherwise, some users may be locked out of your web site when you change over from one certificate to another, because they have slightly different ideas of what time it is. For safety's sake, certificates should be replaced at least 36 hours before they expire.

Some SSL servers allow you to equip them with multiple server certificates. These servers must be running SSL 3.0 or above to download multiple certificates over a single SSL connection.

Wrong Server Address

Web server certificates contain a special field that indicates the Internet hostname of the computer on which the server is running. When a browser opens an SSL connection to a web server, it checks this field to make sure that the hostname in the certificate is the same as the hostname of the computer to which it has opened a connection.

The purpose of this check is to ensure that certificates will be used only on the particular machine for which they are issued. This allegedly provides more security: through an attack called DNS spoofing, it's possible to confuse the client computer's system that translates between domain names and IP addresses. The client thinks it is jumping to a particular web site, like *www.ibm.com*, but it's really jumping to a pirate computer connected to a stolen dialup in Argentina.

This checking of server addresses doesn't really provide any more security, because domain names themselves don't really provide a form of identification. For example, the Sony corporation operates the domain names *sony.com* and *sonystyle.com*, but in July 2001 the domain name *sonyshop.com* belonged to Peter Beerten in Tervuren, Belgium. (Mr. Beerten apparently got the domain in August 1998, as shown in Example 17-4.)

Example 17-4. Sonyshop.com doesn't belong to Sony Corporation, but to Peter Beerten!

```
> whois sonyshop.com
...

Registrant:
Peter Beerten (SONYSHOP-DOM)
```

Example 17-4. Sonyshop.com doesn't belong to Sony Corporation, but to Peter Beerten! (continued)

```
Heide Street #1
Tervuren, Belgium 3080
BE

Domain Name: SONYSHOP.COM

Administrative Contact, Billing Contact:
    Beerten, Peter  (PB6745)  peter.beerten@PANDORA.BE
    Peter Beerten
    Heide Street #1
    Tervuren, Belgium 3080
    BE
    32 2 720 7071 (FAX) 32 2 720 9192
Technical Contact:
    Hostmaster, Verio  (TH941)  VerioHostmaster@VERIO.NET
    560 Gateway Drive
    Napa, CA  94558
    US
    707 521-5400 707 251-3080

Record last updated on 25-Aug-2000.
Record expires on 25-Aug-2001.
Record created on 25-Aug-1998.
Database last updated on 8-Jul-2001 03:05:00 EDT.

Domain servers in listed order:

NSX.NTX.NET              209.1.144.216
NSC.NTX.NET              128.121.247.244
>
```

Instead of validating DNS addresses, web browsers should actually display the distinguished name on the certificate prominently. Sadly, both Netscape and Microsoft have hidden these fields from the certificate in another window that most users don't even know about.

Because SSL validates the checking, you will need a new certificate if you change the name of your web site. For example, if your web site is at *www.company.com*, and you decide the *www* is silly and want to allow people to type just *company.com*, you will need a separate SSL certificate for the *company.com* domain if you intend to use that domain with SSL. An easy way around this is to rig the HTTP server to automatically redirect users who type *company.com* to *www.company.com*.

CHAPTER 18

Securing Your
Web Service

In this chapter:
- Protecting Via Redundancy
- Protecting Your DNS
- Protecting Your Domain Registration

In this chapter, we'll look at technical issues involving entities outside your organization that you need to consider if you hope to offer a reliable web service.

Protecting Via Redundancy

The most powerful technique for providing a reliable service is redundancy: using multiple systems, Internet connections, routes, web servers, and locations to protect your services from failure. Let's look at what can happen if you don't provide sufficient redundancy.

Price and Performance Versus Redundancy

It was Monday, July 10, and all of Martha's Vineyard was full of vacation cheer. But for Simson Garfinkel, who had spent the weekend on the Massachusetts island, things were not so good. At 9:30 a.m., Simson was in the middle of downloading his email when suddenly IP connectivity between his house on Martha's Vineyard and his house on the mainland was interrupted. No amount of pinging, traceroutes, or praying, for that matter, would make it come back.

What had happened to the vaunted reliability of the Walden network that we described in Chapter 2? In a word, it was gone. The Walden network had been decommissioned on June 30, when Simson moved from Cambridge to Belmont. Because Belmont's telephone central office was wired for DSL, Simson was able to move his Megapath Networks DSL line, but Belmont's cable plant had not been upgraded for data, so he had to leave his cable modem behind. So long, redundancy! On the plus side, with the money that Simson saved by canceling the cable modem, he was able to upgrade the DSL line from 384 Kbps to 1.1 Mbps without incurring an additional monthly fee. Moving from 384 Kbps to 1.1 Mbps offered a huge improvement in performance. But the new setup also represented an increase in risk: Simson now only had one upstream provider. Simson had taken a gamble, trading redundancy for performance . . . and he had lost.

Simson caught a 10:45 a.m. ferry from Oak Bluffs to Woods Hole, then drove up to Belmont. With a few more detours and delays, he made it to Belmont at 4:00 p.m. Then he called Megapath Networks, his ISP, and waited on hold for more than 30 minutes. Finally, at 4:45 p.m. a technician answered the phone. The technician's advice was straightforward: turn off the DSL router, wait a minute, then turn it back on. When that didn't work, the technician put Simson on hold and called Rhythms, the CLEC that Megapath had contracted with to provide Simson's DSL service. After another 30 minutes on hold, a Rhythms technician picked up the phone. That engineer did a line test, asked Simson to unplug his DSL router from the phone line, then did another line test. At last the verdict was in: "It seems that your DSL line recently got a whole lot shorter," the engineer said.

How could a telephone line suddenly get shorter? Quite easily, it turns out. Sometimes, when a telephone installer working for the incumbent local exchange company (the ILEC) is looking for a pair of wires to run a telephone circuit from one place to another, the linesman will listen to the line with a telephone set to see if it is in use or not. This sort of practice is especially common in neighborhoods like Cambridge and Belmont, where the telephone wires can be decades old and the telephone company's records are less than perfect. If the telephone installer hears a dial tone or a telephone conversation on a pair of wires, he knows that the pair is in use. But DSL lines don't have dial tones or conversations—they simply have a hiss of data. In all likelihood, a linesman needed a pair for a new telephone that was being installed, clicked onto Simson's DSL line, heard nothing, and reallocated the pair to somebody else.

Two hours later, Simson called Megapath back, which in turn called Rhythms. "Good thing you called!" he was told. Apparently nothing had been done—one of the companies, either Megapath or Rhythms, had a policy of not escalating service outage complaints until the subscriber called back a second time. Rhythms finally made a call to Verizon and was told that a new line would be installed within 48 hours.

Fortunately, things went better the next day. An installer from Verizon showed up at 10 a.m. that morning. That installer discovered that the DSL line had been cut by a junior Verizon employee who was installing Simson's fax line. By 2 p.m. the DSL line was back up. Unfortunately, by that time, Simson's email had already started to bounce, because many ISPs configure their mail systems to return email to the sender if the destination computer is unavailable for more than 24 hours.

Providing for Redundancy

What's the lesson of this story?

If your Internet service provider promises "99% uptime," you should probably look for another ISP. With 365 days in a year, 99% uptime translates to 3 days, 15 hours and 36 minutes of downtime every year. Much better is a commitment of "5 nines" reliability, or 99.999%—that translates to only 5 minutes and 15 seconds of downtime in a year. For many users, 5 minutes of downtime each year is an acceptable level of performance.

Unfortunately, the problem with uptime commitments is that they are only promises—you can still have downtime. Even companies that offer so-called Service Level Agreements (SLAs) can't prevent your network connection from going down if the line is physically cut by a backhoe; all they can do is refund your money or make some kind of restitution after an outage. If Internet connectivity is critical for your service's continued operation, you should obtain redundant Internet connections from separate organizations or provide for backup services that will take over in the event that you are disconnected.

Deploying independent, redundant systems is the safest and ultimately the least expensive way to improve the reliability of your information services. Consider: instead of spending $1000/month for a T1 line that promises less than 6 hours of downtime a month, you could purchase three less-reliable DSL circuits for $200/month from providers that promise 48-hour response time. Not only would save you money, you would actually have a higher predicted level of reliability. In this case, if the T1 were actually down for 6 hours a month, then there would be a 0.83% chance of the line being down on any given hour. For each DSL line, the chance that it would be down on any given hour would be 6.6%. But if the DSL lines are truly independent—coming in from different providers, using different CLECs and different backbones—then the chance that they would all be down for the same hour is 0.029%, making the three DSL lines almost 30 times more reliable than the single T1. The three 1.1 Mbps DSL lines would also offer nearly twice the bandwidth of a single T1 when all are operating normally.

While redundancy is a powerful tool, deploying redundant systems can also be a difficult balancing act. Coordinating multiply redundant systems is both a technical and a managerial challenge. Testing the systems can also present problems. If you are going to deploy redundant systems, here are some things that you should consider:

- Make sure your redundant systems are actually independent! There are many stories of companies that thought they had ordered redundant circuits from separate telecommunications providers, but later discovered that the providers had all partnered with each other and sent all of the circuits down a single fiber-optic conduit! Or you might order one Internet connection over company A's metropolitan fiber ring and a second Internet connection from company B's wireless network, only to later discover that company B was also using company A's fiber ring to interconnect its wireless hubs.

- If you decide to obtain DSL circuits from multiple providers, make sure that each DSL circuit is terminated by a different local carrier.

- If you have multiple upstream Internet connections, you will either have a different set of IP addresses for each connection, or have your own block of IP addresses and use BGP (Border Gateway Protocol) to handle failover.
  - If you use multiple IP addresses, make sure that your DNS servers hand out the appropriate IP addresses depending on the network conditions. One approach is to use DNS round-robin to force users to try each IP address until they find one that works. Another approach is to register two DNS servers, one for each upstream provider, and have each one hand out an IP address on its own network.
  - If you use BGP, monitor your announcements from various parts of the Internet to make sure that your announcements are behaving properly. Remember that some ISPs will not listen to announcements that are smaller than /19 or /20—be sure that both upstream providers can reroute your packets in the event that a line goes down.

  In either case, be aware that multiple upstream connections are for redundancy, and not for load balancing. Each circuit should be able to handle your entire network load on its own. If you have two DS3 circuits to two different upstream providers, and each DS3 circuit routinely runs at 80% of its capacity, then you do not have two redundant circuits—you simply have created two possibilities for catastrophic failure.

- Don't stop at multiple Internet connections: for the greatest reliability, you should have multiple routers, multiple web servers, and—ideally—multiple locations that are simultaneously serving up your content. Figure 18-1 shows various approaches to increasing reliability for web services. Of course, as reliability increases, so do complexity and operating costs.

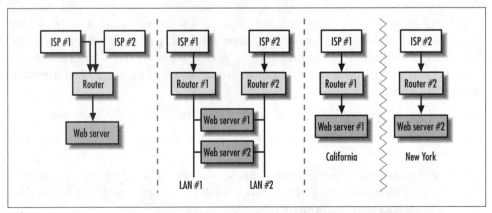

Figure 18-1. You can have multiple upstream providers enter into the same router, which is served by a single web server (left). For increased reliability, have each upstream connection served by its own router, with multiple web servers serving your content (middle). For highest reliability, have multiple, disconnected sites that serve your content to web visitors on the Internet (right).

Protecting Your DNS

All of the redundancy in the world won't keep your web site accessible on the Internet if potential users type in your domain name and it isn't properly translated to the IP address of your servers. Having a Domain Name Server (DNS) that is reliable and accurate is a prerequisite for a reliable web site. Nevertheless, DNS issues are commonly overlooked by many organizations.

There are many reasons DNS does not get the attention it deserves:

- Managers and executives do not understand what DNS does, how it works, and why it is important.
- Because DNS normally functions rapidly and reliably, DNS breakdowns are all the more confusing, unfamiliar, and difficult to diagnose.
- As most ISPs do not explicitly charge for providing DNS service, many users conclude that it must either be simple to provide or not be worth very much.

As we discussed in Chapter 2, DNS is a large distributed database that translates hostnames (e.g., *www.vineyard.net*) into IP addresses (e.g., 204.17.195.100.) When DNS is functioning properly, incoming queries to your nameserver are rapidly replied to with the IP address of your service. Responses contain an assortment of information and an expiration time, better known as a *time to live* (TTL). DNS answers are designed to be cached: if a thousand customers of Earthlink in San Jose all try to access your web site one afternoon, chances are good that your DNS server will see only a single query from Earthlink; the remaining 999 users get their answer from Earthlink's DNS server, which holds onto the information until the TTL expires.

There are many ways DNS can fail. Some of them are catastrophic—for example, your DNS server may have crashed, preventing anybody on the Internet from looking up your IP address. But some DNS failure modes are not so obvious: your DNS server may report that it is *nonauthoritative*, preventing your secondary DNS servers from properly updating their databases and causing them to distribute obsolete or false information.

There are several reasons DNS issues can be exceedingly difficult to diagnose:

- Many of the Internet's diagnostic tools (*ping*, *traceroute*, *nslookup*, *whois*, etc.) depend on DNS.
- Even if your DNS server is down, your secondary DNS servers may continue to answer DNS queries for a time. Thus, your DNS outage may begin hours, days, or even weeks after the primary DNS server fails.
- Different DNS implementations deal with errors in different ways. For example, some DNS implementations attempt to make the best of zone files that contain errors, while other DNS implementations reject them outright.

DNS is also becoming dramatically more complicated. As this book went to press, the Internet Software Consortium's BIND DNS server consisted of more than 100,000 lines of C source code that compiled to more than 500,000 bytes of object code. DNS now has provisions for dynamic updating and cryptographic security. Because the DNS protocol runs on port 53, the DNS server must be started by the superuser on Unix systems.

Most implementations of DNS now allow for remote updates. You should be certain that remote updates on your server are explicitly turned *off* unless you specifically wish to use this feature. If you do wish to use remote updates or dynamic DNS, be sure that update requests are authenticated using the appropriate cryptographic protocol. Do not depend upon IP addresses for authentication, as IP addresses can be spoofed.

Perhaps because of its complexity, BIND has also been the source of several remote exploits. Although the problems in BIND have been rapidly fixed, the widespread use of this software—combined with the fact that many system operators do not even know that it is running on their systems—have allowed the vulnerabilities to persist for a long time. If you run DNS, you should be certain that you are either running the most recent version of the program or running a version so old that nobody knows about its security vulnerabilities anymore (not a gamble that most people want to take). Running a version of BIND that is a year or two out of date is not sound practice.

If possible, you should dedicate a separate computer to DNS service. If this is not possible, you should see if your DNS server can be installed in a "chrooted" environment, or run as a user other than root.

Protecting Your Domain Registration

It's possible for a corporation to spend hundreds of millions of dollars purchasing hardware and software, build multiple redundant data centers, and have multiple upstream connections and backup power systems—yet have its entire network servicing several million customers go offline because it forgot to pay a single $35 annual fee.

It is important to remember that almost every transaction over the Web begins with a DNS query in which some computer somewhere on the Internet asks a top-level domain name server for the IP address of your organization's name servers. If your organization's entry in the *.COM* or *.CO.UK* database has been removed, no amount of redundancy or technical wizardry on your part will allow most users to access your services. For this reason, it is vital to ensure the safety of your domain name registration. Here are some suggestions:

- Know the name of the Internet registrar that maintains your domain name. Although many domain names are registered with Network Solutions, there are now more than a dozen registrars open for business, as well as many national organizations operating in countries other than the United States. Maintain a paper file with the name of the registrar and a printout of your organization's registration.

- Periodically review the registration information for your domain name, making sure that the contact information is up to date and that your bills have been paid.

- Take advantage of any advanced security features that your registrar allows you to put on your registration. Originally, Network Solutions authenticated all domain name change requests by examining the email address of the person making the request to see if it matched the email address of the registration on file. But after a number of high-profile domain names were changed by attackers, Network Solutions implemented its so-called Guardian system which allows its users to either assign a password to their domains or register a PGP key that is used to authenticate domain name change requests.

Besides being stolen by attackers, domain names can also be shut down or suspended by the action of lawyers. Throughout the late 1990s, domain names that were registered to one entity but appeared to impact the trademark of another organization were frequently the target of lawsuits. The Internet Corporation for Assigned Names and Numbers (ICANN) Uniform Dispute Resolution Policy (UDRP) is an attempt to solve these problems; all ICANN registrars are supposed to implement this policy. However, this policy may not be implemented by other nationally chartered registrars, and in any event is secondary to natural laws. Finally, the result of dispute resolution may not go in your favor, no matter how much you believe you are in the right, so it is always a good idea to have multiple domain names.

## CHAPTER 19

Computer Crime

In this chapter:
- Your Legal Options After a Break-In
- Criminal Hazards
- Criminal Subject Matter

In this chapter, we focus on problems and remedies that involve law enforcement organizations. The first part describes what alternatives may be available to you if your site is the subject of an electronic attack. The second part continues our litany of things that can get you in trouble—except this time, the offenses might land you in jail. For additional information on legal matters, see Chapters 23 and 26, which are oriented more to web-content providers.

Your Legal Options After a Break-In

If you suffer a break-in or criminal damage to your system, you have a variety of recourses under the U.S. legal system. This chapter cannot advise you on the many subtle aspects of the law. There are differences between state and federal law, as well as different laws that apply to computer systems used for different purposes. Laws outside the U.S. vary considerably from jurisdiction to jurisdiction; we won't attempt to explain anything beyond the U.S. system.* However, we should note that the global reach of the Internet may bring laws to bear that have their origin outside the U.S.

Discuss your specific situation with a competent lawyer before pursuing *any* legal recourse. Because there are difficulties and dangers associated with legal approaches, you should be sure that you want to pursue this course of action before you go ahead.

In some cases, you may have no choice; you may be required to pursue legal action. For example:

- If you want to file a claim against your insurance policy to receive money for damages resulting from a break-in, you may be required by your insurance company to pursue criminal or civil actions against the perpetrators.

---

* An excellent, although somewhat dated, discussion of legal issues in the U.S. can be found in *Computer Crime: A Crimefighter's Handbook* (O'Reilly), and we suggest you start there if you need more explanation than we provide in this chapter. The book is out of print, but used copies are available.

- If you are involved with classified data processing, you may be required by government regulations to report and investigate suspicious activity.

- If you are aware of criminal activity and you do not report it, you may be criminally liable as an accessory. This is especially true if your computer is being used for the illegal activity.

- If your computer is being used for certain forms of unlawful or inappropriate activity and you do not take definitive action, you may be named as a defendant in a civil lawsuit seeking punitive damages.

- If you are an executive and decide not to investigate and prosecute illegal activity, shareholders of your corporation can bring suit against you.

If you believe that your system is at especially high risk for attack, you should probably speak with your organization's legal counsel *before* you have an incident as part of your security incident pre-planning. Organizations have different policies on when law enforcement should or should not be involved. By doing your homework, you increase the chances that these policies will actually be followed when they are needed.

To give some starting points for discussion, this section provides an overview of a few issues you might want to consider.

Filing a Criminal Complaint

You are free to contact law enforcement personnel any time you believe that someone has broken a criminal statute. You start the process by making a formal complaint to a law enforcement agency. A prosecutor will likely decide if the allegations should be investigated and what charges should be filed, if any.

In some cases—perhaps a majority of them—criminal investigation will not help your situation. If the perpetrators have left little trace of their activity and the activity is not likely to recur, or if the perpetrators are entering your system through a computer in a foreign country, you probably will not be able to trace or arrest the individuals involved. Many experienced computer intruders will leave little tracing evidence behind.*

If you do file a complaint, there is no guarantee that the agency will actually conduct a criminal investigation. The prosecutor involved (federal, state, or local) decides which, if any, laws have been broken, the seriousness of the crime, the availability of trained investigators, and the probability of a conviction. It is important to remember that the criminal justice system is overloaded; new investigations are started only for severe violations of the law or for cases that warrant special treatment. A case in which $200,000 worth of data is destroyed is more likely to be investigated than a

---

* Although few computer intruders are as clever as they believe themselves to be.

case in which someone is repeatedly scanning your home computer through your cable modem.

If an investigation is conducted, you may be involved with the investigators or you may be completely isolated from them. You may even be given erroneous information—that is, you may be told that no investigation is taking place, even though a full-scale investigation is in the works. Many investigations are conducted on a "need to know" basis, occasionally using classified techniques and informants. If you are told that there is no investigation and in fact there is one, the person who gives you this information may be deliberately misinforming you, or they themselves may simply not have the "need to know."

Investigations can place you in an uncomfortable and possibly dangerous position. If unknown parties are continuing to break into your system by remote means, law enforcement authorities may ask you to leave your system open, thus allowing the investigators to trace the connection and gather evidence for an arrest. Unfortunately, if you leave your system open after discovering that it is being misused, and the perpetrator uses your system to break into or damage another system elsewhere, you may be the target of a third-party lawsuit. Cooperating with law enforcement agents is not a sufficient shield from such liability. Investigate the potential ramifications before putting yourself at risk in this way.

Choosing jurisdiction

One of the first things you must decide is to whom you should report the crime. Every state and the federal government currently have laws against some sorts of computer crime, so you have choices. In some cases, state authorities can even prosecute under federal statutes.

Unfortunately, there is no way to tell in advance whether your problem will receive more attention from local authorities or from federal authorities. Here are some recommendations:

- You should first approach local or state authorities, if at all possible. If your local law enforcement personnel believe that the crime is more appropriately investigated by the federal government, they will suggest that you contact federal authorities. Unfortunately, some local law enforcement agencies may be reluctant to seek outside help or to bring in federal agents. This may keep your particular case from being investigated properly.

- Local authorities may be more responsive because you are not as likely to be competing with a large number of other cases (as frequently occurs at the federal level). Local authorities are also more likely to be interested in your problem, no matter how small the problem may be.

- At the same time, although some local authorities are tremendously well-versed in computers and computer crime, local authorities generally have less expertise than state and federal authorities and may be reluctant to take on high-tech investigations. Many federal agencies have expertise that can be brought in quickly to help deal with a problem.

- In general, state authorities may be more interested than federal authorities in investigating and prosecuting juveniles. If you know that you are being attacked by a juvenile who is in your state, you will almost certainly be better off dealing with local authorities. In some cases, you may find that it is better to bypass the legal system entirely and speak with the juvenile's parents or teachers (or have an attorney or friendly police officer speak to them).

Local jurisdiction

In many areas, because the local authorities do not have the expertise or background necessary to investigate and prosecute computer-related crimes, you may find that they must depend on your expertise. You may be involved with the investigation on an ongoing basis—possibly to a great extent. You may or may not consider this a productive use of your time. Your participation may also result in contamination of the case; as the aggrieved party, you could be blamed for falsifying evidence.

Our best advice is to contact local law enforcement before any problem occurs, and get some idea of their expertise and willingness to help you in the event of a problem. The time you invest up front could pay big dividends later on if you need to decide who to call at 2 a.m. on a holiday because you have evidence that someone is making unauthorized use of your system.

Federal jurisdiction

Although you might often prefer to deal with local authorities, you should contact federal authorities if you:

- Are working with classified or military information
- Have involvement with nuclear materials or information
- Work for a federal agency and its equipment is involved
- Work for a bank or handle regulated financial information
- Are involved with interstate telecommunications
- Believe that people from out of the state or out of the country are involved with the crime

Offenses related to national security, fraud, or telecommunications are usually handled by the FBI. Cases involving financial institutions, stolen access codes, or passwords are generally handled by the U.S. Secret Service. However, other federal agents may have jurisdiction in some cases; for example, the Customs Department, the U.S. Postal Service, and the Air Force Office of Investigations have all been involved in computer-related criminal investigations.

Luckily, you don't need to determine jurisdiction on your own. If you believe that a federal law has been violated in your incident, call the nearest U.S. Attorney's office and ask them who you should contact. Often that office will have the name and contact information for a specific agent or an office in which the personnel have special training in investigating computer-related crimes.

Federal Computer Crime Laws

There are many federal laws that can be used to prosecute computer-related crimes. Usually, the choice of law pertains to the type of crime rather than whether the crime was committed with a computer, a phone, or pieces of paper. Depending on the circumstances, laws relating to wire fraud, espionage, or criminal copyright violation may come into play. You don't need to know anything about the laws involved—the authorities will make that determination based on the facts of the case.

Hazards of Criminal Prosecution

There are many potential problems in dealing with law enforcement agencies, not the least of which is their experience with computers, networking, and criminal-related investigations. Sadly, there are still many federal agents who are not well versed with computers and computer crime.* In many local jurisdictions you will find even less expertise. Unless you are specifically working with a "computer crime squad," your case will probably be investigated by an agent who has little or no training in computing.

Computer-illiterate agents will sometimes seek your assistance to try to understand the subtleties of the case. Other times, they will ignore your advice—perhaps to hide their own ignorance, and often to the detriment of the case and the reputation of the law enforcement community.

If you or your personnel are asked to assist in the execution of a search warrant to help identify material to be searched, be sure that the court order directs such "expert" involvement. Otherwise, you might find yourself complicating the case by appearing as an overzealous victim. You may benefit by recommending an impartial third party to assist the law enforcement agents.

The attitude and behavior of the law enforcement officers can sometimes cause major problems. Your equipment might be seized as evidence or held for an unreasonable length of time for examination—even if you are the victim of the crime. If you are the victim and are reporting the case, the authorities will usually make every attempt to coordinate their examinations with you, to cause you the least amount of

---

* However, we have noticed a distinct improvement since the first edition of this book was released. Federal authorities have recognized the need for more training and resources, and have been working to improve the average skill set for their agents.

inconvenience. However, if the perpetrators are your own employees, or if regulated information is involved (bank, military, etc.), you might have no control over the manner or duration of the examination of your systems and media. This problem becomes more severe if you are dealing with agents who need to seek expertise outside their local offices to examine the material. Be sure to keep track of downtime during an investigation as it may be included as part of the damages during prosecution and any subsequent civil suit—suits that may be waged against either your attacker or, in some cases, the law enforcement agency itself.

 Your site's backups can be extremely valuable in an investigation. You might even make use of your disaster-recovery plan and use a standby or spare site while your regular system is being examined.

Heavy-handed or inept investigative efforts may also place you in an uncomfortable position with respect to the computer community. Many computer users harbor negative attitudes toward law enforcement officers—these feelings can easily be redirected toward you if you are responsible for bringing the "outsiders" in. Such attitudes can place you in a worse light than you deserve, and hinder cooperation not only with the current investigation but with other professional activities. Furthermore, they may make you a target for electronic attack or other forms of abuse after the investigation concludes. These attitudes are unfortunate, because there are some very good investigators, and careful investigation and prosecution may be needed to stop malicious or persistent intruders.

For these reasons, we encourage you to carefully consider the decision to involve law enforcement agencies with any security problem pertaining to your system.

- In most cases, we suggest that you may not want to involve the criminal justice system at all unless a real loss has occurred, or unless you are unable to control the situation on your own. In some instances, the publicity involved in a case may be more harmful than the loss you have sustained.

- Once you decide to involve law enforcement, avoid publicizing this fact. In some cases the involvement of law enforcement will act as a deterrent to the attackers, but in other cases it may make you the subject of more attacks.

Be aware that the problem you spot may be part of a much larger problem that is ongoing or beginning to develop. You may be risking further damage to your systems and the systems of others if you decide to ignore the situation.

We wish to stress the positive. Law enforcement agencies are aware of the need to improve how they investigate computer crime cases, and they are working to develop in-service training, forensic analysis facilities, and other tools to help them conduct effective investigations. In many jurisdictions (especially in high-tech areas of the country), investigators and prosecutors have gained considerable experience and have worked to convey that information to their peers. The result is a significant improvement in law enforcement effectiveness over the last few years, with a number of successful investigations and prosecutions. You should very definitely think about the positive aspects of reporting a computer crime—not only for yourself, but for the community as a whole. Successful prosecutions may help prevent further misuse of your system and of others' systems.

The Responsibility to Report Crime

Finally, keep in mind that criminal investigation and prosecution can only occur if you report the crime. If you fail to report the crime, there is no chance of apprehension. Not only does that not help your situation, it leaves the perpetrators free to harm someone else.

A more subtle problem results from a failure to report serious computer crimes: it leads others to believe that there are few such crimes being committed. As a result, insufficient emphasis is placed on budgets and training for new law enforcement agents in this area; little effort is made to enhance the existing laws and little public attention is focused on the problem. The consequence is that the computing milieu becomes incrementally more dangerous for all of us.

Criminal Hazards

If you operate an Internet service provider or web site, or have networked computers on your premises, you may be at risk for criminal prosecution yourself if those machines are misused. This section is designed to acquaint you with some of the risks.

If law enforcement officials believe that your computer system has been used by an employee to break into other computer systems, to transmit or store controlled information (trade secrets, child pornography, etc.), or to otherwise participate in some computer crime, you may find your computers impounded by a search warrant (in criminal cases) or writ of seizure (in civil cases). If you can document that your employee has had limited access to your systems, and if you present that information during the search, it may help limit the scope of the confiscation. However, you may still be in a position in which some of your equipment is confiscated as part of a legal search.

Local police or federal authorities can present a judge with a petition to grant a search warrant if they believe there is evidence to be found concerning a violation of a law. If the warrant is in order, the judge will almost always grant the search warrant. In the recent past, a few federal investigators and law enforcement personnel in some states developed a reputation for heavy-handed and excessively broad searches. In part, this was because of inexperience with computer crime, and it has been getting better with time.

Playing It Safe . . .

Here is a summary of additional recommendations for avoiding possible abuse of your computer. Most of these are simply good policy whether or not you anticipate break-ins:

- Put copyright and/or proprietary ownership notices in your source code and data files. Do so at the top of each and every file. If you express a copyright, consider filing for the registered copyright—this version can enhance your chances of prosecution and recovery of damages.

- Be certain that your users are notified about what they can and cannot do.

- If it is consistent with your policy, make all users of your system aware of what you may monitor. This includes email, keystrokes, and files. Without such notice, monitoring an intruder or a user overstepping bounds could itself be a violation of wiretap or privacy laws!

- Keep good backups in a safe location. If comparisons against backups are necessary as evidence, you need to be able to testify as to who had access to the media involved. Having tapes in a public area will probably prevent them from being used as evidence.

- If something happens that you view as suspicious or that may lead to involvement of law enforcement personnel, start a diary. Note your observations and actions, and note the times. Run paper copies of log files or traces and include those in your diary. A written record of events such as these may prove valuable during the investigation and prosecution. Note the time and context of each and every contact with law enforcement agents as well.

- Try to define in writing the authorization of each employee and user of your system. Include in the description the items to which each person has legitimate access (and the items each person cannot access). Have a mechanism in place so each person is apprised of this description and can understand his or her limits.

- Tell your employees explicitly that they must return all materials, including manuals and source code, when requested or when their employment terminates.

- If something has happened that you believe requires law enforcement investigation, do not allow your personnel to conduct their own investigation. Doing too much on your own may prevent some evidence from being used or otherwise cloud the investigation. You may also aggravate law enforcement personnel with what they might perceive to be interference in their investigation.

- Make your employees sign an employment agreement that delineates their responsibilities with respect to sensitive information, machine usage, electronic mail use, and any other aspect of computer operation that might later arise. Make sure the policy is explicit and fair, and that all employees are aware of it and have signed the agreement. State clearly that all access and privileges terminate when employment does, and that subsequent access without permission will be prosecuted.

—continued—

- Make contingency plans with your lawyer and insurance company for actions to be taken in the event of a break-in or other crime, the related investigation, and any subsequent events.
- Identify law enforcement personnel who are qualified to investigate problems that you may have ahead of time. Introduce yourself and your concerns to them in advance of a problem. Having at least a nodding acquaintance will help if you later encounter a problem that requires you to call upon law enforcement for help.
- Consider joining societies or organizations that stress ongoing security awareness and training. Work to enhance your expertise in these areas.

The scope of each search warrant is usually detailed by the agent in charge and approved by the judge; some warrants are derived from "boilerplate" examples that are themselves too broad. These problems have resulted in considerable ill will, and in the future might result in evidence not being admissible on constitutional grounds because a search was too wide-ranging. How to define the proper scope of a search is an evolving discussion in the courts.

Usually, the police seek to confiscate anything connected with the computer that may have evidence (e.g., files with stolen source code or telephone access codes). This confiscation might result in seizure of the computer, all magnetic media that could be used with the computer, anything that could be used as an external storage peripheral (e.g., videotape machines and tapes), autodialers that could contain phone numbers for target systems in their battery-backed memory, and all documentation and printouts. In past investigations even laser printers, answering machines, and televisions have been seized by federal agents—sometimes apparently with reason, other times as a result of confusion on the part of the agents, and sometimes apparently out of spite.

Officers are required to give a receipt for what they take. However, you may wait a very long time before you get your equipment back, especially if there is a lot of storage media involved, or if the officers are not sure what they are looking for. Your equipment may not even be returned in working condition—batteries discharge, media degrades, and dust works its way into moving parts. Equipment can also be damaged in transport or as a result of the investigation.

You should discuss the return of your equipment during the execution of the warrant, or thereafter with the prosecutors. Indicate priorities and reasons for the items to be returned. In most cases, you can request copies of critical data and programs. As the owner of the equipment, you can also file suit to have it returned,* but such suits

---

* If it is a federal warrant, your lawyer may file a "Motion for Return of Property" under Rule 41(e) of the federal Rules of Criminal Procedure.

can drag on and may not be productive. Suits to recover damages may not be allowed against law enforcement agencies that are pursuing a legitimate investigation.

You can also challenge the reasons used to file the warrant and seek to have it declared invalid, forcing the return of your equipment. However, warrants are frequently sealed to protect ongoing investigations and informants, so this option can be difficult to execute. Equipment and media seized during a search may be held until a trial if they contain material to be used as prosecution evidence. Some state laws require forfeiture of the equipment in the event of a conviction—especially if drug crimes are involved.

At present, a search is not likely to involve confiscation of a mainframe or even a minicomputer. However, confiscation of tapes, disks, and printed material could disable your business even if the computer itself is not taken. Having full backups offsite may not be sufficient protection, because these tapes might also be taken by a search warrant if the police know of their location. If you think that a search might curtail your legitimate business, be sure that the agents conducting the search have detailed information regarding which records are vital to your ongoing operation and request copies from them.

Until the law is better defined in this area, you are well advised to consult with an attorney if you are at all worried that a confiscation might occur. Furthermore, if you have homeowners' or business insurance, check with your agent to see if it covers damages resulting from law enforcement agents during an investigation. Business interruption insurance provisions should also be checked if your business depends on your computer.

Criminal Subject Matter

Possession and/or distribution of some kinds of information is criminal under U.S. law. If you see suspicious information on your computer, you should take note. If you believe that the information may be criminal in nature, you should contact an attorney first—do not immediately contact a law enforcement officer, as you may indirectly be admitting to involvement with a crime merely by asking for advice.

Access Devices and Copyrighted Software

Federal law (18 USC 1029) makes it a felony to manufacture or possess 15 or more access devices that can be used to obtain fraudulent service. The term *access devices* is broadly defined and is usually interpreted as including cellular telephone activation codes, account passwords, credit card numbers, and physical devices that can be used to obtain access.

Federal law also makes software piracy a crime, as well as possession of unlicensed copyrighted software with the intent to defraud. The rental of software without the permission of the copyright holder is also illegal.

Pornography, Indecency, and Obscenity

Pornography thrives on the Internet. With millions of customers and billions of dollars transferred every year, pornography is currently one of the main drivers of e-commerce and broadband residential connections. Pornography has stimulated the development of age verification systems, credit card verification systems, and even forms of electronic currency. Today pornography is one of the main sources of revenue on the Internet for many businesses.

The Internet is a global network. By design, the Internet's content can be accessed from anywhere on the network. But this global feature is at odds with the way that pornography and prostitution have traditionally been regulated in human societies—through local regulation, zoning, and registration. Stories, photographs, sounds, and movies that are considered pornographic or obscene in some communities have long been socially accepted in others, and distributed only to adults in still more.

Thus, there is a tension between the Internet's global nature and the global availability of pornography.

Amateur Action

In 1993, Robert and Carleen Thomas were operating a bulletin board system called the Amateur Action Bulletin Board System in Milpitas, California. The system was accessed by telephone, not the Internet. The BBS contained a wide range of adult fare, and had numerous login screens and banners that clearly indicated that the information the system contained was sexually explicit. To gain access to the system, potential subscribers needed to send AABBS a photocopy of their driver's license (to prove their age) and pay a membership fee of $55 for six months.

In July 1993, a Tennessee postal inspector named Dirmeyer downloaded a number of sexually explicit files from AABBS, after first registering (using an assumed name) and paying the membership fee. The postal inspector was apparently responding to a complaint from a person in his jurisdiction. On the basis of the information that he downloaded, the Thomases were charged with a violation of 18 USC 1465, "knowingly transport[ing] in interstate or foreign commerce for the purpose of sale or distribution . . . any obscene . . . book, pamphlet, picture, film . . . or any other matter."

The outcome of the trial hinged on whether the information that the postal inspector had downloaded was actually obscene or merely sexually explicit. But the standard for obscenity is not defined in U.S. law. In 1973, the United States Supreme Court instead said that obscenity was best judged by local "community standards."

And while the information distributed by AABBS may not have violated the community standards of Milpitas, California, or the standards of the community of dialup bulletin board systems, on July 29, 1994, a jury in the Federal District Court for Western Tennessee ruled that the downloaded images did violate the community standards of Western Tennessee.* (As it turns out, the Thomas' BBS had been previously raided by the San Jose Police Department in 1991; following that investigation, local law enforcement had concluded that the BBS had been acting in a legal manner—at least in California.)

Communications Decency Act

In 1996, the U.S. Congress passed the Communications Decency Act (CDA) as an amendment to the Telecommunications Act of 1996. The purpose of the act was allegedly to protect minors from harmful material on the Internet. But civil libertarians complained that the act was overly broad and that it would actually result in significant limitations on adult users of the network.

Shortly after the act was passed, a coalition of civil liberties groups filed suit against Attorney General Janet Reno, asking the court to enjoin Reno from enforcing the law. The case, *American Civil Liberties Union v. Reno*, was "fast tracked" to a special three-judge court in Philadelphia. That court ruled that two key provisions of the law were an unconstitutional abridgment of rights protected under the First and Fifth Amendments. The first provision struck down was a part of the law that criminalized the "knowing" transmission of "obscene or indecent" messages to any recipient under 18 years of age. The second was a provision that prohibits the "knowin[g]," sending, or displaying to a person under 18 of any message "that, in context, depicts or describes, in terms patently offensive as measured by contemporary community standards, sexual or excretory activities or organs."

The Clinton Administration appealed the ruling in the case *Reno v. ACLU*. The case went to the U.S. Supreme Court, which ruled against the Clinton Administration and the law.† At the time of the ruling, one of the key issues that the Court focused on was the increasing availability of filtering software that could be used to prevent children from accessing pornography. The argument was that if parents wanted to "protect" their children from pornography, all they had to do was to equip their computers with the requisite software; there was no need to restrict everybody else who used the Internet.

---

* More details about the Amateur Action case can be found at *http://www.eff.org/Legal/Cases/AABBS_Thomases_Memphis/Old/aa_eff_vbrief.html*, *http://www.spectacle.org/795/amateur.html*, and *http://www.loundy.com/CDLB/AABBS.html*.

† For details on the CDA, see *http://www.epic.org/cda/* and *http://www.eff.org/Censorship/Internet_censorship_bills/*.

Realizing that it could not regulate the Internet itself, Congress subsequently passed a law requiring that federally supported schools and libraries install filtering software on computers to prevent children from accessing pornography at these places.

Mandatory blocking

Numerous laws now require that schools and libraries install mandatory filtering software on their Internet connections. Of these, the most important is the Children's Internet Protection Act (Pub. L. 106-554), which requires that schools receiving discounted communications services have in place technology that prevents access through computers to visual depictions that are "(I) obscene, (II) child pornography, or (III) harmful to minors."

Child pornography

Today, the harshest punishments in the U.S. legal system for possesion of contraband information are reserved for pornography that involves the sexual depiction of children or pornography that uses children in its creation. The prohibition against child pornography is based on the need to protect children from sexual exploitation. Because the child pornography regulations criminalize the mere posession of child pornography, you can be in serious legal trouble simply by receiving by email an image of a naked minor, even if you don't know what is in the image at the time you fetch it.

Child pornography laws are applied selectively. In several cases, individuals have been arrested for downloading child pornography from several major online service providers. Yet the online service providers themselves have not been harassed by law enforcement, even though the same child pornography resides on the online services' systems.

In recent years, there has been a move to expand the definition of child pornography to include simulated acts of child pornography, computer animations of child pornography, and even textual descriptions of child pornography. Proponents of these expansions argue that besides any harm that may be caused to children in the creation of child pornography, the mere existence of child pornography is criminal.

Devices that Circumvent Technical Measures that Control Access to Copyrighted Works

Passed in 1999, the Digital Millennium Copyright Act (DMCA) described in Chapter 4 makes it a crime to circumvent technical measures that are used to control access to copyrighted works. It also makes it a crime to distribute certain kinds of technical information that may be used to disable copyright control mechanisms.

The DMCA was pushed through the U.S. Congress very quickly by the Clinton Administration at the request of the publishing and entertainment industry, which has long argued that copyright control systems are needed to prevent piracy, and that information regarding the disabling of these systems should be controlled.

But the result of the DMCA's passage means that there is now a whole class of contraband programs—programs that, in many cases, simply allow people to exercise their rights to copyrighted material under the "fair use" provisions of copyright law. For example, if you rent a copy of *The Matrix* on DVD, take it home, and play it on a Mac or on a PC running the Windows operating system, you are not in violation of any law. But if you play it on a PC running the Linux operating system, you are breaking the law. Operating the Linux DVD player is a violation of the DMCA because it was not licensed by the Motion Picture Association of America (MPAA) to decrypt the encrypted bitstream on the DVD that decrypts to be the MPEG-2 files that contain *The Matrix*. Not only is it a violation of the DMCA to run the Linux DVD player, but it may also be a violation to have the program on your hard disk or to distribute it on a web page. And in 2000, a federal court prohibited the magazine *2600* from posting a link on its web site to a second web site that might have a copy of the program.

It's hard to believe that the DMCA won't be found to be a violation of the U.S. Constitution's First Amendment. But until it is, the DMCA is the law of the land. Be careful about the anticopyright programs that are on your web server.

Cryptographic Programs and Export Controls

As we discussed in Chapter 4, U.S. law considers cryptography to be a munition, akin to nuclear materials and biological warfare agents. Although U.S. policy on cryptography has been liberalized in recent years, export of technology and know-how is still regulated by the Defense Trade Regulations.

To export a program in machine-readable format that implements cryptography, you need a license from the Commerce Department; publishing the same algorithm in a book or public paper is not controlled.

Export of cryptographic technology is prohibited to countries considered terrorist countries. As of October 2001, these countries consisted of Taliban-controlled Afghanistan, Cuba, Iran, Iraq, Libya, North Korea, Sudan, and Syria. For further information, please see Chapter 4.

## PART IV

Security for Content Providers

This part of the book focuses on issues surrounding the content of the web server, rather than the mechanics of the web server's operation.

Chapter 20, *Controlling Access to Your Web Content*, looks at techniques for controlling information to "private" areas of your web server.

Chapter 21, *Client-Side Digital Certificates*, expands on the access control techniques described in Chapter 20 by discussing how you can use digital certificates for access control and secure messaging.

Chapter 22, *Code Signing and Microsoft's Authenticode*, shows how you can sign Windows binaries, including ActiveX controls and *.EXE* files, using Microsoft's Authenticode technology.

Chapter 23, *Pornography, Filtering Software, and Censorship*, discusses the politics and the technology of controlling pornography on the Internet.

Chapter 24, *Privacy Policies, Legislation, and P3P*, explores the concept of data protection and discusses legislative and self-regulatory techniques for controlling the use of personal information.

Chapter 25, *Digital Payments*, is a how-to guide for sending and receiving money over the Internet. For those interested in e-commerce history, this chapter also discusses a number of failed digital payment systems.

Chapter 26, *Intellectual Property and Actionable Content*, discusses trademarks, copyright, and patents—all legal structures that can be used to protect information.

## CHAPTER 20

Controlling Access to Your Web Content

Organizations run web servers because they are an easy way to distribute information to people on the Internet. But sometimes you don't want to distribute your information to *everybody*. For instance, you might have:

- Information on your web server intended only for employees of your organization

- An electronic publication that contains articles that are only available to customers who have paid a monthly subscription fee.

- Confidential technical information that is only for customers who have signed nondisclosure agreements

- A web-based interface to your order-entry system that is open to preauthorized users, but should not be open to the general public

These scenarios have different access control requirements. Fortunately, today's web servers have a variety of ways to restrict access to information.

Access Control Strategies

There are a number of techniques that can be used to control access to web-based information:

- Restricting access by using URLs that are "secret"—that is, URLs that are hidden and unpublished

- Restricting access to a particular group of computers based on those computers' hostnames or Internet addresses

- Restricting access to a particular group of users based on their identity

Most web servers can use these techniques to restrict access to HTML pages, CGI scripts, and API-invoking files. These techniques can be used alone or in combination. You can also add additional access control mechanisms to your own CGI and API programs.

Hidden URLs

The easiest way to restrict access to information and services is by storing the HTML files and CGI scripts in hidden locations on your web server.

For example, when Simson's daughter Sonia was born, he wanted to quickly put some photographs of her on the World Wide Web so that his friends and family could see them, but he didn't want to "publish" them so that anybody could look at them. Unfortunately, he didn't have the time to give usernames and passwords to the people he wanted to see the pictures. So Simson simply created a directory on his web server named *http://simson.vineyard.net/sonia/* and put the photographs inside. Then he sent the URL to his parents, his in-laws, and a few other networked friends.

Hidden URLs are about as secure as a key underneath your door mat. Nobody can access the data unless they know where to look; then they have access to all that they want. Furthermore, this information is transitive. You might tell John about the URL, and John might tell Eileen, and Eileen might post it to a mailing list of her thousand closest friends. Somebody might put a link to the URL on another web page—or even register the hidden URL with a web search engine.

Indeed, search engines such as Lycos, AltaVista, and Google pose a special problem for hidden URLs. Most search engines "spider" the Web by retrieving a page, indexing its content, analyzing the page for links, and then repeating the process with every page that is referenced by a link. If you have no links to a "secret" page, the search engines will generally not find it. However, if there is a single link to your page's hidden URL on any other page that is indexed by a search engine, it is likely that your hidden URL will be indexed as well. This can happen even if the page that linked to your hidden URL is later deleted; the links can still be active in the search engine's databanks. We've found lots of interesting and "hidden" pages by searching with keywords such as *secret*, *confidential*, *proprietary*, and so forth.

In general, avoid using secret URLs if you really care about maintaining the confidential nature of your page.

 If you are a user on an Internet service provider, a hidden URL gives you a simple way to get limited access control for your information. However, if you want true password protection, you might try creating a *.htaccess* file (described later in this chapter in the section, "Controlling Access with Apache") and seeing what happens.

Host-Based Restrictions

Most web servers allow you to restrict access to particular directories from specific computers located on the Internet. You can specify these computers by their IP addresses or by their DNS hostnames.

Restricting access to IP-specific addresses or a range of IP addresses on a subnet is a relatively simple technique for limiting access to web-based information. This technique works well for an organization that has its own internal network and wishes to restrict access to people on that network. For example, you might have a network that has the IP addresses 204.17.195.1 through 204.17.195.254; by configuring your web server so that certain directories are accessible only to computers on network 204.17.195, you prevent outsiders from accessing information in those directories. This is a practical technique for many organizations that use Net 10 (10.0.0.0 through 10.255.255.255) behind their firewalls.

RFC 1918 reserves three blocks of IP address space for private addressing. These addresses are shown in Table 20-1.

Table 20-1. Private IP address space designated by RFC 1918

Range	Prefix notation	# of Hosts
10.0.0.0–10.255.255.255	10/8	16,777,214
172.16.0.0–172.31.255.255	172.16/12	10,48,574
192.168.0.0 –192.168.255.255	192.168/16	65,534

According to RFC 1918:

> An enterprise that decides to use IP addresses out of the address space defined in RFC 1918 can do so without any coordination with IANA or an Internet registry. The address space can thus be used by many enterprises. Addresses within this private address space will only be unique within the enterprise, or the set of enterprises which choose to cooperate over this space so they may communicate with each other in their own private internet.

> Because private addresses have no global meaning, routing information about private networks shall not be propagated on inter-enterprise links, and packets with private source or destination addresses should not be forwarded across such links. Routers in networks not using private address space, especially those of Internet service providers, are expected to be configured to reject (filter out) routing information about private networks. If such a router receives such information the rejection shall not be treated as a routing protocol error.

Instead of specifying computers by IP address, most web servers allow you to restrict access on the basis of DNS domains. For example, your company may have the domain *company.com* and you may configure your web server so any computer that has a name of the form *.company.com* can access your web server. Specifying client access based on DNS domain names has the advantage that you can change your IP addresses and you don't have to change your web server's configuration file as well. (Of course, you will have to change your DNS server's configuration files, but you would have to change those anyway.)

The advantage of host-based restrictions is that they are largely transparent to users. If a user is working from a host that is authorized and she clicks on a URL that points to a restricted directory, she sees the directory. If the user is working from a host that is not authorized and she clicks on the URL that points to a restricted directory, the user sees a standard message that indicates that the information may not be viewed. A typical message is shown in Figure 20-1.

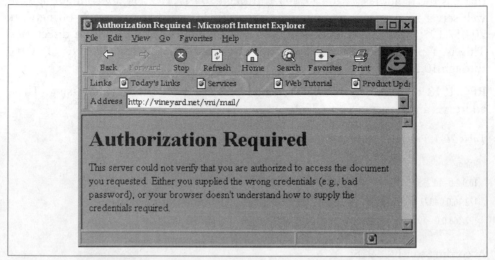

Figure 20-1. Access denied

 Although the standard Domain Name Service protocol is subject to spoofing, security can be dramatically increased by the use of public key encryption as specified in the DNSSEC protocol (described in Chapter 4). Implementations of DNSSEC are now available from a variety of sources, including *ftp://ftp.isc.org/*. To improve the overall security of the Internet's Domain Name Service, DNSSEC should be deployed as rapidly as possible.

Using firewalls to implement host-based access control

You can also implement host-based restrictions using a firewall to block incoming HTTP connections to particular web servers that should only be used by people inside your organization. Such a network is illustrated in Figure 20-2.

Caveats with host-based access control

Host-based addressing is not foolproof:

- IP spoofing can be used to transmit IP packets that appear to come from a different computer from the one they actually do come from. This is not a risk for static content such as HTML files, since the server will be unable to send the response back to the attacker. However, spoofed IP packets are a concern for programs executed by web servers (e.g., CGI and ASP scripts).

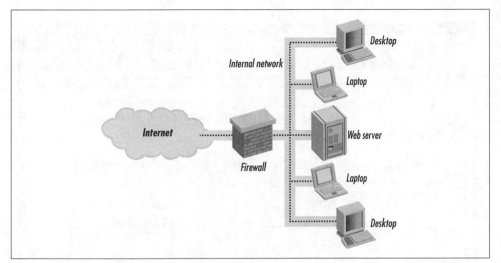

Figure 20-2. Using a firewall to implement host-based restrictions; access to the internal web server is blocked by the firewall.

- Host-based access control will not protect information from attackers who enter an organization's network using a remote-access system such as Carbon Copy, Windows NT RAS, VPNs, or IP tunneling. In these cases, the attacker's computer will appear to be behind your firewall, even though the attacker's computer may actually be located elsewhere.

- Host-based addressing that is based on DNS names requires that you have a secure DNS server. Otherwise, an attacker could simply add his own computer to your DNS domain, and thereby gain access to the confidential files on your web server.

Identity-Based Access Controls

Restricting access to your web server based on usernames is one of the most effective ways of controlling access. Each user is given a username and a password. The username identifies the person who wishes to access the web server, and the password authenticates the person.

When a user attempts to reference an access-controlled part of a web site, the web server requires the web browser to provide a username and password. The web browser recognizes this request and displays a request, such as the one shown in Figure 20-3.

Because passwords are easily shared or forgotten, many organizations are looking for alternatives to them. One approach is to use public key technology. Another approach is to give authorized users a physical token, such as a smart card, which they must have to gain access. Most of these systems merely require that the users

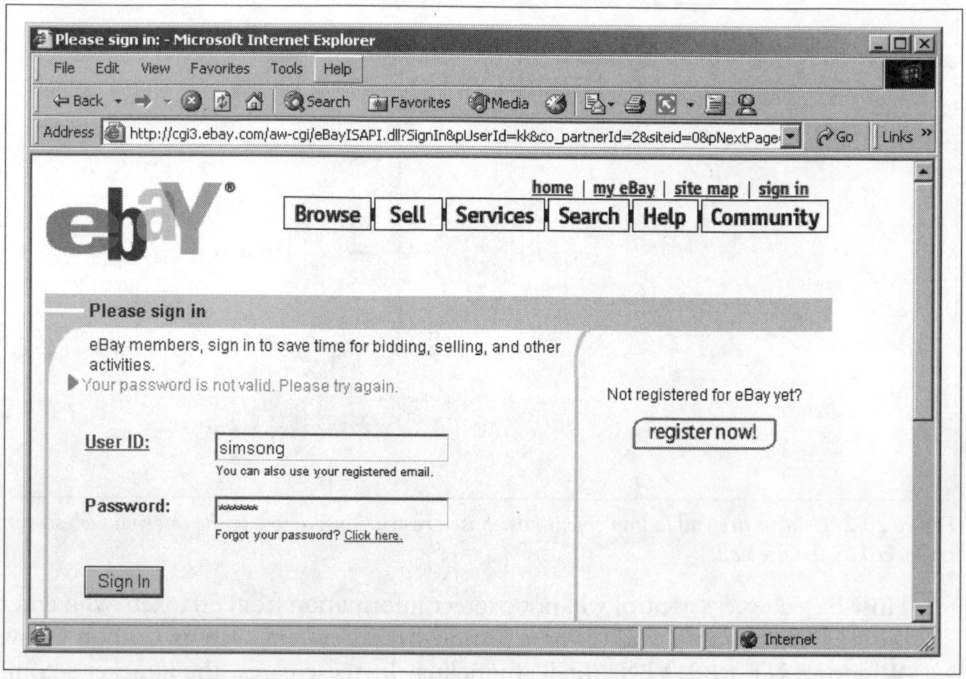

Figure 20-3. Prompt for user's password

enter their normal username and a different form of password. For example, users of the RSA Security SecurID card enter a password that is displayed on their smart cards; the password changes every minute.

One of the advantages of user-based access controls over host-based controls is that authorized users can access your web server from anywhere on the Internet. A sales force that is based around the country or around the world can use Internet service providers to access the corporate web site, rather than having to place long distance calls to the home office. Or you might have a sales person click into your company's web site from a high-speed network connection while visiting a client.

User-based access can also be implemented through the use of cookies (see "Understanding Cookies" in Chapter 8).

Controlling Access with Apache

One of the most common ways to restrict access to web-based information is to protect it using usernames and passwords. Although different servers support many different ways of password-protecting web information, one of the most common techniques is with the <Limit> server configuration directive present in the Apache web server.

Using <Limit>, you can control which files on your web server can be accessed and by whom. The Apache server gives you two locations where you can place your access control information:

- You can place the restrictions for any given directory (and all of its subdirectories) in a special file located in that directory. Traditionally the name of this file is *.htaccess*, although you can change the name in the server's configuration file.

- Alternatively, you can place all of the access control restrictions in a single configuration file. The Apache server allows you to place access control information in the server's single *httpd.conf* file.

Whether you choose to use many access files or a single file is up to you. It is certainly more convenient to have a file in each directory. It also makes it easier to move directories within your web server, as you do not need to update the master access control file. Furthermore, you do not need to restart your server whenever you make a change to the access control list—the server will notice that there is a new *.htaccess* file and behave appropriately.

On the other hand, having an access file in each directory means there are more files that you need to check to see whether the directories are protected. There is also the possibility that an attacker will be able to convince your web server (or another server running on the same computer) to fetch this file directly. Although the attacker's possession of the *.htaccess* file doesn't ruin your system's security, it gives an attacker additional information that might be used to find other holes.

Enforcing Access Control Restrictions with the .htaccess File

Here is a simple file that restricts access to registered users whose usernames appear in the file */ws/adm/users*:

```
% cat .htaccess
AuthType Basic
AuthName Web Solutions
AuthUserFile /ws/adm/users

<Limit GET POST>
require valid-user
</Limit>
%
```

The *.htaccess* file consists of two parts. At the beginning of the file is a set of commands that allow you to specify the authorization parameters for the given directory. The second half of the file contains a <Limit . . .> . . . </Limit> block containing security parameters that are enforced for the HTTP GET and POST commands.

The *.htaccess* file needs to be placed in the directory on the web server that you wish to protect. For example, if your web server is named *www.ex.com* and has a document root of */usr/local/etc/httpd/htdocs*, naming this file in the directory */usr/local/etc/httpd/ htdocs/internal/.htaccess* would restrict all information prefixed by the URL *http:// www.ex.com/internal/* so that it could only be accessed by authorized users.

Enforcing Access Control Restrictions with the Web Server's Configuration File

The access restrictions described in the *.htaccess* file can also be placed in the configuration file of the Apache web server. In this case, the commands would be enclosed within a pair of <Directory *directoryname*> and </Directory> tags. The *directoryname* parameter should be the directory's full pathname and not the directory within the web server's document root or the directory name as referenced by a symbolic link. For example:

```
...
<Directory /usr/local/etc/httpd/htdocs/internal>
AuthType Basic
AuthName Web Solutions
AuthUserFile /ws/adm/users

<Limit GET POST>
require valid-user
</Limit>
</Directory>
...
```

The format of the user account files (*/ws/adm/users* in this example) is similar to the Unix password file, but only contains usernames and encrypted passwords. It is described in detail later in this chapter in the section "<Limit> Examples."

Commands Before the <Limit>. . . </Limit> Directive

The following commands can be placed before the <Limit>. . .</Limit> block of most web servers:

AllowOverride what
> Specifies which directives can be overridden with directory-based access files. This command is only used for access information placed in system-wide configuration files such as *conf/access.conf* or *conf/httpd.conf*.

AuthName name
> Sets the name of the Authorization Realm for the directory. The name of the realm is displayed by the web browser when it asks for a username and password. It is also used by the web browser to cache usernames and passwords.

AuthRealm realm
> Sets the name of the Authorization Realm for the directory; this command is used instead of AuthName by older web servers.

AuthType type

> Specifies the type of authentication used by the server. Most web servers only support "basic," which is standard usernames and passwords.

AuthUserFile absolute_pathname

> Specifies the pathname of the *httpd* password file. This password file is created and maintained with a special password program; in the case of the Apache web server, use the *htpasswd* program. Note that the web server's password file is not stored in the same format as */etc/passwd*. The format is described in "Manually Setting Up Web Users and Passwords" later in this chapter.

AuthGroupFile absolute_pathname

> Specifies the pathname of the *httpd* group file. This group file is a regular text file. Note that this file is not in the format of the Unix */etc/group* file. Instead, each line begins with a group name and a colon and then lists the members, separating the member names with spaces. For example:
>
> ```
> stooges: larry moe curley
> staff: sascha wendy ian
> ```

Limit methods to limit

> Begins a section that lists the limitations on the directory. For more information on the *Limit* section, see the next section of this chapter.

Options opt1 opt2 opt3 . . .

> Turns on or off individual options within a particular directory. Options available are listed in the following table.

Option	Meaning
ExecCGI	Allows CGI scripts to be executed within this directory.
FollowSymLinks	Allows the web server to follow symbolic links within this directory.
Includes	Allows server-side include files.
Indexes	Allows automatic indexing of the directory if an index file (such as *index.html*) is not present.
IncludesNoExec	Allows server-side includes, but disables CGI scripts in the includes.
SymLinksIfOwnerMatch	Allows symbolic links to be followed only If the target of the file or the directory containing the target file matches the owner of the link.
All	Turns on all options.
None	Turns off all options.

Commands Within the <Limit>. . . </Limit> Block

The <Limit> directive is the heart of the Apache access control system. It is used to specify the actual hosts and/or the users that are to be allowed or to be denied access to the directory.

The format of the <Limit> directive is straightforward:

```
<Limit HTTP commands>
directives
</Limit>
```

Normally, you will want to limit both GET and POST commands.

The following directives may be present within a <Limit> block:

order options
> Specifies the order in which allow and deny statements are evaluated. Specify "order deny,allow" to cause the deny entries to be evaluated first; servers that match both the "deny" and "allow" lists are allowed.
>
> Specify "allow,deny" to check the allow entries first; servers that match both are denied.
>
> Specify "mutual-failure" to cause hosts on the allow list to be allowed, those on the deny list to be denied, and all others to be denied.

allow from host1 host2 ...
> Specifies hosts that are allowed access.

deny from host1 host2 ...
> Specifies hosts that are denied access.

require user user1 user2 user
> Only the specified users "user1, user2, and user3 . . ." are granted access.

require group group1 group2 ...
> Any user who is in one of the specified groups may be granted access.

require valid-user
> Any user that is listed in the *AuthUserFile* will be granted access.

Hosts in the *allow* and *deny* statements may be any of the following:

- A domain name, such as *.vineyard.net* (note the leading "." character)
- A fully qualified hostname such as *nc.vineyard.net*
- An IP address such as 204.17.195.100
- A partial IP address such as 204.17.195, which matches any host on that subnet
- The keyword "all", which matches all hosts

<Limit> Examples

If you wish to restrict access to a directory's files to everyone on the 204.17.195 subnet, you could add the following lines to your *access.conf* file:

```
<Directory /usr/local/etc/httpd/htdocs/special>
<Limit GET POST>
order deny,allow
```

```
deny from all
allow from 204.17.195
</Limit>
</Directory>
```

If you then wish to allow only the authenticated users *wendy* and *sascha* to access the files, and only when they are on subnet 204.17.195, you could add these lines:

```
AuthType Basic
AuthName The-T-Directory
AuthUserFile /etc/web/auth
<Limit GET POST>
order deny,allow
deny from all
allow from 204.17.195
require user sascha wendy
</Limit>
```

If you wish to allow the users *wendy* and *sascha* to access the files from anywhere on the Internet, provided they type the correct username and password, try this:

```
AuthType Basic
AuthName The-T-Directory
AuthUserFile /etc/web/auth
<Limit GET POST>
require user sascha wendy
</Limit>
```

If you wish to allow any registered user to access files on your system in a given directory, place this *.htaccess* file in that directory:

```
AuthType Basic
AuthName The-T-Group
AuthUserFile /etc/web/auth
<Limit GET POST>
require valid-user
</Limit>
```

 After modifying your *.htaccess* file, test it by attempting to access the information in the protected directory with both a valid account and an invalid account.

Manually Setting Up Web Users and Passwords

To use authenticated users, you need to create a password file. You can do this with the *htpasswd* program, using the "*-c*" option to create the file. For example:

```
# ./htpasswd -c /usr/local/etc/httpd/pw/auth sascha
Adding password for sascha.
New password: deus333
Re-type new password: deus333
#
```

You can add additional users and passwords with the *htpasswd* program. When you add additional users, do *not* use the "-c" option, or you will erase all of the users who are currently in the file:

```
# ./htpasswd /usr/local/etc/httpd/pw/auth wendy
Adding password for wendy.
New password:excom22
Re-type new password:excom22
#
```

The password file is similar, but not identical, to the standard */etc/passwd* file:

```
# cat /usr/local/etc/httpd/pw/auth
sascha:ZdZ2f8MOeVcNY
wendy:ukJTIFYWHKwtA
#
```

Because the web server uses *crypt*-style passwords, it is important that the password file be inaccessible to normal users on the server (and to users over the Web) to prevent an ambitious attacker from trying to guess passwords using a program like *Crack*.

Advanced User Management

If you need to manage more than a few users, you will want to implement a more sophisticated user management system.

Use a database

Instead of storing users, passwords, and groups in a single file, you can store them in a database such as MySQL. The Apache web server can then be programmed to refer to this database to determine whether users are valid. The user authentication database can be on the same computer as the web server, or it can be located on a central database server.

Use RADIUS or LDAP

RADIUS is a remote authentication protocol originally developed by Livingston and now used widely throughout the Internet industry. Radius provides for centralized username/password management. To use Radius, your web server is configured to validate username/password authentication requests with a remote RADIUS server.

LDAP is a general-purpose directory system that is increasingly being used for remote authentication. As with RADIUS, if you configure your web server to use LDAP for authentication, username/password pairs are sent to the remote LDAP server for validation. LDAP offers considerably more flexibility than RADIUS, such as the ability to manage groups and more easily handle authentication tokens. However, unlike RADIUS, LDAP sends usernames and passwords without encryption. If you wish to use an LDAP server, you need to protect usernames and passwords that are sent by either having them sent on a segregated network or having the transmissions encrypted by using LDAP over SSL.

Use PKI and digital certificates

Instead of using a username and password to authenticate a user, you can use a digital certificate that is stored on the user's hard disk.

To make use of digital certificates, a web site user must first create a public key and a secret key. The public key is then signed by a certification authority, which returns to the user a certificate that consists of the user's public key, a distinguished name (DN), and the certification authority's signature. You then configure your web server so that it will allow access to any user who has a valid certificate.

The advantage of using PKI and digital certificates is that you do not need to distribute valid user accounts to the web server—you only need to distribute the public key for the certification authority and a list of revoked certificates. This isn't a great advantage when you are running a single web server, but it can be tremendously advantageous when you are running hundreds or thousands of web servers.

For further information on digital certificates, see Chapter 21.

Controlling Access with Microsoft IIS

Microsoft's Internet Information Services (IIS) is a web service that is shipped as part of the Windows NT 4, 2000, and XP operating systems. It is a full-featured web server that does just about anything that you could possibly want (other than run on Unix, that is).

Installing IIS

To install IIS, follow these steps:

1. Open the "Add/Remove Programs" control panel.
2. Select "Add/Remove Windows Components."
3. Check "Internet Information Services."
4. Click "Next."

IIS installs the following directories on your system:

\Inetpub
   Root directory for your web server

\Inetpub\wwwroot
   Root document directory for the web server

\systemroot\Help\iisHelp
   Help files

\systemroot\system32\inetsrv
   Program files

The directories containing user content will remain on your system after you completely uninstall IIS.

 As soon as you install IIS, be sure that you go to the Microsoft Windows Update web site and download all relevant patches for IIS before you start the server. If possible, download the patches from behind a firewall. If you fail to install the IIS patches, your Windows server will almost certainly be broken into and compromised. This is true even if you are behind a corporate firewall or are otherwise "protected."

Downloading and Installing the IIS Patches

To install the patches, follow these steps:

1. Log into your Windows system using an account that has Administrator access.

2. Using Microsoft's Internet Explorer, open the URL *http://windowsupdate. microsoft.com/*. On most installations, you can easily open this URL by picking "Windows Update" from the Start menu.

3. You may be prompted as to whether or not you wish to run an ActiveX component that is signed by Microsoft Corporation. You must run this ActiveX applet in order to run the Windows Update feature.

4. Windows Update will search your system and identify which patches need to be updated. In all likelihood, you will need to install the Critical Updates Package. If a new service pack has come out, you will be advised to install that as well.

5. Select the updates you wish to download and click "Download" to download the software.

6. You will be prompted to accept the Supplemental Microsoft End User License Agreement ("Supplemental EULA"). Read the license agreement. You will note that "The entire risk arising out of use or performance of the OS components and any support services remains with you." You will also note that Microsoft disclaims all liability arising from its software for whatever damage that the software may cause, "even if Microsoft . . . has been advised of the possibility of such damages."

7. Click "Yes" to accept the Supplemental EULA.

8. Windows Update will download and install the necessary updates. In all likelihood, your computer will need to be rebooted when the updates are installed.

Controlling Access to IIS Web Pages

After your computer reboots, IIS will be running. If you go to the URL *http://localhost/*, you will be prompted to enter a valid username and password. Enter a username and password for a local administrative user and you will be presented with the IIS *localstart.asp* page. This page will give you information on how to start up the IIS console, how to view the online documentation, and how to create a document root.

Using the IIS snap-in component to the Windows Computer Management application, you can control many aspects of the IIS web and FTP server. To run the component, select "Adminstrative Tools" from the "Control Panel" window. Then double-click on "Computer Management." Expand the "Services and Applications" item in the tree (see Figure 20-4).

Figure 20-4. The Internet Information Services snap-in for the Windows Computer Management control panel allows you to control many aspects of IIS security.

To modify the properties of the web site, select "Default Web Site" and choose the "Properties" item from the Action menu.

Using this interface, you can enable or disable a variety of features, including:

- Whether or not accesses to the web site are logged, and if they are logged, where they are logged.
- The "home directory," or document root, of the web server.
- Whether the directory should be indexed.
- Whether anonymous access is allowed to the directory. (Default is yes.)

- If anonymous access is allowed, the local user that is used for granting anonymous access.
- Which authentication system is used for granting access.
- Whether visitors are allowed read and/or write access to the web server. (Default is read only.)
- Whether directory browsing is allowed. (Default is no.)
- Whether access is allowed to the source code of your scripts. (Default is no.)
- Whether additional headers should be sent with the web pages.
- What the PICS rating is for this web site.

If there are subdirectories in your *wwwroot* directory, you can select them and control their access on a directory-by-directory basis.

Restricting Access to IIS Directories

It is surprisingly easy to create a directory in your IIS web server that will be restricted to a specific set of users over the Internet. Windows IIS integrates with the Windows username directory and Windows directory permissions. Web users are generally users who have local accounts on your computer. For anonymous access, the default IIS installation creates an account named IUSR_*computername* (where *computername* is the name of your computer). If the IUSR_*computername* user has access to read a directory, then the directory can be read over the Internet.

In this example, we will create a directory called *private* and allow access only to a user named *blue* with a password *blueboy*.

1. Create a directory called *private* in the directory *c:\InetPub\wwwroot*.
2. Find the directory in the Computer Management application, select it, and examine its properties. This will display a window titled "private Properties."
3. Select the "Directory Security" tab of the "private Properties" window.
4. In the box titled "Anonymous access and authentication control," click the button labeled "Edit . . .".
5. Uncheck the box that says "Anonymous access."
6. Check the box that says "Basic Authentication" (the password is sent in clear-text). If you do not check this box, IIS will only use Microsoft's proprietary extensions to the HTTP protocol, which make Windows' challenge-response authentication system run over HTTP. (If you do not wish to have usernames and passwords sent in the clear over the Internet, simply use URLs that begin with *https:* instead of *http:*. See Figure 20-5.)
7. Click "Yes" to indicate that you wish to use Basic Authentication.
8. Click "OK" to close the Authentication Methods window.

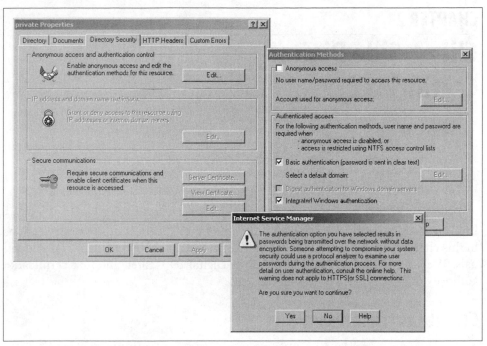

Figure 20-5. Using the Computer Management application to restrict access to a directory

9. Click "Apply" to apply your changes to the directory.

10. In the Computer Management application, select on the "Local Users and Groups" element of the tree.

11. Choose "New User" from the Action menu.

12. Create a new user that has the username *blue* and the password *blueboy*.

The user that you have created will now have access to the directory.

> Be sure to configure your system so that the users you create will not have undue access to your Windows computer. Specifically, you may wish to remove these users from the Users group and place them in a specific group for World Wide Web access. You should also firewall your Windows server so that users on the Internet only have access to ports 80 and 443.

If your *wwwroot* directory is on an NTFS partition, you can use the NTFS directory permissions to control which users have access to the private directory. If your *wwwroot* directory is on a FAT32 partition, all valid users will have access to all files.

For more information on IIS security, refer to the IIS Documentation under the section "Administration → Server Administration → Security."

## CHAPTER 21

Client-Side Digital Certificates

In this chapter:
• Client Certificates
• A Tour of the VeriSign Digital ID Center

In the previous chapter, we looked at the use of digital certificates by organizations. In this chapter, we'll look at how digital certificates can certify the identity of individuals. We'll also walk through the VeriSign Digital ID Center, the first certification authority to offer public services on the Web.

Client Certificates

A *client certificate* is a digital certificate designed to certify the identity of an individual. As with certificates for web sites, client certificates bind a particular name to a particular secret key. They are issued by certification authorities. Client certificates have many uses and benefits:

- Digital certificates can eliminate the need to remember usernames and passwords. You simply sign your digital signature whenever you enter a restricted space (provided that the server accepts your digital signature).

- Instead of deploying a large distributed database, organizations can simply use an authorization digital certificate issued by a particular CA as proof that the individual is authorized to access the resource. (Many organizations use the existence of a valid certificate from a CA as authorization in itself. This works, but it is costly because you then need a different CA for every service that you wish to be able to authorize separately.)

- Because authenticating your identity with a digital certificate requires access to a secret key, it is harder for groups of individuals to share a single digital ID than it is for a group of people to share a username and password. This is because there are technical barriers to sharing secret keys between users, and because users may be unwilling to share a secret key that is used for more than one application. This is interesting to sites that have per-user charges for distributing information over the Internet.

- Because digital certificates contain a person's public key, you can use somebody's digital certificate to send that person encrypted electronic mail.

- Certificates that denote a person's age could be used for restrictions on sexually oriented material or on chat groups, provided that certificates are only issued to adults and that there's a way to prevent adults from sharing private keys with minors.
- Certificates that denote a person's gender could be used to allow access to "women's only" or "men's only" spaces, provided, once again, that there are suitable controls on the issuance of certificates and the transfer of keys.

Why Client Certificates?

By creating strong systems for identifying users, certificates help eliminate anonymity. They do so even more effectively than cookies. A cookie merely leaves a track of where you have been through a web site. A digital certificate, on the other hand, leaves behind your name, email address, or other identifying information that by design can be traced back to you.

Because certificates eliminate anonymity, some Internet users are opposed to certificates on the grounds that they compromise a user's privacy. Well, of course they do: that's their purpose. As currently constructed, however, certificates are never sent by a web browser without the user's knowledge and permission. Furthermore, certificates never contain information that is unknown to the user. Of course, both of these conditions could change in the future.

In the long term, Internet users may change their minds about certificates. It's true that a mark of totalitarian regimes is the issuing of identification cards and strong penalties for the failure to produce those cards when asked. But identification cards also solidify a strong society and good behavior, giving authorities ways of holding people accountable for their actions (and reminding people they can be held accountable). They also permit trust and commerce, which benefit all members of society. Thus, strong identification is likely to become more common on the Internet. Digital signatures are likely to be a part of any identification infrastructure.

Support for Client-Side Digital Certificates

Client-side digital certificates are supported by Microsoft Internet Explorer 3.0 and above, Netscape Navigator 3.0 and above, and many other SSL-based applications. To support client-side certificates, a browser must provide the following functions:

Key creation
: The browser contains code for creating a public/private key pair and sending the public key to a certification authority in the form of an HTTP POST transaction.

Certificate acquisition
: The browser must be able to accept a certificate that is downloaded from the certification authority and to store the certificate in a certificate store.

Challenge/response

> The browser must be able to use its stored secret key to sign a randomly generated challenge supplied by an SSL server.

Secure storage

> The browser must have a secure place to store the secret key. Netscape Navigator allows keys to be stored in either an encrypted file or a cryptographic token, such as a smart card. Internet Explorer uses the Microsoft CryptoAPI, which allows for similar functionality. Figure 21-1 shows Netscape's functions.

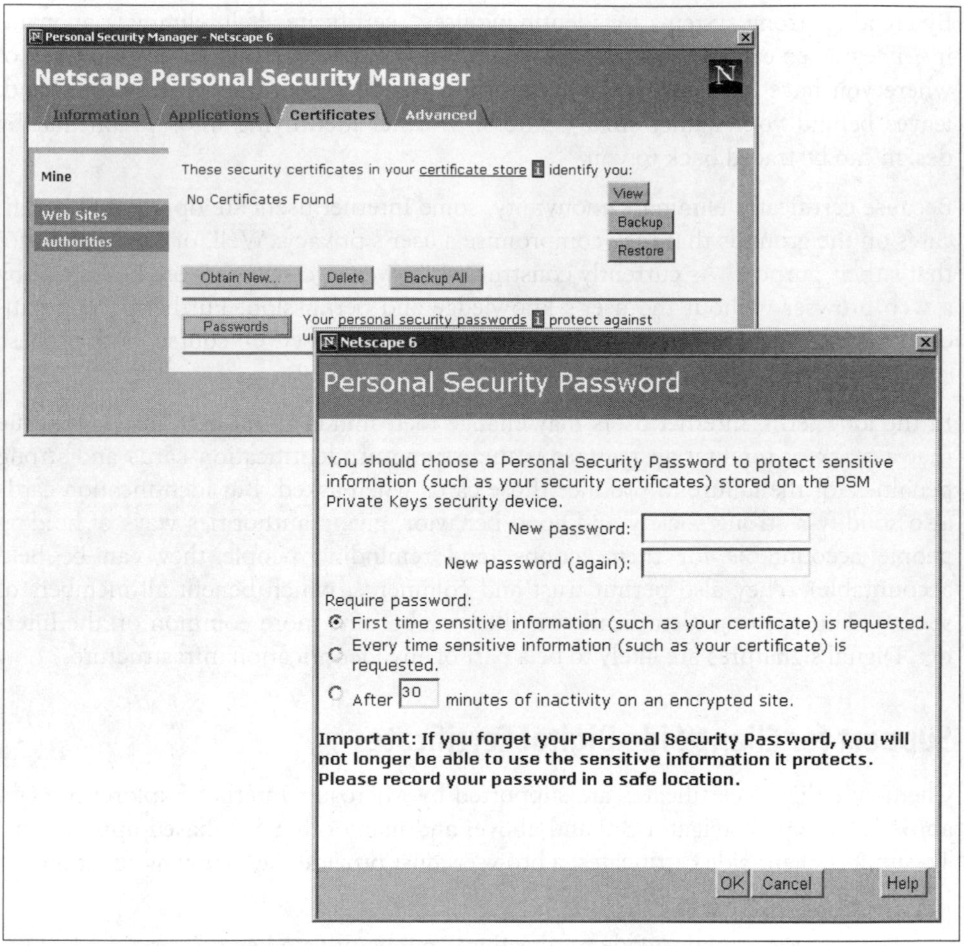

Figure 21-1. Netscape's Personal Security Manager panel allows you to put a password on your secret keys and web site passwords. The password is used as an encryption key to encrypt your information. Netscape can automatically prompt you for the password the first time in a browsing session that the information is needed, each time, or after a set time of inactivity.

A Tour of the VeriSign Digital ID Center

VeriSign opened its Digital ID Center during the summer of 1996. Today VeriSign is the oldest and largest of the world's certification authorities. VeriSign sells certificates for personal use, servers, and code signing. The center is located at *http://digitalid.verisign.com/*. Its home page is shown in Figure 21-2.

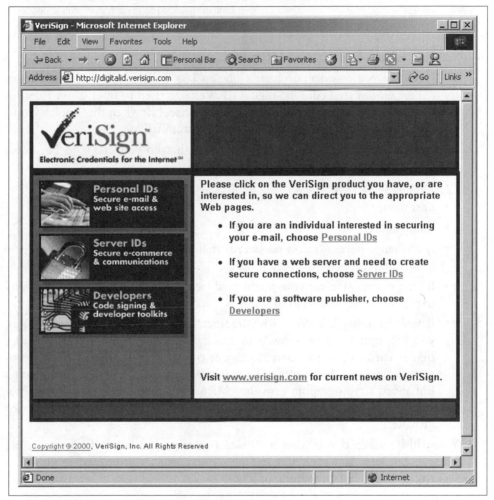

Figure 21-2. The home page for VeriSign's Digital ID Center

Generating a VeriSign Digital ID

VeriSign distributes digital certificates (called *digital IDs* by VeriSign) from its web site. These certificates are standard X.509 v3 public key certificates and can be used with a wide variety of programs, as shown in Table 21-1.

Table 21-1. Some programs that can use client certificates

Program	Purpose
Lotus Notes and Domino Server	Email encryption and digital certification; verify the identity of web users.
Microsoft Internet Explorer	Verifying the identity of a person browsing a web site.
Microsoft Outlook and Outlook Express	Emailing encryption and digital certification.
Netscape Navigator	Email encryption and digital certification; verify the identity of a person browsing a web site.

VeriSign's certificate creation process consists of six steps:

1. You decide if you wish to purchase a single Class 1 digital ID or if you wish to try a "Free 60-day trial edition" digital ID. VeriSign used to offer Class 1 certificates in "bulk" for distribution within an enterprise, but when this book went to press it appeared that this option had been discontinued.

2. You provide identifying information to establish who you claim to be. For a Class 1 digital ID in July 2001, VeriSign required:

   * First name or alias

   * Last name

   * Email address

   * A challenge phrase (i.e., a password) that is used to revoke, replace, renew or set preferences for the digital ID.[*]

   * Billing information for your credit card (required even if you are purchasing the "Free 60-day trial edition").

   * If you are using Windows with Internet Explorer and 128-bit encryption, you will optionally be allowed to specify a cryptographic service provider that is used to generate and store your private key. Service providers supported include Microsoft's Base Cryptographic Provider, Microsoft's Enhanced Cryptographic Provider, Microsoft's Strong Cryptographic Provider, Gemplus GemSAFE Card, and Schlumberger Cryptographic Service Provider.

3. You will be asked if you wish to "Protect your private key." If you are using Internet Explorer and click this checkbox, you will be prompted to choose a security setting of high, medium, or low:

   High

   With this setting, your private key is encrypted and requires the use of a special password every time it is used.

---

[*] Please note the irony that VeriSign protects the security of its customers' digital IDs with a simple passphrase.

Medium

> With this setting, your private key is stored encrypted and you must enter your special password the first time that it is used in any browsing session.

Low

> With this setting, your private key is stored without any specific security procedures (although it may still be scrambled by the Windows login system).

4. You will be asked to read and accept the terms of this statement. (Note that the VeriSign certificate practices statement is a very long and dense legal agreement that almost nobody reads and that has changed from time to time.)

5. VeriSign will send you an email message. The email message contains a URL and a personal identification number (PIN). By copying the PIN from the email message and pasting it into the form contained on the URL that you are provided, VeriSign is able to verify that you can indeed receive email at the address that you provided.

6. VeriSign's web server will locate your digital ID and allow you to install it by pressing the INSTALL button (see Figure 21-3).

Evolution at VeriSign

VeriSign's original plan was to offer several different levels or *classes* of digital IDs for the VeriSign Trust Network (VTN). The lowest levels would offer minimum security and certification, while the higher levels would allow businesses to place higher reliance on the security of the certificates. For the lowest level, Class 1, VeriSign would merely assure that the digital ID mapped to a valid email address. For the highest level, Class 4, an individual would have to appear in person before a VeriSign representative, and the private key would have to be stored in some sort of device that required biometric authentication before it could be used. (Class 4 certificates were publicly discussed, but never offered by the company.)

Alas, VeriSign's grand scheme for digital IDs has not yet come to pass. Today VeriSign sells only a single ID, the Class 1 certificate. VeriSign's Class 1 certificate contains a person's name and email address. All recipients of the Class 1 certificate are listed on the company's public web site. The certificates also come with $1000 worth of VeriSign's "NetSure" insurance to protect "against economic loss caused by corruption, loss, or misuse of your digital ID," although it's really not clear what that means in practice. (VeriSign's representatives would not answer questions as to whether or not a claim had ever been made under the NetSure program.)

It's interesting to see how VeriSign's Class 1 digital ID certificate program has evolved over the past six years. In 2001 VeriSign Class 1 digital IDs cost $14.95 each and are good for a year. Meanwhile, the VTN server certificates do not follow the class system at all. Instead, VeriSign sells the "Secure Site," "Secure Site Pro," "Commerce Site," and "Commerce Site Pro" certificates.

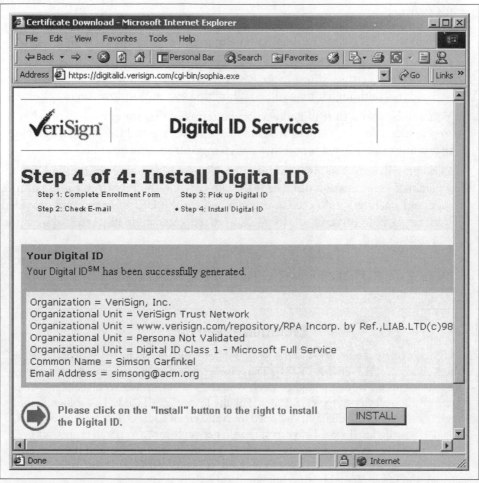

Figure 21-3. After you have verified that your email address works, VeriSign's web site will allow you to retrieve your digital ID.

Your digital ID is now installed. If you wish to view the ID, you can use Internet Explorer's Certificates panel to view the certificate, as shown in Figure 21-4.

 If you create your digital ID with Internet Explorer, you will be unable to use it with Netscape Navigator. Likewise, if you create a digital ID with Netscape Navigator, you will be unable to use it with Microsoft programs.

Finding a Digital ID

VeriSign provides a system for looking up a digital ID by name, email, address, or serial number. The form is located at *http://digitalid.verisign.com/query.htm*, but you

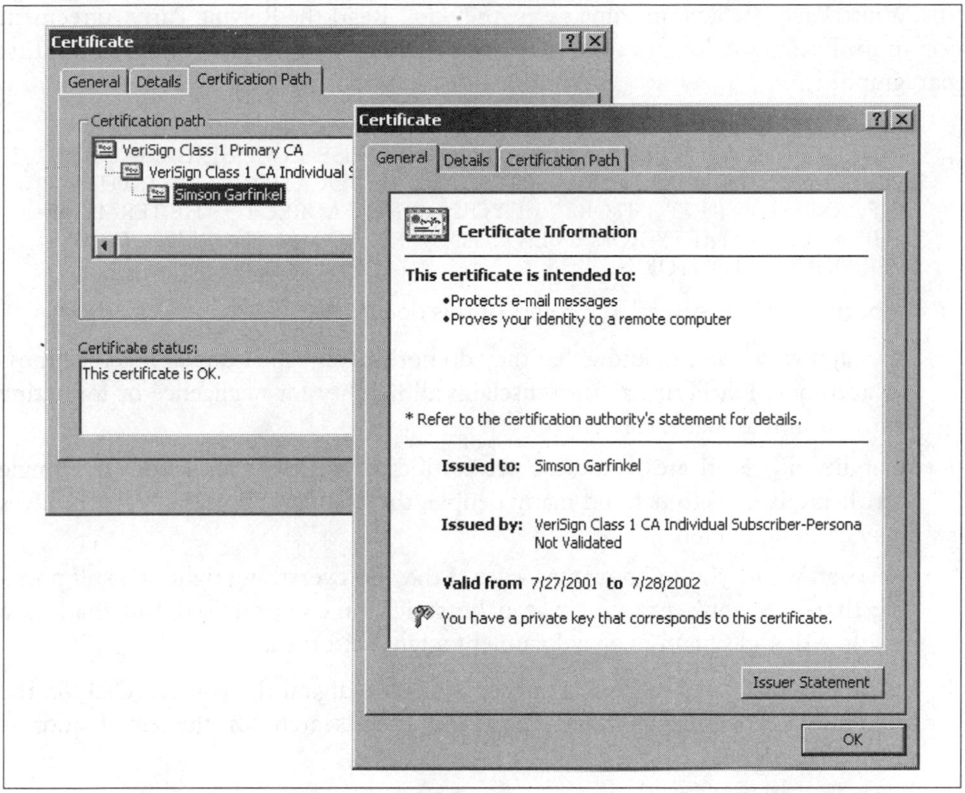

Figure 21-4. The certificate that was created in Figure 21-3, as viewed with the Internet Explorer Certificates . . . panel. Internet Explorer notices that we have a private key that corresponds to the certificate.

can also click on the home page of the VeriSign Digital ID Center. On that page you will find the following text:*

> Search our online database for anyone's Digital ID by entering the name, email address, or serial number and issuer name contained in the Digital ID, and clicking on the SEARCH button. If you cannot locate a Digital ID by email address or name, the owner of the Digital ID may have chosen to "unlist" it when setting Digital ID preferences. In order to find it, you will need to obtain the serial number and issuer name of the Digital ID from its owner.

> You cannot use wildcard characters. By clicking the SEARCH button you accept the terms of our *Relying Party Agreement*.

This page states that looking up a user's digital ID in VeriSign's online database requires that you agree to be bound by VeriSign's Relying Party Agreement. This is sort of like a phone company requiring you to agree to a legal agreement before using

---

* As of autumn 2001.

the White Pages (which, in some cases, they do). Read the Relying Party Agreement for yourself; it is too long to print here in its entirety, but we have included the first paragraph:

> YOU MUST READ THIS RELYING PARTY AGREEMENT BEFORE VALIDATING A DIGITAL IDSM ("CERTIFICATE") OR OTHERWISE ACCESSING OR USING VERISIGN'S DATABASE OF CERTIFICATE REVOCATIONS AND OTHER INFORMATION ("REPOSITORY"). IF YOU DO NOT AGREE TO THE TERMS OF THIS RELYING PARTY AGREEMENT, YOU ARE NOT AUTHORIZED TO USE VERISIGN'S REPOSITORY.

It's important to note several key points of this document:

- VeriSign wants you to know that they do not warrant their digital IDs for fitness or accuracy. Furthermore, they disclaim all liability for negligence or for acting without unreasonable care.

- Liability on certificates is limited per certificate, not per transaction. If a single certificate is used to defraud many people, the compensation that each receives may be quite limited.

- VeriSign wants you to know that, even if they do everything right, it's still possible that a person's private key can be stolen or compromised and that, as a result, a digital signature on a document might be forged.

If you are still interested in finding Simson's Class 1 digital ID, you can click on the word "Find" on VeriSign's home page and then search for the email address *simsong@acm.org*.

When this book was written, such a search displayed two digital IDs:

```
Simson Garfinkel (Valid)
simsong@acm.org
Digital ID Class 1 - Client Authentication Full Service New
Validity period from Jul-28-2001(GMT) to Jul-28-2002(GMT)

Simson L Garfinkel (Expired)
simsong@acm.org
Digital ID Class 2 - Software Validation
Validity period from Nov-06-1996(GMT) to Nov-06-1997(GMT)
```

Revoking a Digital ID

VeriSign provides a system for revoking digital IDs issued to individuals. The system requires that you know a digital ID's serial number and the type of digital ID, and that you give a reason for the revocation. Some of the reasons VeriSign allows you to choose are:

- Forgotten or lost password
- Compromised private key
- Per request of subscriber

- Issuer update
- Overwrote old key pair file and submitted new request
- Corrupted key pair
- Incorrect common name
- Wrong size key pair
- Information may be materially threatened or compromised
- Material fact is known or reasonably believed to be false
- Material certificate issuance prerequisite not satisfied or waived
- CA's private key compromised*
- Per request of subscriber's agent
- Faulty issuance
- Replacement

VeriSign can also revoke digital IDs that it determines were issued fraudulently or for which the subscriber did not, in VeriSign's opinion, follow the terms of the VeriSign CPS. For example, in one case VeriSign revoked the digital ID of a programmer who, in VeriSign's opinion, did not follow the terms of the CPS and the Authenticode pledge (see Chapter 22).

---

* It may seem strange that VeriSign would allow users to revoke their digital IDs because they think that VeriSign's private key has been compromised. However, if a user really does think that VeriSign's private key has been compromised, then presumably that user would want to revoke his or her digital ID.

## CHAPTER 22

Code Signing and Microsoft's Authenticode

In this chapter:
- Why Code Signing?
- Microsoft's Authenticode Technology
- Obtaining a Software Publishing Certificate
- Other Code Signing Methods

Code signing is a technique for signing executable programs with digital signatures. Code signing is designed to improve the reliability of software distributed over the Internet by making it possible to detect very minor alterations to programs. Code signing is also designed to combat the problem of malicious programs, including computer viruses and Trojan horses.

This chapter describes the mechanics of code signing. For a discussion of why code signing might not provide the degree of safety its backers hope for, see Chapter 12.

Why Code Signing?

Walk into a computer store and buy a copy of Microsoft Windows, and you can be pretty sure the box contains a genuine CD-ROM with a computer operating system written by the Redmond software giant. The program, after all, comes shrinkwrapped in a box, with a difficult-to-forge security hologram seal. Inside the box is a CD-ROM that may include its own hologram. You have great confidence that your CD-ROM or floppy disks have the same program as every other CD-ROM or floppy disk sold in every other Windows box. Presumably, the software was checked at the factory, so you have every reason to believe that you've got a legitimate and unaltered copy.

The same can't be said for software downloaded over the Internet. When Microsoft released its 1,264,640-byte Service Pack 1 for Windows 95, the only way to be sure that you had a legitimate and unaltered copy was to download it directly from Microsoft's web site—and then hope the file wasn't accidentally or intentionally corrupted either on Microsoft's site or while it was being downloaded.

What's worse, if you wanted to save yourself some time by copying Service Pack 1 from a friend, there was no way that you could inspect the file and know whether it was good or not: your friend's copy might have been corrupted on his hard disk, or it might have been infected with a virus, or it might not even be the right program. How do you know if it is a true copy, other than trusting your friend at his word?

With Microsoft Windows 95 Service Pack 1, there was no way to electronically certify the contents of code downloaded over the Internet. But starting with Internet Explorer 3.0, Windows users were given a powerful system for trusting the authenticity of their software: digital signatures for executable programs. Called *Authenticode*, the Microsoft digital signature system is specifically designed to allow users to verify that downloaded programs are authentic and unmodified.

Code Signing in Theory

Code signing was supposed to bring the assurance of shrink-wrapped software to the world of software that's distributed electronically. It does this by adding two things to an executable:

- A digital signature that signs the executable with a secret key.
- A digital certificate that contains the corresponding public key, the name of the person or organization to whom that key belongs, and a digital signature signed by a recognized certification authority.

These are shown in Figure 22-1.

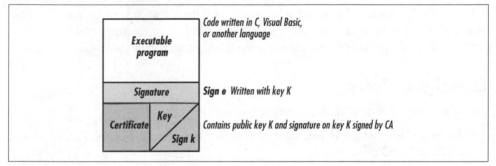

Figure 22-1. A piece of signed code, showing the code's digital signature and the corresponding digital certificate.

To work, code signing presupposes the existence of a working public key infrastructure. Otherwise, there is no way to tell whose signature is on a piece of signed code. Code signing also requires that those individuals and organizations that hold secret keys protect them properly. Otherwise, there is no way to know if a signature was written by an authorized individual or by a malicious attacker who obtained a copy of another's secret key.*

---

* We'll also assume that the algorithms used are strong, that the key is big enough and sufficiently random, and the overall software infrastructure was coded and protected properly. There are many more assumptions, but these should illustrate the point—at some level, you need to trust a lot of things that can go wrong. The reputation and competence of the parties involved help you gain confidence in the structure, or contribute to a lack of confidence.

Microsoft's Authenticode system is used most often with VeriSign's public key infrastructure, although any certification authority key that is approved for code signing and that is in the Internet Explorer key store can be used for verifying Authenticode signatures.

To be useful, the signatures must be verified. Internet Explorer will analyze code after it is downloaded to determine if a signature is or is not present. Later versions of Windows, including Windows 2000, ME, and XP take Authenticode one step further and use it for signing critical parts of the Windows operating system. These signatures are verified every time the Windows operating system starts up. In this way, code signing can detect malicious attempts to modify code, accidental modifications that might result from operating system errors or hardware failure, and unauthorized modification attempts by the user. Thus, code signing can dramatically boost the reliability of today's computer systems by allowing us to detect modifications in programs before those programs are run.

Code signing has also been proposed as a way of creating accountability for people who write programs and distribute them on the Internet. The idea is that Internet users should be taught not to run programs that are unsigned.* Then, if a malicious program is distributed on the Internet, it will be a simple matter to find out who distributed the program and punish them. By establishing significant penalties for people who distribute malicious programs, as well as a reliable technique for tracking those authors, it is thought that the incidence of such programs will be greatly diminished.

Code Signing Today

There are several code signing systems in use today:

- Authenticode, which is Microsoft's system for signing CAB, CAT, CTL, DLL, EXE, and OCX files
- Microsoft Office 2000 and VBA Signing, which allows software publishers to digitally sign Microsoft Office Macros and Visual Basic for Applications objects
- Netscape Object Signing, which can be used to digitally sign Java Archive (JAR) files, Netscape plug-ins, Java programs, and JavaScript programs
- Macromedia Shockwave digital signatures (requires Director 8 Shockwave Studio or Macromedia Flash)
- Marimba Castanet, which supports code signing for certification information distributed over a Castanet Channel
- Sun Java SDK, which supports its own code signing model

---

* If public education fails, system software can always be modified so that unsigned programs cannot run.

Code Signing and Legal Restrictions on Cryptography

In contrast to other encryption technologies, there are no significant legal restrictions on code signing technology. This is because signing does not embed secret messages in the signed documents and because the patents that once covered public key cryptography have now expired.

Beware the Zipper!

The need for code signing was conclusively demonstrated in 1995 and 1996, when a program called *PKZIP30B.EXE* was reportedly uploaded to many software libraries on the Internet. The program appeared to be the 3.0 beta release of PKZIP, a popular disk compression program. But when unsuspecting users downloaded the program and tried to run it, the rogue program actually erased the user's hard disk. That didn't do wonders for the reputation of PKWare, PKZIP's creator.

Digital signatures could have prevented this mishap. If PKWare had previously adopted a policy of signing their programs with the company's digital signature, then bad hackers could never have created the *PKZIP30B.EXE* file and credibly passed it off as being the creation of PKWare. That's because the rogue hackers who distributed the *PKZIP30B.EXE* program couldn't have signed it with PKWare's digital signature.

Of course, PKWare would have to have put in place a policy of signing their programs with their secret key and making sure that the company's public key was in wide distribution. They would also have had to make sure that there was a simple-to-use verification program that was widely available.

How could PKWare have done this? It would have been tough. The company could have created a PGP key, distributed it, and used that key to sign new versions of its program. But how could anybody have trusted the key? Or the company could have built its own public key and the verification program in previous versions of PKZIP. The program could have been equipped with a "verify and upgrade" command that would inspect the digital signature of a proposed patch or upgrade, make sure that it matched, and then perform the necessary upgrade. Not only would this have thwarted the malicious hackers, it would have also assured the company's customers that the upgrades they got from friends were true and unadulterated.

Today such bootstrapping is no longer necessary. Companies can simply obtain a software publisher's certificate from a recognized certification authority and use it to sign the programs that they distribute. Of course, since most users will happily run code that is unsigned, it is not clear that code signing ultimately increases the security of a desktop computer system.

Microsoft's Authenticode Technology

Authenticode is a system developed by Microsoft for digitally signing executable code. Authenticode was publicly announced in June of 1996 as part of Microsoft's Internet Explorer 3.0 and ActiveX technologies. Authenticode now ships as a standard part of all Microsoft operating systems and applications.

Authenticode describes a series of file formats for signing Microsoft 32-bit CAB, CAT, CTL, DLL, EXE, and OCX files. The signed file contains the original unsigned file, the digital signature, and an X.509 v3 digital certificate for the public key needed to verify the Authenticode signature. Authenticode cannot sign Windows COM files or 16-bit EXE files.

Authenticode is closely associated with ActiveX, Microsoft's system for downloading programs from web pages to end user computers. There are considerable security issues associated with ActiveX. Authenticode was designed to mitigate these dangers by making software publishers accountable for programs they write. (ActiveX and the security provided by Authenticode are discussed in detail in Chapter 12.)

According to Microsoft's Authenticode documentation, organizations seeking to obtain software publishing certificates must meet the following criteria:

Identification
> Applicants must submit their name, address, and other material that proves their identity as corporate representatives. Proof of identify requires either personal presence or registered credentials.

The Pledge
> Applicants must pledge that they will not distribute software that they know, or should have known, contains viruses or would otherwise harm a user's computer or code.

Dun & Bradstreet Rating
> Applicants must achieve a level of financial standing as indicated by a D-U-N-S number (which indicates a company's financial stability) and any additional information provided by this service. This rating identifies the applicant as a corporation that is still in business. (Other financial rating services are being investigated.) Corporations that do not have a D-U-N-S number at the time of application (usually because of recent incorporation) can apply for one and expect a response in less than two weeks.*

---

* *http://msdn.microsoft.com/workshop/security/authcode/intro_authenticode.asp*

The "Pledge"

What does it mean when a piece of code is "signed?" It could mean that the program has been analyzed and is certified to do exactly what the manufacturer claims that it will do, no more and no less. Or a program could be signed to indicate that it contains a truthful and accurate copy of a computer virus that destroyed a million computers. By itself, the act of signing a program doesn't mean anything unless the keyholder makes a legal representation that it does.

In the case of Authenticode, Microsoft and VeriSign have tried to create a legal framework that signed code will behave responsibly and not wreck computers or data. This legal framework is called the *Software Publisher's Pledge*. The Pledge is a binding agreement in which the software publisher promises not to sign programs that contain viruses or that will otherwise damage a person's computer.

The Pledge is described in the VeriSign subscriber agreement (previously, it was in the VeriSign CPS). It is reprinted here:

> In addition to the other representations, obligations, and warranties contained or referenced in the certificate application, the [individual] [commercial] software publisher certificate applicant represents and warrants that he, she, or it shall exercise reasonable care consistent with prevailing industry standards to exclude programs, extraneous code, viruses, or data that may be reasonably expected to damage, misappropriate, or interfere with the use of data, software, systems, or operations of the other party.

> This software publisher's pledge is made exclusively by the [individual] [commercial] software publisher certificate applicant. Issuing authorities and VeriSign shall not be held responsible for the breach of such representations and warranties by the [individual] [commercial] software publisher under any circumstance.

The Authenticode Pledge can't make software signed by Authenticode software publisher's keys secure. What the Pledge actually does is give certification authorities grounds for revoking software publisher certificates that are used to sign code that does not comply with the Pledge's terms. Of course, any such revocation is only likely to occur *after* signed code has demonstrated that it is dangerous.

Publishing with Authenticode

To publish with Authenticode, you must have two things:

- A program that you wish to sign.
- A copy of the Microsoft Authenticode Software Developer's Kit (SDK). This kit can be freely downloaded from the Microsoft Developer Network (MSDN) Library web site. Because URLs on MSDN change frequently, we will not print it here; you can probably find the development kit by going to *http://msdn. microsoft.com/* and searching for the term "Authenticode".

For developers, signing an application program represents an additional step that must be followed to publish a program. Complicating matters, signing a program must be the last thing that is done to a program before it is released, because if you make any changes to the program after it is signed, it will need to be signed again. If you distribute your program as part of a self-extracting installer, you should sign both the program itself and the installer.

The Authenticode SDK

The Authenticode SDK consists of eight programs:

MakeCert.exe
> Creates keys and certificates that can be used for testing Authenticode. If you do not wish to create your own private key, you can use MakeCert's built-in "test root" which is issued by "Root Agency" to "Joe's-Software-Emporium."

Cert2SPC.exe
> Creates a test software publishing certificate (SPC) from one or more X.509 certificates. This test certificate can be used for code signing, but it is not needed, as the certificate created by MakeCert can be used for signing code. When you actually sign code for public distribution, you will use an SPC that you obtain from a certification authority.

SignCode.exe
> Signs a program with a certificate and private key that you specify. SignCode can create either "personal" signatures or "commercial" signatures. Internet Explorer will display these signatures differently to convey a different level of trust and authenticity.

ChkTrust.exe
> Checks the signature on a file.

MakeCTL.exe
> Creates a certificate trust list.

CertMgr.exe
> Manages certificates, certificate trust lists, and certificate revocation lists.

SetReg.exe
> Sets registry keys that control the certificate verification process.

MakeCat.exe
> Creates a combined catalog of files. This allows a user to approve a single dialog box, instead of having a separate dialog box for each signed component. Trust catalogs require Internet Explorer 5 or above.

The code signing tools can use certificates and keys that are stored either in files or in certificate stores. A *certificate store* is a service that is provided through the Microsoft Cryptographic API (CAPI). The basic CAPI that ships with Authenticode stores certificates and keys encrypted in the Windows registry. However, other CAPIs can store certificates and keys in smart cards or other high-security devices. Because the Authenticode tools can work directly with certificate stores, they can work with any high-security device that is directly supported by Windows.

In the following examples, we use only certificates and keys that are stored in files.

Making the certificate

In this section and those that follow, we will use the MakeCert program to create a test private key and certificate. We will then add the certificate to our program to create a test certificate and use it to sign a test program.

The first step is to create a self-signed certificate for our code signing CA. Let's make Certificate #100 for the Nitroba Code Signing Authority that is good for 20 years (240 months):

```
C:\hello>makecert -r -n "CN=Nitroba Code Signing Authority" -sv nitroba.pvk -ss
NitrobaStore Nitroba.cer -m 240 -# 100
```

When you run this program, *MakeCert.exe* will bring up a window asking you for a password to protect the private key (Figure 22-2).

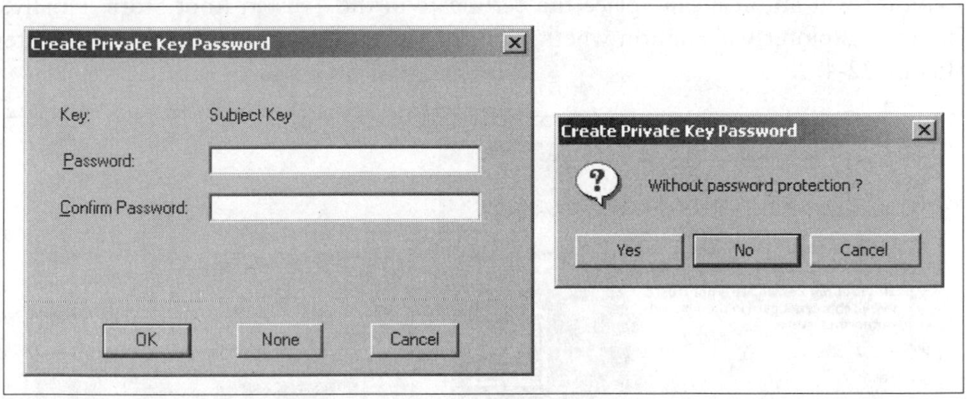

Figure 22-2. The makecert.exe program gives you the opportunity to assign a password to a certificate's corresponding private key. If you choose to enter no password, you will be asked to confirm this decision.

As this is a test certificate, we really don't need to protect the private key. *MakeCert. exe* will ask for confirmation, then put the Nitroba private key into the *nitroba.pvk* file and the certificate in the *nitroba.cer* file:

```
C:\hello>makecert -r -n "CN=Nitroba Code Signing Authority" -sv nitroba.pvk -ss
NitrobaStore Nitroba.cer -m 240 -# 100
Succeeded

C:\hello>dir nitroba.*
 Volume in drive C is 40GB
 Volume Serial Number is 7640-B7AA

 Directory of C:\hello

07/22/2001  01:59p                 332 nitroba.pvk
07/22/2001  01:59p                 406 Nitroba.cer
```

```
        2 File(s)            738 bytes
        0 Dir(s)  27,876,065,280 bytes free
```

C:\hello>

Adding the certificate to the store

To add the certificate to our certificate store, simply double-click on the *nitroba.cer* key in Internet Explorer or use the Windows *start* command:

```
C:\hello>start nitroba.cer
```

c:\hello>

This will bring up the Microsoft Certificate Information panel (Figure 22-3). Press "Install Certificate . . ." to bring up the Certificate Import Wizard. On the next panel, select "Automatically select the certificate store based on the type of certificate." Because we used the "-s" option to create a self-signed certificate, Internet Explorer will automatically place the certificate in the Trusted Root Store. Finally, Internet Explorer will confirm whether or not you really wish to add the certificate (Figure 22-4).

Figure 22-3. The Certificate Information panel can be used to install new certificates.

Signing a program

The program *SignCode.exe* is used to create Authenticode signatures. If the program is run without any arguments, the *SignCode.exe* program runs the Digital Signature

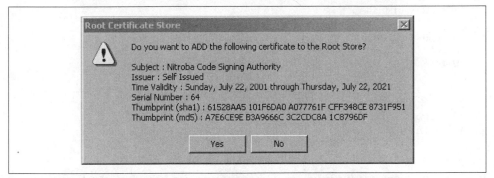

Figure 22-4. Internet Explorer confirms whether or not you wish to add the certificate. Notice that even though we specified certificate Serial Number 100, the serial number that was added is 64.

Wizard (see the following section); *SignCode.exe* can also be run from the command line. The Digital Signature Wizard is useful the first time you use the program. If you wish to have programs signed automatically when they are compiled, you can modify your Makefile so that the *SignCode.exe* program is automatically run after the executable is linked together.

Although Microsoft's Authenticode file format allows for multiple signatures on a single file (cosigners, if you will), the *SignCode.exe* program cannot create such signatures. If you attempt to sign a file that is already signed, the previous signature will be replaced with the new one.

In the following example, we will sign a small program named *hello.exe*. The hello program is the classic C hello program:

```
C:\hello>type hello.c
#include <stdio.h>

int main(int argc,char **argv)
{
        puts("Hello World!");
}

C:\hello>cl hello.c
Microsoft (R) 32-bit C/C++ Optimizing Compiler Version 12.00.8804 for 80x86
Copyright (C) Microsoft Corp 1984-1998. All rights reserved.

hello.c
Microsoft (R) Incremental Linker Version 6.00.8447
Copyright (C) Microsoft Corp 1992-1998. All rights reserved.

/out:hello.exe
hello.obj

C:\hello>dir hello.*
 Volume in drive C is 40GB
 Volume Serial Number is 7640-B7AA
```

```
    Directory of C:\hello

07/22/2001  01:01p                      84 hello.c
07/22/2001  08:22p                     449 hello.obj
07/22/2001  08:22p                  40,960 hello.exe
               3 File(s)         41,493 bytes
               0 Dir(s)  27,871,641,600 bytes free

C:\hello>hello
Hello World!

C:\hello>
```

Running the *SignCode.exe* program without arguments brings up the Digital Signature Wizard (see Figure 22-5.) On the first panel, specify the name of the program that you wish to sign; on the second panel, indicate that you wish "Custom" operation (see Figure 22-6).

Figure 22-5. Running SignCode.exe without arguments brings up the Digital Signature Wizard.

Now that you have selected the program that you wish to sign, you need to choose a certificate to use (see Figure 22-7). After choosing the certificate, you need to choose the private key (see Figure 22-8). Then you will be prompted to choose the hash algorithm to use with the signature—either MD5 or SHA1 (not shown).

Authenticode allows you to include multiple certificates within a single signed file. For example, if a large organization has a single root and an elaborate PKI signing

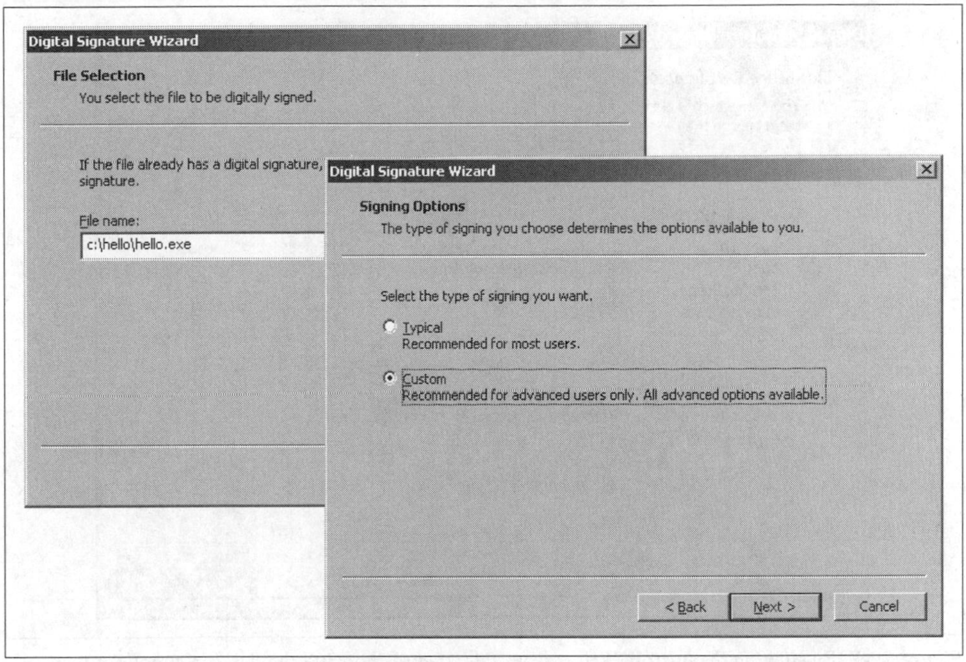

Figure 22-6. To sign a program, you must specify which program will be signed. After you have selected a program, specify "Custom" signing to get access to all of the program's options.

tree, verifying a single signature might require having the organization's root certificate, the certificate for a division, the certificate for a management group, the certificate for a project, and the signature for a particular programmer. By incorporating all of these certificates into the signed executable, you make it possible for the Authenticode system to automatically validate the certificate chain by merely having the organization's root certificate, without forcing the user to download four or more intermediate certificates. The Additional Certificates panel (Figure 22-9) of the Digital Signature Wizard allows you to add these certificates to the binary that you will sign. For most applications, you will choose "No additional certificates."

Authenticode allows you to provide a description and a URL for each signed program. These are created on the Data Description panel (Figure 22-10) of the Digital Signature Wizard. If you provide a URL, you should make sure that the URL will remain valid for as long as your program is available for download or likely to be used. Authenticode also supports timestamping services. These services will digitally sign a hash that is provided over the Web. The purpose of the timestamping service is to allow a digitally signed object to be used after the certificate that was used to sign the object has expired. The secure timestamp lets the client know that the signature was created with a signature that was valid when it was made (Figure 22-11). Finally, the Digital Signature Wizard will display a window that shows all of the options that have been selected. When you press the "Finish" button, the executable will be digitally signed (Figure 22-12).

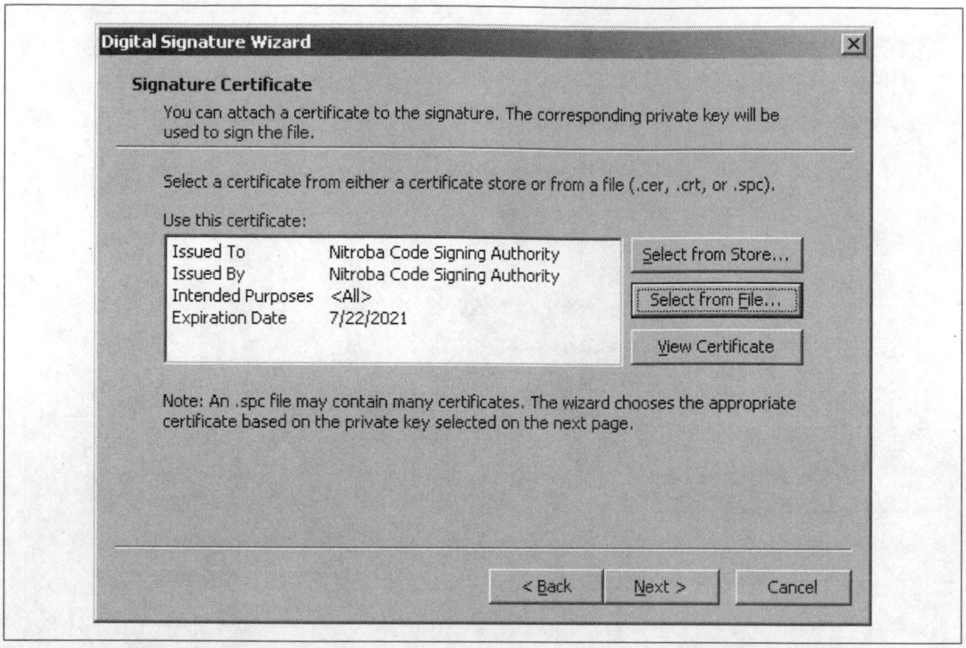

Figure 22-7. By clicking the button "Select from File..." and choosing the key file c:\hello\nitroba. cer, we tell codesign.exe to use the Nitroba Code Signing Authority CA key to sign the program. Although using our CA key for code signing is fine for this example, in practice you might create a separate signing key, sign it with the CA key, and use the signing key to sign your executables.

Signing the *hello.exe* program increases its size by 896 bytes:

```
C:\hello>dir hello.exe
 Volume in drive C is 40GB
 Volume Serial Number is 7640-B7AA

 Directory of C:\hello

07/22/2001  08:22p               40,960 hello.exe
              3 File(s)          40,960 bytes
              0 Dir(s)   27,871,641,600 bytes free

C:\hello>hello
Hello World!

C:\hello>signcode

C:\hello>dir hello.exe
 Volume in drive C is 40GB
 Volume Serial Number is 7640-B7AA

 Directory of C:\hello

07/22/2001  09:21p               41,856 hello.exe
```

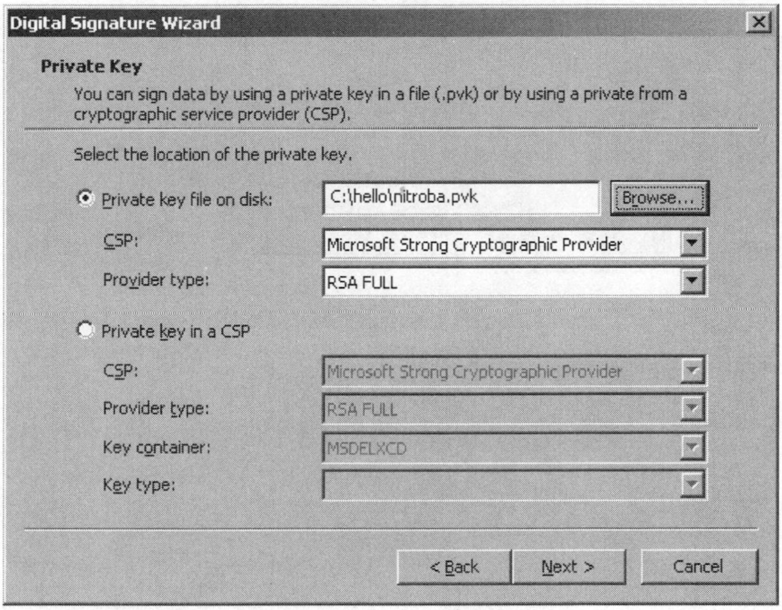

Figure 22-8. After a certificate is chosen, you can choose which private key to use. The private key must match the certificate that was previously chosen.

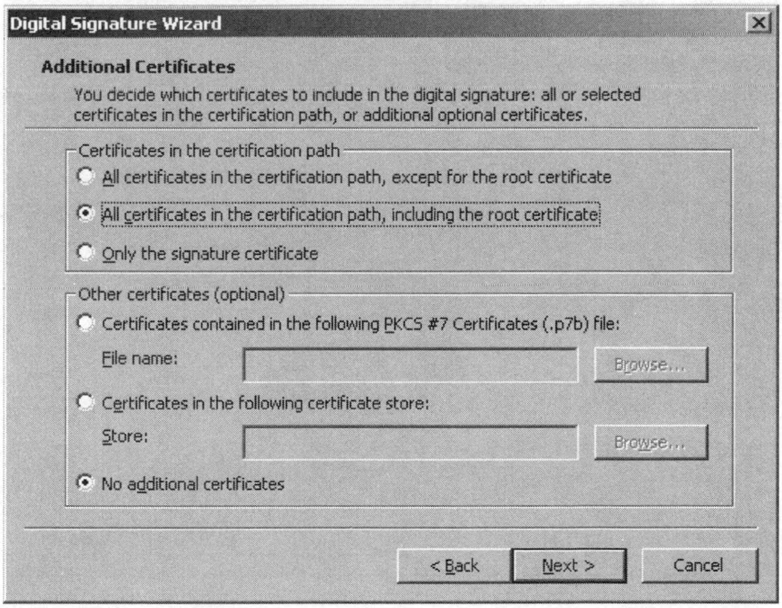

Figure 22-9. The Additional Certificates panel of the Digital Signature Wizard allows you to add multiple certificates to a signed binary.

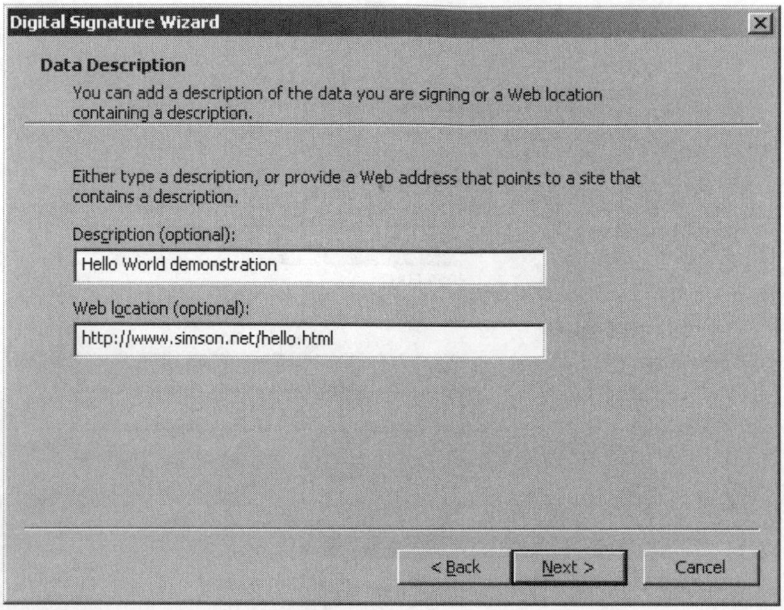

Figure 22-10. Authenticode can give each signed program a description and a web location

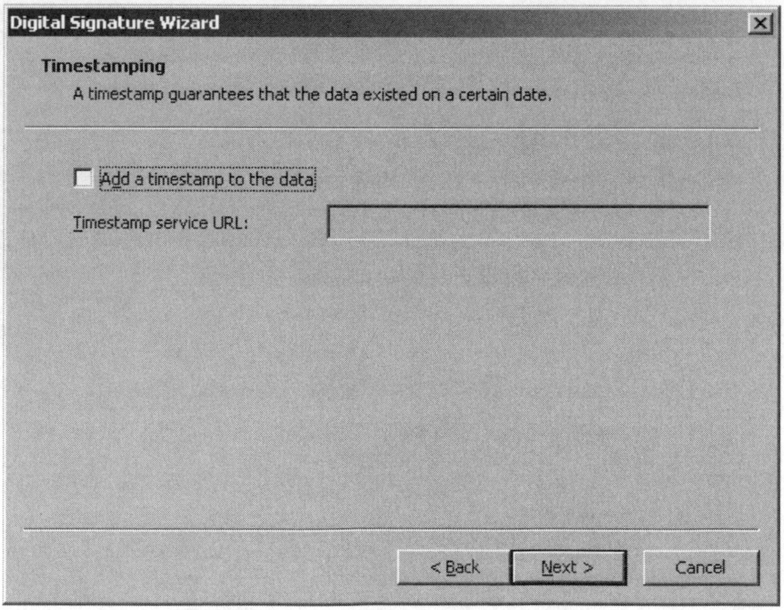

Figure 22-11. Authenticode allows you to digitally timestamp your program using a timestamp service that can be accessed over the Internet. The URL for VeriSign's timestamping service is http://timestamp.verisign.com/scripts/timstamp.dll. For further information on timestamping, see VeriSign's FAQ at http://www.verisign.com/support/signing/authenticode/#7.

Figure 22-12. When you are finished with the Digital Signature Wizard, all of the parameters will be displayed in a scroller

```
       1 File(s)          41,856 bytes
       0 Dir(s)   27,868,987,392 bytes free

C:\hello>
```

Now, if you find the *hello.exe* program in the Windows Explorer and left-click to choose the file's "Properties" panel, you will discover that a new tab called "Digital Signatures" is present. If you attempt to download and run the program with Internet Explorer, the Security Warning panel will indicate that it is digitally signed (see Figure 22-13).

Code signing from the command line

You can also use the *SignCode.exe* program from the command line:

```
C:\hello>signcode -v nitroba.pvk -n "Hello World progarm" -i "http://www.nitroba
.com/" -spc nitroba.spc -t http://timestamp.verisign.com/scripts/timstamp.dll hello.exe
Succeeded

C:\hello>
```

For a list of all of *signcode*'s arguments, use the -? option:

```
C:\hello>signcode -?
Usage:  SignCode [options] [FileName]
Options:
```

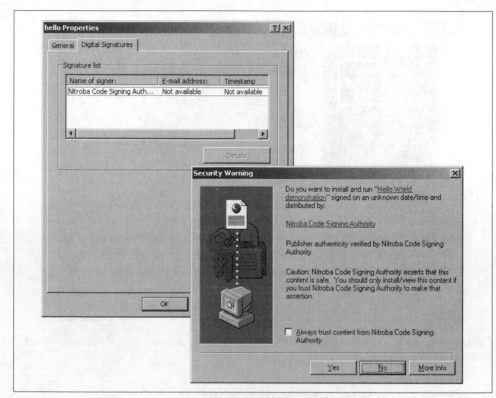

Figure 22-13. The digital signature produced by the Digital Signature Wizard is visible from the Windows Explorer and using the Internet Explorer download feature.

```
-spc  <file>       Spc file containing software publishing certificates
-v    <pvkFile>    Pvk file name containing the private key
-k    <KeyName>    Key container name
-n    <name>       Text name representing content of the file to be signed
-i    <info>       Place to get more info on content (usually a URL)
-p    <provider>   Name of the cryptographic provider on the system
-y    <type>       Cryptographic provider type to use
-ky   <keytype>    Key type
                      <signature|exchange|<integer>>
-$    <authority>  Signing authority of the certificate
                      <individual|commercial>
                      Default to using certificate's highest capability
-a    <algorithm>  Hashing algorithm for signing
                      <md5|sha1>. Default to md5
-t    <URL>        TimeStamp server's http address
-tr   <number>     The # of timestamp trial until succeeds. Default to 1
-tw   <number>     The # of seconds delay between each timestamp. Default to 0
-j    <dllName>    Name of the dll that provides attributes of the signature
-jp   <param>      Parameter to be passed to the dll
-c    <file>       file containing encoded software publishing certificate
```

```
-s      <store>      Cert store containing certs. Default to my store
-r      <location>   Location of the cert store in the registry
                         <localMachine|currentUser>. Default to currentUser
-sp     <policy>     Add the certification path (chain) or add the certification
                     path excluding the root certificate (spcstore).
                         <chain|spcstore>. Default to spcstore
-cn     <name>       The common name of the certificate
-sha1 <thumbPrint> The sha1 hash of the certificate
-x                   Do not sign the file.  Only Timestamp the file

Note:   To sign with a SPC file, the required options are -spc and -v if
        your private key is in a PVK file. If your private key is in a
        registry key container, then -spc and -k are the required options.

C:\hello>
```

Obtaining a Software Publishing Certificate

Although Microsoft's Authenticode technology should work with software publishing digital certificates from any recognized certification authority, when this book went to press the only CA issuing these certificates was VeriSign.

As of July 2001, VeriSign issues two kinds of software publisher's certificates, which the company now calls Code Signing Digital IDs. The CodeSigner Standard ID costs $400 and comes with $50,000 of "NetSure Protection," promises a "Keynote Performance Audit" from 10 cities, and promises 2-day express delivery. For practical purposes, the real difference is that if you pay more money, you can get faster turnaround.

Previously, VeriSign had offered "Personal" certificates for use with Authenticode. These certificates were handy because they cost roughly half as much as the commercial certificates and they were available to individuals, rather than corporations, yet they were as powerful as commercial certificates. Perhaps that is the reason that the personal certificates were discontinued.

Other Code Signing Methods

To close this chapter, we note that there are other ways of signing code to make it trustworthy. For example, for many years, PGP signature certificates have been used for validating programs and announcements distributed over the Internet. There are a few drawbacks to using PGP in this way. Because support for PGP is not built into web servers and browsers, the signature signing and verification must be done as a two-step process. A second drawback is that PGP signatures cannot use the public key infrastructure developed for use with web browsers. A benefit of the use of PGP is that any kind of file, document, or program can be signed with PGP, as PGP signatures can be "detached" and saved in separate locations.

As another alternative, the World Wide Web Consortium's DSig initiative has proposed using PICS 1.1 labels as a tool for digital signatures. Information can be found at *http://www.w3.org/pub/WWW/Security/DSig/Overview.html*.

In this chapter:
- Pornography Filtering
- PICS
- RSACi

CHAPTER 23

Pornography, Filtering Software, and Censorship

As the Web has grown from an academic experiment to a mass medium, parents, politicians, totalitarian rulers, and demagogues have all looked for ways of controlling the information that it contains. What's behind these attempts at control?

- Some people believe that explicit information on the Web about sex and sexuality, drugs, and similar themes is inappropriate for younger people—or for society at large.

- Some politicians believe that writings advocating hate crimes should be banned.

- Some leaders believe that information about free elections, democratic political systems, or successful liberal economies may be destabilizing to their regimes.

- Some special interest groups have sought to limit discussion of religion, ethnic concerns, historical accounts (some of contested accuracy), gender-specific issues, medical procedures, economic material, and a host of other materials.

It is nearly impossible to impose worldwide controls on the creation of content, and on a global network such as the Internet, it will always be possible for those wishing to publish material to find a place to put it. As a consequence, people and organizations trying to suppress the dissemination of information have focused their efforts on programs that automatically detect objectionable content and block it from the end user. This technology is typically called *filtering software*, *blocking software,* or occasionally, *censorware*.

Pornography Filtering

The first and arguably the most important category of blocking software is software that blocks access to web sites that are considered to be pornographic or otherwise harmful to children.* The U.S. Congress has mandated that all schools receiving federal support under the E-Rate program or that purchase computers or Internet access

---

* We note that not everyone defines pornography the same way, nor does everyone believe that exposure to items defined in the law as pornographic is harmful. Such debates are well beyond the scope of this book.

using funds provided under Title III of the Elementary and Secondary Education Act must install software that blocks access to visual depictions that would be considered "obscene, child pornography, or harmful to minors."* Libraries that purchase computers or Internet access using funding provided by the Museum and Library Services Act are similarly required to use filtering technology.

"Harmful to minors" is defined in the Children's Internet Protection Act as:

> Any picture, image, graphic image file, or other visual depiction that—
>
> (i) taken as a whole and with respect to minors, appeals to a prurient interest in nudity, sex, or excretion;
>
> (ii) depicts, describes, or represents, in a patently offensive way with respect to what is suitable for minors, an actual or simulated sexual act or sexual contact, actual or simulated normal or perverted sexual acts, or a lewd exhibition of the genitals; and
>
> (iii) taken as a whole, lacks serious literary, artistic, political, or scientific value as to minors.†

Pornography-filtering software has been installed by many corporations in an attempt to prevent the company's computers from being used for downloading and displaying pornography. This is arguably because viewing pornography is not part of most people's job descriptions. Another reason is that employees downloading pornography may have it visible (or audible) to other employees or customers, which can result in sexual harassment lawsuits by offended parties.

Architectures for Filtering

Filtering software employs a variety of techniques to accomplish its purposes:

Site exclusion lists
> The filtering company makes a list of sites known to contain objectionable content. An initial list is distributed with the filtering software; updates are sold on a subscription basis.

Site and page name keyword blocking
> The filtering software automatically blocks access to sites or to web pages that contain particular keywords in the page's URL. For example, censorship software that blocks access to sites of a sexual nature might block access to all sites and pages in which the word "sex" or the letters "xxx" appear.

Content keyword blocking
> The filtering software can scan all incoming information to the computer and automatically block the transfer of pages that contain a prohibited word.

---

* The legislation was included with the Children's Internet Protection Act (CIPA) that was passed as part of the FCC's end-of-year spending package at the end of 2000. E-Rate recipients are also required to adopt an Internet safety policy after holding a public hearing. For further information, see Section 254(h)(5) of the Communications Act of 1934. The filtering mandate does not apply to institutions receiving E-Rate discounts for purposes other than providing Internet access. CIPA Sec. 1721(a)(5)(A)(ii).

† Secs. 1703(b)(2), 3601(a)(5)(F), 1712(a)(2)(f)(7)(B), and 1721(c)(G).

Image content blocking

The filtering software analyzes the images using image analysis algorithms and recognize those that appear to have too many flesh tones or telltale characteristics, such as obscuring circles surrounded by a region of pink. Currently, image content analysis is not very accurate, but many organizations are actively working on this technology.

Transmitted data blocking

Blocking software can be configured so that particular information cannot be sent from the client machine to the Internet. For example, parents can configure their computers so that children cannot upload their names or their telephone numbers.

Filtering software can be installed at a variety of locations:

- Filtering software can operate at the application level, interfacing closely with the web browser or email client.

- Filtering software can operate at the protocol level, exercising control over all network connections.

- Filtering software can be installed on a firewall or mandatory proxy server. In this configuration, the software automatically applies its filters to all of the computers that rely on the firewall or proxy server.

Each of these models is increasingly more difficult to subvert.

Filtering software can be controlled directly by the end user, by the owner of the computer, by the online access provider, or by the wide area network provider. The point of control does not necessarily dictate the point at which the software operates. For example, America Online's "parental controls" feature is controlled by the owner of each AOL account, but is implemented by the online provider's computers.

Problems with Filtering Software

The biggest technical challenge faced by filtering software companies is the difficulty of keeping the database of objectionable material up to date and of distributing that database in a timely fashion. Presumably, the list of objectionable sites is changing rapidly, with new sites being created all the time and old sites becoming defunct. To make things more difficult, some sites are actively attempting to bypass automated censors. Recruitment sites for pedophiles and neo-Nazi groups, for example, may actually attempt to hide the true nature of their sites by choosing innocuous-sounding names for their domains and web pages.[*]

---

[*] This tactic of choosing innocuous-sounding names is not limited to neo-Nazi groups. "Think tanks" and nonprofit organizations on both sides of the political spectrum frequently choose innocuous-sounding names to hide their true agenda. Consider these organizations: the Progress and Freedom Foundation, the Family Research Council, Fairness and Accuracy in Reporting, People for the American Way. From their names, can you tell what these organizations do or their political leanings?

The need to obtain frequent database updates may be a hassle for parents and educators who are seeking to uniformly deny children access to particular kinds of sites. On the other hand, it may be a boon for stockholders of the filtering software companies.

fAnother problem is the danger of casting too wide a net and accidentally screening out material that is not objectionable. For example, during the summer of 1996, NYNEX discovered that all of the pages about its ISDN services were blocked by censorship software. The pages had been programmatically generated and had names such as *isdn/xxx1.html* and *isdn/xxx2.html*, and the blocking software had been programmed to avoid "xxx" sites. America Online received much criticism for blocking access to breast cancer survivors' online groups because the groups' names contained the word "breast." People with names like "Sexton" and "Cummings" have reported that their email and personal pages have been blocked by overbroad matching rules. Filtering companies may leave themselves open to liability and public ridicule by blocking sites that should not be blocked under the company's stated policies.

Filtering companies may also block sites for reasons other than those officially stated. For example, there have been documented cases where companies selling blocking software have blocked ISPs because those ISPs have hosted web pages critical of the software. Other cases have occurred where research organizations and well-known groups such as the National Organization for Women were blocked by software that was advertised to block only sites that are sexually oriented. Vendors treat their lists of blocked sites as trade secret information; as a result, customers cannot examine the lists to see what sites are not approved.

Finally, blocking software can be overridden by some sophisticated users. A person who is frustrated by blocking software can always remove it—if need be, by reformatting his computer's hard drive and reinstalling the operating system from scratch. But there are other, less drastic means. Some software can be defeated by using certain kinds of web proxy servers or virtual private networks (VPNs), or by requesting web pages via electronic mail. Software designed to block the transmission of certain information, such as a phone number, can be defeated by transforming the information in a manner that is not anticipated by the program's author. Children can, for example, spell out their telephone numbers ("My phone is five five five, one two one two,") instead of typing the number directly. Software that is programmed to prohibit spelled-out phone numbers can be defeated by misspellings.

Parents who trust this software to be an infallible electronic babysitter and allow their children to use the computer without any supervision may be unpleasantly surprised.

PICS

Most filtering software was hurriedly developed in response to a perceived market opportunity and, to a lesser extent, to political need. Access control software was used to explain in courts and legislatures why more direct political limitations on the

Internet's content were unnecessary and unworkable. Because of the rush to market, most of the filtering rules and lists were largely ad hoc, as demonstrated by the example of the blocked ISDN web pages.

The Platform for Internet Content Selection (PICS) is an effort of the World Wide Web Consortium to develop an open Internet infrastructure for the exchange of information about web content and the creation of automated blocking software.

When the PICS project was first launched, it was heralded as a voluntary industry effort that was an alternative to government regulation. When Congress passed the Communications Decency Act, making it a federal crime to put pornography on the Internet where it could be accessed by children,* PICS became the subject of courtroom testimony.

PICS was also by far the most controversial project that the W3C pursued during its first five years. Although PICS was designed as an alternative to state regulation and censorship of the Internet, critics argued that PICS could itself become a powerful tool for supporting state-sponsored censorship. That's because PICS is a general-purpose system that can be used to filter out all sorts of material, from neo-Nazi propaganda to information about clean elections and nonviolent civil disobedience. Critics argued that strong industry support for PICS meant that the tools for censorship would be built into the platform used by billions of people.

Today many of these fears seem overstated, but that is only because the PICS project has largely failed. Although support for PICS is built into Internet Explorer and many proxy servers, the unwillingness of web sites to rate themselves combined with the lack of third-party ratings bureaus has prevented the technology from playing a role in the emerging world of content filtering and control—at least for now.

In the following sections, we'll provide an overview of how PICS was designed to work. Despite its apparent failure, PICS provides valuable insight into how content controls could work. Detailed information about PICS can be found in Appendix D, and on the Consortium's web server at *http://w3.org/PICS/*.

What Is PICS?

PICS is a general-purpose system for labeling the content of documents that appear on the World Wide Web. PICS labels contain one or more ratings that are issued by a *rating service*. Those labels are supposed to contain machine-readable information about the content of a web site, allowing software to make decisions about whether or not access to a web site should be allowed.

---

* The Act was eventually held to violate the First Amendment, and thus unconstitutional. Many members of Congress knew it would be unconstitutional and furthermore could not be enforced against non-U.S. web sites, but voted for it nonetheless so as to appease their constituencies. What is more troubling are the members who either believe that U.S. law governs the whole Internet, or believe that the First Amendment shouldn't apply to the World Wide Web.

For example, a PICS label might say that a particular web page contains pornographic images, or that a collection of pages on a web site deals with homosexuality. A PICS label might say that all of the pages at another web site are historically inaccurate.

Any document that has a URL can be labeled with PICS. The labels can be distributed directly with the labeled information—for example, in the HTTP header or in the HTML body. Alternatively, PICS labels can be distributed directly by third-party rating services over the Internet or on a CD-ROM. John can rate Jane's web pages using PICS—with or without her knowledge or permission.PICS labels can apply to multiple URLs, including a subset of files on a site, an entire site, or a collection of sites. A PICS label can also apply to a particular document or even a particular version of a particular document. PICS labels can be digitally signed for added confidence. PICS labels can be ignored, giving the user full access to the Web's content. Alternatively, labels can be used to block access to objectionable content. Labels can be interpreted by the user's web browser or operating system. An entire organization or even a country could have a particular PICS-enabled policy enforced through the use of a blocking proxy server located on a firewall. Figure 23-1 depicts a typical PICS system in operation.

Software that implements PICS has a variety of technical advantages over simple blocking software:

- PICS allows per-document blocking.
- PICS makes it possible to get blocking ratings from more than one source.
- Because PICS is a generic framework for rating web-based information, different users can have different access-control rules.

PICS needed this amount of flexibility because it was supposed to be the basis of a worldwide system for content control, and people in different countries have different standards for what sort of information should be blocked. But this flexibility ultimately was one of the reasons for the system's failure. Instead of delivering a system for blocking pornography, the W3C created a filtering system construction kit, and nobody ever put it together.

PICS Applications

PICS can be used for assigning many different kinds of labels to many different kinds of information:

- PICS labels can specify the type or amount of sex, nudity, or profane language in a document.
- PICS labels can specify the historical accuracy of a document.*

---

* The attention to historical accuracy and hate speech is largely a response to the Simon Wiesenthal Center, which has argued that web sites that promote hate speech or deny the Jewish Holocaust should not be allowed to exist on the Internet.

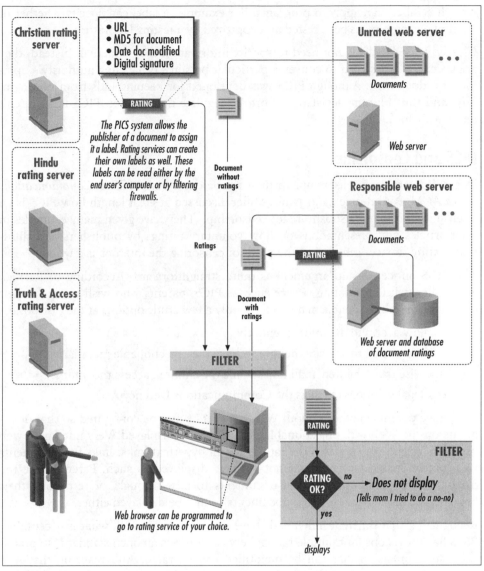

Figure 23-1. A typical PICS system

- PICS labels can specify whether a document is or is not hate speech.
- PICS labels can specify the political leanings of a document or its author.
- PICS labels can rate whether a photograph is overexposed or underexposed.
- PICS labels can indicate the year in which a document was created. They can denote copyright status and any rights that are implicitly granted by the document's copyright holder.
- PICS labels can indicate whether a chat room is moderated or unmoderated.

- PICS labels can apply to programs. For example, a label can specify whether or not a program has been tested and approved by a testing laboratory.

Clearly, PICS labels do not need to specify information that is factual. Instead, they are specifically designed to convey a particular person's or labeling authority's opinion of a document. Although PICS was developed for keeping kids from pornography, and thus blunting legislative efforts to regulate the Internet, PICS labels aren't necessarily for kids.

PICS and Censorship

Does PICS promote censorship? In their article describing PICS in *Communications of the ACM*, Paul Resnick and James Miller discussed at great length how PICS is an open standard that is a substitute for censorship.[*] They have given many examples in their articles and presentations on how voluntary ratings by publishers and third-party rating services can obviate the need for censoring the Internet as a whole.

The PICS anticensorship argument is quite straightforward. According to Resnick and Miller, without a rating service such as PICS, parents who wish to shield their children from objectionable material have only a few crude options at their disposal:

- Disallow access to the Internet entirely
- Disallow access to any site thought to have the objectionable material
- Supervise their children at all times while the children access the Internet
- Seek legal solutions (such as the Communications Decency Act)

PICS gave parents another option. Web browsers could be configured so that documents on the Web with objectionable ratings are not displayed. Very intelligent web browsers might even prefetch the ratings for all hypertext links; links for documents with objectionable ratings might not even be displayed as such. Parents have the option of either allowing unrated documents to pass through, or restricting their browser software so that unrated documents cannot be displayed either.

Recognizing that different individuals have differing opinions of what is acceptable, PICS has provisions for multiple ratings services. PICS is an open standard, so practically any dimension that can be quantified can be rated. And realizing that it is impossible for any rating organization to rate all of the content on the World Wide Web, PICS has provisions for publishers to rate their own content. Parents then have the option of deciding whether to accept these self-assigned ratings.

Digital signatures allow labels created by one rating service to be cached or even distributed by the rated web site while minimizing the possibility that the labels will be

---

[*] See "PICS: Internet Access Controls Without Censorship," October 1996, p. 87. The paper also appears at *http://w3.org/PICSA/tacacv2.html*.

PICS Glossary

This glossary is based on the glossary appearing in the PICS specifications. Definitions from the PICS standard are reprinted with permission.

application/pics-service
> A new MIME datatype that describes a PICS rating service.

application/pics-labels
> A new MIME datatype used to transmit one or more labels, defined in PICS labels.

category
> The part of a rating system that describes a particular criterion used for rating. For example, a rating system might have two categories named "sexual material" and "violence." Also called a *dimension*.

content label
> A data structure containing information about a given document's contents. Also called a *rating* or *content rating*. The content label may accompany the document or may be available separately.

PICS (Platform for Internet Content Selection)
> The name for both the suite of specification documents of which this glossary is a part, and the organization writing the documents.

label bureau
> A computer system that supplies, via a computer network, ratings of documents. It may or may not provide the documents themselves.

rating service
> An individual or organization that assigns labels according to some rating system and then distributes them, perhaps via a label bureau or via CD-ROM.

rating system
> A method for rating information. A rating system consists of one or more categories.

scale
> The range of permissible values for a category.

transmission name (of a category)
> The short name intended for use over a network to refer to the category. This is distinct from the category name inasmuch as the transmission name must be language-independent, encoded in ASCII, and as short as reasonably possible. Within a single rating system, the transmission names of all categories must be distinct.

modified by those distributing them. This would allow, for example, a site that receives millions of hits a day to distribute the ratings of underfunded militant religious organizations that might not have the financial resources to deploy a high-powered Internet server capable of servicing millions of label lookups every day.

Unlike blocking software, which operates at the TCP/IP protocol level to block access to an entire site, PICS can label and therefore control access to content on a document-by-document basis. (The PICS "generic" labels can also be used to label an entire site, should an organization wish to do so.) This is the great advantage of PICS, making the system ideally suited to electronic libraries. With PICS, children can be given access to J. D. Salinger's *Franny and Zooey* without giving them access to *The Catcher in the Rye*. Additionally, an online library could rate each chapter of *The Catcher in the Rye*, giving children access to some chapters but not to others. In fact, PICS makes it possible to restrict access to specific documents in electronic libraries in ways that have never been possible in physical libraries.

Having created such a framework for ratings, Miller and Resnick show how it can be extended to other venues. Businesses, for example, might configure their networks so that recreational sites cannot be accessed during the business day. There have also been discussions as to how PICS can be extended for other purposes, such as rating software quality.

Access controls become tools for censorship

Miller and Resnick argued that PICS didn't promote censorship, but they must have a different definition for the word "censorship" than we do. The sole purpose of PICS appears to be facilitating the creation of software that blocks access to particular documents on the Web on the basis of their content. For a 15-year-old student in Alabama trying to get information about sexual orientation, censorship is censorship, no matter whether the blocking is at the behest of the student's parents, teachers, ministers, or elected officials; whether those people have the right to censor what the teenager sees is a separate issue from whether or not the blockage is censorship.

Resnick said that there is an important distinction to be made between official censorship of information at its source by government and "access control," which he defines as the blocking of what gets received. He argues that confusing "censorship" with "access controls" benefits no one.[*]

It is true that PICS is a technology designed to facilitate access controls. It is a powerful, well thought out, extensible system. Its support for third-party ratings, digital signatures, real-time queries, and labeling of all kinds of documents all but guarantees that it could be a technology of choice for totalitarian regimes that seek to limit their citizens' access to unapproved information and ideas. Its scalability assures that it would be up to the task.

Whatever the claims of its authors, PICS is a technology that remains well-suited for building censorship software.

[*] Personal communication, March 20, 1997.

Censoring the network

Although PICS was designed for blocking software implemented on the user's own machine, any large-scale deployment of PICS really needs to have the content control in the network itself.

The biggest problem with implementing blocking technology on the user's computer is that it is easily defeated. Software that runs on unprotected operating systems is vulnerable. It is unreasonable to assume that an inquisitive 10-year-old child is not going to be able to disable software that is running on an unsecure desktop computer running the Windows or Macintosh operating system. (Considering what some 10-year-old children do on computers now when unattended, disabling blocking software is child's play.)

The only way to make blocking software work in practice is to run it upstream from the end user's computer. This is why America Online's "parental controls" feature works: it's run on the AOL servers, rather than the home computer. Children are given their own logins with their own passwords. Unless they know their parents' passwords, they can't change the settings on their own accounts.

RSACi

The Recreational Software Advisory Council (RSAC) was formed in the mid-1990s in response to several moves within the U.S. Congress to regulate the content of children's video games. Congress was moved to action after a number of video games were produced in which the goal of the game was to brutally murder live-action figures, some of whom were wearing only the scantiest of outfits.* The entertainment industry successfully argued that it could police itself and offered to adopt a voluntary rating system that would let people purchasing a video game determine the levels of gore, violence, and sex that the program contained.

In conjunction with the development of the PICS standard, the World Wide Web Consortium worked with RSAC to develop a modified version of the RSAC rating system—RSACi. Despite the fact that this rating system was designed for rating web sites and was created by the W3C, it still read like a rating system for video games and not for web sites. For example, a web site could be said to "reward injuring non-threatening creatures."

Table 23-1 shows the RSAC ratings that are implemented in Microsoft Internet Explorer 3 and above. Microsoft's Internet Preferences panel is designed to allow parents to create "content advisors" that will prohibit the display of certain kinds of content. Figure 23-2 shows a window from the content advisor. In this case, the content

---

* It has been noted that if the officials were really concerned with the violence, they wouldn't care or need to mention what the characters were (not) wearing.

advisor is loaded with the RSACi content rating system. The browser has been configured so that web pages containing any level of sexual activity may be displayed.

The content advisor can be password-protected, so that it cannot be changed or overridden except by an authorized user.

Table 23-1. RSAC ratings implemented in Microsoft Internet Explorer 3.0

Rating	Description
Language:	
Inoffensive slang	Inoffensive slang; no profanity
Mild expletives	Mild terms for body functions
Moderate expletives	Expletives; nonsexual anatomical reference
Obscene gestures	Strong, vulgar language; obscene gestures; use of epithets
Explicit or crude language	Extreme hate speech or crude language; explicit sexual references
Nudity:	
None	No nudity
Revealing attire	Revealing attire
Partial nudity	Partial nudity
Frontal nudity	Frontal nudity
Provocative display of frontal nudity	Provocative frontal nudity; explicit sexual activity; sex crimes
Sex:	
None	No sexual activity portrayed; romance
Passionate kissing	Passionate kissing
Clothed sexual touching	Clothed sexual touching
Nonexplicit sexual touching	Nonexplicit sexual touching
Explicit sexual activity	Explicit sexual activity; sex crimes
Violence:	
No violence	No aggressive violence; no natural or accidental violence
Fighting	Creatures injured or killed; damage to realistic objects
Killing	Humans or creatures injured or killed; rewards injuring nonthreatening creatures
Killing with blood and gore	Humans injured or killed
Wanton and gratuitous violence	Wanton and gratuitous violence; torture; rape

Internet Explorer's content advisor is not foolproof: it is possible for a skilled user to override the system by deleting key files on a Windows system and reinstalling any necessary software. Additionally, a user can simply download a web browser that does not implement the content controls, such as Netscape Navigator.

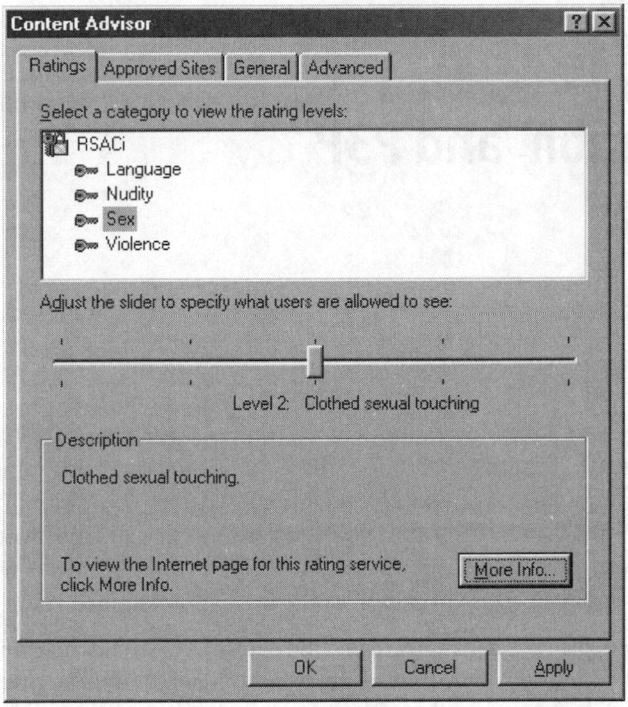

Content Advisor

Ratings | Approved Sites | General | Advanced |

Select a category to view the rating levels:

RSACi
　Language
　Nudity
　Sex
　Violence

Adjust the slider to specify what users are allowed to see:

Level 2:　Clothed sexual touching

Description

Clothed sexual touching.

To view the Internet page for this rating service, click More Info.

[More Info...]

[OK]　[Cancel]　[Apply]

Figure 23-2. Internet Explorer's Content Advisor uses RSACi to allow users to select the maximum permissible rating for each web page that is downloaded.

Conclusion

PICS and RSACi have failed to date, but they continue to be supported by the computer industry—witness their inclusion in IE6. Thus, the specter of these technologies being revived for use for large-scale censorship remains.

CHAPTER 24
Privacy Policies, Legislation, and P3P

In this chapter:
- Policies That Protect Privacy and Privacy Policies
- Children's Online Privacy Protection Act
- P3P

Online businesses know a lot about their customers. An online merchant knows every product that you look at, every product that you put in your "shopping cart" but later take out, and anything that you've ever purchased from them online. Online merchants also know when you shop, if you shop from home or from work, and—if they care—what your credit rating is. Furthermore, unlike the offline world, an online merchant can correlate your shopping profile with your web browsing habits.

Internet service providers can learn even more about their customers because all information that an Internet user sees must first pass through the provider's computers. ISPs can also determine the web sites that their users frequent—and even the individual articles that have been viewed. They can analyze email messages for keywords. By tracking this information, an Internet provider can tell if its users are interested in boats or cars, whether they care about fashion, or even if they are interested in particular medical diseases.

Policies That Protect Privacy and Privacy Policies

What standards should online businesses and organizations follow with regard to the personally identifiable information that they gather?

The Code of Fair Information Practices

History provides strong precedents for helping to understand the rights and responsibilities of online services and providers. These issues of personal information, computers, and large networked databases were first raised in the 1960s. Back then, the consumer reporting industry was embarking on the process of computerizing its vast consumer credit, employment, and insurance files. Much of the data in these files had been assembled over decades without the knowledge or consent of consumers.

Their computerization assured that the files would soon be used more widely than ever before.

At least six subcommittees of the U.S. Congress considered the issue of privacy during the 1960s and early 1970s. Many people testified, including representatives of the companies building these systems and countless individuals who had been harmed by incorrect or inaccurate information that these systems occasionally contained. The U.S. Congress determined that many of these systems provided important services, but decided that the systems needed to operate within a regulatory framework that assured rights to people whose data was archived and recourse for the growing number of people who were being wronged.

One of the most important pieces of legislation, the Fair Credit Reporting Act, was passed by Congress in 1970 and signed into law by President Nixon. This law gave consumers fundamental rights, including the right to see their credit reports; the right to know the third-parties to whom their reports had been disclosed; the right to force credit reporting agencies to re-investigate "errors" detected by consumers; the right to force the agencies to include a statement from the consumer on reports that were in dispute; and a sunset provision requiring credit reporting agencies to purge information on a consumer's report that was more than seven years old (ten years for information regarding bankruptcies).

Elliot Richardson, President Nixon's Secretary of Health, Education, and Welfare, created a commission to study the impact of computers on privacy, and in 1973 that commission issued its report. The most lasting contribution of the report was the creation of the Code of Fair Information Practices (see the sidebar of the same name in this chapter).

Congress continued to pass legislation regulating the use of personal information. But instead of passing comprehensive legislation that would protect all personal information, Congress instead adopted a piecemeal approach. Federal records were covered under the Privacy Act of 1974[*] and the Freedom of Information Act. Student records were protected under the Federal Family Educational Rights and Privacy Act of 1974 (the Buckley Amendment). Banking records, cable subscriber records, and even videotape rental records were all protected by Congressional action. Each of these pieces of legislation were enforced by a different part of the federal government. Some acts, like the antijunk-fax Telephone Consumer Privacy Act, did not have any enforcement mechanism at all other than private lawsuits.

Things were different in Europe. Building on the experience of World War II, during which personal records were misused by the Nazis, most European governments created an institutional framework for regulating the collection and use of personal information. Ironically, much of this work was based on the Code of Fair Information

[*] http://www.usdoj.gov/04foia/privstat.htm

> ## The Code of Fair Information Practices
>
> The Code of Fair Information Practices is based on five principles:
>
> - There must be no personal data record-keeping systems whose very existence is secret.
> - There must be a way for a person to find out what information about the person is in a record and how it is used.
> - There must be a way for a person to prevent information about the person that was obtained for one purpose from being used or made available for other purposes without the person's consent.
> - There must be a way for a person to correct or amend a record of identifiable information about the person.
> - Any organization creating, maintaining, using, or disseminating records of identifiable personal data must assure the reliability of the data for its intended use and must take precautions to prevent misuses of the data.
>
> Source: Department of Health, Education, and Welfare, 1973.

Practices that the United States had formulated in the early 1970s. The Europeans extended these ideas into an overall system that was termed *data protection*.

OECD Guidelines

In 1980, the Organization for Economic Development and Cooperation (OECD) adopted an expanded set of privacy guidelines. These guidelines were designed, in part, to harmonize the growing number of privacy regulations throughout the industrialized world. The guidelines were also specifically designed to deal with the growing problem of *transborder data flows*—the movement of personal information from one country, where that data might be highly protected, to another country that might have lesser protections. The OECD Guidelines on the Protection of Privacy and Transborder Flows of Personal Data* consist of eight principles:

Collection Limitation Principle
> There should be limits to the collection of personal data, and any such data should be obtained by lawful and fair means and, where appropriate, with the knowledge or consent of the data subject.

Data Quality Principle
> Personal data should be relevant to the purposes for which it is to be used, and, to the extent necessary for those purposes, should be accurate, complete, and kept up to date.

---

* *http://www.oecd.org/dsti/sti/it/secur/prod/PRIV-en.HTM*

Purpose Specification Principle

The purposes for which personal data is collected should be specified not later than at the time of data collection and the subsequent use limited to the fulfillment of those purposes or such others as are not incompatible with those purposes and as are specified on each occasion of change of purpose.

Use Limitation Principle

Personal data should not be disclosed, made available, or otherwise used for purposes other than those specified in accordance with the previous principle except:

- With the consent of the data subject; or
- By the authority of law.

Security Safeguards Principle

Personal data should be protected by reasonable security safeguards against such risks as loss or unauthorized access, destruction, use, modification, or disclosure of data.

Openness Principle

There should be a general policy of openness about developments, practices, and policies with respect to personal data. Means should be readily available of establishing the existence and nature of personal data, and the main purposes of their use, as well as the identity and usual residence of the data controller.

Individual Participation Principle

An individual should have the right:

- To obtain from a data controller, or —otherwise, confirmation of whether or not the data controller has data relating to him;
- To have communicated to him, data relating to him:
  - Within a reasonable time;
  - At a charge, if any, that is not excessive;
  - In a reasonable manner; and
  - In a form that is readily intelligible to him;
- To be given reasons if a request made specified as above is denied, and to be able to challenge such denial; and
- To challenge data relating to him and, if the challenge is successful to have the data erased, rectified, completed, or amended.

Accountability Principle

A data controller should be accountable for complying with measures which give effect to the principles stated above.

The OECD Guidelines do not have the force of law, but are instead used as guidelines for each OECD member country when passing its own laws.

Other National and International Regulations

On July 25, 1995, the European Union passed Directive 95/46/EC, the Directive on Protection of Personal Data, aimed at harmonizing the data protection policies of the EU member countries while simultaneously prohibiting the transport of personal information to countries that did not have adequate protections. EU Commissioner Mario Monti said in a press release following the adoption of the legislation:

> I am pleased that this important measure, which will ensure a high level of protection for the privacy of individuals in all Member States, has been adopted with a very wide measure of agreement within the Council and European Parliament. The Directive will also help to ensure the free flow of Information Society services in the Single Market by fostering consumer confidence and minimizing differences between Member States' rules. Moreover, the text agreed on includes special provisions for journalists, which reconcile the right to privacy with freedom of expression. . . . The Member States must transpose the Directive within three years, but I sincerely hope that they will take the necessary measures without waiting for the deadline to expire so as to encourage the investment required for the Information Society to become a reality.

In April 2000, the government of Canada adopted Bill C-6, establishing a data protection framework within Canada by which all nationally charted corporations must abide. The legislation extends itself to all provincially charted corporations in 2003.

"Voluntary Regulation" Privacy Policies

State regulation of personal information used by the business sector has been less successful in the United States. Despite taking an early lead in privacy protection legislation, the United States passed few laws protecting privacy in the last quarter of the 20th century.

With regard to the online collection of personal information, American businesses have fought hard against all suggestions and attempts at federal regulation, arguing that the fledgling world of Internet commerce is simply too immature for meaningful regulation, and that regulation might jeopardize the ability of online businesses to make reasonable profits.

Instead, American businesses have argued that they should be allowed to adopt voluntary codes of conduct and tailor their own policies to suit their business needs. Eager to please its corporate sponsors, the Clinton Administration generally went along with these requests from the business community. Instead of fighting for the passage of meaningful legislation that would protect online privacy, the Clinton Administration instead asked businesses to post voluntary *privacy policies* on their web sites.

Voluntary privacy policies are only that—they are voluntary. No business is forced to post one. However, the Clinton Administration argued, once an organization posted its privacy policy, it would be honor-bound to live up to the rules that it had published on its web site. Companies that violated their own policies would lose customers.

That's where things stood until 1998, when a highly publicized study by Georgetown business professor Mary Culnan revealed that American businesses, despite having asked for the chance to self-regulate, had not risen to the occasion. According to Culnan's study, only 14 percent of the Web's commercial sites were posting any sort of policy regarding the use of personal information. Consumer groups argued that it was time for the federal government to step in and regulate. But business groups asked for more time.

Over the following year, a large number of web sites posted privacy policies. Fearful that regulation might be just around the corner, many businesses focused on the creation of a privacy policy as an end in itself. And in this effort, the businesses were largely successful. A follow-up study in 1999 found that 65.7 percent of web sites were now posting privacy policies. Most importantly, according to Culnan, these web sites made up 98.8 percent of consumer web traffic. Of the top 100 web sites visited by consumers, a whopping 94 percent had posted privacy policies.

Interestingly, studies of many of these online policies revealed problems. One ongoing research effort started in 2000 by Annie Antón and Julie Earp, professors at North Carolina State University, found that many online privacy policies are self-contradictory, incomplete, and often vaguely specified. They identified several instances where online sites clearly stated policies that were also clearly violated, on the very same site.[*]

Seal programs

To enforce voluntary privacy policies, the business community proposed the creation of voluntary membership organizations that would police their member companies. Similar to Underwriters' Laboratories, these organizations would give their members a small logo, or *seal*, that would be displayed on web sites that complied with the organization's own policies.

Two of the most successful seal programs are TRUSTe and the BBBOnline:

TRUSTe

TRUSTe is a membership organization, based in San Jose, California, whose mission "is to build users' trust and confidence on the Internet and, in so doing, accelerate growth of the Internet industry."[†] Founded by the Electronic Frontier Foundation (EFF) and the CommerceNet Consortium, TRUSTe allows member organizations to display TRUSTe's seal, which it calls the *TRUSTe mark*, if the privacy policy contains specific items and if the web site agrees to be audited by TRUSTe or by outside third parties (see Figure 24-1 for an example).

---

[*] Some of these results are in papers at *http://www.csc.ncsu.edu/faculty/anton/publications.html*.

[†] *http://www.truste.org/about/truste/about_faqs.html*

Figure 24-1. The TRUSTe mark and the Click to Verify link.

Because TRUSTe has changed its contract with its member organizations over time, the TRUSTe mark on different web sites actually has different meanings. On the Lycos (*www.lycos.com*) web site, for instance, the TRUSTe mark means that Lycos has agreed to disclose:

- What personally identifiable information or third-party personally identifiable information is collected through the web site.

- The organization collecting the information.

- How the information is used.

- With whom the information may be shared.

- What choices are available to you regarding collection, use, and distribution of the information.

- The kind of security procedures that are in place to protect the loss, misuse, or alteration of information under control of the site.

- How consumers can correct any inaccuracies in the information.[*]

To join TRUSTe, a business needs to create a privacy statement (TRUSTe provides samples on its web site) and submit an application to TRUSTe. Membership dues are on a sliding scale. In April 2001, membership was $299 for a company with an annual revenue of less than $1 million, and $6,999 for an organization with annual revenues of $75 million or more.

It is important to note that a TRUSTe seal does not mean that information collected at a site is kept private! As Professor Antón has noted in presentations and her papers, a company could post a privacy policy stating that they sell collected user information to everyone who asks, that the user has no choices or options as regards collection or sale, that there is no security on the site to speak of to protect information, and that users have no options to correct errors. Although TRUSTe requires that there be statements about each of these issues, there is no requirement that any of the policy statements actually support user privacy protection!

BBBOnline

BBBOnLine is a wholly owned subsidiary of the Council of Better Business Bureaus. According to the organization, "BBBOnLine's mission is to promote

---

[*] *https://www.truste.org/validate/410*

trust and confidence on the Internet through the BBBOnLine Reliability and BBBOnLine Privacy programs."[*]

BBBOnline has several seal programs, all shown in Figure 24-2:

- The BBB Reliability Program seal indicates that a member business has been in business for at least one year, has agreed to abide by BBB standards of truth in advertising, and has committed to work with the BBB to help resolve consumer disputes that arise in conjunction with goods or services promoted or advertised on a web site. Additional requirements can be found at *http://www.bbbonline.org/reliability/requirement.asp*.

- The BBBOnLine "Kid's Privacy Seal" can be posted by sites that are in compliance with the Children's Online Privacy Protection Act and are accepted by the BBBOnLine Kid's Program. Membership in the Kid's Program requires certification that the organization's web site and privacy practices follow a detailed set of requirements that are outlined on the BBBOnLine web site. For details, see *http://www.bbbonline.org/privacy/kid_require.asp*. (See the section later in this chapter, "Children's Online Privacy Protection Act").

- The BBB Privacy Program seal can be used by any business that applies to and is accepted into the BBBOnline Privacy Program. Like the Kid's Program, membership in the Privacy Program requires that the web site implement the provisions of the BBBOnline's model privacy policy. For details, see *http://www.bbbonline.org/privacy/threshold.asp*.

Figure 24-2. BBBOnLine has three seal programs: the BBB Reliability Program, the Kid's Privacy Seal, and the BBB Privacy Program.

FTC enforcement

For customers of companies that have privacy policies, there might even be legal recourse. As privacy policies could be considered a form of advertising, companies that violate their own policies might be found guilty of deceptive and misleading advertisements. Thus, a company that violated its privacy policies might soon find

---

[*] *http://www.bbbonline.org/*

itself the subject of an action by the Federal Trade Commission or one of the state's attorney generals' offices.

Whether or not such legislation passes in the future, web surfers should be aware that information about their activities may be collected by service providers, vendors, site administrators, and others on the electronic superhighway. As such, users should perhaps be cautious about the web pages they visit if the pattern of accesses might be interpreted to the users' detriment.

"Notice, Choice, Access, and Security"

The original code of Fair Information Practices (see the earlier sidebar) identified five principles. The OECD expanded this list to eight principles (see the section "OECD Guidelines" earlier in this chapter). The U.S. government then backtracked. Between 1995 and 1998 staff members at the Federal Trade Commission conducted a series of meetings and workshops to evaluate online privacy issues. At these meetings, they were told that many principles in place in the rest of the world were simply too onerous for American businesses to comply with within the United States proper. After much discussion, the FTC staff put forth a discussion document, "Elements of Effective Self Regulation for the Protection of Privacy and Questions Related to Online Privacy" that dramatically simplified the concept of Fair Information Practices to four key items:

Notice
> Consumers should have a right to know how an organization treats and collects personal information.

Choice
> A consumer should have an option to withhold personal information.

Access
> A consumer should have a right to view personal information that has been collected.

Security
> Online services should employ security measures to prevent the unauthorized release of or access to personal information.

What is missing from these revised items is the principle that people be allowed to challenge incorrect data about themselves. We leave it to you to decide if it is "fair" that incorrect, outdated, or inconsistent personal data about you might be held and repeatedly used without any ability to correct or delete it.

Industry should have been pleased with the FTC's redefinition of the Code of Fair Information Practices. Instead, in testimony before the FTC and the U.S. Senate in the fall of 2000, representatives from Hewlett Packard and America Online said that they could only support the "Notice" and "Choice" provisions, arguing that "Access" and "Security" were too difficult and too elusive to write into regulations.

The Moral High Ground

Here is a simple but workable policy that we recommend for web sites that are interested in respecting personal privacy:

- Do not require users to register to use your site.
- Allow users to register with their email addresses if they wish to receive bulletins.
- Do not share a user's email address with another entity without that user's explicit permission for each organization with which you wish to share the email address.
- Whenever you send an email message to users, explain to them how you obtained their email addresses and how they can get their addresses off your mailing list.
- Do not make your log files publicly accessible.
- Delete your log files when they are no longer needed.
- If your log files must be kept online for extended periods of time, remove personally identifiable information from them.
- Encrypt your log files if possible.
- Do not give out personal information regarding your users.
- Discipline or fire employees who violate your privacy policy.
- Tell people about your policy on your home page, and allow your company to be audited by outsiders if there are questions regarding your policies.

Children's Online Privacy Protection Act

Passed by the U.S. Congress in 1998, the Children's Online Privacy Protection Act (COPPA) seeks to give parents control over how their children's personal information is collected and used on the Internet. Although limited in scope and somewhat awkward to implement, COPPA has had a dramatic impact on both the online community and the children's software industry in general.

Prelude to Regulation

Since the early 1970s, the U.S. database industry has consistently argued against government regulation, saying that "voluntary compliance" was cheaper, more flexible, more effective, and ultimately more in the interest of the American public. These arguments, combined with ample campaign contributions, have largely prevented the U.S. Congress from adopting legislation that would afford wholesale protections to the personal information of most Americans. Fortunately, the same is not true when it comes to protecting the personal information of America's children.

With the birth of the consumer Internet in the mid-1990s, many businesses and marketing firms decided to use the technology as a way to bypass parents and reach out directly to the children of America. In some cases, web sites were created directly for the purpose of extracting personal information from children—information that would later be used to solicit the children to make purchases. In other cases, children were used as an intermediary for gathering financial or demographic information about their parents.

For example, in 1996, the U.S. Federal Trade Commission began an investigation into the web site KidsCom. The site, peppered with cool graphics and free games, required that kids register to play. And registering was no small matter: kids had to fill out elaborate forms reporting age, birth date, sex, size of their family, favorite TV show, favorite TV commercial, favorite musical group, hobbies, how they accessed the Internet, correct email address, email address of their parent or guardian, mailing address, speed of their Internet connection, and career plans. The situation generated a lot of attention in the press: consumer advocates said that KidsCom was targeting children who couldn't make informed decisions about the release of personal information. The site's owners maintained that they asked these questions so they could match up kids in an electronic pen pal program and provide customized content. After a year of investigation, KidsCom voluntarily changed its practices, set up a parent's advisory panel, and adopted a privacy code.

At roughly the same time as the KidsCom investigation, The Walt Disney Company launched its own multimillion-dollar web site whose sole purpose was to promote Disney products and collect marketing information. Unlike KidsCom, Disney did not adopt a strict policy against releasing the names and identities of children. Indeed, the "privacy policy" at the company's web site in 1996 said exactly the reverse: "Information submitted at the time of registration or submission may be used for marketing and promotional purposes by The Walt Disney Company and may be shared with companies that have been pre-screened by The Walt Disney Company."

Congress began a series of hearings on the subject of children's online privacy. As a result of those hearings, in October 1998 Congress passed and President Clinton signed into law the Children's Online Privacy Protection Act. Under the Act, the Federal Trade Commission was charged to write a Rule that would enforce the Act. The FTC's COPPA Rule became effective on April 21, 2000.

COPPA Requirements

In the minds of many lawmakers, marketers had stepped over the line when they directly approached America's children. COPPA was designed to restore the position

---

of parents as the guardians of their children by putting parents in control of the collection and use of their children's personal information.

Who must follow the COPPA Rule?

COPPA applies to operators of commercial web sites and online services that are directed at children under the age of 13, and to operators of general audience sites who discover that they are collecting information from children under the age of 13. Thus, you might have a web site with a mature theme, such as wine tasting, but if you ask people to register with their age, and a subscriber says that he is under 13, COPPA applies to that subscriber.

 According to the FTC's *How to Comply With the Children's Online Privacy Protection Rule*, "to determine whether a web site is directed to children, the FTC considers several factors, including the subject matter; visual or audio content; the age of models on the site; language; whether advertising on the web site is directed to children; information regarding the age of the actual or intended audience; and whether a site uses animated characters or other child-oriented features." *

Basic provisions of COPPA

COPPA applies to all personally identifiable information that might be collected from children online, including:

- Full name
- Home address
- Email address
- Telephone number
- Any information that would allow someone to identify or contact the child
- All information collected from the child, if that information can be tied back to the child's name or identity

Under the terms of COPPA, web site operators must create a privacy policy that clearly states what kind of information is collected and what is done with it. Specifically, the notice must clearly state:

- The name and contact information for all operators collecting or maintaining children's personal information throughout the web site.
- What kind of personal information is collected, and how it is collected.
- How the personal information is used.

---

* *http://www.ftc.gov/bcp/conline/pubs/buspubs/coppa.htm*

- Whether or not information collected from children is disclosed to third parties. If information is disclosed, the notice must describe the general businesses of the third parties, what they do with the information, and whether or not the third parties have agreed to maintain the information's confidentiality and security.
- Finally, a link to the privacy notice must be clearly and prominently placed on the home page of the web site.

The FTC's Rule specifies certain minimum standards that privacy policies must follow, including:

- The operator's privacy policy must give parents the ability to "opt out" of third-party disclosure. That is, it must be possible for children to use the web site without having their information disclosed to others.
- Operators may not require children to "disclose more information than is reasonably necessary to participate in an activity as a condition of participation."
- Parents must have the ability to review a child's personal information, to refuse to have any more information on their children collected or used, and to have the information deleted. The notice must clearly state the procedures that a parent would need to follow.
- Before any information on a child is collected, used, or disclosed, the web site must obtain "verifiable parental consent."
- Parents must have the option of revoking their consent and having the web site operator delete all of their child's personal information at any time.

Verifiable parental consent

Both COPPA and the FTC's COPPA Rule require that web operators obtain consent from the child's parent before any personal information about the child can be collected. This provision is problematic—not because it is hard to verify that a person is giving consent, but because it is difficult (if not impossible) to verify that one online person is the parent of another.

In its initial rule the FTC admitted the difficulty of what Congress had asked it to do. The initial rule adopted a *sliding scale* that specified different levels of consent for different levels of personal information use. The sliding scale is in effect until April 2002; a formal review was planned for October 2001, as this book was going to press.

Under the sliding scale, an email from a parent is sufficient to allow internal uses of a child's personal information within a web site, provided that the web site operator "take additional steps to increase the likelihood that the parent has, in fact, provided consent." Additional steps that the FTC notes would be acceptable include:

- Delayed confirmatory email
- A letter from the parent

- A phone call from the parent

If the child's personal information is going to be publicly disclosed—such as being displayed as a name in a chat room or on a message board—then the FTC requires that the web site operator use "a more reliable method of consent." Typical methods that the FTC notes as acceptable include:

- Getting a signed form from the parent by email or fax
- Having the parent provide a credit card number in connection with a transaction, and having that credit card number verified
- Having a parent call a toll-free number and speak with "trained personnel"
- Receiving an "email accompanied by digital signature"

COPPA exceptions

The FTC's Rule allows several exceptions. These exceptions were designed to cover "many popular online activities for kids, including contests, online newsletters, homework help, and electronic postcards."

Under the FTC's exceptions, parental consent is not required when:

- An email address is collected specifically to provide notice and seek consent.
- An email address is collected to respond to a one-time request from a child, provided that the child's email address is not retained by the web site operator.
- An email address is collected to answer multiple requests or otherwise communicate with the child—for example, for a magazine subscription. However, in these cases, the web site operator must notify the parent about the nature of the communications and give the parent an opportunity to have the communications stop.
- An operator can collect a child's name or contact information "to protect the safety of a child who is participating on the site." However, in these cases, the web site operator must notify the parent to allow the parent "the opportunity to prevent further use of the information."
- An operator can collect a child's name or contact information "to protect the security or liability of the site or to respond to law enforcement."

Enforcement

The Children's Online Privacy Protection Act is enforced by the FTC. In most cases, violations of the Act that are pursued by the FTC will result in a consent agreement between the FTC and the web site in question. In some cases the FTC may prosecute web site operators who violate their written privacy policies under Section 5 of the FTC Act, as a unfair and deceptive trade practice.

P3P

The World Wide Web Consortium's Platform for Privacy Preferences Project (P3P) provides a standard way for web sites to communicate about their practices regarding the collection, use, and distribution of personal information. This section provides a brief introduction to P3P, and Figure 24-3 illustrates the P3P process; Appendix C contains more detailed technical information about the protocol.

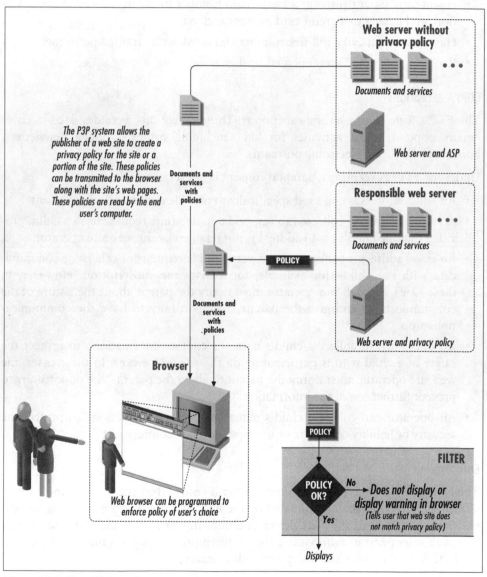

Figure 24-3. How P3P works

P3P and PICS

P3P is an outgrowth of the W3C's earlier work on its web site rating and filtering technology, PICS (see Chapter 23). The idea behind PICS was that web sites would be rated regarding their content, web browsers would download these ratings, and parents could program their children's computers so that web pages that violated the parent's standards would not be displayed.

The P3P system supports many of these concepts. Instead of using the formalisms of PICS to rate their adult content, web sites and online services use the formalisms of P3P to describe their policies regarding data collection and use. These descriptions can be downloaded from the web site to the browser when the web pages are viewed. If the web site's policies do not agree with the policies identified by the user, the browser can either warn the user or disable certain functionality. For example, a web browser could be programmed to discard any cookies from a web site that claims to use cookies for profiling its visitors.

PICS and P3P are similar in many ways:

- Like PICS, P3P doesn't define a specific set of policies or rating techniques. Instead, it describes a generalized vocabulary for describing web site privacy policies.
- Although both the PICS and P3P standards are extensible, both were provided with an initial data schema. In the case of PICS, the schema was the RSACi system, originally developed for rating video games. In the case of P3P, the schema is the base vocabulary. In both cases, it is very unlikely that the base schema will ever be extended, although it is certainly possible.
- Just as having a PICS rating does not imply that a site does or does not contain pornography, having a P3P rating does not imply that a site will or will not protect the privacy of its visitors. To make that determination, you (or your browser) must download the policy and read it.

P3P also differs from PICS in several important ways:

- P3P uses XML instead of LISP S-expressions to define its policies.
- P3P has no provisions for third-party rating services. All P3P policies are downloaded from the web site itself.
- P3P statements are not about the content of a web site, but about its practices. Thus, it is not possible for a user or a third party to verify a P3P statement without conducting a physical audit of the web site's organization.
- Because a web site's P3P statements may be intimately related to a web site's written privacy policy, an organization that treats personal information in a manner that is inconsistent with its P3P statements may be guilty of committing an "unfair trade practice" and may be opening itself up to an enforcement action by the Federal Trade Commision.

When this book went to press, P3P was still in its infancy. Internet Explorer 6.0 contains limited support for P3P (as described in the next section); Netscape Navigator 6.0 contains none.

For information on how to create a P3P policy for your web site, see Appendix C.

Support for P3P in Internet Explorer 6.0

Internet Explorer 6.0 contains limited support for P3P. This support is limited to support for P3P's so-called *compact policies* that describe how a site uses information collected through the use of cookies. IE6 uses this support to determine whether or not the user should accept a cookie from a given web site.

Internet Explorer's P3P implementation is controlled through the "Privacy" tab of the Internet Options control panel (see Figure 24-4). Using this panel, you can specify one of seven default policies to use for all web sites. You can also modify these policies to suit your individual desires. Finally, you can specify a list of web sites to be treated with specific rules.

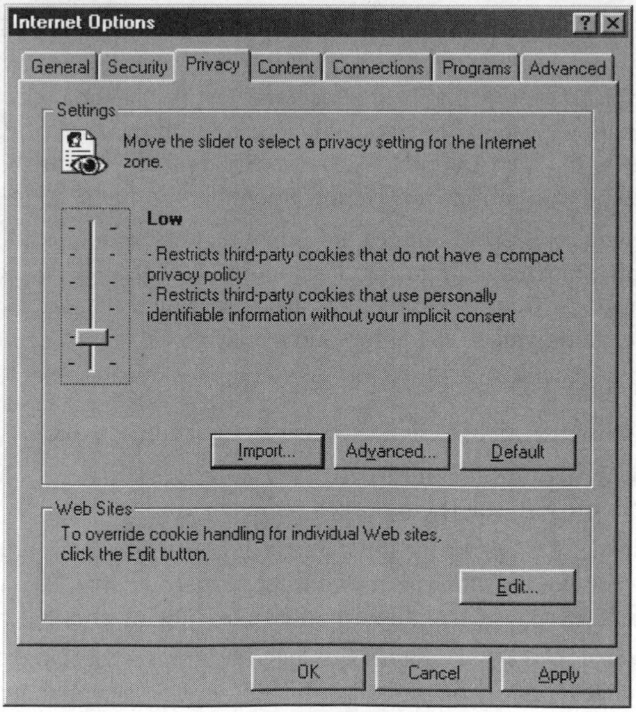

Figure 24-4. Internet Explorer 6.0 has limited support for P3P in the Privacy tab of the Internet Options control panel

Internet Explorer 6.0's P3P implementation is solely concerned with the issue of cookies. The implementation distinguishes between first-party cookies and third-party cookies. The term *first-party cookie* is used to refer to a cookie that is transmitted to your browser in the header of the base HTML page that a browser is viewing. The term *third-party cookie* is used to refer to cookies that are transmitted in the header of included images or frames that come from web sites other than the web site of the base page. In both cases, the browser can be configured to accept or reject cookies depending on whether or not a site has a P3P policy, and on how the policy says the site will handle personally identifiable information (PII).

Several of Microsoft's default policies are concerned with the idea of using PII "without implicit consent." In general, this phrase is used to determine if a web site operator can use personal information that is collected without first asking permission or if permission must be explicitly requested and given.

Internet Explorer 6.0 can "leash" cookies, so that they are only returned to the sites from which they originated. Cookies can also be "downgraded," so that they are automatically deleted when Internet Explorer is exited. The browser also explicitly makes reference to "session cookies;" these are cookies that similarly are deleted at the end of sessions and are not stored on the computer's hard disk.

The default policies are described in Table 24-1.

Table 24-1. Privacy policies in Internet Explorer 6.0

Privacy level	First-party cookies	Third-party cookies
Accept All Cookies	Accepts	Accepts
Low	Accepts	Blocks if no compact P3P policy. "Downgrades" cookies that use PII without *implicit* consent.
Medium	Leashes cookies from sites without P3P policies. Downgrades cookies from sites that allow use of PII without *implicit* consent.	Blocks if no compact P3P policy, or if policy allows use of PII without *implicit* consent.
Medium High	Blocks cookies from sites that use PII without *implicit* consent.	Blocks if no compact P3P policy, or if policy allows use of PII without *explicit* consent.
High	Blocks if no compact P3P policy, or if policy allows use of PII without *explicit* consent.	Blocks if no compact P3P policy, or if policy allows use of PII without *explicit* consent.
Block All Cookies	Blocks all cookies. Cannot read existing cookies.	Blocks all cookies. Cannot read existing cookies.

Conclusion

Although American businesses have argued repeatedly for the chance to police their own actions in the area of privacy and data collection, it appears that few are actually up to the task. Nevertheless, the prospects for federal legislation on this front are dim. Internet users should beware.

CHAPTER 25
Digital Payments

In this chapter:
- Charga-Plates, Diners Club, and Credit Cards
- Internet-Based Payment Systems
- Other Payment Systems
- How to Evaluate a Credit Card Payment System

Digital payment systems are a way to give somebody money without simultaneously giving them gold, coins, paper, or any other tangible item. It's the transfer of value without the simultaneous transfer of physical objects. It's the ability to make a payment in bits rather than atoms.

Digital payments are not a new idea; Western Union devised systems for wiring money by telegraph in the 19th century.[*] Banks have extensively used interbank funds transfers, and consumers have had access to automatic teller machines (ATMs) since the 1960s. Charge cards have been around in some form or another for almost 90 years.

Today credit cards are the most popular way of paying for services or merchandise ordered over the Web, and they are likely to remain the most popular system for quite some time. For that reason, we'll start this chapter with a look at the history of credit cards and see how they are processed. Then we'll look at some of the new digital payment systems developed for the Internet and explore why most of them have failed.

Charga-Plates, Diners Club, and Credit Cards

The *Oxford English Dictionary* lists more than 20 definitions for the word *credit*. Credit is belief, faith, and trust. Credit is trustworthiness. It is reputation. It is power derived from reputation, or from a person's character. It is an acknowledgment of payment by making an entry into an account. It is an amount of money at a person's disposal in the books of a bank:

> Pat deserves *credit* for coming up with that idea. Jane sent in her check and I have posted a *credit* to her account. Ted has no money and must buy those RAM chips on *credit*. Andrea's answer on the test was so absurd I could hardly give her *credit* for it.

---

[*] *The Victorian Internet: The Remarkable Story of the Telegraph and the Nineteenth Century's On-Line Pioneers*, by Tom Standage, Berkeley Publishing Group, 1999.

When used colloquially in the world of commerce, the word credit has all of these meanings, and many more. Perhaps the most important is this: credit is trust in a person's ability and willingness to pay at a later time for goods or services rendered now. Obtaining that trust requires a good reputation for handling debts and a system for keeping accurate accounts.

The credit card is one of the most widely used credit instruments in the United States today. It's also by far the most popular form of payment on today's Internet, according to both the first and second studies of Internet commerce by Global Concepts.[*] Not surprisingly, most systems for placing charges on the Internet today seek to leverage the credit card system, rather than replace it.

A Very Short History of Credit

Credit predates the use of money.[†] References to credit appear in the Code of Hammurabi, circa 1750 BC. Credit is also discussed in the Bible—together with edicts forbidding the charging of interest.

The modern notion of consumer credit dates to the late 18th and early 19th centuries, when liberal British economists argued against laws restricting credit. In the United States, credit took hold after the Civil War, when companies started selling sewing machines, pianos, household organs, stoves, encyclopedias, and even jewelry to consumers on installment plans.

By the early 1910s, many department stores and retailers were extending credit to their wealthier customers: credit allowed a customer to make purchases without having to pay at the point of sale with checks or cash. For many middle-class customers, credit purchases became a natural extension of installment plan purchases.

Oil companies pioneered the use of charge cards in the early 1920s. Called *courtesy cards*, the cards were actually made of paper and were reissued every three to six months. Although oil companies lost money on the cards themselves, they were seen as a way of attracting and retaining customers.

In 1928, the Farrington Manufacturing Company of Boston introduced the *charga-plate*, a small metal plate resembling an army dog tag on which a customer's name and address were embossed. Although charga-plates were initially confined to a particular store, within a few years stores in large urban centers such as New York City had formed cooperative agreements allowing a customer to use a single plate at a variety of stores.

Still, the modern credit card didn't come into existence until one afternoon in 1949, when Alfred Bloomingdale, Frank McNamara, and Ralph Snyder conceived of the

[*] See *http://www.global-concepts.com/* for further information.

[†] This section is largely based on information in *The Credit Card Industry: A History*, by Lewis Mandell, published by Twayne Publishers, Boston, a division of G. K. Hall & Co., 1990.

idea of a universal charge card while having lunch. The trio saw an opportunity for a card that could be used by salesmen for their travel and entertainment expenses, for example, eating at restaurants while entertaining potential clients and paying for hotels and food while on the road. The card, they decided, would be paid for by a monthly fee for the card holders and a seven percent surcharge on all restaurant transactions. They called their card Diner's Club.

In 1958, American Express and Carte Blanche entered the travel and entertainment card business. That same year, Bank of America and Chase Manhattan, the country's first and second largest banks, introduced their own cards. Bank of America's card was called BankAmericard, which changed to Visa in 1976. Chase Manhattan's card was called MasterCharge; the division was sold in 1962 and renamed MasterCard in 1980.

Payment Cards in the United States

Today there are thousands of different kinds of payment cards circulating in the United States. Some of these cards, such as American Express and Diner's Club, are issued by a single financial institution. Others, such as MasterCard and Visa, are in fact large membership organizations. When consumers are issued a MasterCard or Visa, they are actually issued a card from a member bank. Most banks set interest rates and other financial terms, but contract with a bank card processor for the actual running of the computers that maintain the customer and merchant accounts. The service provided by MasterCard and Visa is the setting of systemwide policies and the operation of the interbank network that is used for authorizing and settling charges.

The Interbank Payment Card Transaction

Today the interbank payment card transaction has evolved into a complicated electronic dance among many characters. A typical card transaction involves up to five different parties:

- The consumer
- The merchant
- The consumer's bank, which issued the consumer's charge card
- The merchant's bank (also called the acquiring bank)
- The interbank network

The typical charge card transaction consists of ten steps:

1. The consumer gives her charge card to the merchant.
2. The merchant asks the acquiring bank for authorization.
3. The interbank network sends a message from the acquiring bank to the consumer's bank, asking for authorization.

4. A response is sent on the interbank network from the consumer's bank to the acquiring bank. (The consumer's bank may also place a certain amount of the consumer's credit line on hold, pending the settlement of the transaction.)

5. The acquiring bank notifies the merchant that the charge has been approved.

6. The merchant fills the consumer's order.

7. Some later time, the merchant presents a batch of charges to the acquiring bank.

8. The acquiring bank sends each settlement request on the interbank network to the consumer's bank.

9. The consumer's bank debits the consumer's account and places the money (possibly minus a service charge) into an interbank settlement account.

10. The acquiring bank credits the merchant's account and withdraws a similar sum of money from the interbank settlement account.

This process is illustrated in Figure 25-1.

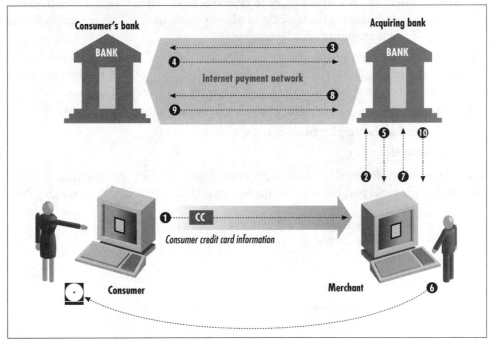

Figure 25-1. The players in a typical charge card transaction

In recent years, the time for a charge card authorization has dropped from nearly a minute to less than five seconds. In the past, many point-of-sale transactions were not authorized: authorizations took so long that banks worried that they would lose more money because of lost sales than they would lose from fraud. Thus, in the

1970s, authorizations were usually reserved for sales above a high threshold: $50 or more. Today in the U.S. virtually all card transactions are authorized. In many other countries, only high-value transactions are authorized.[*]

The charge card check digit algorithm

The last digit of a charge card number is a check digit that is used to detect keystroke errors when a charge card number is entered into a computer. Although the check digit algorithm is public (ISO 2894), it is not widely known.

The algorithm is:

1. Remove any spaces, dashes, and other nonnumeric information from the credit card number. In general, web-based applications should allow people to type spaces or dashes in credit card numbers, because this reduces the chances of a transcription error. That's because it's easier to catch a typo in the entered string "3333 342534 54330" than in the string "333334253454330." Many e-commerce systems do not allow users to type spaces or dashes, or fail silently when these characters are typed. It's best to allow people to type this information and then to have it programmatically removed.

2. Multiply each digit in the charge card by its "weight." If a charge card has an even number of digits, the first digit has a weight of 2; otherwise the digit has a weight of 1. Afterwards, the weights of the digits alternate 1, 2, 1, 2.

3. If any digit has a weighted value that is more than 9, subtract 9.

4. Add together the weights of all of the digits, modulo 10.

5. The result should be 0.

This algorithm is designed to catch transposed digits or other typing errors; it is not designed as a general-purpose security mechanism.[†] Here is the algorithm coded in Perl:

```
sub validate_cc {
        my ($cc) = $_[0];
        my ($digit,$sum,$val);
        my ($weight) = 1;

        $cc = s/[^0-9]//g;

        $weight = 2 if (length($cc) %2 ==0);
```

---

[*] The threshold at which transactions are authorized and which are allowed through without authorization is determined by the cost of local telephone calls within the country and the likelihood of fraud. Different merchants may obviously have different thresholds.

[†] Unfortunately, some businesses have used the algorithm as a low-cost way of "verifying" credit card numbers. For example, some online services have deployed software that creates accounts for any individual presenting a credit card number that passes the algorithm, in an attempt to save the cost of performing millions of verifications.

```
    while($cc ne ""){
        $digit = substr($cc,0,1);
        $cc = substr($cc,1);
        $val = $digit * $weight;
        $val-=9 if ($val>9);
        $sum += $val;
        $weight = ($weight==2) ? 1 : 2;
    }
    return ($sum % 10) == 0;
}
```

Now, let's check it with a charge card randomly taken from Simson's wallet: American Express charge card number 3728 024906 54059.

The charge card has 15 digits. The number 15 is odd, so the first digit has a weight of 1.

To compute the check digit, we multiply:

```
(3 x 1) , (7 x 2) , (2 x 1) , (8 x 2) , (0 x 1) ,
(2 x 2) , (4 x 1) , (9 x 2) , (0 x 1) , (6 x 2) ,
(5 x 1) , (4 x 2) , (0 x 1) , (5 x 2) , (9 x 1)
```

which is:

```
(3) , (14) , (2) , (16) , (0) , (4) , (4) ,
(18) , (0) , (12) , (5) , (8) , (0) , (10) ,
(9)
```

Subtract 9 from every value greater than 9, and add them together:

```
(3) + (5) + (2) + (7) + (0) + (4) + (4) +
(9) + (0) + (3) + (5) + (8) + (0) + (1) +
(9) = 60
```

This gives us a check of 0 (as it should), because:

```
60 mod 10 = 0
```

Remember: don't use Simson's charge card number. It's a felony.

The charge slip

The charge slip tracks charge card transactions. For more than 30 years these charge slips have been paper. Although they were initially returned to the consumer, as with checks, this proved to be too expensive over time. By the mid-1970s, Visa and Master-Card customers were receiving monthly statements summarizing their charges, rather than the original charge slips. In the 1980s, American Express began digitizing charge slips and giving its customers digitized printouts of their charge slips. Today, however, consumers merely receive printed reports listing all of the relevant charges.

Over time, the amount of information on the charge slip has steadily increased. Today there is a large collection of information, including:

- Name of customer
- Customer's charge card number

- Customer's address
- Customer number
- Transaction date
- Transaction amount
- Description of the merchandise or service offered
- Reference number
- Authorization code
- Merchant name

Computerized systems largely mimic the paper-based systems that have been used for more than 20 years. That's because the information on the charge slip has been shown to be useful in consummating transactions and combating fraud. Many computerized systems still use the word "slip." Others refer to the charge or payment "record" or "draft."

Charge card fees

Banks impose a fee anywhere between one percent and seven percent for each charge card transaction. This fee is paid by the merchant. Thus, a consumer who makes a purchase for $100 may see a $100 charge on her credit card statement, but the merchant may only see $97 deposited into his bank account. The difference is split between the acquiring bank, the merchant's bank, and the network.

Some merchant banks additionally charge their merchants a per-transaction fee and an authorization fee, both of which can be anywhere from pennies to a dollar. Merchants can also be charged sign-up fees, annual fees, and rental fees for the use of their charge card terminals.

Merchant fees are determined by many factors, such as the number of charges the merchant processes in a month, the average value of each transaction, the number of charge-backs, and the merchant's own negotiating power.

Issuing banks make money from annual fees that are imposed directly on the consumer and from interest charges on unpaid balances. The cost to banks for servicing an individual consumer ranges between $50 and $200 per year.

Despite the fact that they lose a few percentage points to service fees, most merchants seem to prefer being paid by credit cards to being paid by check or cash. When they are validated with online systems, credit cards provide almost instant assurance that the payment has been made, and the money is deposited directly into the merchant's bank account. Checks, by contrast, sometimes bounce. Cash is sometimes counterfeit. And even when the checks and cash are good, they still represent physical objects that must be dealt with. Most merchants file their credit card charges electronically, storing the credit slips on-site. Thus, merchants may actually save money by accepting credit cards, even though they are paying the service fee.

Refunds and Charge-Backs

Charge cards are actually two-way financial instruments: besides transferring money from a consumer's account into a merchant's, they can also transfer money from a merchant's account back into the consumer's.

A *refund* or *credit* is a reverse charge transaction that is initiated by a merchant. A merchant might reverse a transaction if a piece of merchandise is returned. The consumer can receive either a partial refund or a complete refund. In some cases, the acquiring bank will refund the bank charges as well. For this reason, it's to the advantage of a merchant to issue a refund to a customer's credit card, rather than to simply write a refund check directly to the customer.

Many bank card issuers have rules that state that credits can only be issued in response to charges issued on the same card. That is, if you buy something using an American Express card, and you take it back to the store, the store is supposed to issue a credit on your American Express card, and not on your Discover card or your Visa card. In practice, there are few mechanisms in place to enforce this requirement. However, there is enough auditing of the charge slips that if a merchant were doing a lot of these transactions for fraudulent purposes, that merchant would be leaving quite a paper trail and that would eventually be picked up; at least, that's the way that the system is supposed to work.

Charge-backs are credit operations that are initiated by the customer, rather than by the merchant. A customer might be billed for purchases that were never delivered, for example, or a customer might feel otherwise cheated by the merchant. Federal law allows a customer to dispute charges under a variety of circumstances. Different banks make this process simpler or more difficult. (For example, some banks will allow customers to dispute charges over the phone, while others require disputes to be in writing.) Banks also have different standards for transactions in which there is an actual signature as opposed to transactions that are mail orders or telephone orders: merchants generally have more responsibility for the transaction when they do not have a signature on file, or when merchandise is not shipped to the billing address of the credit card. Charge-backs can also be initiated by the bank itself when fraud is detected.

Makers of computerized credit card processing systems need to build mechanisms into their systems to handle credit card transactions that are initiated by the merchant, the consumer, or the bank. Otherwise, merchants who use these systems will need to constantly enter credit and charge-back transactions by hand into their accounting systems whenever the need arises. Some systems also have built-in checks to protect against common mistakes. For example, some credit card systems will detect duplicate charges and automatically suppress them.

Debit Cards

Many banks are now issuing branded *debit cards*. These may look exactly like a Visa or MasterCard (or other credit card). However, when a purchase is made using a debit card and an online verification is performed, the charge is immediately deducted from the client's checking account. No credit is actually extended to the consumer. The same inter-bank network is used to process the transaction as if the card were a credit card.

These cards are very convenient for the consumer because they are accepted at more places than a check would be. Merchants also like them because they can get an immediate authorization code, thus avoiding the risk of fraud.

Debit cards aren't actually the same as credit cards, however. Even though the card numbers look the same as credit card numbers, debit cards clear over different networks and are covered by different regulations from those that cover credit cards. This has an impact on several aspects of use, including automatic fraud protection and regulations regarding charge-backs in cases of dispute. For example, the consumer is not automatically protected if the card or the account number is stolen. If you have a debit card, *carefully* read the card member agreement to see what you may be risking for the convenience.

Additional Authentication Mechanisms

From the beginning, credit cards have been subject to fraud and misuse. The first Diner's Club cards were cardboard cards that were sent out to every person who had purchased a Rolls Royce from a dealer in Beverley Hills. Many of the recipients of the card thought that it was a gag and threw them away, gave them to friends, or used them without any intention of paying their bills. The resulting losses nearly bankrupted the fledgling company.

Because credit cards are carried in wallets, theft has always been a possibility. For years, credit card companies based their security on the signature strip located on the card's back. The strip was made of a certain material that was designed to clearly show tampering. The theory was that if somebody stole your card, they would have a hard time signing your name exactly the way it was signed on the back of the credit card. As long as the merchant inspected the signature on the back of the card and on the charge strip, fraud could supposedly be prevented or minimized.

The rise of "card-not-present" transactions—transactions in which items were purchased by telephone or mail order—eliminated any security that the signature strip could provide. At first, to initiate a card-not-present transaction, all a crook needed was the name on the credit card, the credit card's number, and the expiration date. (Early on, the crook didn't even need the name or the expiration date.) This information could easily be obtained from credit card receipts, from the carbon paper used to make the receipts, or even from crooked merchants or their employees. Fundamentally, the problem that the credit card companies faced was that the information used by one merchant to initiate a charge could be reused by others.

Since the 1980s, credit card companies have looked for ways to improve the security of their systems without changing the underlying structure of the credit card number itself or the charge clearing system. They have done this by modifying their systems so that consumers could provide additional information to perform a card-not-present transaction, and then charging merchants a higher percentage rate if this additional information was not presented.

Address verification is one such system. With address verification, a consumer must provide his credit card's billing address for a charge to be approved. The problem with address verification is that consumers sometimes do not know the address that their card bills to, and sometimes an address may be inadvertently mistyped. Thus, there is a trade-off: the system can be programmed to require a very exact match, which will probably reduce the chance of fraud, but highly exacting matches will also disallow some genuinely legitimate transactions. Some credit card companies will tell the merchant's computers exactly how much of the address matched—the Zip code, the street number, the street name, or even the telephone number—and then allow the merchant to decide whether to accept the transaction or to disallow it.

Another verification system involves the additional digits that are printed above the credit card account number or printed on the credit card's signature strip. These numbers do not appear on the card's magnetic strip, and because they are not embossed, they do not appear on carbon paper. Thus, if the consumer is able to provide this information in a card-not-present transaction, there is a very good chance that the consumer is holding the credit card.

Using Credit Cards on the Internet

Because many merchants already had mechanisms for handling charge card transactions made by telephone, charge cards were an obvious choice for early Internet-based payment systems.

However, credit cards also present a problem for merchants because credit card numbers are essentially unchanging passwords that can be used to repeatedly charge payments to a consumer's account. Thus, charge card numbers must be protected from eavesdropping and guessing.

In recent years, merchants have experimented with three different techniques for accepting charge card numbers in conjunction with transactions that are initiated over the Web:

Offline

After the order is placed over the Web, the customer calls up the merchant using a telephone and recites the credit card number. This technique is as secure as any other purchase made by mail order or telephone (called MOTO by industry insiders). Although credit card numbers can be found if the phone line is wire-tapped or if a PBX is reprogrammed, it seems to be a risk that merchants, consumers, and banks are willing to take. Furthermore, people basically understand the laws against credit card fraud and wiretapping in cases of this kind.

Online with encryption

The consumer sends the credit card number over the Internet to the merchant in an encrypted transaction.

Online without encryption

The consumer simply sends the credit card number, either in an email message or in an HTTP POST command. Although this technique is vulnerable to eaves-dropping—for example, by a packet sniffer—there has to date been no publicized case of information gain from eavesdropping being used to commit credit card fraud.[*]

Internet-Based Payment Systems

Although most purchases made on the Internet today are made with credit cards, increasingly merchants and consumers are turning their attention to other kinds of Internet-based payment systems. In contrast to credit cards, these new systems seem to promise a number of possible advantages:

Reduced transaction cost

Credit card charges cost between 25 cents and 75 cents per transaction, with a hefty 2 to 3 percent service fee on top of that. New payment systems might have transaction costs in the pennies, making them useful for purchasing things that cost only a quarter.

Anonymity

With today's credit card systems, the merchant needs to know the consumer's name, account number, and frequently the address as well. Some consumers are hesitant to give out this information. Some merchants believe that their sales might increase if consumers were not required to give out this information.

Broader market

Currently, there are many individuals in the world who use cash because they are not eligible for credit cards. Payment systems that are not based on credit might be usable by more people.

---

[*] As of October 2001.

From the consumer's point of view, all electronic payment systems consist of two phases. The first phase is *enrollment*: the consumer needs to establish some sort of account with the payment system and possibly download necessary software. The second phase is the actual *purchase* operation. Some payment systems have a third phase, *settlement*, in which accounts are settled among the consumer, the merchant, and the payment service.

There are several different types of payment systems.

Anonymous

Payment systems can be *anonymous*, in which case it is mathematically impossible for a merchant or a bank to learn the identity of a consumer making a purchase if the consumer chooses to withhold that information. Although many anonymous payment systems have been proposed and tested, to date they have all failed.

Private

Payment systems can be *private*. With these systems, the merchant does not know the identity of the consumer, but it is possible for the merchant to learn the identity by conferring with the organization that operates the payment system.

Identifying

Payment systems can identify the consumer to the merchant in all cases. Conventional credit cards and checks are examples of *identifying* payment systems.

This section describes a variety of payment systems that are used on the Internet today or that have been attempted.

Virtual PIN

In 1994, First Virtual Holdings introduced its *Virtual PIN*, a system for making credit card charges over the Internet. The Virtual PIN was unique among electronic payment systems in that it required no special software for a consumer to make purchases with the system. Instead, payments were authorized by electronic mail.

Typical Virtual PINs were "BUY-VIRTUAL", "YOUR-VIRTUAL-PIN", "SMITH-SAUNDERS", and "SPEND-MY-MONEY".

No encryption was used in sending information to or from the consumer. Instead, the Virtual PIN attained its security by relying on the difficulty of intercepting email. Additional security was provided by the fact that credit card charges could be reversed up to 60 days after they were committed, allowing fraud to be detected and remedied. First Virtual protected itself by not releasing money to merchants until 91 calendar days after a charge was made. Merchants that were creditworthy could apply to get paid within four business days.

Enrollment

To enroll, the consumer needed to fill out and submit a Virtual PIN enrollment form. First Virtual made the form available on its web site and by email. The form included the person's name, address, and the Virtual PIN that she wished to use,* but it did not include the person's credit card number.

Once the form was received, First Virtual sent the user an email message containing her application number and a toll-free 800 number for the user to call. (A non-800 number was also provided for First Virtual consumers who did not live within the United States.) The subscribers called the 800 number, dialed their First Virtual application numbers using a touch-tone telephone and then keyed in their credit card numbers. This automated voice response system was designed in such a way that customer credit card numbers were never sent over the Internet; at the time that First Virtual was deployed, this added bit of security held considerable interest for First Virtual's banking partners.

Several hours after the phone call, First Virtual sent the consumer a second piece of email congratulating her for enrolling and giving the user her final Virtual PIN. This Virtual PIN was the Virtual PIN that the user requested, with another word prepended.

Purchasing

The Virtual PIN purchase cycle consisted of five parts:

1. The consumer gave the merchant his or her Virtual PIN.
2. The merchant transmitted the Virtual PIN and the amount of the transaction to First Virtual for authorization.
3. First Virtual sent the consumer an email message asking if the merchant's charge was legitimate.
4. The consumer replied to First Virtual's message with the words "Yes," "No," or "Fraud."
5. If the consumer answered "Yes," the merchant was informed by First Virtual that the charge was accepted. If the consumer answered "No," the charge was declined. If the consumer answered "Fraud," First Virtual's staff investigated.

Security and privacy

Virtual PINs were not encrypted when they were sent over the Internet. Thus, an eavesdropper could intercept a Virtual PIN and attempt to use it to commit a fraudulent transaction. However, such an eavesdropper would also have to be able to intercept the confirmation email message that is sent to the Virtual PIN holder. Thus, the

---

* First Virtual might prepend a four- to six-letter word to the beginning of a Virtual PIN for uniqueness.

Virtual PIN system relied on the difficulty of intercepting electronic mail to achieve its security. In practice, First Virtual saw little fraud; one of the most significant cases involved a student who had stolen another student's Virtual PIN and was able to intercept his email because they used computers on the same local area network.

First Virtual designed the Virtual PIN to be easy to deploy and to offer relatively good security against systemwide failures. Although it was possible to target an individual consumer for fraud, it would have been very difficult to carry out an attack against thousands of consumers. And any small amount of fraud could be directly detected and dealt with appropriately, for example, by reversing credit card charges.

The Virtual PIN gave the purchaser considerably more anonymity than do conventional credit cards. With credit cards, the merchant knows the consumer's name: it's right there on the card. But with the Virtual PIN, the merchant knew only the Virtual PIN—and the consumer could change his Virtual PIN whenever he wished.

Because each transaction had to be manually confirmed, the Virtual PIN also protected consumers from fraud on the part of the merchant. Consumers who used the system said that they did not consider manually confirming every transaction to be burdensome.

Redux

First Virtual's payment system was the first working digital payment system on the Internet. Unfortunately, while First Virtual's creators thought that the system would be used by all sorts of e-companies, the main reason for interest in First Virtual was for the buying and selling of pornography. Worried about being associated with the smut industry, and failing to realize the size of the market, First Virtual segregated the smut services off its main web site and gradually made it more difficult for the Virtual PIN to be used for that purpose.

Unable to make significant revenue from the Virtual PIN, in the end First Virtual decided to leverage its experience in sending and receiving large amounts of email and became MessageMedia, a company that specializes in sending promotional email over the Internet.

DigiCash

DigiCash was an electronic payment system developed by Dr. David Chaum, the man who is widely regarded as the inventor of digital cash. Also called E-Cash, the system was sold by Dr. Chaum's company DigiCash BV, which was based in Amsterdam. The system was fielded in the United States by the Bank of Mark Twain in 1996.

DigiCash was based on a system of digital tokens called *digital coins*. Each coin was created by the consumer and then digitally signed by the DigiCash mint, which was presumably operated by a bank or a government. Users of the system could exchange the coins among themselves or cash them in at the mint, a process similar to a poker player's cashing in his or her chips at the end of the day.

Enrollment

To enroll with the DigiCash system, a consumer needed to download the DigiCash software and establish an account with an organization that could both mint and receive the DigiCash digital coins. These digital coins were to be backed by some other currency that the bank had on deposit, such as dollars or gold. In theory, though, digital coins could be backed by anything that two parties might find of value—for example, gallons of honey, megawatt hours on the futures market, copies of this book, or even computational time on a network of workstations.

DigiCash accounts consisted of two parts: a deposit account at the financial institution and an electronic wallet that was maintained on the user's computer. To obtain DigiCash, the user's software created a number of electronic coins—blocks of data. Parts of these coins were then *blinded,* or XORed with a random string. The coins were then sent to the mint to be signed. For each dollar of coins that the mint signed, an equal amount was withdrawn from the user's account. The coins were then returned to the user's computer, where they were XORed again. In this manner, it was impossible for the issuing institution to trace back spent coins to the particular user who issued them.

Purchasing

To make a purchase with DigiCash, the consumer needed to be running a small program called the *DigiCash wallet.* The program spoke a protocol that allowed it to exchange coins with a merchant system and with its wallets. Coins could also be sent by email or printed out and sent by other means.

Security and privacy

Chaum developed digital cash systems that offered unconditional anonymity as well as systems that offered conditional anonymity: the consumer always knew the identity of the merchant, and the merchant could learn the identity of the consumer if the consumer attempted to double-spend money.[*]

The DigiCash system is routinely showcased as a model system that respects the privacy of the user. The idea is that DigiCash could be used for a series of small transactions, such as buying articles from an online database, and merchants would be unable to combine information gleaned from those small transactions to build comprehensive profiles of their users.

---

[*] Double-spending is detected at the bank when a merchant attempts to deposit DigiCash coins. As a result, merchants who receive DigiCash are encouraged to deposit it in the bank as soon as possible.

However, an anonymous payment system is not sufficient to assure the anonymity of the consumer. That's because it may be necessary for the merchant to learn identifying information about a consumer to fulfill the consumer's purchase. For example, during a DigiCash trial in 1995, one of the things that could be purchased with DigiCash was a T-shirt. However, to deliver the T-shirt, the merchant needed to know the name and address of the person making the purchase.*

Perhaps one reason that DigiCash did not catch on is that there was never a real market need for the technology. Chaum's original motivation for developing DigiCash was to allow electronic database and library companies such as Lexis/Nexis to sell small pieces of information in a piecemeal fashion—DigiCash would protect people's right to read what they wished in total anonymity. But Lexis/Nexis never wanted a DigiCash-based system. Instead of selling information piecemeal to the public, these companies offer accounts to their customers with different kinds of purchase plans. Some plans have a relatively high cost for occasional use, whereas other plans have a lower cost for higher volumes or for off-hour access. Offering different plans to different kinds of customers allows a database company to maximize its profits while simultaneously using its infrastructure more efficiently. Meanwhile, the users of these services have not demanded the ability to perform their searches and download the results anonymously. Despite the lack of anonymity, users of these services do not seem to worry that their database searches may be scanned by their competitors. At least so far, database vendors seem to realize that customer records must be held in confidence if customers are to be retained.

Redux

Despite a tremendous amount of publicity, DigiCash was never able to create a critical mass. DigiCash eventually ran out of money and was forced to declare bankruptcy. The DigiCash algorithms, on the other hand, are well understood and live on. Despite being protected by various patents, there are numerous individuals who continue to experiment with them.

CyberCash/CyberCoin

CyberCash's first digital payment system was designed to let conventional credit cards be used securely over the World Wide Web. By "securely," CyberCash meant that merchants would never be able to see the credit card numbers of their customers. Instead, the merchant received encrypted credit card numbers and passed them along to their merchant bank. The system was designed to limit the fraud that a mer-

---

* One way around this obvious problem is to put a code number on the box and send it to a fulfillment house. The fulfillment house looks up the code number in a database and sends it to the end user. In this manner, the merchant knows what is in the box but doesn't know where it is going, and the fulfillment house knows where the box is going but doesn't know what is in it.

chant could commit, and thus make it easier for companies to become merchants and accept credit cards.

The CyberCoin system was an adaptation of the technology for small-value transactions. Instead of issuing a credit card charge, the CyberCash server can be thought of as a debit card.

Enrollment

Before using CyberCash, the consumer had to download special software from the CyberCash web site, *http://www.cybercash.com/*. The software was called the *Cyber-Cash wallet*. This software maintained a database of a user's credit cards and other payment instruments.

When the wallet software first ran, it created a public key/private key combination. The private key and other information (including credit card numbers and transaction logs) was stored encrypted with a passphrase on the user's hard disk, with a backup key stored encrypted on a floppy disk.

To use a credit card with the CyberCash system, the credit card had to be enrolled. To create a CyberCoin account, a user had to complete an online enrollment form. The CyberCash implementation allowed money to be transferred into a CyberCoin account from a credit card or from a checking account using the Automated Clearing House (ACH) electronic funds transfer system. Money that was transferred into the CyberCoin account from a checking account could be transferred back out again, but money that was transferred into the account from a credit card could only be spent. (The reason for these restrictions was both to reduce fraud and to deal with the higher cost of using credit cards compared with ACH.) CyberCash allowed the user to close his or her CyberCoin account and receive a check for the remaining funds.

Purchasing

The CyberCash wallet registered itself as a helper application for Netscape Navigator and Microsoft's Internet Explorer. Purchases could then be initiated by downloading files of a particular MIME file type.

When a purchase was initiated, the CyberCash wallet displayed the amount of the transaction and the name of the merchant. The user then decided which credit card to use and whether to approve or reject the transaction. The software could also be programmed to automatically approve small-value transactions. The first version of the software was programmed to automatically approve transactions less than five dollars, raising the danger that merchants might create web pages that stole small amounts of money from web users using the <IMG SRC=> feature without the user's knowledge. (This behavior was changed after the product's launch.)

If the user approved the transaction, an encrypted payment order was sent to the merchant. The merchant could decrypt some of the information in the payment order, but not other information. The merchant's software would add its own payment information to the order, digitally sign it, and send it to the CyberCash gateway for processing.

The CyberCash gateway received the payment information and decrypted it. The gateway checked for duplicate requests and verified the user's copy of the invoice against the merchant's to make sure neither had lied to the other. The gateway then sent the credit card payment information to the acquiring bank. The acquiring bank authorized the transaction and sent the response back to CyberCash, which sent an encrypted response back to the merchant. Finally, the merchant transmitted the CyberCash payment acknowledgment back to the consumer.

CyberCoin purchases were similar to CyberCash purchases, except that money was simply debited from the consumer's CyberCoin account and credited to the merchant's account.

Security and privacy

The CyberCash payment was designed to protect consumers, merchants, and banks against fraud. It did this by using cryptography to protect payment information while it was in transit.

All payment information was encrypted before it was sent over the Internet. But CyberCash further protected consumers from fraud on the part of the merchant: the merchant never had access to the consumer's credit card number.

Digital Money and Taxes

Some pundits have said that digital money will make it impossible for governments to collect taxes such as a sales tax or a value added tax. But that is highly unlikely.

To collect taxes from merchants, governments force merchants to keep accurate records of each transaction. There is no reason why merchants would be less likely to keep accurate business records of transactions consummated with electronic money than they would for transactions consummated by cash or check. Indeed, it is highly unlikely that merchants will stop keeping any records at all: the advent of electronic commerce will probably entail the creation and recording of even more records.

Nor are jurisdictional issues likely to be impediments to the collection of taxes. Merchants already operate under rules that clearly indicate whether or not taxes should be paid on goods and services delivered to those out of the state or the country. What is likely, though, is that many of these rules will change as more and more services are offered by businesses to individuals located out of their home region.

Redux

Despite the security and the convenience of using CyberCash, consumers were slow to adopt the system. One reason offered was the size of the CyberCash client software—several megabytes. At the time, it would have taken most consumers the better part of an hour simply to download the software and install it. Because few consumers had the software, few merchants were interested in spending the money to implement the CyberCash protocols on their own systems. Because few merchants were interested, few banks ever geared up for CyberCash.

CyberCash eventually dropped support for the consumer wallet and instead concentrated on processing credit card orders for merchants that were delivered to merchant web sites using standard web forms and SSL. After a successful initial public offering of its stock, CyberCash made a number of strategic purchases and investments and soon ran out of money. The company was forced into bankruptcy and was eventually purchased by VeriSign.

SET

SET is the Secure Electronic Transaction protocol for sending payment card information over the Internet. SET was designed for encrypting specific kinds of payment-related messages. Because it cannot be used to encrypt arbitrary text messages, programs containing SET implementations with strong encryption have been able to receive export permission from the U.S. State Department.

The SET standard was jointly developed by MasterCard, Visa, and various computer companies. Although the SET initiative appears to be dead, detailed information about SET can still be found on the MasterCard web site at *http://www.mastercard.com/set* and on the Visa web site at *http://www.visa.com/*. It is worth taking a look at how this initiative was intended to work.

According to the SET documents, some of the goals for SET were to:

- Provide for confidential transmission
- Authenticate the parties involved
- Ensure the integrity of payment instructions for goods and services order data
- Authenticate the identity of the cardholder and the merchant to each other

SET uses encryption to provide for the confidentiality of communications and uses digital signatures for authentication. Under SET, merchants are required to have digital certificates issued by their acquiring banks. Consumers may optionally have digital certificates issued by their banks. During the SET trials, MasterCard required consumers to have digital certificates, while Visa did not.

From the consumer's point of view, using SET is similar to using the CyberCash wallet. The primary difference is that support for SET was to be built into a wide variety of commercial products.

Two channels: one for the merchant, one for the bank

In a typical SET transaction, there is information that is private between the customer and the merchant (such as the items being ordered) and other information that is private between the customer and the bank (such as the customer's account number). SET allows both kinds of private information to be included in a single, signed transaction through the use of a cryptographic structure called a *dual signature*.

A single SET purchase request message consists of two fields, one for the merchant and one for the acquiring bank. The merchant's field is encrypted with the merchant's public key; likewise, the bank's field is encrypted with the bank's public key. The SET standard does not directly provide the merchant with the credit card number of the consumer, but the acquiring bank can, at its discretion, provide the number to the merchant when it sends confirmation.*

In addition to these encrypted blocks, the purchase request contains message digests for each of these two fields, and a signature. The signature is obtained by concatenating the two message digests, taking the message digest of the two message digests, and signing the resulting message digest. This is shown in Figure 25-2.

The dual signature allows either the merchant or the bank to read and validate its signature on its half of the purchase request without needing to decrypt the other party's field.

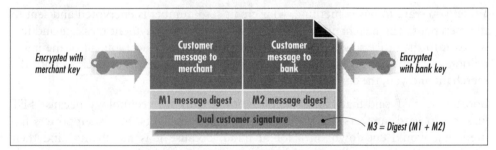

Figure 25-2. The SET purchase request makes use of a dual signature.

Why SET failed

To understand why SET was not successful, consider the system from the consumer's point of view. Before a consumer could purchase something with SET, the consumer needed to follow these steps:

---

* Some merchants have legacy systems that require the consumer's credit card number to be on file. It was easier to build this back-channel into SET than to get merchants to modify their software so that credit card numbers would not be required.

1. The consumer needed to first obtain the digital wallet software. This software was never distributed with web browsers. Instead, it needed to be separately downloaded.

2. The consumer needed to type his credit card number into the wallet software.

3. The consumer needed to obtain digital certificates for each credit card.

4. Finally, the consumer needed to find a web site that was enabled to process SET transactions.

In the end, few customers went to the trouble of downloading the SET wallets. Those who did discovered that there were few merchants on the Internet who supported the protocol. And because SET offered no direct advantage to the consumer—it didn't really speed up purchasing, and it didn't offer a discount—there was no real incentive for ISPs and software publishers to prebundle SET with programs such as web browsers or email clients. Despite the huge support by Mastercard, Visa, Microsoft, and others, SET never really got off the ground.

Before you can use the SET system, you must first enter your credit card number into the electronic wallet software. Most implementations will store the credit card number in an encrypted file on your hard disk or in a smart card. The software also creates a public key and a secret key for encrypting your financial information before it is sent over the Internet.

When you want to buy something, your credit card number is encrypted and sent to the merchant. The merchant's software digitally signs the payment message and forwards it to the processing bank, where the Payment Server decrypts all of the information and runs the credit card charge. Finally, a receipt gets sent back to both the merchant and you, the customer.

Boosters of SET said that banks would be excited by the technology because SET kept credit card numbers out of the hands of the merchants. SET's supporters figured that would cut down on a lot of fraud, because it is merchants (and their employees), and not teenage hackers, who are responsible for much of the credit card fraud in the world today. But in practice, the added security provided by SET was not sufficient to interest many banks, as they had already created sophisticated systems for detecting merchant fraud. Furthermore, most of the early SET implementations ended up providing credit card numbers to the merchant anyway using the SET merchant channel, because the merchant computers required the consumer's credit card numbers so that the legacy software could function properly.

Redux

Instead of being dead, SET may be dormant. In the coming years, SET may be reborn as a protocol for moving credit card transactions that are initiated with smart cards.

PayPal

PayPal is an electronic payment system that can be used to transfer money between any two people on the Internet, provided that both individuals have an email address and a credit card or bank account. PayPal is commonly used to settle purchases made on Internet auction sites such as eBay. In recent years, PayPal has become one of the Internet's most popular payment systems.

PayPal advertises that its payment system can be used to send money to "anybody"—all you need to know is that person's email address. In fact, PayPal can only be used to send money to other PayPal users. If you send money to a person who is not a PayPal user, PayPal will send that person email telling them that they have money waiting; all they need to do is to open a PayPal account. It is this ease of account creation that is largely responsible for PayPal's success.

Besides being used to settle auction payments, PayPal increasingly is hunting for other business opportunities. In 2001, the company started agressively marketing to business customers, saying that PayPal is "the cheapest way to accept payments online. E-commerce has never been easier!" PayPal also has a free shopping cart system (although customers can only settle their accounts with PayPal). The company also has a credit card.

Sending money

Sending money with PayPal is remarkably easy:

1. Assuming that you have a PayPal account, you simply log into PayPal's web site with your username and password.
2. Click the button "Send Money." (See Figure 25-3.)
3. Specify the recipient's email address. (PayPal keeps an address book of people to whom you have recently sent money.)
4. Specify the amount.
5. Specify the reason for the payment. (PayPal allows you to specify payment for Service, Goods, or Quasi-Cash.)
6. Specify a subject line.
7. Specify a note, if you wish.
8. Click Continue.
9. PayPal will display the details of the transaction and allow you to confirm the payment. At this point, you can pick your funding option—you can transfer money from a PayPal account, from a checking account, or from a credit card that you have registered.

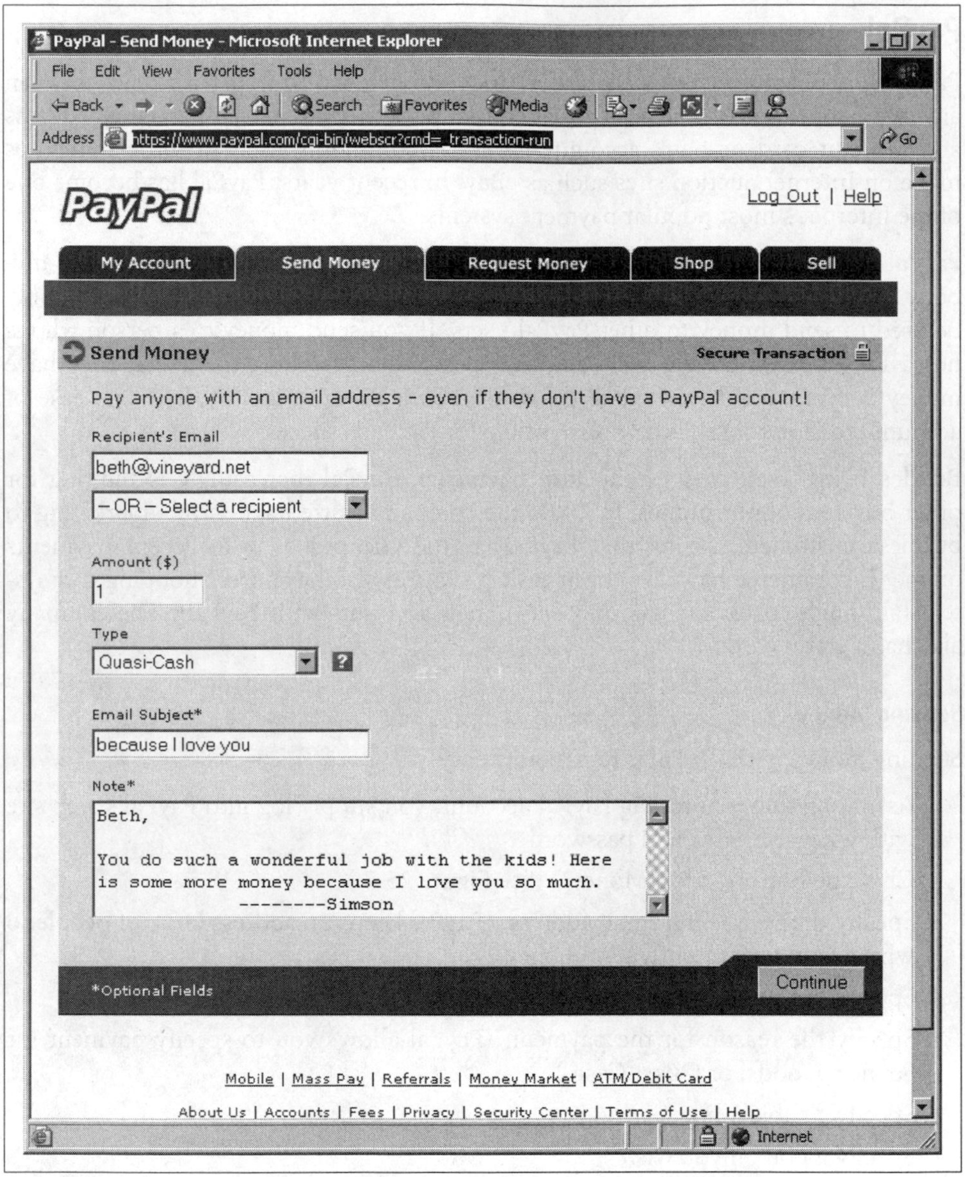

Figure 25-3. Sending money with PayPal is remarkably easy

Once the money is sent, PayPal sends a confirmation email to both the initiator and the recipient of the transaction, as shown in Example 25-1.

Example 25-1. The message sent from PayPal to the initiator of a transaction

```
Return-Path: <payment@paypal.com>
Delivered-To: simsong@r2.nitroba.com
Received: from sandbox.sandstorm.net (user-v3qtgdr.biz.mindspring.com [199.174.193.187])
```

```
        by r2.nitroba.com (Postfix) with ESMTP id 3A2F2E44322
        for <simsong@walden.cambridge.ma.us>; Sun, 23 Sep 2001 21:06:10 -0400 (EDT)
Received: from mail.acm.org [199.222.69.4]
        by sandbox.sandstorm.net with esmtp (Exim 2.05 #2 (Debian))
        id 15lKCH-0005qC-00; Sun, 23 Sep 2001 21:06:09 -0400
Received: from web7.sc5.paypal.com (web7.sc5.paypal.com [216.136.154.243])
        by mail.acm.org (8.9.3/8.9.3) with SMTP id VAA24882
        for <simsong@acm.org>; Sun, 23 Sep 2001 21:05:08 -0400
Received: (qmail 5175 invoked by uid 99); 24 Sep 2001 01:05:11 -0000
Date: Sun, 23 Sep 2001 18:05:11 -0700
Message-Id: <1001293511.5175@paypal.com>
From: service@paypal.com
To: simsong@acm.org
Subject: Receipt for your Payment

This email confirms that you sent $1.00 to beth@vineyard.net.


-------------------------------
Payment Details
-------------------------------

Amount: 1.00
Transaction ID: 9NW39779FC564471A
Subject: because I love you
Note: Beth,

You do such a wonderful job with the kids! Here is some more money because I love you so
much.
                --------Simson

View the details of this transaction online at:
https://www.paypal.com/vst/id=6J173029UP867832W


--------------------------------------------------------------
This payment was sent using your bank account.

By using your bank account to send money, you just:

- Avoided incurring debt on your credit cards.
- Sent money faster than writing and mailing paper checks.
- Received an additional entry in our $10,000 Sweepstakes!

Thanks for using your bank account!

--------------------------------------------------------------

Thank you for using PayPal!

The PayPal Team

Please do not reply to this e-mail. Mail sent to this address
cannot be answered. For assistance, login to your PayPal
account and choose the "Help" link in the footer of any page.
```

Security and financial integration

PayPal's popularity comes from its ease of use, but its strength comes from a remarkably well-thought-out approach to practical financial security.

When a person first signs up to use PayPal, the person will typically provide a credit card. To register the credit card, PayPal requires that the user enter the credit card account number, expiration date, and billing address. This is precisely the same information that is required to process a charge. The operating theory is that if you know enough about a person and her credit card to buy something over the Internet, then you should be able to use that credit card to send people money over the Internet. And besides, credit card charges are reversible, so the whole thing is generally pretty safe—certainly no less safe than credit cards themselves.

When a person registers a bank account with PayPal, the company takes other precautions to make sure that you are an authorized user of the bank account. It would be nice if PayPal could just call up your bank and ask them if their user is authorized to use the account, but how does PayPal know who their user is? There is really no way to be sure. Perhaps more importantly, PayPal really doesn't care who the user is—they just want to be sure that the person is authorized. To find out if you are authorized to use a bank account, PayPal initiates two ACH credits for less than a dollar to the account. PayPal then asks you to call up your bank, get the value of these two transactions, then log back into the PayPal site and enter the dollar amounts. If a person has access to this transaction-level information, the theory goes, then that person must be the authorized user of the account.

If a PayPal account is broken into—if somebody guesses your username and password—then it is hoped that the confirmatory email that PayPal sends out will alert the PayPal user to change his or her password. If not, then again it is hoped that PayPal will be able to reverse any fraudulent transactions. And what if PayPal can't reverse the transaction? What if money was transfered from your bank account to another person's bank account and it was immediately withdrawn? Well, PayPal claims that each of its accounts is automatically insured for up to $100,000 against unauthorized withdrawals by Travelers Insurance.

Gator Wallet

Gator is not a payment system per se, but it is tempting to think of it as such because it offers many of the same conveniences of the SET or DigiCash payment systems.

Gator is a *digital wallet* that runs on Microsoft Windows and is tightly integrated with Internet Explorer. Gator constantly monitors every web page that is displayed in Internet Explorer and scans it for forms that it knows how to fill in (see Figure 25-4). If Gator sees a form asking for your name, address, Zip, or other information, the Gator wallet displays a little tab on the side of your window to let you know that it knows how to fill out the form. If you click on the tab, Gator will fill out the form using information that you previously provided. (See Figure 25-5.)

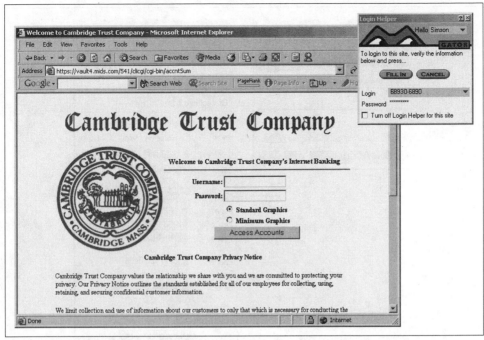

Figure 25-4. Gator Wallet constantly scans the pages displayed in Internet Explorer for forms that it knows how to fill out

Besides your name and address, you can also load one or more credit cards into Gator. If Gator knows your credit card information, you can fill out a "payment" page with the click of a single button. By automatically filling out forms, Gator makes it dramatically easier to spend money online.

To use Gator, it is necessary to go to the Gator web site (*http://www.gator.com/*), create an account, and download the Gator software. Gator account names are email addresses, which guarantees that they will be mostly unique. Once the software is running on your computer, you type in personal information such as your name, address, and credit card numbers. Gator can also memorize the username and password that you provide for each web site that you visit.

Gator stores information on your computer encrypted with a passphrase. (It is not clear what encryption algorithm is used or if the encryption provides adequate security for the information that is provided to the program.) Because people sometimes forget their passphrases, the software has a button labeled "Forgot your password?" Clicking the button and answering some questions will ultimately result in having your Gator password sent by email to the registered email address.

Of course, Gator's willingness to send the user's password to the user's email system mitigates the value of having the personal information stored in an encrypted form.

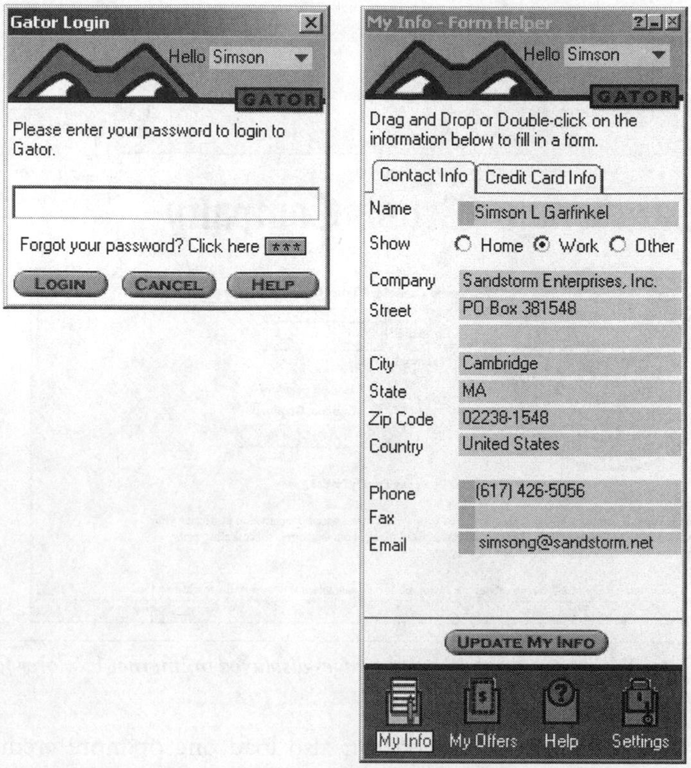

Figure 25-5. Gator fills out forms using information you previously provided

The whole point of using encryption to store the user's personal information, presumably, is so that if somebody gets hold of the user's computer, that person will not have access to highly sensitive information such as the user's credit card numbers. However, if Gator then goes ahead and emails the user's password, it's quite likely that the attacker will be able to use other information on the user's computer (such as a remembered password in an email program) to pick up the victim's email and, as a result, get his Gator password. Gator says that you can send the company email and ask that it never reveal your password, but it is not clear how this mechanism is enforced.

Microsoft Passport

One significant shortcoming with form-filling systems such as Gator is that the wallet program must parse the HTML provided by the remote web site and attempt to figure out the semantic meaning of each field. Sometimes, this job is easy: if there are fields named NAME, ADDRESS, CITY, STATE, and ZIP, it is pretty safe bet that the fields refer to a person's U.S. postal address. Other times, the meaning of the fields can be cryptic: most form-filling programs would be bewildered by those same names translated into Japanese.

At first glance, Microsoft's Passport looks like a an attempt to eliminate the need to fill out forms with shipping and payment information. Instead of filling out this information at each web site, the information is entered once on the Microsoft Passport server (see *http://www.passport.com*). But Passport goes beyond a simple form-filling system. Passport allows web sites to use the Passport service as a single sign-on system. Once a user signs into Passport, that user can jump into any passport-enabled web site without having to enter a name or password.

When a user visits a site that is Passport-enabled, if he has already logged into the Passport system, the Passport-enabled web site has access to the user's name and identifying information. If the user has not logged in, the user can press a "login" button and will be prompted for his username and password. After this information is entered, activity continues as before, except now the user is logged into the Passport system.

Currently, web sites can only use Passport if they are hosted on computers equipped with the Windows operating system and Microsoft's Internet Information Server. It works better with Internet Explorer than with Netscape Navigator.

Passport's design has raised several concerns:

Data theft and appropriation
> Suppose that someone is trying to steal your personal information to commit fraud. Without Passport, they would need to find and then penetrate the computers on which your data is stored. Usually, this means that an attacker needs to find the names of the merchants that you work with, then guess your username, and finally guess your password. With Passport, however, they only need to intercept or guess the password you have selected to protect your Passport account, since the location of Passport's servers are well known and your username is your email address.

Data protection
> All the user data present on the Passport site is potentially vulnerable to attackers. Although Microsoft is committed to protecting the data, there is no guarantee of security. In recent history, there have been several high-profile penetrations and failures of Microsoft sites. Thus, there is a risk that Microsoft's servers will be penetrated and the personal information they contain will be appropriated. Certainly, Passport's servers are sure to be a target of attackers.

Cascading loss of security
> If Passport is successful, many users will be encouraged to use it from locations that aren't secure. For example, a person visiting an Internet cafe might be

tempted to type in his Passport username and password to view his customized news at a financial web site. But the computer at the cafe might not be secure—it could be running a program that automatically records every keystroke that is typed. Because of the Passport design, once the username and password for any web site in the Passport system is compromised, that user's personal information for all web sites is compromised. The result is that Passport users have a greater chance of suffering fraud or privacy loss at multiple web sites when their user-names and passwords are compromised, because the single username and pass-word is used at so many different locations.

Data aggregation and mining

A great deal can be inferred about customers by observing the data and the nature of sites requesting that data. Even more can be learned by combining data from many users visiting many different web sites. Thus, the database of Pass-port users and its authentication logs are potentially quite valuable and would seem to present a wonderful opportunity for people skilled in the art of data mining. Although this data mining seems to run counter to Microsoft's current privacy policy, there is no guarantee that the policy might not change. Nor are there any technical guarantees that the policies against data mining will be strictly observed.

Overall, it remains to be seen whether Passport will be well accepted. Currently, the service is new and has not been widely adopted. A well-publicized security break-in or exposure of personal information might well sink the service, especially as there are familiar and workable alternatives.

Other Payment Systems

In the years to come, the distinction between Internet and non-Internet payment systems is likely to blur or be erased. As PayPal money can be beamed as digital "checks" from one PalmPilot to another, it's likely the future will see the emergence of more payment systems that work equally well in the online and offline worlds.

Smart cards

Smart cards may well be the basis of any future payment system because they offer the security of systems like SET coupled with the convenience of traditional magnetic-strip-based credit cards. Indeed, smart cards look like credit cards except that they store information on microprocessor chips instead of magnetic strips. Compared to conventional cards, smart cards differ in several important ways:

- Smart cards can store considerably more information than magnetic strip cards can. Whereas magnetic strips can hold a few hundred bytes of information, smart card chips can store many kilobytes. Furthermore, the amount of information that can be stored on a smart card is increasing as chip densities increase.

Because of this increased storage capacity, a single smart card can be used for many different purposes.

- Smart cards can be password-protected. Whereas all of the information stored on a magnetic strip can be read any time the magnetic strip is inserted into a reader, the information on a smart card can be password-protected and selectively revealed.

- Smart cards can run RSA encryption engines. A smart card can be used to create an RSA public/private key pair. The card can be designed so that the public key is freely readable, but the private key cannot be revealed. Thus, to decrypt a message, the card must be physically in the possession of the user. This gives high assurance to a user that her secret key has not been copied.

Smart cards have been used for years in European telephones. In the summer of 1996, Visa International introduced a Visa Cash Card at the Atlanta Olympics. Within the coming years, smart cards are likely to be more generally deployed throughout the United States. In 1996, the Smart Card Forum estimated that there would be more than 1 billion smart cards in circulation by the year 2000. That didn't happen, and the Forum has not made public any future projections. Nevertheless, it seems likely that smart cards will continue to proliferate.

Mondex

Mondex is not an Internet-based payment system, but it is one of the largest general-purpose digital payment systems currently in use.

Mondex is a closed system based on a small credit-card-sized smart card that theoretically cannot be reverse-engineered. Mondex uses a secret protocol. Therefore, what is said of Mondex depends almost entirely on statements from the (somewhat secretive) company.

Each Mondex card can be programmed to hold a certain amount of cash. The card's value can be read by placing it in a device known as a *Mondex wallet*. Money can be transferred between two wallets over an infrared beam. Merchants are also provided with a special merchant wallet. Mondex can also be used to make purchases by telephone using a proprietary telephone. The card may be "refilled" using a specially equipped ATM.

In the past, Mondex has claimed that its system offers anonymity. However, Simon Davies of Privacy International has demonstrated that the Mondex merchant system keeps a record of the Mondex account numbers used for each purchase. Despite numerous public trials, Mondex was not widely deployed in the 1990s. It is unclear what the future holds for this technology.

How to Evaluate a Credit Card Payment System

There are many credit card systems being developed for web commerce; any list here would surely be out of date before this book appears in bookstores. Instead, we have listed some questions to ask yourself and your vendors when trying to evaluate any payment system:

- If the system stores credit card numbers on the consumer's computer, are they stored encrypted? They should be. Otherwise, a person who has access to the consumer's computer will have access to personal, valuable, and easily abused information.

- If the system uses credit card numbers, are they stored on the server? They should not be stored unless recurring charges are expected. If the numbers are stored, they should be stored encrypted. Otherwise, anyone who has access to the server will be able to steal hundreds or thousands of credit card numbers at a time.

- Are stored credit card numbers purged from the system after the transaction is completed? If a transaction is not recurring, they should be. Otherwise, a customer could be double-billed either accidentally or intentionally by a rogue employee.

- Does the system test the check digit of the supplied credit card number when the numbers are entered? It should, as it is easier to correct data-entry errors when they are made (and, presumably, while the customer's card is still out), than later, when the charges are submitted.

- Can the system do preauthorizations in real time? This is a feature that depends on your situation. If you are selling a physical good or delivering information over the Internet, you may wish to have instantaneous authorizations. But if you are running a subscription-based web site, you may be able to accept a delay of minutes or even hours between making an authorization request and receiving a result. Some banks may charge a premium for real-time authorizations.

- How does the system handle credits? From time to time, you will need to issue credits onto consumer credit cards. How easy is it to initiate a credit? Does the system place any limits on the amount of money that can be credited to a consumer? Does the system require that there be a matching charge for every credit? Is a special password required for a credit? Are there any notifications or reports that are created after a credit is issued? Issuing credits to a friend's credit card is the easiest way for an employee to steal money from a business.

- How does the system handle charge-backs? If you are in business for any period of time, some of your customers will reverse charges. Does the charge-back automatically get entered into the customer's account, or must it be handled manually?

- What is really anonymous? What is private? Algorithms that are mathematically anonymous in theory can be embedded in larger systems that reveal the user's identity. Alternatively, identity can be revealed through other techniques, such as correlation of multiple log files.

The answers to these questions don't depend solely on the underlying technology: they depend on the particular implementation used by the merchant, and quite possibly also on the way that implementation is used.

## CHAPTER 26

Intellectual Property and Actionable Content

In this chapter:
- Copyright
- Patents
- Trademarks

The Web is a creation of intellect, talent, hard work, and persistence. There are no physical artifacts that can be designated as "the Internet," for it all exists as ephemeral bits stored on disk and displayed on screens. The words, algorithms, programs, images, and designs available on the Net are the product of hard work, and represent an asset to those who have performed the work or commissioned it.

Society labels this work as *intellectual property*. The law recognizes certain forms of protection for intellectual property to protect such assets and encourage their development and use. The three forms of protection most applicable to material on the Web are copyright, patent, and trademark protections. Each covers a slightly different form of material, and in a different manner.

Copyright

Copyright is intended to cover the expression of ideas rather than the ideas themselves. Copyright covers text (including programs), pictures, typefaces, and combinations of these items once they are assembled in some fixed form.[*] Or, as the law phrases it, "A copyright exists in original works of authorship fixed in any tangible medium of expression from which they can be perceived, reproduced, or otherwise communicated, either directly or with the aid of a machine or device."[†]

This definition clearly covers any material entered into a computer and stored on disk, CD-ROM, or tape for display via a web browser. Once it is fixed in form (e.g., saved to disk) it is protected by copyright. Under current law, there is no need to mark such material with a copyright symbol or register the copyright for it to be protected; however, registration and marking of copyright may increase statutory penalties awarded if an infringement occurs.

---

[*] Copyright can also cover performances of music, plays, and movies.

[†] 17 U.S.C. 102

Let's repeat that point—it is very important. Images in your web pages, sound clips played through your web servers, and documents you copied from other sites to pad your own collection all have copyrights associated with them. Online databases, computer programs, and electronic mail are copyrighted as well. The law states that as soon as any of these things are expressed in a tangible form, they have a copyright associated with them. Thus, as soon as the bits are on your disk, they are copyrighted, whether a formal notice exists or not. If you reuse one of these items without appropriate permission, you could be opening yourself up to trouble.

Copyright Infringement

Standard practice on the Internet has been that something exported from a public access server is for public use, unless otherwise noted. However, this practice is not in keeping with the way the copyright law is currently phrased. Furthermore, some items that you obtain from an intermediate party may have had owner and copyright information removed. This does not absolve you of any copyright liability if you use that material.

In particular, rulings in various courts have found that under certain circumstances, system operators can be sued as contributing parties, and thus held partially liable, for copyright infringement committed by users of their systems. Types of infringement include:

- Posting pictures, artwork, and images on FTP sites and web sites without appropriate permission, even if the original items are not clearly identified regarding owner, subject, or copyright.

- Posting excerpts from books, reports, and other copyrighted materials via email, the Web, FTP, or Usenet postings.

- Posting sound clips from films, TV shows, or other recorded media without approval of the copyright holders. This includes adding those sounds to your web pages in any form.

- Posting scanned-in cartoons from newspapers or magazines.

- Reposting news articles from copyrighted sources.

- Reposting of email. As with paper mail, email has a copyright held by the author of the email as soon as it is put in tangible form. The act of sending the email to someone does not give the recipient copyright interest in the email. Standard practice on the Net is not in keeping with the way the law is written. Thus, *forwarding email may technically be a violation of the copyright law.*

The best defense against possible lawsuits is to carefully screen everything you post or make available on your web site to be certain that you know its copyright status. Furthermore, if you are an ISP or you host web pages for others, make all your users aware of the policy you set in this regard, and then periodically audit to ensure that the policy is being followed. Having an unenforced policy will likely serve you as well as no policy—that is, not at all.

Also, beware of "amateur lawyers" who tell you that reuse of an image or article is *fair use* under the law. There is a formal definition of fair use, and you should get the opinion from a real lawyer who knows the issues. After all, if you get sued, do you think that a reference to an anonymous post in the *alt.erotica.lawyers.briefs* Usenet newsgroup is going to convince the judge that you took due diligence to adhere to the law?

If anyone notifies you that you are violating her copyright with something you have on your system, investigate *immediately*. Any delay could cause additional problems. However, we are not necessarily advocating that you pull possibly offending or infringing material from the network any time you get a complaint. Each case must be separately evaluated.

Software Piracy and the SPA

The Software Publishers Association (SPA) is one of several organizations funded by major software publishers. One of its primary goals is to cut down on the huge amount of software piracy that is regularly conducted worldwide. Although each individual act of unauthorized software copying and use may only deprive the vendor of a few hundred dollars at most, the sheer number of software pirates in operation makes the aggregate losses staggering: worldwide losses are estimated in the billions of dollars per year. Figures from various sources indicate that worldwide losses from software piracy alone may be more than $15 billion per year.

Although there are criminal penalties for unauthorized copying, these penalties are only employed against organized software piracy organizations. In contrast, the SPA and others rely on civil law remedies. In particular, the SPA can obtain a court order to examine your computer systems for evidence of unlicensed copies of software. Should such copies be found without supporting documentation to show valid licenses, you may be subject to a lawsuit resulting in substantial damages. Many companies and universities have settled with the SPA in regard to these issues with fines totaling many hundreds of thousands of dollars. This amount is in addition to the many thousands of dollars paid to vendors for any unlicensed software that is found.

Warez

A further danger involves your users if you are an ISP. *Warez* are pirated software programs or activation codes that are made available for other software "pirates" to download without proper license or payment to the legitimate copyright holder.

If some of an ISP's users are running a warez site from its FTP or web server, the SPA or copyright holders might conceivably seek financial redress from the ISP to help cover the loss—even if it does not know about the pirated items and otherwise does not condone the behavior.* The SPA has filed lawsuits against ISPs that appeared to be less than immediately responsive to complaints about customer-run warez servers.

The ISP's best defense in these circumstances is to clearly state to their users that no unlicensed use or possession of software is allowed under any circumstances. ISPs should have this written into their service agreements so they have an explicit statement of intent, and an explicit course of action to follow if there is a violation. Although ISPs don't want to be involved in undue meddling with customers' uses of their services, it is also important they don't become a haven for violators of the law.

Patents

Patents are a type of license granted to an inventor to protect novel, useful, and nonobvious inventions. Originally, these were intended to allow an inventor a fixed time to profit from some new innovation or discovery while also encouraging the inventor to disclose the development behind the patent. Before patents, inventors would try to keep discoveries secret to profit from them and thus impede scientific progress. In some extreme cases, the inventor died before disclosing the discovery, losing it indefinitely.

In recent years, there has been a shift in patent activity to the granting of patents in computing. Firms and individuals are applying for (and receiving) patents on software and algorithms at an astonishing rate. Despite the wording of the Constitution and laws on patents, the Patent Office is continuing to award patents on obvious ideas, trivial advances, and pure algorithms. In the middle of 1995, they effectively granted patent protection to a prime number as well!† Paradoxically, this shift is itself discouraging some scientific progress because it means that the development and use of these algorithms (or prime numbers) is regulated by law.

The danger comes when you write some new code that involves an algorithm you read about or simply developed based on obvious prior work. You may discover, when you try to use your program in a wider market, that lawyers from a large corporation will tell you that you cannot use "their" algorithm in your code because it is covered by their patent. After a patent is granted, the patent holder controls the use of the patented item for 20 years—you aren't even supposed to use it for experimental purposes without their approval and/or license!

---

* Whether they would succeed in such an action is something we cannot know. However, almost anything is possible if a talented attorney presses the case.

† Patent 5,373,560 covering the use of the prime number (in hex) 98A3DF52 AEAE9799 325CB258 D767EBD1 F4630E9B 9E21732A 4AFB1624 BA6DF911 466AD8DA 960586F4 A0D5E3C3 6AF09966 0BDDC157 7E54A9F4 02334433 ACB14BCB was granted on December 13, 1994, to Roger Schlafly of California. Although the patent only covers the use of the number when used with Schlafly's algorithm, there is no other practical use for this particular number, because it is easier (and more practical) to generate a "random" prime number than to use this one.

Many companies are now attempting to build up huge libraries of patents to use as leverage in the marketplace. In effect, they are submitting applications on everything they develop. This practice is sad, because it will have an inhibitory effect on software development in the years to come.* It is also sad to see business switch from a mode of competing based on innovation to a mode of competing based on who has the biggest collection of dubious patents.

Until the courts or Congress step in to straighten out this mess, there is not much you can do to protect yourself (directly). However, we suggest that you be sure to consult with legal counsel in this matter if you are developing new software. Also, consider contacting your elected representatives to make your views on the matter known.

Trademarks

Trademarks are defined by federal law to be any word, name, symbol, color, sound, product shape, or device, or any combination of these that is adopted and used by a manufacturer or merchant to identify goods and distinguish them from those made or sold by anyone else.† *Service marks* are a related concept applying to services as opposed to products; for example, "American Express" is a service mark distinguishing a service rather than a particular product. Traditionally, trademarks were intended to help protect a vendor from imitators confusing customers in a geographic region.‡ Trademarks also help provide a protection against fraud: if someone markets counterfeit goods using a trademark, the trademark holder has some legal recourse. Now that we are involved with multinational corporations doing business on the global Internet, trademarks have become more important as geographical limitations have waned.

Obtaining a Trademark

Trademarks have some similarities to patents and copyrights. Establishing one involves four basic steps:

1. Pick your trademark and establish it in commerce or trade. Trademarks must be based on established use in the marketplace—you cannot think up interesting names for trademarks and "hoard" them for later use or sale. Instead, you need to have an established and ongoing use of the trademark in the marketplace.

---

* Indeed, it already has had negative effects. For instance, the patents on public key encryption have really hurt information security development in recent years. See Chapter 4 for a discussion.

† 15 U.S.C. 1127

‡ Hereafter, we'll use the term "trademark" to refer to both trademarks and service marks.

Simple use of the trademark establishes it, similar to the way that a copyright is established for text once it is in fixed form. However, this form of protection may not provide you with as much protection as you would like in the event of a conflict with someone else. For that, you will want to register it. But first, you will need to take the next step in this list.

2. Research the use of the trademark. Before registering your trademark (and, ideally, before you use it the first time), you should research the trademark to ensure that it is not currently in use by someone else. There are research services that will do this for you, usually associated with a law firm that will also handle the entire registration process for you. You should especially research the lists of already registered trademarks for duplicates or close matches.

   If your search discloses a match of trademark names with one already existing, this does not necessarily mean that you cannot use your choice. Because one of the primary purposes of the trademark is to prevent confusion of products in the minds of consumers, you may be able to duplicate an existing trademark if it is for a product so dissimilar to yours that there could be no confusion in the mind of any reasonable consumer. However, this will need to be agreed upon by the current holder of the trademark, or decided in court.

3. Register the trademark by completing some paperwork and paying a filing fee. You would register your trademark with one or more states where you are likely to do business.* Alternatively, if you are likely to use the trademark in interstate commerce, which is probable if you are using it on the Internet, you could register it as a federal trademark. Federal trademarks are given for 20 years.

4. You must now properly use, display, and defend your trademark to keep it. To keep the trademark valid, you must continue to use it. You must also display it with appropriate marks or designations that it is a trademark (e.g., with a ™ or ® symbol, as appropriate; do not display the ® symbol unless you have a federally registered trademark).

   Most importantly, you must defend your trademark to keep it. If you see or hear of someone else using your trademark improperly, you must take actions to correct them or stop them from using your trademark without credit. If you fail to do so, you may lose your legal protection for the item.

Trademark Violations

Use of trademark phrases, symbols, and insignia without the permission of the holders of the trademark may lead to difficulties. As we noted previously, the holders of those trademarks are expected to protect them, and so they must respond if they discover someone using their trademarks improperly.

---

* All 50 U.S. states have trademark laws.

In particular, to protect yourself against such actions, be careful about putting corporate logos on your web pages. They should be placed with appropriate indications of the trademark holder. Further, you must be careful not to use the logos or names in such a way that they imply endorsement of your product or defame the actual product or holder of the trademark. That means you will probably hear from a corporate attorney if you put the logos for Sun, HP, Xerox, Microsoft, Coca-Cola, or other trademark holders on your web pages—especially if you use them in a way that is uncomplimentary to those companies.

If you have a trademark of your own that you are trying to protect, you must be vigilant for violations. If you learn of anyone misusing your trademark, you must respond quickly. That response may include filing a lawsuit over improper use of your mark. Having a trademark confers some benefits to you, but it also implies some effort and expense to keep it!

Domain Names and Trademarks

Domain names that infringe on trademarks in the United States can be subject to action under either the Internet Corporation for Assigned Names and Numbers (ICANN) Uniform Dispute Resolution Policy (UDRP)* or the Anticybersquatting Consumer Protection Act (ACPA). Both of these regimes specify means by which a trademark owner can take action against a domain name holder for a domain that the trademark owner believes damages the owner's trademark rights. (For information about ICANN, see Chapter 2.)

Under most circumstances, the ICANN UDRP is likely to be the first tool used by any party that believes they are injured by another party's domain name. The UDRP offers the promise of a proceeding that is likely to be faster and cheaper than seeing action under the ACPA. Furthermore, the UDRP is ideally suited to situations that are international in nature—for example, when a domain that is registered by a Chinese company with a registrar that is in Europe violates the trademark of a company that has offices in Honduras.

The UDRP is enforced through contract law. All registrars in the top-level generic domains (currently *.biz*, *.com*, *.info*, *.name*, *.net*, and *.org*) are required to implement the agreement as a condition of their contract with ICANN. These registrars, in turn, pass on the requirements for agreeing to the terms of the UDRP in their agreements with their customers. If you have a domain name, you have agreed to be bound by the rules of the UDRP.

For domain name holders, the key paragraph of the UDRP is paragraph #2, in which the applicant makes the following representations:

---

* *http://www.icann.org/udrp/*

2. Your Representations. By applying to register a domain name, or by asking us to maintain or renew a domain name registration, you hereby represent and warrant to us that (a) the statements that you made in your Registration Agreement are complete and accurate; (b) to your knowledge, the registration of the domain name will not infringe upon or otherwise violate the rights of any third party; (c) you are not registering the domain name for an unlawful purpose; and (d) you will not knowingly use the domain name in violation of any applicable laws or regulations. It is your responsibility to determine whether your domain name registration infringes or violates someone else's rights.

Should you violate any of these representations, you agree to be bound by a "mandatory administrative proceeding." This proceeding can result in your loss of your domain name. The UDRP outlines three specific elements that must be present to result in the loss of a domain name:

1. The domain name is identical or confusingly similar to a trademark or service mark in which the complainant has rights; and

2. The registrant has no rights or legitimate interests in respect to the domain name; and

3. The domain name has been registered and is being used in bad faith.

Fees for the administrative proceeding are paid entirely by the complainant if a panel of three individuals is used to decide the claim; the fees are split 50/50 between the complainant and the domain holder if a single individual is used to decide the claim.

ICANN has gone to great lengths to call its adjudication process an "administrative proceeding" and not an "arbitration hearing." This is so that either party can appeal the results of the administrative proceeding to a court without prejudice. Under the UDRP, either party has ten days to file an appeal.

If you are in the United States, you can file suit against a domain name holder for violation of the ACPA. According to the ACPA:

(1)(A) A person shall be liable in a civil action by the owner of a mark, including a personal name which is protected as a mark under this section, if, without regard to the goods or services of the parties, that person

(i) has a bad faith intent to profit from that mark, including a personal name which is protected as a mark under this section; and

(ii) registers, traffics in, or uses a domain name that--

(I) in the case of a mark that is distinctive at the time of registration of the domain name, is identical or confusingly similar to that mark;

(II) in the case of a famous mark that is famous at the time of registration of the domain name, is identical or confusingly similar to or dilutive of that mark; or

(III) is a trademark, word, or name protected by reason of section 706 of Title 18 or section 220506 of Title 36.

Actionable Content

Computers and networks give us great opportunities for communicating with the world. In a matter of moments, our words can be speeding around the world, destined for a large audience or for someone we have never met in person. Not only is this ability liberating and empowering, it can be very entertaining. Mailing lists, "chat rooms," multi-user dimensions (MUDs), newsgroups, and web pages all provide us with news and entertainment.

Libel and Defamation

Unfortunately, this same high-speed, high-bandwidth communications medium can also be used for less than noble purposes. Email can be sent to harass, news articles can be posted to slander, web pages can contain defaming stories, and online chats can be used to threaten someone with harm.

In the world of paper and telephones, there are legal remedies to harassing and demeaning communication. Some of those remedies are already being applied to the online world. We have seen cases of people being arrested for harassment and stalking online. People have been successfully sued for slander in posted Usenet articles. There have also been cases filed for violation of EEOC (Equal Employment Opportunity Commission at *http://www.eeoc.gov*) laws because of repeated postings that were sexually, racially, or religiously demeaning. Even screensavers with inappropriate images have been the subject of litigation.

Words can hurt others, sometimes quite severely. Often, words are a prelude or indicator of other potential harm, including physical harm. For this reason, ISPs must have policies in place prohibiting demeaning or threatening postings and mailings from the accounts of users. An ISP might even wish to have a policy in place prohibiting any form of anonymous posting or mailing from users. Otherwise, the ISP might be seen by a court as encouraging, at least indirectly, any misbehavior by customers.

As a publisher of web pages, you should also be careful about what you say about others. A false or insulting allegation can land you in a courtroom explaining to a jury what a web page is, and why you shouldn't have all your possessions seized as a judgment because you called someone an untalented idiot in your online review of her web pages. Unlikely? Not necessarily—the law is still evolving in this arena, and electronic media do not have the same protections as print media. But even in print, there are limits on what you can say without being sued successfully.

Liability for Damage

Suppose that you make a nifty new program available via your web page for people to use. It claims to protect any system against some threat, or it fixes a vendor flaw.

Someone at the Third National Bank of Hoople downloads it and runs the program, and the system crashes, leading to thousands of dollars in damages.

Or perhaps you are browsing the Web and discover an applet in a language such as Java that you find quite interesting. You install a link to it from your home page. Unfortunately, someone on the firewall machine at Big Whammix, Inc., clicks on the link and the applet somehow interacts with the firewall code to open an internal network to hackers around the world.

If your response to such incidents is, "Too bad. Software does that sometimes," then you are living dangerously. Legal precedent is such that you might be liable, at least partially, for damages in cases such as these. You could certainly be sued and required to answer in court to such charges, and that is not a pleasant experience. Think about explaining how you designed and tested the code, documented it, and warned other users about potential defects and side effects. And what about the *implied* warranty?

Simply because "everyone on the Net" does an action does not mean that the action will convince a judge and jury that you aren't responsible for some of the mess that the action causes. There have been many times in the history of the United States when people have been successfully sued for activity that was widespread. The mere fact that "everybody was doing it" did not stop some particular individuals from being found liable.

In general, you should get expert legal advice before providing any executable code to others, even if you intend to give the code away.

Protection Through Incorporation

In the U.S. legal system, anyone can sue over basically anything. Even if you are bland and play by all the rules, you can be sued. That doesn't mean you have done anything wrong, or that the plaintiff can succeed in a case. It does mean, however, that you will need to respond. Lawsuits can be used as a harassment tactic. There are some controls on the system, including countersuits over frivolous prosecution. However, you should keep the possibility in mind.

One way to provide partial protection is through incorporation. A corporation is a legal entity. If all the equipment you use is owned by the corporation, and the "publications" that might be at issue are from your corporation, then any lawsuit would be directed at the corporation. This doesn't make such lawsuits any less likely, but it does mean that if you lose, your personal possessions might not be forfeit in a judgment.

There are many other considerations involved with corporations: tax issues, reporting requirements, and operations issues should be carefully considered. Even simple incorporations can add many thousands of dollars to the overall cost of doing business. If your corporation's stock is owned by more than a few people, or if the stock is sold to the general public, the cost of doing business will be higher still.

If you do incorporate, you must be careful to conduct all of your organization's business through the corporation, lest you lose what protection incorporation may grant you. This means that your business should have its own telephone line, and that you should use that phone line for all incoming and outgoing calls that are business-related—and never for calls that are personal. It means that your business should have its own bank account, and these funds should be treated differently from the funds in the bank account of the business's principals. If you use your business to pay all of your personal expenses, you may find your personal assets in jeopardy should litigation arise.

There are many books available on the pros and cons of incorporation. Before proceeding, we repeat our chorus in this chapter: seek the advice of a competent attorney for further discussion and details.

## PART V

Appendixes

This part of the book, is filled with lists and nitty-gritty technical information that is too detailed for the main body of this book.

Appendix A, *Lessons from Vineyard.NET*, is a first-person account of the ISP that offers service exclusively on Martha's Vineyard.

Appendix B, *The SSL/TLS Protocol*, contains more detailed information about the SSL and TLS protocols. This chapter won't give you enough information to write your own SSL or TLS implementation, but it will give you an understanding of what is happening on the wire.

Appendix C, *P3P: The Platform for Privacy Preferences Project*, is a detailed introduction to the P3P specification. This chapter, written by Lorrie Faith Cranor and included with permission, includes information on how to write your own P3P policy.

Appendix D, *The PICS Specification*, provides detailed information on the PICS specification. Although PICS appears largely dead today, a PICS implementation is included in Microsoft's Internet Explorer, so PICS is still there for anybody who wants to use it.

Appendix E, *References*, is a listing of books, articles, and web sites containing further helpful information about web security, privacy, and commerce.

Lessons from Vineyard.NET

The following appendix provides an account of a real-life experience with operating an Internet service provider. It details Simson's experiences starting and operating a small ISP named Vineyard.NET and keeping that ISP secure.

In the Beginning

In May 1995, my wife and I bought a run-down 150-year-old house on Martha's Vineyard, a small island off the coast of Massachusetts with a winter population of roughly 12,000 and a summer population of over 100,000.

Our plan was to live year-round in this somewhat isolated but romantic location. We weren't worried: we would have a 56 kbps connection to the Internet as our main link to the outside world. But when we found out that the cost of our Internet hookup would be roughly $400 a month, we decided to start an Internet cooperative to help pay for it.

We figured we could get together eight people and have them each pay $50/month for a full-time connection. Of course, eight full-time connections meant that we also needed to have some number of dialup lines, increasing our monthly charges by roughly $30 per line. (How many dialup lines did we need? Two? Eight? We didn't know.) Perhaps a better alternative, we realized, would be to get a few dozen people together and charge them each $30/month. As it was unlikely that all of those people would want to go online at the same time, we could probably get away with having only 1 modem for every 5 customers, or perhaps 1 modem for every 10. Our back-of-the-envelope calculations said that we should break even when we got to 30 customers.

As it turned out, we didn't break even until we got to 400 customers, and we couldn't pay our employees a living wage until we hit more than 1000.

This is the story of Vineyard.NET, the Internet service that we created. It's printed here so that others might learn from our experience.

Planning and Preparation

Because they all happened at the same time—the move to Martha's Vineyard, the renovations on the house, and the creation of the Vineyard.NET Internet service provider—they are all intractably tangled together in my mind. Repairing the roof, building a new bathroom, pulling Category 5 network cables to every room, and putting in special grounded outlets for the ISP's computers were all items on the short list of things that needed to be done to make the house habitable. A few months later, when we realized that we had bitten off more than we could chew, the ISP was simply one more reason why we couldn't just leave.

I got Bill Bennett's name out of the phone book. He's an electrician on Martha's Vineyard who had a big advertisement boasting "home theater" and "smart house" systems. Truth be told, Bill is more interested in electronics than electrics. He seemed like an ideal person to help with the wide assortment of electrical tasks that we needed. Bill took the job. He also pointed me to Eric Bates, a carpenter who was also running the computer systems for the town of Oak Bluffs.

Eric moved to Martha's Vineyard after graduating from Dartmouth College. He wanted to crew on the Shenandoah, a topsail schooner in the Vineyard Haven Harbor. Eric went from being boat crew to being a carpenter, and he had been doing that for most of the past decade. Eric had been into computers for years—he even owned one of the original Macintosh computers. But Eric wasn't simply a user, he was a hardcore power geek.

Eric was also the CIO for the town of Oak Bluffs, which meant that he had a part-time job running the town's rag-tag collection of Macs, PCs, and a Unix box. To make this menagerie work together, Eric set up one of the first municipal TCP/IP networks in the country. For years Eric had wanted to set up an Internet connection on the island, but something had always gotten in the way.

Eric and I met and quickly became friends. The idea of a small Internet buyer's club appealed to both of us, and we quickly settled on the name Vineyard Cooperative Networks.

Meanwhile, Bennett Electric had started rewiring the house. It was a big job. The only electricity distribution in the house were a few outlets on the first floor and a few lamps hanging from the ceilings in the second floor bedrooms, all powered by ancient knob-and-tube wiring. Although knob-and-tube is relatively safe as long as you don't touch it, it would never do for the kind of computer equipment that I was thinking of installing.

Bill decided that the best approach would be to pull a 60-amp service from the basement to the second floor and to wire a second panel upstairs. We also wanted to pull Category 5 twisted pairs to every room on every floor, so we could put computers wherever we wanted. And we wanted a traditional four-wire red, green, yellow, black cable to every room for the telephones. The easiest thing to do, we discovered, was to cut 200-foot lengths for all of the wires, bundle them all together with electrician's tape, and pull the whole thing up along one of our chimneys from the basement into the attic. From the attic there were drops into the individual second-floor rooms. The first floor was wired up from the basement. This whole process took two people the better part of a week. When it was done, the house was probably the most wired structure on the island.

Lesson: Whenever you are pulling wires, pull more than you need.

This wiring lesson is well-known in the business world, but it's not very well understood by people who are new to business, or who have only wired residences. Wire is cheap; labor is expensive. So always pull more than you need. Then, when your needs expand, you are prepared.

We made the mistake of pulling a Category 5 and a telephone wire to each room. We figured that we could always use an Ethernet hub to make more Ethernet jacks appear in a room for laptops and the like, and we knew that we would never need more than four wires for the telephone—four wires would handle two telephone lines, and if we ever wanted more than two lines, we would simply get a PBX switch.

In retrospect, we were very wrong. All of those little hubs are a pain to operate: you have to plug them in, get little patch cords, and then they are always running into problems. It's far better to have two or three network connections to each room—one for a desktop, one for a laptop, and one for a guest. If you ever need a plug, there it is.

What's worse, three years after the initial wiring, we purchased a used Merlin 820 telephone system for the house. Total cost was $500 for the system's "brain" and 20 extensions—a real bargain! But the Merlin system, it turned out, uses four pairs of wire instead of two. The upshot is that most of the Category 5 wire that we originally pulled now services the telephones, not the network, and many rooms can have either a phone or a network, but not both. Tremendously annoying.

Lesson: Pull all your wires in a star configuration, from a central point out to each room, rather than daisy-chained from room to room. Wire both your computers and your telephone networks as stars. It makes it much easier to expand or rewire in the future.

Many residences are wired with a single telephone line that snakes in the walls from room to room. This makes it almost impossible to add more than two lines to a house. By pulling each room's telephone line to the basement, we made it easy to put one phone line in one room and another phone line in another room. We run these POTS* lines for faxes or extra modems (useful for testing) in parallel with the Merlin 820.

---

* POTS stands for Plain Old Telephone Service; it's a common abbreviation for analog telephone lines.

Lesson: Use centrally located punch-down blocks for computer and telephone networks.

Before we installed the phone switch, we were constantly changing which telephone lines appeared in which room. To make this job easier, we purchased modular telephone extenders at RadioShack that had a single RJ11 male telephone jack and five female RJ11 plugs. Each telephone extender was put on a different outside line. We could then move telephones around by simply unplugging RJ11 jacks from one module and plugging them into another.

This use of RJ11 jacks was easy enough, but it was space inefficient. What's worse, it was unreliable: RJ11 jacks would occasionally wiggle out of their plug modeling without any indication.

Finally, we ripped out the RJ11s and instead set up a conventional punch-down block for the telephone service. Prior to the arrival of the phone switch, we could establish the dial tones we wanted in each room by simply changing the punch-down configuration. After we got the switch, we still used the punch-down blocks for the residential modem lines, fax lines, and other analog dial tones, as they were needed.

Lesson: Don't go overboard.

We decided against pulling dark fiber along with the Category 5 wires. That's because Category 5 could go at speeds up to 100 Mbits/sec at the time. We couldn't imagine that this would not be fast enough during the time that we would have the house. If we were going to need to have an optical gigabit or ATM network, we would simply have to put it all in the basement!

As it turns out, we were right. The industry didn't move to using fiber optics inside offices. Instead, Category 5/5e/6 became the norm. Five years later, 100 Mbps was common, and gigabit over copper was getting cheap.

Lesson: Plan your computer room carefully; you will have to live with its location for a long time.

Another decision that we made was to put all of the computer and telephone equipment in the basement, rather than in one of the upstairs rooms. We had a lot of reasons for wanting to do this. First and foremost: we didn't want to give up the living space. We also imagined that there would be a lot of people going to and from the machine room, and didn't want them to interfere with the people living up above. The basement had a separate entrance, which became increasingly important as the number of employees in the company expanded.

One problem with the basement, though, was that the floor got pretty wet whenever it rained. We "solved" this problem by building a small computer room within the basement that was on a raised cement slab. That gave us six inches of flood insurance.

Actually, the raised cement slab was largely unintentional. When we bought the house, there was some sort of root cellar in part of the basement. The room had paperboard walls, a dirt floor, and even a dead rat. So we removed the rat, ripped out the walls, poured our own concrete slab, and Eric built a nice stud wall which we finished with plywood and a beautiful handmade door. We ended up with a room that was reasonably secure and moderately dry. It even had a window: a fan provided low-cost cooling in the winter, and a window-mounted air conditioner gave us all the cooling we needed in the summer.

IP Connectivity

One of our first goals was to get the Internet connection up and running.

Lesson: Set milestones and stick to them.

Setting up an Internet service provider and a commercial Internet service is a huge task. I broke the job down into smaller, understandable chunks. Each chunk had its own milestone: a thing that was to be accomplished, and a date by which it was supposed to be accomplished.

On a piece of paper, I sketched out my first set of goals and milestones:

- July 1, 1995—Get leased line installed.
- Mid-July—Get IP connection up and running.
- August 1—Get dialup access working to router.
- August 15—Open up service for a few testers.
- September 1, 1995—Announce service to the community.

The key ingredient to making all of this work was working phone lines—something that the house didn't have when we moved in. Before we closed on the house, we placed an order for four residential phone lines—after all, the house was first and foremost a residence. I had also made arrangements with a mid-level ISP in Cambridge called CentNet for a 56K connection to the Internet that would be delivered over a four-wire DDS frame relay connection. To make this whole thing work I arranged for Cisco to loan me a Cisco 2509 router—a basic router with two high-speed serial ports, eight low-speed asynchronous serial ports, and an Ethernet. I foolishly thought of this router as an "ISP in a box."

Lesson: Get your facilities in order.

I waited for and met the NYNEX telephone installer on the day our residential phone lines were due to be installed. The man wanted to run four separate black two-conductor lines from the telephone pole to the house. I told him that probably wouldn't be enough, as we were having the 56K leased-line installed as well as additional lines as time went on. The installer said that he could bring in a 12-pair cable, which, he thought, would last us for quite a while. I told him that it wouldn't.

A week later, the NYNEX installer was at my front door again, with an order to install 4 lines for the Centrex that we had ordered. He was glad that he put in the 12-pair: eight of the pairs were already in use!

Before the end of the next month, we had saturated the 12-pair cable and we needed more. We were working through a dealer, and we told him that we wanted to have the facility issue resolved for a long time. Thanks to his advocacy with NYNEX, we made arrangements to have a 100-pair cable installed to our house from the street. To have this installed the street needed to be blocked off for half a day and a pair of large telephone company trucks snaked the cable from a junction box three blocks away to my house. We had to cut a large hole in the side of the house to bring in the cable, then set up a space on a plywood wall where the telephone company's termination equipment could be installed.

The 100-pair lasted us for the better part of three years, but we outgrew even that. Unfortunately, at that point, we didn't have any room left in the basement: we had to expand to across the street!

Lesson: Test your facilities before going live.

A week after the installation of the 12-pair, the installer was at my door one more time, this time to put the 56K line in place. I plugged in a CSU/DSU that I bought from CentNet and plugged the Cisco into the CSU/DSU. The first thing that I learned was that my Cisco was running a version of Cisco's operating system that was many months out of date. We downloaded a new version of the operating system over the frame relay connection and set up my network with an IP address in CentNet's CIDR block. Logging into the Cisco router from my laptop, I could telnet to my Unix workstation (an old NeXTstation) that was still at my old house in Cambridge.

Lesson: Provide for backup facilities before, during, and after your transition.

The next day, I moved the NeXTstation from Cambridge to Martha's Vineyard, saying good-bye to my old ISP and hello to my new provider. The house in Cambridge had its own Class C network (204.17.195) and I wanted to keep using those IP addresses. Unfortunately, some sort of strange routing problem cropped up, and I didn't have real Internet connectivity with my old Class C network until the next day. Mail bounced because we didn't have an MX server specified in the DNS configuration.

Commercial Start-Up

Now that the Unix workstation was on the island and the leased line to the Internet was up and running, the next thing to do was to work on our dialup access.

Working with the Phone Company

A friend who ran an ISP in Cincinnati had told me that if I wanted to run a successful dialup operation, I should get a service from the phone company called *circular hunting*. Normally, a bank of telephones is put into what is called a *hunt group*. You might have a block of phone numbers, from 555-1000 to 555-1020. With normal hunting, a phone call to 555-1000 is always taken by the first phone in the hunt group that isn't busy. But with circular hunting, the phone system remembers the last phone that it dialed and automatically dials the next phone number in the hunt group, whether the call to the previous phone number has hung up or not.

Circular hunting sounded like a great idea if you are running dialup access with analog modems. Consider what happens if you have a modem that suddenly fails to answer new calls. If you have circular hunting, then you only lose one modem: the next caller gets the next modem. But if you don't have circular hunting, then every caller will get the ringing modem, and nobody will get any of the other modems in the hunt group that are still good.

Lesson: Design your systems to fail gracefully.

I called NYNEX and tried to order a Centrex system with circular hunting. Unfortunately, nobody at the phone company knew what I was talking about. (A few months later, I learned that the reason nobody knew what I was talking about was that the service has a different name in Massachusetts from the one it has in Ohio. In Massachusetts, the service is called UCD, Uniform Call Distribution.)

Lesson: Know your phone company. Know its terminology, the right contact people, the phone numbers for internal organizations, and everything else you can find out.

I ordered a conventional Centrex system with four lines. Three of the lines, 696-6650, 696-6651, and 696-6652, would be in the hunt group. The fourth line, 696-6653, would not be in the hunt group. That line would be our business line.

Incorporating Vineyard.NET

In mid-August, the Internet cooperative got a third partner: Bill Bennett. Bill had been watching everything that Eric and I had been doing and he wanted a piece of the action. I also owed Bill a tremendous amount of money, because the wiring of the house had cost far more money than I had budgeted. Bill was willing to forgive the loan in exchange for a percentage of the Internet cooperative.

It was quickly becoming clear that running the Internet access provider as a cooperative wasn't going to work in the long run. Unless we could make a profit, there would never be money to purchase new equipment and expand our capacity. Unless we could make a profit to hire somebody else, I would be stuck forever doing technical support. Bill thought that an aggressive commercial service could make a tremendous amount of money. Egged on in part by Bill, in part by my debts, and in part by a spate of Internet-related companies that had initial public offerings in the spring and summer of 1995 (at somewhat obscene valuations), the three of us incorporated Vineyard.NET and embarked on a slightly more aggressive service offering.

Our plans for offering service mimicked many other Internet companies that were starting at the time. We planned to let early adopters use our service free for a few months. Then we hoped to charge a low introductory rate, after which we hoped to raise our prices once again to the actual level.

Initial Expansion

The first things that we needed were more phone lines and modems. That required working again with NYNEX or, in our case, our NYNEX-authorized reseller. We told them that we wanted to have a fiber optic circuit brought from the central office to our location. But NYNEX wouldn't do it: they said that the fiber demultiplexing equipment was not CPE—customer premise equipment. Instead, they brought a cable with 100 pairs of copper to our location. Bringing it required two huge trucks, five men, and shutting down the street for a day. We calculated that the whole operation must have cost NYNEX somewhere between $5,000 and $10,000. All of a sudden, things were getting serious. NYNEX had spent real money in the anticipation that we would be paying our bills. And to do that, we needed to get customers and collect money from them.

I knew that one of the most expensive things for a technology-based company to do is offer technical support to its customers. Tech support is even more expensive than research and development, since research and development costs remain roughly constant while tech support requirements increase along with a company's customer base. Another thing that's incredibly expensive is advertising. Rather than build our own technical support group, we partnered with computer stores on the island. They could sign people up for our Internet service when customers bought computers or came in to buy supplies. It seemed like a win-win situation.

Lesson: Build sensible business partnerships.

The idea of partnering made a lot of sense. The island's computer stores, after all, were already experienced in dealing with computer users on the island—the people who would be our customers. And they were also equipped to sell customers any additional hardware or software that they might need to make their computers Internet-capable. We set up our systems so that our computer store partners would be able to create accounts on our machine. They would also collect sign-up fees. In return, they would get a bounty for each user they brought in, and a set percentage of each user's monthly fee. We also set up a few of the island's computer consultants as resellers.

Once we had our phone lines installed, we needed to figure out what to use for modems. We briefly looked at some rack-mounted modems made by U.S. Robotics and were scared away by the high prices. Although I wanted to use rack-mounted modems, it seemed that all we would be able to afford for a while would be discrete ones.

But which discrete modems? I bought some ZyXEL modems for a lot of money and they were having problems, so we started trying other brands. We settled on Motorola's Lifestyle 28.8 modems. They seemed to work reliably and they didn't give off much heat. Eric built a modem "rack" for them out of wood, with each modem tilted at a 45-degree angle so that the heat would vent out the back side. (Eventually, we switched over to rack-mounted modems manufactured by Microcom.)

We started offering service for free in August 1995. Our plans were for "charter" members—people who signed up before October 1, 1995—to be charged $20/month for the first year. And then anybody who signed up in November would be charged $25/month. We wanted to keep our prices lower than $29/month—that's what The Internet Access Company (TIAC) was charging. TIAC offered dialup access on Martha's Vineyard, and it was important to Eric that we charge less than they did.

Accounting Software

The next thing we realized was that we would need to have some sophisticated software for keeping track of user accounts.

It wasn't my intention to write a complete customer billing and accounting system in Perl. I really only wanted to have a system for keeping track of who had paid their monthly bills and who hadn't. I wanted customers to be able to check their balances from the Web. And I wanted to be able to send customers their bills by email.

I had run a business before, back in 1992, and had used QuickBooks to keep track of the business books. QuickBooks is made by Intuit, the makers of Quicken. QuickBooks can easily keep track of a customer-driven business with hundreds or even thousands of customers. But QuickBooks didn't have any easy way of importing lists of invoices that we might generate on the Unix system, and it didn't have any easy way of exporting the data for view on the Web. In the end, I used QuickBooks for the business's main books, but had to create my own system for managing user accounts.

It turned out that writing our own accounts management system was the right idea: it gave us the power to tailor our business policies and terms however we wished, knowing that we could easily modify our billing software to accommodate our desires.

For instance, we wanted our resellers to be paid a 20 percent commission on the accounts that they owned, but only when their customers actually paid their bills. That wasn't a problem: I simply modified the program that received payment so that when a check was received on a customer's account, the reseller was automatically credited with the commission.

Lesson: Make sure your programs are table-driven as often as possible.

From speaking with my friend in Cincinnati, I realized that we might have dozens of different kinds of accounts and special deals within a few months. It had become an accounting nightmare for him. Rather than repeat his experience of building this logic directly into our accounting system, I created an accounting system that was table-driven. Each customer had a different account type. The account type keyed into a database that included information such as the account's sign-up fee, its monthly fee, the number of hours included in that monthly fee, and the cost for each additional hour.

Lesson: Tailor your products for your customers.

We also created a special kind of account for small businesses called a "group" account. This account allowed a business to have several Internet accounts that would all be charged to a single bill. Businesses were charged on a different scale from residential users—a lower monthly fee, but a higher hourly rate. We did this because many businesses seem more comfortable with a pay-as-you-go approach. (Or perhaps it's because businesses find it easier to let these charges creep up when they are not paying attention.) At any rate, going after business users made sense, because they had a peak usage time between 9 a.m. and 5 p.m., and the peak residential usage time was between 5 p.m. and 12 p.m.

We did not funnel the group accounts through our resellers. Instead, we resolved that we would provide tech support to a single person at each business; this person, in turn, was expected to provide first-line technical support to the other members of his organization. Once again, having built our own account management and billing software made this easy to do—it was just a matter of coding. The final system allowed the group account managers to create or delete accounts for their own organizations without having to bother us. The managers could even change the passwords for people who had forgotten their passwords—but only for people who were in each manager's particular group.

Lesson: Build systems that are extensible.

I wrote all of the software in the Perl 5 programming language. Perl is a great language for building large applications relatively quickly, and it runs reasonably fast. For a customer database, I used the Unix filesystem. A large directory called */vni/accts* has a subdirectory for each user on our system. Inside each user's directory is a series of files, each file containing a different piece of information about that user's account. So the account type for Eric's account was kept in a file called */vni/accts/ericx/account-type*, whereas the name of the reseller that owned Bill's account was kept in a file called */vni/accts/bill/owner*.

As the system evolved, we developed three kinds of Perl programs. The first was a set of library routines that were used by all of the systems. These library routines managed the account database and the billing system. The second was a set of CGI programs that could be used to perform routine chores, like looking at a user's bill or adding an account. The third was a set of Perl programs meant to be run from the command line. These were administrative programs meant to be run by Eric or me.

Lesson: Automate everything you can.

In writing these programs, I had a simple rule. The first time I had to do a task, I would do it manually, simply to be sure that I understood what was wanted. The second time I had to do something, I would do it manually again, to be sure that I was doing it correctly. The third time, I would write a program.

Following this strategy, we soon ended up with dozens of small but useful programs. We didn't forget about them; they were all referenced on a web page. We set up the Vineyard.NET web server so that users, resellers, and administrators would all use the same URL to access the system: *http://www.vineyard.net/start*. The system automatically looked at the username of the person accessing the web page and made the appropriate commands available.

For the first few months, I had a single regret about the design of the system: I wished that instead of using the Unix filesystem, I had used an actual relational database, or at least a Perl DBM file. But as time went on I realized that the decision to use the Unix filesystem as our database was a pretty good one after all. Certainly the filesystem could handle it: I've been on Unix systems with thousands of users, and they store all of the user home directories in a single directory. Furthermore, using the filesystem meant that we could use all of the standard Unix tools, such as *grep* and *find*, to manage our user accounts database. I figured that when we hit 10,000 customers, we would probably have to do something else. But quite possibly, all we would have to do would be to add a second layer of indirection, changing Eric's directory from */vni/accts/ericx/account-type* to */vni/accts/e/ericx/account-type*.

Lesson: Don't reinvent the wheel unless you can build a better wheel.

As it turns out, I was wrong about the scalability of our file-based database: it started to get really slow not at 10,000 customers, but at 600. One of the reasons is the way that the Unix filesystem implements locking on directory inodes. Another problem, though, was that the file-based database had no indexing: searching for all of the accounts that were of type "dialup" or all of the customers for a given reseller required opening hundreds of files, which took a long time.

About three years into the project, it was clear that we needed to change to something new. My first impulse was to revamp my database using Perl DBM files. But my wife said that I would be far better off using a third-party database. After all, if Vineyard.NET ever hired somebody else, there was a remote chance that they might have knowledge about our third-party database, but there was no way whatsoever that they would know how to use "Simson's database." What's more, we might even find other people using the same third-party database, which would mean that there would be somebody we could ask for help.

I looked around and discovered that there were basically three free databases from which to choose: MySQL, mSQL, and PostgreSQL. Not really sure which was best, I wrote a common interface that would work with any of them (I thought that a Perl DBI was too complicated), downloaded them all, and tried them all out. mSQL was the fastest and seemed to be the most powerful, so we started with that one. After a few weeks, we ran into some significant problems with mSQL,, so I moved over to PostgreSQL. Although PostgreSQL had transactions, the lack of multithreading support proved to be a showstopper, so we finally ended up with MySQL. Of course, that was back in 1997. If we had to do it all over again, we might end up with a different database—PostgreSQL now supports multithreading, for example.

Publicity and Privacy

With this basic business idea in place, we called up *The Martha's Vineyard Times*, one of the two newspapers on Martha's Vineyard, and asked them to write an article about us. The *Times* sent over a reporter with a camera, and a few days later the newspaper ran an article about Vineyard.NET with a photograph of Bill, Eric, and me.

The reporter wanted to print a phone number at the end of the article that people could call to get signed up for our service. This free advertising was precisely the reason that we had called the newspaper in the first place!

Lesson: Always be friendly to the press.

Unfortunately, our phone numbers were in a shambles. It was clear that we didn't want to use the number 696-6653 as our office number. First, it was too difficult to remember. Second, it was clear that we wanted as many of the 696-665x numbers as possible to be in our hunt group.

Eventually we picked the number 696-6688 as our office number. But that number wouldn't be installed for more than a week. In the meantime, the company was using my home phone number, which is the number that the newspaper ended up printing.

Lesson: Never give out your home phone number.

Letting the newspaper publish my home phone number was one of the biggest mistakes that I made throughout the entire Vineyard.NET project. For the next year, I received telephone calls on almost a daily basis from people who wanted to find out more about the Internet. It's true, the phone number was only printed once. But people clipped the article. People photocopied the article for friends. They wrote down the phone number, thinking that they would get around to calling it someday. I got those calls during the day, over the weekends, and even in the middle of the night (people who couldn't get to sleep, and who thought that they would be leaving a message on our answering machine).

It turns out that there were many other places that my home phone number had been used as well. My phone number was in the router MOTD (message of the day), because the MOTD had been written before Vineyard.NET became a commercial service, and it had never been changed. NYNEX had my home phone number listed as the official contact number for Vineyard.NET's account, because that was the phone number that I had asked them to call when the Centrex line was first set up. Months later, when Vineyard.NET started billing people's credit cards, my phone number was the phone number that was printed on our customer's bills—because our bank had simply copied down my phone number from their records.

Lesson: It is very difficult to change a phone number. So pick your company's phone number early and use it consistently.

Perhaps I should have changed my home phone number, but I didn't. Still, it was hard not to get angry the thirtieth or fortieth time I got a phone call from somebody wanting information about Vineyard.NET. Indeed, sometimes I did get angry—such as when I got calls at 8 a.m. on a Sunday morning. Unfortunately, every time I got angry at somebody for calling my home phone number, I was hurting the company, because the person at the other end of the line genuinely thought that they were calling the place of business, not my house.

Ongoing Operations

Before Vineyard.NET, I always handled the security of my own computer system with a few simple and reliable policies: don't run any services that might be unsecure; don't give out accounts to people you don't know; disconnect your computer from the Internet when you are not around. The monitoring that I did, insofar as I did any, was haphazard.

Those techniques wouldn't work for a commercial service such as Vineyard.NET. Instead, I needed to design and deploy a system that could be readily maintained, defended, and scaled.

Security Concerns

From the start, Vineyard.NET's security was one of my primary concerns. As the coauthor of several books on computer security, I knew any Internet service that I was involved with might be a target.

But there were other reasons that I was concerned about security. Vineyard.NET was a company that depended on computers that were connected to the Internet. If these computers were broken into and compromised, our reputation would be damaged, we would lose customers, and we would lose time required to put our systems back in order. We might lose so much in the way of customers, reputation, and time, that we might even go out of business.

Because of these problems, we followed a few simple rules for our system and networks: minimize vulnerabilities and plan for break-ins.

Lesson: Don't run programs with a history of security problems.

From the beginning, we avoided running programs that had a history of security problems. The primary offender here is *sendmail*, the Unix SMTP server and mail delivery agent. *sendmail* is an especially dangerous program because it runs as the superuser, has full access to the Unix filesystem, implements a complicated command language, and talks to any other computer on the Internet.

Organizations like the CERT/CC are continually sending out notices of new security problems discovered with *sendmail*. People are advised to download upgrades immediately from their vendors, if possible. Vineyard.NET ran the BSDI operating system, BSD/OS, and BSDI was very good about responding to security problems in a timely manner. But a much better way to deal with the problem is to use *smap*, a *sendmail* proxy, so that programs on the outside world never connect directly to our *sendmail* program.

Over time, we customized *smap*, adding features to deal with Vineyard.NET's authentication system, and then features to deal with spam. Somewhere in there, though, we ran into problems and *smap* started losing mail. Although we tried to find what was wrong with our fixes, in the end we had to abandon the *smap/sendmail* combination and move over to a different mailer. (We checked out both *postfix* and *qmail*.)

Lesson: Make frequent backups.

Another thing we did to protect ourselves was to make frequent backups of our system. These backups protected us against both break-ins and accidents on the part of myself or Eric.

At Vineyard.NET we make two kinds of backups. The first are tape backups. We started out using the GNU *tar* facility, but switched over to Unix *dump* because it ran at nearly twice the speed. Then we switched back to GNU *tar*, because the dump manpages were filled with warnings about the dangers of backing up an active filesystem. Vineyard.NET's disks are always active.

Each day we make a full dump of every file on the system. To accommodate all of the files, we got a DDS-II DAT tape drive. That held 8 GB with compression, and, as we had only 6 GB online, things were okay for a while. Our tapes are labeled Monday, Tuesday, Wednesday, and so on. At the end of each month, we make a "permanent" backup that is taken offsite. (Eventually we had to get a DDS-III drive, then a

DDS-IV drive, as we bought more disks. We always tried to keep one tape per disk for backups.)

We also make daily backups of the entire */usr/local/etc/httpd/htdocs* directory. These backups are kept online in a single compressed *tar* file. The backups are designed to protect us from accidentally deleting a file.

It turns out that we've used all of the backups with more or less successful results. The backups have been quite useful when files have been accidentally deleted. The only time we had a problem that our backups couldn't solve was when we were changing a disk formatting parameter on a disk drive that was being used to store Usenet files. We backed up the entire filesystem to the DAT drive twice, reformatted the disk, and then tried to restore it. It wouldn't. It turns out the Berkeley *restore* command has some hardcoded limits inside it, and it simply couldn't restore 100,000+ files at once. The result: we lost all of our netnews. In retrospect, it was no big deal.

Lesson: Limit logins to your servers.

From the beginning, I decided that Vineyard.NET would not offer "shell" accounts —that is, accounts that allowed people to log into our Unix server. We also resolved that all administration of the web server would be done through the FTP command. Although this was a little awkward for some people, and I think it cost us a few customers, in the end it was the right decision. It is far easier to run a Unix machine securely if you do not allow people to log into it.

Lesson: Beware of TCP/IP spoofing.

TCP/IP spoofing is a rather arcane attack, but it is one that has been successful in at least one widely publicized attack. To protect ourselves against it, we configured our external routers to reject any incoming packets that indicated they were being sent from our internal network.

Lesson: Defeat packet sniffing.

As soon as we could, Eric and I set up *ssh*, the secure shell, so we could log on from one computer to another with the knowledge that our password was not being sent over the network. We also required that friends on the Internet who wanted guest accounts on our machines use *ssh* to access those accounts as well.

As for our home machines, we installed Kerberos on our BSDI box and started using a Kerberized-version of the Macintosh Telnet program. About a year later, we switched to a commercial version of *ssh* sold by Data Fellows. The program was terrible, but it was the only thing available. When Van Dyke came out with Secure-CRT, we switched to that on our PCs; by then, we had stopped using the Macs.

Lesson: Restrict logins.

We configured our Cisco routers so that they could only be logged into from a particular computer on our internal network. Although this slightly increased the difficulty of our administering the system, it dramatically improved the security of the routers. Prior to the configuration change, a person could have broken into our router by trying to guess thousands or millions of passwords. (Cisco's operating system makes this procedure easier than that statement makes it sound.) After the change, the only way to break into the routers was first to identify and break into the one host on the subnet that could telnet to the routers. Still, it would have been better if Cisco had simply added support for Kerberos, S/Key, or *ssh* into their products. (Note that Cisco has since added support for some of these protocols.)

Lesson: Tighten up your system beyond manufacturer recommendations.

In the interest of improved security, we started reducing the access permissions of many directories on our Unix system. Directories that contained programs were changed from mode 755 (read/write access for the superuser, read and *chdir* access for everybody else) to mode 711 (read/write access for the superuser, but only search *chdir* for others). Configuration files were changed from mode 644 (world-readable access) to mode 600 (access only for superuser). The idea of reducing permissions in this manner was to make it harder for somebody who had an account on the system to use that account to probe for further weaknesses.

The revised permissions also protected the privacy of our users. For example, with the original permissions, it was possible for a user to open an FTP connector to our server and list the contents of the */users* directory, effectively giving that user a list of all our customers' email addresses. With the revised permissions, this was no longer possible.

One day we noticed that somebody named *http* had logged into our system and was running an xterm, with the DISPLAY variable set to be somewhere in Texas. Apparently the person had broken into our main computer through the web server and had convinced the program to run an X terminal of his choosing. We immediately modified our firewall to block all packets to or from the attacker's ISP, then used the *gcore* command to look at the memory map of the attacker's shell. This gave us, among other things, a list of every command that the attacker had typed.

We noticed that the attacker had spent two hours uploading various small programs to our computer, compiling them, and then running the programs with various command-line arguments—like "./a 72", "./a 80", "./a 432". We surmised that the attacker had uploaded programs that probe for buffer-overflow exploits and had then tried them with the proper offsets for various operating systems. Poor guy! He thought he had broken into a Linux box, and he was actually on a BSD/OS system. After four hours, he had given up.

We were pleased that he hadn't been able to able to ratchet up his permissions and turn a *http* login into a superuser access. Clearly, something about our security worked. But we shouldn't have made it so easy for him. The next day, we modified our system further, placing the compiler, the */usr/include* files, the linkable libraries, and all of the other program development tools into a separate group. People who weren't in the group would be unable to run those programs.

Lesson: Remember, the "free" in "free software" refers to "freedom."

Although I am an advocate of free software, there were many times in the development of Vineyard.NET that we went with commercially available versions of free programs. For example, we chose to use BSD/OS, a commercial operating system from BSDI, rather than using FreeBSD, NetBSD, OpenBSD, or Linux. We wanted BSDI to track security problems for us and provide us with bug fixes, rather than having to do it ourselves. Likewise, we chose to purchase our web server from Community ConneXion, rather than simply using the freely available Apache web server. Yes, our primary reason for purchasing the Community ConneXion server was to obtain an SSL-enabled web server. But we were also eager to have somebody else tracking reported security problems with the web server and providing us with patches.

The "free" in "free software" refers to freedom, not to price. The actual price that you pay for a program frequently is only a tiny part of your total investment. This became clear to us when we spent many hours trying to get both "free" and commercial software to work. Frequently with the commercial software, we were able to get a service contract and get somebody to help us. The same was not always true with the free stuff.

On the other hand, we were more than happy to use free software on occasions where it was clearly better than the commercial alternative. We replaced the Perl 5 interpreter that came with BSDI with one that we downloaded from the Internet because BSDI's version of Perl 5 was out of date. We used GNU *emacs* as our text editor and GCC as our compiler, rather than purchasing expensive development tools that might not have worked as well.

As time progressed in the history of Vineyard.NET, our attitude towards free versus commercial software changed. We slowly phased out the BSD/OS operating system in favor of FreeBSD, and we switched from Stronghold to Apache with *mod_ssl*. In contrast to others who made similar switches in the late 1990s, the reason for our switch didn't have to do with the apparent quality of the free software, but instead with the drop in both quality and service of the commercial vendors. As both FreeBSD and BSD/OS matured, we discovered that there were many features in FreeBSD that were simply unavailable in BSD/OS. Likewise, the version of Apache that C2 software distributed fell significantly behind the version of Apache that was being distributed from *www.apache.org*. We left the commercial vendors because we wanted advanced features that they were not offering.

Phone Configuration and Billing Problems

We had continual (and continuing) problems with the configuration of our telephone lines. Prudent security practices dictate that lines used for incoming telephone calls should not be able to make outgoing calls—and they certainly should not be able to place long distance calls. Otherwise, somebody who breaks into your computer might use the ability to place long distance calls to charge tens of thousands of dollars in phone calls to your account.

It turns out that Vineyard.NET is particularly vulnerable to this sort of toll fraud, because we have placed Centrex lines in locations such as schools and libraries, so these organizations could call the Vineyard.NET phone lines without having to pay message units. Every few months, we notice between $10 and $30 of phone calls on these lines to other phone numbers.

We have repeatedly asked our phone company, NYNEX, to disable 9+ dialing on both the dialup telephone lines and the phone lines that are located on customer premises. Each time we've been assured by the phone company that the problem has been corrected, yet every time we check, we discover that the phones still can dial local and long distance calls.

Frankly, this is still an unsolved problem. Right now, I'm trying to get a letter from NYNEX saying that our lines cannot place outgoing calls. Then I'm going to wait for another $100 phone bill and refuse to pay it.

Another problem that we had with NYNEX is billing disputes. For several months we were not billed for one of our high-speed serial lines. Then we were double-billed. Payments made were not credited. We were billed for lines after they were disconnected. New phones that were installed were not billed for many months, then we had months of back invoices suddenly posted to our account. And we have never been able to decipher our Centrex bills to our satisfaction.

After having our office manager spend more than 100 hours trying to resolve these problems with NYNEX, we came to the realization that some amount of incorrect billing is probably unavoidable when dealing with NYNEX. So we are careful about what charges we dispute. Some are challenged right away. Others we let slide, because there are only so many hours in the day. (If our billing is that far off, we wonder what it is like for more substantial commercial firms?)

Credit Cards and ACH

One of the biggest problems for any business is getting paid; after we had been operating for a few months, we had more than 200 customers and we were owed more than $10,000 in late fees. We didn't want to make things worse by charging people finance charges. We just wanted our money.

It turned out that a lot of our customers wanted to pay us, they were simply lazy. Writing a check is, after all, a pain. Receiving them was difficult, too; entering each check into the computer, putting it on a deposit ticket, and taking it to the bank all took a considerable amount of time.

Fortunately, we found our savior: a technique for billing people's credit cards and for withdrawing money directly from people's credit cards using a system called ACH (the U.S. Automated Clearing House).

These days, it's quite easy for a legitimate merchant to get a credit card merchant account. You go to your bank, fill out some forms, and wait. A few days later you'll get a phone call from an investigator, who wants to stop by your place of business and make sure that you are legitimate. If that goes well, and it almost always does, you get a machine.

I had a credit card merchant account once before, when I was running a company that was selling computer software. But having to run people's credit card numbers through a machine—and having to do it every month—is a real pain. We probably would have had to hire somebody to do the job, and that would have cost time and money.

Instead I started looking around for software that could charge people's credit cards automatically, and submit all of the charges by modem. My bank gave me a list of companies that sell this software. Most of it runs on PCs, some of it runs on Macs, and perhaps one or two programs run on a Unix-based system. But nothing was quite right.

Then, by chance, I visited a trade show and found out about CheckFree's merchant services. Based in Ohio, CheckFree has made a name for itself in the wireless bill payment business. In fact, I've used CheckFree for years to pay my various bills. I simply type all of the bills into Quicken, type a code, and my computer makes a phone call. CheckFree electronically removes the money from my account and transfers it into my merchant's. If the merchant isn't set up for ACH, CheckFree can write a check on my account. If several CheckFree customers try to pay the same merchant during the same payment period, CheckFree may transfer the money out of my account and into a CheckFree account, then send the merchant a single check for all of the CheckFree customers (with an accompanying statement indicating who paid what).

It turned out that CheckFree also had merchant services and could process credit card transactions for us. Also, CheckFree could do Merchant ACH: we could type in the checking account numbers of our customers and pull the money out directly. Even better, Checkfree had set up a system that allowed merchants to submit charges over the Internet encrypted using PGP.

Clearly, CheckFree's Gateway system was exactly what Vineyard.NET had been looking for. It would allow us to take credit card numbers on our web server, store them online, and then automatically use credit cards and ACH charges to settle our customer's accounts. Unfortunately, when I asked CheckFree to send me a program that implemented their protocols, they sent me a three-ring binder instead. There was no off-the-shelf code that they could provide me.

Lesson: If you have the time to write it, custom software always works better than what you can get off the shelf.

Over the next four months, I wrote a complete implementation of CheckFree's Gateway 3.0 protocols. Although it was a fun experience and I learned a lot about Perl, bank card processing, and the intricacies of the nation's ACH networks, I wished that I had been able to buy off-the-shelf the programs that I was looking for. In fact, there was a freelance computer consultant who sold such a package, but he wanted $1,000 for the software. It was all written in C and I didn't feel comfortable working with the person. So I ended up writing it all myself. Doing this had the added advantage of teaching me a lot about how credit cards are processed, which was useful for writing Chapter 25 of this book.

Lesson: Live credit card numbers are dangerous.

One of the scariest things was working with real live credit card numbers. If we screwed up, we might charge somebody too much money. If we got a sign reversed, we might transfer money from our account into a customer's, rather than the other way around. If we had a break-in, somebody might steal the credit card numbers of our customers, and we could be liable. For the first six months, I went over every credit card batch for half an hour before submitting it to our bank.

Lesson: Encrypt sensitive information and be careful with your decryption keys.

We tried to protect the live credit card numbers the best we could. Perhaps the most important thing we did was to store them encrypted on our web server. To do the encryption, we used PGP. The credit card encryption system has a special public key/private key. The web server and CGI scripts know the public key, but not the secret key. So when people enter their credit card numbers, the numbers are encrypted with the public key. The numbers are only decrypted when an actual billing run happens. We do this once or twice a month. To initiate the billing run, either Eric or I must type the PGP passphrase that decrypts the secret key that, in turn, decrypts the credit card numbers.

Lesson: Log everything, and have lots of reports.

As an added measure of protection, we set up numerous logs and reports that would be created every time a credit card run was processed. Not only did this help us in writing and debugging the software, it also made it easier for us to track down problems when they occurred.

Each time the software runs, Eric and I get sent numerous reports that are issued from CheckFree. We're used to seeing this sequence of reports, and when we don't get them, we know that there is something amiss. The reports have also notified us when the other person runs the billing system.

Lesson: Explore a variety of payment systems.

When customers pay by credit cards, merchants are assessed a surcharge between two and three percent. (Don't think about passing this surcharge on to your customers: that's a violation of your merchant agreement.) Still, despite this surcharge, it's often cheaper for businesses to accept payment by credit cards than by check or cash. That's because it's difficult, and therefore expensive, to handle large amounts of cash or large numbers of checks. And when customers pay by cash or check, there's always a chance that something will go wrong: the check will bounce, or it will get credited to the wrong account, or you'll simply lose the money. (All of these have happened to us at Vineyard.NET.) None of these problems happen when you are charging somebody a monthly fee for a credit card that you've got on file. A further advantage is that you are immediately told if the charge is approved or not. If the charge is approved, it's nearly a sure thing that you will get the money.

We prefer ACH to credit cards. Instead of being charged a fee between two and three percent, we are charged a flat fee of roughly 27 cents. But ACH is not without its problems. Transactions can fail for a variety of reasons, and sometimes we don't hear about failed transactions for up to 10 days. Our ACH system requires more by-hand intervention than our credit card system. Sometimes we receive a Notification Of Change (NOC) on ACH, which means that we have to change somebody's account number. Other times a NOC means that the account has been deleted.

Our enthusiasm for these new electronic payment systems was not shared by our customers. After all, they had been able to pay by check whenever they wanted—and not pay when they didn't. We had essentially been giving our customers zero percent interest loans on the overdue balances.

Lesson: Make it easy for your customers to save you money.

After nearly eight months of asking our customers to pay by ACH because it saved us money, we hit upon a better approach. We started giving a $1 monthly discount for customers who paid by credit card, and a $2 monthly discount for those who paid by ACH. Soon customers were calling us up, volunteering their credit card numbers and their bank account information. They thought they were getting a terrific deal. As far as we were concerned, the $2/month discount was a lot cheaper for us than typing the checks into two accounting systems, taking the checks to the bank, and hounding customers who forgot to make their payments.

Lesson: Have a backup supplier.

Eric and I were so pleased with the CheckFree system, and so hard-pressed for time, that we never seriously explored getting an alternative credit card processor. After all, why look for more work?

Then one day, we got a notice from CheckFree that they were selling their merchant card systems to FirstUSA Paymentech. CheckFree promised us that FirstUSA would continue to offer all of the same services that CheckFree had in the past, but shortly after the acquisition was completed, we received a letter in the mail that said that FirstUSA would no longer be offering the Gateway 3.0 features. We had the choice of moving to a few other systems, including CyberCash and IC Verify. If we wanted to keep using ACH, we had no choice but to move to CyberCash.

Grudgingly, we downloaded the CyberCash software and rewrote our processing system to use the CyberCash gateway. Immediately we had problems with documentation that was incomplete or did not accurately reflect the software that we had downloaded. We were halfway through implementing the system when we discovered that CyberCash had no way to automatically handle charge-backs. We called up CyberCash and asked them what the system did when a consumer reversed a credit card charge. "Oh, somebody will send you a fax or give you a phone call," we were told.

Once we had the CyberCash system finally working, we discovered a serious limitation: we wanted to process transactions in batch, but the CyberCash system couldn't handle batch sizes of more than a few dozen cards—FirstUSA Paymentech took so long to process the cards under these circumstances that the CyberCash software actually timed out. We started lowering the batch size—first to 100 transactions, then to 50, and eventually to 20. Months later, Paymentech complained to us that we were sending too many batches through and demanded that we increase our batch size, even though that made the system less reliable.

Working with both CyberCash and Paymentech proved to be problematic at best. For every transaction, we would create a unique transaction ID and give it to Cyber-Cash, which forwarded it to Paymentech. But Paymentech didn't use this Cyber-Cash ID: they created their own. Tracking transactions through the system thus became more complicated; it was an incredibly difficult and very manual exercise—every time we got one of those faxes from Paymentech telling us that a credit card had been declined or reversed—to actually figure out which customer had initiated the charge-back.

Over time we discovered another problem with the CyberCash system. The software wasn't stable. In an effort to deal with its many problems, CyberCash was continually bringing out new releases to its software. That's good. Unfortunately, many of these releases broke our existing code. Every so often, we would get an email from CyberCash about a mandatory upgrade. We ignored those emails at our peril.

Then on January 1, 2000, we discovered that we were unable to process credit cards. We called up FirstUSA; they denied that they had a Y2K problem. We called up CyberCash; they said the same thing. We decided to wait for a week or so to see if the problem would resolve itself, but of course, it did not. When we finally started going through our code line by line, we discovered that CyberCash had made an undocumented change to their API on January 1. When we called CyberCash to complain, they denied it. But their own code proved otherwise.

Monitoring Software

Vineyard.NET had been operational as a commercial service for about two weeks when I started wondering if we had enough phone lines. Unfortunately, there wasn't any way to know for sure: neither our Unix operating system nor our Cisco routers came with monitoring software that would accurately report usage over time.

One way to plan for capacity is simply to count how many users you have and make an educated guess about how many resources each person requires. For instance, one rule of thumb in the ISP industry is that you need 1 dialup phone line for every 10 customers, for a ratio of 1:10. But another rule of thumb is that you need 1 modem for every 20 customers. And some ISPs have 1 for every 6.

There is not much in the way of good hard data behind these numbers. It depends on a lot of things, such as whether your customers are dialing in from work or from home, what time of the year they are dialing in (usage is higher in the winter, when the nights are longer), whether your customers are married, whether they have children, and whether there is anything especially interesting on the Internet. We might have wanted a lower ratio because there isn't a whole lot to do on Martha's Vineyard after the sun goes down, but have a higher ratio because a lot of the computer users on the island aren't very sophisticated—and thus aren't likely to stay online for extended periods of time. We saw a strong correlation between daylight savings time and modem usage; in the spring, when clocks were set forward an hour, our modem usage dropped dramatically. We guessed that people had better things to do than go online.

Another approach is simply to buy more phone lines when people start getting busy signals. But adding capacity isn't cheap—or fast. The phone company charges us $50 to install each new phone line. Off-the-shelf 28.8 modems can be had for as low as $160 today, but if you don't want a maintenance nightmare you'll buy rack-mounted modems, which cost $600 for the rack (holds 16) and $240 for each modem. Connected to the modems you need a terminal concentrator such as a Livingston Portmaster or a Cisco 2511. We had more experience with the Cisco, so we bought one of those for $3000; it can handle 16 modems at a time. Crunch these numbers and you get a total cost of $515 to install a new port. Then there is the monthly cost of $20 per phone line. And every time you add another phone line, you increase the amount of capacity that's needed for the ISP's connection to the rest of the Internet.

So there is this constant dance between wanting to expand facilities to give better performance and the problem that expanding facilities makes the whole enterprise more expensive to operate. This is the difficulty of managing growth. It's one of the hardest things for a company to do properly.

Lesson: Monitor your system.

It turns out that the only sensible way to gauge your capacity is to monitor how much you are using and make your decisions accordingly. We ended up developing a number of reports to do this.

The first report is a modem report. This report is sent nightly and includes the number of users who dialed up during the last 24-hour period, the number of calls per modem, a histogram of the number of users logged on at a time, and a hourly graph that shows the number of people logged on by time of day. This report is built by examining the login/logout records.

The second report we developed shows the usage of our high-speed connection to the Internet. This report is built by querying our external router every 5 minutes and recording the results.

When we started looking at our reports over time, we were somewhat surprised by the results:

- Dialup usage was steadily increasing, but not because people were staying on significantly longer. Instead, people were calling up more frequently and staying on for roughly the same amount of time.
- Peak usage dropped considerably after daylight savings time kicked in.
- The need for bandwidth may be illusory; we ran an ISP with 32 people dialed up simultaneously and never came near to saturating our connection to the outside Internet.

Example A-1 shows what one of Vineyard.NET's early daily reports looked like.

Example A-1. Vineyard.NET's daily modem report standard example format

```
From: "Mr. Logger" <logger>
Subject: Logger

Generating report for last 24 hours
Total number of calls: 530
Average time per call: 24 minutes
Longest call:          472 minutes (ericx) (16:06 - 23:59)

*** Bad Lines: A-14  (1)

Samples with 0 callers: 0
Samples with 1 callers: 3
Samples with 2 callers: 7
Samples with 3 callers: 27
```

```
Samples with 4 callers: 13
Samples with 5 callers: 14
Samples with 6 callers: 19
Samples with 7 callers: 11
Samples with 8 callers: 6
Samples with 9 callers: 19
Samples with 10 callers: 18
Samples with 11 callers: 20
Samples with 12 callers: 27
Samples with 13 callers: 19
Samples with 14 callers: 21
Samples with 15 callers: 15
Samples with 16 callers: 18
Samples with 17 callers: 11
Samples with 18 callers: 7
Samples with 19 callers: 4
Samples with 20 callers: 4
Samples with 21 callers: 1
Samples with 22 callers: 2
Samples with 23 callers: 1


Sample size: 5 minutes


Line Reports
```

Line	Calls	Short Calls	Total Min.	Average Length	Longest Call
A-01	21	2	7'55'40''	22'39''	2'14'34''
A-02	22	0	8'43'29''	23'47''	1'36'53''
A-03	17	1	10'29'33''	37'01''	7'52'33''
A-04	25	0	6'15'32''	15'01''	1'42'24''
A-05	22	1	10'03'05''	27'24''	2'49'48''
A-06	28	3	7'12'31''	15'26''	1'58'29''
A-07	23	0	7'09'47''	18'41''	1'27'24''
A-08	28	2	9'03'33''	19'24''	1'50'38''
A-09	17	1	6'41'55''	23'38''	1'14'20''
A-10	22	2	7'54'02''	21'32''	1'57'00''
A-11	15	1	11'15'53''	45'03''	6'36'20''
A-12	16	0	11'45'13''	44'04''	3'52'53''
A-13	24	2	7'05'54''	17'44''	1'20'37''
A-15	24	1	7'42'27''	19'16''	1'48'53''
A-16	21	0	8'30'44''	24'19''	1'47'59''
B-01	25	3	6'46'32''	16'15''	1'57'28''
B-02	17	0	7'23'25''	26'05''	2'18'28''
B-03	26	0	6'59'04''	16'07''	1'17'53''
B-04	21	1	9'37'57''	27'31''	3'15'40''
B-05	21	1	6'10'08''	17'37''	1'11'24''
B-06	18	0	10'04'32''	33'35''	2'32'54''
B-07	24	2	8'04'27''	20'11''	1'56'46''
B-08	23	2	8'16'24''	21'34''	3'18'23''

```
C-01        14      0       8'53'42''       38'07''     3'20'50''
C-02        16      1       12'53'02''      48'18''     4'28'25''
Total lines: 25
Short calls are calls that are less than 30 seconds.


Usage by hour:
Time                average number logged in
 0:00 -  0:59       7.6     *************
 1:00 -  1:59       7.1     ************
 2:00 -  2:59       4.7     ********
 3:00 -  3:59       2.2     ***
 4:00 -  4:59       3.1     *****
 5:00 -  5:59       3.1     *****
 6:00 -  6:59       4.2     *******
 7:00 -  7:59       5.2     *********
 8:00 -  8:59      10.1     ******************
 9:00 -  9:59      12.9     ***********************
10:00 - 10:59      15.1     ***************************
11:00 - 11:59      13.0     ************************
12:00 - 12:59      10.3     ******************
13:00 - 13:59      11.2     ********************
14:00 - 14:59      12.5     ***********************
15:00 - 15:59      17.8     *********************************
16:00 - 16:59      14.2     **************************
17:00 - 17:59      16.2     ******************************
18:00 - 18:59      13.4     *************************
19:00 - 19:59      13.5     **************************
20:00 - 20:59       9.8     *****************
21:00 - 21:59       9.4     ****************
22:00 - 22:59      15.4     ****************************
23:00 - 23:59      15.2     ****************************
```

Vineyard.NET also set up a system called MRTG (Multi Router Traffic Grapher) by Tobias Oetiker and Dave Rand to monitor the bandwidth utilization of its external Internet connection (see Figure A-1). Over time we modified MRTG to track the CPU of our servers, our dialup utilization, the amount of free disk space, and the utilization of each of our leased lines. MRTG has since been superseded by RRDTool and MRTG2. We highly recommend these programs.

Redundancy and Wireless

Around Vineyard.NET's third anniversary, I started worrying about the possibility of a fire—and what it would do to our company. At that time, Vineyard.NET was located completely within my house, a 150-year-old wood frame building. One careless night with wine and some candles, and the whole ISP could be history.

I had heard of something called business continuity insurance, so I called my insurance agent and asked what it was all about. He said that I would need to prepare a

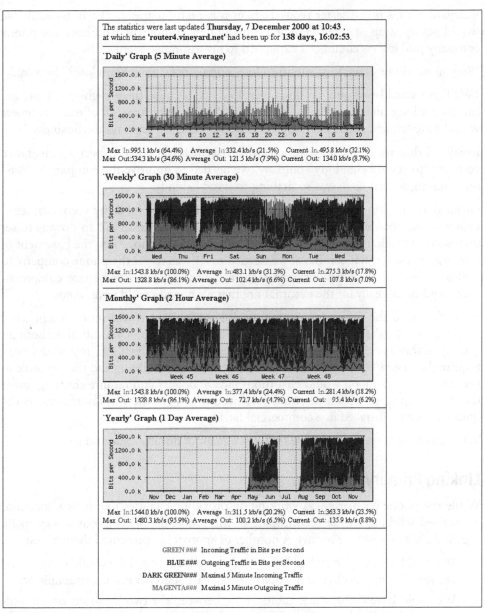

The statistics were last updated **Thursday, 7 December 2000 at 10:43** , at which time **'router4.vineyard.net'** had been up for **138 days, 16:02:53**.

`Daily' Graph (5 Minute Average)

Max In:995.1 kb/s (64.4%) Average In:332.4 kb/s (21.5%) Current In:495.8 kb/s (32.1%)
Max Out:534.3 kb/s (34.6%) Average Out: 121.5 kb/s (7.9%) Current Out: 134.0 kb/s (8.7%)

`Weekly' Graph (30 Minute Average)

Max In:1543.8 kb/s (100.0%) Average In:483.1 kb/s (31.3%) Current In:275.3 kb/s (17.8%)
Max Out: 1328.8 kb/s (86.1%) Average Out: 102.4 kb/s (6.6%) Current Out: 107.8 kb/s (7.0%)

`Monthly' Graph (2 Hour Average)

Max In:1543.8 kb/s (100.0%) Average In:377.4 kb/s (24.4%) Current In:281.4 kb/s (18.2%)
Max Out: 1328.8 kb/s (86.1%) Average Out: 72.7 kb/s (4.7%) Current Out: 95.4 kb/s (6.2%)

`Yearly' Graph (1 Day Average)

Max In:1544.0 kb/s (100.0%) Average In:311.5 kb/s (20.2%) Current In:363.3 kb/s (23.5%)
Max Out: 1480.3 kb/s (95.9%) Average Out: 100.2 kb/s (6.5%) Current Out: 135.9 kb/s (8.8%)

GREEN ### Incoming Traffic in Bits per Second
BLUE ### Outgoing Traffic in Bits per Second
DARK GREEN### Maximal 5 Minute Incoming Traffic
MAGENTA### Maximal 5 Minute Outgoing Traffic

Figure A-1. Vineyard.NET monitors the utilization of its network connection using MRTG; the holes in the graph represent times when the monitoring system was not running.

description of Vineyard.NET for the underwriters, the sort of problems that we could encounter, how much lost revenue each month we would have, and how we would recover after a loss. I chuckled; he was asking me for the very sort of disaster recovery plan that we advocate in earlier chapters of this book.

Vineyard.NET's first disaster recovery plan was pretty pathetic. "Well, basically we would set up shop in a new building, buy all new equipment, and have the phone company pull in new circuits," I explained to my insurance agent.

"So you would be down for a month? How much money would you lose?" he asked.

"Well, we would probably be down for 45 days, because these high-speed circuits can take a long time to get installed," I said. "But by that time, all of our customers would have left and gone elsewhere. So it would basically wipe out the business."

I realized that we didn't have an insurable risk. Before I could expect an insurance company to stand behind my company, we needed to improve the company's disaster planning so that there was something to stand behind.

Given that my primary concern was the possibility of fire, and my secondary concern was the possibility of theft, the logical thing for Vineyard.NET to do was to set up a second machine room in a second building. We had a location: the basement of our largest reseller, Educomp. All we needed to do was to get the phone company to pull a second 100-pair network cable to that location, put some spare equipment there, and be all ready for the eventual fire that we hoped would never come.

A quick call to the phone company revealed that this plan was more complicated than it seemed. NYNEX* said that it would not put facilities in a location without an order. Furthermore, once we placed the order, getting the facilities installed would require that a new conduit be installed between our new building and the manhole in the street; the operation would cost thousands of dollars and require shutting down the street again. And this time, we would need to pay for the work ourselves, as the lines were being installed in a commercial facility.

We thought of this expense as the first installment of our insurance policy.

Linking Primary to Backup

While the phone company was working on providing facilities to our new location, we started working on the second part of the problem—figuring out a way to tie together the two machine rooms. A number of approaches presented themselves:

- We could have a T1 installed between the two locations. This would certainly be the simplest approach, but it would cost at least $600 per month, indefinitely.
- We could have a fiber optic cable strung between the two locations on the utility lines. I checked around and learned that pole rentals were cheap—typically $5/month for each pole passed. The problem with pulling our own fiber was the up-front cost: we would have to have an engineer create a wiring plan and get it approved by the electric company, the phone company, the town, or all three.

---

* Bell Atlantic and NYNEX had merged to become NYNEX.

And once we had the wires up, we would be responsible for the maintenance. If there ever needed to be a repair, we would need to have that done as well. The more we looked into this approach, the more it was clear that this was not the way to go.

- We could set up a wireless link using unlicensed wireless hardware. After all, the two buildings were less than 1000 feet apart, and we could clearly see one from the other.

We decided to go with the wireless approach. The first equipment that we tried came from an Israeli company named Breezecom. This equipment operated at 2.4 GHz using the 802.11 frequency-hopping standard. After a few months of trials, we gave up on the Breezecom equipment: it simply was not reliable enough. Our next try was with hardware from a company called C-Spec. The hardware was basically a 486 PC with a Lucent 915 MHz frequency-hopping Wavelan card and special software that C-Spec had written. The C-Spec equipment cost more than the Breezecom, but it worked without problems.

Building the Backup Site

Vineyard.NET's largest reseller was extremely happy with its new high-speed wireless connection to the Internet; for the previous three years, Educomp's only connection to the Internet had been multiple dialup connections. But for Educomp, getting the wireless to work had been quite easy: the wireless system was an Ethernet bridge, so all we needed to do was to plug one wireless system into Vineyard.NET's Ethernet and plug the second one into Educomp's. Getting the wireless system to be usable for Vineyard.NET required considerably more work.

The first question that we were faced with, of course, was "What do we want to do with the backup site?" We knew that we wanted it to be our backup site, so we decided that we needed a backup computer system there. We took an old PC that we had upgraded, put some big SCSI hard drives on it, and put it in a rack in Educomp's basement. We added to the setup a rack of 16 modems and a Cisco 2516 router. Normally, the Cisco would simply be an access server. But if our main building ever burned, we would have the phone company jumper the T1 to the new location and we could use the 2516 as our upstream router as well.

Once we had the computer at the backup site operational, our next order of business was to make it truly functional. We set up a series of jobs on our primary computer that would automatically back up the hard drives to the backup system on a daily basis. Then we set up another job that would copy over our most critical files—the accounting files, people's email, and so on—on an hourly basis.

Although the backup system was designed to help us survive a fire, we quickly realized that having a secondary system would also make it possible for us to survive a server crash, something that was far more likely. In the event that our primary server crashed, we wanted the backup server to be able to take over from the primary. This meant that it needed to be able to serve web pages, accept mail, and generally pretend to be the primary system.

To make this illusion successful, we gave the backup computer the IP address of our secondary nameserver. We set up a copy of our web server so that the backup computer could serve the web pages for all of our customers. We further modified the system so that some of the scripts would notice if they were running on the backup system and, if so, not execute. We decided that it was simply easier to prevent users from changing their passwords or account options while they were running on the backup server, rather than try to figure out how to propagate the changes from the backup systems back to the primary system.

Finally, we waited.

Failover—and Back!

Over the following two years we had very little use for an online backup server. Whenever we accidentally deleted a file, we could get the backup from the backup computer.

Then in the fall of 1998, our backup system got its first real test. One afternoon, everything on our primary computer started to go haywire. Our *ls* and *du* commands were dumping core. We thought that we were either under attack or had suffered a really serious hardware problem. But then we noticed that other, dramatically more accomplished subsystems were working fine: we were able to log into the computer using *ssh*, and *emacs* still worked perfectly.

We tried to debug the problem with BSDI, but nobody had heard of the problems that we were having. We explained that we clearly had an operating system bug; we needed help. The best help that BSDI could give us, I said, was the source code to the *ls* program. I could then compile the program with debug symbols, see where the crash was, and figure out what we had done to trigger the problem.

But BSDI refused to give us the source code to the system that we had: "We just don't do that," I was told. Vineyard.NET could purchase the source code, but they would not give it to us, not even to help us find an operating system bug.

After an hour of screwing around with BSDI, we decided that we were on our own. For the first time since we had built the system, we switched over to run completely off the backup system. Doing the switchover was far easier than I thought it would be: we simply copied the current mail files from our primary system to the backup system, then we halted the primary system and gave its IP address to the backup. Suddenly Vineyard.NET was up and running again. Our customers never found out that we were running on a machine with a fraction of the capacity of the primary.

An hour later, an engineer at BSDI called me back. He said that he couldn't give me the source code, but he could give me a specially compiled version of the *ls* command with debug symbols left in. I ran the program, it crashed, and I examined the core dump. According to the core dump, the program had crashed when attempting to access a function called the *getgrent()*—a function that reads through the */etc/group* file. I examined the file and discovered that it had some trailing blank lines. I removed the blank lines and the problem went away. Apparently the extra blank lines had tickled a bug in the BSDI shared library. Programs like *emacs* and *ssh* were not affected because our copies of these programs had been compiled and linked before we had upgraded our system to the 3.0 release of the operating system, so they were using the 2.0 shared library, which did not have the bug.

With the problem diagnosed, we now could switch back to our primary system. There was only one problem—we couldn't figure out a way to do this without interrupting service. At 4:00 a.m. that night, we turned off our SMTP server, copied everybody's mail files back to the primary system, and moved back the IP addresses.

The Big Cash-Out

In April 2000, I had a chance meeting with an old friend. My friend was starting up a new Internet service provider and wanted to know if I would be on the advisory board. What was going to make his new ISP different, he said, is that it would offer high-speed service in areas where cable and DSL were not available using unlicensed wireless equipment.

"What a coincidence," I told him. "Vineyard.NET has been using unlicensed wireless equipment for nearly five years! You don't want me on your advisory board—you want to hire me!"

In fact, he didn't only want to hire me; he wanted to hire me, Eric, and the rest of the Vineyard.NET crew, and, while he was at it, he decided that he might as well buy Vineyard.NET.

My friend's company was Broadband2Wireless (BB2W). The firm had more than $6 million in funding and was planning on closing a second round for $25 million or so by September 2000. Over the next few weeks we negotiated with him the purchase of Vineyard.NET by BB2W and guaranteed jobs for all of the Vineyard.NET employees.

Broadband2Wireless was a wild ride. Over the next three months the company grew from 3 employees to more than 60. Instead of planning a validating trial in one city, and then a careful build-out, we decided to launch in 6 cities by September 2000, then be in 20 cities by January 2001, and in 40 cities by January 2002. Why the rush? Because we were told that there was so much competition that if we didn't quickly grab a huge amount of potential market share, we would be unable to raise future money. "Grow big or go home," our venture capital financiers said.

Things did not go smoothly. One of the reasons was the change in the economy. In the spring of 2000, money was readily available—especially for big schemes that promised a huge return on investment from a billion-dollar market. But by the fall of 2000, the economy was cooling off: financiers were much more interested in sustainability than in unrestricted growth.

Amazingly, BB2W was able to close its second round of financing in the fall of 2000, with more than $20 million invested and a post-money valuation of more than $80 million. The company was elated. By the end of 2000, BB2W had an operational network in Boston, Miami, and Los Angeles, with an additional network deployed in New York and Atlanta.

Unfortunately, BB2W's continued growth depended upon the ability to raise additional rounds of funding—and in this endeavor the company was not successful. The business climate had finally caught up with BB2W. Despite having a working network with customers, the company was unable to raise its third round of funding, and BB2W was forced to lay off all of its employees and declare bankruptcy in June of 2001. The company had both grown big and gone home.

As luck would have it, even though BB2W planned to dissolve Vineyard.NET and fold the Vineyard-based operations into the main company, BB2W's staff never quite got around to the job. Vineyard.NET's payroll had been transferred to BB2W, but the rest of the company's contracts, business agreements, and long-term relationships remained otherwise intact. Vineyard.NET's systems had been largely neglected by BB2W—after all, the company was more interested in building a nationwide ISP than in maintaining a dialup ISP on Martha's Vineyard. Over the year, Vineyard.NET had lost a significant number of customers and one of its major resellers. So when BB2W declared bankruptcy, Vineyard.NET's original founders approached the bankruptcy trustee with an offer to repurchase the company. The court asked the trustee to solic offers from other ISPs and to advertise the sale on the Internet. But there were no other takers; apparently, few ISPs were interested in purchasing a dialup-only ISP with fewer than 1,400 customers, an ISP that was still located in my house. With no other offers, the trustee and the court approved the repurchase of Vineyard.NET by its original founders.

Thankfully, service for Vineyard.NET's remaining subscribers was never disrupted.

Conclusion

It's interesting to look back over Vineyard.NET's first six years of operation. On the one hand, we accomplished practically everything we set out to do. We created a self-sufficient company with a fairly large customer base. We created Perl scripts for managing user accounts, generating reports, and even submitting credit card numbers securely over the Internet to our merchant bank for payment. We grew the company to more than a thousand customers. We cashed out. And then we bought it back.

On the other hand, a lot of the diversions that we investigated never panned out. For example, we have that great software for billing credit cards, but we have never been able to sell it to anybody else—we couldn't even give it away. We spent many hours working on proposals for providing network service to schools and various businesses, only to be passed over for political reasons that had nothing to do with our technical capabilities. We deployed a cryptographic web server because our customers told us that we had to have one, and then nobody used it. All of that is pretty frustrating.

I learned a lot about Unix and computer security by running Vineyard.NET. The project added a good 200 pages to *Practical Unix & Internet Security* and was responsible for the creation of the book that you are reading now. On the other hand, running Vineyard.NET kept me from writing who knows how many other books.

As for the value of what we've created, I certainly would have made more money working for somebody other than myself. When Broadband2Wireless bought Vineyard.NET, my annual salary jumped from $30,000 to $140,000. When we bought Vineyard.NET back, my salary was suspended: Vineyard.NET simply could not afford to pay me.

The ultimate lesson that Vineyard.NET teaches is that it takes a lot more than the correct mix of technology to create a successful service. It takes the right people, the market, the customers, the market conditions, and a lot of luck.

APPENDIX B
The SSL/TLS Protocol

This appendix describes the SSL Version 3.0 protocol introduced in Chapter 5. It gives a general overview of the protocol that's appropriate for a semi-technical audience.

The Internet Engineering Task Force (IETF) Transport Layer Security (TLS) working group was established in 1996 to create an open stream encryption standard. The group began working with SSL Version 3.0 and, in 1999, published RFC 2246. "TLS Protocol Version 1.0" RFC 2712 adds Kerberos authentication to TLS. RFC 2817 and 2818 apply to TLS using HTTP/1.1.

TLS is a general-purpose protocol for encrypting web, email, and other stream-oriented information sent over the Internet. But while TLS may eventually supersede SSL, it could be years before this happens. Even once TLS becomes widely used, people may still call it SSL by sheer force of habit.

The charter for the TLS working group can be found at *http://www.ietf.org/html. charters/tls-charter.html*.

History

The SSL protocol was designed by Netscape Communications for use with Netscape Navigator. Version 1.0 of the protocol was used inside Netscape. Version 2.0 of the protocol shipped with Netscape Navigator Versions 1 and 2. After SSL 2.0 was published, Microsoft created a similar secure link protocol called PCT (described briefly in Chapter 5) that it claimed overcame some of SSL 2.0's shortcomings. However, PCT generally annoyed the rest of the industry, which claimed that Microsoft wasn't interested in working with standards bodies and was more interested in doing things its own way. The advances of PCT were incorporated into SSL 3.0, which was used as the basis for the TLS protocol developed by the IETF.

The TLS protocol is arranged in two layers:

- The TLS Record Protocol, which is responsible for transmitting blocks of information called records between the two computers.

- The TLS Handshake protocol, which manages key exchange, alerts, and cipher changes.

These two layers are built on top of a third layer, which is not strictly part of SSL:

- The data transport layer (usually TCP/IP)

These layers are illustrated in Figure B-1.

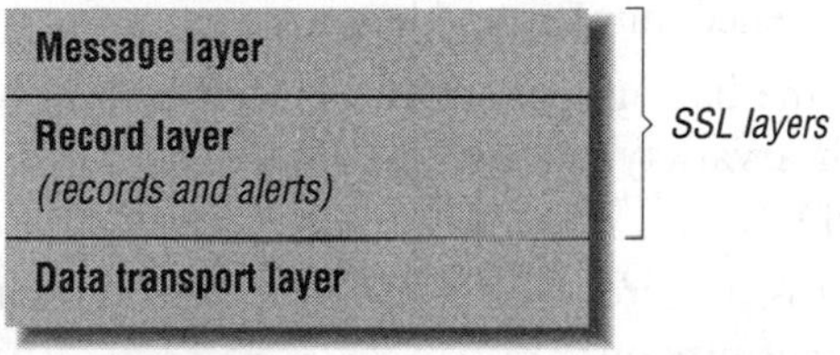

Figure B-1. SSL layers

TLS Record Layer

At the bottom layer of the TLS protocol is the TLS record layer. The record layer sends blocks of data, called *records*, between the client and the server. Each block can contain up to 16,383 bytes of data. Quoting from the original SSL specification and RFC 2246, "Client message boundaries are not preserved in the record layer." This means that if higher-level processes send multiple messages very quickly, those messages may be grouped together into a single record. Alternatively, they might be broken into many records—and they will be broken if they're longer than 16,383 bytes.

Each TLS record contains the following information:

- Content type
- Protocol version number
- Length
- Data payload (optionally compressed and encrypted)
- Message Authentication Code (MAC)[*]

Each record is compressed and encrypted according to the current compression algorithm and encryption algorithm. At the start of the connection, the compression function is defined as *CompressionMethod.null* and the encryption method is TLS_NULL_WITH_NULL_NULL—that is, there is no compression or encryption. Both

---

[*] The Content Type, Protocol Version, Length, and Data Payload are part of the TLSCompressed structure, while the MAC is part of the GenericStreamCipher or GenericBlockCipher structures. They are included together in this explanation for brevity.

the compression and encryption algorithms can be set during the "Hello" and changed during the course of the conversation.

The MAC is calculated using the formula:

```
HMAC_hash( MAC_write_secret, seq_num + TLSCompressed.type + TLSCompressed.version +
TLSCompressed.length + TLSCompressed.fragment))
```

where:

- *seq_num* is the sequence number for the message.
- *HMAC_hash()* is the hashing algorithm. HMAC is a keyed MAC function that can be used with a variety of hashing algorithms. TLS is typically used with either MD5 or SHA-1.
- *MAC_write_secret* is a secret shared between the SSL client and server that is used to validate transmission.
- *TLSCompressed.type* is the type of the record.
- *TLSCompressed.version* is the TLS version number.
- *TLSCompressed.length* is the length of the data fragment.
- *TLSCompressed.fragment* is the data itself.

The record layer provides for data integrity. The use of the MAC prevents replay attacks within a session, because each message has a unique sequence number. And the record layer provides for compression—this is important because once data is encrypted, it cannot be further compressed.

SSL/TLS Protocols

SSL and TLS protocols are specific types of messages that are sent using the record layer. The SSL v3.0/TLS standard defines three protocols:

- The Handshake protocol, which performs the initial key negotiation.
- The Alert protocol, which sends important messages about the state of the SSL/TLS connection from one side to the other.
- The ChangeCipherSpec protocol, which changes the encryption system currently in use.
- The application data protocol, which sends user data.

Handshake Protocol

The SSL Handshake protocol is used to authenticate the SSL server to the client (and optionally the client to the server) and to agree upon an initial encryption algorithm and keys. The Handshake protocol is described in the next major section.

Alert Protocol

Alerts are a specific type of message that can be transmitted by the SSL/TLS record layer. Alerts consist of two parts: an AlertLevel and an AlertDescription. Both are coded as single 8-bit numbers.

The SSL v3.0 and TLS 1.0 specifications define two alert levels.

Alert level	Level name	Meaning
1	Warning	SSL warnings indicate a problem that is not fatal.
2	Fatal	SSL fatal alerts immediately terminate the current SSL session.

SSL v3.0 and TLS 1.0 define the following alerts.

SSL alert number	TLS alert number	Alert name	Meaning
0	0	close_notify	Indicates that the sender will not send any more information. If a close_notify is sent with a warning alert level, the session may be resumed. If a close_notify is sent with a fatal alert level, the session may not be resumed.
10	10	unexpected_message	Inappropriate message was received. This alert should never occur; it indicates an error in one of the SSL implementations participating in the conversation.
20	20	bad_record_mac	Sender received a record with an incorrect MAC. Fatal.
N/A	21	decryption_failed	The received data could not be decrypted.
N/A	22	record_overflow	The decompressed data is larger than 16,383 bytes.
30	30	decompression_failure	Information in the record would not properly decompress. Fatal.
40	40	handshake_failure	Indicates that the sender was unable to negotiate an acceptable set of security parameters—for example, the sender was not satisfied with the encryption algorithms and strengths available on the recipient. Fatal.
41	N/A	no_certificate	Sent in response to a certification request if no appropriate certificate is available.
42	42	bad_certificate	Sent if a certification request fails—for example, if the certificate is corrupted, or the signature did not verify properly.
43	43	unsupported_certificate	Sent if the sender does not support the type of certificate sent by the recipient.
44	44	certificate_revoked	Sent if the sender receives a certificate that was already revoked.
45	45	certificate_expired	Sent if the sender receives a certificate that has expired.
46	46	certificate_unknown	Sent if some other error arises during the processing of the certificate.
47	47	illegal_parameter	Sent if the sender finds that another value in the handshake is out of range or inconsistent. Fatal.

SSL alert number	TLS alert number	Alert name	Meaning
N/A	48	unknown_ca	A valid certificate was provided, but the CA that signed the certificate (or the chain) is not recognized or not trusted.
N/A	49	access_denied	Access is not allowed because of access control restrictions that are in effect.
N/A	50	decode_error	The message could not be decoded because something is out of range.
N/A	51	decrypt_error	A cryptographic handshake failed or an encrypted value could not be decrypted properly.
N/A	60	export_restriction	This session is not in compliance with export restrictions and must be terminated.
N/A	70	protocol_version	The protocol requested by the client is recognized but not supported. (For example, an old protocol may no longer be permitted because of known security problems.)
N/A	71	insufficient_security	The server requires ciphers that are more secure than the client has, so this transaction will not be allowed to continue.
N/A	80	internal_error	Something is wrong—perhaps the client or the server ran out of memory or suffered a crash.
N/A	90	user_canceled	The user has asked to cancel the handshake operation.
N/A	100	no_renegotiation	Either the client or the server does not wish to renegotiate a key. This is a warning.

ChangeCipherSpec Protocol

The ChangeCipherSpec protocol is used to change from one encryption algorithm (called a *strategy* by the specification) to another.

To change the encryption algorithm, the client and server first negotiate a new CipherSpec and keys. They each then send a ChangeCipherSpec message, which causes the receiving process to start using the new CipherSpec and keys.

Although the CipherSpec is normally changed at the end of the SSL/TLS handshake, it can be changed at any time.

SSL 3.0/TLS Handshake

When a client connects to an SSL or TLS server, the SSL/TLS Handshake begins. The Handshake establishes the protocols that will be used during the communication, selects the cryptographic algorithms, authenticates the parties, and uses public key cryptography to create a *master secret*, from which encryption and authentication keys are derived.

The master secret for the session is created by the server using a premaster secret sent from the client.

The master secret is used to generate four more secrets (keys):

- An encryption key used for sending data from the client to the server.
- An encryption key used for sending data from the server to the client.
- An authentication key used for sending data from the client to the server.
- An authentication key used for sending data from the server to the client.

Sequence of Events

The Handshake is performed by a complex exchange between the client and the server. Optional items are indicated in brackets:

1. The client opens a connection and sends the ClientHello.
2. The server sends a ServerHello.
3. [The server sends its certificate.]
4. [The server sends a ServerKeyExchange.]
5. [The server sends a CertificateRequest.]
6. The server sends a ServerHelloDone (TLS only).
7. [The client sends its certificate.]
8. The client sends a ClientKeyExchange.
9. [The client sends a CertificateVerify.]
10. The client and server both send ChangeCipherSpec messages.
11. The client and server both send finished messages.
12. Application data flows.

With the exception of the secrets that are encrypted with the recipient's public key, the entire Handshake is sent unencrypted, in the clear. The secrets are then used to encrypt all subsequent communications.

1. ClientHello

The SSL/TLS ClientHello is a message that contains the information shown in Table B-1.

Table B-1. ClientHello message

Field	Meaning
ProtocolVersion `client_version`	The highest SSL/TLS version understood by the client. 3.0 for SSL 3.0; 3.1 for TLS 1.0.
Random `random`	A random structure (consisting of a 32-bit timestamp and 28 bytes generated by a secure random number generator).

Table B-1. ClientHello message (continued)

Field	Meaning
SessionID *session_id*	The session ID. Normally, this is empty to request a new session. A nonempty session ID field implies that the client is attempting to continue a previous SSL session. The client can specify 0 to force a new session for security reasons.
CipherSuite *cipher_suites*<2..2^{16}-1>	A list of the cipher suites that the client supports.
CompressionMethod *compression_methods* <1..2^{8}-1>	A list of the compression methods that the client supports.

After the client sends the ClientHello, it waits for the ServerHello message.

2. ServerHello

When the SSL/TLS server receives the ClientHello, it responds with either a *handshake_failure* alert or a ServerHello message.

The ServerHello message has the form shown in Table B-2.

Table B-2. ServerHello message

Field	Meaning
ProtocolVersion *client_version*	The SSL version used by the client (3.0).
Random *random*	A random structure (consisting of a 32-bit timestamp and 28 bytes generated by a secure random number generator).
SessionID *session_id*	The session ID. The server may return an empty *session_id* to indicate that the session will not be cached and therefore cannot be resumed. If it matches the *session_id* provided by the client in the ClientHello, it indicates that the previous session will be resumed. Otherwise, the *session_id* of the new session is provided.
CipherSuite *cipher_suite*	The cipher chosen by the server for this session.
CompressionMethod *compression_method*	The compression method chosen by the server for this session.

Notice that the server chooses the cipher suite and compression method to be used for the SSL/TLS connection. If the server does not implement or will not use any of the cipher suites and compression methods offered by the client, the server can simply send a *handshake_failure* alert and terminate the session.

3. Server certificate

After sending the ServerHello, the server may optionally send its certificate. The certificate consists of one or more X.509 v1, v2, or v3 certificates. (If the server uses the Fortezza cipher suite, the server certificate sent is a modified X.509 certificate.)

4. Server key exchange

The server sends the server key exchange message if the server has no certificate or if it has a certificate that is used only for signing. This might happen in one of three cases:

- The server is using the Diffie-Hellman key exchange protocol.
- The server is using RSA, but has a signature-only RSA key.
- The server is using the Fortezza/DMS encryption suite.

The key exchange message consists of the fields shown in Table B-3.

Table B-3. Server key exchange parameters

Field	Meaning
For Diffie-Hellman key exchange:	
ServerDHParams params	The server's Diffie-Hellman public value for p, g, and Ys (SSL only sends Ys).
For RSA:	
ProtocolVersion client_version	The most recent version of the SSL protocol supported by the client.
opaque random[46]	46 random bytes generated with a secure random number generator.
(encrypted with server's RSA public key)	
For Fortezza/DMS (not supported by TLS)	
opaque y_c<0..128>	The client's Yc value used in the Fortezza Key Exchange Algorithm (KEA).
opaque r_c[128]	The client's Rc value used in the KEA.
opaque wrapped_client_write_key[12]	The client's write key, wrapped by the Fortezza's token encryption key (TEK).
opaque wrapped_server_write_key[12]	The server's write key, wrapped by the Fortezza's TEK.
opaque client_write_IV[24]	The initialization vector (IV) for the client write key.
opaque server_write_IV[24]	The IV for the server write key.
opaque master_secret_IV[24]	The IV for the TEK used to encrypt the premaster secret.
block-ciphered opaque encrypted_pre_mater_secret[48]	48 bytes generated with a secure random number generator and encrypted using the TEK.

Signatures may be RSA signatures, DSA signatures, or anonymous (in which case there are no signatures). Servers that have no signatures offer no protection against man-in-the-middle or server substitution attacks.*

SSL 3.0 and TLS define three modes of Diffie-Hellman operations for the initial key exchange:

---

* A server substitution attack is an attack in which somebody replaces your server with theirs.

Anonymous Diffie-Hellman

In this mode, the server generates its Diffie-Hellman public value and the Diffie-Hellman parameters and sends them to the client. The client then sends back its client value. This mode is susceptible to the man-in-the-middle attack, because the server's parameters and public value are not authenticated. (In a man-in-the-middle attack, an attacker could simply conduct anonymous Diffie-Hellman with both parties.)

Fixed Diffie-Hellman

In this mode, the server's certificate contains its fixed Diffie-Hellman parameters instead of an RSA or DSS public key. Because SSL 3.0 allows only one key per server, a server that is configured to operate in fixed Diffie-Hellman mode cannot interoperate with SSL clients that expect to perform RSA key exchanges.

Ephemeral Diffie-Hellman

In this mode, the server generates its own Diffie-Hellman parameters, then uses a pre-existing RSA or DSS public key to sign the parameters, which are then sent to the client. This third mode appears to be the most secure SSL 3.0 operating mode.

Few commercial products implement the Diffie-Hellman SSL/TLS key exchange algorithms.

5. Certificate Request

If the server wishes to authenticate the client, it can send a Certificate Request to the client. Certificate Requests consist of five parts, shown in Table B-4.

Table B-4. Certificate Request message

Field	Meaning
ClientCertificateType certificate_types <1..2^8-1>	The types of certificates requested by the server.
Random random [SSL only]	A random structure (consisting of a 32-bit timestamp and 28 bytes generated by a secure random number generator).
SessionID session_id [SSL only]	The session ID. This field is never empty. If it matches the session_id provided by the client in the ClientHello, it indicates that the previous SSL session will be resumed. Otherwise, the session_id of the new session is provided.
CipherSuite cipher [SSL only]	The cipher chosen by the server for this session.
CompressionMethod compression_method [SSL only]	The compression method chosen by the server for this session.
DistinguishedName certificate_authorities <3..2^16-1> [TLS only]	A list of distinguished names of acceptable certificate authorities.

6. The server sends a ServerHelloDone (TLS only)

This step is performed only for TLS.

7. Client sends certificate

If requested by the server, the client sends any certificates that were requested. If no certificate is available, the client sends the *no certificate* alert.

It is up to the server to decide what to do if a no certificate alert is received. The server could continue the transaction with an anonymous client. Alternatively, the server could terminate the connection by sending a data handshake failure alert.

8. ClientKeyExchange

The client can send one of three kinds of key exchange messages, depending on the particular public key algorithm that has been selected. These are shown in Table B-5.

Table B-5. Server key exchange parameters

Field	Meaning
For Diffie-Hellman key exchange:	
opaque dh_Yc<1..2^16-1>	The client's Diffie-Hellman public value (Yc).
Signature signed_params	The signature for the parameters.
For RSA:	
ServerRSAarams *params*	The server's RSA parameters.
Structure *signed_params*	The signature for the parameters.
For Fortezza/DMS [SSL only]:	
ServerFortezzaParams *params*	The server's Fortezza parameters.

9. CertificateVerify

If the client sends a public certificate that has signing capability (such as an RSA or a DSS certificate), the client now sends a CertificateVerify message. This message consists of two message authentication codes, one calculated with the MD5 algorithm and one calculated with SHA. They are:

```
CertificateVerify.signature.md5_hash
         MD5(ClientHello.random + ServerHello.random + ServerParams);

CertificateVerify.signature.sha_hash
         SHA(ClientHello.random + ServerHello.random + ServerParams);
```

The *handshake_messages* refers to all handshake messages starting with the Client-Hello up to but not including the CertificateVerify message.

10. ChangeCipherSpec

After the CertificateVerify is sent, the ChangeCipherSpec message is sent. After the message is sent, all following messages are encrypted according to the specified cipher suite and compressed according to the compression method.

11. Finished

Finally, both the client and the server send finished messages. The finished message consists of the result of a pseudorandom function (another hash) that takes as arguments the master secret, the *finished_label*, and both the MD5 and SHA-1 of the handshake message.

The finished message verifies that both the client and server are in proper synchronization. If they aren't, then the SSL link is terminated.

12. Application Data

After the finished message is sent, application data is transported. All application data is divided into individual record-layer messages. These messages are then compressed and encrypted according to the current compression method and cipher suite.

P3P: The Platform for Privacy Preferences Project

This appendix was contributed by Lorrie Cranor of AT&T Labs—Research. It is copyright AT&T and reprinted with permission.

The Platform for Privacy Preferences Project (P3P), introduced in Chapter 24, provides a standard way for web sites to communicate about their data practices. Developed by the World Wide Web Consortium (W3C), P3P includes a machine-readable privacy policy syntax as well as a simple protocol that web browsers and other user agent tools can use to fetch P3P privacy policies automatically. P3P-enabled browsers can allow users to do selective cookie blocking based on site privacy policies, as well as to get a quick "snapshot" of a site's privacy policies.

This appendix provides an overview of how P3P works and how you can obtain and use it. For more information about P3P, see *http://www.w3.org/P3P/*. That site includes pointers to the complete P3P specification, lists of P3P software and P3P-enabled web sites, and more detailed instructions for using P3P on your web site. For a complete discussion of P3P and how you can use it to best advantage, see the forthcoming book, *P3P*, by Lorrie Cranor.

How P3P Works

The P3P specification includes a standard *vocabulary* for describing a web site's data practices, a set of *base data elements* that web sites can refer to in their P3P privacy policies, and a protocol for requesting and transmitting web site privacy policies.

The P3P protocol is a simple extension to the HTTP protocol. As shown in Figure C-1, P3P user agents use standard HTTP requests to fetch a P3P *policy reference file* from a "well-known location" on the web site to which a user is making a request.* The policy reference file indicates the location of the P3P *policy file* that

---

* For information about where the "well-known location" resides, see the section later in this chapter, "Helping User Agents Find Your Policy Reference File."

applies to each part of the web site. There might be one policy for the entire site, or several different policies, each of which covers a different part of the site. The user agent can then fetch the appropriate policy, parse it, and take action according to the user's preferences.

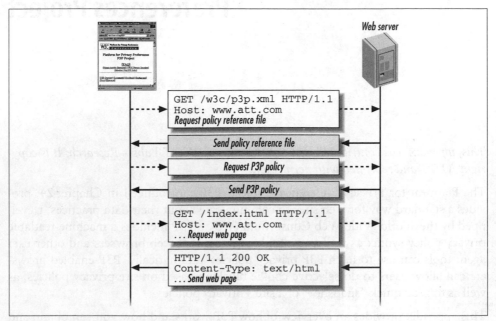

Figure C-1. The basic protocol for fetching a P3P policy.

P3P also allows sites to place policy reference files in locations other than the well-known location. In these cases, the site must declare the location of the policy reference file using a special HTTP header or by embedding a <LINK> tag in the HTML files to which the P3P policies apply.

Here's a plain English example of the kind of disclosure a web site might make in a P3P policy:

> Steve's Store strives to protect your privacy. When you come to our site to browse our catalog, we will not ask you to tell us who you are, and we will use data about your visit only to help us improve and secure our site. When you browse our site, we collect basic information about your computer and connection. We purge this information on a weekly basis. We also collect aggregate information on what pages consumers visit on our site.
>
> Steve's Store is a licensee of the PrivacySealExample Program. The PrivacySealExample Program ensures your privacy by holding web site licensees to high privacy standards and confirming with independent auditors that these information practices are being followed.
>
> Questions regarding this statement should be directed to: Steve's Store, 123 Steve Street, Bethesda, MD 20814 USA, Email: steve@stevesstore.com, Telephone (301)

392-6753. If you are not satisfied with our response to your inquiry, you may contact PrivacySealExample at *http://www.privacyseal.example.org*. Steve's Store will correct all errors or wrongful actions arising in connection with the privacy policy.

And here's what this policy would look like using the P3P syntax and encoding:

```
<POLICIES xmlns="http://www.w3.org/2000/12/P3Pv1">
<POLICY discuri="http://www.stevesstore.com/privacy.html"
 name="policy1">
 <ENTITY>
  <DATA-GROUP>
   <DATA ref="#business.name">Steve's Store</DATA>
   <DATA ref="#business.contact-info.postal.street">
        123 Steve Street</DATA>
   <DATA ref="#business.contact-info.postal.city">Bethesda</DATA>
   <DATA ref="#business.contact-info.postal.stateprov">MD</DATA>
   <DATA ref="#business.contact-info.postal.postalcode">20814</DATA>
   <DATA ref="#business.contact-info.postal.country">USA</DATA>
   <DATA ref="#business.contact-info.online.email">
        steve@stevesstore.com</DATA>
   <DATA ref="#business.contact-info.telecom.telephone.intcode">1</DATA>
   <DATA ref="#business.contact-info.telecom.telephone.loccode">301</DATA>
   <DATA ref="#business.contact-info.telecom.telephone.number">
        3926753</DATA>
  </DATA-GROUP>
 </ENTITY>
 <ACCESS><nonident/></ACCESS>
 <DISPUTES-GROUP>
  <DISPUTES resolution-type="independent"
    service="http://www.PrivacySeal.example.org"
    short-description="PrivacySeal.example.org">
   <IMG src=http://www.PrivacySeal.example.org/Logo.gif
        alt="PrivacySealExample logo"/>
   <REMEDIES><correct/></REMEDIES>
  </DISPUTES>
 </DISPUTES-GROUP>
 <STATEMENT>
  <PURPOSE><admin/><develop/></PURPOSE>
  <RECIPIENT><ours/></RECIPIENT>
  <RETENTION><stated-purpose/></RETENTION>
  <DATA-GROUP>
   <DATA ref="#dynamic.clickstream"/>
   <DATA ref="#dynamic.http"/>
  </DATA-GROUP>
 </STATEMENT>
</POLICY>
</POLICIES>
```

If you are familiar with XML (Extensible Markup Language), this encoding may look familiar to you. It is important to note that P3P policies are not designed to be read by end users. User agents will interpret these policies on a user's behalf. In addition, every policy should contain the URL of the web site's human-readable privacy policy.

Deploying P3P

Some of the first questions webmasters ask when they are considering deploying P3P on their sites are "How long is this going to take?" and "How difficult is this going to be?" The answers to these questions, of course, depend on the details of each particular web site. A small company that already has a privacy policy posted on its site should be able to deploy P3P in a few hours—the technical work may even take less than 15 minutes. A large company may need to have their attorneys spend time reviewing their P3P policy, and they may need to figure out the best way to deploy P3P on a large number of servers around the world. Companies that provide "third-party" web services, such as advertising agencies and content distribution networks, may have some more complicated decisions to make as well.

To help you estimate how much work it will be for you to deploy P3P on your web site, here is an outline of the basic steps involved.

Create a privacy policy.

The privacy policy needs to include enough details to be able to use it to create a P3P policy. If you have already created a detailed policy for your site, you may still have a few questions that you have to revisit when you create your P3P policy, but you will have already done most of the difficult work. If you don't yet have a privacy policy or your policy does not go into much detail about the kinds of data your site collects or how this data is used, you will probably have to get your company's lawyers or policy makers involved in figuring out what your company's privacy policy is.

Determine whether you want to have one P3P policy for your entire site or different P3P policies for different parts of your site.

If you already have multiple privacy policies for your site, then you will probably want to have multiple P3P policies as well. For example, some sites have different policies associated with different types of services they offer. Even if you have a single, comprehensive policy for your entire site, you may want to have multiple P3P policies. For example, your site's privacy policy might include a statement like "We do not collect personally identifiable information from visitors except when they fill out a form to order a product from us." You might wish to create two P3P policies: one for use on most of your site where there are no forms, and the other for use specifically on the parts of the site where visitors fill out forms to order products.

Create a P3P policy (or policies) for your site.

You can use one of the P3P policy generator tools to easily create a P3P policy without having to learn XML. You will need to have a detailed understanding about the kinds of data your site collects and how they are used—but most of this should be documented in your site's privacy policy.

Create a policy reference file for your site.

Most of the policy generator tools will help you create a policy reference file for your site too. This file lists all of the P3P policies on your site and the parts of your site to which they apply. In most circumstances you will have just one policy reference file for your entire site. However, if you have a very large number of policies on your site or if you don't wish to provide information that would reveal the structure of your site (perhaps due to security considerations if parts of your site are password protected), you may wish to have multiple policy reference files.

Configure your server for P3P.

On most sites this can be done by simply placing the P3P policy and policy reference files on the web server in the proper locations. However, some sites will want to configure their servers to send a special P3P header with every HTTP response, and some will want to add <LINK> tags to their HTML content. Some sites will also want to send compact versions of P3P policies with SET_COOKIE requests.

Test your site to make sure it is properly P3P enabled.

The W3C P3P Validator tool can be used to test your site and report back a list of any problems it finds. Of course, this tool cannot verify that your P3P policy matches your privacy policy or that either policy conforms to your actual practices. But it can make sure that your policy and policy reference files are syntactically correct and that you've configured everything properly. You can try the W3C P3P Validator at *http://www.w3.org/P3P/validator/*.

Creating a Privacy Policy

Your policy should include enough detail to answer the questions you will have to answer to create a P3P policy. Here's a basic outline of the points that you should cover:

- The name and contact information for your company or organization.

- A statement about the kind of access you provide (do you let people find out what information you hold about them, and if so, how can they get this access?).

- A statement about what privacy laws you comply with, what privacy seal programs you participate in, and other mechanisms available to your customers for resolving privacy disputes. This statement may also describe what remedies you offer should a privacy policy breach occur.

- A description of the kinds of data you collect. If your web site uses cookies, be sure to mention this too and explain how the cookies are used.

- A description of how collected data is used, and whether individuals can opt-in or opt-out of any of these uses.

- Information about whether data may be shared with other companies, and if so, under what conditions and whether or not consumers can opt-in or opt-out of this.

- Information about your site's data retention policy, if any.

- Information about how consumers can take advantage of opt-in or opt-out opportunities.

P3P doesn't cover web site security practices, but most privacy policies also include a statement about the site's commitment to security. And web sites with content aimed at children often describe their policy with respect to children's data.

Generating a P3P Policy and Policy Reference File

If your privacy policy is fairly simple (or if you happen to enjoy writing XML), you may want to write your P3P policy and policy reference file by hand in XML, perhaps cutting and pasting from one of our examples. However, most people will probably opt to use a P3P policy generator program.

One good P3P policy generator you may want to try is the P3P Policy Editor from IBM. This tool features a drag-and-drop interface, shown in Figure C-2, that lets you edit P3P policies by dragging icons representing P3P data elements and data categories into an editing window. The tool also has pop-up windows that let you set the properties associated with each data element (purpose, recipient, etc.) and also fill out general information about the site's privacy practices. You can view the XML that has been created as you add each data element, as well as a corresponding human-readable version of the policy. There is also a useful errors tab that indicates problems with your policy, such as leaving out information in required fields. The tool comes with good documentation and a set of templates for typical web sites. This tool can also create policy reference files. It is available for free download from the IBM Alphaworks web site at *http://www.alphaworks.ibm.com/tech/p3peditor*.

Helping User Agents Find Your Policy Reference File

The P3P specification has designated */w3c/p3p.xml* as the "well-known location" for policy reference files. P3P user agents will check this location automatically for a policy reference file at every site they visit. If they can't find a policy reference file at a site, they will keep rechecking once every 24 hours if the user returns to that site.

Most web sites should be able to place their policy reference file at the well-known location without a problem. However, for sites that do not wish to do this, two alternatives are offered: sites can be configured to send a special P3P header with every HTTP response, or <LINK> tags can be embedded in HTML documents that give the location of the policy reference file.

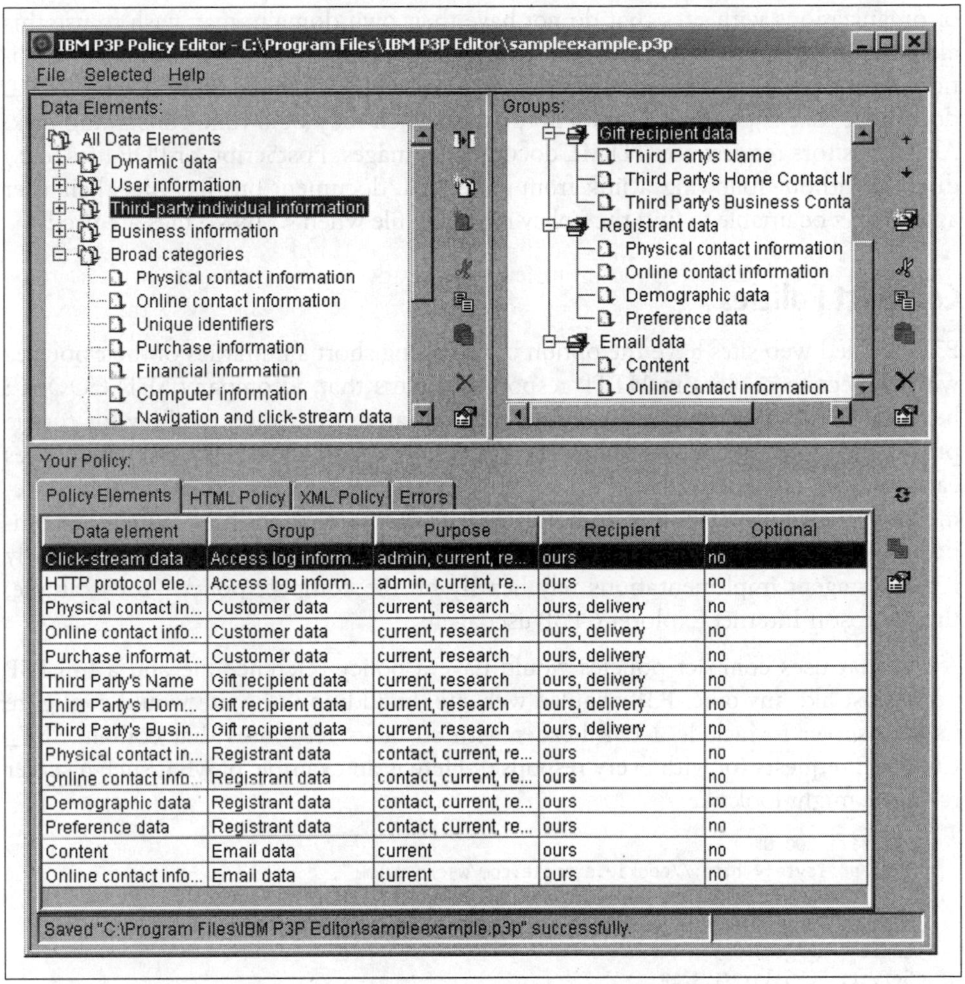

Figure C-2. The IBM P3P Policy Editor features a drag-and-drop interface.

The HTTP header alternative is most useful for sites that have decided to use multiple policy reference files. It allows sites to send a pointer to the policy reference file applicable to each request. The downside of using the HTTP header instead of the well-known location is that there is no way for a user agent to know a site's policy before requesting a resource. Thus, some user agents may suppress cookies, referer headers, or other information until they receive the P3P response header.

The HTML <LINK> tag alternative was designed primarily for sites in which content providers have access only to a designated area of the web server (which does not include the */w3c* directory) and do not have the ability to configure the server to send extra HTTP response headers. For example, students who wish to provide a privacy policy on a personal home page hosted on a university server, or individuals or organizations with sites that do not have their own domain, may wish to use this alternative. This alternative has the same drawbacks as the HTTP header. In addition, sites that wish to use this alternative must add a <LINK> tag to every HTML document that is covered by the P3P policy, which may be a time-consuming task. Also, if visitors request non-HTML documents (images, PostScript, or PDF files, etc.) directly without following a link from an HTML document on that site, their user agents may be unable to find the policy reference file when <LINK> tags are used.

Compact Policies

P3P-enabled web sites have the option of providing short summaries of their policies with respect to cookies in HTTP response headers that accompany SET_COOKIE headers. These compact policies are designed as an optimization to allow for cookie processing to proceed at the same time that a full P3P policy is being evaluated. Sites can only use compact policies if they set cookies, and if their cookie-related statements in their full P3P policy do not include mandatory extensions. While the compact policy is entirely optional for P3P-enabled web sites, note that some of the early P3P user agent implementations rely heavily on the compact policy—for example, the Microsoft Internet Explorer 6 P3P user agent.

A site that uses compact policies would have a policy reference file and a full P3P policy just like any other P3P-enabled web site. In addition, the site would configure its web server to include a P3P header with all of its responses that contain SET_ COOKIE requests (or with every response). Here is an example of what such a server response might look like:

```
HTTP/1.1 200 OK
P3P: policyref="http://cookie.example.com/w3c/p3p.xml",
    CP="NON DSP ADM DEV PSD CUSo OUR IND STP PRE NAV UNI"
Content-Type: text/html
Content-Length: 8934
Server: CC-Galaxy/1.3.19
```

Most of the P3P policy generator tools will also generate compact policies.

Simple P3P-Enabled Web Site Example

Many sites, including personal home pages and sites designed primarily to provide information (as opposed to those designed to sell things or provide interactive services), have very simple privacy policies. They tend to collect minimal amounts of data, and generally will either commit to using that data in very limited ways, or make no commitment that might limit future use of that data. Furthermore, for these simple sites one P3P policy is probably sufficient for the entire site.

Example C-1 is a policy reference file for a simple site named Example.Com that has one policy for the entire site. This policy reference file is placed at the well-known location (*/w3c/p3p.xml*). This file also includes the site's P3P policy. The policy reference file and policy expiry are set to 10 days. The policy for this site also applies to all the cookies set by this site. Example.com keeps typical web logs. These logs are kept indefinitely and are used to diagnose problems with the web site. They are not shared with other companies; however, they are sometimes analyzed in order to gain insights into how people are using the web site.

Example C-1. A policy reference file for a simple site that includes an inline policy

```
<META xmlns="http://www.w3.org/2000/12/P3Pv1">
  <POLICY-REFERENCES>
    <EXPIRY max-age="864000"/> <!-- 10 days -->
    <POLICY-REF about="#policy1">
      <INCLUDE>/*</INCLUDE>
      <COOKIE-INCLUDE>* .example.com *</COOKIE-INCLUDE>
    </POLICY-REF>
  </POLICY-REFERENCES>
  <POLICIES>
  <POLICY discuri = "http://www.example.com/privacy/policy.html"
    name="policy1">

    <EXPIRY max-age="864000"/> <!-- 10 days -->
    <ENTITY>
      <DATA-GROUP>
        <DATA ref="business.name">Example Corp.</DATA>
        <!-- it's a good idea to include an email address or
             other contact information here as well -->
      </DATA-GROUP>
    </ENTITY>
    <ACCESS><nonident/></ACCESS> <!-- no identified data is collected -->
    <!-- if the site has a dispute resolution procedure that it follows,
         a DISPUTES-GROUP should be included here -->
    <STATEMENT>
      <PURPOSE><current/><admin/><develop/></PURPOSE>
      <RECIPIENT><ours/></RECIPIENT>
      <RETENTION><indefinitely/><RETENTION>
      <DATA-GROUP>
        <DATA ref="#dynamic.clickstream"/>
        <DATA ref="#dynamic.http"/>
      </DATA-GROUP>
    </STATEMENT>
  </POLICY>
  </POLICIES>
</META>
```

APPENDIX D

The PICS Specification

The PICS specification introduced in Chapter 23 consists of two parts:

- A specification for the protocols that must be supported by a rating service. This specification is located at *http://w3.org/PICS/services.html*.

- A specification for the format of the labels themselves. This specification is located at *http://w3.org/PICS/labels.html*.

An excellent article describing PICS is "PICS: Internet Access Controls Without Censorship," by Paul Resnick and James Miller, *Communications of the ACM,* October 1996, p. 87. The online version of the article is at *http://w3.org/PICS/iacwcv2.html*.

Rating Services

The PICS rating service specifications are designed to enable many different kinds of ratings services on the World Wide Web. A rating service is any person, organization, or other entity that issues ratings. Ratings can be distributed with the document being rated, by a third-party site, on a CD-ROM, or by any other electronic means.

The PICS standard specifies a syntax for text files that describe the different kinds of ratings that a rating service can issue. This lets computer programs automatically parse the kinds of ratings that a service provides.

In their article describing PICS, Resnick and Miller create a sample PICS rating service based on the MPAA's movie-rating scheme:

```
((PICS-version 1.0)
  (rating-system "http://moviescale.org/Ratings/Description/")
  (rating-service "http://moviescale.org/v1.0")
  (icon "icons/moviescale.gif")
  (name "The Movies Rating Service")
  (description "A rating service based on the MPAA's movie rating scale")
  (category
   (transmit-as "r")
   (name "Rating")
```

```
(label (name "G") (value 0) (icon "icons/G.gif"))
(label (name "PG") (value 1) (icon "icons/PG.gif"))
(label (name "PG-13") (value 2) (icon "icons/PG-13.gif"))
(label (name "R") (value 3) (icon "icons/R.gif"))
(label (name "NC-17") (value 4) (icon "icons/NC-17.gif"))))
```

This rating description indicates a location where information about the rating system and service can be found, gives it a name, and creates a single rating category called *Rating*. Rated objects can have one of five different ratings: *G, PG, PG-13, R,* or *NC-17*. The standard gives each of these ratings a value and an associated icon to be displayed with the rating.

The PICS rating service description is defined to have a MIME file type *application/ pics-service*. The file is formatted as a list.

The PICS format makes extensive use of name/value pairs. These are formatted as *(name value)*. They are interpreted as "*name* has the value of *value*." For example, *(min 0.0)* means that the particular object being described has a minimum value of 0.0.

The following names are used to describe the ratings services themselves:

PICS-version aVersion
> The version number of the PICS standard being supported. Should be 1.1.

rating-system aURL
> A URL that indicates the location of a human-readable description of the categories, scales, and intended criteria for assigning ratings.

rating-service aURL
> A URL that denotes the location of information used by the rating service itself. This URL is used as the basic URL for all icons and database queries.

icon aString
> An icon associated with the particular object that is being described.

name aName
> A human-readable name of the object being described.

description aDescription
> A human-readable description of the object being described.

category
> Introduces a list of elements used to denote a particular category that is supported by this rating service.

If a list begins with the atom *category*, then the list contains a list of name/value pairs that are used to describe a particular ratings category. The following are supported:

transmit-as aString
> The name of the category when it is transmitted in a PICS label.

name aName
> The name of the category itself.

min aNumber
> The minimum value that a label in this category can have.

max aNumber
> The maximum value that a label in this category can have.

multivalue aBoolean
> Indicates that an object can have more than one label in the category. Has a value of true or false.

unordered aBoolean
> Indicates that the order in which labels are reported has no significance. Can be true or false.

label
> Introduces a list of elements that describe a particular label.

Integer
> Indicates that the label is transmitted as an integer. By default, PICS ratings are not integers.

Each PICS label is further described by a collection of name/value pairs:

name aValue
> The name of the label and its value.

Ratings services can operate label bureaus. A label bureau is "a computer system which supplies, via a computer network, ratings of documents. It may or may not provide the documents themselves."

PICS Labels

The PICS label specification defines the syntax for document labels. Labels can be obtained over the Web from a search service using an HTTP extension defined in the PICS standard. Alternatively, labels can be automatically included with a document, as part of the document's header.

Here is a PICS label that ranks a URL using the service described in the previous section:

```
(PICS-1.0 "http://moviescale.org/v1.0"
 labels
  on "2002.6.01T00:01-0500"
  until "2002.12.31T23:59-0500"
  for "http://www.missionimpossible.com/"
  by "Simson L. Garfinkel"
  ratings (r 0))
```

This label describes the web site for the Paramount movie *Mission: Impossible* using the fictitious labeling service described in the previous section. The label was created on June 1, 2002, and is valid until December 31, 2002. The label is for information stored at the URL *http://www.missionimpossible.com/*. The label was written by Simson L. Garfinkel. Finally, the label gives the rating "(r 0)."

Although the movie *Mission: Impossible* had a rating of "R," the web site has a rating of "G." (The value "G" is transmitted with 0 using the *http://moviescale.org/v1.0* rating service.)

Ratings may include more than one transmitted value. For example, if a rating service defined two scales, a label rating might look like this: "(r 3 n 4)."

Labels can be substantially compressed by removing nearly all information except the ratings themselves. For example, the previous label could be transmitted like this:

```
(PICS-1.0 "http://moviescale.org/v1.0"
 r 0)
```

Labels can optionally include an MD5 message digest hash of the labeled document. This allows software to determine if the fetched document has been modified in any way since the label was created. Labels can also have digital signatures, which allows labeling services to sign their own labels. That would allow a site to distribute labels for its content that were created by a third-party labeling service and give users the assurance that the labels have not been modified in any way.

Here is a complete description of all of the fields in revision 5 of the label format.

Information about the document that is labeled

at quoted-ISO-date
> The modification date of the item being rated. The standard proposes using the modification date "as a less expensive, but less reliable, alternative to the message integrity check (MIC) options."

MIC-md5 "Base64-string"
or MD5 "Base64-string"*
> The MD5 hash value of the item being rated

Information about the document label itself:

by name
> The name of the person or organization that rated the item. The *name*, like all strings in the label specification, may be either a human-readable quoted name or a Base64 encoded string.

for URL
> The URL of the item to which this rating applies.

---

* The names "MIC-md5" and "MD5" are synonyms. According to Miller, the standard allows the use of either "MIC-md5" or "MD5" in a label so that the label's author may choose between completeness and compactness. Others might reasonably infer that allowing both of these synonyms to be present in the standard was the result of an argument between members of the PICS committee as to which tag should be used.

generic boolean

If Boolean is "true," the label applies to all items that are prefaced by the "for" URL. This is useful for rating an entire site or set of documents within a particular directory. If false, the rating applies only to this document.

on quoted-ISO-date

The date on which the rating was issued.

signature-RSA-MD5 "Base64-string"

An RSA digital signature for the label.

until quoted-ISO-date
exp quoted-ISO-date

The date on which this rating expires.

Other information:

comment acomment

A comment. It's not supposed to be read by people.

complete-label quotedURL
full quotedURL

A URL of the complete label. The idea of this field is that an abridged label might be sent with a document in the interest of minimizing transmission time. Then, if a piece of software wants the complete label, that software can get it from the quotedURL.

extension quotedURL data

Extensions are a formal means by which the PICS standard can be extended. The *extension* keyword introduces additional data that is used by an extension. Each extension must include a URL that indicates where the extension is documented. This is designed to avoid duplication of extension names. For example, both China and Singapore could adopt "monitoring" extensions that might be used to transmit to the web browser a unique serial number used to track every download of every labeled document. However, the two countries might adopt slightly different monitoring extensions. As one extension would have a URL of *http://censorship.gov.cn/monitoring.html* and the other would have a URL of *http://censorship.gov.sg/monitoring.html*, the two extensions would not conflict even though they had the same name. A list of extensions currently in use appears at *http://w3.org/PICS/extensions*. There were no such extensions at the time this book was published.

Labeled Documents

The PICS standard allows for PICS labels to be automatically transmitted with any message that uses an RFC 822 header. These headers are used by Internet email, HTTP, and Usenet news protocols. This allows for convenient labeling of information transmitted over these systems.

The PICS RFC 822 header is PICS-Label. The format is:

```
PICS-Label: labellist
```

For example, the following email message might contain some explicit, racy material. Or, it might be about some medical experiments. Or maybe it has to do with one roommate playing a joke on another after a party. Or it could be an exercise in surreal literature. Whatever it may be, we can use the PICS label to determine something about content and whether we should avoid reading the full text, thereby saving ourselves from shock and embarrassment. (Alternatively, we could use the labels to quickly scan a mail archive and zero in on the "good ones"):

```
To: saras@ex.com
From: wendy@ex.com
Date: Tue, 26 Nov 2002 14:05:55 -0500
Subject: Last Night
PICS-Label: (PICS-1.1 "http://www.rsac.org/1.0/" v 0 s 4 n 4 l 4)

Dearest Sara,

You passed out last night before the action really got started, so I wanted to send
you a detailed description of what we did ...
```

Requesting PICS Labels by HTTP

PICS defines an extension to the HTTP protocol that allows you to request a PICS header along with the document. The extension requires that you send a Protocol-Request command after the HTTP GET command. The Protocol-Request command contains a tag that allows you to specify which PICS service labels you wish.

For example, to request a document using HTTP with the RSAC labels, a client might send an HTTP request such as this:

```
GET / HTTP/1.0
Protocol-Request: {PICS-1.1 {params minimal {services "http://www.rsac.org/1.0"}}}
```

The keyword "minimal" in the HTTP request specifies the amount of information that is requested. Options include minimal, short, full, and complete-label.

A PICS-enabled HTTP server might respond with this:

```
Date: Fri, 29 Nov 1996 21:43:40 GMT
Server: Stronghold+PICS/1.3.2 Ben-SSL/1.3 Apache/1.1.1
Content-type: text/html
PICS-Label: (PICS-1.1 "http://www.rsac.org/1.0/" v 0 s 0 n 2 l 0)

<HTML>
<HEAD>
<TITLE>Welcome to Deus Ex Machina Software, Inc.</TITLE>
...
```

Requesting a Label from a Rating Service

The PICS standard also defines a way to request a label for a particular URL from a rating service. A rating service might be run by anybody. In 1996, the Simon Wiesenthal Center conducted a campaign asking Internet service providers to block access to Nazi hate literature that was on the Web; an alternative recommended by Resnick and Miller is that the Simon Wiesenthal Center could run a rating service, rating documents on the Web based on their view of the historical accuracy and propaganda level. SurfWatch, a vendor of blocking software, might run its own rating service that indicated the amount of nudity, sex, violence, and profane language based on each particular document. Fundamentalist religious groups could rate pages on adherence to their particular beliefs. And militia groups could run a rating service that would put up increasing numbers of little black helicopter icons for pages they suspect have fallen under United Nations control. The potential is limited only by one's free time.

Rating services are supposed to respond to HTTP GET requests that encode database lookups in URLs. URLs should look like this:[*]

```
http://service.net/Ratings?opt=generic&u="http://www.some.com/somedoc.html"&s="http:/
/www.some.rating.company/service.html"
```

Several options are defined:

opt=normal
> This indicates that the label for the URLs specified should be sent. If no label is available for the specific URL, the server may send a generic URL or a URL for an ancestor URL. Omitting the opt completely has the same result.

opt=tree
> This requests a tree of labels—that is, all of the labels for the site or for the requested subpart of the site.

opt=generic+tree
> This requests a generic label for the specified tree.

u=objectURL
> This specifies the URL for which a label is desired. More than one URL may be requested by including multiple u= specifications.

s=serviceURL
> This specifies the URL for the particular rating service that is desired. If multiple services are requested, a label is returned for each.

---

[*] When the URL is actually sent an HTTP GET request, it must be properly encoded. For example, the characters %3A must be used to represent a ":" and the characters %2F must be used to represent a "/". This encoding is specified by RFC 1738.

format=aformat

> Specifies which format of labels are requested.

extension=aString

> Specifies an extension that should be in effect for the label that is requested.

Thus, if a web browser were communicating with a rating service, the actual message sent to port 80 of the web server at *service.net* would be:

```
GET /Ratings?opt=generic&u="http%3A%2F%2Fwww.some.com%2Fsomedoc.html"
&s="http%3A%2F%2Fwww.some.rating.company%2Fservice.html" HTTP/1.0
```

This message would be sent as a single line without a break or space.

References

The field of web security, and computer security in general, is large and growing larger every day. Rather than attempting to list all of the many useful references, we'll note the ones we think especially appropriate. For a more extensive and up-to-date listing of references, we recommend that you pursue an online reference such as the CERIAS hotlist (cited below). Appendixes D through F of *Practical Unix & Internet Security*, although somewhat dated, still contain a great deal of highly useful material. The CERIAS hotlist has thousands of references to Internet-based sources of security information; the *PUIS* book has almost 50 pages of references to journals, organizations, books, papers, and other resources in the indicated appendixes.

Electronic References

There is a certain irony in trying to include a comprehensive list of electronic resources in a printed book such as this one. Electronic resources such as web pages, newsgroups, and mailing lists are updated on an hourly basis; new releases of computer programs can be published every few weeks. Books, on the other hand, are infrequently updated.

We present the following electronic resources with the understanding that this list necessarily can be neither complete nor completely up to date. What we hope, instead, is that it is expansive. By reading it, we hope that you will gain insight into places to look for future developments in web security. Along the way, you may find some information you can put to immediate use.

Mailing Lists

There are many mailing lists that cover security-related material. We describe a few of the major ones here. However, this is not to imply that only these lists are worthy of mention! There may well be other lists of which we are unaware, and many of the lesser-known lists often have a higher volume of good information.

Never place blind faith in anything you read in a mailing list, especially if the list is unmoderated. There are a number of self-styled experts on the Net who will not hesitate to volunteer their views, whether knowledgeable or not. Usually their advice is benign, but sometimes it is quite dangerous. There may also be people who are providing bad advice on purpose, as a form of vandalism. And certainly there are times when the real experts make a mistake or two in what they recommend in an offhand note posted to the Net.

There are some real experts on these lists who are (happily) willing to share their knowledge with the community, and their contributions make the Internet a better place. However, keep in mind that simply because you read it on the network does not mean that the information is correct for your system or environment, does not mean that it has been carefully thought out, does not mean that it matches your site policy, and most certainly does not mean that it will help your security. *Always* carefully evaluate the information you receive before acting on it.

Following are some of the major mailing lists.

Bugtraq

Bugtraq is a full-disclosure computer security mailing list. This list features detailed discussion of Unix security holes: what they are, how to exploit them, and what to do to fix them. This list is not intended to be about cracking systems or exploiting their vulnerabilities (although that is known to be the intent of some of the subscribers). It is, instead, about defining, recognizing, and preventing use of security holes and risks. To subscribe, send "subscribe bugtraq" in the body of a message to *bugtraq-request@securityfocus.com* or use the form at *http://www.securityfocus.com/forums/bugtraq/intro.html*.

CERT-advisory

New CERT/CC (Computer Emergency Response Team Coordination Center) advisories of security flaws and fixes for Internet systems are posted to this list. This list makes somewhat boring reading; often the advisories are so watered down that you cannot easily figure out what is actually being described. Nevertheless, the list does have its bright spots. Send subscription requests to *cert-advisory-request@cert.org* or use the form at *http://www.cert.org/contact_cert/certmaillist.html*.

Archived past advisories are available from *info.cert.org* via the Web at:

> *http://www.cert.org/advisories/*

CIAC-notes and C-Notes

The staff at the Department of Energy CIAC (Computer Incident Advisory Capability) publish helpful technical notes on an infrequent basis. These are very often tutorial in nature. To subscribe to the list, send a message with "subscribe ciac-notes yourname" in the message body to *ciac-listproc@llnl.gov*. Or, you may simply wish to browse the archive of old notes:

http://www.ciac.org/cgi-bin/cnotes

Firewalls

The Firewalls mailing list is the primary forum for folks on the Internet who want to discuss the design, construction, operation, maintenance, and philosophy of Internet firewall security systems. To subscribe, send a message to *firewalls-request@lists.gnac.net* with "subscribe firewalls" in the body of the message.

The Firewalls mailing list is high volume (sometimes more than 100 messages per day, although usually it is only several dozen per day). To accommodate subscribers who don't want their mailboxes flooded with lots of separate messages from Firewalls, there is also a Firewalls-Digest mailing list available. Subscribers to Firewalls-Digest receive daily (more frequent on busy days) digests of messages sent to Firewalls, rather than each message individually. Firewalls-Digest subscribers get all the same messages as Firewalls subscribers; that is, Firewalls-Digest is not moderated, just distributed in digest form.

Subscription information and archives can be found at:

http://lists.gnac.net/firewalls/

NTBugTraq

NTBugTraq is a mailing list dedicated to discussion of exploits in the Windows NT operating system. To subscribe, send "subscribe ntbugtraq firstname lastname" to *listserv@listserv.ntbugtraq.com*:

http://www.ntbugtraq.com/

NT-security

The NT-security mailing list is for discussions of problems with Windows NT security. It is hosted by ISS. To subscribe, send "subscribe ntsecurity" or "subscribe ntsecurity-digest" to *request-ntsecurity@iss.net*.

RISKS

RISKS is officially known as the ACM Forum on Risks to the Public in the Use of Computers and Related Systems. It's a moderated forum for discussion of risks to society from computers and computerization. Send email subscription requests to *RISKS-Request@csl.sri.com*.

Back issues are available from *crvax.sri.com* via anonymous FTP and HTTP:

ftp://crvax.sri.com/risks/
http://catless.ncl.ac.uk/Risks

RISKS is also distributed as the *comp.risks* Usenet newsgroup, and this is the preferred method of subscription.

Usenet Groups

There are several Usenet newsgroups that you might find to be interesting sources of information on network security and related topics. However, the unmoderated lists are the same as other unmoderated groups on the Usenet: repositories of material that is often off-topic, repetitive, and incorrect. Our warning about material found in mailing lists, expressed earlier, applies doubly to newsgroups.

alt.security
   Alternative discussions of computer and network security

comp.admin.policy
   Computer administrative policy issues, including security

comp.protocols.tcp-ip
   TCP/IP internals, including security

comp.risks (moderated)
   As described previously

comp.security.announce (moderated)
   Computer security announcements, including new CERT/CC advisories

comp.security.unix
   Unix security

comp.security.misc
   Miscellaneous computer and network security

comp.security.firewalls
   Information about firewalls

comp.unix.admin
   Unix system administration, including security

comp.unix.wizards
   Unix kernel internals, including security

comp.virus (moderated)
   Information on computer viruses and related topics

netscape.public.mozilla.security
netscape.public.mozilla.crypto
   Information on JavaScript security and SSL in Netscape and Mozilla

sci.crypt
   Discussions about cryptology research and application

sci.crypt.research (moderated)
   Discussions about cryptology research

Web Pages and FTP Repository

There are dozens of security-related web pages with pointers to other information. Some pages are comprehensive, and others are fairly narrow in focus. The ones we list here provide a good starting point for any browsing you might do. You will find most of the other useful directories linked into one or more of these pages, and you can then build your own set of "bookmarks."

Attrition.org

There is information about hacking available at:

http://www.attrition.org/

CERIAS

CERIAS is the world's foremost university center for multidisciplinary research and education in areas of information security (computer security, network security, and communications security), and information assurance. It is intended to function with close ties to researchers and engineers in major companies and government agencies. COAST focuses on real-world research needs and limitations.

CERIAS contains information about software, companies, FIRST teams, archives, standards, professional organizations, government agencies, and FAQs (frequently asked questions)—among other goodies. The web hotlist index at COAST is the most comprehensive list of its type available on the Internet at this time. Check out the "WWW Security" and "Java Security" sections of the COAST list.

http://www.cerias.purdue.edu/

CERIAS also maintains a large FTP repository of software, papers, and computer security tools.

ftp://cerias.purdue.edu/

CIAC

The staff of the CIAC keep a good archive of tools and documents available on their site. This archive includes copies of their notes and advisories, and some locally developed software.

http://www.ciac.org/ciac/

DigiCrime

Your full-service criminal computer hacking organization. This tongue-in-cheek site demonstrates some very real web security issues.

http://www.digicrime.com/

FIRST

The FIRST (Forum of Incident Response and Security Teams) Secretariat maintains a large archive of material, including pointers to web pages for other FIRST teams.

http://www.first.org/

IETF

The Internet Engineering Task Force is the primary standards-making body of the Internet. The IETF's web site hosts charters of the IETF working groups, final versions of the IETF "Request For Comments" series, as well as Internet drafts, recommendations, policy documents, archives of some mailing lists, and other information.

http://www.ietf.org/

Mozilla

The Mozilla project maintains an up-to-date set of web pages on JavaScript and SSL Security.

http://www.mozilla.org/projects/security/components/index.html

NIH

The web index page at NIH (National Institutes of Health) provides a large set of pointers to internal collections and other archives.

http://www.alw.nih.gov/Security/security.html

NIST CSRC

The National Institutes of Standards and Technology Computer Security Resource Clearinghouse. This center seeks to distribute complete and accurate information about computer security issues to government and the general public.

http://csrc.ncsl.nist.gov/

Princeton SIP

These pages follow the ongoing efforts of the Princeton SIP (Secure Internet Programming) group in finding problems with Internet programming systems and solutions for making these systems more reliable.

http://www.cs.princeton.edu/sip

Radius.Net Cryptography Archives

This site is the largest list of cryptographic programs and software that are freely redistributable.

http://crypto.radiusnet.net/

RSA Data Security

This is RSA Data Security's home page.

http://www.rsa.com/

OpenSSL

These pages are for the OpenSSL project, a free implementation of the SSL protocol.

http://www.openssl.org/

SecurityFocus

SecurityFocus is a for-profit web site that tracks news and current events about computer security.

http://www.securityfocus.org/

System Administration, Networking, and Security (SANS) Institute

SANS is a for-profit educational organization that runs conferences, sends out mailings, and publishes books that are generally dedicated to the topics of system administration, networking, and security. SANS sends out customized email alerts on a regular basis that are a general distillation and summary of all important advances and alerts in the field. Highly recommended.

http://www.sans.org/

World Wide Web Consortium (W3C)

The World Wide Web Consortium is one of two standards-making bodies for the Web (the other being the Internet Engineering Task Force). At the W3C's web site you can find many information about current web security standards and practices, projects, and current security issues.

http://www.w3c.org/

WWW Security

This is Lincoln D. Stein's FAQ about web security. It contains a lot of good, practical information, and it is updated on a regular basis.

http://www.genome.wi.mit.edu/WWW/faqs/www-security-faq.html

Software Resources

This section describes some of the tools and packages available on the Internet that you might find useful in maintaining security at your site. Many of these tools are mentioned in this book. Although this software is freely available, some of it is restricted in various ways by the authors (e.g., it may not be permitted to be used for commercial purposes or be included on a CD-ROM, etc.) or by the U.S. government (e.g., if it contains cryptography, it may not be able to be exported outside the United States). Carefully read the documentation files that are distributed with the packages. If you have any doubt about appropriate use restrictions, contact the author(s) directly. Although we have used most of the software listed here, we can't take responsibility for ensuring that the copy you get will work properly and won't cause any damage to your system. As with any software, test it before you use it!

 Some software distributions carry an external PGP signature. This signature helps you verify that the distribution you receive is the one packaged by the author. It does not provide *any* guarantee about the safety or correctness of the software, however. Because of the additional confidence that a digital signature can add to software distributed over the Internet, we strongly encourage authors to take the additional step of including a standalone signature. We also encourage users who download software to check multiple sources if they download a package *without* a signature. This may help in locating malicious modifications.

chrootuid

The *chrootuid* daemon, by Wietse Venema, simplifies the task of running a network service at a low privilege level and with restricted filesystem access. The program can be used to run gopher, HTTP, WAIS, and other network daemons in a minimal environment: the daemons have access only to their own directory tree and run with an unprivileged user ID. This arrangement greatly reduces the impact of possible security problems in daemon software.

You can get *chrootuid* from:

ftp://ftp.porcupine.org/pub/security/

COPS (Computer Oracle and Password System)

The COPS package is a collection of short shell files and C programs that perform checks of your system to determine whether certain weaknesses are present. Included are checks for bad permissions on various files and directories, and malformed configuration files. The system has been designed to be simple and easy to verify by reading the code, and simple to modify for special local circumstances.

The original COPS paper was presented at the summer 1990 USENIX Conference in Anaheim, CA. It was entitled "The COPS Security Checker System," by Dan Farmer and Eugene H. Spafford. Copies of the paper can be obtained as a Purdue technical report by requesting a copy of technical report CSD-TR-993 from:

Technical Reports
Department of Computer Sciences
Purdue University
West Lafayette, IN 47907-1398

COPS can be obtained from:

ftp://coast.cs.purdue.edu/pub/tools/unix/cops

In addition, any of the public USENIX repositories for *comp.sources.unix* will have COPS in Volume 22.

Kerberos

Kerberos is a secure network authentication system that is based upon private key cryptography. The Kerberos source code is integrated into many operating systems, including FreeBSD, NetBSD, OpenBSD, Linux, and Windows 2000. The papers are available from the Massachusetts Institute of Technology. Contact:

MIT Software Center
W32-300
20 Carlton Street
Cambridge, MA 02139
(617) 253-7686

You can use anonymous FTP to transfer files over the Internet from:

ftp://athena-dist.mit.edu/pub/kerberos

MRTG

The Multi Router Traffic Grapher (MRTG) is a tool that generates web pages with graphs of data about your network. Originally, it was designed to show data from routers, gathered with SNMP, but it is easy to use it to show any data that can be gathered via SNMP, and only slightly harder to adapt it for other ways of getting numeric values. It provides historical data (that is, it shows values over time), but it updates the web pages in real time, as information comes in. These graphs are very useful for recognizing patterns and trends in network usage—especially for detecting and diagnosing cases of misuse.

http://ee-staff.ethz.ch/~oetiker/webtools/mrtg/mrtg.html

portmap

The *portmap* daemon, written by Wietse Venema, is a replacement program for Sun Microsystem's *portmapper* program. Venema's *portmap* daemon offers access control and logging features that are not found in Sun's version of the program. It also comes with the source code, allowing you to inspect the code for problems or modify it with your own additional features, if necessary.

You can get *portmap* from:

ftp://ftp.porcupine.org/pub/security/

Venema's *portmap* daemon is included as the standard *portmap* daemon with most versions of free Unix and Linux.

rsync

rsync is a synchronization system that uses checksums to determine differences (instead of relying on modification dates) and does partial file transfers (transferring only the differences instead of the entire files). *rsync* was developed by Andrew Tridgell and Paul Mackerras. *rsync* can use SSH for tunneling, and you should run it that way.

http://rsync.samba.org/rsync

SATAN

SATAN, by Wietse Venema and Dan Farmer, is the Security Administrator Tool for Analyzing Networks.* Despite the authors' strong credentials in the network security community (Venema is from Eindhoven University in the Netherlands and is the author of the *tcpwrapper* package and several other network security tools; Farmer is the author of COPS), SATAN was a somewhat controversial tool when it was released. Why? Unlike COPS, Tiger, and other tools that work from within a system, SATAN probes the system from the outside, as an attacker would. The unfortunate consequence of this approach is that someone (such as an attacker) can run SATAN against any system, not only those that he already has access to. According to the authors:

> SATAN was written because we realized that computer systems are becoming more and more dependent on the network, and at the same time becoming more and more vulnerable to attack via that same network.

> SATAN is a tool to help systems administrators. It recognizes several common networking-related security problems, and reports the problems without actually exploiting them.

---

* If you don't like the name SATAN, it comes with a script named *repent* that changes all references from SATAN to SANTA: Security Administrator Network Tool for Analysis.

For each type of problem found, SATAN offers a tutorial that explains the problem and what its impact could be. The tutorial also explains what can be done about the problem: correct an error in a configuration file, install a bug-fix from the vendor, use other means to restrict access, or simply disable service.

SATAN collects information that is available to everyone with access to the network. With a properly configured firewall in place, that should be near-zero information for outsiders.

The controversy over SATAN's release was largely overblown. SATAN scans are usually easy to spot, and the package is not easy to install and run. Most response teams seem to have more trouble with people running ISS scans against their networks.

From a design point of view, SATAN is interesting in that the program was among the first to use a web browser as its presentation system. The source may be obtained from:

ftp://ciac.llnl.gov/pub/ciac/sectools/unix/satan/

Source, documentation, and pointers to defenses may be found at:

http://www.cs.purdue.edu/coast/satan.html

SOCKS

Originally written by David Koblas and Michelle Koblas, SOCKS is a proxy-building toolkit that allows you to convert standard TCP client programs to proxied versions of those same programs. There are two parts to SOCKS: client libraries and a generic server. Client libraries are available for most Unix platforms, as well as for Macintosh and Windows systems. The generic server runs on most Unix platforms and can be used by any of the client libraries, regardless of the platform.

You can get SOCKS from:

http://www.socks.nec.com/

SSH

The SSH program is the secure shell. This program lets you log into another computer over the network over a cryptographically protected link that is secure from eavesdropping. SSH also provides for secure copying of files and for secure X Window System commands. SSH is meant as a replacement for *rlogin*, *rsh*, and *rcp*. It can also be used to replace Telnet and FTP.

There are many programs available that implement the SSH protocol, including the original SSH, OpenSSH, *putty*, SecureCRT, and others.

More information about SSH can be found in the SSH FAQ at:

http://www.uni-karlsruhe.de/~ig25/ssh-faq/

The SSH Security home page is located at:

http://www.ssh.fi/

You can get OpenSSH from:

http://www.openssh.com/

Swatch

Swatch, by Todd Atkins of Stanford University, is the Simple Watcher. It monitors log files created by *syslog*, and allows an administrator to take specific actions (such as sending an email warning, paging someone, etc.) in response to logged events and patterns of events. You can get Swatch from:

ftp://stanford.edu/general/security-tools/swatch
ftp://coast.cs.purdue.edu/pub/tools/unix/swatch/

tcpwrapper

The *tcpwrapper* is a system written by Wietse Venema that allows you to monitor and filter incoming requests for servers started by *inetd*. You can use it to selectively deny access to your sites from other hosts on the Internet, or, alternatively, to selectively allow access.

The *tcpwrapper* system is built into most versions of Free Unix and Linux on the market today as either a standalone program or as a linkable library that is part of programs such as *inetd* and *sshd*. If you are using a free version of Unix you probably don't need to specially download *tcpwrapper*, but if you want it, you can get it from:

http://oit.ucsb.edu/~eta/swatch/

Tiger

Tiger, written by Doug Schales of Texas A&M University (TAMU), is a set of scripts that scans a Unix system looking for security problems, in a manner similar to that of Dan Farmer's COPS. Tiger was originally developed to provide a check of the Unix systems on the A&M campus that users wanted to be able to access off-campus. Before the packet filtering in the firewall would be modified to allow off-campus access to the system, the system had to pass the Tiger checks.

You can get Tiger from:

ftp://net.tamu.edu/pub/security/TAMU/

TIS Internet Firewall Toolkit

The TIS Internet Firewall Toolkit (FWTK), from Trusted Information Systems, Inc., is a useful, well-designed, and well-written set of programs for controlling access to Internet servers from the Internet. FWTK includes:

- An authentication server that provides several mechanisms for supporting nonreusable passwords

- An access control program (wrapper for *inetd*-started services), *netac*
- Proxy servers for a variety of protocols (FTP, HTTP, gopher, *rlogin*, Telnet, and X11)
- A generic proxy server for simple TCP-based protocols using one-to-one or many-to-one connections, such as NNTP
- A wrapper (the *smap* package) for SMTP servers such as *sendmail* to protect them from SMTP-based attacks. You should install *smap* if you run *sendmail* at your site.

The toolkit is designed so that you can pick and choose only the pieces you need; you don't have to install the whole thing. The pieces you do install share a common configuration file, however, which makes managing configuration changes somewhat easier.

You can get the toolkit from:

ftp://ftp.tis.com/pub/firewalls/toolkit/

Tripwire

Tripwire, originally written by Gene H. Kim and Eugene H. Spafford of the COAST project at Purdue University, is a file integrity checker, a utility that compares a designated set of files and directories against information stored in a previously generated database. Added or deleted files are flagged and reported, as are any files that have changed from their previously recorded state in the database. Run Tripwire against system files on a regular basis. If you do so, the program will spot any file changes when it next runs, giving system administrators information to enact damage-control measures immediately.

After Kim graduated from Purdue, he helped start Tripwire, Inc., which is commercializing the Tripwire technology. The Tripwire.org is an open source version of the product.

You can get Tripwire from:

http://www.tripwire.com/
http://www.tripwire.org/

UDP Packet Relayer

This package, by Tom Fitzgerald, is a proxy system that provides much the same functionality for UDP-based clients that SOCKS provides for TCP-based clients.

ftp://coast.cs.purdue.edu/pub/tools/unix/udprelay-0.2.tar.gz

Paper References

There are many excellent books and articles available on web security and computer security in general. We are personally familiar with those listed here and can recommend them.

Computer Crime and Law

Arkin, S. S., B. A. Bohrer, D. L. Cuneo, J. P. Donohue, J. M. Kaplan, R. Kasanof, A. J. Levander, and S. Sherizen. *Prevention and Prosecution of Computer and High Technology Crime*. New York, NY: Matthew Bender Books, 1989. A book written by and for prosecuting attorneys and criminologists.

BloomBecker, J. J. Buck. *Introduction to Computer Crime*. Santa Cruz, CA: National Center for Computer Crime Data, 1988. (Order from NCCCD, 408-475-4457.) A collection of essays, news articles, and statistical data on computer crime in the 1980s.

BloomBecker, J. J. Buck. *Spectacular Computer Crimes*. Homewood, IL: Dow Jones-Irwin, 1990. Lively accounts of some of the more famous computer-related crimes of the 1970s and 1980s.

Cook, William J. *Internet & Network Law*. A comprehensive volume which is updated regularly; the title may change to reflect the year of publication. For further information, contact the author at:

> Willian Brinks Olds Hofer Gilson and Lione
> Suite 3600, NBC Tower
> 455 N. Cityfront Plaza Dr.
> Chicago, IL 60611-4299

Icove, David, Karl Seger, and William VonStorch, *Computer Crime: A Crimefighter's Handbook*, Sebastopol, CA: O'Reilly & Associates, 1995. A popular rewrite of an FBI training manual.

Power, Richard. *Current and Future Danger: A CSI Primer on Computer Crime and Information Warfare, Second Edition*. San Francisco, CA: Computer Security Institute, 1996. An interesting and timely summary.

Computer-Related Risks

Leveson, Nancy G. *Safeware: System Safety and Computers. A Guide to Preventing Accidents and Losses Caused by Technology. Reading*, MA: Addison-Wesley, 1995. This textbook contains a comprehensive exploration of the dangers of computer systems, and explores ways in which software can be made more fault tolerant and safety conscious.

Neumann, Peter G. *Computer Related Risks*. Reading, MA: Addison-Wesley, 1995. Dr. Neumann moderates the Internet RISKS mailing list. This book is a collection of the most important stories passed over the mailing list since its creation.

Nissenbaum, Helen, and Deborah G. Johnson, editors. *Computers, Ethics & Social Values*. Englewood Cliffs, NJ: Prentice Hall, 1995. A fascinating collection of readings on issues of how computing technology impacts society.

Peterson, Ivars. *Fatal Defect*. New York, NY: Random House, 1995. A lively account of how computer defects kill people.

Schneier, Bruce. *Secrets and Lies: Digital Security in a Networked World*. New York, NY: John Wiley & Sons, 2000. Covers digital attacks, security, risk assessment in companies, implementation of security policies and coutermeasures, and more.

Computer Viruses and Programmed Threats

Communications of the ACM, Volume 32, Number 6, June 1989 (the entire issue). This whole issue was devoted to issues surrounding the Internet Worm incident.

Denning, Peter J. *Computers Under Attack: Intruders, Worms, and Viruses*. Reading, MA: ACM Press/Addison-Wesley, 1990. One of the two most comprehensive collections of readings related to these topics, including reprints of many classic articles. A "must-have."

Ferbrache, David. *The Pathology of Computer Viruses*. London, England: Springer-Verlag, 1992. This is probably the best all-around book on the technical aspects of computer viruses.

Hoffman, Lance J., *Rogue Programs: Viruses, Worms, and Trojan Horses*. New York, NY: Van Nostrand Reinhold, 1990. The other most comprehensive collection of readings on viruses, worms, and the like. A must for anyone interested in the issues involved.

Cryptography

Denning, Dorothy E. R. *Cryptography and Data Security*. Reading, MA: Addison-Wesley, 1983. The classic textbook in the field.

Garfinkel, Simson. *PGP: Pretty Good Privacy*. Sebastopol, CA: O'Reilly & Associates, 1994. Describes the history of cryptography and the history of the program PGP, and explains PGP's use.

Hoffman, Lance J. *Building in Big Brother: The Cryptographic Policy Debate*. New York, NY: Springer-Verlag, 1995. An interesting collection of papers and articles about the Clipper chip, Digital Telephony legislation, and public policy on encryption.

Kaufman, Charles, Radia Perlman, and Mike Speciner. *Network Security: Private Communications in a Public World*. Englewood Cliffs, NJ: Prentice Hall, 1995. A technical but readable account of many algorithims and protocols for providing cryptographic security on the Internet. The discussion of the Web is very limited.

Schneier, Bruce. *Applied Cryptography: Protocols, Algorithms, and Source Code in C, Second Edition*. New York, NY: John Wiley & Sons, 1996. The most comprehensive, unclassified book about computer encryption and data privacy techniques ever published.

General Computer Security

Amoroso, Edward. *Fundamentals of Computer Security Technology*. Englewood Cliffs, NJ: Prentice Hall, 1994. A very readable and complete introduction to computer security at the level of a college text.

Anderson, Ross. *Security Engineering*. New York, NY: Wiley & Sons, 2001. A general overview of security engineering and practice.

Carroll, John M. *Computer Security, Second Edition*. Stoneham, MA: Butterworth Publishers, 1987. Contains an excellent treatment of issues in physical communications security.

Mandia, Kevin and Chris Prosise. *Incident Response: Investigating Computer Crime*. New York, NY: McGraw-Hill Professional Publishing, 2001. Describes the methods and techniques necessary to perform a professional and successful response to computer security incidents.

Northcutt, Stephen and Judy Novak. *Network Intrusion Detection: An Analyst's Handbook, Second Edition*. Indianapolis, IN: New Riders, 2000. A training aid and reference for intrusion detection analysts.

Pfleeger, Charles P. *Security in Computing, Second Edition*. Englewood Cliffs, NJ: Prentice Hall, 1996. A good introduction to computer security.

Van Wyk, Kenneth R. and Richard Forno. *Incident Response*. Sebastopol, CA: O'Reilly & Associates, 2001. Shows both the technical and administrative aspects of building an effective incident response plan.

System Administration, Network Technology, and Security

Network Technology

Comer, Douglas E. *Internetworking with TCP/IP, Third Edition*. Englewood Cliffs, NJ: Prentice Hall, 1995. A complete, readable reference that describes how TCP/IP networking works, including information on protocols, tuning, and applications.

Hunt, Craig. *TCP/IP Network Administration, Second Edition*. Sebastopol, CA: O'Reilly & Associates, 1998. This book is an excellent system administrator's overview of TCP/IP networking (with a focus on Unix systems), and a very useful reference to major

Unix networking services and tools such as BIND (the standard Unix DNS server) and *sendmail* (the standard Unix SMTP server).

Stevens, Richard W. *TCP/IP Illustrated*. Volume 1, *The Protocols*. Reading, MA: Addison-Wesley, 1994. This is a good guide to the nuts and bolts of TCP/IP networking. Its main strength is that it provides traces of the packets going back and forth as the protocols are actually in use, and uses the traces to illustrate the discussions of the protocols.

Secure Programming

Gundavaram, Shishir, Scott Guelich, and Gunther Birznieks. *CGI Programming with Perl, Second Edition*. Sebastopol, CA: O'Reilly & Asscociates, 2000. An excellent discussion of using CGI on the Web.

McGraw, Gary, and Edward W. Felten. *Securing Java: Getting Down to Business with Mobile Code, Second Edition*. New York, NY: Wiley Computer Publishing, 1999. A book on web browser security from a user's point of view.

Musciano, Chuck and Bill Kennedy. *HTML & XHTML: The Definitive Guide, Fourth Edition*. Sebastopol, CA: O'Reilly & Associates, 2000. Truly is the definitive guide covering everything you need to know about HTML and the newer XHTML.

Oaks, Scott. *Java Security, Second Edition*. Sebastopol, CA: O'Reilly & Associates, 2001. Focuses on the Java platform features that provide security—the class loader, bytecode verifier, and security manager—and recent additions to Java that enhance this security model: digital signatures, security providers, and the access controller.

Viega, John and Gary McGraw. *Building Secure Software*. Reading, MA: Addison-Wesley, 2001. Describes how to determine an acceptable level of risk, develop security tests, and plug security holes before shipping software.

Security and Networking

Bellovin, Steve, and Bill Cheswick. *Firewalls and Internet Security*. Reading, MA: Addison-Wesley, 1994. The classic book on firewalls. This book will teach you everything you need to know about how firewalls work, but it will leave you without implementation details unless you happen to have access to the full source code to the Unix operating system and a staff of programmers who can write bug-free code.

Zwicky, Elizabeth, D., Simon Cooper, and D. Brent Chapman, *Building Internet Firewalls, Second Edition*. Sebastopol, CA: O'Reilly & Associates, 2000. A superb how-to book that describes in clear detail how to build your own firewall. Covers Unix, Linux, and Windows.

Unix System Administration

Albitz, Paul, and Cricket Liu. *DNS and BIND, Third Edition*. Sebastopol, CA: O'Reilly & Associates, 1998. An excellent reference for setting up DNS nameservers.

Costales, Bryan, with Eric Allman and Neil Rickert. *sendmail, Second Edition*. Sebastopol, CA: O'Reilly & Associates, 1997. Rightly or wrongly, many Unix sites continue to use the *sendmail* mail program. This huge book will give you tips on configuring it more securely.

Frisch, Æleen. *Essential System Administration, Second Edition*. Sebastopol, CA: O'Reilly & Associates, 1995. A fine discussion of the most important aspects of Unix system administration.

Garfinkel, Simson and Gene Spafford. *Practical Unix & Internet Security, Second Edition*. Sebastopol, CA: O'Reilly & Associates, 1996. Nearly 1000 pages of Unix and network security, with many helpful scripts and checklists.

Honeynet Project (Ed). *Know Your Enemy: Revealing the Security Tools, Tactics, and Motives of the Blackhat Community*. Reading, MA: Addison-Wesley, 2001. Describes the technical skills needed to study a blackhat attack and learn from it. The CD includes examples of network traces, code, system binaries, and logs used by intruders from the blackhat community.

Killelea, Patrick. *Web Performance Tuning*. Sebastopol, CA: O'Reilly & Associates, 1998. Gives concrete advice for quick results—the "blunt instruments" for improving crippled performance right away. The book also approaches each element of a web transaction—from client to network to server—to examine the weak links in the chain and how to strengthen them.

Nemeth, Evi, Garth Snyder, Scott Seebass, and Trent R. Hein. *UNIX System Administration Handbook, Third Edition*. Englewood Cliffs, NJ: Prentice Hall, 2000. An excellent reference on the various ins and outs of running a Unix system. This book includes information on system configuration, adding and deleting users, running accounting, performing backups, configuring networks, running sendmail, and much more. Highly recommended.

Prestin, W. Curtis. *Unix Backup and Recovery*. Sebastopol, CA: O'Reilly & Associates, 1999. Provides a complete overview of all facets of Unix backup and recovery and offers practical, affordable backup and recovery solutions for environments of all sizes and budgets.

Stein, Lincoln, *Web Security, a Step-By-Step Reference Guide*. Reading, MA: Addison-Wesley, 1998. An excellent all-around book on web security topics.

Windows System Administration

Albitz, Paul, Matt Larson, and Cricket Liu. *DNS on Windows NT*. Sebastopol, CA: O'Reilly & Associates, 1998. This version of the book provides an explanation of the details of how Internet name service works on Windows NT.

Cox, Philip, and Tom Sheldon, *Windows 2000 Security Handbook*, New York, NY: McGraw-Hill Professional Publishing, 2000. An excellent book on Windows 2000 security issues. Provides step-by-step instructions on how to locate and plug security holes and backdoors, authenticate users, and defend against the latest methods of attack in Windows 2000.

Grimes, Roger. *Malicious Mobile Code: Virus Protection for Windows*. Sebastopol, CA: O'Reilly & Associates, 2001. Reveals what destructive programs (including viruses, worms, trojans, and rogue Internet content) can and can't do and how to recognize, remove, and prevent them. Readers learn effective strategies, tips, and tricks for securing any system.

Norberg, Stefan, *Securing Windows NT/2000 Servers for the Internet*. Sebastopol, CA: O'Reilly & Associates, 2000. A concise and excellent checklist–oriented guide to hardening Windows bastion hosts. Also provides some information on OpenSSH, TCP wrappers, VNC, and Cygwin.

Security Products and Services Information

Computer Security Buyer's Guide. San Francisco, CA: *Computer Security Institute*. (Order from CSI, 415-905-2626.) Contains a comprehensive list of computer security hardware devices and software systems that are commercially available. The guide is free with membership in the Institute. The URL is at *http://www.gocsi.com*.

Miscellaneous References

Miller, Barton P., Lars Fredriksen, and Bryan So. "An Empirical Study of the Reliability of UNIX Utilities," *Communications of the ACM*, Volume 33, Number 12, December 1990, 32–44. A thought-provoking report of a study showing how Unix utilities behave when given unexpected input.

Index

Symbols

' (backquote function), 440

Numbers

8mm video tape, 290

A

absolute identification, 125
Absolute Software Corporation, 297
access( ), 446
access.conf file, 542
access control, 78, 533–538
  Apache web servers, 539
  authorizations databases, 544
  directoryname parameter, 540
  host-based restrictions, 534–537
  IIS, 545–549
  <Limit>...</Limit>, 540
  passwords (see passwords)
  physical, 376
  physical tokens for, 127
  PKI, using, 545
  user-based, 537
  (see also identification)
accidents, 375
  (see also natural disasters)
ACH (Automated Clearing House), 626, 672
  online security of, 112
ACK packets, 29
ACPA (Anticybersquatting Consumer
      Protection Act), 648

ActiveX controls, 308–318
  Authenticode, 311
  CLSID (Class Identifier), 309
  hijacking by attackers, 323
  Java, and, 310
  known risks of, 318
  misconceptions, 314
  <OBJECT> tags, 311
  security issues, 316
  uses, 308
ad blockers, 265
  available programs, 268
address munging or mangling, 254
address verification, 619
addressing, 19
  internal, 25
Adleman, Leonard M., 66
administrative logins, 429
AdSubtract, 268
Advanced Research Projects Agency
      (ARPA), 14
aggregate information, 206
air ducts, 376
air filters, 370
alarms (see detectors)
alerts, 691
algorithmic attacks on encryption, 70
AllowOverride command, 540
Amateur Action Bulletin Board System, 527
America Online (see AOL)
American Civil Liberties Union v. Reno, 528
American Registry of Internet Numbers
      (ARIN), 41

We'd like to hear your suggestions for improving our indexes. Send email to *index@oreilly.com*.

Andreessen, Mark, 20
animals, 372
anonymity, 206
    certificates and, 551
    digital payment systems and, 620, 623,
        624
anonymized information, 206
Anonymizer.com, 272
    secure tunneling services, 273
anonymous web browsing, 268–275
    services for, 271
    techniques, 270
AOL (America Online), 581, 589
    anonymous browsing and, 270
    identity theft, and, 257
Apache web servers, xxii
    access controls, 539
        using databases, 544
    CAs, creating for, 484–487
    FreeBSD, on, 478–481
        directory structure, 481
    httpd.conf configuration file, 489–491
    installation, 478–481
        keys and certificates for, 496
        verification of, 481
    mod_ssl configuration file, 489–495
    origins, 477
    SSL, and, 474
APIs (Application Program Interfaces), 436
    extensibility of, 436–443
    programming guidelines, 443–448
Apple Macintosh, security and, 412
application/pics-labels encoding, 587
application/pics-service encoding, 587, 709
appropriation, 204
architecture, room, 376
archiving information, 286
    (see also logging)
ARIN (American Registry of Internet
        Numbers), 41
ARPA (Advanced Research Projects
        Agency), 14
arpwatch, 383
asymmetric key algorithms, 50
Atkins, Derek, 70
AT&T Labs—Research, 699
attackers, 400–403
attacks, 397–400
    automation of, 400
    growing problem of, 399
    host-based restrictions, against, 536
    legal options regarding, 517–523

Mafiaboy, 401
    mirror-world, 358
    packet sniffing, 669
    reconstructing, 324
    recovery from, 325
    remote, 398
    social engineering, 354
    software tools for, 404
attacks, cryptographic, 50
    against hardware-based cryptographic
        systems, 63
    on message digests, 76
    on symmetric encryption
        algorithms, 60–65
    on public key algorithms, 69
    (see also cryptography)
Audiotex Connection, Inc., 301
audits, 419
authentication, 80, 120
    message digests, 71–76
    of new users, 543
    offline systems, 132
    online systems, 132
    PGP, using, 140
    RADIUS protocol, 544
    SSH RSA keys, 147
    token-based, 424
    two-factor authentication, 128
Authenticode, 311, 561, 562, 564–577
    ActiveX, and, 564
    certificate qualification, 564
    evaluation, 314
    Internet Exploder, and, 316
    MD5, use of, 72
    publishing with, 565
    security issues, 316
    signed files, structure of, 564
    Software Developer's Kit (SDK), 566
    Software Developer's Kit (SDK), online
        source, 565
    uses, 313
    VeriSign public key infrastructure,
        and, 562
authorization, 80, 120
    environment variables for, 455
    <Limit> directive and, 540
AUTH_TYPE variable, 455
AutoComplete feature, clearing, 251
autologout shell variable, 391
automated checking systems, 420
automatic memory management, 332
automatic power cutoff (see detectors)

B

back doors, 54, 398
Back Orifice, 242, 404
backquote function, 440
backups, 284–295, 417, 668
    for archiving information, 286
    criminal investigations, and, 522, 526
    encryption of, 385
    keeping secure, 292–294
    laws concerning, 294
    planning, 287
    purpose of, 285
    retention of, 290
    rotating media, 289
    theft of, 385
    types of, 288
    verifying, 385
BankAmericard, 612
base data elements, 699
Basic Input Output System (see BIOS)
BB2W (Broadband2Wireless), 686
BBBOnLine, 598
beacon GIFs, 225
Berkeley "r" commands, 413
Berners-Lee, Tim, 19, 477
best practices, 12
bind, 86
    vulnerabilities, 398, 515
biological threats, 372
biometrics, 128
    identification systems, 128–130
    limitations, 129
BIOS (Basic Input Output System), 20
block algorithms, 53
blocking advertisments, 265
blocking software (see filtering software)
Blowfish, 58
bootstrap loader, 21
bots, 404
branded debit cards, 618
Brandeis, Louis, 204
Brands, Stefan, 172
breaking running scripts, 351
break-ins (see attacks)
BrightMail, 252, 255
browser alerts, SSL, 118
browser cache, 244
    configuring for privacy, 244
    Internet Explorer, management, 244
    Netscape Navigator, management, 244
browsers (see web browsers)

brute force attacks, 50, 55, 61
    and computing power, 56
BSafe SSL-C, 477
buffer overflow, 398
buffers
    printer buffers, security risks, 389
bug tracking, 406
bugs, 408–410
    Bugtraq mailing list, 717
    Java runtime system, 344
    Macromedia Shockwave plug-in, 358
    MS Access ActiveX, 318
bugs (biological), 372
bulk erasers, 386
Bureau of Export Administration (BXA), 98
bytecode, 331
    Java, 336

C

C language, programming guidelines, 456
C shell (see csh)
cables, network, 378, 384
    routing of, 374, 378
    tampering detectors for, 382
    wiretapping, 382
CAPI (Cryptographic API), 566
carbon monoxide, 370
Card Shark, 299
CAs (certification authorities), 84, 160
    certificates for, 168
    certificates, included in browsers,
        inconsistencies, 184
    certificates, obtaining from, 503
    competition of, 176
    creating for Apache web servers, 484–487
    history, 174
    multiple certificates offered by, 182
    need for, 193
    private keys, protections of, 475
    quality control problems of, 183–187
    RSA Certification Services, 176
    types of services, 160
    X.509 v3 certificates, 163–168
    (see also digital certificates)
CDA (Communications Decency Act), 528
CDP (CRL distribution point), 172
ceilings, dropped, 376
cellular telephones, 373
censorship, 586
censorware (see filtering software)

CERN (European Laboratory for Particle Physics), 19
CERT (Computer Emergency Response Team), 407, 717
   CERT/CC, PGP signature, 141
Cert2SPC.exe, 566
Certificate Requests, 696
certificate stores, 566
certificates, 84, 112
   certification authorities, for, 168
   client-side, 550–559
   managing users with, 545
   obtaining from CAs, 503
   renewing, 507
   revoking, 558
   short expiration times, 507
   software publisher's, 577
   SSL, causes of invalidation in, 507
   VeriSign Digital ID Center, 553–559
   web servers under SSL, 475
   (see also digital certificates, CAs)
CertificateVerify message, 697
certification authorities (see CAs)
certification of public keys, 146
CertMgr.exe, 566
cgi-bin directory, 437
CGI (Common Gateway Interface), 435, 467
   example script, 437–443
   extensibility of, 436–443
   programming guidelines, 443–448
   programs to exclude from, 437
challenge-response, 151
change detection tools, 419
ChangeCipherSpec, 692
characters, filtering, 442
charga-plates, 611
charge-backs, 617
charge slips, 615
chargen utility, 412
Chaum, David, 623
check digit algorithm
   Perl encoding, 614
check digits, 614
CheckFree services, 673
checking (see verification)
child pornography, 529
Children's Internet Protection Act, 529, 580
Children's Privacy Protection Act (see COPPA)
ChkTrust.exe, 566
chosen plaintext attacks, 62
chrootuid daemon, 723

CIAC (Computer Incident Advisory Capability), 717
ciphers (see encryption)
circular hunting, 661
Clark, Jim, 20
class loader, Java, 331, 335
clear GIFs, 225
client certificates, 550
ClientHello, 693
clients, 17
   client-side digital certificates, 550–559
client/server model, 17
"client-sniffing" code, 349
Clipper chip, 56, 95
CLSID (Class Identifier), 309
COCOM (Coordinating Committee for Multilateral Export Controls), 101
Code of Fair Information Practices, 593
code signing, 560–577
   Authenticode, 564–577
   current systems, 562
   DSig, 577
   PGP, with, 577
   vulnerabilities, 321
cold, impact on hardware, 372
commerce
   identification and, 121
   Internet-based payment systems, 620–636
   merchant fees, 616
   reverse charge transactions, 617–618
Communications Decency Act (CDA), 528
compact policies, 608, 706
computer failure, 285
computer forensics, 242
computer networks, 17, 21
computer security, 3
   physical, 380
   references for, 731
   unattended systems, 390–391
Computer Security Resource Clearinghouse (CSRC), 721
computer theft, preventing, 295–297
   laptop locks, 295
   precautions, 297
   recovery software and services, 297
   tagging, 295
computer vacuums, 370
computer vandalism (see vandalism)
computer worms (see worms)
computers, environmental threats to, 367–375

Computrace, 297
confidentiality, 80
configuration files, 6
confiscation of property, 525
connectors, network, 379
consistency checking, 445
content types
    application/pics-labels, 587
    application/pics-service, 587, 709
content updating, 426–429
contingency planning, 365
continuity of identification, 125
cookies, 216–217
    applications, 216
    cookie jars, 221
    crushing, 266
    disabling, 224
    implementation and uses, 219
    Internet Explorer 6.0, and, 609
    privacy, and, 220
    profiles, creating with, 219
    protocol, 217
    removal, 247–248
        Internet Explorer, from, 247
        Netscape Navigator, from, 247
    RFC 2109, 222
    secure generation and decoding, 453
    security, 222
    security advantages over hidden
            fields, 451
    third-party cookies, 218
cookies.txt file, 221
COPPA (Children's Online Privacy
            Protection Act), 601–605
    exceptions, 605
    FTC, and, 605
    jurisdiction, 603
    parental consent, and, 604
    provisions, 603
copper network cables, routing of, 374
COPS (Computer Oracle and Password
            System), 723
copy protection systems, 8
copyright, 642–645
    email forwarding, and, 643
    infringement, 643
core dumps, security of, 446
core files, 446
corporations, 651
Council of Better Business Bureaus,
            BBBOnLine, 598

Council of Europe, 102
courtesy cards, 611
CPS (certification practices statement), 162
    maintenance, problems with, 184
    viewing, 184
CPU attacks, 353
CPU time limits, 447
crackers, profiles of, 400–403
Cranor, Lorrie, 699
credit, 610
    history, 611
credit card sniffers, 299
credit cards, 610–620, 672–675
    authentication mechanisms, 618
    check digits, 614
    evaluating system for, 640
    fees, 616
    Internet, usage on, 619
    SET protocol for, 628–629
    United States, use in, 612
credit reports, monitoring, 258
crimes, xi–xvi
criminal laws, 517–523
CRL (certificate revocation list), 172
crushing cookies, 266
cryptanalysis, 62
Crypto Law Survey, 99
cryptographic protocols, 81
    offline, 81–84
    online, 84–88
cryptographic systems, 81
    strength, 54
cryptographically enabled web servers, 11
cryptography, 46–53
    applications, 48
    attacks against, 50
    domestic use restrictions, 103
    dual signatures, 629
    export controls, and, 530
    government regulation of, 94–106
    history, 47
    import/export restrictions, 103
    international agreements, 102
    Internet, use in securing, 78–81
    legal restrictions, 90–106
    limitations, 88–90
    message digests, 71–76
    patents, 90–92
    public keys, 50, 65–70
    roles in information systems, 80

cryptography *(continued)*
    securing information sent to web
        applications, 451
    symmetric key algorithms, 50–64
    trade secret laws, 92
csh (C shell), autologout variable, 391
.cshrc file, 391
CSRC (Computer Security Resource
        Clearinghouse), 721
custom software, 674
cvsup command, 479
CyberCash system, 625
cybercrime (see crimes)

D

DAT (Digital Audio Tape), 290
Data Encryption Standard (see DES)
data integrity, 80
data protection, 7, 285, 381–392, 594
    in transit, 8
    theft, from, 287, 380
database servers, 6
david.exe, 301
Davies, Simon, 639
deadlock conditions, 446
debit cards, 618
    online security of, 112
decryption, 46
    (see also cryptography)
defamation, 650
Defense Trade Regulations, 94
denial-of-service attacks, 9
    Gibson Research Corp., 401
    JavaScript, 351
DES (Data Encryption Standard), 49, 58, 90
    key length, 55
    weakness of, 50
designing programs (see programming,
        guidelines for)
desktop, 21
destroying media, 387
detecting changes, 419
detectors
    cable tampering, 382
    carbon-monoxide, 370
    humidity, 375
    smoke, 369
    temperature alarms, 372
    water sensors, 375
dialers, 22
dialup servers, unprotected, 397

differential attacks, 63
Diffie, Bailey Whitfield, 65
Diffie-Hellman key exchange, 66
    patents, 91
DigiCash system, 623–625
DigiCrime web site, 352
Digital Audio Tape (DAT), 290
digital certificates, 112, 153
    browser-bundled certificates,
        inconsistencies, 184
    current deficiencies of, 191
    fraudulent certificates, 172
    liability insurance for, 182
    PGP, and, 153
    potential uses of, 169
    preinstalled, Internet Explorer, 177–180
    preinstalled, Netscape Navigator, 180
    privacy, and, 193
    real-time validation, 173
    revocation, 172
    short-lived certificates, 174
    software publishing, 577
    types, 168
    Windows operating system, uses by, 170
    X.509 v3 certificates, 163–168
digital coins, 623
Digital IDs (see certificates)
Digital Millennium Copyright Act (see
        DMCA)
digital money
    taxation, and, 627
digital notary, 192
digital payment systems, 610
Digital Signature Wizard, 568–575
digital signatures, 51, 66, 67, 69
    advantages and drawbacks, 153
    Authenticode system, 312
    DSS (Digital Signature Standard), 66, 72
    PGP, example, 141
    validation, 134
digital watermarking, 8
Diner's Club card, 612
Directive 95/46/EC, Directive on Protection
        of Personal Data, 596
directories, backing up by, 289
disable Java setting, Internet Explorer, 340
disaster planning, 364, 365
disclosure of private facts, 204
diskettes (see backups; media)
dispersal of resources, 379
disposing of materials, 387–388
distributed denial-of-service, 403

DLLs (dynamic linked libraries), 305
DMCA (Digital Millennium Copyright
   Act), 99–101
 copyright protections, disabling of,
   and, 529
DNS (Domain Name Service), 25–28, 412
 distributed database, 26
 DNS logs, 215
 DNS requests, 26
 name server, protecting, 514
 Network Solutions, domination by, 42
 remote root exploit, 398
 spoofing, 508
 SSL certificates and, 476
DNSSEC (Domain Name Service
   Security), 86
doctrine of equivalence, 90
document authentication using PGP, 140
document retention and destruction
   policies, 281
domain names, 25
 IP addresses, and, 25
 trademarks, and, 648
domain name registration, 40
 licensing authority for, 44
 security and maintenance, 515–516
Domain Name Service Security
   (DNSSEC), 86
Domain Name Service (see DNS)
domains and ports, 27
downloaded code, risks, 318
downloaded software, privacy issues, 243
downloading files, 389
drink, 376
dropped ceilings, 376
DSA algorithm and PGP, 136
DSL (Digital Subscriber Loop), 21
dual signatures, 629
ducts, air, 376
due care, 12
dumpster diving, 388
dust, 370
dynamically assigned IP addresses, 24

E

earthquakes, 370
eavesdropping, 381–384, 393
 password sniffing, 424–426
 private keys, 151
E-cash (see DigiCash system)
echo command, 412

edit detections, 419
EES (Escrowed Encryption Standard), 95
EFT (Electronic Funds Transfer), online
   security of, 112
Eich, Brendan, 346
8mm video tape, 290
electrical fires, 369
 (see also fires; smoke)
electrical noise, sources of, 372
electronic mail, 412
 authorizing payments by, 621–623
 forwarding, copyright law and, 643
 message digests, 71–76
electronic money, 610
 CyberCash system, 625
 debit cards, 618
 DigiCash system, 623–625
 Mondex system, 639
 SET protocol for, 628–629
 Virtual PIN system, 621–623
elliptic curve cryptosystems, 66
email, 275
 destruction systems, 281
 durability of, 280
 I LOVE YOU worm, 302
 privacy of, ensuring, 277
 security aspects of, 275–283
 spam, preventing, 253
embedded scripting languages, 436
embedded web servers, 436
encoding
 application/pics-labels, 587
 application/pics-service, 587, 709
encrypted messaging, 67
encryption, 8, 46, 380, 674
 attacks on, 50
  (see also attacks, cryptographic)
 of backups, 293
 escrowing keys, 293
 offline systems, 81–84
 online systems, 84–88
 public keys, 50, 65–70
 symmetric key algorithms, 50–64
  (see also cryptography)
encryption algorithms, 49
Engelschall, Ralf S., 478
enrollment, 621
environment variables, CGI/API and, 455
erasing disks, 386–387
errors, 286
 human, 291
errors, programming (see bugs)

escrow agents, 95
Escrowed Encryption Standard (EES), 95
escrowing encryption keys, 293
/etc directory, backup of, 289
/etc/passwd file, 544
Ethernet
    packet sniffers, and, 320
Ethernet cables (see cables, network)
European Laboratory for Particle Physics
        (CERN), 19
European Union privacy protections, 596
ExecCGI option, 541
explosions, 371
export controls and cryptography, 530
extensibility, 436–443

F

failures, computer, 285
Fair Credit Reporting Act, 593
fair use, 644
"fair use" provisions, copyright law, 530,
    644
false negatives and positives, biometrics, 129
Farmer, Dan, 420
faults (see bugs)
Federal Family Educational Rights and
        Privacy Act of 1974, 593
federal jurisdiction, 520
federal laws, 521
federal trademarks, 647
fees, charge card, 616
Felten, Edward W., 344, 354
fiber optic cables, advantages and
        disadvantages, 384
    (see also cables, network)
File Transfer Protocol (see FTP)
files
    access to (see access control)
    core files, 446
    log (see logging)
    temporary, 457
filing criminal complaints, 518–521
filtering invalid characters, 442
filtering software, 579–582
    application, protocol, and firewall
        levels, 581
    censorship, 586
    database currency, 581
    disabling of, 582
    overbroad filtering criteria, 582
    pornography, for, 579

techniques used, 580
technology and censorship concerns, 583
filtering software and pornography, 529
filters, air, 370
FIN bit, 31
finger, 19
finger gateway, 439
    securing, 442
    security hole in, 440
finger protocol, 412
finished_label, 698
fires, 367–370, 393
    extinguishers, 367
firewalls, 17, 431
    host-based restrictions, using, 536
    LANs, protection with, 433
    mailing list for, 718
    NAT support, 432
    packet-filtering, 431
    proxy firewalls, 432
    VPN support, 432
    web servers, protection with, 433
FIRST teams, 721
First Virtual Holdings, 299, 621
first-party cookie, 609
Flash, 358
floods (see water)
floors, raised, 376
FollowSymLinks option, 541
food risks to hardware, 376
forgery-proof identification, 124
format of SSL certificates, 475
forwarding email messages, 643
fraud, electronic funds transfer, 319
free software, 671
FreeBSD, 23
    Apache, installation under, 478–481
    SSL servers, creating with, 477–501
Freedom anonymizers, 273
Freedom Internet Privacy Suite, 268
Freedom of Information Act, 593
FTP (File Transfer Protocol), 19, 412, 427
full backup, 288
function keys, 390

G

gas-charged fire extinguishers, 367
glass walls, security aspects, 377
Gosling, James, 330
Graff, Michael, 70
Graphical User Interface (see GUIs)

guest logins, 429
GUIs (Graphical User Interfaces), 352

H

Halon gas, 368
handshake_failure alert, 694
handshake_messages, 697
handshakes, SSL/TLS, 692–698
harassment, 650
hard disks, difficulty of sanitizing, 386
hardware
    failure of, 286
    food and drink threats, 376
    physical security of, 366
    smoke, effects on, 369
    temperature, influence on, 372
hash functions, 71
heat, impact on hardware, 372
Hellman, Martin E., 65
helper applications, 304–308
    history, 304
hidden fields, 449
hidden URLs, 534
high safety setting, Internet Explorer, 340
history command, web browsers, 351
holograms, 124
Honeynet Project, 400
host name resolution, 26–28
host security, 396, 397–434
    attacks, increase in, 399
    automated attacks, 400
    backups, 417
    change-detecting tools, 419
    compromised systems, attacks from, 403
    eavesdropping, prevention of, 424
    encryption, systems with, 425
    implementation, 405–433
    intrusion detection systems, 421
    log servers, 415
    logging, 414
    malicious programs, 398
    patches, updating, 406
    policies, implementing, 405–411
    remote attacks, 398
    security tools, 418–421
    services, restriction of, 411
    sniffing, prevention, 424–426
    social engineering, 399
    software installation, 410
        logging, 411
    software inventory, 410
    static auditing, 419
    system inventory, 410
    vendor issues, 407
        evaluation web site, 408
    vulnerabilities and attacks, 397
host-based restrictions, 534–537
    attacks, against, 536
hosts, 17
Hotmail, 277
.htaccess file, 539
HTML (Hypertext Markup Language), 20
    embedded JavaScript, 346
    forms, validating, 449
    <LINK> tag and P3P, 705
    refer links, 213
htpasswd program, 543
HTTP (Hypertext Transfer Protocol)
    proxies
        encrypted traffic, and, 264
        requesting PICS labels by, 713
httpd.conf, 489–491
    access control information, 539
    VirtualHost, 491
HTTPS_RANDOM variable, 455
Hudson, Tim, 114, 477
human error and backups, 291
humidity, 374
hunt groups, 661
Hushmail, 277
hybrid public/private cryptosystems, 53
Hypertext Markup Language (see HTML)
Hypertext Transfer Protocol (see HTTP)

I

I LOVE YOU worm, 302
IANA (Internet Assigned Numbers
        Authority), 42
ICANN (Internet Corporation for Assigned
        Names and Numbers), 41
    incorporation, 43
    UDRP (Uniform Dispute Resolution
        Policy), 516, 648
ICMP ECHO packets, 26, 28
IDEA (International Data Encryption
        Algorithm), 59
identification, 119–122
    access based on, 537
    computer-based, 124–130
    digital certificates for (see certificates)
    location-based, 130
    paper-based systems, 122–124
    public keys, and, 130–138
    smart cards for (see smart cards)

identity authentication, 134
identity theft, 256–261
   consequences, 257
   prevention, 258
   Social Security Administration, corruption
     in, 256
identity vs. identification, 188–191
identity.pub file, 148
IETF (Internet Engineering Task Force), TLS
     working group, 688
IIS (Internet Information Server), xxii
   access control, 545–549
   directories, restricting access to, 548
   installing, 545
   patches, downloading and installing, 546
   SSL certificates, installing, 501–504
   web pages, controlling access to, 546
image content blocking, 581
implementation strength, 71
Includes option, 541
IncludesNoExec option, 541
incorporation, 651
incremental backup, 288
Indexes option, 541
industrial spies, 402
information
   asking users for, 354
   censorship of, 586
   on charge slips, 615
   secure content updating, 426–429
information theft, 320–321
informational privacy, 205
input, verifying, 444
insects, 372
installing
   cables, 378
integrity, 80, 344
intellectual property, 642–648
interbank payment card transaction, 612
interest on credit, 616
Intermediate Certification Authorities, 177
International Data Encryption Algorithm
     (IDEA), 59
Internet, 33
   addressing, 19
   credit cards on (see credit cards)
   domain names, conversion to IP
     address, 25
   electronic theft, 302
   payment systems on, 620–636
   pornography, and, 527
   programs that spend money, 319

   security aspects, 78
   vulnerability to scam programs, 299
Internet Corporation for Assigned Names
     and Numbers (ICANN), 41
Internet Exploder, 316
Internet Explorer
   AutoComplete feature, clearing, 251
   browser cache, management, 244
   browser history, clearing, 249
   browser preferences and SSL, V. 6.0, 118
   client certificates, support of, 551
   cookie storage, 221
   cookies, disabling, 224
   cookies, removing, 247
   digital certificates, preinstalled, 177–180
   Java, disabling in restricted security
     zone, 341
   Java security policies, 340–343
   P3P support, 608
   plug-ins, 305
   privacy protections, V. 6.0, 608
   ratings implemented in, 590
   security zones, 338–340
   trusted CAs, installation of
     certificates, 496
Internet Information Server (see IIS)
Internet Junkbuster Proxy, 268
Internet registrars, 40
Internet service providers (see ISPs)
Internet zone, 339
intrusion, 204
intrusion detection programs, 421
invalid characters, 442
invisible GIFs, 225
IP (Internet Protocol), 16
   access restriction by address, 534–537
   connectivity, 659
   IP addresses, 24
     conversion from domain names, 25
     hiding, 270
     internal addressing, 25
     monitoring for security, 383
     private networks, 535
     static, 24
IP numbers and packets, monitoring, 383
IPsec, 87
IPv4, 16
IPv6, 16, 87
ISDN (Integrated Services Digital
     Network), 21
ISPs (Internet service providers), 33
   anonymous browsing from, 271

choosing, 230
copyright and, 644
harassment policies, 650
management, 655–687
privacy policies of, 231
ITAR (International Traffic in Arms
    Regulation), 94

J

Java, 329–346
    bytecode verifier, 336
    Class Loader, 331, 335
    cross-platform capabilities, 331
    design purpose, 336
    history, 330
    JVM (Java virtual machine), 331
    Microsoft products, support in, 343
    Oak, 330
    safety of, 332
    sandbox, 334
    security aspects of, 333
    security deficiencies, 343
    security policies, 336
        Internet Explorer, 340–343
        Netscape Navigator 6.0, setting
            in, 342
    self-defending applet killer, 346
    SSL support, 114
    syntax, 331
JavaScript, 346–358
    alert( ) method windows attacks, 352
    Back button function execution, 352
    capabilities, 347
    denial-of-service attacks, 351
    security aspects, 349
    security flaws, 350
    spoofing attacks, 354
JavaScript Graph Builder library, 347
Joe accounts, 233
JSAFE, 114
JScript, 349
jurisdiction, 519

K

Kerberos, 87, 724
key escrow, 95
    risks of, 97
key length, 55
    and brute force attacks, 56
    and cryptographic security, 56

strength relative to crypographic
    algorithms, 67
key recovery, 95
    risks of, 97
key ring, 83
key search attacks, 50, 55
key signing parties, 159
key switches, 391
keyboard monitors, 384
keyboard sniffers, 241
KeyKatch, 241
kcys, 46
    OpenSSL, creation with, 488
    web servers, maintenance for, 474
keystroke recorders, 241
keyword blocking, 580
KidsCom web site, 602
knapsack algorithm, 91
known plaintext attacks, 54, 62
Koops, Bert-Jaap, 99
ksh (Korn shell), TMOUT variable, 391

L

labels, PICS (see PICS)
LaDue, Mark, 346
LANs (local area networks), 22, 23
    firewalls, protection with, 433
laptops, prevention of theft, 381
    laptop locks, 295
Law Enforcement Access Field (LEAF), 95
laws and legal issues
    backups, 294
    after break-in, 517–523
    circumstances requiring legal action, 517
    compromised networks, hazards of
        ownership, 523–526
    criminal complaints, filing, 518–521
    criminal prosecution, risks of
        pursuing, 521–523
    identification, 121
    intellectual property, 642–648
    jurisdiction, 519–521
    law enforcement, 518–523, 524
    liability for defective software, 650
    libel, 650
    precautions, 524
LDAP, 544
LEAF (Law Enforcement Access Field), 95
Lenstra, Arjen, 70
level-zero backup, 288
Leyland, Paul, 70
liability, 650

libel, 650
lightning, 367, 373
Limit command, 541
<Limit> directive, 538
limiting access (see access control)
links, 19
Linux
    SSL-enabled web servers, and, 474
LiveScript (see JavaScript)
loadable modules, 436
loans, credit (see credit cards)
local HTTP proxy, 264
local intranet zone, 338
local storage, 389–390
location-based identification, 130
lock programs, 391
lock-down, 383
locks, 295
log files, 210
log in, 21
log servers, 415
logging, 286, 414, 674
    browser, 211–214
    criminal investigations, and, 524
    exclusion of sensitive information, 445
    software installations, 411
    Swatch program, 727
    Unix systems, facilities for, 415
    Windows 2000, 416
logins and security, 429
logins, limiting, 669
logout, 391
Love Bug, xii, 302

M

Macintosh, security and, 412
Macromedia Shockwave
    digital signatures, 562
    plug-in bug, 358
MACs (message authentication codes), 73
    address filtering, 383
    CertificateVerify message, 697
    TLS, 690
MAEs (Metropolitan Area Exchanges), 35
Mafiaboy, 401
mail clients, 17
mail logs, 215
mail servers, 17
mailing lists, 716–719
make install command, 479, 480
MakeCat.exe, 566

makecert.ca script, 484–487
MakeCert.exe, 566, 567
MakeCTL.exe, 566
malicious code, 299–304, 398
    phone charge scams, 300
    PKZIP30B.EXE, 563
    Quiken wire transfer program, 302
    Visual Basic scripts, 302
man-in-the-middle attacks and SSL, 110
Marimba Castanet code signing, 562
marshalling, 452
master secret, 692, 698
MasterCard, 612
Maxim, xi
Maxus Credit Card Pipeline, xi
McCool, Rob, 477
McCurley, Kevin, 352
MD2, MD4, MD5 functions, 71
media, 387–388
    damage by smoke, 369
    destroying, 387
    failure of, 289
    overwriting, 387
    print through process, 385
    rotating for backups, 289
    sanitizing, 386–387
medium safety setting, Internet
        Explorer, 341
meet-in-the-middle plaintext attacks, 58
merchant fees, 616
message digests, 53, 71–76
Metcalfe, Robert, 78
Metropolitan Area Exchanges (MAEs), 35
Microsoft
    Access, ActiveX bug, 318
    ActiveX controls (see ActiveX controls)
    Authenticode (see Authenticode)
    certificates, faking of, 316
    Cryptographic API (CAPI), 566
    Internet Explorer, xxiii
    Java, support for, 343
    JScript, 349
    Office 2000
        UA Control vulnerability, 318
    Office 2000, code signing system of, 562
    OLE/COM Object Viewer, 310
    software authentication, 561
    Software Publisher's Pledge, 565
    Windows NT 4.0, vulnerabilities, 398
    Internet Information Server (see IIS)
Miller, James, 586, 588, 708

MIME (Multipurpose Internet Mail Extensions), 84
minimal disclosure certificates, 171
mirror worlds, 358
mirroring RAID systems, 285
mkstemp( ), 457
mobile code, 298
    interpreted languages, 327
mod_ssl, 478
    configuration file, 489–495
    httpd.conf configuration file, 489–491
    installation on FreeBSD, 478–481
Mondex system, 639
money stealing software, 302
monitoring software, 677–680
Monti, Mario, 596
Mozilla, 20
    Network Security Services system, 113
Multipurpose Internet Mail Extensions, 84
Museum and Library Services Act, 580
My Computer zone, 339

N

names and web server certificates, 508
nameservers, 26
    querying, 38
    root, 28, 36–40
        ownership, 37
    top-level, 36–40
name/value pairs, PICS, 709
NAPs (Network Access Points), 35
NAT (Network Address Translation), 432
    converters, 25
National Center for Supercomputer Applications (NCSA), 20
National Telecommunications and Information Administration (see NTIA)
natural disasters, 287, 292
    accidents, 375
    earthquakes, 370
    fires, 367–370
    lightning, 367, 373
    (see also physical security)
natural gas, risks to hardware, 371
Naughton, Patrick, 331
nc, 404
NCSA (National Center for Supercomputer Applications), 20
Netbus, 404

netcat, 404
Netscape Communications, 20
Netscape Navigator, xxiii, 20
    ActiveX controls, and, 311
    browser cache, management, 244
    browser history, clearing, 250
    client certificates, support of, 551
    cookies, 216–217
        disabling, 224
        storage, 221
    cookies, removal from, 247
    digital certificates, preinstalled, 180
    Java policies, setting, 342
    Password Manager, 252
    plug-ins, 311
        security warnings, 305
    SSL, browser preferences, 116
    trusted CAs, installation of certificates, 500
Netscape Object Signing, code signing system, 562
netstat, 405
Network Access Points (NAPs), 35
network connections, securing, 382
Network Solutions, 42
networks
    blocking software and, 589
    cables for, 378
    connectors for, 379
    NFS, 428
    security references, 733
    wiring installation for, 657
newsyslog, 416
NFS (Network File System), 428
NIST CSRC (National Institutes of Standards and Technology Computer Security Resource Clearinghouse), 721
Nitroba CA certificate, 487
    Internet Explorer, installation on, 496
    Netscape Navigator, installation on, 500
nonce, 150
nonrepudiation, 80
nonreusable passwords, 424
Norton Internet Security, 268
NSA (National Security Agency), 55
NSS (Network Security Services), 113
    online resources, 115
NTIA (National Telecommunications and Information Administration), 41
    ICAAN, incorporation of, 43
nyms, 274

O

Oak, 330
<OBJECT> tags, 311
OECD (Organization for Economic Development and Cooperation), privacy guidelines, 594
offline authentication systems, 132
offline encryption systems, 81–84
OLE/COM Object Viewer, 310
Omniva Policy Systems, 281
one-way hash functions, 71
online accounts, establishing, 621
online authentication systems, 132
online cryptographic protocols, 84–88
online fraud, types of, 319
online resources
  ad blockers, 268
  ICANN web site, 41
  Java SSL, 114
  Microsoft Authenticode Software Developer's Kit, 565
  NSS (Network Security Services), 113
  OpenSSL, 114
  Privacy Foundation on web bugs, 227
  software, 723–728
  SSL, 115
  SSL open source programs, 478
  SSL/TLS, 115
  stopping spam, 255
  trinoo, 404
  Walden Network, 23
  web pages and FTP sites, 720–722
  Web Security, Privacy & Commerce, xxiv
online stalking, 650
online transactions, security of, 112
OpenPGP, 82
OpenSSL, 114
  command line, operation from, 488
  makecert.ca script, 484–487
  online resources, 115
  origins of, 477
  services, securing with, 501
Opera, xxiii
operating systems, restriction of users, 437
optic cables (see cables, network)
optical vampire taps, 384
Options command, 541
organized crime, 403
OSI (Open System Interconnection), 14
outsourced certification authorities, 161
overwriting media, 387

P

P3P (Platform for Privacy Preferences Project), 606–609, 699–707
  base data elements, 699
  compact policies, 608, 706
  deploying, 702–706
  enabled web site, example, 706
  HTTP responses, P3P headers, 704
  Internet Explorer, support by, 608
  policy reference files, 699, 704
    <LINK> tags, 704
    well-known locations, 704
  privacy policy, creating, 706
  PrivacySealExample program, 700
packets, 15
  ACK packets, 29
  acknowledgment or retransmission, 31
  byte count, 29
  displaying text, 29
  DNS requests, 26
  size, 17
  SYN packets, 28
  SYN/ACK packets, 29
packet sniffers
  Ethernet interfaces, and, 320
packet sniffing, 669
packet switching, 14–16
packet-filtering firewalls, 17, 431
paper
  shredders for, 388
  throwing out, 387
parity RAID systems, 285
partitions
  backup by, 289
  root (see root directory)
passwords, 125, 231–241, 537
  bad passwords, characteristics, 232
  choosing, 234
  classes, bases, and rotation, 237
  good passwords, characteristics, 233
  hit lists of, 232
  ISPs, requirements for, 233
  management, multiple passwords, 236
  nonreusable, 424
  password files, setting up, 543
  password keepers, 237
  password sniffers, 240, 424–426
    protocols, secure against, 240
  sharing of, 238
  spoofing requests for, 354
  theft of, 399
  writing down, 235

patches, 407
patents, 645
patents, cryptographic systems, 90–92
PCT (Private Communications
    Technology), 86, 108
peering agreements, 35
PEM certification format, example, 487
performance
    C programs, 456
    monitoring resources, 678
    (see also resources)
Perl programming language, 454
    scripts, filtering, 442
    system function, 443
    tainting, 454
PERL.EXE and the cgi-bin directory, 437
personal certificates, 168
personal information, 205
    ISPs, available to, 230
personally identifiable information (see PII)
personnel, security aspects of, 392
PGP (Pretty Good Privacy), 82–83, 132
    digital certificates, and, 153
    document authentication, 140
    DSA algorithm, and, 136
    fraudulent keys, 155
    key certification, 156
    key-pair generation, 136
    keys, certification, 155
    public keys and digital certificates, 154
    signatures, 141–147
      certification, 146
    software signature, 723
phf script, 437
phishing (identity theft scams), 257
phone charge scams, 300
physical security, 363–395
    access control, 376
    of backups, 292–294
    plan, 364
physical tokens, 127
PICS (Platform for Internet Content
    Selection), 583–589, 708–715
    HTTP label requests, 713
    label specification, 710
    MPAA movie-rating example, 708
    name/value pairs, 709
    rating services, label requests from, 714
    RFC 822 header, document labeling
      with, 712
PII (personally identifiable
    information), 206, 609

ping, 26
    ping of death, 398
piracy of software, 527, 644
PKI (public key infrastructure), 153,
    174–187
    barriers to development, 187–200
PKZIP virus, 563
plaintext, 58, 62
Platform for Internet Content Selection
    (see PICS)
Platform for Privacy Preferences Project
    (see P3P)
plug-ins, 304–308, 436
    history, 304
    installation, 305
    Internet Explorer, 305
    Netscape plug-in security warning, 305
    security aspects, 307–308
    security concerns, 359
Polaroid Corporation, identification
    products, 124
policy reference files, 699, 704
    well-known locations, 704
policy, security, 406
pornography and the Internet, 527
    child pornography, 529
    filtering software, 529, 579
portmap service, 725
portrayal of information in false light, 204
ports, 27
    SSL on TCP/IP, 110
    updating, 479
POSIX specification, system calls, 445
Postel, Jon, 41
power surges, 367, 373
    (see also lightning)
PPP (Point-to-Point Protocol), 21
preventing theft, 379
Princton University Secure Internet
    Programming group, 343
print through process, 385
printer spoolers, security risks, 389
printers, security risks, 389
privacy, 204, 666–667
    cookies, and, 220
    digital cash systems, 621, 622, 624
    digital certificates, and, 193
    downloaded software, from, 243
    email and, 277
    JavaScript and, 350
    protecting, 230–261
    torts, 204

privacy (*continued*)
    violations, refer link field, 213
    web browser extensions, from, 243
Privacy Act of 1974, 593
Privacy Foundation
    web bugs, guidelines for use, 227
privacy policies, 209
    P3P, deploying, 702–706
privacy protections
    American business, self regulation, 596
    Canada, 596
    Code of Fair Information Practices, 593
    COPPA, 601–605
    early US legislation, 592
    European legislation, 593–596
    European Union, 596
    Fair Credit Reporting Act, 593
    Internet Explorer 6.0, built into, 608
    OECD guidelines, 594
    seal programs, 597
privacy-protecting technologies, 262
PrivacySealExample Program, 700
Private Communications Technology
    (PCT), 86
private information, 205
private keys, 50
    generation and storage, 135
    management, 134–140
privileges, CGI scripts and, 467
profiles, 219
programmed threats, 730
programming
    errors (see bugs)
    guidelines for, 443–457
    references for, 732
programs that spend money, 319
Promo Line, Inc., 301
proprietary encryption algorithms, 92
protocols, 16
proxies, 17
proxy firewalls, 432
proxy servers, 213, 263
public key cryptography
    algorithms, attacks on, 69
    authentication using SSH, 147–152
    challenge-response, 151
    digital certificates, 154
    Hushmail, 277
    key certification
      Web of Trust, 156
    patents, 91
    PGP, key generation with, 136

    private key management, 134–140
    public key systems, 50–53
      computational expense, 53
    real-world examples, 140
    replay attacks, preventing, 132
public keys, 50, 51
    cryptographic algorithms, 65–70
    identification, using for, 130–138
    PGP, 132
    smart cards, and, 135
public libraries and anonymous
    browsing, 270
public terminals, security risks, 242
publicity, 666–667
public/private key pairs for web servers, 474
punch-down blocks vs. RJ11 plugs, 658
purchasing over Internet, 620–636

Q

quantum computing, 57
Quicken wire transfer program, 302

R

"r" commands, 413
race conditions, 446
radio eavesdropping, 383
radio interference and computers, 372
RADIUS (Remote Authentication Dial-In
    User Service), 214, 544
RAID (Redundant Arrays of Inexpensive
    Disk) systems, 285
rain (see water)
raised floors, 376
RAM, theft of, 380
RASC (Recreational Software Advisory
    Council), 589
rating services, 587, 708–715
    RSACi, 589
RC2, RC5, and RC4 algorithms, 59
rcp program, 427
rdist program, 427
real-time validation of certificates, 173
recommended books, xviii
records, 689
Recreational Software Advisory Council
    (RASC), 589
redundancy, 24
    protection using, 510–513
refer links and refer link fields, 213
refunds, 617–618
Regulations E and Z, 112

relative humidity, 374
relative identification, 125
remote attacks, 398
remote content updating, 426–429
REMOTE_ variables, 455
renewing certificates, 507
replay attacks, 111, 130
    public key cryptography, preventing
            with, 132
    SSL, level of security from, 110
Requests for Comments (RFCs), 42
Resnick, Paul, 586, 588, 708
resources
    GUIs and, 352
    monitoring, 678
restricted sites zone, 339
restricting access (see access control)
retention, 210
    of backups, 290
reverse charge transactions, 617–618
revocation of digital certificates, 172, 558
RFCs (Requests for Comments), 42
    RFC 1918, 25, 535
    RFC 2109, 222
    RFC 602, 78
    RFC 822 header, 712
.rhost file, 428
Rinjdael (AES) algorithm, 56, 59
    key length, 58
risk analysis, 10
Rivest, Ronald L., 66, 71
RJ11 plugs vs. punch-down blocks, 658
root (/) directory, backups of, 289
root kits, 404
root nameservers (see nameservers)
rotating backup media, 289
rotation, 210
routers, 17
RSA algorithm, 59, 66
    patents, 91
    PGP, and, 136
    SSH, authentication, 147
    SSL, and, 477
RSA Data Security, 175
RSA Data Security Inc.
    BSafe-SSL-C, 477
    certificates, SSL support, 113
    certification services, 176
    factoring challenges, 70
RSACi rating system, 589

S

safeWeb, 275
    Triangle Boy service, 276
sandbox, Java, 334
sanitizing media, 386–387
SATAN, 420, 725
saving backup media, 290
    (see also archiving information; backups)
scp program, 427
screen savers
    password-protected, 391
screensavers
    security risks, 299
script kiddies, 401
<script> tags, 346
scripts, 6, 346, 435
    breaking, 351
    using time-outs, 447
    writing in security, 443
search warrants, 521, 525
secret key algorithms, 50
secrets, 108
Secure Electronic Transaction (SET), 86
secure email, 275–283
Secure Hash Algorithms (SHA, SHA-1), 72
Secure Shell (SSH), 88
Secure Sockets Layer (see SSL)
Secure Tracking of Office Property, 296
secure tunneling, 273
secure web servers, 11
Secure/MIME, 84
securing the web server, 6
security, 364
    against eavesdropping, 424
    design principles, 444
    disabling cookies, 224
    evaluating credit card systems, 640
    evaluating site security, 418–421
    holograms, 124
    intrusion detection programs, 421
    message digests, 74
    policies, implementing, 405–411
    programming guidelines, 443–448
    protecting backups, 292–294
    servers' physical environment, 363–395
    web applications, and, 435–471
security holes
    mailing list for, 717
security mailing lists, 407
security perimeter, 364

security plan
   confidentiality of, 365
security policies, Java, 336
security risks
   data storage, 389–??
   function keys, 390
   personnel, 392
   real world examples, 392
   single-user boot up, 391
   vendor supplied screensavers, 391
   X Windows terminals, 390
security tools, 418–421
security zones, 338–340
SecurityManager class (Java), 334
sensors (see detectors)
sequence conditions, 446
server certificates, 168
server key exchange message, 695
ServerHello, 694
servers, 17
   access to (see access control)
   log files, 211–214
   physical security of, 363–395
   proxy, 213
services, minimizing, 7
session cookies, 609
session hijacking, 425
session keys, 53
SET (Secure Electronic Transaction)
        protocol, 86, 628–629
Set-Cookie header, 217
SetReg.exe, 566
settlement, 621
setuid( ) and setgid( ), 468
sexygirls.com, 300
SHA, SHA-1 (Secure Hash Algorithms), 72
Shamir, Adi, 66
shell scripts, 457
Shockwave, 358
   plug-in, 358
shredders, 258, 388
signature authentication with PGP, 141–147
SignCode.exe, 566, 568–575
   command line operation, 575–577
Sims, Joe, 41
single-user boot up, 391
SIP (Secure Internet Programming)
        group, 343
site exclusion lists, 580
site inspection, 392
site security
   evaluating, 418–421

S/Key system, 424
SLAs (Service Level Agreements), 512
smart cards, 537, 638
smart cards and public keys, 135
S/MIME (Secure/MIME), 84
smoke, effects on computer equipment, 369
"Snake Oil" self-signed certificate, 480
snapshots, 419
social engineering, 387, 399
   employee phonebooks, and, 387
social engineering attacks, 239, 354
SOCKS, 726
software
   custom, 674
   free, 671
   liability (see liability)
   for monitoring, 677–680
   patents, 645
   piracy, 527
   publishing, 565, 577
software failure, 286
software key escrow, 95
software patents, 90
software piracy, 644
Software Publishers Association (SPA), 644
Software Publisher's Pledge, 565
software publishing certificates, 169, 309
   obtaining, 577
SomarSoft, 421
source address, 15
SPA (Software Publishers Association), 644
spam
   preventing, 252
      address munging, 254
      anti-spam software and services, 255
Spam Exterminator, 255
SpamCop, 255
SpammerSlammer, 255
spies, 402
spoofing
   DNS spoofing, 508
   forgery-proof identification, 124
spoofing attacks, 354, 669
sprinkler systems, 368
   (see also water)
SRI-NIC, 42
SSH (Secure Shell), 88, 147, 726
   nonce challenge, 150
   public key authentication, 147–152
   RSA authentication, 147
   viewing the key, 150
ssh-keygen program, 148

SSL Hello, 108
SSL (Secure Sockets Layer), 8, 85, 107–108
    browser alerts, 118
    browser preferences, 116–118
    certificates, format, 475
    certificates, installation on IIS, 501–504
    certificates, supported, 113
    history of, 688
    implementations of, 113
    invalid certificates, causes of, 507
    invention by Netscape, 175
    Java, support in, 114
    key-caching, 114
    MD5, use of, 72
    NSS, 113
    open source programs, online
            resources, 478
    OpenSSL, 114
    performance, 114
    RSA public key algorithm, and, 477
    security deficits, 111, 115
    server addresses,checking, 508
    server certificates, deploying, 472–509
    servers
        choosing, 473
        FreeBSD, creation with, 477–501
        planning, 472
        supporting packages, 473
    SSLRef, 113
    TCP/IP, ports used on top of, 110
    transparency to user, 109
    Unix daemons, adding encryption to, 501
    Version 3.0, 688–698
    web server
        VirtualHost, 491
SSLeay, 114, 477
SSL/TLS, 108–111, 688–698
    alerts, 691
    ChangeCipherSpec protocol, 692
    compression support, 111
    handshake protocol, 692–698
        Certificate Reaquests, 696
        CertificateVerify message, 697
        ClientHello, 693
        client/server exchange, 693
        server key exchange message, 695
        ServerHello, 694
    online resources, 115
    protocols, 690–692
    (see also SSL, TLS)
sslwrap program, 501
stack attacks, 353

static audits, 419
static electricity, 373
static IP addresses, 24
stolen property (see theft)
stolen usernames and passwords, 399
storage, 389–390
storing private keys, 136
stream algorithms, 53
strength, cryptographic, 54
strength of cryptographic systems, 54
string command, 391
strings(1) command, 29
striping, 285
subject.commonName field, wildcards, 476
substitution ciphers, 47
SUID and SGID privileges, 467
Sun Java SDK
    code signing system, 562
Sun Microsystems, 330
Superincreasing Knapsack Problem, 70
Surety Technologies, Inc., 192
surge suppressors, 373
surges (see power surges)
Swatch program, 727
SymLinksIfOwnerMatch option, 541
symmetric key algorithms, 50–64
    common schemes, 58
symmetric keys
    exchange, problems with, 51
    security issues, 51
    uniqueness, problems with, 51
SYN packets, 28
SYN/ACK packets, 29
syslog, 445
system administration
    errors by, 286
    references on, 732
    sanitizing media, 386
system calls, checking return codes
        from, 445
systems-based crytpographic attacks, 64

T

tagging, 295
tainting Perl, 454
tamper-proofing of documents, 124
tandem backup, 289
tax collection and digital money, 627
tcpdump, 26–28
    three-way handshakes, 28

TCP/IP (Transmission Control
        Protocol/Internet Protocol), 17, 107
    connections, 28
    spoofing, 669
tcpwrapper system, 727
telephone billing fraud, 319
telephones, cellular, 373
Telnet service, 413
temperature, impact on hardware, 372
TEMPEST system, 383
temporary files, 457
terrorists, 402
testing (see verifying)
theft, 393
    of backups, 385
    information theft, 320–321
    prevention, 379
    RAM, 380
third-party certification authorities, 162
third-party cookies, 218, 609
Thomas, Robert and Carleen, 527
threats
    to backups, 292–294
    biological, 372
    computer failures, 285
    criminal prosecution, risks of
            pursuing, 521–523
    disposed materials, 387–388
    inability to break running scripts, 351
    mailing list for, 718
    media failure, 289
    mirror worlds, 358
    programmed, 730
    race conditions, 446
    spoofing (see spoofing)
    SUID and SGID privileges, 467
    trademark violation, 647
    unattended terminals, 390–391
    vandalism, 377–379
three-way handshakes, 29
Thwate Holdings, 176
Tiger, 727
Tiger utility, 419
Time Warner, 330
timeouts, 447
TIS Internet Firewall Toolkit (FWTK), 727
Title III, Elementary and Secondary
        Education Act, 580
TLS (Transport Layer Security), 108,
        688–698
    MACs (message authentication
            codes), 690

origins, 107
record layer, 689
(see also SSL, SSL/TLS)
TMOUT variable, 391
/tmp directory, security of, 447
tobacco smoke, effects on computer
        equipment, 369
token-based authentication, 424
tokens, 127
top-level nameservers (see nameservers)
tort of privacy, 204
traceroutes, 36
tracing programs, 297
trade secret law and cryptography, 92
trademarks, 646–648
    domain names, and, 648
    establishing a trademark, 646
    infringement, 647
    registration, 647
traffic, 34
traffic analysis, 55
transborder data flows, 594
transit, 36
transit agreements, 35
Transmission Control Protocol/Internet
        Protocol (see TCP/IP)
transmitted data blocking, 581
transmitters, radio, 373
transposition ciphers, 47
trashing, 388
Triangle Boy, 276
triangulation, 207
trinoo, 404
Triple-DES algorithm, 58
Tripwire, 420, 728
Trojan horses, 398
trust, 157
    domains, 356
    Java applets, 354
trust hierarchies, 174
TRUSTe, 597
Trusted Root Certification Authorities, 178
trusted sites zone, 339
tunnels, 88
two-factor authentication, 128
two-key cryptography, 51

U

UCD (Uniform Call Distribution), 661
UDP (User Datagram Protocol), 17
    Packet Relayer, 728

UDRP (Uniform Dispute Resolution Policy), 516, 648
unattended terminals, 390–391
uniform resource locators (see URLs)
uninterruptable power supply (UPS), 368
United States
  federal computer crime laws, 521
  federal jurisdiction, 520
  payment cards in, 612
Unix
  logging, 415
    pruning of log files, 416
  newsyslog command, 416
  programming references, 732
  shell scripts, 457
  sslwrap program, 501
  strings(1) command, 29
Unix shell, security vulnerabilities, 440
unroutable IP addresses, 25
unsecure hosts, 397
unspoofable areas, 357
updating content securely, 426–429
uploading stored information, 389
UPS (uninterruptable power supply), 368
URLs (uniform resource locators), 19
  hidden, 534
  mirror worlds, 358
Usenet groups, 719
user education, 10
user error, 286
usernames
  doubling as passwords (Joes), 233
  theft of, 399
users
  access based on, 537
  asking for information/action, 354
  authenticating, 543
  biometric identification systems, 128
  checking values from, 444
  cookies for, 220
  operating system restrictions of, 437
  spoofing/impersonating (see spoofing)
  unattended terminals, 390–391

V

vacuums, computer, 370
validity, 157
vampire taps, 384
vandalism, 377–379
VBA signing, 562

VC-I video encryption algorithm, 64
vendors, choosing, 407
  evaluation web site, 408
Venema, Wietse, 420
ventilation
  air ducts, 376
  holes (in hardware), 378
  (see also dust; smoke)
verification
  credit card check digit, 614
  Java bytecode, 336
  user input, 444
  (see also authentication)
verifying
  backups, 385
VeriSign, 160, 176, 553–559
  digital certificates of, 182–183
  software publishing and, 565, 577
vibration, 374
video tape, 290
vigilantes, 402
Vineyard.NET, 655–687
Virtual PIN system, 621–623
virtual private networks (VPNs), 87
VirtualHost, 491
viruses, 398
  references on, 730
Visa, 612
voltage spikes, 373
VPNs (Virtual Private Networks), 87, 432
VTN (VeriSign Trust Network), 160

W

W3C (see World Wide Web Consortium)
Walden Network, 23
Walt Disney Company, collecting information on children, 602
warez, 644
Warren, Samuel, 204
Wassenaar treaty, 102
water, 375
  humidity, 374
  sprinkler systems, 368
  sprinkler systems (fire suppression), 369
  stopping fires with, 368
web applications
  securing of, 435–471
  security risk, 436
  technologies used in, 435

web browsers
  advertising, and, 262
  cache, 244
  convenience features, security risks, 250
  cookies, 216–217
  extensions, privacy issues, 243
  history, clearing, 248–250
  log files of, 211–214
  shopping cart vulnerability, 449
  spoofing status of, 356
  vulnerabilities, 9
web bugs, 225–228
  Privacy Foundation's usage
    guidelines, 227
  uses, 228
  web pages, on, 225
web forms, assuring security of fields, 449
web logs
  DNS logs, 215
  information stored in, 211
  limiting data transfer to, 213
  mail logs, 215
  RADIUS, 214
Web of Trust, 156, 157
web profiles, 219
web security, 3–5
  primary elements, 3
Web Security, Privacy & Commerce
  book web site, xxiv
  summary of content, xviii–xxi
web servers, xxii
  access control, 533–538
  attacks on, examples, 6
  flawed distributions, 437
  private keys, maintaining, 474
  restricting access, 7
  secure web servers, 11
  securing, 6
  SSL, planning, 472
web services
  prevention of outages, 510–516
web sites
  secure updating, 426–429
  security, evaluating, 418–421
  security levels, assignment to, 337
web-based email services and privacy, 277
WebWasher, 268
Westin, Alan, 205
whitelist, 255
wildcards, subject.commonName field, 476
Windows
  certificates, 170

  keystroke monitoring screensavers, 299
  logging, Windows 2000, 416
  mailing list, Windows NT, 718
  SSL-enabled web servers, and, 474
  Windows 98, file sharing weakness, 400
windows, attacks on, 352
windows (glass), security aspects, 377
wireless LANs, security of, 383
wiretapping, 382
wiring buildings for networks, 657
wiring, configuration of, 657
World Wide Web, 19
  convenience vs. security, xvi
  cookies, 216–217
  crime, xi–xvi
  history command, 351
  impact, xi
  mirror worlds, 358
  refer links, 213
  references on, 720–722
  security aspects, 78
World Wide Web Consortium
  code signing certificates, 577
  P3P protocol (see P3P)
  PICS (Platform for Internet Content
    Selection), 583
worms, 10, 398
write-protecting backups, 293
writing programs (see programming,
  guidelines for)

X

X Window System, security aspects, 390
X.509 v3 certificates, 163–168
  renewal, 507
  selective disclosure, and, 192

Y

Yahoo Mail, 277
Young, Eric A., 114, 477

Z

Zero Knowledge Systems, 172
  Freedom anonymizer, 273

About the Author

Simson Garfinkel is a journalist, entrepreneur, and international authority on computer security. Garfinkel is Chief Technology Officer at Sandstorm Enterprises, a Boston-based firm which develops state-of-the-art computer security tools. Garfinkel is also a columnist for *Technology Review Magazine* and has written for more than 50 publications, including *Computerworld, Forbes,* and *The New York Times.* He is the author of *Database Nation, PGP: Pretty Good Privacy,* and six other books. With Gene Spafford, he is the coauthor of *Practical Unix & Internet Security.*

Gene Spafford is a professor at Purdue University, and Director of CERIAS, the world's premier multidisciplinary academic center for information security. Spaf is a Fellow of the AAAS, ACM, and IEEE, and has additionally been recognized for his research and teaching in infosec with the National Computer Systems Security Award, the William Hugh Murray Medal of the NCISSE, election to the ISSA Hall of Fame, and the Charles Murphy Award at Purdue. He was named as a CISSP, honoris causa in 2000. He is the coauthor of *Practical Unix & Internet Security* and was the consulting editor for *Computer Crime: A Crimefighters Handbook.*

Colophon

Our look is the result of reader comments, our own experimentation, and feedback from distribution channels. Distinctive covers complement our distinctive approach to technical topics, breathing personality and life into potentially dry subjects.

The animal on the cover of *Web Security, Privacy & Commerce, Second Edition* is a whale shark. Sharks have lived on the Earth for over 300 million years, and populate all the oceans of the world (as well as some freshwater lakes and rivers). They are related to skates and rays, differing from ordinary bony fish in having a cartilaginous skeleton that makes their bodies unusually flexible. Unlike bony fish, sharks give birth to live young, in small litters.

A common misconception about sharks is that they need to keep swimming at all times. While they do need to move their fins constantly in order to stay afloat, many species of sharks like to rest on the bottom of the ocean floor.

Sharks make excellent predators because of their well-developed sensory system (not to mention their big, sharp teeth). They have excellent eyesight and an unusually keen sense of smell; they are known to be able to locate prey from a single drop of blood. Sharks can also sense electrical currents in the water indicating the presence of other fish. They retain several rows of teeth, which roll outward to replace those that are lost.

The whale shark, on the other hand, is a kinder, gentler shark. Whale sharks (*Rhinocodon typus*) have a large flat head, a wide mouth, and tiny teeth. As a filter feeder, they feed primarily on plankton and small fish. They have distinctive spotted markings on their fins and dorsal sides. Whale sharks are so named because of their size: they may weigh more than 18 metric tons and measure up to 60 feet long. They are the largest species of fish alive today.

Whale sharks live in tropical and temperate seas. They pose little or no risk to humans. In fact, whale sharks are considered a particular treat to divers, since they are impressive in size but are slow-moving and not aggressive.

Colleen Gorman was the production editor and the copyeditor for *Web Security, Privacy & Commerce, Second Edition*. Melanie Wang and Sue Willing were the proofreaders. Matt Hutchinson provided quality control. Mary Brady, Phil Dangler, Maureen Dempsey, Derek Di Matteo, Catherine Morris, and Edie Shapiro provided production support. John Bickelhaupt wrote the index.

Edie Freedman designed the cover of this book. The cover image is a 19th-century engraving from the Dover Pictorial Archive. Emma Colby produced the cover layout with QuarkXPress 4.1 using Adobe's ITC Garamond font.

David Futato designed the interior layout. Neil Walls updated the files to FrameMaker 5.5.6 using tools created by Mike Sierra. The text font is Linotype Birka; the heading font is Adobe Myriad Condensed; and the code font is Lucas-Font's TheSans Mono Condensed. The illustrations that appear in the book were produced by Robert Romano and Jessamyn Read using Macromedia FreeHand 9 and Adobe Photoshop 6. The tip and warning icons were drawn by Christopher Bing. This colophon was written by Linda Mui.

Whenever possible, our books use a durable and flexible lay-flat binding. If the page count exceeds this binding's limit, perfect binding is used.

More Titles from O'Reilly

Web Administration

Webmaster in a Nutshell, 2nd Edition

By Stephen Spainhour & Robert Eckstein
2nd Edition June 1999
540 pages, ISBN 1-56592-325-1

This indispensable book takes all the essential reference information for the Web and pulls it together into one volume. It covers HTML 4.0, CSS, XML, CGI, SSI, JavaScript 1.2, PHP, HTTP 1.1, and administration for the Apache server.

Apache: The Definitive Guide, 2nd Edition

By Ben Laurie & Peter Laurie
2nd Edition February 1999
388 pages, Includes CD-ROM
ISBN 1-56592-528-9

Written and reviewed by key members of the Apache group, this book is the only complete guide on the market that describes how to obtain, set up, and secure the Apache software on both Unix and Windows systems. The second edition fully describes Windows support and all the other Apache 1.3 features. Includes CD-ROM with Apache sources and demo sites discussed in the book.

Web Performance Tuning

By Patrick Killelea
1st Edition October 1998
374 pages, ISBN 1-56592-379-0

Web Performance Tuning hits the ground running and gives concrete advice for improving crippled web performance right away. For anyone who has waited too long for a web page to display or watched servers slow to a crawl, this book includes tips on tuning the server software, operating system, network, and the web browser itself.

Building Internet Firewalls, 2nd Edition

By Elizabeth D. Zwicky, Simon Cooper,
& D. Brent Chapman
2nd Edition June 2000
894 pages, ISBN 1-56592-871-7

Completely revised and much expanded, this second edition of the highly respected and best-selling *Building Internet Firewalls* now covers Unix, Linux, and Windows NT. It's a practical and detailed guide that provides step-by-step explanations of how to design and install firewalls, and how to configure Internet services to work with a firewall. It covers a wide range of services and protocols. It also contains a complete list of resources, including the location of many publicly available firewalls construction tools.

Apache Pocket Reference

By Andrew Ford
1st Edition June 2000
110 pages, ISBN 1-56592-706-0

The *Apache Pocket Reference*, a companion volume to *Writing Apache Modules with Perl and C* and *Apache: The Definitive Guide*, covers Apache 1.3.12. It provides a summary of command-line options, configuration directives, and modules, and covers Apache support utilities.

Web Programming

ActionScript: The Definitive Guide

By Colin Moock
1st Edition May 2001
720 pages, ISBN 1-56592-852-0

ActionScript: The Definitive Guide is for
web developers and web authors who want
to go beyond simple Flash animations to create enhanced Flash-driven sites. Regardless
of your level of programming expertise, this
combination of ActionScript fundamentals,
applications, and handy quick-reference will have you scripting
like a pro.

CGI Programming with Perl, 2nd Edition

By Shishir Gundavaram
2nd Edition July 2000
470 pages, ISBN 1-56592-419-3

The Common Gateway Interface (CGI) is one
of the most powerful methods of providing
dynamic content on the Web. CGI is a generic
interface for calling external programs to
crunch numbers, query databases, generate
customized graphics, or perform any other
server-side task. Based on the best-selling *CGI Programming on
the World Wide Web*, this edition has been completely rewritten
to demonstrate current techniques available with the CGI.pm
module and the latest versions of Perl.

Dynamic HTML: The Definitive Reference

By Danny Goodman
1st Edition July 1998
1088 pages, ISBN 1-56592-494-0

Dynamic HTML: The Definitive Reference
is an indispensable compendium for web
content developers. It contains complete reference material for all of the HTML tags, CSS
style attributes, browser document objects,
and JavaScript objects supported by the vari-
ous standards and the latest versions of Netscape Navigator and
Microsoft Internet Explorer.

JavaScript: The Definitive Guide, 4th Edition

By David Flanagan
4th Edition November 2001 (est.)
960 pages (est.), ISBN 0-596-00048-0

To stay on top of their work, web professionals need the most up-to-date, complete
reference available on the core JavaScript
language, which is growing more and more
essential for effective web design and development. This new edition covers JavaScript
1.5, the latest version of the language. The book's comprehensive
reference section documents every object, property, method,
event handler, function and constructor used by client-side
JavaScript.

Programming ColdFusion

By Rob Brooks-Bilson
1st Edition August 2001
974 pages, ISBN 1-56592-698-6

Programming ColdFusion covers everything
you need to know to create effective web
applications with ColdFusion, a powerful tool
for rapid web site development. The book
starts with the basics and quickly moves to
more advanced topics, providing numerous
examples of common web application tasks, so you can learn by
example.

Programming Web Services with SOAP

By James Snell, Doug Tidwell & Pavell Kulchenko
1st Edition December 2001 (est.)
352 pages (est.) ISBN 0-596-00095-2

In typical O'Reilly fashion this book moves
beyond the theoretical and explains how to
build and implement SOAP web services.
The book begins with a solid introduction to
SOAP, detailing its history and structure,
followed by an introduction to the three
major types of SOAP applications: SOAP-RPC, SOAP-Messaging,
and SOAP-Intermediaries. Each SOAP application is illustrated
with an in-depth implementation.

Web Programming

Webmaster in a Nutshell, 2nd Edition

By Stephen Spainhour & Robert Eckstein
2nd Edition June 1999
540 pages, ISBN 1-56592-325-1

This indispensable book takes all the essential reference information for the Web and pulls it together into one volume. It covers HTML 4.0, CSS, XML, CGI, SSI, JavaScript 1.2, PHP, HTTP 1.1, and administration for the Apache server.

ASP in a Nutshell, 2nd Edition

By A. Keyton Weissinger
2nd Edition July 2000
492 pages, ISBN 1-56592-843-1

ASP in a Nutshell, 2nd Edition, provides the high-quality reference documentation that web application developers really need to create effective Active Server Pages. It focuses on how features are used in a real application and highlights little-known or undocumented features.

JavaServer Pages

By Hans Bergsten
1st Edition December 2000
572 pages, ISBN 1-56592-746-X

JavaServer Pages shows how to develop Java-based web applications without having to be a hardcore programmer. The author provides an overview of JSP concepts and illuminates how JSP fits into the larger picture of web applications. There are chapters for web authors on generating dynamic content, handling session information, and accessing databases, as well as material for Java programmers on creating Java components and custom JSP tags for web authors to use in JSP pages.

Web Database Applications with PHP & MySQL

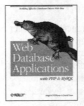

By Hugh E. Williams & David Lane
1st Edition December 2001 (est.)
400 pages (est.), ISBN 0-596-00041-3

This book offers both theoretical and practical guidance for creating web database applications. The detailed information on designing relational databases and the web application architectures that interact with them will be especially useful to readers who have worked with or built database-backed web sites before. The book implements a sample web application using PHP and MySQL on the Apache platform.

Java Servlet Programming, 2nd Edition

By Jason Hunter with William Crawford
2nd Edition April 2001
780 pages, ISBN 0-596-00040-5

The second edition of this popular book has been completely updated to add the new features of the Java Servlet API Version 2.2, and new chapters on servlet security and advanced communication. In addition to complete coverage of the 2.2 specification, we have included bonus material on the new 2.3 version of the specification.

Designing Active Server Pages

By Scott Mitchell
1st Edition September 2000
360 pages, ISBN 0-596-00044-8

Designing Active Server Pages is written for developers who have already mastered the basics of ASP application development and are ready to take the next logical step. It is sure to become an indispensable part of every web developer's library.

How to stay in touch with O'Reilly

1. Visit Our Award-Winning Web Site

http://www.oreilly.com/

★ "Top 100 Sites on the Web" —PC Magazine
★ "Top 5% Web sites" —Point Communications
★ "3-Star site" —The McKinley Group

Our web site contains a library of comprehensive product information (including book excerpts and tables of contents), downloadable software, background articles, interviews with technology leaders, links to relevant sites, book cover art, and more. File us in your Bookmarks or Hotlist!

2. Join Our Email Mailing Lists

New Product Releases
To receive automatic email with brief descriptions of all new O'Reilly products as they are released, send email to:
ora-news-subscribe@lists.oreilly.com
Put the following information in the first line of your message (not in the Subject field):
subscribe ora-news

O'Reilly Events
If you'd also like us to send information about trade show events, special promotions, and other O'Reilly events, send email to:
ora-news-subscribe@lists.oreilly.com
Put the following information in the first line of your message (not in the Subject field):
subscribe ora-events

3. Get Examples from Our Books via FTP

There are two ways to access an archive of example files from our books:

Regular FTP
• ftp to:
  ftp.oreilly.com
  (login: anonymous
  password: your email address)
• Point your web browser to:
  ftp://ftp.oreilly.com/

FTPMAIL
• Send an email message to:
  ftpmail@online.oreilly.com
  (Write "help" in the message body)

4. Contact Us via Email

order@oreilly.com
To place a book or software order online. Good for North American and international customers.

subscriptions@oreilly.com
To place an order for any of our newsletters or periodicals.

books@oreilly.com
General questions about any of our books.

cs@oreilly.com
For answers to problems regarding your order or our products.

booktech@oreilly.com
For book content technical questions or corrections.

proposals@oreilly.com
To submit new book or software proposals to our editors and product managers.

international@oreilly.com
For information about our international distributors or translation queries. For a list of our distributors outside of North America check out:
http://www.oreilly.com/distributors.html

5. Work with Us

Check out our website for current employment opportunites:
http://jobs.oreilly.com/

O'Reilly & Associates, Inc.
1005 Gravenstein Hwy North
Sebastopol, CA 95472 USA
TEL 707-829-0515 or 800-998-9938
    (6am to 5pm PST)
FAX 707-829-0104

Titles from O'Reilly

International Distributors

http://international.oreilly.com/distributors.html • international@oreilly.com

UK, EUROPE, MIDDLE EAST, AND AFRICA (EXCEPT FRANCE, GERMANY, AUSTRIA, SWITZERLAND, LUXEMBOURG, AND LIECHTENSTEIN)

INQUIRIES
O'Reilly UK Limited
4 Castle Street
Farnham
Surrey, GU9 7HS
United Kingdom
Telephone: 44-1252-711776
Fax: 44-1252-734211
Email: information@oreilly.co.uk

ORDERS
Wiley Distribution Services Ltd.
1 Oldlands Way
Bognor Regis
West Sussex PO22 9SA
United Kingdom
Telephone: 44-1243-843294
UK Freephone: 0800-243207
Fax: 44-1243-843302 (Europe/EU orders)
or 44-1243-843274 (Middle East/Africa)
Email: cs-books@wiley.co.uk

FRANCE

INQUIRIES & ORDERS
Éditions O'Reilly
18 rue Séguier
75006 Paris, France
Tel: 33-1-40-51-71-89
Fax: 33-1-40-51-72-26
Email: france@oreilly.fr

GERMANY, SWITZERLAND, AUSTRIA, LUXEMBOURG, AND LIECHTENSTEIN

INQUIRIES & ORDERS
O'Reilly Verlag
Balthasarstr. 81
D-50670 Köln, Germany
Telephone: 49-221-973160-91
Fax: 49-221-973160-8
Email: anfragen@oreilly.de (inquiries)
Email: order@oreilly.de (orders)

CANADA
(FRENCH LANGUAGE BOOKS)
Les Éditions Flammarion ltée
375, Avenue Laurier Ouest
Montréal (Québec) H2V 2K3
Tel: 1-514-277-8807
Fax: 1-514-278-2085
Email: info@flammarion.qc.ca

HONG KONG
City Discount Subscription Service, Ltd.
Unit A, 6th Floor, Yan's Tower
27 Wong Chuk Hang Road
Aberdeen, Hong Kong
Tel: 852-2580-3539
Fax: 852-2580-6463
Email: citydis@ppn.com.hk

KOREA
Hanbit Media, Inc.
Chungmu Bldg. 210
Yonnam-dong 568-33
Mapo-gu
Seoul, Korea
Tel: 822-325-0397
Fax: 822-325-9697
Email: hant93@chollian.dacom.co.kr

PHILIPPINES
Global Publishing
G/F Benavides Garden
1186 Benavides Street
Manila, Philippines
Tel: 632-254-8949/632-252-2582
Fax: 632-734-5060/632-252-2733
Email: globalp@pacific.net.ph

TAIWAN
O'Reilly Taiwan
1st Floor, No. 21, Lane 295
Section 1, Fu-Shing South Road
Taipei, 106 Taiwan
Tel: 886-2-27099669
Fax: 886-2-27038802
Email: mori@oreilly.com

INDIA
Shroff Publishers & Distributors Pvt. Ltd.
12, "Roseland", 2nd Floor
180, Waterfield Road, Bandra (West)
Mumbai 400 050
Tel: 91-22-641-1800/643-9910
Fax: 91-22-643-2422
Email: spd@vsnl.com

CHINA
O'Reilly Beijing
SIGMA Building, Suite B809
No. 49 Zhichun Road
Haidian District
Beijing, China PR 100080
Tel: 86-10-8809-7475
Fax: 86-10-8809-7463
Email: beijing@oreilly.com

JAPAN
O'Reilly Japan, Inc.
Yotsuya Y's Building
7 Banch 6, Honshio-cho
Shinjuku-ku
Tokyo 160-0003 Japan
Tel: 81-3-3356-5227
Fax: 81-3-3356-5261
Email: japan@oreilly.com

SINGAPORE, INDONESIA, MALAYSIA, AND THAILAND
TransQuest Publishers Pte Ltd
30 Old Toh Tuck Road #05-02
Sembawang Kimtrans Logistics Centre
Singapore 597654
Tel: 65-4623112
Fax: 65-4625761
Email: wendiw@transquest.com.sg

AUSTRALIA
Woodslane Pty., Ltd.
7/5 Vuko Place
Warriewood NSW 2102
Australia
Tel: 61-2-9970-5111
Fax: 61-2-9970-5002
Email: info@woodslane.com.au

NEW ZEALAND
Woodslane New Zealand, Ltd.
21 Cooks Street (P.O. Box 575)
Waganui, New Zealand
Tel: 64-6-347-6543
Fax: 64-6-345-4840
Email: info@woodslane.com.au

ARGENTINA
Distribuidora Cuspide
Suipacha 764
1008 Buenos Aires
Argentina
Phone: 54-11-4322-8868
Fax: 54-11-4322-3456
Email: libros@cuspide.com

ALL OTHER COUNTRIES
O'Reilly & Associates, Inc.
1005 Gravenstein Hwy North
Sebastopol, CA 95472 USA
Tel: 707-829-0515
Fax: 707-829-0104
Email: order@oreilly.com

O'REILLY®